Social Work Practice With African Americans in Urban Environments

Rhonda Wells-Wilbon, DSW, MSW, LICSW, LCSW-C, is a tenured associate professor and former chair, Masters of Social Work Program; she currently serves as a faculty member in the PhD Program, School of Social Work, Morgan State University, Baltimore, MD. She is the founder and chief executive officer (CEO) of Asili Consultants LLC. Her professional articles have appeared in the *Journal of Family Strengths, Journal of Black Studies, Black Women, Gender and Families,* and *Journal of Teaching Social Work,* to name a few. She has contributed to the professional literature with training curriculums, research reports, conference presentations, and book chapters. Her primary practice and research areas include domestic violence and adult survivors of child sexual abuse and sexual assault. Her active board memberships include the Council on Social Work Education's Women's Council, National Association of Black Social Workers, the House of Ruth Maryland, and Morgan State University's Head Start Program, and she is the founding chair of the board of trustees for the Richard Wright Public Charter School in Washington, DC.

Anna R. McPhatter, PhD, MSW, LCSW, is dean and professor, School of Social Work, Morgan State University, Baltimore, MD. With 35 years of teaching experience in undergraduate and graduate social work programs, she is an expert on child welfare, human behavior in the social environment, social group work, family treatment, culturally competent social work practice, and clinical social work with Black families. She is currently commissioner on the Commission on Accreditation, Council on Social Work Education; a member of the National Association of Social Workers (NASW); president of the board of directors for Helping Children Grow, a child welfare agency located in Washington, DC; and board member for the Govans Ecumenical Development Corporation (GEDCO), an agency that provides sustainable housing for the elderly, the homeless, and consumers dealing with substance abuse; and formerly a commissioner for the Baltimore City Department of Social Services. She serves on the editorial boards of the *Journal of Health Care for the Poor and Underserved* and *Health and Social Work.* Her journal and book chapter publications are numerous.

Halaevalu F. Ofahengaue Vakalahi, PhD, MSW, MEd, is professor and associate dean, School of Social Work, Morgan State University, Baltimore, MD. Her areas of teaching include human behavior and the social work environment, social policy, organizational leadership, and cultural diversity. Her contribution to the profession and community includes serving in the Council on Social Work Education, National Association of Social Workers, and the Baltimore City Commission on Aging. Her areas of scholarship include Pacific Islander culture and community, specifically in relation to aging and intergenerational transmission of cultural values, beliefs, and practices, and the experiences of women of color in academia. Her publications in these areas of scholarship include numerous peer-reviewed articles, chapters, references, and coedited–coauthored books, including her most recent work titled *Transnational Pacific Islanders and Social Work* and *The Collective Spirit of Aging across Cultures.*

Social Work Practice With African Americans in Urban Environments

Rhonda Wells-Wilbon, DSW, MSW, LICSW, LCSW-C
Anna R. McPhatter, PhD, MSW, LCSW
Halaevalu F. Ofahengaue Vakalahi, PhD, MSW, MEd

Editors

SPRINGER PUBLISHING COMPANY
NEW YORK

Springer Publishing Company, LLC
11 West 42nd Street
New York, NY 10036
www.springerpub.com

Acquisitions Editor: Sheri W. Sussman
Production Editor: Michael O'Connor
Composition: Newgen KnowledgeWorks

ISBN: 978-0-8261-3074-7
e-book ISBN: 978-0-8261-3075-4
Instructors' Materials: Qualified instructors may request supplements by e-mailing textbook@springerpub.com:
Instructors' Manual ISBN: 978-0-8261-3768-5
Instructors' PowerPoints ISBN: 978-0-8261-3769-2

15 16 17 18 19/ 5 4 3 2 1

The author and the publisher of this Work have made every effort to use sources believed to be reliable to provide information that is accurate and compatible with the standards generally accepted at the time of publication. The author and publisher shall not be liable for any special, consequential, or exemplary damages resulting, in whole or in part, from the readers' use of, or reliance on, the information contained in this book. The publisher has no responsibility for the persistence or accuracy of URLs for external or third-party Internet websites referred to in this publication and does not guarantee that any content on such websites is, or will remain, accurate or appropriate.

Library of Congress Cataloging-in-Publication Data
Social work practice with African Americans in urban environments / Rhonda Wells-Wilbon, Anna R. McPhatter, Halaevalu F. Ofahengaue Vakalahi, editors.
    pages cm
 ISBN 978-0-8261-3074-7
 1. Social work with African Americans. 2. Urban African Americans—Services for. 3. Urban African Americans—Social conditions. I. Wells-Wilbon, Rhonda.
 HV3181.S6145 2016
 362.84'96073—dc23   2015022553

Special discounts on bulk quantities of our books are available to corporations, professional associations, pharmaceutical companies, health care organizations, and other qualifying groups. If you are interested in a custom book, including chapters from more than one of our titles, we can provide that service as well.

For details, please contact:
Special Sales Department, Springer Publishing Company, LLC
11 West 42nd Street, 15th Floor, New York, NY 10036–8002
Phone: 877-687-7476 or 212-431-4370; Fax: 212-941-7842
E-mail: sales@springerpub.com

Printed in the United States of America by McNaughton & Gunn.

It is indeed an honor to dedicate this work to the late Dr. Jay Carrington Chunn, our colleague, mentor, friend, and proverbial giant among the shakers and movers of our time. From his time as the dean of the Howard University School of Social Work, to his presidency at Medgar Evans College, and to his developing and directing the National Center for Health Behavioral Change, and being senior administrator and doctoral professor at Morgan, Jay lived and thrived on motivating others and getting that next project, publication, or book, done. Likewise, he was the thrust we needed to complete this book for which we will be eternally grateful. The entire School of Social Work at Morgan State University will forever remember and uphold the legacy of Dr. Chunn and his sense of urgency about every effort to move the needle toward social and economic change for marginalized people everywhere. It is our hope that he would be proud of this work as its goal is to better prepare urban social workers and human service practitioners to work with African Americans.

Anna McPhatter

Contents

SECTION I: CONCEPTUALIZING URBAN SOCIAL WORK

SECTION II: CHILDREN, YOUTH, AND FAMILIES

SECTION III: PUBLIC HEALTH, HEALTH, AND MENTAL HEALTH

SECTION VI: NAVIGATING THE URBAN BUILT ENVIRONMENT

Contributors

Timothy Akers, PhD   Assistant Vice President for Research Innovation & Advocacy, Division of Research & Economic Development, Morgan State University, Baltimore, Maryland

Paul Archibald, PhD, MSW, LCSW-C   Professor, School of Social Work, Morgan State University, Baltimore, Maryland

Sandra Austin, EdD, MSW   Associate Professor, School of Social Work, Morgan State University, Baltimore, Maryland

Tricia Bent-Goodley, PhD, MSW, LICSW Director, Howard University Interpersonal Violence Prevention Program; Professor and Director, Doctoral Program, Howard University School of Social Work, Washington, District of Columbia

Errol S. Bolden, PhD, MSW, MPH   Associate Professor of Social Work, Department of Social Work, Coppin State University, Baltimore, Maryland

LaPricia Lewis Boyer, BS, LPN   Senior Research Program Coordinator, Division of Internal Medicine, Johns Hopkins University School of Medicine, Baltimore, Maryland

Marquis Chandler, MSW   Doctoral Candidate, Morgan State University, Baltimore, Maryland

Sandra S. Chipungu, PhD, MSW   Chair, PhD Department, School of Social Work, Morgan State University, Baltimore, Maryland

Kevin Daniels, PhD, MSW   Professor, School of Social Work, Morgan State University, Baltimore, Maryland

Linda Darrell, PhD, MSW, LCSW-C   Assistant Professor, MSW Program, School of Social Work, Morgan State University, Baltimore, Maryland

Anthony Estreet, PhD, MSW, LCSW-C, LCADC Assistant Professor, School of Social Work, Morgan State University, Baltimore, Maryland

Yvonne V. Greene, MSW, BS, LCSW-C Chairperson, BSW Department, School of Social Work, Morgan State University, Baltimore, Maryland

Warren W. Hewitt, DrPH, MS Chief Executive Officer, HKJ Behavioral Health Services, Baltimore, Maryland

Lori James-Townes, MSW, LCSW-C Chief of Social Work Division and Services, Maryland Office of Public Defender, Baltimore, Maryland

Kimberly Y. Johnson, PhD, MSW, LCSW-C Director, Title IV-E Public Child Welfare Program, School of Social Work, Morgan State University, Baltimore, Maryland

Kenya Jones, PhD, MSW Assistant Professor, The Whitney M. Young Jr. School of Social Work, Clark Atlanta University, Atlanta, Georgia

Saanjh Aakash Kishore, PhD, MA, CPhil Doctoral Candidate, University of California, Los Angeles, California

Iris Carlton LaNey, PhD, MSW Professor, School of Social Work, University of North Carolina at Chapel Hill, Chapel Hill, North Carolina

Claudia Lawrence-Webb, DSW, MSW, LCSW-C Adjunct Professor, School of Social Work, Morgan State University, Baltimore, Maryland

Margaret Lombe, PhD, MSW Associate Professor, Graduate School of Social Work, Boston College, Chestnut Hill, Massachusetts

Isiah Marshall Jr., PhD, MSW Associate Professor of Social Work and MSW Program Director, Department of Sociology and Social Work, Daemen College, Amherst, New York

Denise McLane-Davison, PhD, MSW Assistant Professor, MSW Department, School of Social Work, Morgan State University, Baltimore, Maryland

Anna R. McPhatter, PhD, MSW, LCSW Dean and Professor, School of Social Work, Morgan State University, Baltimore, Maryland

Jarrell J. McRae, MSW, LCSW-C Program Director, Baltimore Teens in Transition, Baltimore, Maryland

Merissa R. Munford, MSW, LGSW   Founder, Actively Aging to Perfection, Towson, Maryland

Von E. Nebbitt, PhD, MSW   Associate Professor, Jane Addams College of Social Work, University of Illinois at Chicago, Chicago, Illinois

Margaret E. Pittman, MSW   Doctoral Candidate, Professor, School of Social Work, Morgan State University, Baltimore, Maryland

Thelma Rich, MSW, LCSW   Director, Field Education, School of Social Work, Morgan State University, Baltimore, Maryland

Leeza M. Scheidt, MSW, LGSW   Regional Manager, Meals on Wheels of Central Maryland, Inc., Baltimore, Maryland

Marni N. Seyyid, PhD, MSW, LCSW-C   Chief Executive Officer/Lead Trainer, Souldier Seyyid Solutions, LLC, Baltimore, Maryland

Tanya L. Sharpe, PhD, MSW   Assistant Professor, School of Social Work, University of Maryland, Baltimore, Maryland

Gaynell M. Simpson, PhD, MSW   Assistant Professor, School of Social Work, University of Alabama, Tuscaloosa, Alabama

Michael M. Sinclair, PhD, MSW   Assistant Professor, Morgan State University, Baltimore, Maryland

Laurens G. Van Sluytman, PhD, MSW, LCSW-C   Assistant Professor, School of Social Work, Morgan State University, Baltimore, Maryland

Belinda Davis Smith, PhD, MSW   Assistant Professor, School of Social Work, Morgan State University, Baltimore, Maryland

Stacy A. Smith, MSW   Managing Partner, Urban Business Center, Baltimore, Maryland

Kim Dobson Sydnor, PhD   Dean/Associate Professor, School of Community Health and Policy, Morgan State University, Baltimore, Maryland

Colette Walker Thomas, MSW, LCSW-C   Proprietor, Walker & Thomas Clinical Associates, P.A., Windsor Mill, Maryland

Denise Torres, MSW, LCSW   Doctoral Candidate, Graduate Center of the City University of New York, New York

Dawn Thurman, PhD, MSW   Assistant Professor, School of Social Work, Morgan State University, Baltimore, Maryland

M. Taqi Tirmazi, PhD, MSW   Assistant Professor, School of Social Work, Morgan State University, Baltimore, Maryland

Halaevalu F. Ofahengaue Vakalahi, PhD, MSW, MEd   Professor and Associate Dean, School of Social Work, Morgan State University, Baltimore, Maryland

Rhonda Wells-Wilbon, DSW, MSW, LICSW, LCSW-C   Associate Professor, PhD Program, School of Social Work, Morgan State University, Baltimore, Maryland

Dana Burdnell Wilson, PhD, MSW, LCSW   Director, Student Affairs and Admissions, School of Social Work, Morgan State University, Baltimore, Maryland

Foreword

This foreword is being written during the unfolding of urban turmoil in the City of Baltimore, Maryland, in response to systemic injustices faced by African American men across the nation. In 1951, Langston Hughes, through poetry, posed the following question, "What happens to a dream deferred?" He ends his sociopolitical poem with yet another profound question–truth, "Does it explode?" Across the nation's urban centers, we are mourning deaths of young men like Freddie Gray, and bracing for what can happen to others who languish from the cumulative disadvantages that have yet to be addressed by social policies that mend rather than reform social welfare. The founding dean of the Howard University School of Social Work, Dr. Inabel Burns Lindsay, in her 1967 centennial address to the university, alluded to the difficulty of reform and the role of social work. She stated that "the process may be uncomfortable, disillusioning, and at times probably disheartening. But if social work is to realize its unlimited potential, the challenge of the future must be accepted." In his book, *Community Social Work Practice in an Urban Context*, Delgado (1999) asserts that the future of social work is inextricably linked to how well it addresses urban issues related to urban communities of color. The editors and contributors to this book have indeed responded to the challenge to provide context for practice in urban environments that are swollen with untended injustices and interventions that are too often color-blind or misguided. This valuable contribution, "*Social Work Practice With African Americans in Urban Environments*," brings focus to the unique needs of urban individuals and communities. It is a resource for social work educators and practitioners at micro-, mezzo-, and macro-levels.

Urban areas are defined as densely developed residential, commercial, and other nonresidential areas. The Census Bureau reports that in the last decade, urban population has grown by more than 12%. These areas now account for 80.7% of the U.S. population, up from 79.0% in 2000 (U.S. Census Bureau, 2012). The Census Bureau identifies two types of urban areas: "urbanized areas" of 50,000 or more people and "urban clusters" of at least 2,500 and less than 50,000 people (U.S. Census Bureau, 2012). Taken together, they had an overall population density of 2,534 people per square mile. These data clearly document the importance of specialized urban practice that is a community-based and strengths perspective utilizing a variety of indigenous efforts that heavily rely on empowerment strategies using both informal and formal resources. Delgado (2010) acknowledges that social work literature has not kept pace with urban contexts and the related complexity of urban life. African Americans are largely concentrated in urban areas. The authors of this book are affiliated with Morgan State University, a historically Black college and university (HBCU) located in Baltimore, Maryland. According to the 2010 census, Baltimore has the second highest percentage (65%) of Blacks or African Americans in the nation. This is important given that many of the authors have practiced and researched in the City of Baltimore, thus adding authenticity based on their experience and scholarship with urban African Americans and organizations and institutions involved in service delivery. It is important to note, however, that there are clear differences among cities (Black, Kolesnivoka, & Taylor, 2010); however, the authors have presented content that is transferrable, given this recognition of uniqueness.

African Americans have exhibited extraordinary resiliency in surviving the lingering effects of the pernicious U.S. institution of slavery, and thriving. Although many families have navigated this terrain and made extraordinary gains, others are still crippled by the cumulative years of inequality. These individuals often make up the caseloads of human service agencies and organizations. Social workers in these organizations provide critically important support to individuals across the life span who exhibit a range of problems. According to the U.S. census (2013/2015), African Americans make up 13.2% of the U.S. population, yet they are disproportionately represented with chronic disease, health disparities, poverty, unemployment, wealth, and many more variables related to quality of life. Racism continues to play a significant role in determining the outcomes and quality of life of African Americans. To address these problems that often intersect, social work practice must focus on the complexity of the lives of African Americans and identify interventions that are culturally responsive and consistent with the core values of the social work profession. Urban-based and urban-driven issues (Delgado, 2010) that uniquely impact African Americans require sensitivity that is born out of the Black experience. Contemporary social work practice cannot ignore this landscape and is thirsty for scholarship and interventions, such as the ones in this book, that are not ahistorical and recognize the enormous gains from Civil Rights for many while simultaneously acknowledging what Dean Emeriti Douglas Glasgow of the Howard University School of Social Work calls *The Black Underclass*. In his seminal book, Glasgow (1981) asserts that antipoverty programs and other social programs failed to uplift certain segments of the population. It is this segment of the population that most requires the culturally competent interventions that are addressed in this book.

The National Association of Social Workers (NASW) states that the core values of social work are service, social justice, dignity and worth of the person, importance of human relationships, integrity, and competence (NASW, 2008). Effective practice of social work insists on these core values being honored. In addition to adhering to the core values of the profession, competent practice must also consider the context of practice and employ related knowledge, skills, and abilities to address the needs of the client system(s). To ensure that context is inextricably linked to social work education and practice, the Council on Social Work Educational Policy Statement gives primacy to it and defines it as encompassing "the mission of the institution in which the program is located and the needs and opportunities associated with the setting" (Council on Social Work Education [CSWE], 2008).

The book begins with a rich overview that addresses critical perspectives, concepts, and theories that provide an understanding of why the unique focus on urban social work practice with African Americans is absolutely essential to competent social work practice. This book also aligns itself with the context of practice through insightful chapters that cover a range of contemporary practice arenas including child welfare, aging, public health, mental health, substance use, domestic violence, faith-based, and school settings. Chapters also examine work with specific populations such as adolescents, immigrants, sexual minorities, HIV/AIDS, caregivers, victims of violence, and urban gangs. Additionally, the book provides a sociohistorical lens through an in-depth review of African American social work pioneers who have paved the way for many of our successful programs and culturally relevant interventions. The book ends with policy implications that build on the strengths, resilience, and cultural values of African Americans.

Collectively, the authors provide an understanding of both the challenges and strengths that African Americans face residing in urban communities. The chapters include evidence-based practice, research, and case studies to acquaint the reader with the subject matter. Some authors provide assignments that can be used to stimulate the learning of students related to the topics. Others stimulate critical thinking about the nature of oppression and discrimination. This can be used to enrich the knowledge of students and practitioners. They present a number of theoretical frameworks including African-centered, Africentric, critical race, feminist, womanist, intersectionality, and modern social work. Additionally, strengths and ecological, historical, and international perspectives are used by authors. Cultural competence is the overarching lens used by the authors present relevant practice knowledge and skills.

In the seminal book, *Social Work and the Black Experience*, Martin and Martin (1995, p. 1) stated two decades ago, "Social work literature seldom treats black individuals as a unique people with unique cultural and historical experiences." They go on to state the danger in lumping people of color together because of the missed nuances. This book avoids this pitfall. By focusing specifically on the African American community, the authors have deepened our knowledge of both the within-group differences and shared experiences. They help explain not only the challenges but offer interventions and strategies that can serve as a bridge to success in working with African American individuals, families, groups, and communities. Building on seminal works such as Solomon's (1976) *Black Empowerment: Social Work in Oppressed Communities* and Robert Hill's *Strengths of Black Families* (1972) and *Strengths of Black Families Revisited Twenty-Five years Later* (1999), this new resource is a welcomed addition to social work literature. As a former social worker in public housing in an urban metropolitan area, I truly understand the value of this book. Social work programs, especially those located in urban centers will find the value of this book in preparing culturally competent social workers who strongly embrace social justice and strengths-based practice.

Sandra Edmonds Crewe, PhD, MSW, ACSW
Dean and Professor
Howard University School of Social Work
Washington, DC

REFERENCES

Black, D. A., Kolesnikova, N., & Taylor, L. J. (2010). African-American economic progress in urban areas. Retreived April 27, 2015, from http://www.google.com/url?sa=t&rct=j&q=&esrc=s&source=web&cd=3&ved=0CDEQFjAC&url=http%3A%2F%2Fwww.research-gate.net%2Fprofile%2FDan_Black2%2Fpublication%2F228267791_African-American_Economic_Progress_in_Urban_Areas_A_Tale_of_14_American_Cities%2Flinks%2F02e7e52 1ec758080de000000.pdf&ei=FKhFVZXFPMungwTpr4CIDQ&usg=AFQjCNExZgrqUiJKc1 r6HO2PllWozJbfag&bvm=bv.92291466,d.eXY

Council on Social Work Education. (2008). *Educational policy and accreditation standards.* Alexandria, VA: Author.

Delgado, M. (1999). *Community social work practice in an urban context: The potential of a capacity-enhancement perspective.* New York, NY: Oxford University Press.

Delgado, M. (2010). Urban practice. In T. Mizrahi & L. Davis (Eds.), *Encyclopedia of social work* (pp. 251–254). Oxford, UK: Oxford University Press.

Glasgow, D. (1981). *The black underclass.* New York, NY: Vintage Books.

Hill, R. B. (1972). *The strengths of black families.* New York, NY: Emerson Hall.

Hill, R. B. (1999). *The strengths of black families: Twenty-five years later.* Lanham, MD: University Press of America.

Hughes, L. (1951). *Harlem: A dream deferred.* Retrieved April 28, 2015, from http://www.cswnet.com/~menamc/langston.htm

Hughes, L. (1990). *Selected poems of Langston Hughes.* New York, NY: Random House.

Martin, E. P., & Martin, J. M. (1995). *Social work and the black experience.* Washington, DC: NASW Press.

National Association of Social Workers. (2008). *Code of ethics.* Washington, DC: Author.

Solomon, B. (1976). *Black perspective: Social work in oppressed communities.* New York, NY: Columbia Press.

U.S. Census Bureau. (2012). *Growth in urban population outpaces rest of nation, Census Bureau reports.* Washington, DC: Author.

Preface

This is the cutting-edge diversified urban human services book we have all been waiting for. Although many social workers and other human service professionals work in urban settings, few have been educated in programs that deliberately focus on urban environments, and even fewer emphasize the unique experiences of African Americans in those environments. Compiling and managing the process for publishing this book has been a true labor of love. Our final nudge came from our mentor and colleague, Dr. Jay Carrington Chunn, who transitioned only a few weeks after we submitted the successful book proposal to Springer Publishing Company. Several of us were planning an urban social work book, but CSWE accreditation and building a school of social work became such a huge task that no one had time to even think about it, but Dr. Chunn! He literally pushed us for a couple of years and would not let it fade from our view, and finally we were ready to move forward with an idea that had been brewing for years.

Over the course of the past 20 years, I have had a unique opportunity to participate in the process for building a school of social work at an institution designated as the State's Urban University. When I arrived on the campus of Morgan State University as a newly appointed assistant professor in what was then the department of social work, it was an exciting, yet grueling time. My department chair at the time, Anna McPhatter had just arrived the year before. The department, a BSW Program that was started in the early 1970s, had a long history with many graduates, but it had become stagnant with a small faculty that had all worked in the department for 20 plus years. Well, Anna McPhatter does not do stagnant! I remember that when she saw me doing well over my share of advising students or chairing too many department committees, she would say, "it won't always be like this." It was that promise, and the energy and excitement that were exchanged in the classroom with my students that formed the initial foundation for the reasons I stayed.

Later, when an opportunity presented itself, we were asked to develop an MSW and PhD Program, but even before then we knew we had something pretty special going on. With courses on diversity, social and economic justice, and Black families in our BSW Program, our graduates had earned a solid reputation in the public and private human service agencies throughout the Baltimore and Washington, DC, metropolitan area. Students would often recall situations in the field placement agency in which the MSW students from other institutions would rely on them for their knowledge and skills when working with various client populations. We knew we were doing something unique, but I do not think we really knew how important it was, until our students and graduates and agencies continuously confirmed it for us over and over again.

The something different is a unique perspective as social work educators on how to engage clients in urban environments, particularly African Americans. You will find that unique perspective weaved throughout our course syllabi in all three of our social work programs. And that unique perspective is reflected throughout every chapter in this book.

What we know for sure is that fear can never be a factor when engaging the populations we serve. Because many of our students come from the various communities we prepare them to serve, they are a valuable resource in the classroom and in creating a curriculum that best meets the needs of the urban community. We also believe that urban social work cannot be divided into micro, mezzo, and macro, but that urban social workers need skills in all areas in order to meet the needs of complex urban populations. Urban social workers have to constantly be thinking outside the box, working with other professionals on interdisciplinary teams, and with residents of the community in their neighborhoods, churches, schools, and homes in order for transformation to take root. Meeting people where they are is not just a social work slogan we add to our lectures when we do not know what else to say, it is a skill that we teach our students to use, so they can do their very best work.

This book should be used with any group of students being prepared to be comfortable working in and negotiating urban centers, and those who want to realize the unique experiences and challenges faced by African Americans in those environments. It can be used at the undergraduate and graduate level. And there are some interesting topics and perspectives you have not read about before that will certainly challenge your worldview. It addresses the challenges of urban social work in regard to public health, health, and mental health; substance abuse, criminal justice, and violence prevention; navigating the urban built environment; and the intersection between African Americans and other diverse groups.

The experiences of African Americans in urban communities are unique, and require an in-depth appreciation of the interface between micro- and macro-level factors to be truly understood. This text, an outgrowth of an actual urban social work curriculum with a focus on the African American experience, field education, community engagement, and practice, presents a framework for urban social work practice that encompasses a deep understanding of the challenges faced by this community. From a perspective based on empowerment, strengths, resilience, cultural competence, and multiculturalism, this book delivers proven strategies for social work practice with the urban African American population.

As additional aids in preparing students in the understandings, perspectives, and competencies necessary for practice in the urban African American environment, qualified instructors can request both an Instructors' Manual and chapter based PowerPoint presentations by emailing textbook@springerpub.com.

Rhonda Wilbon

Acknowledgment

The editors would like to thank Ms. Erin Harris for her commitment and assistance with the many tasks associated with editing a book. We would never have met our goals and time lines without all your hard work.

CHAPTER   **1**

Urban Social Work With African Americans: Critical Perspectives, Concepts, and Theories

Anna R. McPhatter

Conceptualizing social work within an urban context with a specific population is a multifaceted endeavor that demands much thought and reflection. As a school of social work within a 150-year-old historically Black university, designated as the state's urban research university, the task becomes even more daunting as efforts are made to clarify the essentials of this endeavor for our own program within the local context as well as make a meaningful contribution to the broader urban community contexts. To facilitate the task at hand, the profession of social work offers foundational elements such as accreditation standards and codes of ethics on which to build a conceptual framework for examining the human experience in context. The Council on Social Work Education's 2008 Educational Policies and Accreditation Standards (EPAS, 2008) states that "context encompasses the mission of the institution in which the program is located and the needs and opportunities associated with the setting. Programs are further influenced by their historical, political, economic, social, cultural, demographic, and global contexts." Reflecting the significance of a mission relative to context, Morgan State University's mission states that the university:

> Serves the community, region, state, nation, and world as an intellectual and creative resource by supporting, empowering and preparing high-quality, diverse graduates to lead the world. The University offers innovative, inclusive, and distinctive educational experiences to a broad cross section of the population in a comprehensive range of disciplines at the baccalaureate, master's, doctoral, and professional degree levels. Through collaborative pursuits, scholarly research, creative endeavors, and dedicated public service, the University gives significant priority to addressing societal problems, particularly those prevalent in urban communities. (Morgan State University, 2012)

Derived from this university-level mission, the School of Social Work's mission at the Morgan State University is "To fully prepare urban social work leaders who are committed to the alleviation of human suffering, social justice, and the improvement of the quality of life for diverse urban populations."

The discussion in this chapter reflects the experiences of our school as we have worked to bring our social work programs in concert with the urban context in which we educate and train our students. In this discussion, the conceptualization of urban social work with African Americans emerges from contextual, historical, cultural, social, demographic, political, economic, and global parameters. The education and training of social work students include perspectives, concepts, and theories that have proven critical to effectively work with African American people and communities. Following a brief discussion of the underlying assumptions, beliefs, and principles that undergirded the analysis of the school and resulted in refocusing and reframing a long-term urban social work emphasis, further description of concepts, perspectives, and theories that have been found critical for the practice of social work in urban environments is provided. Also discussed are examples of relevant courses and curriculum content included to describe critical knowledge, values, and skills that are essential in preparing urban social workers.

UNDERLYING ASSUMPTIONS, BELIEFS, AND PRINCIPLES

In the substantive review of our Bachelor of Social Work and Master of Social Work curriculums, considerable time was spent in discussing principles, beliefs, and assumptions, which would prove important in this arduous process. Viewing Morgan's School of Social Work as a case example, it is hoped that these will be helpful for others engaging in a similar process. These beliefs and principles include:

Society is not color-blind; therefore race, ethnicity, culture, gender, disability, language of origin, and sexual orientation, always matter. Since the founding of this country and the import of slaves into America, the history of racism has continued to permeate every aspect of U.S. society. One does not have to look far for recent examples, such as Ferguson, Missouri, and the killing of Michael Brown, a young African American man, by a White police officer who suffered no consequence or retribution. Over the past year, the criminal justice system has shown many examples of how the color of one's skin determines the value of one's life and that this practice continues nationally with impunity. In practicing with African Americans in urban communities, this reality must always be at the forefront of the urban social worker's thoughts, together with well-developed methods of assessment and interventions to address the presenting needs of these communities.

Eurocentric values, worldviews, traditions, development and dissemination of knowledge, and practice interventions do not reflect the history and life experiences of people of African descent, and therefore are largely ineffective as currently practiced within the broad arena of professional social work. Much of social work history, theory development, and practice perspectives, although acknowledging the importance of culturally competent social work practice, rarely pursue cultural competence as a critical goal with the forthrightness and depth required when working with African Americans and other people of color. The roles of history, race, and culture in psychosocial–spiritual development and in individual, family, and community experiences unfortunately do not have a place of prominence in most social work practice (McPhatter, 2004). Schiele (1997, 2010) vigorously challenges both the validity of Eurocentric social and behavioral science as the singular way of knowing and the effectiveness of intervention approaches that derive therefrom.

Engagement with African Americans within an urban context by necessity includes the environmental context; history; experiences of structural oppression; classism; internalized oppression, as well as strengths and resilience. Since its inception, the profession of social work has touted the importance of the environmental context in serving people. Unfortunately, the profession has waned in its emphasis on these contextual factors, especially in what is most often conceptualized as "clinical social work" and the tendency to isolate social work as either micro or macro. Most social workers in the United States choose micro social work, also known as direct or clinical practice, and fail to see macro practice as an essential component to micro or mezzo practice. This failure alone denies persons of African descent the importance of the totality of their experiences in the United States. The nature of oppression and discrimination and how it impacts African Americans both individually and institutionally, and strategies for addressing these are absolutely a priority in any interaction in which social workers engage with this population (McPhatter, 1997; McPhatter & Ganaway, 2003). Moreover, urban social workers must be knowledgeable about the role they may play in exercising their own privilege and be committed to giving up those privileges to attain the goal of social justice. Social workers must also understand the dynamics of internalized oppression and how this dynamic perpetuates oppression as well as proscribe negative self-concepts and low self-esteem. Additionally, although the profession of social work expresses a propensity toward the incorporation of strengths and resilience in their approach to practice, by its failure to not only be knowledgeable about these as they play out in African American lives and collective communities, social workers still predominantly utilize deficit-oriented models inherent in conceptualizations of clinical social work practice. The historic resilience and strengths of African American communities must be elucidated in practice and also used as starting points for personal and collective empowerment (Hill, 1972; Martin & Martin, 2002).

Urban social workers have an ethical obligation to know and understand the landscape that makes up the lives of the people they serve and must always work toward the goal of cultural competency and effectiveness in carrying out their professional roles. This principle applies to any context and any area of social work practice; it is particularly important when the people served by the social worker are culturally, racially, and ethnically different from the social worker, their colleagues, and the agencies within which they practice. As McPhatter (1997) queries, "what would be the purpose of attempting to serve people one is unwilling to learn about?" Urban social workers simply do not have an option to not spend the time and effort to become thoroughly immersed in the culture of people of African descent and all of the nuances they bring to the service encounter (Martin & Martin, 2002).

Individuals and families residing in inner cities and urban environments are heavily impacted by the seemingly insurmountable social and economic problems they face. Working to help urban individuals and families must be approached equally within the context of working to help communities become well. It is our belief that urban people can rarely achieve wholeness when their communities are not whole. Simply stated, the work of urban social workers must always be about partnering and collaborating with urban communities for the larger common good. This, by necessity, includes an advocacy, social justice, and empowerment emphasis in the perspectives and practice approaches of urban social work. While individual, family, and small group interventions are certainly important, they must always be undertaken with a broader and more societal and global view as the context (McPhatter, 2004).

These beliefs, assumptions, and principles have served as a critical guide to Morgan School of Social Work's approach to educating and training social workers. They inform the school's thinking, they reflect curricula models, and they serve as the basis for conceptualization of urban social work with African Americans. Although commonly used social work theories, perspectives, and practice approaches are not excluded, subjecting these to the scrutiny of the appropriateness for African Americans in urban communities similar to the one that makes up the urban context is common practice in our program. With optimism, the principles and frameworks tried, tested, and adopted in Morgan's School of Social Work will be relevant to and used by other urban programs and be seen as pertinent to social work regardless of where it is practiced.

CRITICAL CONCEPTS, PERSPECTIVES, AND THEORIES

The following theories, concepts, and perspectives serve as the foundation for urban social work as integrated in the programs at Morgan's School of Social Work. Undoubtedly, other perspectives might have been selected, but the ones selected have been found to be grounded both historically and practically for the population for which students are being prepared. These include African-centered perspective, cultural competence, advocacy and empowerment, and strengths and resilience.

African-Centered Perspective

The Afrocentric paradigms emerged from several African American psychologists and other social scientists who had grown weary and frustrated with the deficit-oriented views of African American life and who documented the inconsistencies of these views with the reality of life experiences of people of African descent (Akbar, 1984; Asante,

1988; Schiele, 1996, 1997, 2010). Eurocentric worldviews reflected a belief system that placed the European American worldview, culture, and behavior as the norms and certainly preferred if not superior to others, specifically those of African American people, which are often described as dysfunctional and as never quite measuring up to the Eurocentric yardstick. Moreover, Asante (1987, 1988), who is credited with coining the term Afrocentricity, indicates that Afrocentric frameworks solidly place the study of people of African descent within African cultural values and worldviews. This theoretical perspective then would challenge social workers to view human behavior and functioning of African Americans and thus tailor their practice interventions within the African cultural context and traditions.

Schiele (1997) defines Afrocentric social work as "a method of social work practice based on traditional African philosophical assumptions that are used to explain and to solve human and societal problems" (p. 803). African-centered social work includes knowledge, values, and skills that evolve from a foundation of historical and cultural aspects of West Africa from which slavery predominantly emanated and survived over time, but these life experiences of African descendants most often are used as strengths in contemporary African American communities. This approach is indeed rooted in the values of ancient African experiences that survived in the DNA of people of African descent and are easily identified by social workers when they are knowledgeable about these experiences.

The African-centered perspective has three major foci (Schiele, 2010): (a) It promotes an alternative social science paradigm toward one that most reflects the cultural and political reality of African Americans and away from paradigms that are staunchly Eurocentric in ideology; (b) the African-centered perspective moves toward the removal of negative distortions, preconceived notions, and damaging theoretical and practice approaches toward people of African ancestry, and legitimizes a worldview more particular to that carried in the minds, hearts, and practices of everyday life experiences of African Americans; and (c) the African-centered perspective promotes a worldview that fosters human and societal transformations inclusive of universal needs for spiritual, moral, and humanistic endeavors. The African-centered perspective is essential as a theoretical concept that forces urban social workers to think differently and reflectively about the African American experience in the United States and how that experience evolves from deeply rooted cultural values, folkways, family structures, and individual and community behaviors. It reminds the social worker that African American people are not, in fact, "willy-nilly" mimicking the White world and that African American culture, language, dialects, child-rearing practices, and civic and social institutions of support are historic, well developed, and thoughtfully executed every single day despite the obstacles that exist in the communities. Moreover, the African-centered perspective enables the urban social worker to draw on a number of approaches for working with African American individuals, families, and communities (Bent-Goodley, 2005).

Bent-Goodley describes a number of African-centered principles that inform practice with victims of domestic violence but can be used as belief systems and approaches for a broader perspective on practice with people of African ancestry. These principles are briefly summarized as follows:

Fundamental goodness—This principle states that people are inherently good and are not predisposed toward harming or hurting others. Adopting this principle will help urban social workers begin to see people who have been vilified in media and other societal arenas as worthy and valuable members of the society.

Self-knowledge—This principle essentially denotes the importance of the social worker being conscious of his or her own self and nature, recognizing areas of deficit and needs for growth and healing, and acknowledging, for example, his or her own privileged status and how that status often contributes to maintaining structures that oppress others. The worker must come to grips with his or her lack of knowledge about the experiences of urban African Americans and commit to begin the process of remedying this void in his or her education and practice experiences; and it is most critical regarding self-knowledge for the worker to honestly assess the extent to which his or her work is damaging to the individual and community empowerment that must occur in his or her practice with African Americans.

Communalism—This principle describes communalism by Harvey (2001; Harvey and Hill, 2004) as the "sensitivity to the interdependence of people and the notion that group concerns transcend individual strivings." Much of what is taught in social work focuses on the individual and often negates the familial, let alone community, context in which individual functioning and behavior occur. This tragedy is amplified with African Americans in urban communities daily, without any thought to the interdependence of individuals and the impact of extended families and neighborhoods. Students in social work education cannot be allowed to miss this fundamental principle as they structure their work with people in the urban environment, particularly people of color.

Interconnectedness—This principle further highlights the connections African Americans make in collective struggles for survival, to respond to oppression, and to work toward the health and well-being of the collective. There is rarely a single African American who does not understand what the "hook up" means and the context in which it is expressed. This is a colloquialism that essentially says, "I am looking out for you," and is stated to express mutuality.

Spirituality—This principle is a major component of African-centered theory and occupies a place of centrality among most, if not all, of the contemporary scholars of Afrocentricity (Harvey, 2001; Martin & Martin, 1995, 2002; Schiele, 1997, 2010). Spirituality, although having different meanings for different people, essentially recognizes the existence of a universal "God," a sacred or divine force on which people can rely for guidance, healing, and survival. Although African Americans are predominantly connected with organized religious traditions, the role of spirituality in their daily life existence can never be understated. Martin and Martin (1995) eloquently described the traditions of people of African descent to utilize spirituals and blues, that is, "Moanin"—identifying the problem; "Mourning"—examining and identifying pain and suffering and the path needed for healing through collective empathy, support, and hope; and "Morning"—an indication through spirituals and the early morning connection with Jesus that they were on the verge of a breakthrough. The wider social work profession has come to accept and embellish the role of spirituality in human development and behavior and the subsequent practice of social work. However, social workers who practice with African Americans will need to not only grasp the significance of spirituality and religion to this group, but be cognizant and conversant with them about the role of the pastor and the Black church in any social work intervention.

Self-reliance—This principle refers to the ability of the individual to develop the kind of life skills that enable them to make contributions to the whole through their own efforts. This principle implies that strengthening oneself in all personalized arenas is not targeted at self-realization alone but a deep expectation is that others participate in this effort of self-development and they expect to benefit from individual contributions as well. An example of this principle is the case in which whole African American communities contribute to the educational success of a young man or woman from their community, with the explicit understanding that the person will come back to the community to contribute in whatever manner he or she can.

Language and oral tradition—This principle, which is reflected in the African-centered paradigm, refers to West African traditions of multiple methods of communication, including rhythms expressed in drums, music, dance, blues, hip hop, dialects, and other tools used to communicate or confuse outsiders. In contemporary America, communication has become increasingly complex with the advent of social media, which demands that the urban social worker be ever vigilant regarding intergenerational communication differences, the intention of communication, the target of messages, the integrity of the messages, and the effectiveness of communication that comes from trust developed in the relationship.

Cultural Competence

Cultural competence was selected by the school as one of the pillars for urban social work practice. Cultural competence has been defined as the ability to transform knowledge and cultural awareness into health and/or psychosocial interventions that support and sustain healthy client system functioning within the appropriate cultural context (McPhatter, 1997). Green (1995) indicates that the culturally competent practitioner conducts professional work in a way that is congruent with the behavior and expectations that members of a distinctive culture recognize as appropriate among themselves. It is from these perspectives that the following guiding principles derive:

1. Culturally competent social work practice is a mandate that all practitioners and agencies must pursue.

2. Achieving the goal of cultural competence is a multilevel, multisystemic effort that includes individual, interprofessional, and organizational activities.

3. Becoming culturally competent requires commitment from the top level of the organization and must be reflected in the organizational mission and values, as well as fiscal and human resources. Just as agencies develop strategic plans for carrying out their overall mission with measurable outcomes, cultural competence as a goal must be held to a similar standard of measure.

4. Cultural competence is a protracted endeavor and should never be treated as a one-time initiative or as an afterthought; failure to include cultural competence as a priority in the overall purpose, mission, goals, and objectives of the organization sends a message to practitioners as well as those served by the organization that cultural competence is not important and even minimal efforts by a few committed individuals will fall short.

The urban social worker must always be on the journey of becoming culturally competent. Lacking knowledge, values, and skills to practice effectively within a cultural context essentially limits the practitioner's work to minimal usefulness. Social workers who work within every geographic and demographic area must have cultural competency as a high priority in their work. This means that there is a working familiarity with the culture of the population in which the worker practices, along with an ongoing commitment to learn about the values, beliefs, family orientations, strengths, religious orientations, and other values of a population. McPhatter (1997) proposed a Cultural Competence Attainment Model that includes the following components:

- *Enlightened consciousness*—restructuring one's worldview to include acceptance of other cultures and beliefs to be as valuable and acceptable as one's own. This is often a difficult and painful process as one is often challenged to reject socialization, values and norms of his or her own family, his or her formal education, and that of the wider society that places value on people based on their race, ethnicity, and/or gender. This work is critical as one engages the cultural competence protracted process.
- *Grounded knowledge base*—examining and adapting formal as well as informal education to reject the Eurocentric bias, which is the foundation of our learned history, mythology, values, and science, toward incorporating a comprehensive range of information from diverse communities, disciplines, religions, social institutions, family structures, and communities; and analysis of theoretical constructs with an emphasis on strength-based and resilience concepts. This knowledge base is inclusive of how institutional structures historically impede the well-being of communities of color.
- *Cumulative skill proficiency*—engaging in a skill development process that builds proficiency through focused reflection and evaluation in addition to knowledge. Ability to intervene at the individual, family, organizational, community, and policy levels to achieve not only needed resources and services, but also social justice and system change.

Social work attracts practitioners, who most often have altruistic intentions, selfless spirits, and the motivation to make a difference. Good intentions, however, must not stand in the way of an honest self-appraisal, and the willingness to embark on a sustained journey of continued development toward cultural competence. The increasingly diverse children, families, groups, and communities we serve deserve nothing less.

Cultural competence may be viewed from a client-centered or an organizational perspective. McPhatter (1997, 2004) stated: "Achieving cultural competence is a dynamic protracted and developmental change process that requires genuine commitment on the part of chief executive staff, mid-level managers, direct service workers and support staff...the organization is actively pursuing identifiable and measurable outcomes." The goals for a culturally competent organization include a diverse workforce, a well-developed strategic plan for achieving cultural competence, partnership with diverse communities, a structure for facilitating professional cultural competence goal attainment, cultural competence performance goals in employee evaluations and provision of knowledge, and training toward a continuous journey that enhances the organization (McPhatter, 1997, 2004). Cultural competence enhances practice effectiveness and sets up a circular process whereby culturally diverse clients are successfully served. Likewise, urban practitioners experience success and pride in meaningful ways while impacting the lives of others. In addition, the organization itself achieves its mission in a manner that positively impacts the larger community.

Empowerment and Advocacy

Similar to the African-centered perspective and cultural competence, advocacy and empowerment are viewed as critical endeavors in which students must be adept. Empowerment and advocacy have been included in the social work methods of intervention and as guiding principles for achieving social justice for several decades. Empowerment is defined by Whitmore (1988) as "an interactive process through which people experience personal and social change, enabling them to take action to achieve influence over the organizations and institutions which affect their lives and the communities in which they live" (p. 13). This point of view acknowledges that the primary goal of empowerment at the individual level is to help clients gain power and reduce powerlessness over anything that blocks their ability to lead healthy fulfilling lives. It aims to increase self-confidence, and is an interpersonal as well as collaborative process. Social work pursues empowerment as a global endeavor and as a way of addressing oppression and discrimination inherent in the structures and institutions of the larger society. Anderson, Wilson, Lengwe-Katembula, and Osei-Hwedie (1994) developed a model of empowerment in Africa that included five practice dimensions: personal, social, educational, economic, and political. Social workers practice within these realms one at a time or all at the same time. While practitioners most often work in the personal dimension with individual clients, it is critical for urban social workers to always include all five dimensions in their areas of function. Urban social workers are challenged by complex environmental issues that are unrelenting in the lives of people who live in inner cities. The urban social workers must be absolutely as competent in addressing personal issues of powerlessness as they are in engaging agencies and institutions that block opportunities for large segments of the urban community. For example, helping clients address low self-esteem and lack of basic resources may occur at the micro- or mezzo level; assisting a neighborhood with recalcitrant landlords would require macro-level engagement and collaboration to bring forth educational, economic, and political dimensions of empowerment.

At the core of empowerment and advocacy is the representation of the interests of powerless people and through the utilization of the people's own voices work to achieve social justice and equality. Whether advocacy occurs at the case level or identifies a larger cause as the focus, urban social workers do not have the luxury of choosing one or the other. It is their role to always keep at the forefront of their work these larger issues that demand their knowledge and skills and that impact individuals and families. Lord and Hutchinson (1993) developed the following Empowerment Principles for Community Practice based on the research and experience of vulnerable people who were engaged in efforts of gaining power over their lives and communities:

1. In order to understand empowerment, citizens who are devalued must be seen as oppressed and marginalized by society, not simply as clients to be served. Sources of oppression range from poverty and abuse to social isolation and lack of access to valued resources.

2. Service systems must give up their control over people who are currently devalued. This means eliminating the power relationships that exist between professionals and citizens by ensuring collaboration and supporting consumer-controlled initiatives.

3. For a power transfer to occur, citizens must be the ones to identify the problems and solutions to personal and community issues and must have direct access to funding that normally only goes to service agencies.

4. Although power cannot be given to people by professionals, concerned professionals (urban social workers) can work to eliminate the systematic barriers that have been created, which oppress, control, and disempower vulnerable citizens.

5. Listening to the concerns, stories, feelings, experiences, and hopes of people who feel powerless is the basis for broadening people's awareness of their oppression. The language of professionalism, which encourages dependency and control, needs to be replaced by dialogue, which supports mutuality and reciprocity.

6. Build on the strengths and capacities of citizens and avoid a focus on deficits. This is critical for building self-esteem, which is both an outcome and part of the empowerment process.

7. Participation in community life at three levels is critical for the empowerment of individuals: working on issues that affect their own lives; connecting with others who have had similar experiences; and being involved in a range of community groups and activities.

8. Encourage and support citizens to make ongoing contributions to their communities through access to valued social roles, such as employee, volunteer, mentor, advocate, or friend.

9. Citizens who are consumers of services should have control over the resources and personal supports they need to live with dignity.

10. It is possible to learn important strategies about prevention from studying the process of empowerment, for example, as people become more empowered, they rely less on formal service systems and more on informal support networks. These learnings can be used as important principles for proactively empowering potentially vulnerable individuals and groups.

Strengths and Resilience

Strengths and resilience are critical additional dimensions to the previously discussed perspectives essential to urban social work. Social work has embraced a strengths perspective as an important way of viewing people, their personal and social problems in favor of the deficit and pathology orientation, which has been characteristic of the profession since its early beginnings. A focus on what is wrong with people rather than their strengths limits a multitude of opportunities for people to grow interpersonally as well as within their social context. Weick (1992) suggests that "every person has an inherent power that may be characterized as life force, transformational capacity, life energy, spirituality, regenerative potential, and healing power…that can guide personal and social transformation" (p. 24). In this, the assumption is that within each of us there is a capacity to learn, relearn, grow, and change. Saleebey (1992) adds that "individuals and groups have vast, often untapped and frequently unappreciated reservoirs of physical, emotional, cognitive, interpersonal, social, and spiritual energies, resources and competencies" (p. 6). People not only survive difficult traumas and life experiences, but often learn and grow from these experiences finding them to be of great benefit.

The strengths perspective when applied to African Americans often refers to their ability to not only survive slavery, oppression, discrimination, profiling in the justice system, and socioeconomic disadvantage but also to thrive in spite of these insidious attacks. Black families, for example, rely heavily on extended family, fictive kin, informal social networks, the Black church, and self-help and civic societies as buffers for challenging and stressful life events. Hill (1972) and Hines and Boyd-Franklin (1996) describe strengths of Black families to include loyal and strong kinship bonds; flexible family roles; deep religious faith; and orientations toward work, education, and achievement. These dimensions of Black family life are too often overlooked by social workers who maintain narrow practice perspectives and interventions steeped in pathology, preconceived ideas, and a focus on their own cultural yardstick. A strengths perspective requires that an urban social worker be extremely knowledgeable about the numerous services and resources available in urban communities at both the informal and formal institutional levels. They must be knowledgeable about policies and programs that are culturally competent, accessible, and beneficial to urban people. Moreover, they absolutely must be skilled at both assisting clients and in removing barriers to service provision through their own advocacy. Partnering and collaborating with clients or consumers and modeling strategic and effective interventions with these systems leave lasting lessons on empowerment at both the individual and community levels. Urban social workers do not fall prey to economic or political systems that have left out the voices of urban people but become major allies with urban dwellers in challenging these systems that do not behave in the best interest of people of color.

Saleebey (2002) developed an extensive list of questions that may be used in assessing strengths. For example: How have you managed thus far given all the challenges you have had to contend with? What have you learned about yourself and your world during your struggles? Which people have given you special understanding, support, and guidance? When things were going well in life, what was different? What, now, do you want out of life? What are your hopes, visions, and aspirations? What is it about your life, yourself, and your accomplishments that gives you real pride? These questions and similar others assist the social worker in moving the emphasis toward the capture of personal and social strengths and in essence remind people of the inherent resilience that they already possess.

Resilience refers to people's innate capacity to respond to challenging and adverse events they encounter over their life course, reducing the chance that these events will result in negative or debilitating outcomes. All people have this inherent quality but whether it is used effectively to ward off difficult life issues depends on the extent to which people recognize and are aware of this capacity and the extent to which people have relied on this capacity in past life events. Resilience includes personal qualities and environmental resources that facilitate health and overall well-being. A resilience perspective requires the social worker to pursue and focus on what works and why. Understanding what helps people respond effectively to adversity gives clues for new social work interventions that can be used for future adaptations to traumatic or stressful events. Bachay and Cingel (1999) in a qualitative analysis of minority women, found that self-efficacy, well-defined faith lives, and the ability to reframe barriers and obstacles were important protective factors that enhanced their resilience. Others have identified family cohesion and higher satisfaction with social support (Carbonell, 1996), community closeness, faith in people, compassion, and spirituality (McMillen and Fisher, 1998) as buffers and protective factors for negative life issues, whether related to normal biopsychosocial development or unanticipated crises. A strong racial and cultural identity has also been found to enhance resilience. Altogether, these personal characteristics and environmental assets present important avenues for urban social workers to tap into as they incorporate these strengths into personal and community empowerment (Carlton-LaNey, 2001).

CONCEPTUALIZING A SOCIAL WORK CURRICULUM: CASE STUDY

The program completed an in-depth analysis and review of the vision, mission, and goals for the social work programs. We developed the aforementioned assumptions, beliefs, and values, and then agreed that the curriculum would be grounded in the previously discussed theories, concepts, and perspectives. We certainly did not consider these to be exhaustive, but rather a starting point for ongoing deliberations and change. For example, we continue to embrace ecological perspective and generalist practice as foundational and significant in our conceptualization of culturally competent social work practice. We are vigilant, nonetheless, in our emphasis on the African-centered paradigms—cultural competence as an ever-present goal, empowerment, strengths, and resilience—which is absolutely critical for practice with African Americans who reside in urban environments. The discussion that follows will provide examples of our curriculum, which we believe are in concert with our overall contextual practice framework. The school's goals also frame the curriculum and will also be included.

SCHOOL OF SOCIAL WORK GOALS

1. To prepare social work leaders, activist scholars, and practitioners committed to solving urban social and economic problems and enhancing the quality of life of urban populations and communities.

2. To develop a cadre of social work professionals who are culturally competent, knowledgeable, and skilled in addressing all forms and mechanisms of social injustice, oppression, and discrimination.

3. Through varied social research and knowledge development and dissemination, contribute to best practices with African American families, communities, and organizations and other historically disenfranchised and marginalized populations and communities.

4. Utilizing democratic values, social work values and ethics, a global perspective, and critical pedagogy, socialize graduates with compassion and commitment to service civic and community engagement with particular emphasis on addressing issues of poverty, human suffering, and socioeconomic disadvantage.

5. To develop an appreciation for the historical and contemporary contributions of African Americans to the field of social welfare and social work as the context for urban social work practice.

The curriculum that was subsequently developed evolved from the school's goals and included, for example, some of the following required and/or elective courses. (See Table 1.1 for a complete list of courses.)

TABLE 1.1 MSW Curriculum Sample

Foundation Curriculum Courses (All Required)	
SOWK 501: Generalist Social Work Practice (Practice I)	3
SOWK 502: Neighborhood Advocacy and Development in Poor Urban Communities (Practice II)	3
SOWK 503: Foundation Practicum I (16 hours/week) (Field I)	3
SOWK 504: Foundation Practicum II (16 hours/week) (Field II)	3
SOWK 505: Life Course Development and Issues (HBSE I)	3
SOWK 506: Urban Organizations, Neighborhoods and Communities (HBSE II)	3
SOWK 507: Social Welfare and Urban Economics (Policy I)	3
SOWK 509: Chemical Dependency and Community Violence: Urban Perspectives	3
SOWK 510: Research and Urban Social Problems (Research I)	3
Advanced Curriculum Core Courses (All Required)	
SOWK 601: Psychopathology and Clinical Intervention (Practice III)	3
SOWK 602: Social Work Practice With Urban Black Families (Practice IV)	3
SOWK 603: Advanced Field Practicum III (24 hours/week) (Field III)	3
SOWK 604: Advanced Field Practicum IV (24 hours/week) (Field IV)	3
SOWK 608: Organizational Policy and Leadership in Human Services (Policy II)	3
SOWK 610: Evaluation Research of Urban Social Problems, Services and Interventions (Research II)	3
Concentration Courses and Recommended Electives **Gerontology (* Indicates Required Courses for Concentration)**	
SOWK 620: Urban Social Work Practice With the Aged and Their Families*	3
SOWK 621: Social Forces Affecting Older Adults and Their Families*	3
SOWK 622: Coping With Losses and Grief*	3
SOWK 623: Implications of Intergenerational Issues for Urban Adults	3
Urban Children, Youth and Families (* Indicates Required Courses for Concentration)	
SOWK 630: Urban Child Welfare*	3
SOWK 631: Child Abuse and Neglect*	3
SOWK 632: Juvenile Justice: Prevention, Development and Intervention*	3
SOWK 643: Popular Youth Culture	3
School Social Work(* Indicates Required Courses for Concentration)	
SOWK 640: Social Work in Urban Schools*	3
SOWK 641: Schools in Communities*	3
SOWK 642: Urban School Social Work and Special Education*	3
SOWK 643: Popular Youth Culture	3
Public Health Social Work(* Indicates Required Courses for Concentration)	
SOWK 650: Social Work Practice in Health and Disease Prevention*	3
SOWK 651: Epidemiology*	3

(continued)

TABLE 1.1 MSW Curriculum Sample   (*continued*)

SOWK 652: Maternal and Child Health Macro Practice, Programs and Policies	3
SOWK 653: Public Health Policy, Urban Health Services, Issues and Planning*	3
Other Electives	
SOWK 670: Spirituality, Religions and the Helping Tradition	3

Required Courses

- Advocacy and development in poor underserved communities
- Generalist practice in urban communities
- Chemical dependency and community violence
- Clinical intervention with Black families

Elective Courses

- Spirituality, religions, and the helping tradition
- Coping with grief and loss across the life span
- Juvenile justice and delinquency prevention
- Popular youth culture
- Social work in urban schools

The competencies that follow also include a sample from the various courses that reflect not only the underlying belief structure discussed earlier but also the theoretical and conceptual constructs discussed. The course competencies are critical for urban social work and serve as examples of knowledge, values, and skills students are expected to acquire on completion of the program:

1. Demonstrate a comprehensive knowledge of the *Diagnostic and Statistical Manual of Mental Disorders* (5th ed.; *DSM–5*; American Psychiatric Association, 2013) and understand the evolution of the *DSM-5* and the forms and mechanisms of oppression and discrimination.

2. Demonstrate knowledge of traditional West African family formation and functioning prior to the onset of the international slave trade, including an understanding of basic concepts, definitions, and trends, and the identification of cultural values and historical forces that have shaped life experiences of African–Black families, including extended and aged kin, from slavery to the current era.

3. Critically analyze major theoretical perspectives that have developed over the past 100 years on Black families' structures and functioning, applying best practices for assessment, intervention, and evaluation.

4. Demonstrate an understanding of basic social problems African–Black families have experienced over time and common results–reactions to adversity in urban centers.

5. Develop and apply advanced skills in assessing African–Black families' strengths, resources, and potentialities, and demonstrate clinical skills for the assessment, diagnosis, and treatment of Black families in urban environments.

6. Develop an ability to analyze social policy and its impact on the lives of African–Black families—particularly those who reside in urban environments—from a historical and contemporary perspective.

7. Identify, critique, and analyze the contributions of African American social welfare pioneers to the field of social work, social work practice, social justice, and public policy, and their impact on the current social work practice context that influences the life experiences of African–Black families.

8. Acquire new knowledge and understanding of theories and values of planned organization change in the context of social services to African Americans and other urban minority families, children, other organizations, and communities.

9. Understand the barriers to equitable participation of all persons who, because of labels, are denied access to basic social rights and privileges as clients and providers in human service organizations and an ability to apply this knowledge to policy designs and intervention strategies.

10. Recognize and assess the historical context and the connection of discrimination across the life span and the implications for those oppressed groups as they age.

11. Recognize the importance of religion and spirituality among diverse populations in shaping life experiences related to mourning practices and the role of grief and loss at the same time as they are facing a range of social problems with the intent of gaining awareness, combating oppression and discrimination, and encouraging the unique coping skills within such marginalized groups.

12. Comprehend how the interdependence of generations across the life course recognizes the contributions of all age-group members to strengthen communities and organizations.

13. Respect and promote older adults' rights to dignity and self-determination; and assess and address the adverse impacts of aging policies on historically disadvantaged populations.

14. Understand relationships among poverty, race, culture, gender, class, and the dynamics of oppression, and how these contribute to overrepresentation of African American and other children of color in the child welfare system.

15. Identify and differentiate appropriate approaches and strategies for culturally competent practice with African American children and their families and other oppressed inner-city school populations while demonstrating an understanding of and sensitivity to the role of poverty and oppression in the lives of disadvantaged inner-city children and their families.

16. Demonstrate an ability to negotiate urban communities, organizations, and public and private agencies for the benefit of urban youth with an emphasis on understanding and interpreting the role of micro, mezzo, and macro-practice models in the promotion of organizational change on behalf of urban youth, including developing a sense of responsibility for activism to promote such change.

17. Identify and critically reflect on urban African American and other diverse spiritual perspectives and experiences.

IMPLICATIONS

This chapter has presented what are believed to be critical theories, concepts, and practice perspectives essential for effective practice with African Americans within the urban context. Although these reflect promising practices among African American scholars and practitioners, nonetheless, they are not exhaustive. It is strongly believed that if urban social workers pursue these theoretical and practice perspectives, they are much more likely to be effective in their work with African Americans who live in urban communities. More importantly, a lack of understanding of these critical areas most assuredly perpetuates culturally ineffective practice, which will frustrate the worker, increase chances of burnout, and, even worse, result in negative or damaging outcomes for a substantial population of Americans.

To begin with, the urban practice community must commit to becoming culturally competent as individuals, interpersonally, and organizationally. This would include a critical examination of the underlying assumptions, values, and beliefs hereto described. Undoubtedly, if an honest examination occurs, the need for further knowledge, values, and skills will become apparent. This very simply requires an acknowledgment that "typical" social work knowledge, values, and skills taught in many schools of social work that continue to be Eurocentric in their orientation do not meet the needs of African Americans in urban communities as they also do not do so for other historically marginalized groups. We willingly acknowledge that some of these traditional perspectives do have value, but we do not believe that they provide the depth that is required for competent practice with these oppressed groups. Moreover, our experiences have been that social workers, even during this time in our history, still have trouble freely and honestly addressing issues that impact African Americans, such as racism, or serving as models for addressing individual and structural discrimination for their students. It is our fervent hope that this work will serve as an impetus for once again making what seem to be difficult topics to embrace a priority, with the goal of making a real difference in the lives and communities of a substantial population in our country. Inability to do so will continue to have serious negative implications on social work practice for African Americans, other people of color, as well as the broader social work community. Still needed in order to further strengthen the constructs herein embraced is practice-related research, which can possibly add to what has already been developed, predominantly by scholars of African descent. This requires, however, some commitment to developing and disseminating new knowledge that acknowledges and is grounded in the cultural values representative of people of African descent. These principles should undergird any practice or research endeavors taken on by the profession of social work that is targeted at African Americans or other oppressed groups. The implications of commitment to this work are profound and should be approached with the immediacy demanded if global social work goals are to be reached. The whole of society will certainly be better off if the profession of social work is able to make significant strides in effectively addressing the needs of communities that are still on the margins of achieving equality and social justice.

FOR FURTHER STUDY

Suggested Readings

Akbar, N. (1984). Africentric social sciences for human liberation. *Journal of Black Studies, 14*, 395–414.

Asante, M. K. (2003). *Afrocentricity, the theory of social change*. Chicago, IL: African American Images.

Asante, M. K. (2007). *An Afrocentric manifesto: Toward an African Renaissance*. New York, NY: Polity.

Asante, M. K. (2011). *Afrocentric idea revised*. Philadelphia, PA: Temple University Press.

Bent-Goodley, T. B. (2003). Policy implications of the criminal justice system for African American families and communities. In T. B. Bent-Goodley (Ed.), *African American Social Workers and Social Policy* (pp. 137–161). New York, NY: Routledge.

Carlton-LaNey, I. B. (Ed.). (2001). *African American leadership: An empowerment tradition in social welfare history*. Washington, DC: NASW Press.

Carlton-LaNey, I. B. (2005). *African Americans aging in the rural south: Stories of faith, family and community*. Durham, NC: Sourwood Press.

Carlton-LaNey, I. B., & Alexander, S. C. (2001). Early African American social welfare pioneer women: Working to empower the race and the community. *Journal of Ethnic and Cultural Diversity, 10*(2), 67–84.

Carlton-LaNey, I. B., & Burwell, N. Y. (2014). *African American community practice models: Historical and contemporary responses*. Binghamton, NY: Routledge.

Chipungu, S. S. (2003). Child welfare policies and African-American families. In T. B. Bent-Goodley (Ed.), *African American Social Workers and Social Policy* (pp. 55–68). New York, NY: Routledge.

Everett, J., Chipungu, S. S., & Leashore, B. R. (Eds.). (2004). *Child welfare revisited: An Africentric perspective*. Piscataway, NJ: Rutgers University Press.

Freeman, E. M., & Logan, S. L. (Eds.). (2004). *Reconceptualizing the strengths and common heritage of black families: Practice, research, and policy issues.* Springfield, IL: Charles C Thomas.

Green, J. W. (1999). *Cultural awareness in the human services: A multi-ethnic approach* (2nd ed.). Boston, MA: Allyn and Bacon.

Hill, R. B. (1999). *The strengths of African American families: Twenty-five years later.* Lanham, MD: University Press of America.

Hill, R. B. (2003). *The strengths of black families* (2nd ed.). New York, NY: University Press of America.

Logan, S. L., Freeman, E. M, & McRoy, R. G. (1990). *Social work practice with black families: A culturally specific perspective.* New York, NY: Longman Publishing Group.

Martin, E. P., & Martin, J. M. (1995). *Social work and the black experience.* Washington, DC: NASW Press.

Martin, E. P., & Martin, J. M. (2002). *Spirituality and the black helping tradition in social work.* Washington, DC: NASW Press.

Martin, J. M., & Martin, E. P. (1985). *The helping tradition in the black family and community.* Silver Spring, MD: National Association of Social Workers.

McAdoo, H. P. (Ed.). (2006). *Black families.* Thousand Oaks, CA: Sage.

McAdoo, H. P., & McAdoo, J. L. (2002). The dynamics of African American fathers' family roles. In H. P. McAdoo (Ed.), *Black children: Social, educational, and parental environments* (2nd ed., pp. 3–11). Thousand Oaks, CA: Sage.

Harriette Pipes McAdoo (Ed.). (2002). *Black children: Social, educational, and parental environments.* Thousand Oaks, CA: Sage.

Saleebey, D. (Ed.). (2002). *The strengths perspective in social work practice.* Boston, MA: Allyn and Bacon.

Schiele, J. H. (1996). Afrocentricity: An emerging paradigm in social work practice. *Social Work, 41*(3), 284–294.

Schiele, J. H. (2013). *Human services and the Afrocentric paradigm.* London: Routledge.

Schiele, J. H., & Hopps, J. G. (2009). Racial minorities then and now: The continuing significance of race. *Social Work, 54*(3), 195.

Solomon, B. B. (1976). Black empowerment: Social work in oppressed communities.

Solomon, B. B. (1987). Empowerment: Social work in oppressed communities. *Journal of Social Work Practice, 2*(4), 79–91.

Velazquez, J., McPhatter, A., & Yang, K. (2003). Perspectives on cultural competence: A special issue of CWLA's *Child Welfare Journal. Child Welfare Journal* LXXXII(2) (March–April)

REFERENCES

Akbar, N. (1984). Africentric social sciences for human liberation. *Journal of Black Studies, 14*, 395–414.

American Psychiatric Association. (2013). *Diagnostic and statistical manual of mental disorders* (5th ed.). Arlington, VA: American Psychiatric Publishing.

Anderson, S. C., Wilson, M. K., Lengwe-Katembula, M., & Osei-Hwedie, K. (1994). Empowerment and social work education and practice in Africa. *Journal of Social Development in Africa, 9*(2), 71–86. Cited in Payne, M. (1997). *Modern social work theory* (2nd ed.). Chicago, IL: Lyceum Books, Inc.

Asante, M. K. (1987). *The Afrocentric idea.* Philadelphia, PA: Temple University Press.

Asante, M. K. (1988). *Afrocentricity.* Trenton, NJ: Africa World Press.

Bachay, J. B., & Cingel, P. A. (1999). Restructuring resilience: Emerging voices. *AFFILIA: Journal of Women and Social Work, 14*(2), 162–175.

Bent-Goodley, T. (2005). An African-centered approach to domestic violence. *Families in Society, 86*(2), 197–206.

Carbonell, D. M. (1996). *Resilience in late adolescence: Young people at risk who have positive functioning* (Dissertation). Simmons College, April.

Carlton-LaNey, I. B. (Ed.). (2001). African American leadership: An empowerment tradition in social welfare history. Washington, DC: NASW Press.

Green, J. W. (1995). *Cultural awareness in the human services: A multi-ethnic approach.* Boston, MA: Allyn and Bacon.

Harvey, A. R. (2001). Individual and family intervention skills with African Americans: An Africentric approach. In R. Fong & S. Furuto (Eds.), *Culturally competent practice: Skills, interventions and evaluations* (pp. 225–240). New York, NY: Haworth.

Harvey, A. R., & Hill, R. B. (2004). Africentric youth and family rites of passage program: Promoting resilience among at-risk African American youth. *Social Work, 49*(1), 65–74.

Hill, R. B. (1972). *The strengths of Black families.* New York, NY: Emerson Hall.

Hines, P. M., & Boyd-Franklin, N. (1996). African American families. In M. McGoldrick, J. Giordana, & J. K. Pearce (Eds.), *Ethnicity and family therapy* (2nd ed., pp. 66–84). New York, NY: Guilford Press.

Lord, J., & Hutchinson, P. (1993). The process of empowerment: Implications for theory and practice. *Canadian Journal of Community Health, 12*(1), 5–22.

Martin, E. P., & Martin, J. M. (1995). *Social work and the black experience.* Washington, DC: National Association of Social Workers.

Martin, E. P., & Martin, J. M. (2002). *Spirituality and the black helping tradition in social work.* Washington, DC: NASW Press.

McMillen, J. C., & Fisher, R. H. (1998). The perceived benefit scales: Measuring perceived positive life changes after negative events. *Social Work Research, 22*(3), 173–186.

McPhatter, A. R. (1997). Cultural competence in child welfare. *Child Welfare, 77*(1), 255–278.

McPhatter, A. R. (2004). Modeling culturally competent practice. In M. Austin & K. Hopkins (Eds.), *Supervision as collaboration in the human services* (Chapter 5). Thousand Oaks, CA: Sage.

McPhatter, A. R., & Ganaway, T. (2003). Beyond the rhetoric: Strategies for implementing culturally effective practice with children, families and communities. *Child Welfare, 82*(2), pp. 103–124.

Saleebey, D. (1992). Introduction: Power in the people. In D. Saleebey (Ed.), *The strengths perspective in social work practice,* pp. 3–17. New York, NY: Longman.

Saleebey, D. (2002). *The strengths perspective in social work practice* (3rd ed.). New York, NY: Allyn and Bacon.

Schiele, J. H. (1996). Afrocentricity: An emerging paradigm in social work practice. *Social Work, 41*(3), 284–294.

Schiele, J. H. (1997). The contour and meaning of Afrocentric social work. *Journal of Black Studies, 27*(6), 803–804.

Schiele, J. H. (2010). *Human services and the Afrocentric paradigm.* New York, NY: Routledge.

Weick, A. (1992). Building a strengths perspective for social work. In D. Saleebey (ed.), *The strengths perspective in social work practice.* New York, NY: Longman.

Whitmore, E. (1988). *Empowerment and the process of inquiry.* A paper presented at the annual meeting of the Canadian Association of Schools of Social Work, Windsor, Ontario. Cited in Lord and Hutchison (1993). The process of empowerment: Implications for theory and practice. *Canadian Journal of Community Health, 12*(1), 5–22.

CHAPTER 2

African American Pioneers of Urban Social Work

Iris Carlton-LaNey

African American pioneers in social work developed their own unique system of social welfare for the African American community. Denied access to the myriad social work and social welfare organizations emerging at the turn of the 20th century, African Americans relied on each other for support and aid, and, thus, developed a parallel social welfare system. The mutual beneficence that provided the impetus for African American social welfare development had its origins in African culture and history, which promulgated the interconnectedness of all things and taught the significance of the collective over the focus on individuals.

The widespread social and economic problems in rural communities during the early 1900s prompted African Americans to begin a migratory trek from the rural South to urban areas of the North, Midwest, and West; the Great Migration would last for more than 30 years. A wide range of factors contributed to this migration, including Jim Crowism, lynching, peonage, convict leasing, extremely poor living conditions, and multiple years of failing crops due to floods, depleted soil, and the ravages of the cotton boll weevil. The few positive factors contributing to the migration were related to the industrial and commercial innovations in the urban centers that promised employment opportunities. However, the cities were neither prepared nor willing to accept the hordes of African Americans who were inundating their boundaries. Instead, these new migrants were greeted with blatant race and gender discrimination. African Americans were paid the lowest wages, denied membership in trade unions, herded into the poorest quality of housing, and victimized by an unscrupulous urban system that saw no value in them beyond their unskilled, low-skilled, and cheap labor.

The African American social welfare leadership of the Progressive Era included members of the "talented tenth"[1] as well as those individuals who assumed positions of leadership because of the sheer vastness of need and their inability to sit idly by and wait. African Americans were able to respond to these intense problems through hard work and frugality as well as a strong understanding of and reliance on shared values and the imperative of collective actions.

Lack of formal resources confronted urban dwellers in subtle and blatant ways. Issues critical to the quality of life among African American urban dwellers were marked by what was lacking, including the lack of health care, child care, employment, educational access, and safe and affordable housing. These problems were addressed in myriad ways by women's clubs, sororities and fraternities, philanthropists, health care professionals, business women and men, educators, and social workers. These individuals and organizations shared a focus on individual and group uplift, middle-class mores, and a determination to mentor and model acceptable behavior that provided a foundation that undergirded their impetus to work. These reformers used a variety of approaches to meet the needs of the African Americans in urban communities such as establishing social welfare organizations, schools, old folks' homes, orphanages, and settlement houses. In addition, magazines, newsletters, newspapers, tracks, scholarly research, and the power of oratory formed the mechanisms for gathering data, disseminating information, and motivating action and interaction.

These various methods of communications between those in need and those developing and providing services were critical to the development of informal and formal social welfare systems. The emergence of a social welfare system was particularly significant to families migrating from rural agrarian areas to urban communities where the mutual beneficence of their small rural communities was no longer available. Furthermore, the racial discrimination in the urban environments created even more complications for migrant families trying to transition to urban life. These families experienced crowded, dilapidated, and ill-suited housing in the blighted urban centers (Wolfinger, 2009). Money was scarce and the work that was available to African American men did not provide sufficient income for them to care adequately for their families. In general, African American women were forced to seek work outside their homes where they found few employment opportunities other than low-wage domestic and personal service jobs. Children and youth were particularly vulnerable to the risks of the urban environment because they were often left without supervision as their parents scrounged out a living in the parsimonious and punitive work environment of cities. Few formal social services were available to youth. Yet, through the initiative of African American race women and race men, a system of social service delivery was designed and implemented to meet the needs of these communities, to serve families, and to protect the vulnerable.

WOMEN'S CLUB

African American women's clubs proliferated during the late 1800s and early 1900s. These women's groups began to establish social welfare services in response to the social problems that inundated the segregated urban African American communities.

Women's clubs were established by an array of organizations, ranging from faith-based groups to secret societies (Evans, 2007). These organizations consisted of church groups such as the National Baptist Association of Colored Women and various faith-based ladies' auxiliaries. Secret fraternal organizations were also part of the Women's Club Movement, including the Order of the Eastern Star, the Grand United Order of Salem, the Daughters of Zion, and Greek letter sororities. Sororities organized by college women began in 1908 with the founding of the Alpha Kappa Alpha Sorority at Howard University. Other sororities soon followed, including Delta Sigma Theta (1911) and Zeta Phi Beta (1920), both of which were also founded at Howard. Finally, in 1922, the Sigma Gamma Rho Sorority was founded at Butler University in Indianapolis (Terborg-Penn, 2005).

Multidimensional professional women's groups can also be counted as part of the club movement and included groups such as the National Association of Colored Graduate Nurses, which was founded in 1907 in New York City, and the Madam C. J. Walker Hair Culturist Union of America, which was established in 1906. These women's groups worked to provide direct services to their members and to bring a voice and political power to the African American community (Carlton-LaNey, 2011).

Perhaps the most prominent club among all the African American women's groups was the National Association of Colored Women's Clubs, founded in 1896. This organization has been described by Hine (1989, p. 917) as the "largest and most enduring protest organization" in African American history. Evans's (2007) description of these women's clubs lauds their political energy and their focused determination. Moreover, Evans (p. 64) noted that these women "carried out administrative coups, filibustered and stonewalled reminiscent of the most powerful board rooms and staterooms." The women's skillful mediating abilities served them well and enabled them to organize and strategize in service to their community. They served small towns as well as the largest urban communities. These reformers were astute political players who understood the politics of change and the necessity of their engagement.

THE POLITICS OF REFORM

The women and men who formally entered the political arena often did so without actually running for political office, although many eventually did, including community leaders such as Elizabeth Ross Haynes, who was elected as coleader of the 21st Assembly District in Harlem, New York, in 1935. Although Ida B. Wells-Barnett ran for the Illinois State Senate in 1930, she never held elected office. These women understood the power of the vote and advocated that African Americans exercise their right to influence laws that governed them. Wells-Barnett strongly encouraged African American political involvement; to further that end, she founded the Alpha Suffrage Club, which was the first political club for African American women in Illinois (Bay, 2009). Wells-Barnett used the Alpha Suffrage Club to "demonstrate the significance of the ballot to the masses of black women in Chicago" (Hendricks, 1994, p. 176).

Although women were often discouraged from political involvement, some women garnered positive public attention and support for their efforts in the political arena, which in turn, served to increase their political power and group support. For example, in Richmond, Virginia, Maggie Lena Walker was selected to run for the position of superintendent of public instruction on that state's Lily Black Republican ticket. Walker was also an active member of the Virginia Federation of Colored Women's Clubs and a strong supporter of the Virginia Industrial School for Colored Girls. This web of affiliations was common among pioneer social workers and reformers. When the state took over the Industrial School's management, Walker accepted a gubernatorial appointment to serve on the school's board (Marlowe, 1993). For many of the African American reformers, their oratorical and negotiating skills served them well politically and brought them national and international notoriety. For example, a White Illinois Republican Congresswoman, Ruth Hanna McCormick, sought out well-known Washington, DC–based Mary Church Terrell "to run her campaign to female black voters" (Bay, 2009, p. 325). Terrell was an internationally known activist, a skilled and highly sought after public speaker, and a prominent club woman who dedicated her life to race work. She was also a well-connected and influential part of the urban elite.

Other political leaders, whose work had an urban focus, became members of President Franklin Roosevelt's Black Cabinet, including Eugene Kinckle Jones, the field secretary and second executive director of the National Urban League (NUL), and Mary McLeod Bethune, club woman and founder of Bethune Cookman College. Although the Black Cabinet has been described as being somewhat impotent, its existence demonstrated organized group advocacy for and by African Americans. Bethune was the only female member of the Black Cabinet, and she was appointed to head the Office of Minority Affairs of the National Youth Administration, a position she held for 8 years from 1936 to 1944.

SETTLEMENT HOUSES

African American reformers used their influence and support to establish settlement houses in their communities to help meet the needs of the rapidly growing African American urban population. These segregated settlement houses were poorly financed but, nonetheless, provided a plethora of services and programs that benefited African Americans who had migrated to urban centers such as Chicago, New York, Minneapolis, Philadelphia, Washington, DC, as well as cities across the country. By 1913, Chicago had four settlement houses for African Americans: the Wendell Phillip Settlement, the Frederick Douglass Center, the Enterprise Institute, and Ida B. Wells-Barnett's Negro Fellowship League and Reading Room. These settlements houses were established to facilitate community uplift by providing clubs, lectures, community improvement projects, kindergartens, reading materials, and affordable boarding rooms.

Philadelphia's African American community grew very rapidly during the Progressive Era, and by the early 1930s was the third largest in the country behind

New York City and Chicago (Wolfinger, 2009). Housing was one of the worst problems for residents of North Philadelphia, the area where large numbers of migrants resided. Philadelphia was also home to the famed Wharton Center, which was a settlement house that provided recreational and community social services. In addition, the Wharton Center focused on housing and strategies for addressing neighborhood issues. Without an initial overt political agenda, the Wharton Center fostered self-awareness and empowerment among residents. The settlement leaders organized neighborhood beautification projects and worked to change the area into usable and productive spaces such as playgrounds and areas for special social events (Wharton Center, n.d.).

Another prominent settlement house, the Phyllis Wheatley[2] House, opened in Minneapolis in 1924. The Wheatley House, under the leadership of well-trained and charismatic head, W. Gertrude Brown, offered four departments: recreation, education, music, and dramatics. Through these departments, men, women, and children could engage in wholesome leisure programs. The settlement also had "transient bedrooms" that were made available to noted African Americans artists who were not allowed to rent rooms in the local racially segregated hotels. African American students who were admitted to the University of Minnesota, but who were not allowed to reside on campus, also found housing at the Phyllis Wheatley (Karger, 1986).

Settlement houses were not as successful among African Americans as they were in the White immigrant community; yet, the settlement houses were a critical part of social welfare programs' discourse on the urban social problems created by the rapid urbanization of African Americans. Organized leisure activities were especially desirable and were seen as a way to divert the new urban residents from the vice of red light districts that permeated their communities.

THE NATIONAL URBAN LEAGUE

The NUL epitomized urban social work among African Americans. George Edmund Haynes, along with Ruth Standish Baldwin, founded the NUL in 1911. The NUL became a social movement akin to the social settlement house movement and was part of the Progressive Era's response to urban poverty and need. Under Haynes's executive leadership from 1911 to 1918, the NUL provided social services to African American migrants in cities across the United States. Haynes's research and scholarship provided the NUL with a firm foundation on which to design and build the services and programs for this new urban population. The NUL's goals included serving and protecting children, women and girls, and families. Interracial cooperation was also a key feature of the NUL's strategy for service development and delivery. NUL's mission was multifaceted, and included a range of activities from ensuring the availability of wholesome recreation (e.g., by working to provide playgrounds, clean places of amusement, boys' and girls' clubs) to promoting neighborhood unions, and to preparing workers for employment opportunities (Carlton-LaNey, 1983, 1994).

Investigating conditions of city life and securing and training African American social workers were significant to the NUL's service delivery plan. The NUL fellowship program, also under George Haynes's leadership, was open to promising African American students who had completed college and who wanted a career in social work. Candidates were selected by a Fellowship Committee composed of NUL Executive Board members, and then placed in various schools of social work for training (Carlton-LaNey, 1994).

Haynes was at the epicenter of discourse on African American urban migration. A doctoral graduate from Columbia University and the first African American graduate of the New York School of Philanthropy, Haynes spent much of his early career studying the urban migration and work situations of African Americans as they moved from the South to cities in the North and the Midwest. His dissertation, *The Negro at Work in New York City: A Study in Social Progress*, was published in 1912. This study painted a rather bleak picture of employment among African Americans in cities, noting their opportunities for joining unions were severely limited and the few African Americans who were allowed to join trade unions did not receive union wages due to widespread racial discrimination. Haynes also noted the necessity of women's employment, although their low wages did not provide enough income for their families to live in safe, decent housing. Instead, these families were forced to take in lodgers; this situation, along with the absence of the working mothers, was believed to have a negative impact on the children and the family structure, leaving these families vulnerable to physical and moral disruption (Carlton-LaNey, 1983).

Although taking in lodgers contributed to a home's overcrowding and was not always ideal for family stability, it was a way for families to support each other as well as the extended family and fictive kin network. In many cases, the lodgers were family, friends, or distant relatives who were migrating to cities and in need of temporary housing. Women largely supported this migratory stream, encouraging family to move North and help each new migrant to become acclimated to city life (Hine, 1991).

The conditions of urban slum dwellers, whether immigrants from European countries or African American migrants from the Southern states, were the focus of tremendous discourse and scientific scrutiny. Like Haynes, other sociologists, social workers, and reformers turned their attention to the causes of and solutions to problems that befell African Americans in urban communities. For example, in his study of African Americans in Boston, Daniels (1914, p. 176) wrote that the necessity of women working outside the home imposed severe "obstacles to home-building" and "retard[ed] the formation of a strong and healthy Negro community" (p. 177). Similarly, Ovington (1911, p. 38), a dedicated civil rights activist, suffragist, and journalist, expressed grave concern about the African American infant mortality rate. She noted that, "Negro mothers, owing to the low wage earned by their husbands . . . leave their home [for employment] but . . . sacrifice the lives of many of their babies." Ovington was often the only White person in the neighborhoods where she chose to live and work, and found "the poorer the family . . . the more enviable appears the fortune of the anti-social class," and consequently, the children of the poor who grow up "pure in thought and deed" do so in spite of their surroundings (1911, p. 38). The bleakness of Ovington's forecast was in synchrony with the general discourse of social workers and reformers who decried the widespread practice of taking in boarders as a way to supplement the family's income as the "lodger evil" (Park & Kemp, 2006, p. 716).

Club women, settlement house workers, and social reformers considered the community's moral well-being as part of their responsibility, and therefore, their purview included modeling appropriate behavior, developing programs to teach healthful and productive living, and cautioning residents against unbecoming and destructive living practices. For example, Lugenia Burns Hope's Atlanta Neighborhood Union included four departments, one of which was the Moral and Educational Department. Within this department, an investigation committee operated with the goal of "improving the moral fiber of the communities" (Rouse, 1984, p. 120). Members of the investigation committee kept a close eye on their neighborhood and reported back to the director anything that looked suspicious or that might pose a risk to community moral cleanliness (Rouse, 1984). Although the goals of the Neighborhood Union articulated neighborliness and inclusiveness, these oversight and reporting practices served to reinforce invidious distinctions. The club women were part of Atlanta's urban culture and were intolerant of those who failed their test of moral uprightness. The club women focused little on the fallen individuals and instead concentrated on prevention as a strategy for community betterment.

Many club women expended tremendous time and energy on teaching and educating as a strategy for improving the race. Charlotte Hawkins Brown, founder of Palmer Memorial Institute, a private school for upper class African Americans, was convinced that suitable behavior and social graces were essential for African Americans to become acceptable to Whites. In an effort to reach that goal, in 1941, Brown published her seminal work, *The Correct Thing to Do, to Say, to Wear*. To ensure that Palmer Memorial Institute students were prepared to negotiate the world on graduation, students were required to read and practice the directives prescribed in the book. However, Brown did not completely reject poor and lower class African Americans, as was evident from her work with the Efland Home for Girls (North Carolina), which was a training school for girls who had run-ins with the criminal justice system.

Many other African Americans who were also part of the urban elite refused to denigrate the less fortunate of their race, and instead engaged in compassionate outreach. For example, George Edmund Haynes believed that rescuing and serving those who had become victims of vice and crime were part of his duty as a social worker and as a Christian. When the police closed a local brothel in Nashville leaving the African American sex workers homeless, Haynes did not disparage them for their work, but stepped in to ensure that the women had safe alternative housing available to them. He responded similarly to the poor families who were victims of the East Nashville Fire in 1916. Haynes began to identify possible problem-solving approaches even before the fire was brought under control (Carlton-LaNey, 1996).

HOUSING IN THE CITIES

Large numbers of single men and women also migrated to cities in the North and Midwest. Several gender-related themes permeate the scholarship on African American urban migration. Young unattached women were particularly vulnerable. These young women faced delimited job options, isolated lives without family and children, and lacked personal–private living space. In general, the same types of jobs that they left in the South were waiting for them in Northern and Midwestern cities. However, in the cities, these women had fewer employment opportunities and sometimes faced greater discrimination than they had in the South. Why then did single women leave the rural Southern communities in such large numbers? Hine (1991) posits that personal self-sufficiency and the imperative to escape sexual victimization from both African American and White men were their motivations for migration. Many of these women were mothers who made the difficult decision to leave their children with kin while they took the opportunity to migrate. Live-in maid positions were easy transitions for the women and often the only opportunity for employment. Even though the women expected to work in personal service, most were, nonetheless, disappointed to find their opportunities so circumscribed.

Many social welfare efforts targeted this population of women. African American social reformers were themselves closely connected to the women they helped. They shared similar life experiences circumscribed by the same foreboding rules of seg-regation and discrimination. Housing was one of the primary obstacles facing these new migrants. Reformers were especially concerned about migrant women's housing situations.

Working girls' homes were established in urban centers throughout the North and Midwest. Victoria Earle Matthews founded the White Rose Mission and Industrial Association in 1897 in New York City. The White Rose Mission was established as a home for African American working girls and women where they could be educated and trained following the principles of "right living" and mutual aid. The Mission's goal was to protect independent African American girls who were moving to New York alone. The White Rose Mission became a refuge and haven for young single women (Waites, 2001).

Nearly 20 years later, Jane Edna Hunter opened the Phyllis Wheatley Home in 1913 in Cleveland, Ohio. Hunter recalled her own struggle with securing reputable, safe hous-ing when she migrated from her home state of South Carolina to Cleveland. By 1927, the home had grown from a small rented house to a 11-story residence that was eventu-ally renamed the Phyllis Wheatley Association (Jane Edna Hunter Papers, n.d.; Jones, 1993), and served as a model for other cities struggling with the problem of housing for women who were migrating to cities alone. Hunter's successful advocacy for women and girls made her a prominent figure in local politics and a role model for others across the country who embraced a similar mission.

Chicago also had a Phyllis Wheatley Home for Women, which was opened in 1908 with the same goals of protecting young women migrating to the city without friends

or family by providing safe housing in a healthy enviro
Home for Women offered a Christian influence, employr
(Jackson, 1978).

The nation's capital had two settlement houses that se
women migrating to Washington, DC: the Sojourner Trut
and Girls and the Home for Friendless Colored Girls (I
founded with the help of the First Lady Frances Clevela
working women (Miller Center, 2014).

Providing safe and accessible housing for migrants moving to cities was a major
chore and one to which several reformers dedicated their lives. Circumstances of urban
migration and life in the city left other groups vulnerable as well. Orphans and the elderly
were also in need of safe and sanitary housing. The housing needs of these groups were
addressed by secret orders, churches, women's clubs, and philanthropists who established
old folk's homes and orphanages. Homes for indigent aged were established in Atlanta,
St. Paul, Philadelphia, New Orleans, and other major cities. In Atlanta, the Carter's Old
Folks Home was established by the Friendship Baptist Church under the leadership of
Reverend Edward R. Carter. Other examples of the private efforts to house and care for
indigent elders and orphans include the Attucks Industrial School, Orphanage, and Old
Folks Home in St. Paul, Minnesota; the Negro Baptist's Old Folks Home in Richmond,
Virginia; the Home for Aged and Infirm Colored People in Chicago, Illinois; and Lafon's
Old Folks' Home in New Orleans, Louisiana (Carlton-LaNey, 1989; Jackson, 1978).
Philanthropist Thomy Lafon of New Orleans, for whom the Lafon Old Folks' home
was named, and business woman Eartha Mary Magdalene White were instrumental
in providing housing for the aged. White established the Mercy Hospital for the Aged
in Jacksonville, Florida and later replaced it with the M. M. White Nursing Home, a
122-bed facility named in honor of her mother (Johnson, 1993).

African American children were also affected profoundly by the migration of and
urbanization of African Americans. In many cases, elderly family members and young
children were left behind as young adults migrated to the North, Midwest, and West.
These family members' needs were exasperated by their isolation and lack of caregiver
attention. Establishing facilities in southern cities was often the response to these groups'
needs. In addition to housing the elderly in old folks' homes, social workers and reformers also focused on providing child care and support for indigent children.

TAKING CARE OF CHILDREN AND YOUTH

Concern for the welfare and supervision of children and youth was a significant issue
among urban dwellers. In response to the needs of the burgeoning number of children
and youth in the cities, the social reformers led the way in opening kindergartens, day
nurseries, schools, orphanages, boys' and girls' clubs, and training schools. The financial
necessity for African American mothers to work outside of the home meant that these
women either had to arrange child care or the children were left alone and unsupervised.

Sometimes a lodger who was an elder family member would take the responsibility of child care while parents worked. Unfortunately, many children were often left at home alone, and many suffered the dire and deadly consequences. Unwilling to accept this level of child endangerment, social workers and social reformers devised responses.

Ida Barbour, a teacher and community activist in Portsmouth, Virginia, founded the Miller Home and Day Nursery in 1910. This facility provided a safe space for children while their mothers worked. The facility also provided temporary housing for children whose parents were detained by the judicial system. When the influenza pandemic inundated Portsmouth in 1918, the Miller Home provided care for ill children whose mothers were working. The Miller Home and Day Nursery was unique in its provision of temporary housing for children and their parents. This was a critical need, especially for those women who were live-in maids and had no housing aside from their quarters in the employers' homes (Fairfax, 2007).

Other Virginians also committed their lives to the welfare of the state's children. Janie Porter Barrett's interest in the welfare of young girls began with a series of weekly meetings in her home in Hampton. Barrett was concerned about the young girls' futures and life chances, and worked to transform these informal gatherings into the more formally organized Locust Street Settlement. Through the settlement, the National Health Week was established with the goal of bringing attention to improving the health and well-being of the community, particularly its children.

After an incident in the local community in which a very young girl was at risk of being sent to prison, Barrett was motivated to establish a formal alternative to prisons for girls who were found guilty of crimes. Subsequently, she became one of the founders of the Virginia Industrial School for Colored Girls. The Virginia School provided an alternative to prison for girls who found themselves in trouble with the law or were deemed to be delinquents. The school's goal was to rehabilitate delinquents girls by building character and teaching self-discipline, "with the expectation that, when ready, a girl could be 'paroled' to a private family in the Richmond area and work for normal wages" (Social Welfare History Project, 2014, para. 2). Barrett and the women of the Virginia Federation of Colored Women raised money to build a facility to protect and train these young girls and to give them an opportunity for a meaningful future. The Virginia School became a model using the most up-to-date information for reform available. Barrett became the head of the School, a position she held until she retired in 1940 at the age of 75 years (Peebles-Wilkins, 2001; Scott, 1993).

Modeled after the Virginia Industrial School for Colored Girls, the Efland Home for Girls was founded by the North Carolina Federation of Negro Women in Efland, North Carolina. Under the leadership of Charlotte Hawkins Brown, the home, also known as the North Carolina Industrial Home for Colored Girls, was opened in 1921. The general neglect of delinquent African American girls in the state and the club women's mission to "uplift" African American women provided the impetus for establishing this home (White, 1998). Similar to the Virginia Industrial School and others established to serve delinquents, the Efland Home was not located in an urban community, but many of the girls were from the larger, more urban communities throughout the state. Because Efland

Home was the only such facility in North Carolina, it served African American girls from across the state.

The Efland Home for Girls was privately funded and received only a small stipend from the state of North Carolina. However, the state had similar facilities for White boys and girls and African American boys who were more adequately funded by the state. Determined that African American girls should not be neglected and subjected to terms of incarceration in the adult prisons, the North Carolina Federation of Negro Women developed programs to prepare these girls for productive lives through religious instruction, "an improved social environment, industrial training, and character building" (Brice, 2005, p. 306).

Efforts to serve boys and to address their needs were also critical. Settlement house programs generally included a person in the role of "boy's worker," who designed and implemented programs specifically targeting boys, their interests, and their preparation for adulthood. Birdye Haynes, executive director of New York's Lincoln House in 1915, was particularly attuned to the needs of boys and was emphatic that the settlement house would not turn away the boys who were criticized as troublemakers and nuisances in the neighborhood. Instead, Haynes insisted that the settlement house's boys would become so polished and refined that they would be looked on as assets that the neighborhood would be pleased to have around. Haynes seemed to delight in the boys' energy and helped to plan programs that would divert their forces and provide active and constructive roles for them in the house (Carlton-LaNey, 1994).

Using a similar approach as Haynes's, Atlanta's Neighborhood Union planned a series of services and programs for girls and boys in the community. With assistance from young college men attending Morehouse College, the Neighborhood Union was able to expand its programming to include training in military tactics, and athletics (Rouse, 1984).

Responding to the "consequences of urbanization on men" in the North Carolina mountain community of Asheville, a group of African American men worked to interrupt the culture that they believed "stunted the growth of a respectable black manhood" (Hornsby, 2001, p. 277). The concept of *respectable black manhood* was a complex construct in urban communities during the early 1900s. For African American males, the line between boyhood and manhood was blurred by strict rules of segregation and institutional racism. African American men learned to exist in a segregated space circumscribed by both formal and informal legal, economic, social, and political practices. Violations of those practices could mean certain death. Yet, the African American men in Asheville believed that existing social programs had failed African American boys, and that they had to act on behalf of all African American manhood.

The result of their initiative was the Young Men's Institute (YMI). The YMI was intended to provide a wholesome diversion for boys that would nurture them and keep them from drifting into dangerous and destructive life styles. The YMI worked to develop temperance in behavior and thought while teaching the boys to live useful, virtuous, and wholesome lives. The YMI programs resembled the goals of the YMCA and the settlement houses, and provided social outlets for the boys in the community.

The YMI building provided a segregated space for African American men to exert their manhood and to model character and expectations for the community's boys. Although the threat of mob violence and lynching was omnipresent, the founders of the YMI used the segregated and gendered space to serve boys. A variety of social service programs were housed in the YMI building including "a boarding house, gymnasium, kindergarten, school of domestic science for girls, and a bathing department" (Hornsby, 2001, pp. 293–294). Although the YMI was designed to serve the boys of the community, it provided an important service to the entire Asheville African American community. For example, even though the building was a gendered space where men and boys were given preferential treatment, women and girls were also an integral part of the services delivered through the YMI.

DISCUSSION

The social work or welfare activities of urban communities during the Progressive Era involved both social betterment and social protest initiatives. Social betterment efforts focused on developing human capital and protecting the most vulnerable members of the community. Social protest aimed to secure a more equitable distribution of societal resources and to ensure access to societal participation (O'Donnell, 1996). These two approaches did not exist as separate entities, but were seamlessly integrated into the social welfare community.

The self-help ideology embraced by the African American community fueled their development of services and programs to meet persistent and evolving needs of the community. These services and programs targeted needs that spanned from the concrete provision of safe, sanitary housing to the more abstract aspects of character building. Neighbors served each other's immediate needs as illustrated through the Atlanta Neighborhood Union. At the same time, national leaders and organizations orchestrated and organized social protest to call attention to problems, and to demonstrate the African American community's unrest and unwillingness to accept continued systemic exclusion. The delimitations of institutionalized racism, the success of social programs along with the realization of incremental change seemed to provide the indefatigable determination that fueled Progressive Era reform among African Americans.

IMPLICATIONS

This brief examination of African American social work/welfare historical antecedents suggests significant implications for contemporary practice. The social work or welfare pioneers understood the social problems that needed to be addressed and devised plans of attack. Many of the social problems of the turn of the 1900s continue to plague the African American community and many of their services and programs continue to provide models for dealing with these contemporary urban problems. Today urban social work practice tends to focus on and intervene at the individual and family levels. Early African American social workers had a strong community focus and believed that their responsibility was to ensure the growth and sustainability of the larger community. This reflects commitment to the collective over the individual.

Essentially their work had a "we" focus. Their various organizations' mottos reflected this focus and approach. For example, the National Association of Colored Women's Clubs motto of "lifting as we climb" and the NUL's "not alms, but opportunity" both suggest a focus on the collective over the individual. The National Association of Black Social Workers' (NABSW) mission embraces the pioneers' legacy of community well-being. As encouragement to contemporary practitioners, the NABSW states in part, "If a sense of community awareness is a precondition to humanitarian acts, then we must use our knowledge of the Black community, our commitment to its self-determination, and our helping skills for the benefit of Black people as we marshal our expertise to improve the quality of life of Black people" (Hamilton-Mason & Gonzalez-Ramos, 2006; NABSW, 1968).

This strong community focus suggests to contemporary social workers that we need to reacquaint ourselves with the communities that we serve. We need to reinvest in those communities, get to know the resources therein, and call on the community for direction and support. Furthermore, these austere and politically conservative times call for a renewed commitment to service and to creative approaches to meeting human needs.

Our pioneers were able to accomplish a great deal with very little funding. Their commitment seemed to drive them along with their willing to contribute personal resources of professional skills, political power, and financial assets. Our historical antecedents approach to practice also suggests the importance of fostering and cultivating informal community networks.

FOR FURTHER STUDY

Suggested Assignments

1. The *Intellectual Biography* is a good assignment for students to examine a pioneer social work or welfare leader's intellectual contributions using primary data. With this assignment, students will enhance their research and analytical skill along with their critical thinking abilities as they examine an aspect of the pioneer's life and contributions using documents that the pioneer wrote or that were written during the time that the pioneer lived and worked. This is NOT a biography. This assignment is discussed in some depth in Carlton-LaNey (1990).

2. *Small group exercise*: Students review details of a historical event such as the *Wilmington Insurrection of 1898* (also known as the *Wilmington Massacre*

of 1898) or the *Red Summer of 1919* and discuss how and why African American pioneers in social work might have responded to those major racial incidences.

3. *Historical implications for contemporary practice*: Students engage with each other in identifying and discussing how history impacts contemporary issues that individuals, families, and communities face. For example, accumulated wealth is clearly related to history and societal access granted or denied. Discuss ways that this knowledge might impact contemporary social work practice?

Suggested Readings

Bent-Goodley, T. (2006). Oral histories of contemporary African American social work pioneers. *Journal of Teaching in Social Work, 26*(1–2), 181–199.

Brice, T., & Scales, L. (2013). The first and the last: A confluence of factors leading to the integration of Carver School of Missions and Social Work, 1955. *Journal of Sociology & Social Welfare, 40*(1), 85–102.

Carlton-LaNey, I. (2011). African American club women's resistance to oppressive public policy in the early 20th century. In J. Schiele (Ed.), *Social welfare policy: Regulation and resistance among people of color* (pp. 43–62). Los Angeles, CA: Sage.

Carlton-LaNey, I., & Brice, T. (2010). *African Americans—Oxford bibliographies online research guide*. Retrieved from http://ebookstore.sony.com/ebook/iris-carlton-laney/african-americans-oxford-bibliographies-online-research-guide/_/R-400000000000000235873

Gordon, L. (1991). Black and White visions of welfare: Women's welfare activism, 1890–1945. *The Journal of American History, 78*(2), 559–590.

Higginbotham, E. (1992). African-American women's history and the metalanguage of race. *Signs, 17*(2), 251–274.

Lasch-Quinn. E. (1993). *Black neighbors: Race and the limits of reform in the American settlement house movement, 1890–1945*. New York, NY: Haworth Press.

Phillips, N. K. (2006). Growing up in the urban environment: Opportunities and obstacles for children. In N. K. Phillips, & L. A. Straussner (Eds.), *Children in the urban environment: Linking social policy and clinical practice* (2nd ed., pp. 5–28). Springfield, IL: Charles C. Thomas.

Sabbath, T. (1994). Social work services and social work training for African Americans in Philadelphia 1900–1930. *Journal of Sociology and Social Welfare, 21*(1), 83–95.

Simon, B. (1994). The empowerment tradition in American social work: A history. New York, NY: Columbia University Press.

NOTES

1. The Talented Tenth was a concept put forth by W. E. B. Du Bois (1868–1963), an African American educator, author, and civil rights activist, who was among the most influential African Americans of the Progressive Era and the first half of the 20th century. Du Bois used the term *talented tenth* when advocating for postsecondary education for the most able 10% of African Americans. He considered higher education as the best means of developing the leadership capacity of the African American community, and a pathway to achieve equality. Du Bois emphasized the need for African Americans to follow educational paths that lead to professional careers

because he feared overemphasis on vocational training would artificially constrain the social development of African Americans.

2. Several cities had settlement houses named in honor of Phyllis Wheatley, who had been sold into slavery, but became a poet and the first published African American woman. The various settlement houses bearing her name were independent of each other.

REFERENCES

Bay, M. (2009). *To tell the truth: The life of Ida B. Wells*. New York, NY: Hill and Wang.

Brice, T. (2005). Disease and delinquency know no color: Syphilis and African American female delinquency. *Affilia, 20*, 300–315. doi:10.1177/0886109905277753

Brown, C. (1941). *The correct thing to do, to say, to wear*. Boston, MA: Christopher Publishing House.

Carlton-LaNey, I. (1983). Notes on a forgotten Black social worker and sociologist George Edmund Haynes. *Journal of Sociology & Social Welfare, 10*(3), 530–539.

Carlton-LaNey, I. (1989). Old folks' homes for Blacks during the Progressive Era. *Journal of Sociology & Social Welfare, 43*, 43–60.

Carlton-LaNey, I. (1990). The intellectual biography: A mechanism for integrating historical content. *Arete, 15*, 46–51.

Carlton-LaNey, I. (1994). Training African American social workers through the NUL Fellowship Program. *Journal of Sociology & Social Welfare, 21*, 43–53.

Carlton-LaNey, I. (1996). George and Birdye Haynes' legacy to community practice. *Journal of Community Practice, 2*(4), 27–48. doi:10.1300/J125v02n04_03

Carlton-LaNey, I. (2011). African American club women's resistance to oppressive public policy in the early 20th century. In J. Schiele (Ed.), *Social welfare policy: Regulations and resistance among people of color* (pp. 43–62). Los Angeles, CA: Sage.

Daniels, J. (1914). *In freedom's birthplace*. Boston, MA: Houghton Mifflin.

Evans, S. (2007). *Black women in the Ivory Tower 1850–1954: An intellectual history*. Gainesville: University of Florida Press.

Fairfax, C. (2007). The African American child-saving legacy of Ida Barbour: An alternative to foster care policy and practice. *Arete, 31*(1/2), 73–85.

Hamilton-Mason, J., & Gonzalez-Ramos, G. (2006). Urban children living in poverty. In N. K. Phillips & S. L. A. Straussner (Eds.), *Children in the urban environment: Linking social policy and clinical practice* (2nd ed., pp. 29–49). Springfield, IL: Charles C. Thomas.

Harley, S. (1982). Beyond the classroom: The organizational lives of Black female educators in the District of Columbia, 1890–1930. *Journal of Negro Education, 51*(3), 254–265. doi:10.2307/2294693

Haynes, G. (1912). *The Negro at work in New York City*. New York, NY: Longmans, Green, Agents.

Hendricks, W. (1994). "Vote her the advantage of ourselves and our race." The election of the first Black alderman in Chicago. *Illinois Historical Journal, 87*, 171–184.

Hine, D. C. (1989). Rape and the inner lives of Black women in the Middle West. *Signs, 14*, 912–920. doi:10.1086/494552

Hine, D. C. (1991). Black migration to the urban Midwest: The gender dimension 1915–1945. In J. Trotter (Ed.), *The great migration in historical perspective: New dimensions of race, class & gender* (pp. 127–146). Bloomington: Indiana University Press.

Hornsby, A. (2001). "The boy problem": North Carolina race men groom the next generation 1900–1930. *Journal of Negro History, 86*(3), 276–304. doi:10.2307/1562448

Jackson, P. (1978). Black charity in Progressive Era Chicago. *Social Service Review, 52*(3), 400–417. doi:10.1086/643652

Jane Edna Hunter Papers, Series II. (n.d.). Documents of the Phyllis Wheatley Association. Retrieved from http://ead.ohiolink.edu/xtf-ead/view?docId=ead/OCLWHi0149.xml;query=;brand=default

Johnson, A. (1993). White, Eartha Mary Magdalene White (1876–1974). In D. Hine, E. Brown, & R. Terborg-Penn (Eds.), *Black women in America: A historical encyclopedia* (Vol. 1, pp. 1256–1257). Bloomington: University of Indiana Press.

Jones, A. L. (1993). Hunter, Jane Edna (1882–1971). In D. Hine, E Brown, & R. Terborg-Penn (Eds.), *Black women in America: A historical encyclopedia* (Vol. 1, pp. 592–594). Bloomington: University of Indiana Press.

Karger, H. (1986). Phyllis Wheatley House: A history of the Minneapolis Black settlement house, 1924 to 1940. *Phylon, 47*(1), 79–90. doi:10.2307/274697

Marlowe, G. (1993). Walker, Maggie Lena (c. 1867–1934). In D. Hine, E. Brown, & R. Terborg-Penn (Eds.), *Black women in America: An historical encyclopedia* (pp. 1214–1219). Bloomington: Indiana University Press.

Miller Center, University of Virginia. (2014). *American president: Reference resource Rose Cleveland, Francis Cleveland.* Retrieved from http://millercenter.org/president/cleveland/essays/firstlady

National Association of Black Social Workers. (1968). *Code of ethics.* Washington, DC. Author.

O'Donnell, S. (1996). Urban African American community development in the Progressive Era. *Journal of Community Practice, 2*(4), 7–26. doi:10.1300/J125v02n04_02

Ovington, M. (1911). *Half a man.* New York, NY: Schocken Books.

Park, Y., & Kemp, S. (2006). "Little Alien Colonies": Representations of immigrants and their neighborhoods in social work discourse, 1875–1924. *Social Service Review, 80*(4), 705–734. doi:10.1086/507934

Peebles-Wilkins, W. (2001). Janie Porter Barrett and the Virginia Industrial School for Colored Girls: Community response to the needs of African American children. *Child Welfare, 74*(1), 143–161.

Phillips, N. K. (2006). Growing up in the urban environment: Opportunities and obstacles for children. In N. K. Phillips, & L. A. Straussner (Eds.), *Children in the urban environment: Linking social policy and clinical practice* (2nd ed., pp. 5–28). Springfield, IL: Charles C. Thomas.

Rouse, J. (1984). The legacy of community organizing: Lugenia Burns Hope and the Neighborhood Union. *Journal of Negro History, 69*(3/4), 114–133. doi:10.2307/2717617

Scott, A. (1993). Barrett, Janie Porter (1865–1948). In D. Hine, E. Brown, & R. Terborg-Penn (Eds.), *Black women in America: An historical encyclopedia* (pp. 90–91). Bloomington: Indiana University Press.

Social Welfare History Project. (2014). *Virginia Industrial School for Colored Girls.* Retrieved from http://www.socialwelfarehistory.com/organizations/the-virginia-industrial-school-for-colored-girls/

Terborg-Penn, R. (2005). Sororities movement. In D. Hine (Ed.-in-chief), *Black women in America* (2nd ed., vol. 3, pp. 163–168). New York, NY: Oxford University Press.

Waites, C. (2001). Victoria Earle Matthews: Residence and reform. In I. Carlton-LaNey (Ed.), *African American leadership: An empowerment tradition in social welfare history* (pp. 1–16). Washington, DC: NASW Press.

Wharton Center. (n.d.). *Wharton Centre (Philadelphia, Pa.) records.* Retrieved from http://library.temple.edu/scrc/wharton-centre-philadelphia-pa

White, D. (1998). *Too heavy a load: Black women in defense of themselves, 1894–1994.* New York, NY: W.W. Norton.

Wolfinger, J. (2009). The limits of Black activism: Philadelphia's public housing in the Depression and World War II. *Journal of Urban History, 35*, 787–814. doi:10.1177/0096144209339556

CHAPTER 3

Child Welfare in Urban Environments

Kimberly Y. Johnson and Sandra S. Chipungu

Trends in child welfare practices and policies in the United States are presenting special challenges for urban communities, children, and their families. Some of the trends are decreasing caseloads in foster care and declining Title IV-E penetration rates, disproportionately for racial and ethnic groups. These trends have led to both positive and negative outcomes for families. Another special challenge is addressing the traumatic exposure that impacts families and professional helpers.

Child welfare agencies are also influenced by the larger societal problems such as the sustained recession, unemployment, poverty, homelessness, affordable housing, substance abuse, HIV/AIDS, and incarceration of parents. Child welfare agencies must take into account the financial and human resources, legal mandates, and unique challenges of the geographic area in which child welfare services are provided. The population, demographics, and wealth may all affect the type and amount of services available to help families and children. The number of children in the foster care system also remains crucial and requires a discussion of its current state.

This chapter provides an overview of the trends in child welfare in general and the trends in child welfare in a state in the northeastern area of the United States. There is a national trend within child welfare agencies to focus on the impact that trauma has on families and children involved in the child welfare system. Thus, the latter part of this chapter highlights some of the child welfare workforce issues with a focus on the traumatic experiences of children, families, and child welfare professionals. Trauma preventions and strategies will be highlighted leading to a discussion on the implications for social work policy, education, and practice.

RECENT TRENDS IN FOSTER CARE

Recent statistics indicate that the number of children in foster care and those enter-ing foster care have been decreasing. According to Child Welfare Information Gateway (2013), there were an estimated 399,546 children in foster care. Of these, more than a quarter (28%) were in relatives' homes, and nearly half (47%) were in nonrelative foster family homes. About half (53%) had a permanency plan of reunification with their fam-ilies. About half (51%) of the children who left foster care in fiscal year (FY) 2012 were reunited with their parents or primary caregivers. Close to half of the children (46%) who left foster care in FY 2012 were in care for less than a year (Foster Care Statistics, 2012).

From FY 2012 to 2013, the numbers of children in foster care on September 30 and the numbers of children who entered care during the latter year decreased. There has been an almost continuous decline in the number of children in fos-ter care on the last day of each federal FY (September 30) between FY 2002 and 2012 (Administration on Children Youth and Families, Children's Bureau, 2013). In FY 2005, the number of entries into foster care reached its highest point to date with 307,000 entries reported. Since that time, however, the number of entries has declined and appears to be leveling off over the last 2 years. The number of exits, which increased between FY 2002 (278,000) and 2006 (295,000), had been on a continual decline to 241,000 in FY 2012 (Administration on Children Youth and Families, Children's Bureau, 2013).

DEMOGRAPHIC TRENDS IN FOSTER CARE

Over the past decade, the U.S. foster care population has undergone a substantial reduc-tion in size and experienced a shift in its racial and ethnic composition. The num-ber of children in foster care on the last day of the federal FY declined by almost a quarter (23.7%) between 2002 and 2012, from 523,616 to 399,546 (Administration on Children Youth and Families, 2013). While numbers declined among all major non-Hispanic racial groups, reductions among African American children were the most dramatic, declining by 47.1% between 2001 and 2012 and accounting for nearly three quarters (74%) of the overall decline. According to Adoption and Foster Care Analysis and Reporting System (U.S. Department of Health and Human Services, 2013), of the estimated 399,546 children in foster care on September 30, 2012, 42% were White, 26% were Black or African American, 21% were Hispanic (of any race), 9% were of other races or multiracial, and 3% were unknown or unable to be determined. The per-centage of Black children in care on September 30 decreased between FY 2003 and 2012, whereas the percentages of White children, Hispanic children, and children of other races or multiracial children increased (U.S. Department of Health and Human Services, 2013).

DEMOGRAPHIC TRENDS IN MARYLAND

Maryland had 6,905 children placed in foster care (U.S. Department of Health and Human Services, 2010), of whom 2,163 (31%) were placed in relative family foster care, and 3,095 (45%) were placed in nonrelative family foster care, while 1,039 (15%) were placed in group homes or institutions (Kids Count Data Center, 2011). According to the Child Welfare League of America (2013) in Maryland, 6,098 children in Maryland lived apart from the families in out-of-home care in 2010, compared to 7,052 in 2009. The number of children living apart from their families in out-of-home care has decreased (32.6%) in comparison to the number of children in out-of-home care in 2006 (Child Welfare League of America [CWLA], 2013). Of the number of Maryland children in out-of-home care in 2010, 23.9% were White, 65.6% Black, 3.9% Hispanic, 0.0% American Indian/Alaskan Native, 0.3% Asian or Pacific Islander, and 3.9% of more than one race or ethnicity (CWLA, 2013).

Of the 3,649 children exiting foster care in Maryland in 2010, 39.7% were reunited with their parents or other family members. In 2010, 644 children were legally adopted through the public children welfare agency in Maryland, a 12.3% decrease from 734 in 2009. Of the 6,098 children in out-of-home care, 883 or 14.5% were waiting to be adopted, and 2,037 were living with relatives while in care. Of all Maryland children in kinship care in 2010, 27.9% were White, 59.9% Black, 4.1% Hispanic, 0.0% American Indian/Alaskan Native, 0.4% Asian or Pacific Islander, and 59.9% of more than one race or ethnicity. In 2010, 753 children aged out of out-of-home care—exited foster care to emancipation in Maryland (CWLA, 2013).

DISPROPORTIONALITY: CHILD WELFARE

There is disproportionality of certain racial and ethnic groups in child welfare in the United States (Chipungu, 2004; Hill, 2004). The disproportionality rates vary by states, cities, and counties, but, in general, African American, Hispanic, and Native American children represent a higher proportion of children in foster care than those in the larger population or local population figures. The reasons for disproportionality have been higher maltreatment rates, class status, and biases in the decision making within the child welfare system (Hill, 2004).

Others argue that disproportionality is attributed to institutional racism within the child welfare system. Hill argued that institutional racism is a form of racism known as "structural discrimination." Structural (or unintentional) discrimination refers to the disparate adverse consequences of societal trends and institutional policies on racial minorities that may not have been explicitly designed to have racially discriminatory effects (Hill, 2004). The greater percentage of African American children in foster care in Maryland (67%), compared to that of Whites (24%), is an example of disproportionality by race.

Maryland has a disproportional index of children in foster care by race for 2000 to 2012 of 2.4 for African American children (National Council of Juvenile and Family Court Judges [NCJFCJ], 2014). In 2000, African American children represented 38% of the foster care population, while they comprised only 16% of the general child population, indicating a disproportionality index of 2.5 (i.e., African American children were disproportionately represented in foster care at a rate 2.5 times their rates in the general population; NCJFCJ, 2014). In 2012, 12 years later, these numbers have changed. Although the disproportionality rate increased between 2000 and 2004, African American disproportionality has now decreased to 2.0 from 2.5 nationally (NCJFCJ, 2014).

FINANCING CHILD WELFARE: PENETRATION RATES

States are facing a challenge in the funding of child welfare services due to decreases in caseloads and the penetration rate in Title IV-E financing. Casey (2013) argued for changes in the financing of child welfare. One part of the proposal calls for the "phased in elimination of the income eligibility requirement with reduced federal match." Casey argue that the federal share of foster care expenses is declining (17%) decline in penetration rate between 2000 and 2010. The Congressional Budget Office (CBO) projects a 45% decline in federal outlays for maintenance payments over the next decade. Twenty-seven states currently have penetration rates less than 50%, including Maryland (Casey, December 2013).

The Child and Family Services Improvement and Innovation Act reauthorized and expanded an existing authority to grant waivers to provisions of Title IV-E of the Social Security Act. There is an urgent need for comprehensive financing reform of the child welfare system to address the situation (Casey, 2014). Lessons learned from waivers demonstrate how dollars can be invested in the kinds of evidence-based and evidence-informed practices to improve the outcomes for children and families (Casey, 2014). Trauma-informed practice is the current evidence-based practice being implemented within child welfare systems across the nation.

TRAUMA: CHILD WELFARE

Children come to the attention of the child welfare system due to child abuse and neglect, which are known to be traumatic experiences. Children are beaten; shaken; burned; molested; raped; victims of incest; trafficked for sex; and emotionally, physically, and educationally neglected. African American children who live in impoverished urban communities are significantly more at risk of being maltreated (Collins et al., 2012).

African American children across the diaspora are exposed to trauma, especially in South Africa, where there is a large AIDS-orphaned population, which places children at risk of posttraumatic stress disorder (PTSD; Culver, Fincham, & Seedat, 2009). Community and family violence may also result in mental health diagnoses of PTSD or anxiety. For example, as a child welfare worker, the author worked with a 4-year-old African American girl who lived in a high-crime urban neighborhood. At only 4 years of age, she was diagnosed with having anxiety disorder and enuresis as a result of being exposed to the sounds of nightly gunshots outside of her bedroom window.

Children are also at risk of being vulnerable to more traumas while in out-of-home placements or due to system-induced trauma (Pence, 2012). For example, parents are entitled to visitation with their children and may experience trauma due to limited visitation arrangements (New York Initiative of Children of Incarcerated Parents: A Special Project of the Osborne Association [n.d.]). Incarcerated parents are entitled to visits by their children, which is significant for permanency planning. Many children come to the attention of the child welfare system due to their parents' substance abuse and mental health issues. During visitation with the incarcerated parent, children have the cognitive and emotional intelligence to observe their parents' state of mind and they out of disappointment with their parents' motivation to change, they become withdrawn, which can also lead to trauma. All these traumatic exposures can lead to maladaptive behaviors in children, and workers must remain sensitive to the underlying cause of acting-out behaviors (Mercer, 2011).

Parents and guardians of abused and neglected children often have child abuse and neglect histories (Pence, 2012). In many families, there is a generational cycle of child abuse and neglect. During a family involvement meeting (FIM), a parent once became angry and kicked the caretaker of her son because she blamed him for the abuse she encountered from him as a child. She argued that she used drugs and had mental health issues because of being abused and neglected by him.

Once families and children become involved in the child welfare system, little attention is centered on their traumatic experiences. The focus of local departments of social services is to complete multiple forms and never-ending checklists although many child welfare agencies have adopted a "systems of care" (SOC) model through Family-Centered Practice. In schools of social work, students are taught to have empathy, engage, and assess the needs of families and children. Social workers in local departments of social services often proclaim that they do not have enough time to engage with families and do not believe that they work for a child welfare agency. A child welfare worker who is a licensed graduate social worker at a local urban department of social services states that, "it's not about the families and children, it's more about meeting deadlines and counts." Daley (1979) argues that not being able to follow up with families because of these deadlines impeded on child welfare workers' psychological health.

Most social workers employed in child welfare agencies really want to understand the impact that trauma has on families and children. However, the mandates and directives from the administration supersede workers' desire to explore the traumatic experiences of families and children. Workers report not having a choice to meet the mandates and directives of the administration due to consequences of severe disciplinary action, while ignoring the true needs of the family. They have little autonomy and feel that their social work training has little value. For example, an African American social worker was given a directive to cancel all appointments with families and work on getting forms completed for compliance. The social worker was told that if she did not have the form completed by the end of the day, then she would be referred to personnel for disciplinary action.

This type of practice further causes harm to families and children by compromising established relationships and rapport building. Families and children may feel that they cannot trust and share the traumatic experiences due to worker inconsistency and insensitivity by not showing up. In this model of working with families and children, child welfare agencies adopt a functional service model of practice that focuses on agency requirements and could result in a vast number of workforce issues.

WORKFORCE ISSUES

In 2003, the General Accounting Office (GAO) report documented that staff shortages, high caseloads, high worker turnover, and low salaries impinged on delivering services to achieve permanence and well-being of children (CWLA, 2013). According to the 2003 GAO report, the average caseload for child welfare–foster care caseworkers was 24 to 31 children; these high caseloads contributed to high worker turnover and insufficient services being provided to children and families. CWLA recommends that foster care caseworkers have caseloads of 12 to 15 children (CWLA, 2013).

The National Child Welfare Workforce Institute identified pressing workforce issues and proposed strategies for addressing them. They are as follows: (a) destructive child welfare agency environment; (b) limited pool of qualified and committed applicants for child welfare positions; (c) ineffective selection processes that result in questionable hires; and (d) high turnover rates among qualified and experienced staff.

The goals of child welfare agencies are to reduce the number of children entering out-of-home placement and to prevent children from reentering the system. To prevent children from reentering the child welfare system and exiting healthy, the underlying issues that brought children into care must be fully addressed by competent child welfare workers who understand the traumatic experiences of families and children. The lack of attention in addressing the traumatic needs of families and children is particularly alarming because African American families and children are disproportionately represented in the child welfare system, have poorer outcomes, and receive inadequate services (Boyd-Webb, 2006; Chipungu, 2004; Mercer, 2011).

In addition to limited attention to addressing the traumatic needs of families and children, even less attention is given to the secondary traumatic stress (STS) that child welfare workers experience as a result of vicarious trauma (Cunningham, 2003; Jankoski, 2010). Child welfare workers work under hazardous conditions and are exposed to severe emotional discomfort due to interviewing and assessing the maltreatment of children. Child welfare workers may be required to conduct home assessments in environments that may be deemed inhabitable for human beings, which may also induce stress.

Clark, Craig, and Sprang (2009); Conrad and Kellar-Guenther (2006); Hopkins, Cohen-Callow, Kim, and Hwang (2010); and Van Hook & Rothenburg (2009) refer to STS as an "occupational hazard" and Jankoski (2010) describes that caring for others is an "occupational hazard" (p. 117). Child welfare workers may be assigned cases where fatalities have occurred and may have to case manage drug-exposed newborns and children who have severe physical and behavior diagnoses. Child welfare workers are expected to engage and work with those individuals who have maltreated children and remain emotionally "put together" (Courage and William, 1986).

TRAUMA TYPOLOGIES

Trauma is defined as an "emotional wound caused by frightening and painful experiences" (Boyd-Webb, 2006, p.14). In Boyd-Webb (2006), Lenore Terr (1991) argues that trauma is categorized as Type I trauma and Type II trauma. Type I trauma is described as witnessing a single event, such as homicide, and Type II trauma involves multiple frightening experiences such as physical or sexual abuse. *STS, also referred to as compassion fatigue,* is the reexperiencing of increased arousal and/or avoidance symptoms with rapid onset, following at least one indirect exposure to traumatic material. *Vicarious trauma* is a concept that describes the emotionally shocking images of horror and suffering experiences by clinicians who work with victims of sexual assault and that exposure to clients' trauma over a period of time can lead to cognitive disruptions and impact affect (McCann & Pearlman, 1990).

TRAUMA AND ATTACHMENT ISSUES FOR CHILDREN

Children who experience Type II trauma and when the pain is inflicted by parents or caregivers are more likely to have difficulty engaging in treatment (Cunningham, 2003; Herman, 1992) and clinicians are likely to experience more stress. Trauma may also contribute to children having attachment and separation issues. This may be particularly significant for children who have secure attachments to their parents, especially because parents' roles are to love, nurture, and protect (Mallon, 2012).

TRAUMA AND MENTAL HEALTH

The Diagnostic and Statistical Manual of Mental Disorders (5th edition.; *DSM-5*; American Psychiatric Association, 2013) is the guide to diagnosing mental health disorders. PTSD has been found to be a common diagnosis of traumatized foster care youth. Griffin et al. (2012) state that, "it is important for the child welfare community to understand that the PTSD diagnosis does not adequately capture the full picture of childhood trauma" (p. 71). According to the National Center for PTSD (2015), "the current PTSD diagnosis does not fully capture the psychological harm that occurs with prolonged, repeated trauma" (para. 1) of the National Center for PTSD also explains that, "the current PTSD diagnosis does not capture the severe psychological harm that occurs with prolonged and repeated trauma" (p. 2). Herman (1992) argues that individuals who experience long-term sexual and physical abuse situations should be given a diagnosis of complex PTSD (CPTSD).

Collaboration from child welfare agencies and the mental health community is necessary to improve appropriate diagnosis and treatment. This collaboration would include specialized training, consultation, and teaming, which would assist in developing appropriate individualized case plans, and service agreements (Boyd-Webb, 2006). Griffin et al. explain that, "treatment for mental illness is different than treatment for trauma and cautions clinicians in diagnosing a mental health disorder before treating the trauma" (p. 86).

The mental health of child welfare professionals is equally important and must be acknowledged and addressed. Gold (1998) explains that, "child welfare workers often report having mood swings, anger, depression, fearfulness, anxiety, paranoia, low self esteem, and nightmares about being chased and murdered" (p. 712).

TRAUMA AND WELL-BEING

Families' and children's well-being should always be paramount. Child welfare practice is guided by the three federal child welfare outcomes of safety, permanency, and well-being. Prior to the Adoptions Safety Family Act of 1997 (ASFA), achieving permanency was paramount, which put children's safety at risk, which resulted in further harm to children. Certainly, safety should always be first, but where does that leave the well-being of children. There has been a strong focus on safety and permanency with less emphasis on well-being (Samuels, 2012).

Well-being encompasses mental health, physical health, community health, and education, which are compromised as a result of maltreatment. Children can achieve permanency through reunification, relative placement for custody and guardianship, adoption, or another permanent planned living arrangement (APPLA). Child welfare workers are required to practice concurrent permanency planning, which means working on more than one permanency plan at the same time. The same should be practiced regarding safety, permanency, and well-being as they are equally important for long-lasting positive outcomes. Safety ensures that children will be free from abuse and neglect, permanency provides a loving and nurturing environment for children forever, and well-being ensures that children have long-lasting social and emotional health.

More attention is needed to address the social and emotional health of children who have experienced trauma because of maltreatment. Children who come to the attention of child welfare experience various levels of trauma. In the state of Illinois alone, data from children's comprehensive assessment revealed that, "one-quarter of the children in foster care exhibited clinical levels of trauma symptoms" (Samuels, 2012, p. 21).

The National Survey of Child and Adolescent Well-Being (NSCAW II) is a longitudinal study that captures the functioning of children who come in contact with the child welfare system and from February 2008 to April 2009, 5,873 children, ranging in age from birth to 17. 5 years, in 83 counties, were sampled. Children between the ages of 8 and 17 years responded to the Trauma Symptom Checklist for Children (TSCC, $N = 1,530$; Briere, 1996), which evaluates posttraumatic symptomatology and the effects of child abuse and neglect, interpersonal violence, and witnessing trauma.

The findings from the study revealed that, regardless of the placement setting, all children experienced some level of trauma. Placement settings included (a) in-home care, (b) kin care, (c) foster care, and (d) group home or residential programs. Surprisingly, children in kin care (12.7%) scored higher in the clinical range for PTSD symptoms compared to those in in-home care (11.6%); foster care (7.3%); and group home or residential programs (7.6%). Males (13%) presented a higher percentage of PTSD symptoms than females (10.4%). Children between the ages of 8 and 10 years (18%) were more likely to present with PTSD symptoms compared to those between the ages of 11 and 17 years (8.7%); White children (13.4%) scored higher than Black children (10.5%) for PTSD symptoms (Casanueva, Ringeisen, Wilson, Smith, & Dola, 2011).

Similar findings (Griffin et al., 2012) show that youth entering foster care experienced trauma and trauma symptoms, which increased with the child's age. All children regardless of placement setting, gender, age, and race experienced some symptoms of trauma. If these traumatic experiences are left untreated and unaddressed, the outcomes are dismal and may put children at further risk of harm or immediate danger. For example, Mallon (2012) describes the life of 4-year-old Robert, who came into foster care because his mother's boyfriend held his hands over oven top burners with flames so high that his skin melted away. Robert's hands were undoubtedly disfigured, but he survived the physical trauma. Although Robert endured such an unimaginable trauma early in life, he managed to age out the foster care system with a high school diploma, and obtained an apartment and employment. This is deemed in many child welfare agencies to be a success. After only 2 years of aging out of the foster care system, at age 22 years, Robert shot and killed himself. Trauma is similar to mental injury in that it has no observable physical indicators. More attention is needed in helping children in care to emotionally heal from childhood trauma.

Even less research has been conducted to assess trauma exposure and emotional and behavioral functioning of youth placed in treatment foster care (TFC) placements. TFC is considered to be a more restricted placement that provides higher levels of case management and social work services. TFC placements are also more costly to child welfare agencies and often work toward a goal of "stepping children down" to a less restricted placement such as regular foster care or kinship care. However, if this goal is to be successful, evidence-based trauma-informed interventions in working with this population are needed. Children in TFC placements are known to have low levels of behavioral and emotional functioning and their foster parents are expected to undergo specialized training to meet their behavioral and emotional needs.

Burns et al. (2012) conducted a study and found that 85% of their 229 participants in TFC placements had experienced trauma as a result of emotional abuse and 65.4% from being a witness to domestic violence. Surprisingly, the study findings revealed that TFC foster parents had little knowledge about the traumatic impact of sexual abuse and domestic violence. The Culver et al. (2009) study findings revealed that support from caregivers is instrumental in reducing PTSD symptoms. Therapeutic mentoring (TM) can also provide support for foster parents who care for foster care youth (Johnson & Pryce, 2004). Recognizing the importance of the trauma and maltreatment, policy makers passed federal legislation through the Child and Family Services Improvement and Innovation Act (P.L. 112–34) and Promoting Safe and Stable Families Program (2011; Griffin et al. 2012). These enacted policies require states to implement plans to identify and address trauma that is associated with maltreatment and a child's removal from the home.

TRAUMA: HELPING THE CHILD WELFARE PROFESSIONAL

In colleges and universities that offer social work programs, it is found that the mission statements in essence are centered around helping, healing, and providing hope to the individual, family, and community at large. There is little literature centered on how the social work curriculum will prepare aspiring social workers to work with traumatized children, families, and communities (Pence, 2012). Some professors will have a discussion on self-help, countertransference, and burnout, but because of the nature of work that social workers carry out, particularly in child welfare, a curriculum centered on helping the child welfare social worker cope with STS and vicarious traumas should be implemented and mandated by the Council on Social Work Education (CSWE). In a trauma informed case management investigative (TIFCMI) training, STS was of little discussion; however, trainees could not help but to reflect on the emotional discomfort of working with abused and neglected children. Trainees expressed the need to spend more time in the training to help process the trauma they experienced in investigating maltreatment (Pence, 2012), which resulted in a recommendation to include an STS in the curricula.

Once students graduate with a bachelor's or master's degree in social work and are licensed, they are required to engage in continuing education credits (CEUs), which are set by state licenses governing boards. Additionally, many government and nongovernment agencies and organizations require their social workers to engage in CEUs. Particularly, if a social worker is employed in a child welfare position, a minimum of three CEUs should be focused on STS or vicarious trauma. There is also limited knowledge in the body of literature around the emotional trauma that child welfare workers experience when engaging with abused and neglected children. Much of the literature regarding the stress on the child welfare worker is studied under "burnout" (Jayaratne, Chess, & Kunkel, 1986) and countertransference (Cunningham, 2003), which does not address the emotional impact that workers experience from working with cases involving maltreatment.

Dane (2000) explored the emotional impact of working with maltreated children on child welfare professionals. Data were gathered through two focus groups consisting of 10 child welfare staff. Six of the 10 participants were African Americans and mostly women who worked in a metropolitan area of the city. Some of the research questions included the following: (a) If your case involved trauma to the child, how did it affect you personally, professionally, and spiritually? (b) Tell us about your support system personally and professionally. (c) What would you like to do differently to help you cope with stress and trauma on the job? Some of the themes that emerged from the study were coping; secondary trauma; and child fatalities. Participants discussed being excited about entering the field of child welfare after leaving college. However, they also explained the trauma they encountered when experiencing the death of a child. Child welfare workers experience additional stress of a child dying in the system, which is often exacerbated by the media, family members, and society at large. Blaming the child welfare worker for outcomes is a common practice and brings about additional emotional distress. However, many of the child welfare outcomes are not within the workers' control; nonetheless, workers develop self-blame, which may ultimately lead to burnout. Gold's (1998) study on the physical and mental health of female social workers in child welfare reveals that lack of control was a major issue for workers. For example, workers reported having no control over court decisions and lack of resources, which could have prevented them from removing children and a contributor to their job stress. A participant from Gold's study (1998) describes her experience:

> Removing children from their families is painful for everybody, including the workers…You have all this pain coming at you, and it keeps hitting you and hitting you and hitting you. That's the root of the stress. (p. 708)

When students graduate from social work programs, they often describe one of their roles as empowering others. Dane (2000) offers some suggestions to help child welfare workers cope with trauma exposure from working with abused and neglected families.

1. Social work education should integrate trauma across the curriculum.

2. Institutional mission and procedures should be reassessed.

3. A national training model on the effects of secondary trauma on child welfare workers should be developed.

Cunningham (2003), in a study to explore a relationship between working with traumatized clients and indicators of vicarious traumatization, also suggests that vicarious trauma be more infused in the social work curriculum. Jankoski (2010), also concerned with the impact of vicarious trauma on child welfare professionals, conducted four focus groups with participants from both rural and urban child welfare agencies. Findings from the study revealed that vicarious trauma was the reason for turnover and not burnout or countertransference issues. Child welfare workers presented with PTSD symptoms. For example, a participant reported, "I will never forget how that baby looked. I'm a man but I wake up crying at night; I can still smell that baby's burnt buttocks. It's terrible" (p. 115). One of the study's recommendations also suggests including a trauma curriculum to educate students about the impact of vicarious trauma.

TRAUMA-INFORMED PRACTICE AND INTERVENTIONS

A paradigm shift is necessary to address the traumatic experiences of children and families who come in contact with child welfare agencies. Additional helping strategies are needed for child welfare professionals to cope with stress when working with traumatized children and families. Trauma-informed practices and interventions are becoming more prominent and the new narrative in child welfare practice.

Interventions: Children and Families

The National Child Traumatic Stress Network (NCTS) has been instrumental in helping child welfare administrators lobby for policies that promote trauma-informed practice, which resulted in legislative testimony from former Commissioner Samuels of the

Administration on Children, Youth and Families (Griffin et al., 2012). NCTS is one of the most recognized organizations that address the impact of trauma on children and highlight several evidence-based trauma-informed treatments and interventions. Some of these interventions include trauma focused behavioral therapy (TF-CBT), parent–child psychotherapy (CPP), cognitive behavioral intervention for trauma in schools (CBITS), trauma affect regulation: Guide for education and therapy (TARGET), and Real Life Heroes, which have been proven to be effective in treating diverse populations (Black-Pond, Coryn, Henry, Richardson, & Unrau, 2012).

Additional interventions found to be effective include trauma-informed case management (TICM) designed to reduce resistance and help facilitate engagement (Pence, 2012) and TM with an aim to reduce trauma symptoms in those in foster care who experience complex trauma (Johnson & Pryce, 2004). Researchers Johnson and Pryce (2004) examined the effectiveness of TM in reducing trauma of foster care youth. They sampled 262 youth who were placed through a private agency in an urban area with 76% of the foster youth being African Americans. Engagement was an important component of TM and raters used the Child and Adolescent Needs and Strengths (CANS), which measures well-being. Raters included Systems of Care (SOC) clinicians and therapeutic mentors. Two of the CANS domains focus on trauma. The findings revealed that TM helped to reduce trauma symptoms; however, CANS trauma domains did not decrease. The researchers consider it a limitation that SOC clinicians rate the CANS rather than the mentors who would be able to assess the improved skills of foster youth.

Samuels (2012) further discusses the importance of providing evidence-based trauma-informed interventions and highlights family connection (FC), also referred to as trauma adapted family connection (TA-FC). He purports that this model addresses the needs of multigenerational trauma exposure and provides a manual to address symptomology, family functioning, and prevention of child abuse and neglect. Samuels (2012) explained the importance of developing screening and assessment instruments that would examine a child's history of trauma prior to out-of-home care, given that many children are exposed to trauma before entering care. Pence (2012) explained that, "while gathering and interpreting facts is essential to the investigative process, an investigation that is not informed by the context and consequences of trauma may unwittingly make things worse" (p. 52). Understanding the depth of children's trauma must be paramount in order to produce long-lasting positive outcomes. A participant who took part in Trauma Informed Case Management Investigation (TICMI) training now states, "I will consider the trauma a child has experienced prior to my involvement and how that affects my investigation" (Pence, 2012, p. 57).

Collins et al. (2005) also discuss the need for evidence-based trauma interventions and highlight TA-FC as a tool to address trauma specifically related to children in urban communities. The principles of TA-FC are centered on "theories of attachment, neglect, trauma, family interaction & community/family based intervention and has a public health social work framework" (p. 32). Social workers are one of the primary service providers who work with maltreated children whether it is in child welfare, mental health, school social work, or advocates in the community. Social workers are everywhere (Anna McPhatter, 2012, personal communication) and are important change agents, especially in African

American communities. One of the main concepts of TA-FC is engagement, which is also a core principle of social work practice. Students in schools of social work are trained on the skills of engagement as they matriculate through the social work curricula. TA-FC also incorporates engagement throughout the three-phase intervention process, which involves 2 months of treatment for each phase, which is provided in the family's home or community. Families are serviced through an empowerment framework that delineates that the family is the "expert," which is very similar to the model of family-centered practice, which is practiced in child welfare agencies across the nation. The family-centered practice model also points out that the family "knows the family best" and is the "expert."

> Phase 1—Involves trauma-informed engagement, assessment, service planning, helping to connect families to resources in their communities to meet their basic needs.
> Phase 2—Centered on family psychoeducation, emotional identification, affect regulation, building family cohesion, communication, and strengthening family relationships.
> Phase 3—Includes developing family—shared meaning of trauma, case closure, and endings (Collins et al., 2012).

Strengthening the family's protective capacities can also aid in reducing traumatic experiences within families and keeping families safely together in urban communities. The Indian Child Welfare Act of 1978 (ICWA, Public Law 95–608, 1978) is centered on preserving families, but few strategies exist to help child welfare workers carry out the law and Native children are also disproportionately represented in the child welfare system. A vast majority of Native Americans live in urban areas and experience family and community challenges similar to African Americans, including trauma.

Bussey and Lucero (2013) discuss the importance of trauma-informed interventions in working with Native American children and families who reside in urban communities and examine direct and systemic models of practice. These practice models are implemented through the Denver Indian Family Resource Center (DIFRC), which has a collaborative approach, provides intensive case management, and is culturally responsive. The DIFRC fosters systemic changes through its collaboration with child welfare agencies in providing training for child welfare staff. Engagement is also a core component of the DIFRC and utilizes team decision-making meeting (TDM), which is also the cornerstone of Family-Centered Practice. Some of the goals of the TDM in the DIFRC are to develop trauma-informed assessments and address mental health issues such as PTSD.

It is essential to understand the overwhelming traumatic experiences that groups of people have generationally endured. Bussey and Lucero (2013) state that, "a trauma informed approach includes respecting the trauma that families have experienced and the historical trauma they may bring up in narratives about their family background" (p. 95). This important recognition can also be used in working with African American families who have traumatic family histories and backgrounds due to slavery and racism. Supervision has also been demonstrated to be helpful in educating child welfare staff on the importance of trauma-informed practice.

The courts also have an important role to play in understanding the dynamic traumas that exist with maltreated children and their families. Parents of maltreated children often have substance abuse issues, which may be the underlying cause of the abuse and neglect. Recognizing the significance of alcohol and other drugs (AOL) in child abuse and neglect, the Pima County Family Drug Court (FDC) includes trauma as a component of treatment. Dolce, Powell, Sinclair, Smith-Sweenson, and Stevens (2012) studied the outcomes of the Pima County FDC by examining the relationship between receiving trauma treatment and child reunification rates. The results revealed that participants (51%) who were referred for trauma treatment achieved reunification at 86% compared to those who were not referred for trauma treatment (41%), who achieved reunification at 28%. The authors point out that additional research is needed to examine various types of trauma and treatment effectiveness in participants who exhibit higher levels of mental health symptoms.

Interventions: Child Welfare Professionals

There is little information in the literature on programs, strategies, and interventions designed to help child welfare workers cope with trauma. Supportive supervision is emotionally comforting for the child welfare worker, and Clark et al. (2009) suggest using a model of reflective supervision to allow workers to process their distress in working with maltreated children. Jankoski (2010) suggests that, "organizations have in place a debriefing mechanism in which outside referrals must be made available" (p. 117) and that supervisors receive specialized training on vicarious trauma. Just as children and families face challenges in addressing trauma experiences, so do child welfare professionals. Child welfare workers report coping with trauma by eating, drinking, reading, and shopping. However, other coping strategies, such as improving the autonomy of the child welfare worker, are correlated with reduced stress (Clark et al., 2009; Gold, 1998).

There has been a dramatic decline among African American children in foster care; however, they are still disproportionately represented in the child welfare system.

As discussed in the chapter, the number of children in foster care has been decreasing through reunification with parents or primary caregivers. The data also show that children are spending less time in out-of-home placement. When removal is necessary, children are more likely to be placed with a family member. Importantly, there has been a drastic decrease in the number of children who are placed in congregate care.

IMPLICATIONS FOR POLICY

Recently, states have experienced a decrease in funding for child welfare services due to a continuous decline in the federal penetration rate. The decline in the federal penetration rate is directly related to the decrease in the number of children entering out-of-home care and children whose parents do not meet the income reimbursement requirements for Title IV-E eligibility. The current penetration rate provides evidence that child welfare agencies across the nation are preserving families by keeping children safely in their homes. The current penetration rate is based on the 1997 Aid to Families with Dependent Children (AFDC) regulations, which are outdated. The implications of applying outdated regulations may result in an eligible case being ineligible for Title IV-E reimbursement. Once birth parents are determined to be Title IV-E ineligible, the case can never become eligible. An eligible determination would provide increased financing for child welfare services. Policy makers and advocates must continuously analyze how outdated policies influence child welfare funding and service delivery.

IMPLICATIONS FOR SOCIAL WORK EDUCATION

There is an urgent need to emotionally prepare social work students to work with traumatized clients regardless of their selected concentration. Social work graduates will inevitably engage client(s) who have experienced some type of trauma at the micro and macro levels of practice. These graduates will go on to conduct social science research in their fields of practice, which may require them to collect data from vulnerable populations who have experienced trauma. Exposure to study participants' trauma may put social workers at risk of compassion fatigue or STS, and vicarious trauma, thus leading to burnout or leaving the field of social work altogether. Social workers in general, and in particular in child welfare, have a goal to help preserve the family. In order to preserve families, SOC must continuously assess the stability and emotional needs of families and provide ongoing support. A similar preservation model may be useful to help social workers cope with trauma exposures and decrease worker turnover.

IMPLICATIONS FOR PRACTICE

The chapter also highlights the implications of adopting a child welfare trauma-informed practice for families, children, as well as the child welfare professionals. An alternative response to assessing abuse and neglect has to be the new narrative for child welfare. Even if children must be removed from their parents, a trauma-informed practice approach must be utilized from case opening to case closure regardless of the selected permanency plans. An emerging concern now exists in assisting out-of-home placement providers to become trauma informed and skilled in providing trauma-informed interventions to children in their care.

FOR FURTHER STUDY

Suggested Assignments

1. Use the World Wide Web to create a book of social policies relevant to child welfare.
2. Analyze these selected policies using a policy analysis framework.

3. Review the below links to resources for working with traumatized populations:
   http://www.samhsa.gov/nctic
   https://www.childwelfare.gov/responding/trauma.cfm
   http://www.nasmhpd.org/TA/nctic.aspx
   http://www.nctsn.org/resources/topics/creating-trauma-informed-systems
   http://childwelfaresparc.org/wp-content/uploads/2013/11/Implementing-
      Trauma-Informed-Practices.pdf
   http://www.traumainformedcareproject.org
   http://www.acestudy.org/download
   http://www.cdc.gov/violenceprevention/acestudy

4. Are you at risk of compassion fatigue? Print and complete the Compassion
   Fatigue Self-Assessment at www.myselfcare.org.

Suggested Readings

Boyd, N. (2006). *Working with traumatized youth in child welfare: Social work practice with children and families*. New York, NY: Guilford Press.

Bride, B. E. (2004). The impact of providing psychosocial services to traumatized populations. *Stress, Trauma, and Crises, 7*, 29–46.

Bride, B. E. (2007). Prevalence of secondary traumatic stress among social workers. *Social Work, 52*(1), 63–70.

Cunningham, M. (2003). Impact of trauma work on social clinicians: Empirical findings. *Social Work, 48*(4), 451–459.

Dane, B. (2000). Child welfare workers: An innovative approach for interacting with secondary trauma. *Journal of Social Work Education, 36*, 27–38.

Einarsen, S. (1999). The nature and causes of bullying at work. *International Journal of Manpower, 20*(1/2), 16–27.

Figley, C. R. (1989). *Helping traumatized families*. San Francisco, CA: Jossey-Bass.

Gold, N. (1998). Using participatory research to help promote the physical and mental health of female social workers in child welfare. *Child Welfare, 77*(6), 701–724.

Prather, W., & Golden, J. A. (2009). A behavioral perspective of childhood trauma and attachment issues: Toward alternative treatment approaches for children with a history of abuse. *International Journal of Behavioral Consultation and Therapy, 5*(1), 56–74.

Pryce, D., Pryce, J., & Shackelford, K. (2007). Secondary traumatic stress and the child welfare professional. Chicago, IL: Lyceum Books, Inc.

Toland, M. (2008). *She aint angry for nothin': An intervention & behavior modification curriculum*. Morals & Values Press.

Walker, A. T. (2006). And then came GOD: Your secret's safe with me. Kingston Springs, TN: Westview.

REFERENCES

Administration on Children, Youth and Families. (2013). Recent demographic trends in foster care (Data Brief 2013-1). Retrieved from https://www.acf.hhs.gov/sites/default/files/cb/data_brief_foster_care_trends1.pdf.

Administration on Children, Youth and Families, Children's Bureau. (2013). Child welfare outcomes 2008–2011: Report to Congress. Retrieved from https://www.acf.hhs.gov/sites/default/files/cb/cwo08_11.pdf.

American Psychiatric Association. (2000). *Diagnostic and statistical manual of mental disorders* (4th ed., text rev.). Washington, DC: Author.

Boyd-Webb. (2006). The impact of trauma on youth in families in the child welfare system. In Boyd-Webb (Ed.), *Working with traumatized youth in child welfare* (pp. 13–26). New York, NY, London: Guilford Press.

Briere, J. (1996). *Trauma symptom checklist for children: Professional manual.* Odessa, FL: Psychological Assessment Resources.

Burns, B., Cox, J., Dorsey, S., Farmer, E., Southerland, D., & Wagner, R. (2012). Prior trauma exposure for youth in treatment foster care. *Journal of Child and Family Studies,* 21, 816–824. doi:10.1007/s10826–011-9542–4

Bussey, M., & Lucero, N. (2013). A collaborative and trauma informed practice model for urban Indian child welfare. *Child Welfare, 91*(3), 89–111. Retrieved from Child Welfare Information Gateway (2013).

Casanueva, C., Ringeisen, H., Wilson, E., Smith, K., & Dola, M. (2011). *NSCAWII baseline report: Child well-being [OPRE Report #2011–27b].* Washington, DC: Office of Planning, Research, and Evaluation, Administration for Children and Families, U.S. Department of Health and Human Services.

Casey Family Programs. (2013) Smarter investments Keep children safe: The Child and Family Services Improvement Act expanded the Title IV-E. *Smarter investments keep children safe.* Retrieved from http:www.casey.org/waiver-hone-action-progress/

Child Welfare Information Gateway. (2013). *Foster care statistics 2012.* Washington, DC: U.S. Department of Health and Human Services, Children's Bureau.

Child Welfare League of America. (2013). *Maryland's children 2012.* Washington, DC: CWLA. Retrieved from www.cwla.org.

Chipungu, S. S. (2004). The impact of child welfare policies on African American families: In S. S. Chipungu, J. Everett, & B. Leashore (Eds.), *Child welfare revisited* (pp. 77–92). New Brunswick, New Jersey, and London: Rutgers University Press.

Clark, J., Craig, C., & Sprang, G. (2009). *Secondary traumatic stress and burnout in child welfare workers: A comparative analysis of occupation distress across professional groups. Child Welfare, 90*(6), 149–168.

Collins, K., Clarkson-Freeman, P., Strieder, F., DePanfilis, D., Greenberg, P., Linde, L., & Tabor, M. (2012). Trauma adapted family connections: Reducing developmental and complex trauma symptomatology to prevent child abuse and neglect. *Child Welfare,* 90(6), 29–47.

Collins, K., Strieder, F., DePanfilis, D., Tabor, M., Freeman-Clarkson, P., Linde, l., & Greendber, P. (2005). Trauma adapted family connections: Reducing developmental and complex trauma symptomatology to prevent child abuse and neglect. *Child Welfare,* 90(6), 29–47.

Conrad, D., & Kellar-Guenther, Y. (2006). Compassion fatigue, burnout, and compassion satisfaction among Colorado child protection workers. *Child Abuse & Neglect,* 20(10), 1071–1080.

Courage, M., & William, D. (1986). An approach to the study of burnout in professional care to the study of burnout in professional care providers in human service organizations. *Journal of Social Service Research, 10*(1), 7–21.

Culver, L., Fincham, D., & Seedat, S. (2009). *Journal of Traumatic Stress, 22*(2), 106–112.

Cunningham, M. (2003). Impact of trauma work on social work clinicians: Empirical findings. *Social Work, 48*(4), 451–459.

Daley, R. (1979). Burnout: A smoldering problem in protective services. *Social Work, 25,* 375–379.

Dane, B. (2000). Child welfare workers: An innovative approach for interacting with secondary trauma. *Journal of Social Work Education, 36*(1), 27–38.

Dolce, B., Powell, C., Sinclair, K., Smith-Sweenson, C., & Stevens, S. (2012). Outcomes of a trauma-informed Arizona family drug court. *Journal of Social Work Practice in the Addictions, 12,* 219–241. doi: 10.1080/1533256X.2012.702624

Gold, N. (1998). *Using participatory research to help promote the physical and mental health of female social workers in child welfare.* New York, NY: Child Welfare League of America.

Griffin, G., Holzberg, M., Kisiel, C., Maj, N., McClelland, G., & Stolbach, B. (2012). *Addressing the impact of trauma before diagnosing mental illness in child welfare. Child Welfare,* (90), 69–89.

Herman, J. (1992). Complex PTSD: A syndrome in survivors of prolonged and repeated trauma. *Journal of Traumatic Stress, 5*(3), 377–391.

Hill, R. (2004). Institutional racism in child welfare. In J. E. Everett, S. S. Chipungu, & B. R. Leashore (Eds), *Child welfare revisited: An Africentric perspective.* New Brunswick, NJ: Rutgers University Press.

Hopkins, K., Cohen-Callow, A., Kim, J., & Hwang, J. (2010). Beyond intent to leave: Using multiple outcome measures for assessing turnover in child welfare. *Children & Youth Services Review, 32*(10), 1380–1387.

Jayaratne, S., Chess, W., & Kunkel, D. (1986). Burnout: Its impact on child welfare workers and their spouses. *Social Work, 31,* 53–59.

Jankoski, J. (2010). Is vicarious trauma the culprit. *Child Welfare, 89*(6), 105–120.

Johnson, S. B., & Pryce, J. M. (2004). Therapeutic mentoring: Reducing the impact of trauma for foster youth. *Child Welfare, 92*(3), 9–25.

Kids Count Data Center. (2011). Data snapshot on foster care placement. Retrieved from http://www .aecf.org/m/resourcedoc/AECF-DataSnapshotOnFosterCarePlacement-2011.pdf

Mallon, G. (2012). Trauma informed child welfare practice—Remembering Robert. *Child welfare, 90*(6), 7–10.

McCann L., & Pearlman, L. A. (1990). Vicarious traumatization: A framework for understanding the psychological effects of working victims. *Journal of Traumatic Stress, 3*(1), 131–149.

Mercer, B. (2011). Psychological assessment of children in a community mental health clinic. *Journal of Personality Assessment, 93,* 1–6. doi: 10.1080/00223891.2011.528741.

National Center for PTSD. (2015). U.S. Department of Veteran Affairs, Complex PTSD Retrieved from http://www.ptsd.va.gov/professional/PTSD-overview/complex-ptsd.asp.

National Council of Juvenile and Family Court Judges. (2014). *Disproportionality rates for children of color in foster care (Fiscal year 2012): Technical assistance bulletin, May 2014.* Reno, Nevada: University of Nevada.

New York Initiative of Children of Incarcerated Parents: A Special Project of the Osborne Association. (n.d). Retrieved from http://www.osborneny.org/images/uploads/printMedia/Initiative%20 CIP%20Stats_Fact%20Sheet.pdf

Pence, D. (2012). Trauma-informed forensic child maltreatment investigations. *Child Welfare, 90*(6), 49–68.

Richardson, M., Black-Pond, C., & Unrau, Y. (2012). Development and evaluation of trauma informed system change instrument: Factorial validity and instrument for use. *Child Adolescent Social Work Journal, 29,* 167–184. doi: 10.107/s10560–012-0259-z

Samuels, B. (2012). Addressing trauma to promote social and emotional well-being: A child welfare imparative. *Child Welfare, 90*(6), 19–28.

U.S. Department of Health and Human Services. (2010). *The AFCARS report: Preliminary FY 2009 estimates as of July, 2010, No. 17.* Retrieved from http://www.acf.hhs.gov/sites/default/files/cb/ afcarsreport17.pdf

U.S. Department of Health and Human Services. (2013). *The AFCARS report: Preliminary FY 2012 estimates as of November, 2013, No. 20.* Retrieved from http://www.acf.hhs.gov/sites/default/ files/cb/afcarsreport20.pdf

Van Hook, M., & Rothenburg, M. (2009). Quality of life and compassion satisfaction/fatigue and burnout in child welfare workers: A study of the child welfare workers in community-based care organizations in central Florida. *Social Work and Christianity, 36,* 36–54.

CHAPTER 4

Engaging Urban African American Adolescents in Treatment

Michael M. Sinclair and Belinda Davis Smith

Over the last two decades, mental health professionals have witnessed a significant increase in treatment outcome studies for children and adolescents with emotional and behavioral problems (Bors, Sanders, & Dadds, 2002; Clarke-Rohde, DeBar, & Lewinsohn, 2003; Kendall, 1996; Southam-Gerow & Prinstein, 2014; Weisz et al., 2014). Despite the advances in clinical studies of evidence-based treatment (EBT) with minorities, there is a paucity of literature that reflects efforts to determine if or how currently available treatments and interventions developed for one cultural group can be used effectively with yet another cultural group.

Invariably, clinical interventions do not work equally well with all clinical problems or client groups (Liddle, Rowe, Dakof, Ungaro, & Henderson, 2004). For example, Kadzin, Stolar, and Marciano (1995) examined treatment among 279 White and Black children attending outpatient treatment and found that Black children were 59.6% more likely to drop out of treatment than their White counterparts. In yet another study, Belgrave, Nguyen, Johnson, and Hood (2011) examined aggressive behavior among African American adolescents and found that boys are more likely to engage in aggressive acts and are more likely to be perceived by their peers as aggressive. Consequently, urban adolescents may be at a disadvantage when seeking mental health treatment because racial and ethnic mismatch between clients and therapist, psychological misdiagnosis, and cultural mistrust (Awosan, Sandberg, & Hall, 2011).

In a recent national study conducted by Gibbs et al. (2013), they found that African Americans were more likely to be given a more severe mental health diagnosis than their non-Hispanic White counterparts. Gibbs et al. further suggest that historical racism, lack of access to resources, and culturally biased assessment instrumentation and interpretation may place African Americans at a disadvantage. Given these background factors, clinical social workers face enormous challenges in developing culturally congruent and effective engagement interventions with urban adolescents. Whether this challenge arises from the treatment modalities and culture or from the client characteristics irrespective of culture, or from some combination of the two is yet to be determined. The need for clinical social workers to gain competency in working with this population is evident.

Therefore, the purpose of this chapter is to examine culturally relevant strategies that may be useful to effectively engage African American adolescents in treatment. This chapter will be presented in three major sections: (a) culturally competent practice with urban adolescents, (b) urban adolescent culture, and (c) theories of working with urban adolescents.

CULTURALLY COMPETENT PRACTICE WITH URBAN ADOLESCENTS

Culturally competent social workers have a responsibility to become knowledgeable about different cultural values, norms, and customs of urban adolescents. Although several models have emerged to guide practitioners through the process of cultural adaptations of standard EBT, it should be used with great caution (Barrera & Castro, 2008; Castro, Barrera, & Holleran-Steiker, 2010; Wingood & Clemente, 2008). Many of these models emphasize using a combination of data and theory to make selective modifications. Popular treatment models such as brief solution-focused treatment, and psychodynamic or family systems theory models are often used by social workers in assisting urban youth deal with a variety of clinical problems (Bromfield, Gillingham, & Higgins, 2007; Weiss et al., 2012). Prior to making any modifications, there should be sufficient evidence that a specific treatment protocol is either inappropriate or ineffective with the targeted population and the specific clinical problem. Resnicow, Soler, Brathwaite, Ahluwalia, and Butler (2000) contend that these types of modifications typically occur on two levels: surface and deep structure. *Surface*-level modifications are essentially adjusting treatment materials and messages to accommodate a specific target group. In contrast, *deep structure* adaptions require a thorough understanding of the group's norms, cultural values, and stressors (environmental, social, economic, and historic) to make targeted changes to the treatment protocols. Currently, surface structure modifications have been used much more frequently, although it has become evident that some deep structure adaptions may be required to work with urban adolescents (Galinsky, Fraser, Day, & Richman, 2013). For culturally competent social workers to be effective in their modifications, they should understand the difference among (a) cultural attunement, (b) cultural tailoring, and (c) cultural adaptations (Barrera, Castro, Strycker, & Toobert, 2013).

Modifying evidence-based models requires social workers to demonstrate cultural sensitivity. As such, it is important for social workers to understand the difference among (a) cultural attunement; (b) cultural tailoring; and (c) cultural adaptations. *Cultural attunement*, also known as cultural sensitivity, occurs when culturally relevant themes are added to existing treatment protocols in order to enhance engagement and retention of specific ethnic minority groups (Falicov, 2009). Using cultural idioms and addressing culturally specific barriers to participation are examples of how many social work practitioners enhance the attractiveness of treatment for many urban adolescents. *Cultural tailoring*, on the other hand, utilizes a more individualized method for modifying existing treatment protocols. Culturally tailored treatment protocols are designed to meet the needs of a specific client rather than an entire ethnic group (Kreuter & Skinner, 2000). The practitioner often collects information about the adolescent's personal connection to his or her cultural background as it relates to the youth's targeted therapeutic goal. According to Bernal et al., *cultural adaptation* is the systematic modification of an EBT protocol to consider language, culture, and context in a way that it is compatible to the adolescent's own cultural patterns, meanings, and values (Bernal, Jiminez-Chafey, & Domenech Rodriguez, 2009). Many social workers find it much easier to make surface-level modifications when addressing the needs of urban minority youth; however, there is very little literature to support the efficacy of this process (Hwang, 2009).

THE URBAN ADOLESCENT

Adolescence is a time marked with rapid biological and interpersonal changes (Lee & Styne, 2013). As children make the transition into adolescence, they experience major changes in their physiology as well as their self-concept and their identity (Mendle, Harden, Brooks-Gunn, & Graber, 2010). Social workers, psychologists, and other social scientists have struggled to understand the racial–ethnic dynamics of urban culture and adolescent development (Williams et al., 2014). Social workers have also called for a strength-based view of urban adolescents and pushed to integrate explicit attention to race and culture into mainstream models of development (Williams, Tolan, Durkee, Francois, & Anderson, 2012) and to counter deficit-oriented explanations of functioning (Cabrera, Beeghly, & Eiseberg, 2012).

Although many social scientists are dedicating more time to the study of youth in general, a comprehensive study of urban youth culture demands more rigorous forms of analysis. It can be argued that urban youth have more access to information through television, radio, Internet, and other media sources than any other time in history. The nationwide response to the Trayvon Martin and Michael Brown cases was largely youth driven through the use of social networks such as Facebook, Twitter, and Instagram. Such factors change the way we as a society perceive youth. The old notion that urban youth are often passive, misguided, and economically useless have to be reexamined. Urban youth have proven themselves to be a major force in the economic train of this country, and have emerged as a political force to contend with in relation to social issues of the day. Recognizing these paradigm shifts, parents, educators, and social workers are now encouraged to engage youth in a more egalitarian form of interaction (Steinberg, 2007).

Urban adolescents are often confronted with some unique stressors (e.g., interpersonal and/or institutional discriminations and cultural incongruence between family practices and institutional demands), and given that adolescence is a time in which identity exploration is key, many social workers have focused their attention on healthy identity development as a quintessential factor in fostering adaptive outcomes for urban adolescents of color (Swanson, Spencer, Harpalani, & Spencer, 2002). The impact of discrimination and oppression may be most evident in impoverished ethnic minority families (Boyd-Franklin & Karger, 2012), whereas all adolescents living in urban communities have the potential to encounter stress; African American and Latino adolescent males are more likely to experience both interpersonal and institutional discrimination (Gonzales et al., 2012). Notably, there is growing evidence to suggest that beyond racial–ethnic-related stressors like discrimination, other broader stressors such as poverty, community violence, substance abuse, family structure, and supports have all exacerbated the risks for negative behavioral and psychological outcomes for urban adolescents (Williams, Aiyer, Durkee, & Tolan, 2013).

POVERTY

Urban youth are more likely to spend a larger proportion of their childhood in poverty than nonminority youth (Lambert, Nylund-Gibson, Copeland-Linder, & Ialongo, 2010). According to a recent report, approximately 16 million children in the United States live in poverty. Addy, Englehardt, and Skinner (2013) stated that based on U.S. Census Bureau 2010 data there are more than 10,312,400 African Americans who are living in poverty. According to the Children's Defense Fund (December, 2014), 597 African American children are born each day into poverty. By 2012, the poverty rate for African Americans reached 28.1% (U.S. Census Bureau, 2014). If put in its proper context, more than one in every four African American families are living in poverty. Also, the highest rate of poverty, 47.5%, is found in African American families with children younger than 18 years and headed by single mothers, while the poverty rate for married African American families is 8.4%. Furthermore, African Americans represent 11.5% of those residing in government housing; 13.6% receive temporary assistance to needy families (TANF); and more than 25% receive Supplemental Nutrition Assistance Program (SNAP) benefits. Additionally, approximately 12,853,100 Latino families live in poverty. According to the Pew Research Institute, the income gap between African American families and White Non-Hispanic families is currently 59.2%. The Bureau of Labor statistics reported that the African American unemployment rate (12.6%) was more than double that of their White Non-Hispanic counterparts (6.6%) in October 2014.

FAMILY STRUCTURE

In 2010, African American families accounted for 8.4 million families in the United States. However, less than one half were married and 45% were headed by women with no spouse present. In 2010, the Census Bureau further reports that within the African

American community, 5.6 million children lived in households headed by relatives other than their parents. African American families historically had a number of strengths such as adaptive family roles and strong religious, achievement, and work orientations (Bell-Tolliver, Burgess, & Brock, 2009). Yet and still, almost two thirds of the children lived in a household headed by a grandparent. These shifts in urban family composition have had a deleterious effect on our families. Additionally, African American families relied heavily on informal networks of extended family and fictive kinfolk to cope with scarce community resources. These informal resources often provided financial support, child care, and encouragement (Belle & Benenson, 2014; Martin & Martin, 1985).

In 2010, the annual report from the U.S. Department of Health and Human Services (USDHHS, 2010) indicated that young minorities represent almost 55% of the youth in foster care. Multiple studies have suggested that there is a disproportionate amount of minority youth placed in the child welfare system (Villegas, Rosenthal, O'Brien, & Pecora, 2014). African American youth are 44 times more likely than their White counterparts to be placed in out-of-home care. Adolescents living in the foster care system are less able to depend on family members for shelter, adult guidance, and financial support (Unrau, Font, & Rawls, 2012).

As a result of the alarming statistics mentioned previously, there seems to be little doubt as to why so many urban youth search for resources other than their families to support themselves. For many adolescents living in urban environments, peer groups and gangs are essentially performing the functions traditionally provided by families (Gilman, Hill, Hawkins, Howell, & Kosterman, 2014). Gangs often provide both financial and emotional support, along with protection, encouragement, access to intimacy, respect, and guidance that many youth crave. Many youth feel alienated and misunderstood by their families, and the choice of gang involvement may reflect weak community and family structures (Boxer, 2014).

COMMUNITY VIOLENCE

In the United States, youth experience violence rates 30 times greater than those of other industrialized countries (Javdani, Adil, Suarez, Nichols, & Farmer, 2014). Violence—encompassing a variety of intentional or unintentional acts of harm such as stabbings, shootings, rapes, assaults, physical abuse, vandalism, robberies, and homicides—is a critical social problem confronting urban adolescents (Banks, Hogue, Timberlake, & Liddle, 1996). According to the findings from the National Victimization Survey conducted by the Bureau of Justice Statistics, American adolescents between the ages of 16 and 19 years are at greatest risk of victimization from violent crimes, such as aggravated assault, sexual assault or rape, and robbery (Reed et al., 2014). The study's findings also revealed that homicide was the leading cause of death among African American men between the ages of 10 and 24 years of age. According to

Spano, Rivera, Vazsonyi, and Bolland (2012), one third of inner city youth are victims of violence (e.g., assault, robbery) and more than 90% have been exposed to severe forms of violence within the community, such as shootings and stabbings (Spano, Rivera, & Bolland, 2011).

Youth who are exposed to community violence are disproportionately impacted by a host of mental health problems including traumatic stress and disruptive behavior disorders (Javdani et al.). Exposure to community violence has been linked to post-traumatic stress disorder (PTSD), traumatic stress, juvenile delinquency, conduct disorder, and oppositional defiance disorder among urban youth (Garbarino, Kolsteny, & DuBrow, 1991; Schwartz & Gorman, 2003).

SUBSTANCE ABUSE

There is strong evidence regarding the association of substance abuse, mental health, and violence among urban adolescents (Cuevas, Finkelhor, Clifford, Ormond, & Turner, 2010; McElroy & Hevey, 2014). A high incidence of adverse childhood experiences is associated with mental health and substance abuse among youth (Lee & Kim, 2011). Substance abuse is an important risk factor associated with urban adolescents (Epstein-Ngo et al., 2013; McNaughton-Reyes, Foshee, Bauer, & Ennet, 2014; Rothman, Johnson, Azrael, Hall, & Weinberg, 2010). In one study, 71% of urban 12th graders have reported using alcohol, 42.2% using tobacco cigarettes, and 48.2% using other illicit drugs (Bohnert et al., 2014). The same study by Bohnert et al. further suggests that cannabis was the most commonly used illegal drug; however, there is a growing concern about the popularity of the use of prescription drugs within urban communities.

Although there are a number of individual risk factors that may impact urban adolescent substance use (e.g., family history of addiction), sensation-seeking orientation, poor impulse control, and persistent problems with risky behavior (Robbins & Bryan, 2004; Yanovitzky, 2005), there are a significant number of family factors and community factors that put urban adolescents at greater risk of abusing illicit drugs and alcohol (Clark, Nguyen, Belgrave, & Tademy, 2011).

Wallace and Muroff (2002) contend that family risk factors such as family conflict, poor family management practices, dysfunctional family communication patterns, sibling drug use, and poor parent–child bonding may be more of a powerful predictor of drug use among African American urban youth than individual characteristics (Anthony, Alter, & Jenson, 2009). In yet another study of 291 urban African American adolescents by Clark, Belgrave, and Nasim (2008), it was found that peer drug use was a strong predictor of past-30-day alcohol use and marijuana use. Additionally, they found economic deprivation and neighborhood disorganization. Low neighborhood attachment rates, high crime rates, and high population density were also contributing factors to urban adolescent drug abuse.

ENGAGING THE AFRICAN AMERICAN ADOLESCENT

Establishing a Rapport

In most instances, adolescents are not self-referred (Yeh et al., 2002). Quite often, they become clients primarily because they were referred by a caring adult. As such, being an involuntary client may not be uncommon for adolescents. This undoubtedly means that one has to make a concerted effort to develop a working rapport, a nonjudgmental relationship, and a sense of trust with adolescents. In order to do that successfully, a social worker must consider the adolescent's development. Although many adolescents, as a group, are developing their own autonomy, it is still important for many to have a positive and supportive relationship with an idealized adult figure who can help them work through many transitional issues in a safe, nurturing, nonjudgmental environment.

Social workers who work with African American youth from urban communities must become familiar with the patterns of style and behaviors within a specific urban enclave, being mindful that urban youth culture morphs rapidly and what is vogue or acceptable today may quickly change tomorrow (Cauce et al., 2002). Additionally, social workers must understand that cultural norms may be specific to certain blocks, neighborhoods, housing projects, school districts, and communities (Cohen, 2013). Many urban youth can discern one's authenticity or familiarity with their environment by studying a worker's use of common colloquial terms and expressions.

Language and Communication Patterns

The language that a social worker uses in treatment of adolescents may vary from client to client depending on the adolescent's development needs. Social workers must be able to speak to the adolescent on his or her level. Although one must be genuine in his or her language, style, and interactions with urban adolescents, it is equally important for one to develop a style of communication that is conducive to develop a therapeutic alliance with youth. Developing a common language for ongoing interactions is one of the first tasks of working with an urban adolescent.

Social workers must remain abreast of current neologisms by learning from youth both directly and indirectly. A good place to start is listening to the music that many urban youth enjoy, ranging from rap, reggae, calypso, and house, to merengue and salsa. Urban youth often embrace hip hop as a culture because it embodies the attitudes, dress, language, and gestures associated with street culture (Keyes, 1996). Social workers who work with this population should be familiar with fashion because it provides a lens to understand adolescents within the context of their association with their peer group. For example, a client may have a new pair of expensive sneakers, which may suggest that the youth may value fashion and may place a large emphasis on material acquisitions. Also, urban youth who wear the same colors frequently could indicate his or her affiliation with a community gang. Therefore, it is important for a social worker to explore these fashion expressions while remaining nonjudgmental and open-minded.

Another feature of language used by many urban African Americans adolescents is the development of new systems of communication via texting. A text code can be considered a more complex system that is not limited to vocabulary, per se, but includes other levels of language and rules of production (Tulane, Vaterlaus, & Beckert, 2014). The development of texting codes, in which adolescents have played an important role, for different adaptations of conventional writing is experienced in the use of mobile short message systems (SMS). In the case of SMS texting, adolescents have become true innovators of an entirely new language comprising symbols, acronyms, and emoticons. These codes were created, perhaps, by a practical desire for brevity in their peer or parent communication or to create an exclusive language that defies conventional practices of communication, thereby creating an "in group" versus others.

One of the fundamental skills in social work is the ability to keenly listen to your clients (Koprowska, 2014). Listening is a quintessential part of communication. The act of listening can be further separated into two parts: verbal communication and nonverbal communication. Accordingly, *verbal communication* can further be dichotomized into two more parts; *manifest content* and *latent content*. *Manifest content* is the verbal material that is direct, conscious, and clear-cut. For example, adolescents may indicate that they feel angry or upset with their parents' decision to invoke a curfew. This is clear, unambiguous, and straightforward. Conversely, *latent material* is concerned with a deeper emotional meaning or symbolism that may contribute to the manifest content or could possibly be the source of the presenting problem. Over time, the additional meanings may emerge through further dialogue and rapport. Although the adolescent explicitly stated that he or she felt angry, it is equally important to understand the latent material presented. As such, he or she may, in fact, harbor some temporary resentment toward his or her parent for treating him or her like a child, but may be too reticent to say this aloud. Nonverbal communication consists of listening with not only your ears but also your eyes. Social workers who pick up on metaphysical cues of stress, fear, disappointment, and frustration are able to further explore these feelings with the adolescent. Skilled workers may notice a subtle incongruence in what the client said and the body language that was observed.

Social workers need to familiarize themselves with the adolescent subculture. Although this subculture may not be a monolithic group, it may be wise for social workers working with adolescents to regularly refresh their understanding of colloquial terms, neologisms, SMS acronyms, and gestures. Additionally, social workers also need to be able to listen and tend to what their adolescent communicates, both manifest and latent communication.

Assessment

Assessment is a critical process in social work practice. An inaccurate assessment or incomplete assessment can lead to inappropriate goals being set and inappropriate interventions being used. Assessments are more productive and helpful if they are performed in the language of the adolescent's "strengths" and "needs" rather than the adolescent's "problems" and "deficits." When a practitioner focuses on the adolescent's strengths, it empowers the client, and individual assessments should include the client's relationship to his or her culture, ethnicity, religion, and other group affiliations.

Positive support systems can be invaluable resources and can provide nurturance as well as further enhance self-esteem. It is important for social workers to understand the experience of the adolescents in the context of their unique cultural paradigm. Many urban adolescents experience poverty, oppression, and exclusion in varying degrees. Although applying traditional biopsychosocial assessments provides a multidimensional view of the adolescent, once the practitioner identifies the adolescent's strengths, it may be wise to incorporate those strengths in treatment plans that reflect the adolescent's culture (Strier, 2009).

Theoretical Frameworks to Work With Urban Adolescents

There is no universal approach applicable to all clinical situations. Hence, it is not uncommon for social workers to become knowledgeable and proficient in utilizing multiple theoretical perspectives to assess, to intervene, and to utilize as a practice approach when working with urban adolescents. Using the same treatment or theoretical approach is not recommended because it leads to faulty assumptions and generalizations that may significantly limit the effectiveness of treatment (Hubble, Duncan, & Miller, 1999). Later in this chapter, specific attention will be given to the examination of cognitive behavioral theory (CBT) and rap therapy. It is the contention of the authors that the use of these theoretical frameworks will provide a lens for assessment, engagement, and intervention with urban adolescents.

Cognitive-Behavioral Theory (Therapy)

Several studies indicate the efficacy of using cognitive behavioral treatment with urban minority adolescents with both anxiety disorders and mood disorders (Rohde, Stice, Shaw, & Briere, 2014; Runyon, Deblinger, & Steer, 2014; Wolk, Kendall, & Beidas, 2014). Ginsburg and Drake (2002) reported using a contextually modified form of cognitive-behavior treatment with African American adolescents with anxiety disorders. Another study conducted by Cooley-Strickland, Griffin, Darney, Otte, and Ko (2011) also found that modified cognitive behavioral programs have been effective with urban African American adolescents with anxiety. Rosselló, Bernal, and Rivera-Medina (2012) and Cardemil, Reiveich, and Seligman (2002) suggest cognitive behavioral treatment is effective in working with African American youth with depression. The Lochman and Wells (2004) study showed the effectiveness of cognitive behavioral treatment with African American adolescents with disruptive behavioral problems.

Cognitive behavioral theory/therapy (CBT) is a theoretical approach that includes cognitive and behavioral theory in a relatively short-term structured format. Recognizing that thoughts and behaviors are intimately connected, CBT addresses both in a structured therapeutic model. There are many different forms of CBT, all of which employ learning principles in attempting to alter dysfunctional behaviors (McMahon et al., 2013). Social workers should make a careful assessment of presenting problems, environmental factors, and the cognitive antecedents of the problematic behaviors. If the social worker believes that the adolescent's maladaptive thoughts are leading to the maladaptive behavior, then the intervention emphasizes helping the adolescent change his or her negative thoughts through self-instructional training. These negative thoughts are often referred to as "self-talk." Social workers should seek to "change a person's irrational or faulty thinking and behaviors by educating the person and reinforcing positive experiences which may ultimately lead to fundamental changes in the client's perception and their capacity to cope effectively." Hence, by learning to shift or alter one's thinking processes, clients can think more clearly about the choices they make and the behaviors in which they engage. It is sometimes essential to acknowledge that there may be environmental factors that appear to be contributing to the persistence of a behavior pattern. Subsequently, intervention techniques such as positive reinforcement of desired behaviors and negative consequences of maladaptive or problematic behaviors and the use of tokens are often employed to support behavioral change (Donaldson, DeLeon, Fisher, & Kahng, 2014).

Case Study (Cognitive Behavioral Therapy)

Tamika is a 15-year-old African American girl who was brought into therapy because of her grandmother's concerns about her depression. Tamika has been living with her maternal grandparents and younger brother and sister in a two-bedroom apartment complex in a low-income neighborhood. She has little contact with her father who is currently incarcerated for possession and sale of controlled substances. Tamika's mother is currently attending a recovery program downtown. Tamika is not a self-referral and rejects the idea of seeing a therapist. Tamika states that the therapist has been condescending and paternalistic. Tamika has been suspended from school after being found in possession of a concealed weapon. She has had a series of altercations with her peers this year, which has led to an arrest for disorderly conduct and resisting arrest. Despite Tamika's legal problems, she contends that she does not require therapy and feels as if her grandmother has been exaggerating her self-destructive behaviors.

Tamika describes herself as a leader of her peers. She says that she does not take any mess from anyone and cautions that if people piss her off, they will undoubtedly suffer from her wrath. Tamika had very little interest in school, but boasted that she was a very good singer. After several sessions, Tamika revealed that she believed much of her irritability and problems were related to her recent weight gain. She believed that her lack of exercise and poor eating habits made her unattractive and the brunt of many jokes. Over time, we were able to discuss

(continued)

(*continued*)

Tamika's ideas about weight, exercise, and the extent to which she was motivated to make changes in her lifestyle.

Tamika decided how she would approach her weight loss program. She decided that she would jog in the morning before she attended school. She agreed that she would journal how far she ran in a weekly log. She was a bit anxious about using the scale to monitor progress. She said that, in the past, she became easily frustrated and would eventually give up exercising. We agreed that she would measure her progress by the clothes that she could fit.

Tamika was an adolescent suffering from low self-esteem, poor self-image, obesity, and perhaps mild depression. Nevertheless, she was able to identify specific goals that she was willing to work on while attending her therapy sessions. Eventually, Tamika was able to open up and share some of her feelings regarding her relationships, her life, and her reflections on her aggressive behaviors. Cognitive behavioral treatment was not only useful in helping her structure her goals but it also served as a foundation to help her solve some of her life's other problems.

RAP THERAPY

Rap therapy, also known as hip hop therapy, is the purposeful integration of elements of hip hop culture in a therapeutic setting to achieve catharsis and facilitate psychosocial development. Since the early 2000s, social scientists and practitioners have explored the efficacy of using rap therapy in a variety of milieus and through different modalities. Numerous empirical studies have found rap therapy to be highly effective in improving therapeutic experiences and mental health outcomes, particularly among urban African American adolescents (Allen, 2005; DeCarlo & Hockman, 2004; Tyson, 2006). In 2000, Don Elligan coined the term rap therapy in his article documenting his use of rap in a clinical setting. Although this may be the first written documentation of the use of rap music to address mental health stressors, hip hop has been used as a cathartic release and a form of expression since its inception in the late 1970s, helping to address the harsh conditions of urban life in New York City. Through rap, graffiti, break dancing, and "dj-ing," urban youth were able to cope with stress, build group supports, and speak out against oppression, poverty, and gain a sense of identity.

Although many critics of rap music often are quick to point out that rap music is often violent, misogynistic, and glorifies the use of drugs and alcohol they fail to recognize that many of the youthful listeners of rap music often can relate to the experiences expressed by the rap entertainer. Additionally, rappers are often viewed as icons within the urban community. The chosen few artists have been seemingly able to escape the overarching arms of poverty and escape the immediate chase of the legal system while simultaneously giving voice to the multitude of young urban adolescents and their respective struggles. Rappers have become more than role models, they have become urban folklore. To many young people in urban centers across the country, rappers appear to be the modern-day Robin Hoods. This "rags to riches" theme is appealing to those adolescents who are searching for identity, expression, power, and, most importantly, hope. Embedded, in the fluid discourse is the belief that if you are a creative wordsmith, a young person can rise above his or her environment and grasp fame and all the spoils of wealth. Hope is essential for young people surrounded by despair and constant reminders of failure. Without hope, African American adolescents living in urban impoverished communities are more likely to become discouraged and as a result more vulnerable to the omnipresent risk factors that surround them.

Far too many youth enter the mental health systems with negative labels that often pathologize their behaviors and emphasize the youth's problems and deficits rather than paying equal attention to the adolescent's strengths. A competent social worker will engage the "whole young person" and embrace the adolescent's interests and talents. To bridge the gap and improve mental health outcomes for many African American adolescents, social workers and other mental health practitioners must change the way that clinical services are offered. They need to draw directly from the lives and culture of young people. Considering the far-reaching cognitive influence rap music has on the development of many urban youth, it is imperative for social work practitioners to use rap music in therapy when working with clients heavily influenced by rap. Rap music and its videos continue to define issues around masculinity, values, ethics, relationships, honor, codes of conduct, dress, language, finance, education, drug use, parenting, legal trends, and responsibilities among many inner city African American youth (Kobin & Tyson, 2006).

A culturally competent social worker should explore the many genres of music to which the African American adolescent frequently listens. Today this is much easier because many adolescents carry their music with them on their phones, iPods, and other music storage devices. If the social worker finds that the adolescent listens to rap music sporadically or has a fleeting interest in hip hop culture, rap therapy may not be the most appropriate treatment strategy. However, if the adolescent has a substantial interest in hip hop culture and listens to a preponderance of rap, the practitioner should consider using rap therapy.

Rap therapy is very effective in establishing a working rapport with many adolescents. It should be noted that many adolescents may be wary of sharing their music with the therapist if they believe that they will be judged. It may be wise to inquire about their favorite artist and performers first and then later, as the relationship strengthens, to discuss what specific songs are appealing and why. If the client has several favorite artists, the social worker can ask about the similarities and differences of the artists. As the therapeutic alliance is strengthened, the social worker can begin to challenge the adolescent to deconstruct the lyrics to gain insights into how the lyrics have impacted his or her thoughts and feelings about certain topics. As clients become more aware of their cognitions, they also may gain a greater appreciation of the complexities of the music, the artists, and themselves. They may begin to recognize that they may agree with parts of the song but disagree with other parts. This often becomes a transformative experience because the adolescent may begin to examine aspects of cognitive dissonance, which is often present in many close personal relationships. The youth could then be prompted to consider the complex subtleties of other relationships, which he or she had regarded as all or nothing.

Finally, adolescents who have deconstructed lyrics could be asked to compose their own lyrics and tell their own stories. For instance, an adolescent male who is 15 years old could be asked to write a rap describing how he can better manage his behavior in class. The client may show tremendous insight into his own behavior and may lay the groundwork for the social worker to explore the proposed solutions. Even if the proposed solutions are not viable, the client should be acknowledged for his investment and his effort. Some young people may lack the capacity to gain further insight into their behavior; in this case, the social worker can use hypothetical situations.

Incorporating rap music into therapy is a creative process that utilizes many of the inherent strengths of urban adolescents. Furthermore, it encourages many adolescents who abhor mental health treatment to become active participants in their own treatment and take ownership of their solutions (Mezzacappa & Buckner, 2010).

Case Study (Rap/Hip Hop Therapy)

Yusef is a 17-year-old African American male who has lived in a residential group home in an urban community for the last 20 months. Yusef has been diagnosed with bipolar disorder and has been attending an outpatient rehabilitation program weekly. Yusef is a single child and decided to leave his mother's house when he was 15 years old because he felt that she was unaccepting of his behavior and his lifestyle choices. Yusef does not attend school and believes that he will be able to take the General Equivalency Examination next spring when he turns 18 years old. When Yusef attended his last high school, he was asked not to return because of excessive absences. He admits that he did not apply himself in school and felt like he could not relate to much of the material he was required to learn.

Yusef is required to participate in group sessions as a condition of his stay at the group home. Yusef has a cordial relationship with the four other young men in the home. Yusef occasionally plays a pickup game of basketball at the local park, but spends a majority of his time listening to music and playing dice with older men.

Yusef attended his first individual session with me wearing an expensive pair of headphones and refused to take them off during the session. Rather than asking him to take the headphones off, I allowed him to keep them on under one condition, that he share what he likes about the song. Yusef explained that the artist he was listening to was an underground rapper whom he could identify with. He later suggested that he liked the rapper's "flow" and suggested that his image was of being a misunderstood "baller." I cautiously asked about the similarities he saw in his life. Yusef pointed out some similarities suggesting that he had some insight on his own behavior. Additionally, he felt that the plot of the lyrics was the soliloquy that every man

(continued)

(continued)

can go from rags to riches. I asked Yusef to explain what the lyrics meant to him and he responded in one word: HOPE! He later elaborated that he believed that although his life is not turning out as he had planned, he believed that if he was to become a rapper, producer, or artist, he would become wealthy and, more importantly, happy.

After a few sessions of allowing Yusef to discuss music appreciation, we created a therapeutic alliance. Yusef was eager to share newer songs and deconstruct their meanings. He felt empowered because he felt like he was an expert and I was the tyro. Yusef would be eager to expose me to a variety of different songs that exemplified his moods during the course of the week. One song he shared discussed anger and despair, yet another represented a "happy-go-lucky" carefree life. Yusef stated that he could relate to these songs and the artists. During a session, I asked Yusef to write a few bars of his original works. He initially resisted, saying that he was not a rapper, but then took a few moments to codify some of his thoughts and feelings. I praised him for his efforts and let him know that it takes courage to take risks and try new things. Through Yusef's rap, we were able to identify his feelings of rejection by his family, ambivalence within his own sexual identity, and fear of being out on his own. Yusef made significant steps in sharing his feelings and was able to do so in the group setting with other adolescent boys within his group home.

IMPLICATIONS

Many practitioners are not adequately prepared to work effectively with urban African American adolescents. It is imperative in working with urban African American adolescents to consider the individual characteristics of the client, current research on EBT, and promising practices. Adolescence is a time marked with rapid biological and interpersonal changes. Minority adolescents living in poor urban communities have particularly high mental health needs and limited access to appropriate mental health services (Lindsey, Chambers, Pohle, Beall, & Lucksted, 2013). The problem of engaging young urban adolescents has been well documented (dos Reis et al., 2009). Among the many barriers to the treatment of urban youth, cultural incongruence remains a leading factor (Merikangas et al., 2010). Culturally appropriate interventions to address this growing need still remain underdeveloped. Research has shown that clinical interventions do not work equally well across all cultural groups (Liddle et al., 2004). Social workers and other social scientists have attempted to make modifications and cultural adaptations to current EBT cautiously.

Social workers recognize that urban adolescents are confronted with a plethora of social dilemmas. The impact of discrimination and oppression is apparent in impoverished ethnic minority families (Boyd-Franklin & Karger, 2012). Moreover, urban adolescents experience other stressors such as poverty, community violence, substance abuse, family structure, and supports that have consequently exacerbated the risks for negative behavioral and psychological outcomes for urban adolescents (Williams et al., 2013). This chapter described four community concerns that have an impact on urban African American youth: poverty, family structure, community violence, and substance abuse.

To use an old adage, "we must think outside of the box" when working with adolescents. Adolescent culture is ever evolving. Styles, trends, and colloquialisms all seem to change every few months in urban communities. Social workers must stay abreast of the trends and subtle cultural paradigm shifts if they want to understand adolescents. The hip hop culture, often associated with urban adolescents, has its own unique set of values, norms, and language. We must become somewhat like social anthropologists when we view urban adolescent cultures. We must strive to understand the spoken word and the innovative lexicon of digital communication. Failure to get a full grasp of urban adolescent culture can lead to practitioners establishing inappropriate goals and inaccurate assessments.

Finally, this chapter explored the use of two therapeutic interventions that research has shown to be effective when working with urban African Americans: cognitive behavioral theory and rap therapy. Case vignettes were offered to illuminate the usefulness of each distinct approach.

FOR FURTHER STUDY

Suggested Assignments

1. Students will be asked to create an urban glossary. Each student will be asked to write a list of 10 colloquialisms, idioms, or expressions that are currently being used by our youth in urban settings. Students should make an effort to listen to Hip Hop/Rap music, and actually speak to youth and people who work with youth to gain an understanding of the terms and how they are used.

2. Students will investigate one of the multiple media and technology modalities that have become part of urban adolescents' daily lives: television, film, music, social networking websites and platforms (i.e., Facebook, Instagram, Twitter, text messaging), video games, and so on. You will then write a one- to two-page critique that addresses how this modality can increase your understanding of urban youth and how the integration of these modalities can enhance engagement of urban minority youth.

3. Students will review the case vignettes and describe how they would develop and manage a treatment plan for the adolescent client. Students will discuss behavioral, pharmacological, family, and social treatments that can be utilized, as well as barriers to treatment including but not limited to parental resistance, societal bias and stigma, legal limitation, and insurance.

4. Students will be asked to select several preselected classic rap songs, such as JayZ's "Where I'm From" (track 13 on the *In my Lifetime*, Vol. 1 album),

Eminem's "Beautiful" (track 17 on the *Relapse* album), Lupe Fiasco "Bitch Bad" (on the *Food & Liquor II* album), or Ghostface Killah's "All I Got Is You" (track 15 on the *Ironman* album), and deconstruct the lyrics of the song by identifying thematic messages including but not limited to messages of economic oppression, love/intimacy, empowerment, substance abuse, mental illness, grief/loss, and family values. Students should pay close attention to the use of metaphors, similes, and symbolisms and their meaning to an urban subculture. It may be helpful to direct students to http://genius.com for printed lyrics.

5. Students will design a "Vision Board" with urban images of artwork and fashion by using magazine clippings. Students will present their "Vision Board" and discuss the stereotypes that are often associated with urban youth. Then discuss the myth versus reality of the presented work.

Suggested Readings

Edelman, P. B., Holzer, H. J., & Offner, P. (2006). *Reconnecting disadvantaged young men*. Washington, DC: The Urban Institute.

Johnson, W. E., Jr. (Ed.). (2010). *Social work with African American males: Health, mental health, and social policy*. New York, NY: Oxford University Press.

Marshall, C. L. (2009). *Black man heal*. Washington, DC: Institute for African Man Development Press.

Mincy, R. B. (Ed.). (2006). *Black males left behind*. Washington, DC: The Urban Institute.

Monell, J. S. (2010). *Pop culture, and delinquency: Generation why*. Charlotte, NC: CPCC Press.

REFERENCES

Addy, S., Engelhardt, W., & Skinner, C. (2013). *Basic facts about low-income children: Children under 3 years, 2011*. New York, NY: National Center for Children in Poverty.

Allen, N. M. T. (2005). Exploring hip-hop therapy with high-risk youth. *Building on Our Foundations, 5,* 30–36.

Anthony, E. K., Alter, C. F., & Jenson, J. M. (2009). Development of a risk and resilience-based out-of-school time program for children and youths. *Social Work, 54*(1), 45–55.

Awosan, C. I., Sandberg, J. G., & Hall, C. A. (2011). Understanding the experience of Black clients in marriage and family therapy. *Journal of marital and family therapy, 37*(2), 153–168.

Banks, R., Hogue, A., Timberlake, T., & Liddle, H. (1996). An Afrocentric approach to group social skills training with inner-city African American adolescents. *Journal of Negro Education, 4,* 414–423.

Barrera, M., & Castro, F. (2008). A heuristic framework for the cultural adaptation of interventions. *Clinical Psychology Science Practice, 13,* 311–316.

Barrera, M., Jr., Castro, F. G., Strycker, L. A., & Toobert, D. J. (2013). Cultural adaptations of behavioral health interventions: A progress report. *Journal of Consulting and Clinical Psychology, 81*(2), 196.

Belgrave, F. Z., Nguyen, A. B., Johnson, J. L., & Hood, K. (2011). Who is likely to help and hurt? Profiles of African American adolescents with prosocial and aggressive behavior. *Journal of Youth and Adolescence, 40*(8), 1012–1024.

Belle, D., & Benenson, J. (2014). Children's social networks and well-being. In B-A Asher, F. Casas, I. Frones, & J. E. Korbin (Eds.), *Handbook of child well-being* (pp. 1335–1363). Dordrecht, the Netherlands: Springer.

Bell-Tolliver, L., Burgess, R., & Brock, L. J. (2009). African American therapists working with African American families: An exploration of the strengths perspective in treatment. *Journal of Marital and Family Therapy, 35*(3), 293–307.

Bernal, G., Jiménez-Chafey, M. I., & Domenech Rodríguez, M. M. (2009). Cultural adaptation of treatments: A resource for considering culture in evidence-based practice. *Professional Psychology: Research and Practice, 40*(4), 361.

Bohnert, A. S., Ilgen, M. A., Trafton, J. A., Kerns, R. D., Eisenberg, A., Ganoczy, D., & Blow, F. C. (2014). Trends and regional variation in opioid overdose mortality among veterans health administration patients, fiscal year 2001 to 2009. *The Clinical Journal of Pain, 30*(7), 605–612.

Bors, W., Sanders, M., & Markie-Dadds, C. (2002). The effects of Triple P-Positive Parenting Program on preschool children with co-occurring disruptive behavior and attentional/hyperactive difficulties. *Journal of Abnormal Child Psychology, 30*, 571–579.

Boxer, P. (2014). Youth gangs and adolescent development: New findings, new challenges, and new directions: Introduction to the special section. *Journal of Research on Adolescence, 24*(2), 201–203.

Boyd-Franklin, N., & Karger, M. (2012). Intersections of race, class, and poverty: Challenges and resilience in African American families. In F. Walsh (Ed.), *Normal Family Processes: Growing Diversity and Complexity* (4th ed., 273–296). New York, NY: Guilford Press.

Bromfield, L. M., Gillingham, P., & Higgins, D. J. (2007). Cumulative harm and chronic child maltreatment. *Developing Practice: The Child, Youth and Family Work Journal, 19*, 34–42.

Cabrera, N. J., Beeghly, M., & Eisenberg, N. (2012). Positive development of minority children: Introduction to the special issue. *Child Development Perspectives, 6*(3), 207–209.

Cardemil, E. V., Reivich, K. J., & Seligman, M. E. (2002). The prevention of depressive symptoms in low-income minority middle school students. *Prevention & Treatment, 5*(1), 8a.

Castro, F. G., Barrera Jr., M., & Steiker, L. K. H. (2010). Issues and challenges in the design of culturally adapted evidence-based interventions. *Annual Review of Clinical Psychology, 6,* 213.

Cauce, A. M., Domenech-Rodríguez, M., Paradise, M., Cochran, B. N., Shea, J. M., Srebnik, D., & Baydar, N. (2002). Cultural and contextual influences in mental health help seeking: A focus on ethnic minority youth. *Journal of Consulting and Clinical Psychology, 70*(1), 44.

Clarke, G., DeBar, L., & Lewinsohn, P. (2003). Cognitive-behavioral group treatment for adolescent depression. In A. Kadzin & J. R. Weisz (Eds.), *Evidence-based psychotherapies for children and adolescents* (pp. 120–134). New York, NY: Guilford Press.

Clark, T. T., Belgrave, F. Z., & Nasim, A. (2008). Risk and protective factors for substance use among urban African American adolescents considered high-risk. *Journal of Ethnicity in Substance Abuse, 7*(3), 292–303.

Clark, T. T., Nguyen, A. B., Belgrave, F. Z., & Tademy, R. (2011). Understanding the dimensions of parental influence on alcohol use and alcohol refusal efficacy among African American adolescents. *Social Work Research, 35*(3), 147–157.

Cohen, A. P. (2013). *Symbolic construction of community.* London, England: Routledge.

Cooley-Strickland, M. R., Griffin, R. S., Darney, D., Otte, K., & Ko, J. (2011). Urban African American youth exposed to community violence: A school-based anxiety preventive intervention efficacy study. *Journal of Prevention & Intervention in the Community, 39*(2), 149–166.

Cuevas, C., Finkelhor, D., Clifford, C., Ormrod, R., & Turner, H. (2010). Psychological distress as a risk factor for re-victimization of children. *Child Abuse & Neglect, 34*, 235–243.

DeCarlo, A., & Hockman, E. (2004). RAP therapy: A group work intervention method for urban adolescents. *Social Work with Groups, 26*(3), 45–59.

Donaldson, J. M., DeLeon, I. G., Fisher, A. B., & Kahng, S. (2014). Effects of and preference for conditions of token earn versus token loss. *Journal of Applied Behavior Analysis, 47*(3), 537–548.

Dos Reis, S., Mychailyszyn, M. P., Evans-Lacko, S. E., Beltran, A., Riley, A. W., & Myers, M. A. (2009). The meaning of attention-deficit/hyperactivity disorder medication and parents' initiation and continuity of treatment for their child. *Journal of Child and Adolescent Psychopharmacology*, *19*(4), 377–383.

Epstein-Ngo, Q. M., Cunningham, R. M., Whiteside, L. K., Chermack, S. T., Booth, B. M., Zimmerman, M. A., & Walton, M. A. (2013). A daily calendar analysis of substance use and dating violence among high risk urban youth. *Drug and Alcohol Dependence*, *130*(1), 194–200.

Falicov, C. J. (2009). Commentary: On the wisdom and challenges of culturally attuned treatments for Latinos. *Family Process, 48*(2), 292–309.

Galinsky, M. J., Fraser, M. W., Day, S. H., & Richman, J. M. (2013). A primer for the design of practice manuals four stages of development. *Research on Social Work Practice, 23*(2), 219–228.

Garbarino, J., Kostelny, K., & Dubrow, N. (1991). What children can tell us about living in danger. *American Psychologist, 46*(4), 376.

Gibbs, T. A., Okuda, M., Oquendo, M. A., Lawson, W. B., Wang, S., Thomas, Y. F., & Blanco, C. (2013). Mental health of African Americans and Caribbean Blacks in the United States: Results from the national epidemiological survey on alcohol and related conditions. *American Journal of Public Health, 103*(2), 330–338.

Gilman, A. B., Hill, K. G., Hawkins, J. D., Howell, J. C., & Kosterman, R. (2014). The developmental dynamics of joining a gang in adolescence: Patterns and predictors of gang membership. *Journal of Research on Adolescence, 24*(2), 204–219.

Ginsburg, G. S., & Drake, K. L. (2002). School-based treatment for anxious African-American adolescents: A controlled pilot study. *Journal of the American Academy of Child & Adolescent Psychiatry, 41*(7), 768–775.

Gonzales, N. A., Dumka, L. E., Millsap, R. E., Gottschall, A., McClain, D. B., Wong, J. J., & Kim, S. Y. (2012). Randomized trial of a broad preventive intervention for Mexican American adolescents. *Journal of Consulting and Clinical Psychology, 80*(1), 1.

Hubble, M. A., Duncan, B. L., & Miller, S. D. (1999). *Introduction*. Washington, DC: American Psychological Association.

Hwang, W. C. (2009). The formative method for adapting psychotherapy (FMAP): A community-based developmental approach to culturally adapting therapy. *Professional Psychology: Research and Practice, 40*(4), 369.

Javdani, S., Abdul-Adil, J., Suarez, L., Nichols, S. R., & Farmer, A. D. (2014). Gender differences in the effects of community violence on mental health outcomes in a sample of low-income youth receiving psychiatric care. *American Journal of Community Psychology, 53*(3–4), 235–248.

Kadzin, A. E., Stolar, M. J., & Marciano, P. L. (1995). Risk factors for dropping out of treatment among White and Black families. *Journal of Family Psychology, 9*(4), 402.

Kendall, P. (1996). Long-term follow-up of a cognitive-behavioral therapy for anxiety-disordered youth. *Journal of Consulting and Clinical Psychology, 64*(4), pp. 724–730.

Keyes, C. L. (1996). At the crossroads: Rap music and its African nexus. *Ethnomusicology, 40*, 223–248.

Kobin, C., & Tyson, E. (2006). Thematic analysis of hip-hop music: Can hip-hop in therapy facilitate empathic connections when working with clients in urban settings? *The Arts in Psychotherapy, 33*(4), 343–356.

Koprowska, J. (2014). *Communication and interpersonal skills in social work.* London: Learning Matters.

Kreuter, M. W., & Skinner, C. S. (2000). Tailoring: What's in a name?" *Health Education Research, 15*(1), 1–4.

Lambert, S. F., Nylund-Gibson, K., Copeland-Linder, N., & Ialongo, N. S. (2010). Patterns of community violence exposure during adolescence. *American Journal of Community Psychology, 46*(3–4), 289–302.

Lee, Y., & Kim, S. (2011). Childhood maltreatment in South Korea: A retrospective study. *Child Abuse & Neglect, 35*, 1037–1044.

Lee, Y., & Styne, D. (2013). Influences on the onset and tempo of puberty in human beings and implications for adolescent psychological development. *Hormones and Behavior, 64*(2), 250–261.

Liddle, H. A., Rowe, C. L., Dakof, G. A., Ungaro, R. A., & Henderson, C. E. (2004). Early intervention for adolescent substance abuse: Pretreatment to posttreatment outcomes of a randomized clinical trial comparing multidimensional family therapy and peer group treatment. *Journal of Psychoactive Drugs, 36*(1), 49–63.

Lindsey, M. A., Chambers, K., Pohle, C., Beall, P., & Lucksted, A. (2013). Understanding the behavioral determinants of mental health service use by urban, under-resourced Black youth: Adolescent and caregiver perspectives. *Journal of Child and Family Studies, 22*(1), 107–121.

Lochman, J. E., & Wells, K. C. (2004). The coping power program for preadolescent aggressive boys and their parents: Outcome effects at the 1-year follow-up. *Journal of Consulting and Clinical Psychology, 72*(4), 571.

Martin, J. M., & Martin, E. P. (1985). *The helping tradition in the Black family and community.* Washington, DC: National Association of Social Workers.

McElroy, S., & Hevey, D. (2014). Relationship between adverse early experiences, stressors, psychosocial resources and wellbeing. *Child Abuse & Neglect, 38*(1), 65–75.

McMahon, S. D., Todd, N. R., Martinez, A., Coker, C., Sheu, C. F., Washburn, J., & Shah, S. (2013). Aggressive and prosocial behavior: Community violence, cognitive, and behavioral predictors among urban African American youth. *American Journal of Community Psychology, 51*(3–4), 407–421.

McNaughton-Reyes, H. L., Foshee, V. A., Bauer, D. J., & Ennett, S. T. (2014). Proximal and time-varying effects of cigarette, alcohol, marijuana and other hard drug use on adolescent dating aggression. *Journal of Adolescence, 37*(3), 281–289.

Mendle, J., Harden, K. P., Brooks-Gunn, J., & Graber, J. A. (2010). Development's tortoise and hare: Pubertal timing, pubertal tempo, and depressive symptoms in boys and girls. *Developmental Psychology, 46*(5), 1341.

Merikangas, K. R., He, J. P., Burstein, M., Swanson, S. A., Avenevoli, S., Cui, L., & Swendsen, J. (2010). Lifetime prevalence of mental disorders in US adolescents: Results from the National Comorbidity Survey Replication–Adolescent Supplement (NCS-A). *Journal of the American Academy of Child & Adolescent Psychiatry, 49*(10), 980–989.

Mezzacappa, E., & Buckner, J. C. (2010). Working memory training for children with attention problems or hyperactivity: A school-based pilot study. *School Mental Health, 2*(4), 202–208.

Reed, E., Lawrence, D. A., Santana, M. C., Welles, C. S. L., Horsburgh, C. R., Silverman, J. G., & Raj, A. (2014). Adolescent experiences of violence and relation to violence perpetration beyond young adulthood among an urban sample of Black and African American males. *Journal of Urban Health, 91*(1), 96–106.

Resnicow, K., Soler, R., Brathwaite, J., Ahluwalia, J., & Butler, J. (2000). Cultural sensitivity in substance use prevention. *Journal of Community Psychology, 28*(3), 271–290.

Robbins, R. N., & Bryan, A. (2004). Relationships between future orientation, impulsive sensation seeking, and risk behavior among adjudicated adolescents. *Journal of Adolescent Research, 19*(4), 428–445.

Rohde, P., Stice, E., Shaw, H., & Brière, F. N. (2014). Indicated cognitive behavioral group depression prevention compared to bibliotherapy and brochure control: Acute effects of an effectiveness trial with adolescents. *Journal of Consulting and Clinical Psychology, 82*(1), 65.

Rosselló, J., Bernal, G., & Rivera-Medina, C. (2012). Individual and group CBT and IPT for Puerto Rican adolescents with depressive symptoms. *Cultural Diversity and Ethnic Minority Psychology, 14*, 234–245.

Rothman, E. F., Johnson, R. M., Azrael, D., Hall, D. M., & Weinberg, J. (2010). Perpetration of physical assault against dating partners, peers, and siblings among a locally representative sample of high school students in Boston, Massachusetts. *Archives of Pediatrics & Adolescent Medicine, 164*(12), 1118–1124.

Runyon, M. K., Deblinger, E., & Steer, R. A. (2014). PTSD symptom cluster profiles of youth who have experienced sexual or physical abuse. *Child Abuse & Neglect, 38*(1), 84–90.

Schwartz, D., & Gorman, A. H. (2003). Community violence exposure and children's academic functioning. *Journal of Educational Psychology, 95*(1), 163.

Southam-Gerow, M. A., & Prinstein, M. J. (2014). Evidence base updates: The evolution of the evaluation of psychological treatments for children and adolescents. *Journal of Clinical Child & Adolescent Psychology, 43*(1), 1–6.

Spano, R., Rivera, C., & Bolland, J. M. (2011). Does parenting shield youth from exposure to violence during adolescence? A 5-year longitudinal test in a high-poverty sample of minority youth. *Journal of Interpersonal Violence, 26*(5), 930–949.

Spano, R., Rivera, C., Vazsonyi, A. T., & Bolland, J. M. (2012). Specifying the interrelationship between exposure to violence and parental monitoring for younger versus older adolescents: A five year longitudinal test. *American Journal of Community Psychology, 49*(1–2), 127–141.

Steinberg, L. (2007). Risk taking in adolescence new perspectives from brain and behavioral science. *Current Directions in Psychological Science, 16*(2), 55–59.

Strier, R. (2009). Class-competent social work: A preliminary definition. *International Journal of Social Welfare, 18*(3), 237–242.

Swanson, D. P., Spencer, M. B., Harpalani, V., & Spencer, T. R. (2002). Identity processes and the positive youth development of African Americans: An explanatory framework. *New Directions for Youth Development, 2002*(95), 73–100.

Tulane, S., Vaterlaus, J. M., & Beckert, T. E. (2014). An A in their social lives, but an F in school adolescent perceptions of texting in school. *Youth & Society, 41*(4), 346–352. Advance online publication. doi: 10.1177/0044118X14559916

Tyson, E. H. (2006). Rap-music attitude and perception scale: A validation study. *Research on Social Work Practice, 16*(2), 211–223.

Unrau, Y., Font, S., & Rawls, G. (2012). Readiness for college among students who have aged out of foster care. *Children and Youth Service Review, 1*(34), 76–83.

U.S. Department of Health and Human Services. (2010). The AFCARS report: Preliminary estimates FY 2010. USDHHS, Administration for Children and Families Report. Retrieved from http://www.nationalfostercare.org/uploads/8/7/9/7/8797896/afcars_report18.pdf

Villegas, S., Rosenthal, J., O'Brien, K., & Pecora, P. J. (2014). Educational outcomes for adults formerly in foster care: The role of ethnicity. *Children and Youth Services Review, 36*, 42–52.

Wallace, J. M., Jr., & Muroff, J. R. (2002). Preventing substance abuse among African American children and youth: Race differences in risk factor exposure and vulnerability. *Journal of Primary Prevention, 22*(3), 235–261.

Weiss, N. H., Tull, M. T., Davis, L. T., Dehon, E. E., Fulton, J. J., & Gratz, K. L. (2012). Examining the association between emotion regulation difficulties and probable posttraumatic stress disorder within a sample of African Americans. *Cognitive Behaviour Therapy, 41*(1), 5–14.

Weisz, J. R., Krumholz, L. S., Santucci, L., Thomassin, K., Ng, M. Y., & Rutt, C. (2014). Tailoring evidence-based youth psychotherapies to clinical care contexts. *Annual Review of Clinical Psychology, 11*(1), 139–163.

Williams, J. L., Aiyer, S. M., Durkee, M. I., & Tolan, P. H. (2014). The protective role of ethnic identity for urban adolescent males facing multiple stressors. *Journal of Youth and Adolescence, 43*, 1728–1741.

Williams, J. L., Anderson, R. E., Francois, A. G., Hussain, S., & Tolan, P. H. (2014). Ethnic identity and positive youth development in adolescent males: A culturally integrated approach. *Applied Developmental Science, 18*(2), 110–122.

Williams, J. L., Tolan, P. H., Durkee, M. I., Francois, A. G., & Anderson, R. E. (2012). Integrating racial and ethnic identity research into developmental understanding of adolescents. *Child Development Perspectives, 6*(3), 304–311.

Wingood, G., & DiClemente, R. (2008). The ADAPT-ITT model: A novel method of adapting evidenced based HIV interventions. *Journal of Acquired Immune Deficiency Syndromes, 47,* 40–16.

Wolk, C. B., Kendall, P. C., & Beidas, R. S. (2014). Cognitive-behavioral therapy for child anxiety confers long-term protection from suicidality. *Journal of the American Academy of Child & Adolescent Psychiatry, 54,* 175–179.

Yanovitzky, I. (2005). Sensation seeking and adolescent drug use: The mediating role of association with deviant peers and pro-drug discussions. *Health communication, 17*(1), 67–89.

Yeh, M., McCabe, K., Hurlburt, M., Hough, R., Hazen, A., Culver, S.,... Landsverk, J. (2002). Referral sources, diagnoses, and service types of youth in public outpatient mental health care: A focus on ethnic minorities. *The Journal of Behavioral Health Services & Research, 29*(1), 45–60.

CHAPTER 5

Coming to America: Black Immigrants in Urban Communities

Belinda Davis Smith, Isiah Marshall Jr.,
Dana Burdnell Wilson, and Errol S. Bolden

The United States has a long-standing history of being recognized as a "melting pot" of immigrants hoping to find a pathway to a better life in America. As a result of the Immigration and Nationality Act of 1965, the influx of immigrants with diverse racial and ethnic cultural backgrounds increased (Rong & Fitchett, 2008). Each year, nearly a million immigrants migrate to the United States, with Hispanics representing the fastest-growing and largest ethnic or racial minority group. Recently, the growing number of immigrant children and youth from bordering countries desperately seeking to escape dismal conditions in their country of origin has saturated the news. According to the U.S. Census Bureau (2012), 52 million Hispanics currently reside in the United States. Given the rapid increase, it is predicted that by 2050 there will be 132.8 million Hispanics in this county, representing 30% of the national population.

Black immigrants from African and Caribbean countries are not addressed in scholarly literature or media to the extent of other immigrant groups. However, they have become an increasing part of the influx of diverse racial and ethnic groups that contribute to the transformation of the United States (Kent, 2007). According to Hernandez (2012), the presence of Black immigrants in the United States has doubled over the past 20 years. Currently, there are more than 1.7 million Black Caribbeans and up to 1.4 million Black Africans residing in the United States. Although outnumbered by other immigrant groups, Black immigrants are among the fastest-growing number of immigrants in this country, which clearly has implications for social work education, policy, and practice. Although considerable attention has been paid to the Latino immigration issues, similar issues facing Black immigrants have been absent from the literature.

Scholars studying Black immigrants noted that during the 1980s and 1990s, there was a 200% increase in the number of Black immigrants, which decreased to 100% in the 21st century (Capps, McCabe, & Fix, 2012; Kent, 2007). Similar to other immigrant groups in the United States, most Black immigrants are in search of a better life than they experience in their war-torn countries of origin and have aspirations to avail themselves of educational and employment opportunities, political asylum, or family reunification.

This chapter summarizes characteristics of Black immigrant groups and their immigration history and patterns; addresses U.S. immigration policies and their influence on Black immigrant groups in urban areas; examines the Black immigrant family structure and Black immigrant group interactions with urban systems (e.g., schools and the judicial system); and explores mezzo- and macro-level formal and informal support systems among Black immigrants in urban communities. The chapter concludes with implications for social work practice with immigrants in urban communities and a classroom group exercise.

It is important that social work students and practitioners expand their knowledge of cultural differences among Black immigrants from African and Caribbean countries in order to provide culturally relevant programs and services that maintain cultural heritage and strengthen adaptation and adjustment to American society.

BLACK IMMIGRANTS DEFINED

Black immigrants typically come from the African continent and the Caribbean islands, with each group having its own historical background and experiences in the United States. History records the forced departure of Africans to the United States during the slave trade in the early part of the 17th century through the beginning of the 19th century (Kent, 2007; Rong & Fitchett, 2008; Shaw-Taylor & Tuch, 2007). For more than 150 years, restrictive immigration laws did not allow non-Whites legal entry to the United States. During this period, a majority of the immigrants (76%) were Whites from European countries.

Despite barriers that were designed to exclude Blacks from entry, Caribbean Blacks have a long history of immigration to the United States, through both slavery and voluntary migration. For example, in the 18th century, Blacks from the Caribbean represented about 20% of South Carolina's slaves, many of whom were transported to New York (Hodges, 1999).

The first voluntary group of Black immigrants from the Caribbean migrated to the United States during the early 1900s (Kent, 2007; Thomas, 2012; Toso, Prins, & Mooney, 2013). Most came under contract to work in agriculture and construction, with a large number working on construction of the Panama Canal. However, a group of educated professionals and elite-class Black Caribbean immigrants, generally known as West Indians, settled in Harlem, New York.

Harlem and other urban communities became the destinations of choice for Blacks from the Caribbean during the early 20th century, much as they did for the African American migration to the north (Hine, Hine, & Harold, 2006). Throughout the

20th century, Black Caribbean immigrant rates increased significantly, but at a lesser level. Immigration rates fell about 4% from 2006 to 2009 due to the economic recession in the United States. Despite the changing immigration trends, 1.7 million Black Caribbean immigrants represent the largest Black immigrant group (Thomas, 2012).

African immigration was infrequent until the late 20th century (Capps et al., 2012; Fulwood, III, 2013). According to Kent (2007), the number of Black African immigrants dramatically increased, nearly sevenfold, between 1960 and 1980. With the increase in African immigration, the overall number of black immigrants between 1980 and 2005 nearly tripled, and immigrants as a proportion of all Blacks in the United States increased from 1% to 8%. Many African immigrants entered the United States through the diversity visa program, a mechanism to allow immigrants from underrepresented countries to emmigrate to the United States. Although 70% of Black African immigrants come from 10 countries, Nigeria and Ethiopia have the largest numbers of immigrants to the United States. The immigrants from Caribbean and African nations differ by gender: Most Caribbean immigrants are female, but more than half of the African immigrants are male.

With the influx of Black voluntary immigrants to U.S. urban cities, understanding the heterogeneous composition of the nearly 3 million residents residing in urban communities is essential for culturally competent social work practice.

BLACK CARIBBEAN IMMIGRANTS

In 2009, there were a total 3.5 million Caribbean immigrants (half of whom self-identified as Hispanic) residing in the United States, representing 9% of the foreign-born population (McCabe, 2011). Over the past 50 years, the United States has experienced a 17-fold increase in the Caribbean immigrant population. Caribbean immigrants represent more than 15 nations; 90% of those who self-identify as Black came from Cuba, the Dominican Republic, Jamaica, Haiti, or Trinidad/Tobago (Migration Institute, 2011). There is significant group diversity among Caribbean immigrants, reflected in language variation: English, Spanish, French, and Dutch, as well as dialects such as French Creole, are commonly spoken (Rong & Fitchett, 2008; Toso et al., 2013).

According to Kent (2007), more than 80% of Black Caribbean immigrants come to the United States because of family connections and the proximity of the Florida coast to the Caribbean. A majority of Caribbean immigrants (69%) settle in Florida or New York. However, increasingly, they have migrated to other states, including New Jersey, Massachusetts, Georgia, Connecticut, Pennsylvania, and California. Between 2006 and 2008, 49% were reported as legally authorized residents, 28% had a legal status, 6% were unauthorized immigrants, 7% had entered as temporary residents, and 1% had a legal temporary status (McCabe, 2011). Similar to European immigrant groups during the Progressive Era, contemporary Black Caribbean immigrants have settled in concentrated urban communities or within close proximity to metropolitan areas. Neighborhoods of immigrants with similar cultural backgrounds and language patterns have always been considered significant to immigrants' adaptation and adjustment in the United States (Logan, Alba, & Zang, 2002).

Because 90% of Black Caribbean immigrants are from English-speaking countries, this may explain their high rate of participation in the labor force, estimated at 75%. In fact, Black Caribbean immigrants generally are less educated than African immigrants and native African Americans but tend to earn more. Most Caribbean immigrants have at least a high school education and are employed mainly in service-oriented jobs, construction, extraction, and transportation, as well as administrative support (McCabe, 2011). Thomas (2012) reported gender disparities among Caribbean women in the labor force. Although the females have higher rates of immigration and 73% are participants in the labor force, they tend to lag in earnings by 9% to 13%, which creates economic challenges.

Despite their long-standing immigration history to the United States, Black Caribbean immigrants remain a vulnerable population due to racism and anti-immigrant attitudes; although these attitudes have improved, they continue to permeate the landscape of American society. Toso, Prins, and Mooney (2013) identified health challenges, lower educational levels, employment barriers, and higher rates of female single-parent households as challenges that are faced by Black Caribbean immigrants. Zhou (2003) noted that children of Caribbean immigrants experience arduous challenges as a result of living in urban neighborhoods, such as social isolation from America's mainstream, exposure to a ghetto culture, and an attitude of materialism due to excessive consumption of television. Communities with depleted resources, inadequate schools, and higher rates of community violence increase the level of vulnerability for Black Caribbean immigrant children and their families.

Black immigrants, particularly those in urban communities, maintain that their Caribbean identity is important to them in buffering the challenges of living in urban neighborhoods. Undoubtedly, collectivism and maintained cultural identity must be considered as strengths when working with Black immigrant families. Recognizing cultural competence is a continuum; social workers must diligently strive to develop knowledge of Black Caribbean immigrants' historical background, cultural traditions, values, and beliefs, avoiding the tendency to make generalizations.

AFRICAN IMMIGRANTS

Within the social work literature, only limited attention is given to Black immigrants in the United States. Mukenge and Mukenge (2005) argued that, although there has been an increase in examination of Black immigrants, most of the empirical studies have assumed that Blacks are culturally homogeneous and that Black immigrants from Africa are often excluded and deemed an "invisible minority" in empirical studies. Also, there is a dearth of literature that specifically focuses on Black immigrants in urban communities. Although Caribbean Black immigrants have a long-standing history of voluntary migration to the United States, Black African immigrants have resided in the United States for a shorter period of time.

Notably, though, Black immigrants from the Cape Verde Islands, located on the coast of Senegal in Africa, have a longer history of voluntary immigration to the United

States than other Black immigrants from Africa. Halter (1993) estimated that 20,000 Black Cape Verdeans immigrated to the United States and settled in Massachusetts from 1860 to 1940. Scholars have recognized Cape Verdeans as being the first and largest group of Black Africans to immigrate to the United States voluntarily in the late 19th century and to the middle of the 20th century (Halter, 1993; Kent, 2007; Shaw-Taylor & Tuch, 2007). Given the undeniable presence of racism, oppression, and discriminatory immigration laws, African immigration to the United States was an anomaly. Unlike the Caribbean, which is closer to U.S. shores, the distance between Africa and America added to the difficulty of immigrating to the United States.

Regarding immigration trends, Shaw-Taylor and Tuch (2007) cited data from the 2003 *Statistical Yearbook of the Immigration and Naturalization Service* indicating 74,610 voluntary Black African immigrants from 1891 to 1970. Trends in African immigration to the United States significantly increased after reforms were made in immigration laws in 1965. From 1971 to 2003, immigration rose to 805,564. The authors highlighted that the number of immigrants from Africa during this period included not only Black Africans from the sub-Saharan region but also Arab North Africans.

The pilgrimage that African Americans undertook as part of the exodus from the South to the North in the United States began during the Progressive era from 1910 to 1940 and from 1940 to 1970. Similarly, African immigrants began the pilgrimage from Africa to America during the mid and late 20th century, which reflects the transformative period of U.S. history, particularly the development of urban communities and ethnic conclaves.

During the later years of the 20th century and throughout the early 21st century, Black Africans from Nigeria, Ethiopia, and Ghana immigrated to the United States. Kent (2007) described how the end of colonial rule by European nations led to the emergence of independent nation-states in many areas of the sub-Saharan region, causing many White Africans to flee to several countries, including the United States. During the 1970s, the demise of the economy, political turmoil, government corruption, widespread poverty, and the eruption of violence led to the first wave of Black Africans immigrating to the United States.

URBAN BLACK IMMIGRANTS: IMMIGRATION AND SOCIAL POLICY

Like the majority of immigrant groups who came to America, Black immigrants migrated to this county in search of better opportunities for their families and themselves. During the early waves (1892–1954) of migration to the United States, many European immigrants were processed through Ellis Island in New York and subsequently settled in large cities (e.g., New York, Buffalo, Cleveland, Boston, Detroit, and Chicago; Brown, Mott, & Malecki, 2007). Many Black immigrant groups, primarily Africans and Caribbeans, settled in these urban areas to reap the stable economic and employment opportunities that the United States offered.

HISTORICAL ANALYSIS

Prior to 1958, Blacks could not immigrate to the United States. Due to the racial climate of the United States, especially after the end of the slave trade in 1808, non-Whites were not allowed to enter the country.

In 1965, the passage of the Immigration and Nationality Act of 1965, also known as the Hart–Celler Act, allowed emigration from any part of the world. The policy emphasized family reunification and the need for professional qualifications. The intent of the law was not only to benefit individuals but also to reunify families (Kent, 2007). This act, along with the Immigration and Nationality Act Amendments of 1976, allowed visas to international students to attend U.S. universities. Because of the ease in obtaining the study visa and permission to come to the United States through these policies, Black immigrants seized the opportunity and moved to New York, Miami, and Chicago and established themselves as residents and business owners.

Although many Black immigrants embraced American principles, they formed tight-knit communities and strong alliances through neighborhood block clubs, churches, businesses, social clubs, credit unions, schools, and other outlets that allowed them to maintain their ethnic and cultural heritage (Gooden, 2008). Examples of such communities in New York are Jamaica/Southwest Queens, Washington Heights (Dominican), and Flatbush (Haitian); Chicago has North Rogers Park (Caribbean) and Miami has Lemon City (Little Haiti).

Many Black immigrants had been educated through their home countries' educational systems, which prepared them fully for college and employment. In addition, many had attended leading universities in Europe. Therefore, their educational–professional qualifications met the needs of the United States for experts in science, finance, and other specialized fields, which made immigration an attractive option (Kent, 2007).

When Black immigrants arrived in the 1960s, racial relations had begun to improve. Many Black immigrants in urban areas took advantage of the Civil Rights Act of 1964 and subsequent affirmative action laws, which in theory provided work opportunities in professional arenas. Nevertheless, many Black immigrants without skills and education were employed in service or domestic trades.

In subsequent years, the United States passed several immigration-focused policies that increased the number of immigrants allowed into the county, which benefited Black immigrants and increased the rate of immigration.

The Refugee Act of 1980, allowed refugees who were under attack in their countries to enter the United States. The act increased the number of refugees permitted to enter from 17,400 to 50,000 per year (Kent, 2007). With the increase in immigrant populations, the need for sustainable employment increased; however, the United States now wanted to crack down on illegal immigration. In 1986, the Immigration Reform and Control Act (IRCA) required immigrants who had been in the country prior to 1982 to produce documentation of their status and made it an offense for employers to hire undocumented persons. The Immigration Act of 1990 increased the limits on legal immigration to the United States, revised all grounds for exclusion and deportation, authorized temporary protected status (TPS) to aliens from designated countries, revised and established new nonimmigrant admission categories, revised and extended the Visa Waiver Pilot Program, and revised naturalization authority and requirements.

These policies allowed a large number of Africans to immigrate to the United States, due in part to the oppressive political climate, genocide–ethnic cleansing, and extreme poverty in many African nations, especially those in sub-Saharan Africa. Between 1998 and 2006, people from this region received 27% of the diversity visas awarded by the United States. Although other Black immigrant groups, such as Haitians and Cubans, received diversity visas, the visa did not benefit other Caribbean countries because the U.S. State Department ruled that the quotas for those countries had been reached (Kent, 2007).

CONTEMPORARY POLICIES

Immigration policies put forth by the United States in the 20th century allowed Black immigrants to enter this county in large numbers. As mentioned, foreign-born Black populations rose sevenfold between 1960 and 1980. The number of Haitians—the second-largest Caribbean group—nearly quadrupled between 1980 and 2005, and the number of Jamaicans—the largest Caribbean group—more than doubled. The number of Ethiopians in 2005 was 13 times the number in 1960. African immigrants accounted for a sizable majority of these immigrants. Nigerians and Ethiopians led the number of foreign-born Blacks, and more Africans entered the United States between 2000 and 2005 than entered in the previous decade (Kent, 2007).

Although some Black immigrant groups have benefited from contemporary immigration policies, others, such as Haitians, have been marginalized and unfairly treated. For example, Haitian immigrants, like other immigrant groups such as Cubans and Venezuelans, had suffered under the political and economic oppression of dictators in their countries. When Congress passed the Refugee Act of 1980, which permitted Central Americans to obtain legal immigration status, Haitians were omitted from the regulation. Later, when a law was passed specifically for Haitians, the Immigration and Naturalization Service (INS) delayed issuing regulations regarding who could qualify (Haitian Migration, 2005; Wasem, 2010).

While Cuban and Venezuelan immigrants entered the United States (legally and illegally) in ever larger numbers, Haitian immigrants were captured, detained, and returned to their country. In the 1960s through 1980s, the U.S. government, supporting the Duvalier dictatorship because he stood with the United States against Cuba and Fidel Castro (Haitian Migration, 2005), instituted tight patrols, intercepted boats, and captured and returned Haitian would-be immigrants to their country.

Haitian immigrants also faced false accusations from community leaders and legislators in South Florida. According to Farmer (1990), South Florida and national officials have repeatedly identified Haitians as a health threat; in the 1970s, tuberculosis was allegedly endemic among them. In the early 1980s, the Centers for Disease Control and Prevention identified Haitians as one of the primary groups at risk of AIDS. In spite of their removal from that list, the Food and Drug Administration in the late 1980s refused to accept donations of blood from individuals of Haitian origin.

According to Rong and Fitchett (2008), Black immigrants are challenged by xenophobia, or discrimination based on being a foreigner, as well as discrimination, due to racial identity. False accusations based on stereotypes have a far-reaching impact on the Haitian immigrant's ability to gain employment, which affects the overall quality of life in urban centers of Haitian immigrants, such as Miami and New York.

According to Civic Impulse (2015), Haitian immigrants have been allowed to enter and stay in the country in higher numbers due to the amendments to immigration policy and the passage of the Haitian Refugee Immigration Fairness Act of 1998. In January 2010, Haiti experienced a devastating earthquake that was estimated to have killed more than 300,000 people (A Call to Action, 2010). For many months, the country remained in dire straits as global aid trickled in; cholera became a public health epidemic. According to Wasem (2010), Secretary Janet Napolitano granted TPS until 2013 to Haitian immigrants who were already in the country. Also, Haitian immigrants who arrived a year after the earthquake received TPS. Although this was beneficial to Haitian immigrants and their families in Haiti, many Haitian rights groups claim that the United States discriminates against Haitians and continues to administer standards different from those afforded to other immigrant groups.

It appears that current immigration legislation focuses solely on people of Latino descent. As stated previously, there appears to be blatant discrimination by the United States against Black immigrant groups and no voice for Black immigrants on social policy and advocacy. Special interest groups such as the Black Immigration Network (BIN) have been lobbying Congress on behalf of these groups for several years. The mission of BIN is to contribute to the social and economic well-being of U.S.-born Blacks, and Black immigrants (throughout this chapter, the word "immigrants" includes refugees) by organizing in communities, developing leadership among Black people, and advocating for policies that benefit Black communities. BIN is a national network of organizations and individuals that works at the intersection of race, immigration, and globalization. BIN seeks to build alliances with other organizations and networks in immigrant communities and communities of color for mutual benefit (BIN, 2014). The work of advocacy groups such as BIN gives hope that there will be fair and equitable immigration policy that will serve all immigrant groups well.

ECOLOGICAL FRAMEWORK IN UNDERSTANDING BLACK IMMIGRANT FAMILIES

Like other immigrant groups, Black immigrants face many obstacles when they arrive in the United States. Many experience challenges with language, understanding laws and regulations, and settling into the various cultural milieus of an urban city. Although many immigrant groups in these areas set up federations, clubs, and businesses to assist with the transition to the new culture, many Black immigrants may experience issues with child-rearing practices, crime and policing, and education/schooling within the urban framework.

The family is known to be the most important unit in Black immigrant groups (Lum, 2000; Swigart, 2001). In their home countries, the extended family was also very significant. The extended family serves as a network for support with child care, employment, communal living, and socialization. When the immediate family moves away from this extensive extended family network in the home country, many feel isolated when they move to a major urban center. Stories of crime, poverty, and blight that they heard before arriving add to their fears. Therefore, when many Black immigrant groups arrive in urban areas, they tend to be insular in nature, not associating with residents of their new communities. The characteristic of being insular may be heightened if the Black immigrant group represents an unfamiliar religious sect with strict practices, such as Islam.

BLACK IMMIGRANT FAMILY SYSTEMS AND CHILD REARING

The Black immigrant home is traditionally headed by a patriarch, whose responsibility is to care for the welfare of his family (Williams, 2011). The patriarch handles all financial dealings inside and outside the home; however, over the years, these familial traditions have changed to include immigrant women taking on new and diverse roles outside of the home (Foner, 1997). Usually, the patriarch works to provide for the family, while it is the mother's or wife's responsibility to care for the children and the home. Because many Black immigrant families attempt to maintain cultural traditions and identities in urban areas, many of their practices, such as child rearing, may be viewed by Westerners as archaic and insensitive. Furthermore, because urban areas are densely populated, their close proximity and interactions with dominant cultures may magnify these practices.

Yenika-Agbaw (2009) pointed out several concerns about raising an African child in the diaspora, noting that adjustment is extremely difficult for these children and that Black immigrant children must navigate school and social interactions that can undermine their heritage, even as they carefully maintain the values of their African heritage. The author identified food, language in the home, education, media, and grounding the culture as issues faced by African families.

In fact, food and language may be the last symbols of the family's African heritage. Because the United States is a consumer-driven society, mainstream culture prefers fast-food, but African families prefer to cook culturally traditional meals with a great amount of work put into the preparation. African parents may demand that their children speak only the native language in the home as a means for preserving cultural heritage.

Outside the home, education, social events, and media are explored by African children. Africans (as well as other Black immigrants) place high value on education; however, in mainstream U.S. culture, education and social activities are equally important. Many African parents do not know how to navigate parent–teacher groups or how to be the class parent; however, if they do not attend to these roles, they will be viewed as irresponsible and not committed, which can embarrass the child or harm the child's academic progress.

African parents are very concerned with the images to which their children are exposed. They censor what their child views or hears on radio, television, or the Internet. The messages that are conveyed in mainstream media may undermine cultural heritage or values that are espoused in the home.

It is perfectly acceptable to maintain one's African heritage; however, it is important that parents participate in mainstream culture with their children to understand the context of the culture. What is acceptable with regard to child-rearing practices in the home country (e.g., corporal punishment) may be a violation of the child welfare laws in the mainstream U.S. culture.

CRIME AND POLICE INTERACTION

Many Black immigrants arrive in this country with little to no resources and may have to live in unsafe urban areas and be subjected to criminal activity; they may have issues with understanding laws or police regulations, written or unwritten. Overall, Black immigrant relations with police have been strained. Most of their experiences are an extension of what African Americans have endured for more than 150 years. Most Black immigrants attempt to distance themselves from African Americans; however, they fail to recognize that racism does not identify accent or geography, but only color (Kamya, 1997; Okonofua, 2013; Waters, 1994). The court cases of Amadou Diallo and Abner Louima are examples of Black immigrant victimization by police in urban areas. Both were cases of mistaken identity by the New York Police Department officers (NYPD). Amadou Diallo died after being shot more than 40 times. Abner Louima was beaten and sodomized by officers after an alleged incident at a night club. In both cases, the officers were found not guilty; however, both families sued the city of New York and received financial restitution.

Another case of victimization in the early 1990s strained Jewish–Black relations in Crown Heights, New York. Two Guyanese children were playing when a car driven by a Hassidic Jew struck another car, causing his car to knock down a concrete building column. The column pinned two children, and one, Gavin Cato, died from his injuries. The incident spurred outrage in the predominantly African and African American neighborhood, touching off days of rioting and crimes against Hassidic Jews. Black immigrants in urban areas have encountered similar brutality to that experienced by African Americans, whose lives are commonly devalued. Frustration and tension lead to uprisings.

Many Black immigrants are subjected to crime and criminal activity merely by their presence. In Cincinnati and other large urban cities, Black immigrants are often resettled by international social welfare agencies. Most of the resettlement takes place in poor, crime-infested areas of the city because of the lower cost of living and surplus of housing. Many Black immigrants have been preyed on by criminals because of their "routine activities": the repeated patterns of their day that make it easier for them to be targeted. Due to the insular nature of some Black immigrant groups, their businesses have been targets of vandalism and violence (Dolnick, 2009).

To combat this issue and make community policing more visible, many city law enforcement agencies have made efforts to reduce crime in Black immigrant communities. For example, the twin cities of Minneapolis and St. Paul have the largest Somali population in the nation, and they have found that many Somali youth are involved in crimes. The police department, Federal Bureau of Investigation (FBI), and the Somali community are working together through a multimillion-dollar grant to serve youth aged 8 to 14 years, utilizing the YWCA to perform mentoring, basic skills, and life skills programs for ages 8 to 22 years, crime prevention activities for the community, and identification and intervention for persons at risk of radicalization, gang involvement, or violent crime. Black immigrants living in urban areas face some of the same issues that most African Americans face. It is fortunate that the police have reached out to this group, not only to protect them, but to understand their culture.

EDUCATION

Education appears to be an important value in the Black immigrant community. Black immigrants see education as the catalyst to propel them beyond current circumstances. Many Black immigrants who arrived in the 1960s and 1970s were highly trained and educated. Today, Black immigrants are still the most educated immigrant group in the United States. Even with limited English (writing and speaking) abilities, Black immigrants have surpassed native Blacks on proficiency tests (Massey, Mooney, Torres, & Charles, 2006; Rosenthal, 2011).

At one point in time, Black immigrants such as Africans came to this country in search of educational opportunities that would enrich not only themselves but their home country as well. Former Liberian President Kwame Nkrumah attended Lincoln University; many other prominent Black immigrants have attended historic Black colleges such as Howard University, Hampton University, and Tuskegee University, and predominantly White colleges such as Harvard University, The University of Pennsylvania, and Yale University. Today, because most immigrants do not feel that race is important, many young Black immigrants are choosing to attend more selected colleges and universities (Massey et al., 2006).

According to Koelsch (2007), on arrival in urban areas, many Black immigrants may not utilize the public school system because they feel that these students receive a substandard education and they want their children to compete with students in mainstream colleges and universities. Also, many consider discipline to be too relaxed in public schools, undermining the discipline experienced in the home. The moment Black immigrants can move to the outskirts of a predominantly minority urban area, they utilize the public school because of its diversity and academic reputation; moreover, even if they have to sacrifice, many Black immigrant families send their children to a diverse public school. Koelsch performed a survey of Detroit Public Schools and found a smaller number of Black immigrants represented in urban public schools than in suburban schools.

MEZZO- AND MACRO-LEVEL ENVIRONMENTS

Interactions with groups and communities appear to be a very important facet for Black immigrants in urban communities. In this chapter, we have pointed out various difficulties that this group of immigrants face. Many Black immigrants may not have family support in the urban community; many live with extended family or fictive kin as a means of socialization and bonding in the new environment. Although this extended family may provide various forms of support during adjustment to the new experience, many Black immigrants must interface with groups (cultural and noncultural) and communities that may or may not represent their interests or needs. Navigating the mezzo- and macro-level environments has proven to be difficult for many Black immigrants.

HELP-SEEKING BEHAVIORS

The literature explains that ethnic minority groups have a difficult experience in accessing services (Drachman, Hwon-Ahn, & Paulino, 1996; Leclere, Jensen, & Biddlecom, 1994; Williams et al., 2007). Immigrants face barriers to health care, immigration services, and educational programs. Many do not know how to enroll in and use services that are critical to them because of language, immigration status, and lack of understanding of how to navigate bureaucratic systems. Also, social stigma and cultural beliefs continue to weigh heavily on Black immigrant decision making about receiving assistance for problems through conventional or unconventional means. Black immigrants are no exception to this phenomenon; moreover, there appears to be little to no research on help-seeking behaviors among Black immigrants in urban areas.

Many Black immigrants first seek help from within their families or groups. Social work pioneer Jane Addams is credited as the founder of Chicago's Hull House in the early 1900s. Hull House served as a settlement house where people lived and received services. Many of those who utilized the services of Hull House were immigrants from Italy, Germany, France, or Ireland. Addams wanted to improve the lives of those who entered the doors of Hull House through education, illness prevention, and culture. Addams sponsored ethnic group activities so that cultural heritages could be restored and maintained (Addams, 2014). Similarly, many Black immigrant groups in urban communities founded their own clubs and federations.

FORMAL AND INFORMAL SUPPORT SYSTEMS

According to Shaw-Taylor and Tuch (2007), *social capital* is a cumulative community resource. These scholars examined arguments by Schultz (1961) and Becker (1975) that suggested that training, education, knowledge, and skills can be viewed as measurements of human capital. *Cultural capital* is central to becoming acculturated to dominant culture values, gained through educational institutions, family ties, and informal gatherings. Bourdieu (1986) identified an intersection between human and cultural capital that manifests in the form of educational, academic, and vocational attainment (Shaw-Taylor & Tuch, 2007). *Economic capital* may be the most important capital, as income and wealth serve as a pathway to opportunity. Thus, social relationships and human and economic resources are significant factors that influence Black immigrants' adaptation and acculturation to living in the United States.

Among Black immigrants, social networks serve as an anchorage to buffer the challenges of settlement in the United States. Similar to values espoused by African Americans who migrated to the north during the Progressive Era and even into the mid-20th century, mutual aid has been a normative practice among migrants and immigrants. Kent (2007) described the prevalence of mutual aid organizations to help newly arrived immigrants from Africa and the Caribbean to adjust to their new environment. These formal organizations, established by immigrants with longer residence in the United States, typically serve as a social service support system to provide concrete and supportive services related to housing, jobs, and financial assistance. Black immigrants historically have established social, political, and economic organizations that serve as both formal and informal support systems. Although these organizations are helpful to newly arrived immigrants, they also serve as an information resource to maintain connection to the home country. For many Black immigrants, maintaining a transnational perspective is important to the transformative process (Shaw-Taylor & Tuch, 2007). Social workers who work with Black immigrant families must strive to develop a sociocultural understanding of this diverse population.

Another formal support system is the Black church. Historically, the Black church has served as a spiritual, religious, and social network for African Americans, particularly during slavery and the civil rights movement (Billingsley & Rodriguez, 2007; Martin & Martin, 1985). Affiliation with a religious institution and regular church attendance is viewed as paramount to religious beliefs and practices by Black immigrants. The church is significant to Black immigrants because it serves as a cultural resource for cognitive, relational, and material well-being (Mukenge & Mukenge, 2005).

In an effort to maintain cultural identity, social events such as carnivals began in Harlem in 1950 by Caribbean immigrants. Over the past 60 years, these cultural celebrations have expanded to include cities such as Washington, Baltimore, Miami, and Atlanta. These events with parades and festivals have become an integral part of Black immigrants' efforts to showcase their cultural traditions in the form of music, dress, food, and celebration (Kent, 2007). Hosting such events serves as an informal support system to Black immigrants to mitigate the push–pull factors that come with the concept of adaptation, adjustment, and assimilation in the host country, which involves maintaining a transnational worldview.

IMPLICATIONS

The social work profession has historically been influenced by social, political, and economic factors. With an increase in the number of immigrants in cities and urban areas, there is a clear need to develop knowledge of cultural diverse groups and skills to effectuate change through advocacy.

CULTURAL COMPETENCE

Despite current contentious debates involving immigration policy, Black immigrants, especially those from African countries, remain the fastest growing and most educated groups of immigrants in the United States. Myriad challenges face Black immigrants related to settlement, adaptation, and adjustment in a new country. Immigration status is a determinant of eligibility to receive services, particularly government-sponsored programs such as health care, housing, and public assistance. Problems are compounded by the propensity to give greater attention to immigrants' racial identity as Black, along with misguided assumptions about cultural differences based on country of origin. These difficulties call for action by social workers to ensure that culturally appropriate programs and services are provided.

Equally important is a need for social work educational programs and human service agencies to recruit Black immigrants to pursue social work degrees and become an integral part of the profession. Beyond the academy, agencies and professional development programs in schools of social work in urban areas must create professional development programs and offer workshops, brown bag forums, and training that culminate in continuing education units to be used for licensure. Such efforts help to expand social work professionals' knowledge and enhance their skills to work effectively with diverse Black immigrant populations.

In the historical intersection between African Americans, Africans, and Afro-Caribbean groups, tensions between native Blacks and Black immigrants result from mutual stereotyping (Shaw-Taylor & Tuch, 2007; Waters, 1999). Perceptions of Black immigrants as "model immigrants by the broader society" and employers' propensity to employ Black immigrants based on perceived attributes and traditional values that are viewed as lacking in native Blacks serve to widen the chasm between native Blacks and Black immigrants. Invariably, increased efforts are necessary to examine within-group cultural differences. With a growing trend toward Black immigrants working in service-oriented fields in long-term care facilities, hospitals, and congregate care facilities, there is a need for cross-cultural workshops and training to enhance the quality of service that is provided and received.

Yanca and Johnson (2008) contended that social workers must develop diversity competence to work effectively with diverse populations. Although diversity competence expands beyond race and ethnicity, it provides a lens to understand within-group differences among people of African descent. The social work literature is limited in the focus on Blacks from Africa and Caribbean countries. Equally important is diversity among Black immigrants. Yanca and Johnson provided an outline to guide social workers' efforts to develop diversity competence: (a) understanding self, (b) understanding societal influence, (c) understanding a diverse group, and (d) developing diversity practice skills.

ADVOCACY

The National Association of Social Workers (NASW) *Code of Ethics* has identified core values that serve as a professional compass to guide ethical behavior by social workers: (a) service, (b) social justice, and (c) dignity and worth of the person. Advocacy is central to social workers' professional identity, regardless of the field or level of practice. According to Kirst-Ashman and Hull (2015), "Advocacy is representing, championing, or defending the rights of others" (p. 371). The authors described two types of advocacy: cause advocacy and case advocacy. *Cause advocacy* involves a macro-approach to address issues that affect groups of people, whereas *case advocacy* focuses on micro- and mezzo practice that pertain to individuals and families. They contended that the emergence of cause advocacy typically results from case advocacy.

Reamer (2009) provided a historical lens to highlight hallmarks of the social work profession that began with Mary Richmond's focus on the *case*, which involved helping the individual client to address problems related to functioning and well-being. In contrast, Jane Addams is noted for her contribution to the focus on the *cause*, which considers environmental factors of social injustice and disparities that affect vulnerable populations. Multiple periods of social history point to the social work profession's involvement with cause advocacy to advocate for the rights of those discriminated against based on race, gender, age, socioeconomic status, mental, cognitive, or physical disability (Kirst-Ashman & Hull, 2015). Reamer noted the intersection of the unique attributes of the social work profession's attention to the intersection of the person-in-environment involving concern for the well-being of individuals, families, groups, and communities.

Most of the attention in the media regarding immigration policy has focused on the Latino population, with less attention directed to Black immigrants. According to Capps, McCabe, and Fix (2012), although African immigrants represent smaller numbers of immigrants compared to other groups, they are among the fastest-growing group of immigrants. Hernandez (2012) reported that the population of Black immigrants from African and Caribbean countries has doubled over the past 20 years.

Hernandez contended that Black immigrants with lesser immigration histories, unable to speak English, and a refugee background are generally more disadvantaged.

However, within the social work literature, there is a paucity of conceptual articles and empirical studies that examine Black immigrants in the United States. Experiences and challenges faced by Black immigrants call for action by the social work profession to demonstrate continued efforts to advocate for better policies and services by agencies, organizations, and communities at the local, state, and federal levels of government. With an increase in the number of Black immigrants' migration and settlement in cities or surrounding communities, there is a clear need to advance the body of knowledge and to enhance skills to engage in competent social work practice.

This chapter has presented an overview of Black immigrants and their evolution in urban communities. Other immigrant groups, such as Latinos and Asians, have received a disproportionate share of attention by researchers, legislators, educators, and media outlets, and even though Black immigrants represent the fastest growing group of immigrants in the United States (Capps et al., 2012), they appear to not have fared well in several key social areas.

Although Black immigrants are clearly different in culture, heritage, dialect, and experience, society tends to merge them with other Black groups and does not respect nor adequately explore their diversity. For example, no distinction is made between African or Caribbean Blacks and Black Americans. Some Black immigrants came because the United States needed their skilled expertise in science, technology, or economics, but many came in search of better opportunities and others came to escape political and economic persecution by a dictatorship. Although U.S. immigration policies have allowed large numbers of Black immigrants at various points in time, some immigration policies have clearly failed Black immigrants and prohibited them from entering the country, creating a double standard among immigrant groups.

Black immigrants have been met with myriad social, political, educational, and economic barriers to their success. Nonetheless, they have utilized strength and resiliency to build churches, schools, community centers, credit unions, and shopping districts to create community as a support mechanism for Black immigrants. Many Black immigrants, because of their close connections with each other, have maintained cultural practices such as child rearing and carnival; in addition, they have excelled in the education arena and represent some of the brightest minds in the United States. Although much success can be credited to Black immigrants and their progress, discriminatory practices, police brutality, and crime have tainted their experiences.

It is of the utmost importance that social workers seek and produce research and information for communities and entities that serve Black immigrants. Although the literature reports that Black immigrants have surpassed native-born Blacks in education and will probably rise economically over the next few years, Black immigrants must still grapple with issues of poverty, educational attainment, and equitable immigration policies.

FOR FURTHER STUDY

Suggested Assignments

This group assignment is designed to increase awareness of the experiences of Black immigrant families with origins from African and Caribbean countries who settle in urban communities. Developing and understanding Black immigrant families provides a beginning lens of knowledge acquisition pertaining to culturally diverse group values, beliefs, and experiences. Students can be placed in groups and select a subgroup to conduct research and prepare a graphic presentation. Each group should have 30 minutes to present and respond to questions from peers. Creativity is encouraged, but content should include the following:

- Provide a brief overview of the Black immigrant's country of origin and its characteristics that may influence reasons for immigration.
- Describe the urban areas and regions of the United States where Black immigrants are most likely to settle. Discuss the impact of immigration on family life in urban communities. What are some of the challenges that Black immigrants encounter?
- Describe the role of men and women based on their country of origin values, beliefs, and traditions and push–pull factors that they experience as part of adaption and adjustment.
- Identify the most common type of family structure, and compare it to that of other immigrants and mainstream Americans.
- Describe dating, marriage customs, and family formation patterns. Discuss Black immigrants' views on same-gender relationships.
- Describe child-rearing practices. How are children viewed? What challenges do Black immigrant youth face?
- Describe the role of elders in Black immigrant families. Discuss whether multigenerational families are an integral aspect of Black immigrant families.
- Discuss some of the strengths of Black immigrants that help with their settlement in the United States. Identify cultural similarities and differences between Black immigrants across the African diaspora and native Blacks.
- Discuss the implications for social work practice in terms of policy, programs, and services at the micro-, mezzo-, and macro-levels.

Learning Outcomes

1. Understand within-group diversity among Africans, Afro-Caribbean, and African Americans.

2. Understand Black immigrants' reason for migration, settlement patterns, and adaptation and adjustment in urban communities within the United States.

3. Understand the use of an ecological framework to work with Black immigrant families.

4. Understand the significance of immigration and social welfare policy on Black immigrants' experience.

5. Understand the importance of cultural competency and advocacy with culturally diverse Black immigrant families.

Suggested Websites

Census Bureau: www/census.gov
Immigration Policy Center: www.immigrationpolicy.org
Migration Policy Institute: www.migrationpolicy.org
Pew Research Center: www.pewresearch.org

Suggested Readings

Fulwood, III, S. (2013, February). *Race and beyond: Overlooked story of Black immigrants in the United States deserves attention.* Washington, DC: Center for American Progress.

Hernandez, D. J. (2012, April). Changing demography and circumstances for young black children in African and Caribbean immigrant families. *Migration Policy Institute,* 1–34. Retrieved October 2, 2014, from www.migrationpolicy.org

Jannson, B. S. (2014). *Becoming an effective policy advocate: From policy practice to social justice* (7th ed.). Belmont, CA: Brooks/Cole.

Shaw-Taylor, Y., & Tuch, S. A. (2007). *The other African Americans: Contemporary African and Caribbean immigrants in the United States.* Lanham, MD: Rowman & Littlefield.

Yenika-Agbaw, V. (2009). African child rearing in the diaspora: A mother's perspective. *The Journal of Pan African Studies, 3*(4), 3–16.

REFERENCES

Addams, L. J. (2014). The Biography.com website. Retrieved September 29, 2014, from http://www.biography.com/people/jane-addams-9176298

Becker, G. S. (1975). *Human capital: A theoretical and empirical analysis, with special reference to education.* New York, NY: National Bureau of Economic Research.

Billingsley, A., & Rodgriguez, B. M. (2007). The black family in the twenty-first century and the church as an action system: A macro perspective. In L. A. (Lee) See (Ed.), *Human behavior in the social environment from an African-American perspective* (pp. 57–74). Binghamton, NY: The Haworth Press.

Black Immigration Network. (2014). Retrieved August 15, 2014, from http://blackimmigration.net/

Bourdieu, P. (1986). The form of capital. In J. Richardson (Ed.), *Handbook of theory and research for the sociology of education* (pp. 241–258). New York, NY: Greenwood.

Brown, L. A., Mott, T. E., & Malecki, E. J. (2007). Immigrant profiles of US urban areas and agents of Resettlement. *The Professional Geographer, 59*(1), 56–73.

Capps, R., McCabe, K., & Fix, M. (2012, April). *Diverse streams: Black African migration in the United States.* Washington, DC: Migration Policy Institute, pp. 1–21.

Civic Impulse. (2015). S. 1504-105th Congress: Haitian Refugee Immigration Fairness Act of 1998. Retrieved from https://www.govtrack.us/congress/bills/105/s1504

Dolnick, S. (2009). For African immigrants, Bronx culture turns violent. *New York Times*, October 19.

Drachman, D., Kwon-Ahn, Y. H., & Paulino, A. (1996). Migration and resettlement experiences of Dominican and Korean families. *Families in Society: The Journal of Contemporary Social Services, 77*(10), 626–638.

Farmer, P. (1990). *AIDS and accusations: Haiti and the geography of blame*. Berkeley, CA: University of California Press.

Foner, N. (1997). The immigrant family: Legacies and cultural changes. *International Migration Review, 31*(4), 961–974.

Fulwood, III, S. (2013, February). *Race and beyond: Overlooked story of black immigrants in the United States deserves attention*. Washington, DC: Center for American Progress.

Gooden, A. (2008). Community organizing by African Caribbean in Toronto, Ontario. *Journal of Black Studies, 38*(3), 413–426.

Haitian Migration: 20th Century. (2005, January 1). Retrieved September 7, 2014, from http://www .inmotionaame.org/migrations/landing.cfm;jsessionid=f8301022111411982127002?migration =12&bhcp=1

Halter, M. (1993). *Between race and ethnicity: Cape Verdean American immigrants*. Urbanna, VA: University of Illinois Press.

Hernandez, D. J. (2012, April). Changing demography and circumstances for young black children in African and Caribbean immigrant families. *Migration Policy Institute, 1–34*. Retrieved October 2, 2014 from www.migrationpolicy.org

Hine, D. C., Hine, W. C., & Harrold, S. (2006). *The African-American odyssey* (3rd ed.). Upper Saddle River, NJ: Prentice Hall.

Hodges, G. R. (1999). *Root and branch: African Americans in New York and East Jersey, 1613–1863*. Chapel Hill: University of North Carolina Press.

Kamya, H. A. (1997). African immigrants in the United States: The challenge for research and practice. *Social Work, 45*(2), 154–165.

Kent, M. M. (2007). Immigration and America's black population. *Population Bulletin, 62*(4), 1–16.

Kirst-Ashman, K. K., & Hull, G. H., Jr. (2015). *Generalist practice with organizations and communities* (6th ed.) Stamford, CT: Cengage Learning.

Koelsch, D. C. (2007). *Voices of concern, voices of hope: Experiences of African immigrants in Detroit*. The Warren Institute. Report published on the website of the Berkeley School of Law. Located at "http://www.law.berkeley.edu/files/Koelschpaper.pdf%3e" http://www.law.berkeley. edu/files/Koelschpaper.pdf

Leclere, F.B., Jensen, L., & Biddlecom, A. E. (1994). Healthcare utilization, family context, and adaptation among immigrants to the United States. *Journal of Health and Social Behavior, 35*(4), 370–384.

Logan, J. R., Alba, R. D., & Zang, W. (2002). Immigrant enclaves and ethnic communities in New York and Los Angeles. *American Sociological Review, 67*, 299–322.

Lum, D. (2000). *Social work practice and people of color: A process-stage approach*. Belmont, CA: Brooks/Cole.

Martin, M. J., & Martin, E. P. (1985). *The helping tradition in the Black family and community*. Silver Spring, MD: National Association of Social Workers.

Massey, D. S., Mooney, M., Torres, K. C., & Charles, C. Z. (2006). Black immigrants and Black natives attending selective colleges and universities in the US. *American Journal of Education, 113*(2), 243–271.

McCabe, K. (2011, April). Caribbean immigrants in the United States. *Migration Policy*. Retrieved October 2, 2014 from http://www.migrationpolicy.org

Mukenge, T., & Mukege, I. R. (2005). Children in French-speaking African immigrant families; assessing health disparities, cultural, resources, and health services. *Challenge, 11*(2), 80–107.

Okonofua, B. A. (2013). I am blacker than you: Theorizing conflict between African immigrants and African Americans in the United States. *Sage Open, 3*(2).

Reamer, F. G. (2009). *Eyes on ethics: From case to cause in social work.* Retrieved September 22, 2014, from http://www/socialworktoday.com/news/eoe_081409.shtml

Rong, X. L., & Fitchett, P. (2008). Socialization and identify transformation of black immigrant youth in the United States. *Theory into Practice, 47*(1), 35–42.

Rosenthal, B. M. (2011). Alarming new test score gap discovered in Seattle schools. *Seattle Times,* December 18. Available at: http://www.seattletimes.com/seattle-news/alarming-new-test-score-gap-discovered-in-seattle-schools

Schultz, T. W. (1961). Investment in human capital. *American Economic Review, 51*(1), 1–17.

Shaw-Taylor, Y., & Tuch, S. A. (2007). *The other African Americans: Contemporary African and Caribbean immigrants in the United States.* Lanham, MD: Rowman & Littlefield.

Swigart, L. (2001). *Extended lives the African immigrant experience in Philadelphia.* Philadelphia: Historical Society of Pennsylvania.

Thomas, K. (April, 2012). A demographic profile of Black Caribbean immigrants to the United States. Pennsylvania State University and Migration Policy Institute, April 2012. Retrieved June 18, 2014, from http://www.migrationpolicy.org/research/CBI-demographic-profile-black-caribbean-immigrants

Toso, B. W., Prins, E., & Mooney, A. (2013). The changing face of immigrants in the U.S.: Implications for adult education. *Journal of Lifelong Learning, 22,* 1–21.

U.S. Census Bureau Newsroom Archives. (2012). Retrieved September 29, 2014, from https://www.census.gov/newsroom/releases/archives/facts_for_features_special_editions/cb12-ff19.html

Wasem, R. E. (2010). *U.S. immigration policy on Haitian migrants.* Congressional Research Service 7–5700/RS 21349. Washington, DC: Government Printing Service.

Waters, M. C. (1994). Ethnic and racial identities of second generation black immigrants in New York City. *International Migration Review, 28*(4), 795–820.

Waters, M. C. (1999). *Black identities: West immigrant dreams and American realities.* New York, NY: Russell Sage Foundation and Harvard University Press.

Williams, D. R., Gonzalez, H. M., Neighbors, H., Nesse, R., Ableson, J. M., Sweetman, J., & Jackson, J. S. (2007). Prevalence and distinction of major depressive disorder in African American, Caribbean Blacks, and Non-Hispanic Whites. *Archives of General Psychiatry, 64*(4), 485–494.

Williams, N. (2011). A critical review of the literature: Engendering the discourse of masculinities matter for parenting African refugee men. *American Journal of Men's Health, 5*(2), 104–117.

World Vision Australia. (2010, July 12). *A Call to Action: Haiti at 6 months.* Available at: http://www.worldvision.com.au/Libraries/HEA_reports/A_Call_to_Action_-_Haiti_at_6_months.pdf, 2014.

Yanca, A. J., & Johnson, L. (2008). *Generalist social work practice with families* (1st ed.). Boston, MA: Allyn & Bacon.

Yenika-Agbaw, V. (2009). African child rearing in the diaspora: A mother's perspective. *The Journal of Pan African Studies, 3*(4), 3–16.

Zhou, M. (2003). Urban education: Challenges in educating culturally diverse children. *Teachers College Record, 105,* 208–255.

CHAPTER 6

That Is So Queer: Building a Foundation for Working With African American Lesbian, Gay, and Transgender Individuals in the Community[1,2,3]

Laurens G. Van Sluytman, Denise Torres,
and Saanjh Aakash Kishore

In "I Am Your Sister: Black Women Organizing Across Sexualities," Audre Lorde (2009) wrote, "When I weaned my daughter in 1963 to go to Washington in August to work in the coffee tents along with Lena Horne, making coffee for the marshals because that was what most Black women did in the 1963 March on Washington, I was a Black Lesbian. . . . When I picketed for welfare mothers' rights, and against the enforced sterilization of young Black girls, when I fought institutionalized racism in the New York City schools, I was a Black Lesbian. But you did not know it because we did not identify ourselves, so now you can say that Black Lesbians and Gay men have nothing to do with the struggles of the Black Nation. And I am not alone." Lorde ends the essay declaring that she does not want to be tolerated. She wants to be recognized. Black gay, lesbian, and transgender (BGLT) individuals have played an important role in United States and Black American history, though these histories are by no means separate, despite facing complex systems of inequality and discrimination. Bruce Nugent, a luminary of the Harlem Renaissance, wrote about same-gender desire as early as 1926 in the short story, *Smoke, Lilies, and Jade*. In the 1928 song *Prove It on Me Blues*, Ma Rainey sang about her same-sex relationships, crooning, *"Went out last night with a crowd of my friends. They must've been women, 'cause I don't like no men."* Activist Bayard Rustin, an influential civil rights adviser, fought for racial equality despite the antigay criticisms of many of his contemporaries and his arrest for "homosexual acts." When the

1969 riot at the Stonewall Inn galvanized the modern gay liberation movement, several gay, lesbian, and transgender (GLT) people of color, including African American transgender activist Marsha P. Johnson, were on the front lines. It is no wonder, then, that in 1970, Black Panther cofounder Huey P. Newton highlighted the revolutionary potential of Black homosexual men and women and condemned the party's use of homophobic slurs. Indeed, many of the most influential voices for justice across racial, economic, sexual orientation, and gender lines have been those of BGLT artists, activists, and warriors, such as James Baldwin, Angela Davis, Alvin Ailey, Alice Walker, Lavern Cox, and Janet Mock.

Although attitudes are changing with support for same-sex relationships increasing from 43% to 64% between 1977 and 2014 (Gallop, 2014), legal recognition of same-sex unions in several states, and marginal improvements at the federal level, social workers must question the ingrained assumptions regarding "normal" and "pathological" identity that persist and inform their daily work. For example, although homosexuality and transgender identities are no longer psychiatric disorders, the diagnosis of gender dysphoria remains in the *Diagnostic and Statistical Manual of Mental Disorders*, Fifth Edition (*DSM-5*; American Psychiatric Association, 2013). Although this diagnosis was developed to help ensure individuals would not be denied access to medical care, such a compromise nevertheless frames the individual as the "problem" and leaves unaddressed the structural, political, and economic factors that impact the experiences of BGLT people in ways that social workers and other providers have not readily trained to identify and intervene. For instance, the multiple jeopardy–advantage (MJA) hypothesis (Jeffries & Ransford, 1980; Ransford & Miller, 1983) posited that the intersection of various social status positions, such as class, sexual orientation, race, gender identity, and disability, may result in risk and resilience. For instance, the intersection of two high-status positions such as male and heterosexual may result in substantial advantages, whereas, two or more low-status positions (e.g., lesbian and disabled) may expose the individual to disadvantages as well as psychological distress associated with exposure to discrimination due to those statuses. Thus, we may encounter LGT youth who have been rejected by their families and who contemplate and attempt suicide at rates much higher than their heterosexual counterparts (Russell & Joyner, 2001). Hence, potential future gains in marriage benefits—such as tax incentives, pensions, social security and inheritances, the right to visit loved ones in hospitals, and to make decisions for partners who are incapacitated—are fragile and must be seen within the context of discriminatory efforts to contain civil rights advances.

Discrimination faced by BGLT individuals is complex and may be based on their sexual orientation, age, gender, gender presentation, or race—or all of these—so that the cumulative effects of multiple forms of discrimination impact levels of distress and the capacity to function (Huebner, Rebchook, & Kegeles, 2004; Williams, Neighbors, & Jackson, 2003). Racial discrimination within the larger GLT community, for example, may contribute to psychological distress among GLT people of color (Van Sluytman, 2015). Because racial discrimination occurs within society at large as well as within the GLT community (Boykin, 1996; Harper, 1992; Herek & Capitanio, 1995; Riggs,

1991) and because discrimination due to sexual orientation and gender identity occur both broadly and within Black communities (Pettiway, 1996; Poussaint, 1990; Roberts, 1986), BGLT individuals contend with compounded stress related to identity stigma.

To reduce the phenomenon of hiding in plain sight and to improve the capacity of social workers to create contexts that will reduce the stigma and discrimination BGLT individuals face, after a brief discussion of practice competencies, this chapter gives voice to their experiences and recognizes their contribution to and enrichment of the urban social landscape. In each section, our aim is to synthesize relevant information on population size, identity formation, key stressors, and resiliencies within the population. Adhering to a biopsychosocial or person-in-environment perspective, we give special attention to BGLT youth and elders, as the developmental stress associated with these periods increases their potential involvement in the formal systems in which social workers practice. Further, case studies are used to expose the reader to clinical, evaluation, advocacy, and research practices with BGLT populations.

RELEVANT CORE COMPETENCIES (EDUCATIONAL POLICY AND ACCREDITATION STANDARDS)

Although the Educational Policy and Accreditation Standards (EPAS) promulgated by the Committee for Social Work Education (CSWE, 2013) require the development of core competencies through awareness and practice, we recognize that not all students will serve the members of the BGLT population during their field experience. The chapter provides an overview of the challenges and strengths within these communities to raise awareness and promote a professional understanding of the responsibility to provide services in ways that support the dignity and worth all people, especially those who are marginalized (Competency 1—Ethical and Professional Behavior). The chapter encourages engagement in critical thinking and reflexive practice by using an intersectional lens to examine how combinations of age, class, culture, disability, ethnicity, gender, gender identity and expression, race, sex, and sexual orientation inform identity and shape experience (Competency 2—Diversity and Difference). To advance the profession's quest for human rights and social and economic justice, we discuss the communities' needs within the context of macro- and micro-forms of oppression and mechanisms of discrimination (Competency 3—Social Justice and Human Rights), including how policies are implemented (Competency 4—Policy Practice) and the need to translate research into practice (Competency 5). Case studies are used to highlight practice as ongoing dynamic processes of engagement, assessment, intervention, and evaluation (Competency 6, 7, 8, and 9, respectively) that considers changes in environments (macro- and meso-levels), populations (older members), and emerging societal contexts (histories of disease).

The authors of this chapter developed case studies designed to elucidate the core practice of social work, advocacy, and policy (*GLT Youth Case study*), evaluation (*Black Gay Male Case study*), and individual practice (*Transgender Population Case study*). They are designed to increase the students' exposure to a variety of experiences and to increase capacity to adjust to practice with members of the lesbian, gay, bisexual, and transgender (LGBT) community. The case studies represent consumer and worker experiences that may occur within the work environment. They are intended for use by the instructor to increase students' skills in the following areas:

- Interpreting critically
- Identifying assumptions
- Assessing and decision making
- Communicating ideas and defending decisions.

Most significantly they are intended to encourage analysis, discussion, and recommendations, as a class, in small groups, or as individual projects.

IN THE LIFE: BLACK GAY AND LESBIAN LIVES

Discussing Black gay and lesbian sexual orientation is complicated by the history of stereotyping of Black sexualities in the United States. Black men's masculinity has been characterized paradoxically: On the one hand, they are described as less than manly, dependent, and incapable of protecting their families, and on the other, as hypermasculine, sexually insatiable, and predatory (Cooper, 2005). Similarly, scholars have argued that Black women's femininity has been measured by their capacity to appropriately perform the roles of family and sexuality, even though many of these family functions have been denied to Black women because of historic race-based state sanctions (Collins, 2000). For "failing" to perform these tropes of femininity, Black women have stereotypically been viewed as promiscuous and aggressive (Freydberg, 1995; Hancock, 2004; Roberts, 1997). Hence, Black women and men, regardless of sexual orientation, gender identity, or gender expression, are caught in a Catch-22, with limited and polarizing demands on their sexuality. Understanding stereotypes of Black sexuality may therefore be paramount in understanding views on same-sex desire, relationships, and unions in Black communities. Indeed, research has found that members of Black communities were the least tolerant of the GLT community (Ohlander, Batalova, & Treas, 2005) and were more likely to voice homophobic viewpoints than non-Black Americans (Newman, Dannenfelser, & Benishek, 2002), in part due to religious conservatism within the Black Church (Staples, 1990; Ward, 2005). These findings may speak to the overall tensions surrounding sexuality and gender in Black communities that give rise to greater expressions of homophobia. That is, historic White supremacy and patriarchy likely have a lot to do with the contemporary homophobia that Black gays and lesbians face in their racial–ethnic communities.

Many Black gays and lesbians often live within communities that share their racial–ethnic identities, but coming or being "out" is not necessarily the norm. Although revealing one's sexual orientation may result in greater intimacy within some families, enhancing the development of social networks and access to resources (Van Sluytman,

Braine, Acker, Friedman, & Des Jarlais, 2013), this same act of self-disclosure may be seen as an act of racial betrayal by assigning greater salience to one's gender identity and/or sexual orientation than one's racial identity (Blackman & Perry, 1990). In such cases, disclosure may result in alienation or expulsion from places of residence and employment. Fear of such rejection can result in concealment of sexual orientation from family and kinship networks, thereby depriving the individual of validation and protection from abuse, victimization, and poverty. Similarly, silence, secrecy, and early experiences of discrimination contribute to avoidance of seeking health care (Hiestand, Horne, & Levitt, 2007; Levitt & Horne, 2002; O'Hanlan, Cabaj, Schatz, Lock, & Nemrow, 1997; Szymanski, 2006; Tracy, Lydecker, & Ireland, 2010) as well as engaging in high-risk behaviors that can result in psychological distress and aid the spread of sexually transmitted infections (Van Sluytman et al., 2014).

Stigma and Risk Health/Mental Health

The minority stress model (Meyer, 2003) asserts that stress resulting in morbidity is associated with repeated experiences of oppression by dominant factions of the society. Further, discrimination and stigma associated with sexual orientation from both their communities of origin and the society at large may result in victimization; microaggressions in education, employment, and housing; and verbal and physical abuse for Black gays and lesbians. Although intimate partner violence has begun to receive some attention (Balsam & Szymanski, 2005; Balsam, Rothblum, & Beauchaine, 2005; Duke & Davidson, 2009; Hassouneh & Glass, 2008), very little research examines its occurrence within Black same-sex relationships. Those who experience violence due to their sexual orientation or by intimate partners may resist reporting the incidence as they fear a lack of sensitivity by police authorities, which reinforces shame and underreporting (Anderson, 2005).

Traditional health literature has grouped LGBT people, ignoring the differing health needs of each group, whereas the health disparities literature has only recently begun to examine gender-based differences beyond inequalities that are so extreme as to be endemic. Such is the case with HIV/AIDS, which continues to represent a significant source of distress for Black communities. Well into the fourth decade of the fight against HIV/AIDS, Black gay men disproportionately comprise newly diagnosed cases of HIV infections (Centers for Disease Control and Prevention [CDC], 2015). Although the reasons for this are part of a vigorous debate, HIV/AIDS, as with other disparities, must be viewed environmentally and as a product of multiple social forces—poverty, discrimination, and stigma among others—that may lead Black gay men to engage in high-risk behavior or avoid testing (The World Health Organization [WHO], 2011).

Black lesbians are underrepresented populations in current research on health disparities. For example, smoking, obesity, and poverty are more prevalent among Black lesbians than in non-Black populations, placing these women at risk for various health concerns such as cancer and sepsis (Cawthorn, 2008; Lantz, Weigers, & House, 1997). For all Black women, education and discrimination can act as barriers to routine health screening (Mouton et al., 2010) supporting contemporary researchers' contention that cancers (cervical and uterine corpus cancer) are an overlooked health disparity impacting Black lesbians (Brown & Tracy, 2008). Lesbians also report greater anxiety, anger, depressive symptoms, self-injury, and suicidal ideation and attempts (Hughes, McCabe, Wilsnack, West, & Boyd, 2010) and social and behavioral risk factors for a number of diseases than heterosexual women.

Resilience

Despite risk factors, all humans have the capacity for resilience, a pattern of behaviors, competencies, and cultural capacities that can be deployed during times of adversity (Fredriksen-Goldsen, 2007). Lorde (1984), hooks (1984, 1992), and Hall and Fine (2005) each asserted the concept of positive marginality—wisdom is garnered through observing the margins. Such observations inaugurate the capacity to contextualize the marginality, power, status, and resistance. Resilience is dynamic: A resilience approach emphasizes the life experiences of Black lesbians and gay men and places their mental and physical health behaviors and outcomes within the context of adversity and competency (Yates & Masten, 2004). Examples include the positive effects of education and the experience of fewer incidences of discrimination on Black women's likelihood to obtain Pap tests and colonoscopies (Mays, Yancey, Cochran, Weber, & Fielding, 2002). In addition, extensive social supports and networks may help individuals to better cope with adverse conditions (Ajrouch, Reisine, Lim, Sohn, & Ismail, 2010).

Furthermore, one's presentation of self may differ at times under various conditions to achieve desired outcomes or avoid undesired consequences. Employing a strategy known as double consciousness (Du Bois, 1897; Gravely, 1982) or code switching (Cross & Strauss, 1998; Greene & Walker, 2004; Guiffrida, 2003), many Black lesbians and gays can create a sense of safety by managing who they disclose to and under which conditions. For both Black lesbian and gay men, gender presentation serves multiple purposes—presenting as prescribed by societal norms accrues middle-class respectability and suitable morality that has often been denied of Black people in general and their sexuality, specifically. At other times for Black lesbians, gender presentation shapes relationships with both intimate and larger social environment—signifying boundaries and expectations in social settings, while asserting control of one's sexuality (Moore, 2006). Furthermore, with increased visibility, legislation scaling back sexual orientation discrimination, and curricula and interventions designed to reduce stigma and improve access to resources, many younger Black lesbians and gay men present themselves openly, rejecting stereotypes and confronting both macro- and micro-aggressions, by contesting their invisibility, rejecting their erasure, and reclaiming terms previously used to disparage them, such as queer, dyke, butch, and fem queen.

Interventions and Evaluation

Numerous interventions to reduce the rates of HIV transmission that provide culturally, gender, age, and urban-specific content have been designed and demonstrated to be effective when they address the concerns and social realities of the population and are created in collaboration with the target community (Jones et al., 2008). The CDC has compiled a list of evidence-based interventions comprising biomedical (medication adherence); structural (condom distribution); behavioral (Diffusion of Effective Behavioral Interventions [DEBI]); public health (counseling, testing, and referral); and social marketing interventions. Recently, an effort to create a media-based social marketing campaign to address the need for cancer screening among lesbians generated so much public outcry at use of the word lesbian that it almost failed (Phillips-Angeles et al., 2004), demonstrating the barriers for Black lesbians. Yet, a recent meta-analysis of campaigns targeted to women of color demonstrates that access-enhancing and cultural strategies significantly increase testing although few Pap interventions engage community members in this process (Han et al., 2011). Finally, while the minority stress model that suggests BGLT individuals experience greater psychological distress because of prejudice and discrimination has empirical support, practitioners must continue to build the capacity of clients to act as resilient agents while working against larger social forces (Meyer, 2003 in Meyer & Northridge, 2007).

BLACK GAY MALE CASE STUDY—EVALUATION RESEARCH

Reticence among African Americans concerning research and medical treatment has been informed by multiple abuses. The "founder of gynecology," James Marion Sims, refined his methods by performing painful surgeries on Black women without sedation during the 19th century. The Tuskegee Syphilis Experiments conducted between 1932 and 1972, by the U.S. Public Health Service (PHS) exposed Black men to tertiary syphilis, resulting in blindness, insanity, and death. And upon her death from cancer in October 1951, neither Mrs. Lacks nor her family knew that the cells found in a sample of her tumors, taken without permission, would contribute to the research and development of medications to treat multiple diseases and generate millions in profits. Despite reticence and distrust, the disproportionate negative health outcomes for all Black men and elevated rates of HIV infection among Black men who have sex with men, require examining factors contributing to disparities, developing effective evidence-based practice models, and implementing research-informed services that involve the population under study throughout the process. Research *with* communities rather than *on* them, promotes opportunities for interaction and planning within the community and expands the involved members and their constituencies' knowledge and capacity to acquire information that can prove valuable to enhancing and developing effective interventions.

"We Are Part of You.org" is part of a larger campaign entitled The Campaign for Black Men's Lives, initiated by The New York State Black Gay Network. The campaign responded to persistent elevated rates of HIV infection among African American/Black men who have sex with men (MSM) and several incidents of violence against Black gay men in New York. The campaign sought to mobilize African American gay men and their community allies against homophobia and the continued struggle against HIV/AIDS in the community. During initial meetings with community stakeholders and affected individuals, attendees developed strategies to increase involvement of those affected and their representatives and gained access to and knowledge of key organizational and local–national change agents. As the size of the group increased, stakeholders began the process of identifying common interests, including those outside the scope of the organization's capacity, while establishing clarity by developing ground rules of engagement, goals, and identifying methods of goals attainment. Providing equal access to information about the size of the population and ethical research methods of data collection and dissemination, members gained an equal footing in the dialogue, especially in discussions related to potential outcomes, and established sufficient trust to negotiate and build common understandings.

Negative representations are associated with negative self-evaluations (McDermott & Greenberg, 1984) and inaccurate public perceptions (Mahtani, 2001). Accordingly, members of the group decided to employ a social marketing campaign that would feature several images prominently displaying, on billboards, the message that Black gay men are present in divergent aspects of Black community life (e.g., religious, recreational, and familial).

The billboard campaign directed observers to the "We Are Part of You.org" website, which provides additional information concerning homophobia, health, HIV transmission, and resources. Evaluation of the campaign demonstrates the community's desire for greater information, the diversity of the community, and the importance of enlisting community partners in issues concerning African American or Black gay men. Many reported that the campaign made them want to get involved, others wanted to talk about it: wishing to spread the word or seeking further guidance to resources. Respondents indicated that they knew gay men either as friends, coworkers, and/or family members. However, many reported that they had witnessed instances of physical and verbal abuse against Black gay men.

There are few social work interventions designed specifically for women with same gender desire creating conflict over how best to help (Throckmorton & Yarhouse, 2006). Increasingly, interventions have begun to draw on intersectionality: sexual identity therapy was developed in the early 2000s resulting from a call for mental health professionals to provide more culturally sensitive interventions for lesbian, gay, bisexual, transgender, and queer (LGBTQ) clients. Clients experiencing conflict may face a number of problems as the result of being unable to resolve what are seen as irreconcilable differences between their values, attitudes, and sexuality (Schuck & Liddle, 2001). Intersectionality is also found in the fusion of public health with traditional social work practice. Issues such as violence and health behaviors are viewed through an ecological lens, focusing on the roles that societal oppression plays in the interpersonal and individual levels

(Messinger, 2012). An example of the intersection of public health and social work is the Spirit Health Education Program (SHE), a psychoeducation program integrating arts and Yoruba principles. SHE, and programs like it, are designed to address the intersecting identities of urban and lesbian and bisexual women of color (SHE Circle, 2005).

YOUTH AND OLDER GLT LIVES

Studying human behavior in the social environment requires examining individuals over the course of time. Knowledge of the risks and protective factors across various points in human development is critical to developing effective and developmentally appropriate interventions. These must also be culturally appropriate for Black lesbian and gay youth and older adults and transgender individuals who face distinct challenges associated with age and gender identity.

Youth

Over a decade ago, Mallon (1999) noted that it is difficult to truly know the size of the LGBTQ youth population because they must hide their identity within rejecting and hostile environments. Although the actual number is not known, advocates estimate between 5% and 7% of American youth—or 2.25 and 2.7 million—identify themselves as LGBTQ[5] (Human Rights Watch, 2001), with a 2003 study suggesting that 2.7 million adolescents identify themselves as LGB (Harris et al., 2003).

Albeit researchers have found no significant differences between or among LGBTQ White youth and youth of color in urban centers in terms of when they come out to others (Grov, Bimbi, Nanin, & Parsons, 2006; Rosario, Scrimshaw, & Hunter, 2004), youth of color have been found to be more discrete than White youth so that Black youth engage in fewer queer identified activities, express less comfort with disclosure, and come out to others less often (Rosario et al., 2004). Although Rosario, Scrimshaw, and Hunter (2004) offered that cultural factors lengthened the process of identity development, they suggest Black youth had greater increases in and greater surety of their sexual identity across time than their White counterparts. Nevertheless, as a race comparative design, the time needed to consolidate identity was compared to a White male ideal, viewing gender and racial differences as deficit based (Akerlund & Cheung, 2000; Cooper, Jackson, Azmitia, & Lopez, 1998; Savin-Williams & Diamond, 2001).

Stigma and Victimization

The experience of stigma, discrimination, and victimization among Black LGBTQ is unique even as compared with other racial and sexual minority youth. As young persons with multiple minority statuses—age, ethnic, racial, and sexual orientation and/or gender identity—the complexity of the oppression and stigma they face is multiplicative and causal factors are difficult to parse. Few intersectional analyses of their needs and experiences are available, even as there is greater awareness regarding the need for studies that elucidate the processes underlying and contributing to the inequities and barriers they face (Hatzenbuehler, 2009).

Managing family relations can be difficult for any teen and may be especially tense for LGBTQ youth who must grapple with years of family gender role socialization and sexual orientation expectations (Mallon, 1999). For Black LGBTQ youth, race comparative research suggests that rather than race or ethnicity, the level of adherence to traditional values (defined as religiosity, heterosexual marriage, offspring, and a language other than English spoken at home) may have a greater impact on disclosure and response (Newman & Muzzonigro in Merighi & Grimes, 2000). Given the role of the "Black Church" in the Black community, the issue of religious and moral attitudes toward nonconforming identities may contribute to familial strain and rejection (Herek, Chopp, & Strohl, 2007; Ward, 2005) and the diminished likelihood of Black youth to come out to their parents as compared to their Latino or White counterparts (60% vs. 71% and 80%, respectively; Grov et al., 2006).

Because the "experiences and needs of gay, lesbian and transgender students of color remain largely unexplored in existing research" (Diaz & Kosciw, 2009, p. 2) in 2007, Gay Lesbian & Straight Education Network (GLSEN, 2009) specifically examined the intersections of race–ethnicity, sexual orientation, and gender identity and found that almost half of the lesbian and gay youth of color experienced verbal harassment and over a fifth experienced physical violence due to their combined orientation and racial–ethnic identity. Diaz and Kosciw (2009) also reported that when LGBTQ Black youth were a racial minority, they are three times more likely to feel unsafe and almost twice as likely to experience verbal harassment. LGBTQ Black youth are also vulnerable to sexual abuse and victimization (Higa et al., 2012).

System Involvement—Child Welfare, Juvenile Justice, and Homelessness

Although pathways are complex, hostile interpersonal environments coupled with equally insensitive providers and few queer and trans affirming systems of care substantially contribute to homelessness, and involvement in the juvenile justice and foster care systems, sectors that Black youth are already disproportionately represented in given poverty and racial–ethnic policy legacies (Green, 2002; Mastin, Metzger, & Golden, 2013). For example, because Blacks are overrepresented among individuals experiencing homelessness, it is not surprising that Black LGBTQ youth are disproportionately homeless in New York City (Ferguson-Colvin & Maccio, 2012), NY State, Detroit, Ann Arbor, Denver, and Waltham, Massachusetts (cf. Ray, 2006). LGBTQ youth have greater vulnerability to a range of behavioral health conditions, such as depression, anxiety, eating disorders, and suicide, with parental and social rejection significant in negative outcomes (Garofalo, Deleon, Osmer, Doll, & Harper, 2006; Hershberger & D'Augelli, 1995; Higa et al., 2012). Even as rates of suicide are lower in the Black population as compared to the general population, among Black respondents of the National Transgender Discrimination Survey (NTDS), 49% reported having attempted suicide (Grant, Mottet, et al., 2011). And, once homeless, LGBTQ youth are more likely to experience mental distress and suicidality (Cochran, Stewart, Ginzler, & Cauce, 2002; Whitbeck, Chen, Hoyt, Tyler, & Johnson, 2004), to use substances and engage in HIV risk behaviors (Cochran et al., 2002); to be victimized (Aratani, 2009; Cochran et al., 2002); and face discrimination, assault, and harassment (Grant et al., 2011).

Interventions

In practice with Black lesbian and gay youth, the need to create supportive safe spaces where youth can be actors and agents in their learning and development is vital. Second, for LGBTQ Black youth—especially those in institutional settings—oppression informs multiple areas of their lives. Moreover, when we shift our role from one of expert on "the problem" to that of partners in discovery and social change, social workers create opportunities for "intravention," whereby the organic processes within communities themselves become interventions that help move cultures of risk to cultures of support (Friedman et al., 2004). Given that research indicates that sexual identity consolidation is very much tied to and dependent on successful racial–ethnic identity consolidation, with life satisfaction, self-esteem, and greater surety significantly related to the latter rather than the former (Crawford, Allison, Zamboni, & Soto, 2002; Della, Wilson, & Miller, 2002; Rosario et al., 2004), and given Black youth's greater reticence around coming out, a focus on general antibias training may be more culturally syntonic. A crucial support for many Black families is the Black Church, a vital transmitter of cultural history that offers networks and connectedness crucial to developing a sense of racial–ethnic identity (Swanson, Spencer, Harpalani, & Spencer, 2002; Ward, 2005) and personal self-esteem (Sullivan & Wodarski, 2002). Although the Black Church has begun to "intravene" by launching affirming churches (Ward, 2005), houses of worship of all types can provide invaluable support because spirituality–faith practice acts as a buffer for Black youth exposed to high levels of community violence or substance use (Fowler et al., 2006 in Toro, Dworsky, & Fowler, 2007) and against heterosexism (Della et al., 2002). As social workers working with Black LGBTQ youth and their families, it is important that we do not assume these lifelines are rejecting or unavailable.

GLT YOUTH CASE STUDY—ADVOCACY AND POLICY

As a service-learning field instruction assignment, a master of social work (MSW) student was asked to develop a group with a marginalized or underserved population that had been a focus of research during her first year. The student chose LGBTQ youth in residential care, given her research on bullying and interest in effecting policy change in the child welfare system related to these issues. Based on her research, foundation year course work, and her position within child welfare, the student framed the problem as a need for knowledge and skills around bullying and an educationally focused group curriculum was developed. During group facilitation, however, the student learned that the youth were quite knowledgeable about bullying and appropriate responses and engaged in significant self-advocacy. In time, the student understood that what the youth needed most was a safe space to share and process their feelings and thoughts about these experiences with an ally. In response, the group was transitioned from an educational group to a mutual-aid or support group that addressed a fuller range of discrimination, oppression, power, and voice. With such support, the LGBTQ youth were able to make larger social and institutional links, to identify needed changes within their school and residential settings, and to problem solve around initiating these changes. Thus, the need to reconfigure the group was a profound lesson for the student in paternalism and pathologization: rather than passive recipients to a service, the youth became cocreators of the group and instead of an expert, the student was a partner and ally.

BGLT OLDER LIVES

Approximately 13.7% or about 41 million of the more than 300 million Americans are people 65 years and older (U.S. Census Bureau, 2014). Black elders represent approximately 9% of the population or roughly 3 million. If estimates stating that GLT seniors represent between 3.8% and 7.6% of the population (Grant, 2010) are true, then between 135,000 and 270, 000 of the total elder GLT population are African American. Although not a large population, special attention should be given to the intersection of race, poverty, and age: U.S. Census Bureau (2013) poverty rates among Blacks were 25.8% as compared to 14.3% in the general population and the finding from the Williams Institute at the University of California Los Angeles, School of Law found that when compared to White same-sex couples, African Americans were three times more likely to live in poverty (Sears & Badgett, 2012).

Stigma and Risk

In working with elder gays and lesbians, it is important to acknowledge that many members of this community have lived lives in secrecy, fearing recrimination from both the larger society and Black communities (Van Sluytman et al., 2013). Living in silence often results in isolation and avoidance of seeking needed services. Discrimination related to gender presentation may result in lack of access to universal housing and entitlements just as discrimination in employment experienced over lifetimes may result in ineligibility for income-based benefits or rights-afforded spouses. Some have found that many health disparities among older adult transgender, lesbian, and bisexual women are related to perceived abuse or neglect by health care providers (for discussion, see Kishore, 2013; Rice, 2013). For example, a transgender man may still be at risk for breast cancer, but his health care provider may not be knowledgeable enough to appropriately assess risk. Similarly, ageism reduces the likelihood that providers will inquire about an older person's sexuality, including histories and current activities, whereas heterosexism and relying on a history of heterosexual activity reduce the likelihood of cancer screening for older lesbians (Rice, 2013). For many older African Americans, engaging with adult children involves changing roles concerning dependence and interdependence within an extended family network (Ajrouch et al., 2010; Cohen & Wills, 1985; Kawachi & Berkman, 2001). This is also the case with many older GLT persons (Averett, Yoon, & Jenkins, 2011; Brotman et al., 2007; Goldberg, Sickler, & Dibble, 2005; Hash, 2006; Jones & Nystrom, 2002) who may lose valuable resources as well as the opportunity to perform valued family roles should the family reject the older adult due to sexual orientation. Deprived of engagement, such as meaningful relationships with both biological and fictive kin, social capital is lost and the elder is unable to perform roles critical to well-being and healthy aging. Given that these elders face discrimination based on race (Beam, 1983, 1986; Bonilla & Porter, 1990; Boykin, 1996; Harper, 1992; Herek & Capitanio, 1995; Riggs, 1991; Simmons, 1991) and age (Barker, Herdt, & de Vries, 2006; deVries, 2008; Gay, lesbian, and transgender MAP & SAGE, 2010; Hostetler, 2004; Schope, 2005) in GLT social networks, and reduced social networks and consequent isolation are an important factor in mental health and well-being, social work practice that is reflective, culturally humble, well informed, and attentive to issues of stigma and social inclusion is necessary to improve aging outcomes for BGLT older adults.

Interventions

As GLT individuals of color age, they contend with agism, racism, and heterosexism. However, understanding that aging is an ongoing process, the authors of this chapter suggest that all models of interventions targeting the BGLT community must be designed to engage milestones associated with individual and group development that are particular to the demands of Black communities. Interventions must access critical information resulting in increased engagement. Further, ongoing training allows for deeper understanding of the lives of African American LGBT people. Such training engages participants in increasing their awareness while questioning their biases, privilege (e.g., race, class, gender, sexual orientation, immigration status, and other identities), histories of oppression, and the manner by which they may act as deterrent to engagement among GLT consumers. Such awareness encourages building alliances that are safe and accepting through accountable change-oriented risk taking with African America GLT youth, adults, and elder. Kishore (2013, emphasis added) offered "A basic understanding of terminology can help practitioners feel more competent...but this must be coupled with a willingness to ask relevant questions. It may be helpful to ask Who do you consider family? rather than Are you married/do you have children? because the former question leaves room for a variety of family and support structures" (National Association of Social Workers [NASW], 2000, p. 145). Van Sluytman and Torres (2014) state that meeting the needs of older BGLT adults requires a transformative antiracist stance that joins this population in questioning the context-rich factors that render them invisible. Situating the person in the environment, social workers must adopt an intersectional lens to promote and restore wellness among those who face multiple oppressions.

GLT ELDER CASE STUDY—PROGRAM DEVELOPMENT

Research indicates that the quality and stability of social support influence mental health functioning (Horowitz, Reinhardt, Boerner, & Travis, 2003). Organizations such as GRIOT Circle have developed a creative intervention program called Buddy-2-Buddy, which offers strategic engagement among and between elders. Buddy-2-Buddy is also a component of social work–case management service as it counters isolation and restricted mobility among members, thereby promoting independence and self-reliance among elders.

One participant provides a vivid portrait of the challenges faced by elders. Lillie, an 89-year-old African American, recalls the death of her partner of 47 years. She revealed that she had no GLT friends because she and her partner lived together as cousins and were not out about their sexuality or their relationship. Lilly discovered GRIOT's Buddy-2-Buddy program and now proudly claims a vibrant circle of friends—14 to be exact. They visit regularly bringing her news and conversation while affirming to Lillie and the staff of the nursing home that she is truly not alone.

Buddy-2-Buddy provides an array of services, including hospital and home visits, escort services, telephone calls, and assistance with cleaning and shopping. The intervention emphasizes the importance of supportive relationships established among members of GRIOT. Buddy-2-Buddy distinguishes itself in work with elders of color who are often reticent about discussing personal problems with "strangers." Employing cultural humility, buddies are often able to meet each other where they address fears and needs without damaging their sense of dignity or independence. The intervention is volunteer based. Buddies are recruited through mailings, phone calls, gatherings at GRIOT, and word of mouth. When an individual expresses an interest in being a Buddy, he or she details their needs and reviews expectations of the program. The applicant is entered into the Buddy database, containing Buddies' personal information, contact information, interests, skills, and other relevant information. When an appropriate match is found, the Buddies are then paired, and services can commence. Should a pairing become unsatisfactory, Buddies can inform the Volunteer Coordinator, and a new match can be made.

GRIOT attempts to remove financial strain from its Buddies, many of whom are low income, in several different ways; providing transportation at no cost, community potluck meals, and assistance with acquiring free cell phone services to ensure a means of connection. Many of the participants who are homebound or have limited mobility, use the telephone as their primary means of communication. However, others also pay home visits or accompany one another on social outings and errands. The participants are free to decide for themselves the style and frequency of their interactions.

Among other innovations, the program makes use of social gatherings with Buddy-2-Buddy "Parties," where Buddies and other GRIOT members come together to eat and socialize, as well as to assess participants' experiences and opinions about the program. Buddy-2-Buddy has reached nearly 150 individuals and fostered 89 partnerships each week to enhance socialization and support.

TRANSGENDER LIVES

Transgender is an umbrella term that is used to describe individuals whose gender identities and/or expressions differ from the sex they were assigned at birth (Kirk & Kulkarni, 2006). Although this term is often used interchangeably with *transsexual*, a term that describes a specific subset of transgender individuals who undergo surgery, hormone treatment, or other procedures to better align the physical body and gender identity (Haas et al., 2010), transgender encompasses a wide range of gender identities and expressions that may or may not be accompanied by medical procedures. More recently, younger people have used the terms *gender queer* and *gender nonconforming* to describe gender identities and expressions that are neither male nor female, but between or outside of this dichotomy. By contrast, the term *cisgender* has been used to identify those members of society for whom gender identity and gender expression generally align with society's expectations of gender based on assigned sex at birth.

Population-based estimates of the transgender population in the United States are scarce, but various estimates suggest that between 0.1% and 2% of the population is transgender, depending on methods of estimation and the definition of transgender that is used (Gates, 2011). Smaller estimates refer to the number of people who identify as a transgender man or woman, while larger estimates refer to people who may identify with a wide variety of cross-gender behaviors and identities.

Gender Identity Formation

A few process (Mason-Schrock, 1996) and stage models (Devor, 2004; Lev, 2004; Nuttbrock, Rosenblum, & Blumenstein, 2002) have been proposed for understanding transgender and transsexual identity. These models range from 4 to 14 stages or processes, with some degree of overlap. The shortest model, proposed by Nuttbrock, Rosenblum, and Blumenstein (2002), suggests that transgender individuals move through four stages of transgender identity development, including identity awareness, identity performance, identity congruence, and identity support. At the other extreme, Devor's (2004) model suggests that transgender people navigate 14 stages of identity development through processes of *witnessing,* or being seen as oneself by others, and *mirroring,* or feeling seen as oneself by others like oneself. Unfortunately, because empirical research on transgender identity formation is still nascent, frameworks for understanding transgender identity development in the context of racial, ethnic, and sexual identity development do not currently exist. Rather, clinicians and researchers who work with transgender people of color must create opportunities to understand these experiences.

Psychosocial Experiences

The extant literature on the psychosocial experiences of transgender populations in the United States is sparse at best, perhaps in part due to the difficulties in defining and accessing this population. Rather, attempts to capture potential exposure to trauma, psychosocial stress, and health issues among transgender people are largely limited to nonrandom samples of convenience with little information on differences based on race or ethnicity, socioeconomic status, or location (i.e., data on specific racial or ethnic groups, broken down by urban, suburban, rural contexts; Shipherd, Maguen, Skidmore, & Abramovitz, 2011; Williams & Freeman, 2007). Nevertheless, it is evident that transgender people—and transgender people of color in particular—live in the context of pervasive discrimination at the interpersonal and structural levels, putting them at risk for poor health outcomes and a diminished sense of well-being. In fact, the recently conducted NTDS demonstrated that while the transgender population as a whole faces high levels of discrimination relative to the general population, Black transgender people and other transgender people of color experienced the especially devastating impact of racism and anti-transgender discrimination in society (Grant et al., 2011).

Stigma, Abuse, and Victimization

Transgender and gender nonconforming people are often targets of fatal hate and violence, and a large proportion of hate crime fatalities are transgender people of color (Stotzer, 2008). In addition, Black transgender people face nonfatal forms of harassment and abuse in many arenas of everyday life (Grant et al., 2011). Whether in school, the workplace, or in encounters with the police and prison systems, Black transgender individuals reported frequent experiences of harassment, physical assault, and sexual assault, with a clear impact on psychosocial well-being. These traumas occurred at the hands of peers and authority figures alike, with teachers, employers, and police officers failing to protect against or even perpetrating violence against Black transgender respondents. Not surprisingly, these frequent reports of violence in schools and in the workplace are accompanied by the over-policing of Black transgender people. More than one third of the Black respondents to the NTDS reported being arrested or held in a cell due to bias.

High levels of harassment, abuse, and assault across multiple domains of society make Black transgender people especially vulnerable to unemployment, homelessness, and poverty. Indeed, results from the NTDS indicate that Black transgender respondents experienced an unemployment rate that was twice that of transgender respondents of other races and quadruple that of the general population (Grant et al., 2011). In addition to employment discrimination, extreme poverty, and homelessness, they also face the additional burdens of being denied access to shelters due to gender identity or expression, as well as harassment, physical assault, and sexual assault within shelters.

Health and Mental Health

While no comprehensive study exists on transgender health risks by ethnicity, it is likely that Black transgender people are vulnerable to many of the chronic and life-threatening illnesses that are elevated in the Black population, metabolic health problems and certain types of cancers being among these (e.g., Keppel, 2007). Disproportionate rates of substance use in this population may compound risk of illness, while fear of discrimination and refusal of care due to bias may delay treatment of serious medical conditions, ultimately worsening prognoses (Clements-Nolle, Marx, Guzman, & Katz, 2001; Grant et al., 2011). According to the NTDS, Black transgender individuals endorsed extremely high rates of HIV, with 20% endorsing positive status compared to 2.64% of transgender people of other races, 2.4% of the general Black population, and only 0.6% of the general U.S. population. Nearly half of all Black transgender respondents to the NTDS also endorsed a suicide attempt, compared with only 1.6% of the general U.S. population.

Activism as Intervention

Despite the substantial impact of pervasive racism and gender-based discrimination on health and well-being, Black transgender individuals also share powerful stories of resilience and are at the forefront of many liberation efforts across the nation. Few, if any, services are known to specifically address the needs of Black transgender and gender nonconforming individuals, but agencies in some major U.S. cities do provide significant resources to this population. For example, the Minority AIDS Project (www .minorityaidsproject.org) in Los Angeles, CA, and the Positive Health Project (http:// harmreduction.org/connect-locally/new-york/positive-health-project/) in New York, NY, aim to address HIV and AIDS within Black and Latino communities in those cities. As an extension of their work to provide housing, treatment, counseling, information, and vocational training for individuals with HIV and AIDS, these organizations serve a large proportion of Black transgender and gender nonconforming individuals. The Sylvia Rivera Law Project (SRLP, srlp.org) is another important resource for Black transgender people, as it provides legal resources and advocacy around issues that most directly impact low-income transgender people of color. SRLP also provides guides for community organizing and self-advocacy on their websites to help empower transgender people. In this same vein, smaller grassroots organizations in a few U.S. cities use leadership development and community mobilization to address racial- and gender-based inequalities. Examples of these include Gender Justice LA in Los Angeles, CA; the Audre Lorde Project's TransJustice project in New York, NY; and the Brown Boi Project in Oakland,

CA. Although relatively few, organizations like those mentioned here aim to empower low-income transgender people of color to fight for the right to self-determination and freedom from gender-, economic-, and race-based oppression.

TRANSGENDER POPULATION CASE STUDY—INDIVIDUAL PRACTICE

Respondent 1

Early Life

It started when I was at least 4 or 5 years old. I was aware of the fact that my physical body did not match my identity spiritually or mentally. I would tell everyone who would listen that I would grow up into this androgynous figure who blurred gender lines, was beautiful, feminine, glamorous, and was loved, adored, and desired by both men and women. I hated labels, only because I liked to be able to exist in a fluid manner.

Naming Trans Identity

When I was 20, I met a woman named K who became my first trans friend. She showed me that it was okay to identify as trans and as a woman, and it was okay to explore my femininity. Up until meeting her, I knew vaguely of "trans" identity, but I could not connect my journey with that of being trans. Once I made the connection, the fear I faced as a trans individual seemed to lessen. From that moment, I decided I would transition on my comfort level, and define womanhood and what it meant to be trans on my terms. It has been hard. It is hard. So many people have their own ideas and their own misconceptions about me, my path, my journey. A lot of people whom I love and whose opinions I cherish deeply have, in one way or another, tried to steer me down the path they saw fit.

Intersectionality and Lived Experience

Being a Black trans person, I am constantly facing the stereotypes that come with being both trans *and* Black. I have a job where I have authority and stability. I have my own apartment, benefits, steady income. I have been able to bypass much of the struggle, but not the stigma and the stereotypes. I still experience so many prejudices that exist against both trans people as well as Black people and people who live at the intersection of both. I am solicited for sex and accosted. I have been sexually assaulted on more than one occasion, and am constantly harassed. I try to not let it affect me personally when men attempt to victimize me, degrade me, sexually assault me. I have grown, because it has made me stronger, but it is more of a struggle than anything.

Resilience

As a Black trans woman, I live to break every stereotype. I do that by living my life, and not stopping because of prejudice or discrimination. I continue to break down any wall put up in front of me because of people's ignorance. I continue to shine through my identity and my gender and sex expression, even as I bend and play with the fluidity of that expression.

Respondent 2

Early Life

Growing up in a poor, Black community in the south, I was just open. I liked to catch worms, play with my cousin, Darren—we would roughhouse, play ninja turtles, and sometimes Barbie dolls. When I was 10, all the girls decided to get training bras, and I thought that was the dumbest idea. I would parade around the locker room with my shirt off saying "I feel free." I would take my shirt off at home, too, until my mother told me it was inappropriate. She would try to dress me up in girly stuff, but I would say "I just want to be comfortable. I'm not a *girl*, I'm *comfortable*." My childhood was so open and then a closing happened through socialization.

Naming Trans Identity

I went to a women's college, which also brought up issues around race and class, but I met a few masculine-of-center folks there. One night we were hanging out and one of them asked if we ever felt like maybe we were guys. I was scandalized to be having that conversation out loud with somebody else, but it was such an affirming moment for me. When I talk about my gender now, that sentiment I expressed to my mom about wanting to be comfortable still sticks. I think of gender as a language. To understand me best is to understand me through masculinity, but that does not really fully capture me. I have to communicate something to you, but there are things unexpressed through binaries.

Intersectionality and Lived Experience

I am Black, queer, and trans—it all shows up in the world at the exact same time. In a way, my life has felt like a series of unsafe places. Early on, I became very attuned to other people in order to survive. I learned to notice people's movements, breathing, everything, and I felt closed off from others. I have experienced community violence. I have been attacked randomly in the streets. I have been attacked by White people who layer on racial epithets in the midst of gender-based violence. I have been attacked by people within the Black community who layer on transphobia, homophobia, and misogyny. I feel the weight of it every day, in everything I do. When I wake up each day, I think about how I will gather the strength to navigate through the world. There have been times in my life when I thought I would not survive my experience, that my mind, soul, and spirit could not bear it.

Resilience

I have found relationships in which I can be loved and accepted. The secure, loving relationship with my psychotherapist allowed me to break through some of the trauma and feel things I had not felt before, while generative somatics reintroduced me to the wisdom of my body. These experiences told me for the first time that everything about me gets to be here in the world at once—I get to be Black, and queer, and trans, and my story matters. My trauma—with healing and wisdom—becomes my gift. As a therapist myself, I have some anxiety about being Black, queer, trans, and a healer because I know each new client is going to project a lot on me. I have to get my shame in check before I go into the room and remember why I am there. At the same time, clients are forced to read my gender in a way they have seldom had to before. It brings us very quickly to what is core about being human.

Of course, it is dynamic. The trauma is ongoing, simply because I wake up every day. It hurts every day, and it breaks my heart every day. In the long term, I need community—people who also know what it is like to live in a world that tells you you are not real, and who can reach out and say, "you matter." Trans and queer people of color activism creates this because so many of us carry a story of being expelled from our communities; yet, we are committed to them and to each other—we know we need to change the systems and conditions that create the need for people to divide and conquer one another. Ultimately, I think we have a lot to tell the world about forgiveness.

IMPLICATIONS

Through the political action of many GLT activists, representations of gay men and lesbians and to a lesser extent transgender individuals, have become more visible in multiple social environments. Further, the Internet has increased access to resources among sexual minorities. However, multiple factors including gender and gender representation, race, class, and social and geographic locations, among others, continue to uniquely impact the lives and well-being of BLGT individuals. First, as with other Black men, women and children, many struggle with the challenges of income insecurity and disproportionate rates of incarceration. Second, the feminization of poverty and women's longer life spans means lesbians are at greater risk of living in poverty than their male counterparts, (Cawthorn, 2008) and because the risk of living in poverty increases greatly as women age, elder Black lesbians are at substantial risk. Third, a paucity of resources in urban communities (Fullilove & Fullilove, 1999) across the United States has resulted in losses of jobs, opportunities, resources, and social capital that previously sustained marginalized communities (Wilson, 1978). Fourth, in many urban communities, the transformation of larger economic forces such as deindustrialization has led to concentrated poverty, diminished social capital, and heightened surveillance by the criminal justice system. Finally, members of the African American community who are LGBT live in a society that marginalizes Black skin and age and stigmatizes gender nonconformity and nonheterosexual orientations. Given these issues, the particular needs and concerns of BGLT individuals and their families may go largely unaddressed if social workers focus solely on racial or sexual orientation issues without recognition of how subjugated identities intersect and are given salience. The profession's ethical code demands an understanding of the impact of race, ethnicity, national origin, age, marital status, and physical ability—among others—on oppression and diversity (NASW, 2000, p. 151). Furthermore, it is incumbent on social workers to strengthen the relationships that enhance individual, family, and social group well-being (NASW, 2000, p. 145). Ignoring or minimizing the complexity of these ethics renders GLT members of the community invisible.

To redress the historical and systemic erasure of oppressed communities, social workers must assess policies and procedures that reinforce silences and act as barriers to full disclosure by clients. Though disclosure must always be voluntary, assumption of a heterosexual orientation or gender presentations based on dichotomies (e.g., male and female) must be interrogated. The scope of psychosocial assessment must increase to examine social forces (e.g., stigma) that make disclosure hazardous and presentation management a necessary strategy for GLT individuals. Similarly, advocacy and outreach efforts should actively confront heteronormativity, sexism, agism, and racism. The lives of BGLT individuals involve negotiating interactions based on race and gender identity and expression grounded in essentialist beliefs concerning what is Black and what is masculine and feminine (Malebranche, Peterson, Fullilove, & Stackhouse, 2004). Fear of discrimination related to sexual orientation and gender identities may impact health-seeking behaviors, thereby exacerbating existing disparities.

However, there are recognized resiliencies among BGLT people. Shippy (2007) reported that GLT individuals may not be estranged from their biological families even as many may also have "families of choice" including members of social networks beyond biological families. Accordingly, engaging family calls for a reframing of traditional notions of family (Fredriksen-Goldsen & Hooyman, 2007) and examination of the roles of both formal and informal members of the biological and choice families. This is particularly relevant to African American communities where reliance on family of origin networks may mitigate the impact of discrimination (Ajrouch et al., 2010; Cohen & Wills, 1985; Kawachi & Berkman, 2001).

The complexity of African American GLT individuals' lives and identity construction requires social work to prepare all clinicians to serve clients in culturally appropriate ways. Tools must include GLT affirming competencies across the life course and self-reflective practice. Competency concerning sexual orientation and gender identity and expression should be measured as with other forms of competency. Improving competency includes raising awareness of issues unique to any population as well as examining the literature.

Van Sluytman and Torres (2014) argue that transformations in society, including increase in the number of people of color in general as well as changes in public policy, require "invit[ing] persons of color into difficult dialogues" that employ an intersectional lens to give voice to the experience of GLT individuals, to challenge prevailing forms of structural discrimination, and increase their visibility and participation.

FOR FURTHER STUDY

Suggested Assignments

1. Identify and describe an employment, health, or housing issue affecting members of the community who are LGBT:

   a. Describe how widespread the issue is (prevalence, incidence);

    b. Suggest *evidence-based interventions social workers can use in organizations* that work with LGBT youth to address the issue; and

    c. Identify *appropriate technological resources* that can inform social work strategies–interventions.

2. Give an informal but prepared 10-minute talk about their past, present, and future in relation to social work with members of the community who are LGBT.

3. Write an agency plan on adapting organizational policies, procedures, and resources to facilitate the provision of services to members of the community who are LGBT older adults and their family caregivers.

Suggested Reading

Gay and Lesbian

Beam, J. (1986). *In the life: A Black gay anthology.* Boston, MA: Alyson Publications.

Boykin, K. (1996). *One more river to cross: Black and gay in America.* New York, NY: Anchor Books/ Doubleday.

Burin, Y., & Sowinski, E. A. (2014). Sister to sister: Developing a black British feminist archival consciousness. *Feminist Review, 108*(1), 112–119.

Clarke, C. (1983). The failure to transform: Homophobia in the Black community. In B. Smith (Ed.), *Home girls: A black feminist anthology* (pp. 197–208). New Brunswick, NJ Rutgers University Press.

Collins, P. H. (2002). *Black feminist thought: Knowledge, consciousness, and the politics of empowerment.* New York, NY: Routledge.

Ferguson, R. A. (2004). *Aberrations in black: Toward a queer of color critique.* Minneapolis: University of Minnesota Press.

Frilot, S. (1995). Black nations/queer nations. San Francisco: California Newsreel.

Hammonds, E. (1994). Black (w) holes and the geometry of black female sexuality. *DIFFERENCES-BLOOMINGTON, 6,* 126.

Hemphill, E. (Ed.). (1991). *Brother to brother: New writings by Black gay men.* Boston, MA: Alyson Publications.

Johnson, E. P., & Henderson, M. G. (Eds.). (2005). *Black queer studies: A critical anthology.* Durham, NC: Duke University Press.

Lorde, A. (1997). Age, race, class, and sex: Women redefining difference. *Cultural Politics, 11,* 374–380.

Moore, M. R. (2006). Lipstick or Timberlands? Meanings of gender presentation in Black lesbian communities. *Signs: Journal of Women in Culture and Society, 32*(1): 113–139.

Reid-Pharr, R. (2001). *Black gay man: Essays.* New York: NYU Press.

Richardson, M. U. (2003). No more secrets, no more lies: African American history and compulsory heterosexuality. *Journal of Women's History, 15*(3), 63–76.

Rupp, L. J. (2003). Women's history in the new millennium: Adrienne Rich's "Compulsory heterosexuality and lesbian existence": A retrospective. *Journal of Women's History, 15*(3), 9–10.

Simms, D. C. (Ed.). (2001). *The greatest taboo: Homosexuality in Black communities.* Boston: Alyson.

Smith, B. (Ed.). (1983). *Home girls: A black feminist anthology.* New Brunswick, NJ: Rutgers University Press.

LGBT Youth

Chesir-Teran, D., & Hughes, D. (2009). Heterosexism in high school and victimization among lesbian, gay, bisexual, and questioning students. *Journal of Youth and Adolescence, 38*(7), 963–975.

Davidson, M. (2008). Rethinking the movement: Trans youth activism in New York City and beyond. In S. Driver (Ed.), *Queer Youth Cultures* (pp. 243–260). Albany, NY: SUNY Press.

Goodenow, C., Szalacha, L., & Westheimer, K. (2006). School support groups, other school factors, and the safety of sexual minority adolescents. *Psychology in the Schools, 43*(5), 573–589.

Grossman, A. H., & D'Augelli, A. R. (2007). Transgender youth and life-threatening behaviors. *Suicide and Life-Threatening Behavior, 37*(5), 527–537.

Heck, N. C., Flentje, A., & Cochran, B. N. (2011). Offsetting risks: High school gay-straight alliances and lesbian, gay, bisexual, and transgender (LGBT) youth. *School Psychology Quarterly, 26*(2), 161.

Kosciw, J. G., Greytak, E. A., & Diaz, E. M. (2009). Who, what, where, when, and why: Demographic and ecological factors contributing to hostile school climate for lesbian, gay, bisexual, and transgender youth. *Journal of Youth and Adolescence, 38*(7), 976–988.

McCreery, P. (2008). Save our children/let us marry: Gay activists appropriate the rhetoric of child protectionism. *Radical History Review, 2008*(100), 186–207.

Talburt, S. (2004). Constructions of LGBT youth: Opening up subject positions. *Theory Into Practice, 43*(2), 116–121.

Transgender

Dutton, L., Koenig, K., & Fennie, K. (2008). Gynecologic care of the female-to-male transgender man. *Journal of Midwifery & Women's Health, 53*(4), 331–337.

Garofalo, R., Deleon, J., Osmer, E., Doll, M., & Harper, G. W. (2006). Overlooked, misunderstood and at-risk: Exploring the lives and HIV risk of ethnic minority male-to-female transgender youth. *Journal of Adolescent Health, 38*(3), 230–236.

Kenagy, G. P., & Hsieh, C. M. (2005). The risk less known: Female-to-male transgender persons' vulnerability to HIV infection. *AIDS Care, 17*(2), 195–207.

Nemoto, T., Operario, D., Keatley, J., Han, L., & Soma, T. (2004). HIV risk behaviors among male-to-female transgender persons of color in San Francisco. *American Journal of Public Health, 94*(7), 1193–1199.

Phillips, G., Peterson, J., Binson, D., Hidalgo, J., Magnus, M., & YMSM of color SPNS Initiative Study Group. (2011). House/ball culture and adolescent African-American transgender persons and men who have sex with men: A synthesis of the literature. *AIDS Care, 23*(4), 515–520.

Rachlin, K., Green, J., & Lombardi, E. (2008). Utilization of health care among female-to-male transgender individuals in the United States. *Journal of Homosexuality, 54*(3), 243–258.

Rowniak, S., Chesla, C., Rose, C. D., & Holzemer, W. L. (2011). Transmen: The HIV risk of gay identity. *AIDS Education and Prevention, 23*(6), 508–520.

Suggested Websites

Gay and Lesbian

Blacklight: A Site for African American Lesbians and Gay Men, http://www.blacklightonline.com

Nia Collective, http://www.niacollective.org

National Black Justice Coalition, http://nbjc.org

The Audre Lorde Project, http://alp.org

United Lesbians of African Heritage

ZAMI for Lesbians of African Descent, http://www.zami.org

Zuna Institute, http://www.zunainstitute.org

LGBT Youth

Resources for LGBT Youth and Their Friends

Gay, Lesbian, and Bisexual Teens: Facts for Teens and Their Parents, https://www
.healthychildren.org/English/ages-stages/teen/dating-sex/Pages/Gay-Lesbian-and-
Bisexual-Teens-Facts-for-Teens-and-Their-Parents.aspx

StopBullying.gov: Information for LGBT Youth, http://www.stopbullying.gov/at-risk/
groups/lgbt/

The Trevor Project: Crisis Intervention and Suicide Prevention, http://www
.thetrevorproject.org/

Resources for Parents and Family Members

Advocates for Youth (AFY): GLBTQ Issues Info for Parents, http://www
.advocatesforyouth.org/lgbtq-issues-info-for-parents

Gay, Lesbian, and Bisexual Teens: Facts for Teens and Their Parents

**Helping Families to Support Their LGBT Children,http://store.samhsa.gov/product/A-
Practitioner-s-Resource-Guide-Helping-Families-to-Support-Their-LGBT-Children/
PEP14-LGBTKIDS**

KidsHealth.org: Sexual Attraction and Orientation, http://kidshealth.org/teen/sexual_
health/guys/sexual_orientation.html

Parents, Families, Friends, and Allies of Lesbians and Gays (PFLAG), https://community
.pflag.org

Parents' Influence on the Health of Lesbian, Gay, and Bisexual Teens: What Parents and
Families Should Know, http://www.cdc.gov/healthyyouth/protective/pdf/parents_
influence_lgb.pdf

Sexual Orientation: Families Are Talking, http://www.siecus.org/index.
cfm?fuseaction=page.viewPage&pageID=632&nodeID=1

StopBullying.gov: Information for Parents, http://www.stopbullying.gov/what-you-can-do/
parents

Supportive Families, Healthy Children: Helping Families with Lesbian, Gay, Bisexual,
and Transgender Children, https://sait.usc.edu/lgbt/files/Supportive%20Families%20
Healthy%20Children.pdf

Technology and Youth Violence: Electronic Aggression, http://www.cdc.gov/
violenceprevention/youthviolence/electronicaggression

The Trevor Project: Education and Resources for Adults

Understanding Sexual Orientation and Gender Identity, http://www.plannedparenthood.org/
learn/sexual-orientation-gender

Transgender

Transgender Visibility Guide, http://www.hrc.org/resources/entry/transgender-visibility-guide

A National Crisis: Anti-Transgender Violence, http://www.hrc.org/resources/entry/a-national-
crisis-anti-transgender-violence

Equality Rising, http://www.hrc.org/resources/entry/equality-rising

NOTES

1. The chapter makes use of same-gender desire interchangeably with gay and homosexual. Many
Black men and women with same-gender desire do not refer to themselves as gay or homosexual or bisexual. Use of the term same gender refers to those whose self-perception of their gender
matches their assigned sex at birth or cisgender and cissexual.

2. We recognize that bisexual individuals face multiple stigmas, assumptions of duplicity, and pro-miscuity. Discussions and portrayals of bisexuality tend to eroticize bisexuality among women. Bisexuality among White men is often viewed as an outcome of the society's constraints (Pitt, 2006) such as the star-crossed lovers in "Brokeback Mountain." This latter view is not similarly extended to Black men. Instead, for them, bisexuality is often viewed as a threat to masculinity, uncontrolled lust, and a disease transmission vector. This chapter is grounded in the belief that sexual desire occurs along a continuum ranging from exclusive homosexual to exclusive hetero-sexual sexual desire. Those who identify as bisexual face these dichotic sexual orientations and frequently lack institutional supports (Conerly, 1996). Consequently, they socialize in environ-ments (exclusively homosexual, heterosexual, and mixed environments) that endorse their pre-sentation or the assumption–appearance of their sexual orientation, sharing both the challenges and opportunities in these communities.
3. We thank Dr. Tiffany Rice for her contribution to this chapter.
4. Q is included here to represent both queer and questioning, given a continuum of experience, as recognition that identity during this period undergoes dynamic shifts, and generational nomen-clature differs.

REFERENCES

Ajrouch, K., Reisine, S., Lim, S., Sohn, W., & Ismail, A. (2010). Perceived everyday discrimination and psychological distress: Does social support matter? *Ethnicity & Health, 15*(4), 417–434.

Akerlund, M., & Cheung, M. (2000). Teaching beyond the deficit model: Gay and lesbian issues among African Americans, Latinos, and Asian Americans. *Journal of Social Work Education, 36*(2), 279.

American Psychiatric Association. (2013). *Diagnostic and statistical manual of mental disorders* (5th ed.). Arlington, VA: American Psychiatric Publishing.

Anderson, K. L. (2005). Theorizing gender in intimate partner violence research. *Sex Roles, 52*(11–12), 853–865.

Aratani, Y. (2009, September). *Homeless children and youth: Causes and consequences.* New York, NY: National Center for Children in Poverty.

Averett, P., Yoon, I., & Jenkins, C. L. (2011). Older lesbians: Experiences of aging, discrimina-tion and resilience. *Journal of Women & Aging, 23*(3), 216–232. doi:10.1080/08952841.2011.587742

Balsam, K. F., Rothblum, E. D., & Beauchaine, T. P. (2005). Victimization over the life span: A com-parison of lesbian, gay, bisexual, and heterosexual siblings. *Journal of Consulting and Clinical Psychology, 73*(3), 477.

Balsam, K. F., & Szymanski, D.M. (2005). Relationship quality and domestic violence in women's same-sex relationships: The role of minority stress. *Psychology of Women Quarterly, 29*(3), 258–269.

Barker, J. C., Herdt, G., & de Vries, B. (2006). Social support in the lives of lesbians and gay men at midlife and later. *Sexuality Research & Social Policy, 3*(2), 1–23.

Beam, J. (1983). Racism from a black perspective. In M. Smith (Ed.), *Black men/white men* (pp. 57–63). San Francisco, CA: Gay Sunshine Press.

Blackman, I., & Parry, K. (1990). Skirting the issue: Lesbian fashion for the 1990s. *Feminist Review, 34*, 67–78.

Bochenek, M., & Brown, A. W. (2001). *Hatred in the hallways: Violence and discrimination against lesbian, gay, bisexual, and transgender students in US schools.* Human Rights Watch.

Bonilla, L., & Porter, J. (1990). A comparison of Latino, Black, and non-Hispanic White attitudes toward homosexuality. *Hispanic Journal of Behavioral Sciences, 12*, 437–452.

Boykin, K. (1996). *One more river to cross*. New York, NY: Anchor Books.

Brotman, S., Ryan, B., Collins, S., Chamberland, L., Cormier, R., Julien, D., & Richard, B. (2007). Coming out to care: Caregivers of gay and lesbian seniors in Canada. *The Gerontologist, 47*(4), 490–503.

Brown, J. P., & Tracy, J. K. (2008). Lesbians and cancer: An overlooked health disparity. *Cancer Causes and Control, 19*, 1009–1020.

Cawthorn, A. (2008). The straight facts on women in poverty. Retrieved from http://www.american-progress.org/issues/women/report/2008/10/08/5103/the-straight-facts-on-women-in-poverty

Centers for Disease Control. (2015). HIV Among African Americans. Retrieved from http://www.cdc.gov/HIV/RISK/RACIALETHNIC/AA/FACTS/INDEX.HTML.

Clements-Nolle, K., Marx, R., Guzman, R., & Katz, M. (2001). HIV prevalence, risk behaviors, health care use, and mental health status of transgender persons: Implications for public health intervention. *American Journal of Public Health, 91*(6), 915.

Cochran, B. N., Stewart, A. J., Ginzler, J. A., & Cauce, A. M. (2002). Challenges faced by homeless sexual minorities: Comparison of gay, lesbian, bisexual, and transgender homeless adolescents with their heterosexual counterparts. *American Journal of Public Health, 92*(5), 773–777.

Cohen, S., & Wills, T. A. (1985). Stress, social support, and the buffering hypothesis. *Psychological Bulletin, 98*, 310–357.

Collins, P. H. (2000). *Black feminist thought* (2nd ed.). New York, NY: Routledge.

Conerly, G. (1996). The politics of Black lesbian, gay, and bisexual identity. In B. Beemyn & M. Eliason (Eds.), *Queer studies: A lesbian, gay, bisexual, & transgender anthology* (pp. 133–145). New York, NY: NYU Press.

Cooper, C. R., Jackson, J. F., Azmitia, M., & Lopez, E. M. (1998). Multiple selves, multiple worlds: Three useful strategies for research with ethnic minority youth on identity, relationships, and opportunity structures. In V. C. McLoyd & L. Steinberg (Eds.), *Studying minority adolescents: Conceptual, methodological, and theoretical issues* (pp. 111–125). Mahwah, NJ: Lawrence Erlbaum.

Cooper, F. R. (2005). Against bipolar black masculinity: Intersectionality, assimilation, identity performance, and hierarchy. *UC Davis School of Law—Law Review, 39*, 853.

Crawford, I., Allison, K. W., Zamboni, B. D., & Soto, T. (2002). The influence of dual-identity development on the psychosocial functioning of African-American gay and bisexual men. *Journal of Sex Research, 39*(3), 179–189.

Cross, W. E., Jr., & Strauss, L. (1998). The everyday functions of African American identity.

Della, B., Wilson, M., & Miller, R. L. (2002). Strategies for managing heterosexism used among African American gay and bisexual men. *Journal of Black Psychology, 28*(4), 371–391.

Devor, A. H. (2004). Witnessing and mirroring: A fourteen stage model of trans-sexual identity formation. *Journal of Gay and Lesbian Psychiatry, 8*(1/2): 41–67.

Diaz, E. M., & Kosciw, J. G. (2009). *Shared differences: The experiences of lesbian, gay, bisexual, and transgender students of color in our nation's schools*. New York, NY: GLESN.

Ferguson-Colvin, K., & Maccio, E. M. (2012). Toolkit for practitioners/researchers working with lesbian, gay, bisexual, transgender, and queer/questioning (LGBTQ) runaway and homeless youth (RHY). Retrieved from http://www.dccourts.gov/internet/system/headlines/2012_family_court_conference/articles/Toolkit%20September%202012.pdf.

Fredriksen-Goldsen, K. I. (2007). HIV/AIDS caregiving: Predictors of well-being and distress. *Journal of Gay and Lesbian Social Services, 18*, 53–73.

Fredriksen-Goldsen, K. I., & Hooyman, N. R. (2007). Caregiving research, services, and policies in historically marginalized communities: Where do we go from here? *Journal of Gay & Lesbian Social Services, 18*(3/4), 129–145.doi:10.1300/J041v18n03–08

Freydberg, E. H. (1995). Saffires, spitfires, sluts, and superbitches: Aframericans and Latinas in contemporary American film. In K. M. Vaz (Ed.), *Black women in America* (pp. 222–243). Thousand Oaks, CA: Sage.

Friedman, S. R., Maslow, C., Bolyard, M., Sandoval, M., Mateu-Gelabert, P., & Neaigus, A. (2004). Urging others to be healthy:"Intravention" by injection drug users as a community prevention goal. *AIDS Education and Prevention, 16*(3), 250–263.

Fullilove, M. T., & Fullilove, R. E. (1999). Stigma as an obstacle to AIDS action. *American Behavioral Scientist, 42*(7), 1117.

Gallup (2003). RELIGION AND SOCIAL TRENDS. Retrieved from http://www.gallup.com/poll/8413/six-americans-say-homosexual-relations-should-recognized-legal.aspx.

Garofalo, R., Deleon, J., Osmer, E., Doll, M., & Harper, G. W. (2006). Overlooked, misunderstood and at-risk: Exploring the lives and HIV risk of ethnic minority male-to-female transgender youth. *Journal of Adolescent Health, 38*(3), 230–236.

Gates, G. J. (2011). How many people are lesbian, gay, bisexual and transgender. Retrieved from http://williamsinstitute.law.ucla.edu/wp-content/uploads/Gates-How-Many-People-LGBT-Apr-2011.pdf

Gay Lesbian & Straight Education Network. (2009). *Research brief: Teaching respect-LGBT inclusive curriculum and school climate.* New York, NY: Author.

Goldberg, S., Sickler, J., & Dibble, S. L. (2005). Lesbians over sixty: The consistency of findings from twenty years of survey data. *Journal of Lesbian Studies, 9*(1–2), 195–213.doi:10.1300/J155v09n01_18

Grant, J. M. (2010). *Outing age 2010: Public policy issues affecting lesbian, gay, bisexual and transgender elders.* Washington, DC: National Gay and Lesbian Task Force Policy Institute.

Grant, J. M., Mottet, L. A., & Tanis, J. (2011). *Injustice at every turn: A look at Black respondents in the National Transgender Discrimination Survey.* Washington, DC: National Center for Transgender Equality.

Grant, J. M., Mottet, L., Tanis, J. E., Harrison, J., Herman, J., & Keisling, M. (2011). Injustice at every turn: A report of the National Transgender Discrimination Survey. National Center for Transgender Equality. Retrieved from http://www.thetaskforce.org/injustice-every-turn-report-national-transgender-discrimination-survey

Gravely, W. B. (1982). The dialectic of double-consciousness in Black American Freedom celebrations, 1808–1863. *Journal of Negro History, 67*(4), 302–317.

Green, M. Y. (2002). Minorities as majority: Disproportionality in child welfare and juvenile justice. *Children's Voice, 11*, 8–13. Retrieved from http://www.cwla.org/articles/cv0211minorities.htm

Greene, D. M., & Walker, F. R. (2004). Recommendations to public speaking instructors for the negotiation of code-switching practices among Black English-speaking African American students. *Journal of Negro Education, 73*(4), 435–442.

Grov, C., Bimbi, D., Nanin, J., & Parsons, J. (2006). Race, ethnicity, gender, and generational factors associated with the coming out process among gay, lesbian, and bisexual individuals. *Journal of Sex Research, 43*(2), 115–121.

Guiffrida, D. A. (2003). African American student organizations as agents of social integration. *Journal of College Student Development, 44*(3), 304–319.

Hall, R. L., & Fine, M. (2005). The stories we tell: The lives and friendship of two older black lesbians. *Psychology of Women Quarterly, 29*(2), 177–187.

Han, H. R., Kim, J., Lee, J. E., Hedlin, H. K., Song, H., Song, Y., & Kim, M. T. (2011). Interventions that increase use of Pap tests among ethnic minority women: A meta-analysis. *Psycho-Oncology, 20*(4), 341–351.

Hancock, A. (2004). *The politics of disgust and the public identity of the "Welfare Queen."* New York: New York University Press.

Harper, P. B. (1992). Eloquence and epitaph: Black nationalism and the homophobic impulse in responses to the death of Max Robinson. In M. Warner (Ed.), *Fear of a queer planet: Queer politics and social theory* (pp. 230–263). Minneapolis: University of Minnesota Press.

Harris, K. M., Florey, F., Tabor, J., Bearman, P. S., Jones, J., & Udry, J. R. (2003). The National Longitudinal Study of Adolescent Health [Online]. Retrieved from http://www.cpc.unc.edu/addhealth

Haas, A. P., Eliason, M., Mays, V. M., Mathy, R. M., Cochran, S. D., D'Augelli, A. R.,…Clayton, P. J. (2010). Suicide and suicide risk in lesbian, gay, bisexual, and transgender populations: Review and recommendations. *Journal of homosexuality, 58*(1), 10–51.

Hash, K. (2006). Caregiving and post-caregiving experiences of midlife and older gay men and lesbians. *Journal of Gerontological Social Work, 47*(3/4), 121–138.

Hassouneh, D., & Glass, N. (2008). The influence of gender role stereotyping on women's experience of female same-sex intimate partner violence. *Violence Against Women, 14,* 310–325.

Hatzenbuehler, M. L. (2009). How does sexual minority stigma "get under the skin"? A psychological mediation framework. *Psychological Bulletin, 135*(5), 707.

Herek, G. M., & Capitanio, J. P. (1995). Black heterosexuals' attitudes toward lesbians and gay men in the United States. *The Journal of Sex Research, 32,* 95–105.

Herek, G. M., Chopp, R., & Strohl, D. (2007). Sexual stigma: Putting sexual minority health issues in context. In I. H. Meyer & M. E. Northridge (Eds.), *The health of sexual minorities: Public health perspectives on lesbian, gay, bisexual and transgender populations* (pp. 171–208). New York, NY: Springer Publishing.

Hershberger, S. L., & D'Augelli, A. R. (1995). The impact of victimization on the mental health and suicidality of lesbian, gay, and bisexual youths. *Developmental Psychology, 31*(1), 65.

Hiestand, K. R., Horne, S. G., & Levitt, H. M. (2007). Effects of gender identity on experiences of healthcare for sexual minority women. *Journal of LGBT Health Research, 2,* 150–127.

Higa, D., Hoppes, M. J., Lindhorst, T., Mincer, S., Beadnell, B., Morrison, D. M.,…Mountz, S. (2012). Negative and positive factors associated with the well-being of lesbian, gay, bisexual, transgender, queer, and questioning (LGBTQ) youth. *Youth and Society, 446*(5), 663–687.

hooks, b. (1984). *From margin to center*. Boston, MA: South End.

hooks, b. (1992). *Black looks: Race and representation* (p. 101). Boston, MA: South End Press.

Horowitz, A., Reinhardt, J., Boerner, K., & Travis, L. (2003). The influence of health, social support quality and rehabilitation on depression among disabled elders. *Aging& Mental Health, 7*(5), 342–350.

Hostetler, A. J. (2004). Old, gay, and alone? The ecology of well-being among middle-aged and older single gay men. In G. Herdt & B. de Vries (Eds.), *Gay and lesbian aging: Research and future directions* (pp. 143–176). New York, NY: Springer Publishing.

Hughes, T., McCabe, S. E., Wilsnack, S. C., West, B. T., & Boyd, C. J. (2010). Victimization and substance use disorders in a national sample of heterosexual and sexual minority women and men. *Addiction, 105,* 2130–2140.

Huebner, D. M., Rebchook, G. M., & Kegeles, S. M. (2004). Experiences of harassment, discrimination, and physical violence among young gay and bisexual men. *American Journal of Public Health, 94*(7), 1200–1203.

Jeffries, V., & Ransford, H. E. (1980). *Social stratification*. Boston, MA: Allyn & Bacon.

Jones, K. T., Gray, P., Whiteside, Y. O., Wang, T., Bost, D., Dunbar, E.,…Johnson, W. D. (2008). Evaluation of an HIV prevention intervention adapted for Black men who have sex with men. *American Journal of Public Health, 98*(6), 1043–1050.

Jones, T. C., & Nystrom, N. M. (2002). Looking back…looking forward: Addressing the lives of Lesbians 55 and older. *Journal of Women & Aging, 14*(3–4), 59–76. doi:10.1300/J074v14n03_05

Kawachi, I., & Berkman, L. F. (2001). Social ties and mental health. *Journal of Urban Health, 78,* 458–467.

Keppel, K. G. (2007). Ten largest racial and ethnic health disparities in the United States based on healthy people 2010 objectives. *American Journal of Epidemiology, 166*, 97–103.

Kirk, S. C., & Kulkarni, C. (2006). The whole person: A paradigm for integrating the mental and physical health of trans clients. In M. D. Shankle (Ed.), *The handbook of lesbian, gay, bisexual and transgender public health: A practitioner's guide to service* (pp. 145–174). New York, NY: Harrington Park Place.

Kishore, S. A. (2013). Dying with dignity: Considerations for treating elder transgender people of color. Retrieved from http://www.asaging.org/blog/dying-dignity-considerations-treating-elder-transgender-people-color

Lantz, P. M., Weigers, M. E., & House, J. S. (1997). Education and income differentials in breast and cervical cancer screening: Policy implications for rural women. *Medical Care, 35*, 219–236.

Lev, A. I. (2004). *Transgender emergence: Therapeutic guidelines for working with gender variant people and their families.* Binghamton, NY: The Haworth Press.

Levitt, H. M., & Horne, S. G. (2002). Explorations of lesbian–queer genders. *Journal of Lesbian Studies, 6*, 25–39.

LGBT Movement Advancement Project & Services and Advocacy for Gay, Lesbian, Bisexual and Transgender Elders. (2010). *Improving the lives of LGBT older adults.* Denver, CO: LGBT MAP.

Lorde, A. (1984). *Sister outsider: Essays and speeches by Audre Lorde.* Freedom, CA: Crossing.

Lorde, A. (2009). I am your sister: Black women organizing across sexualities. In R. P. Byrd, J. B. Cole, B. Guy-Sheftall (Eds.), *I am your sister: Collected and unpublished writings of Audre Lorde* (pp. 57–63.69–70). New York, NY: Oxford University Press.

Mahtani, M. (2001). Representing minorities: Canadian media and minority identities. *Canadian Ethnic Studies, 33*(3), 99–133.

Malebranche, D. J., Peterson, J. L., Fullilove, R. E., & Stackhouse, R. W. (2004). Race and sexual identity: Perceptions about medical culture and healthcare among black men who have sex with men. *Journal of the National Medical Association, 96*(1), 97–107.

Mallon, G. P. (1999). *Let's get this straight: A gay and lesbian affirming approach to child welfare.* New York, NY: Columbia University Press.

Mason-Schrock, D. (1996). Transsexuals' narrative construction of the" true self". *Social Psychology Quarterly,* 176–192.

Mastin, D., Metzger, S., & Golden, J. (2013, April). *Foster care and disconnected youth: A way forward for New York.* New York, NY: Community Service Society & The Children's Aid Society.

Mays, V. M., Yancey, A. K., Cochran, S. D., Weber, M., & Fielding, J. E. (2002). Heterogeneity of health disparities among African American, Hispanic, and Asian American women: Unrecognized influences of sexual orientation. *American Journal of Public Health, 92*, 632–639.

McDermott, S., & Greenberg, B. (1984). Parents, peers and television as determinants of Black children's esteem. *Communication Yearbook, 8*, 164–177.

Merighi, J. R., & Grimes, M. D. (2000). Coming out to families in a multicultural context. *Families in Society: The Journal of Contemporary Social Services, 81*(1), 32–41.

Messinger, J. (2012). Antibisexual violence and practitioners' roles in prevention and intervention: An ecological and empowerment-based approach in public health social work. *Journal of Bisexuality, 12*, 360–375.

Meyer, I. H. (2003). Prejudice, social stress, and mental health in lesbian, gay, and bisexual populations: Conceptual issues and research evidence. *Psychological Bulletin, 129*, 674–697.

Meyer, I. H., & Northridge, M. E. (2007). *The health of sexual minorities: Public health perspectives on lesbian, gay, bisexual and transgender population.* New York, NY: Springer Publishing.

Moore, M. R. (2006). Lipstick or timberlands? Meanings of gender presentation in black lesbian communities. *Signs, 32*(1), 113–139.

Mouton, C. P., Carter-Nolan, P. L., Makambi, K. H., Taylor, T. R., Palmer, J. R., Rosenberg, L., & Adams-Campbell, L. L. (2010). Impact of perceived racial discrimination on health screening in black women. *Journal of Health Care for the Poor and Underserved, 21*(1), 287.

National Association of Social Workers. (2000). *Code of ethics of the National Association of Social Workers*. Washington, DC: Author.

Newman, B., Dannenfelser, P., & Benishek, L. (2002). Assessing beginning social work and counseling students' acceptance of lesbian and gay men. *Journal of Social Work Education, 38*, 273–288.

Newton, H. P. (2001). Manifesto Issued by the Black Panthers (A Letter from Huey to the Revolutionary Brothers and Sisters about the Women's Liberation and Gay Liberation Movements). In C. Bull. (Ed.). *Come out fighting: A century of essential writing on gay and lesbian liberation* (pp. 89–91). New York, NY:Thunder's Mouth Press/Nation Books.

Nuttbrock, L., Rosenblum, A., & Blumenstein, R. (2002). Transgender identity affirmation and mental health. *International Journal of Transgenderism, 6*(4), 97–103.

O'Hanlan, K. A., Cabaj, R. P., Schatz, B. S., Lock, J., & Nemrow, P. (1997). A review of the medical consequences of homophobia with suggestions for resolutions. *Journal of the Gay and Lesbian Medical Association, 1*(1), 25–39.

Ohlander, J., Batalova, J., & Treas, J. (2005). Explaining educational influences on attitudes toward homosexual relations. *Social Science Research, 34*, 781–791.

Pettiway, L. (1996). *Honey, honey, missthang: Being Black, gay, and on the streets*. Philadelphia, PA: Temple University Press.

Phillips-Angeles, E., Wolfe, P., Myers, R., Dawson, P., Marrazzo, J., Soltner, S., & Dzieweczynski, M. (2004). Lesbian health matters: A pap test education campaign nearly thwarted by discrimination. *Health Promotion Practice, 5*(3), 314–325.

Poussaint, A. F. (1990, September). An honest look at Black gays and lesbians. *Ebony*, 124(126), 130–131.

Ransford, H. E., & Miller, J. (1983). Race, sex, and feminist outlooks. *American Sociological Review, 48*, 46–59.

Ray, N. (2006). *Lesbian, gay, bisexual and transgender youth an epidemic of homelessness*. New York, NY: National Gay and Lesbian Task Force Policy Institute and the National Coalition for the Homeless.

Ream, G. L., Barnhart, K. F., & Lotz, K. V. (2012). Decision processes about condom use among shelter-homeless LGBT youth in Manhattan. *AIDS Research and Treatment, 2012*. Article ID 659853.

Rice, T. (2013). Cervical cancer in elder Black lesbian and bisexual women. Retrieved from http://www.asaging.org/blog/cervical-cancer-elder-black-lesbian-and-bisexual-women

Riggs, M. (1991). Tongues untied. In E. Hemphill (Ed.), *Brother to brother: New writings by Black gay men* (pp. 200–205). Boston, MA: Alyson Publications.

Roberts, D. E. (1997). *Killing the black body: Race, reproduction, and the meaning of liberty*. New York, NY: Pantheon Books.

Roberts, J. C. (1986). A light that failed. In J. Beam (Ed.), *In the life: A Black gay anthology* (pp. 87–92). Boston, MA: Alyson Publications.

Rosario, M., Schrimshaw, E. W., & Hunter, J. (2004). Ethnic/racial differences in the coming-out process of lesbian, gay, and bisexual youths: A comparison of sexual identity development over time. *Cultural Diversity and Ethnic Minority Psychology, 10*(3), 215.

Russell, S. T., & Joyner, K. (2001). Adolescent sexual orientation and suicide risk: Evidence from a national study. *American Journal of Public Health, 91*, 1276–1281.

Savin-Williams, R. C., & Diamond, L. M. (2000). Sexual identity trajectories among sexual-minority youths: Gender comparisons. *Archives of Sexual Behavior, 29*(6), 607–627.

Schope, R. D. (2005). Who's afraid of growing old? Gay and lesbian perceptions of aging. *Journal of Gerontological Social Work, 45*(4), 23–39. doi:10.1300/J083v45n04_03

Schuck, K. D., & Liddle, B. J. (2001). Religious conflicts experienced by lesbian, gay, and bisexual individuals. *Journal of Gay and Lesbian Psychotherapy, 5*, 63–82.

Sears, B., & Badgett, L. (2012). Beyond stereotypes. Retrieved February 17, 2014, from http://williamsinstitute.law.ucla.edu/headlines/beyond-stereotypes-poverty-in-the-lgbt-community/

Shipherd, J., Maguen, S., Skidmore, W., & Abramovitz, S. (2011). Potentially traumatic events in a transgender sample: Frequency and associated symptoms. *Traumatology, 17*, 56–67.

Shippy, R. A. (2007). We cannot go it alone: The impact of informal support and stressors in older gay, lesbian and bisexual caregivers. *Journal of Gay & Lesbian Social Services, 18*(3-4), 39–51.

Simmons, R. (1991). Tongues untied: An interview with Marlon Riggs. In E. Hemphill (Ed.), *Brother to brother: New writings by Black gay men* (pp. 50–53). Boston, MA: Alyson Publications.

Spirit Health Education Circle Online. (2005). About us. Retrieved from http://www.shecircle.org/about.php

Staples, R. (1990). Race, masculinity, and sexuality: An insider's perspective. In F. Abbot (Ed.), *Men and intimacy: Personal accounts exploring the dilemmas of modern male sexuality* (pp. 103–110). Freedom, CA: The Crossing Press.

Stotzer, R. (2008). Transgender identity and hate crimes: Violence against transgender people in Los Angeles county. *Sexuality Research & Social Policy, 5*, 43–52.

Sullivan, M., & Wodarski, J. S. (2002). Social alienation in gay youth. *Journal of Human Behavior in the Social Environment, 5*(1), 1–17.

Swanson, D. P., Spencer, M. B., Harpalani, V., & Spencer, T. R. (2002). Identity processes and the positive youth development of African Americans: An explanatory framework. *New Directions for Youth Development, 2002*(95), 73–100.

Szymanski, D. M. (2006). Does internalized heterosexism moderate the link between heterosexist events and lesbians' psychological distress? *Sex Roles, 56*(3/4).

Throckmorton, W., & Yarhouse, M. A. (2006). Sexual identity therapy: Practice framework for managing sexual identity conflicts. Retrieved from http://sitframework.com/wp-content/uploads/2009/07/sexualidentitytherapyframeworkfinal.pdf

Toro, P. A., Dworsky, A., & Fowler, P. J. (2007). Homeless youth in the United States: Recent research findings and intervention approaches. In D. Dennis, G. Locke, & J. Khadduri (Eds.), *Towards understanding homelessness: The 2007 National Symposium on Homelessness Research* (pp. 61–633) Washington, DC: Department of Health & Human Services and U.S. Department of Housing and Urban Development, September.

Tracy, J. K., Lydecker, A. D., & Ireland, L. (2010). Barriers to cervical cancer screening among lesbians. *Journal of Women's Health, 19*, 229–237.

U.S. Census Bureau. (2013). Poverty rates for selected detailed race and Hispanic groups by state and place. 2007–2011. Retrieved February 17, 2014, from http://www.census.gov/prod/2013pubs/acsbr11–17.pdf

U.S. Census Bureau. (2014). State & county quick acts. Retrieved February 17, 2014, from http://quickfacts.census.gov/qfd/states/00000.html

Van Sluytman, L. G., Braine, N., Acker, C. J., Friedman, S., & Des Jarlais, D. C. (2013). Migration narratives: Expanding methods to examine the interaction of person and environment among aging gay men. *Journal of Gerontological Social Work, 56*(3), 219–236.

Van Sluytman, L. G., & Torres, D. (2014). Hidden or uninvited? A content analysis of elder LGBT of color literature in gerontology. *Journal of Gerontological Social Work, 57*(2–4), 130–160

Van Sluytman, L., Spikes, P., Nandi, V., Van Tieu, H., Frye, V., Patterson, J., & Koblin, B. (2015). Ties that bind: Community attachment and the experience of discrimination among Black men who have sex with men. *Culture, Health & Sexuality,* (ahead-of-print), 1–14.

Ward, E. G. (2005). Homophobia, hypermasculinity and the US black church. *Culture, Health & Sexuality, 7*(5), 493–504.

Whitbeck, L. B., Chen, X., Hoyt, D. R., Tyler, K. A., & Johnson, K. D. (2004). Mental disorder, subsistence strategies, and victimization among gay, lesbian, and bisexual homeless and runaway adolescents. *Journal of Sex Research, 41*, 329–342.

Williams, M., & Freeman, P. (2007). Transgender health: Implications for aging and caregiving. *Journal of Gay and Lesbian Social Services, 18*(3/4), 93–108.

Wilson, W. J. (1978). *The declining significance of race: Blacks and changing American institutions.* Chicago, IL: University of Chicago Press.

World Health Organization. (2011). Prevention and treatment of HIV and other sexually transmitted infections among men who have sex with men and transgender people. Recommendations for a public health approach 2011. Retrieved from: http://www.who.int/hiv/pub/guidelines/msm_guidelines2011/en

World Health Organization. (2012). What do we mean by "sex" and "gender"? Retrieved from http://www.who.int/gender/whatisgender/en

Yates, T. M., & Masten, A. S. (2004). Fostering the future: Resilience theory and the practice of positive psychology. In P. A. Linley & S. Joseph (Eds.), *Positive psychology in practice* (pp. 521–539). Hoboken, NJ: John Wiley.

CHAPTER 7

Social Work and Health—Understanding the Contexts of Social Work and Public Health

Paul Archibald and Kim Dobson-Sydnor

From its early roots in the 1888 settlement movement, highlighted by the work of Jane Addams, to the establishment of the National Association of Social Work in 1954, which standardized ethics and principles of the profession, to the current day, social work has been at the forefront of meeting the social welfare needs of individuals and families "where they are." The levels of engagement in addressing the social problems that plague individuals and families range from the micro to the macro and the areas of focus have considerable breadth that incorporates the critical elements that contribute to the social well-being including employment, housing, justice, and health (Glicken, 2011). A slogan used by social work leadership is "social workers are everywhere," which would aptly capture the scope of the profession. What the social work profession is best and most commonly known for is providing services to those in need. Thus, the need for practices and models of intervention that can help address the needs of the many, including those living in urban communities.

In *Social Work in the 21st Century: An Introduction to Social Welfare, Social Issues, and the Profession*, Glicken (2011) provides a chronology of the historic highlights of social work in the United States. The chronology includes not only benchmarks in the development of the profession, but key social policy milestones that have signaled a shift in the availability of social goods for individuals. Noteworthy is the last event in the chronology, the passing of *Obamacare*, more appropriately entitled the Affordable Care Act (ACA). When the history and work of the social work is examined, it is no surprise that health policy would be considered a sentinel moment. From the early work in advocating for policies to improve living conditions for those with mental illness to the specialized training of public health social workers, health has been a consistent thread for the profession. Social workers have been involved in public health practice since the early

20th century as they practiced their skills in the settlement houses, worked on issues related to communicable disease control, and assisted with maternal and child health promotion (Popple & Leighninger, 2004). The social work and public health missions are similar in that both seek to enhance well-being through social and economic justice as a means of eradicating social health problems. The WHO defines health as "a state of complete physical, mental and social well-being and not merely the absence of disease or infirmity" (World Health Organization, 1946, p. 100). With both the history of social work and the broadened definition of health, at no time has the link between the social welfare of individuals and health been more clearly apparent.

THE SOCIAL WORK PUBLIC HEALTH FRAMEWORK

Public health social work (PHSW) has recently been defined as the prevention and health promotion practice of social work that utilizes epidemiology to promote health, social justice, and the overall well-being of the community being served. In fact, the National Association of Social Workers (NASW) has developed a working definition, standards, and competencies for PHSW (NASW, 2006). The overlap of public health within the profession is distinctly reflected in the PHSW framework. This framework incorporates the epidemiological approach to problem analysis and incorporates a prevention framework alongside the intervention model that is inherent in social work. The public health model is one that begins with defining the problem; identifies the contributing risk–protective factors linked to the problem; develops, implements, and evaluates prevention–intervention strategies based on the assessment; and then, where effectiveness has been shown, seeks to facilitate adoption of the program at a broader population level. The public health approach is buttressed by the ecological framework that conceptualizes individual health outcomes as being encapsulated and influenced by factors at the micro- (relational/familial), mezzo (community), and macro- (societal) levels (Fielding, Teutch, & Breslow, 2010). Social work has utilized the public health approach when developing interventions in areas such as substance abuse and violence prevention.

The mezzo level of influence has increasingly achieved prominence in the public health sector as the centrality of community contexts in producing overall health has been well documented. This recognition of the social contributors to health is reflected in the long-term goals for the population's health as specified in Healthy People 2020 and in the focus on community-level prevention and intervention supported the ACA: A brief discussion of each of these federal agenda is provided as context.

HEALTHY PEOPLE 2020

The goal of having a healthier nation has been set by the federal government and implemented by the Department of Health and Human Services through the Healthy People initiatives, starting with Healthy People 1990. The Healthy People goals provide benchmarks to be achieved in improving the health of the nation as well as encouraging strategies and practices to help achieve those goals. A new benchmark plan for the nation's health is designed for each subsequent decade (Fielding et al., 2010). The current goals are codified in Healthy People 2020 (HP 2020). Its development was grounded in the public health ecological framework and a broad determinants understanding of what produces health. HP 2020 envisions health as being produced over the life course—thus, it incorporates a developmental approach with emphasis on both intervention and prevention for individuals and communities (www.healthypeople.gov/2020/Consortium/HP2020Framework.pdf).

THE ACA

The Patient Protection and Affordable Care Act (ACA; Public Law 111–148) (http://housedocs.house.gov/energycommerce/ppacacon.pdf) passed in 2010 is, as previously mentioned, more generally known as the Affordable Care Act or "Obamacare." The law is a consolidation of existing health policy with reforms. The law has 10 sections designed to expand health insurance coverage to those who are uninsured or under-insured, improve the quality of care, reduce the costs of care, and enhance patients' rights. Notable among the 10 domains are Title IV (Prevention of Chronic Disease and Improving Public Health) and Title V (Health Care Workforce). Title IV targets preventive services that are community based, with specific reference to achieving healthier communities. Title V makes a commitment to build the public health workforce (broadly described) through training and fellowships, and expansion of the workforce through support of community health workers. These two areas of focus evidence the degree to which community has achieved a central place in the redressing of population health issues (www.hhs.gov/healthcare/rights/law/index.html).

These two federal imperatives with far-reaching consequences are, at their core, social welfare documents that reflect an understanding of health as a social good and a social responsibility. Additionally, they both, in their respective ways, emphasize the importance of community in addressing issues of health. As such, the ACA and HP 2020 are important documents for social work and lay a foundation for current work that intersects with public health.

THE SOCIAL DETERMINANTS OF HEALTH AND HEALTH DISPARITIES

It would be difficult to understand the importance of the role of communities in addressing health without clarifying what is meant by the social determinants of health. The WHO defines social determinants as "the circumstances in which people are born, grow up, live, work and age, and the systems put in place to deal with illness. These circumstances are in turn shaped by a wider set of forces: economics, social policies, and politics." In other words, place (physical, geographical, social, political) matters (www.who.int/social_determinants/final_report/key_concepts_en.pdf?ua=1). This perspective drives the mandate to address health beyond the medical setting and to consider the following, as examples,

- The influence of socioeconomic conditions, including income, education, and employment.
- The critical contexts of the life course, including home life, family, school, workplace, and neighborhoods.
- The health status of individuals and communities, including physical, mental, social, and spiritual health.
- The differential impact of social systems, including social justice and health, income, and racial equity.

The social determinants of health are closely aligned with the notion of social good and social responsibility as they help to explain the inequities in health that are pervasive in the United States and indeed, around the world. The term "inequity" implies not just lack of equivalence but both an unjust and an undesirable set of conditions. The inequities in health are evidenced in the data regarding health disparities in the United States. Based on 2011 data, African Americans' age-adjusted all-causes death rate was the highest among all races and ethnicities (Hoyert & Yu, 2012). With regard to specific diseases, African Americans had the highest age-adjusted death rate for cancer, diabetes, heart disease, and HIV/AIDS (National Center for Health Statistics, 2012). More generally speaking, African Americans have greater rates of death from heart disease, higher prevalence of high blood pressure, obesity, and diabetes, greater rates of infant death and shorter life spans as compared to Whites. Research indicates that African Americans have a shorter life expectancy in every state in the United States, with White females expected to live 5 years longer than African American females and White men expected to live 7 years longer than African American males. Health care has been identified as playing a major role in life expectancy disparity (Bharmal, Tseng, Kaplan, & Wong, 2012). Accompanying these differences in disease and death experiences, Africans Americans have a higher percentage of uninsured and a higher percentage of living in poverty (Centers for Disease Control and Prevention [CDC], 2013). In fact, in 2011, the poverty rates for African Americans exceeded the national average, with 25.7% of African Americans, compared to 11.6% of Whites identified as being poor (DeNavas-Walt, Proctor, & Smith, 2012). These are persistent disparities. Factors such as discrimination, cultural barriers, and lack of access to care—all intertwined social variables—play a role in producing these inequities ultimately.

A PLAN FOR ACTION

The broad scope of the social work discipline, the implementation of social welfare policies in the form of the ACA and the HP 2020 strategic plan, the recognition of the multifaceted nature of health, the emerging enlightenment regarding the social determinants of health, the importance of community as a space for intervention and prevention, and the persistent disparities point to a moment rife with the opportunity for social workers to engage in collaborative strategies for meeting the needs of people and communities, especially urban communities where need has always been concentrated. The UN World Urbanization Prospects (2008) has projected that, by 2030, there will be more people in developing countries living in urban areas rather than rural areas. In the United States, more African Americans populate 15 out of the 20 largest urban areas—New York (61%); Philadelphia (53%); Boston (46%); Baltimore (51%); Houston (49%); Chicago (54%); Detroit (60%); San Diego (56%); Phoenix (45%); and Los Angeles (40%); relative to all other race populations (U.S. Census Bureau, 2011). This process of urbanization is understood in terms of the increase in the number of cities and urban population that includes psychological changes and is associated with mental health status (Tayfun & Asli, 2008). These psychological changes are introduced through the pathways of increased life stressors such as poverty, high levels of violence, and health issues. The growth in resources needed to adequately service the people in urban areas is incongruent with the increase in the population. This work will require in-depth theoretical and practical understanding of health issues to emerge with effective models. In this chapter, we take a look at one health issue, African American mental health, as an example of the kind of analysis that will be needed to bring to bear on the multiple health issues that impact communities.

SOCIAL WORK PUBLIC HEALTH ANALYSIS: AFRICAN AMERICAN MENTAL HEALTH STATUS

The mental health status of African Americans living in urban communities has a long and varied history in the United States. The classic ecological studies conducted by Harburg et al. (1973) found that living in stressful urban areas is characterized by factors such as low median income, little formal education, residential instability, marital instability, and crime, all of which adversely affect mental health. There are multifaceted and complex contributing factors that produce mental health, largely linked to stress exposures. An understanding of the stress process will be useful in comprehending the dynamics that broadly shape the mental health of African Americans as well as other communities of color.

Stress and Coping: A Theoretical Model

Stress and coping theories propose that when individuals are confronted with a stressor, they resort to a wide range of coping strategies to help alleviate the stress (Lazarus & Folkman, 1984). The life stress process as conceptualized by Pearlin et al. (1981) identified three core components: stressors, moderators (social and psychological resources), and outcomes (mental health). According to Pearlin (2005), stressors refer to:

> problems, hardships, or threats that challenge the adaptive capacities of people; moderators are the social and personal resources that people can mobilize to contain, regulate, or

otherwise ameliorate the effects of the stressors; and outcomes refer to the effects of the stressors that are observed after the moderating resources are taken into account. (p. 3)

In this theoretical model, each component of the life stress process is interrelated. To further elaborate, stress can be operationalized as the combined relationship of stressors and the individual's response to the stressors. Stress responses are the ways that an individual reacts to the stressors; psychologically, physiologically, and behaviorally (e.g., depression).

African American Stress Exposure

The risk factors associated with mental health status are exacerbated by the conditions in which African Americans living in economically depressed inner city or urban neighborhoods are exposed. Adverse urban influences include low socioeconomic status, low educational attainment, unstable living arrangements, marital instability, and criminal activity (Geronimus, Hicken, Keene, & Bond, 2006), all serving as potential stressors that can undermine mental, as well as physical, health.

African Americans are victims of crimes of violence at a rate higher than any other ethnic or racial group (Bureau of Justice Statistics, 2013). African Americans are not only at higher risk of being a victim of a physical violence but also at higher risk of knowing someone who has suffered violence (American Psychological Association Presidential Task Force on Violence and the Family, 1996). In 2012, African Americans were victims of a violent crime at a rate of 34.2 per 1,000 compared to 25.2 per 1,000 for Whites and 24.5 per 1,000 for Hispanics. The rate of exposure to serious violence was 11.3 per 1,000 for African Americans compared to 9.3 per 1,000 for Hispanics and 6.8 per 1,000 for Whites (Bureau of Justice Statistics, 2013).

Stress is a widespread issue. *Mental Health America* conducted an attitudinal survey in fall 2006 that included measures of perceived stress. This survey was conducted through telephone interviews and the Internet among a nationally representative sample of 3,040 respondents aged 18 years and older. Figure 7.1 shows that survey respondents report finances (48%), health (33%), and employment (32%) as the most common sources of stress. Figure 7.2 shows that when stress was examined by race, the combined and quantified, proportions show that African Americans reported greater stress than Whites (38% vs. 30%).

Race-Specific Exposures

The disproportionality illustrated in Figure 7.2 provides an implication that stressful events, although affecting everyone, may have greater import for African Americans because of the sheer quantity of exposures (Miranda & Green, 1999; Turner, Wheaton, & Lloyd, 1995; Wilson, 1987), including race-specific exposures. Several researchers have documented that race-related stress is positively associated with poor mental health and occurs more frequently in African Americans than Whites (Seaton, 2003). Plummer and Slane (1996) defined race-related stress as the psychological discomfort that occurs

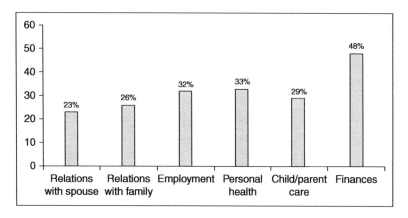

FIGURE 7.1 Percentage of life stressors reported in Mental Health America Attitudinal Survey, October 2006.

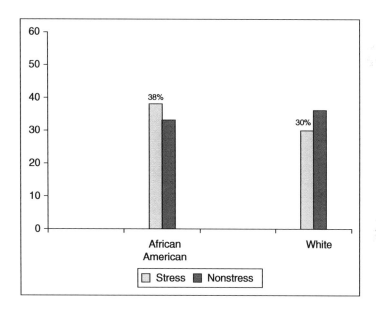

FIGURE 7.2 Prevalence of stress by race reported in Mental Health America Attitudinal Survey, October 2006.

when a situation is appraised as stressful, secondary to racism, racial prejudice, racial discrimination, or racial isolation. The lifetime prevalence of discrimination was 50% for African Americans and 31% for Whites. Only 3% of Whites reported experiencing day-to-day perceived discrimination as compared to 25% of African Americans (Kessler, Mickelson, & Williams, 1999). An analysis of the data for victims of single-bias hate-crime incidents from the Uniformed Crime Reporting Program showed that more than half of the incidents were racially motivated; 66.1% of the victims were African Americans who were offended because of anti-Black bias compared to 22.4% of Whites who were offended due to anti-White bias (U.S. Department of Justice Federal Bureau of Investigation, 2013).

Minority Status Hypothesis

African Americans can be viewed through the racialized lens of a minority construct, which is usually linked with inferiority and powerlessness (Aponte, Rivers, & Wohl, 1995). Within this perspective, minorities are viewed as occupying disadvantaged positions in society, and the chronic social stressors associated with these positions produce psychological distress. This would be consistent with the work that has been cited. Consequently, the *minority status hypothesis* predicts much higher rates of mental disorders for African Americans than for Whites at all levels of socioeconomic status, as a result of African Americans' greater stress exposure (Halpern, 1993; Nazroo, 2003).

Although these correlations should work to substantiate a minority status hypothesis, findings from five epidemiologic community surveys—the National Institute of Mental Health Epidemiologic Catchment Area Study (Robins & Reiger, 1991); the National Comorbidity Survey (Kessler et al., 1994); the National Survey of American Life (Jackson et al., 2005); the National Epidemiologic Survey of Alcohol and Related Conditions, 2001 to 2002 (Hasin, Goodwin, Stinson, & Grant, 2005); and the 2008 National Health Interview Survey, present the *minority mental health status dilemma*. These five national studies indicate that the mental health status of African Americans is comparable to, and possibly better than, those of Whites. Furthermore, independent of the relative health of African Americans, this racial group's mental health status is better than might be expected based on the prevalence of stressors alone. The disproportionate rate of stress and the lower than expected rates of mental disorders among African Americans have raised a number of questions regarding the additional factors related to their mental health.

One area to consider is in racial differences noted in stress coping responses. African Americans seem to take an active role in dealing with stressors rather than avoiding them (Broman, 1996); an active response tending to produce stress reduction. Research has suggested that African Americans make an effort to attempt to handle the stressor on their own more frequently than Whites (Sussman, Robins, & Earls, 1987). African Americans seem to appraise stressful situations as changeable more frequently than Whites (Halstead, Johnson, & Cunningham, 1993). Figure 7.3 shows that Whites were more likely to engage in unhealthy coping skills when they felt stressed.

Twenty-four percent of African Americans, compared to 28% of Whites, noted that they smoke, drink, or use drugs when they feel stressed. African Americans were more likely than Whites to engage in healthy coping skills. For instance, 56% of African Americans as compared to 52% of Whites noted that they exercise when they are stressed. African Americans (82%) were more likely than Whites (59%) to use prayer or meditation as a way to deal with stress.

Stress and Coping From a Cultural Perspective

Culture influences mental health status and seems to play a role in how people cope with stressors (Cameron & Lalonde, 1994). In an attempt at identifying the coping capacity of African Americans, Edwards (1999) conducted a qualitative study to examine the

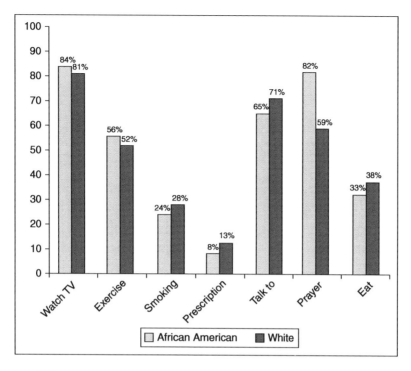

FIGURE 7.3 Differential coping styles of African Americans and Whites reported in Mental Health America Attitudinal Survey, October 2006.

self-defined components of psychological health for African Americans and found that two identified cultural resources (spirituality and racial identity) may help shed some light on *the minority mental health status dilemma*. Figure 7.4 shows the proposed pathway of "the cultural resilience life stress paradigm."

The cultural resilience life stress paradigm, in this context, attempts to explain the capacity to which a cultural group capitalizes on its resources to reduce psychological distress in the presence of life stressors. As identified by Johnson (2002), the evidence of capacity (conscious or unconscious) to mitigate the effects of life stressors on psychological distress serves as a protective factor for African Americans. This process includes such culture-resilient resources as spirituality and racial identity that help restrict the scope and intensity of life stressors and help protect African Americans, who follow the "cultural norm" of the racial group, from the depressive effects of life stressors.

Spirituality–Coping

Spirituality is recognized as a cultural resource utilized by African Americans when coping with life stressors (Boyd-Franklin, Kelly, & Durham, 2008) and as a way of understanding and giving meaning to stress and adversity (McGoldrick, Giordano, & Garcia-Preto, 2005). Racial identity has also been identified as a cultural coping strategy among the African American population (Azibo, 2006; Hall, 2001) and has been

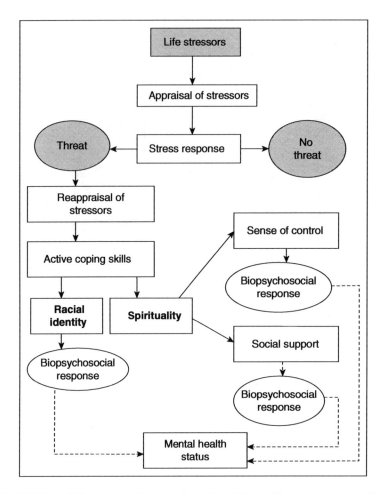

FIGURE 7.4 Diagram of the cultural resilient life stress paradigm.
Adapted from Archibald (2010).

associated with the psychological health and well-being of African Americans (Franklin-Jackson & Carter, 2007; Pieterse & Carter, 2010). Mattis et al. (2004) asserted that African Americans oftentimes interpret the world, appraise their life stressors, and cope with those stressors through the lens of a varied spirituality that is expressed primarily through the vehicle of the "Black church" and is shaped from historical African religions and slavery. This culture of African American spirituality incorporates a mechanism for both sense of control and social support to be revealed.

Research has indicated a direct and significant positive relationship between spirituality and sense of control (Archibald, 2010; Archibald, Sydnor, Daniels, & Bronner, 2013; Jang & Johnson, 2004). Hence, participants high in spirituality may perhaps have had an increased feeling of autonomy in reference to their level of mastery and understanding of perceived constraints and available resources which in turn possibly affected how they reappraised their life stressors. When African Americans are initially exposed to life stressors, and when it has been identified that their available resources are low, they may assume a low sense of control (Brown & Jackson, 2004). However, during the reappraisal phase of the life stress process, it is plausible that this low external view of sense of control activates a high internal view of sense of control through spirituality. Schieman, Pudrovska, and Milkie (2005) developed a conceptual framework termed *personal empowerment,* asserting that as individuals identify that they are unable to adequately control or change the outcome of certain life's problems, they engage in a collaborative relationship with God in an attempt to solve these problems. This collaborative relationship enhances their feelings of personal effectiveness and reduces uncertainties (Pargament et al., 1988). Individuals who embrace this collaborative relationship now attach new meaning to life problems based on what is expected of them from God, which, in turn, provides more favorable outcomes of their sense of control and affects their mental health status (Chatters, Taylor, Jackson, & Lincoln, 2008; Holt & McClure, 2006). Simply put, as African Americans are confronted with life stressors, they resort to spirituality strategies to help interpret, comprehend, and alleviate the stress which in turn activates their sense of control. These spirituality strategies include engaging in high religious cognition and commitment; subjective religious practice; religious guidance; and attending church, praying, or looking to God for strength, guidance, and support (Archibald, 2010; Chatters et al., 2008; Eliassen, Taylor, & Lloyd, 2005; Ellison, Boardman, Williams, & Jackson, 2001; Holt & McClure, 2006; Jang & Johnson, 2004). This sense of control activation counteracts feelings of powerlessness, which allows them to restrict the scope and intensity of life stressors and help protect them from the depressive effects.

Research reveals a direct and significant positive relationship between spirituality and social support (Archibald, 2010; Eliassen et al., 2005; Holt & McClure, 2006; Jang & Johnson, 2004). Social support related to spirituality accounted for a significant amount of the influence on the predicted levels of depressive symptoms and reduced the effect of the positive relationship between life stressors and depression. It has been shown that the African American culture places great value on relationships and connection with others (Holt & McClure, 2006). Windle (1992) reported that how an individual perceives their level of acceptance and value in their interpersonal environment increases their esteem, confidence, and efficacy, which reduce the impact of depression. Social support seems to cause the effect of spirituality that produces an increased feeling of being cared for and valued by others and an increased feeling of self-confidence and self-efficacy, which in turn possibly affects how life stressors are reappraised. Hence, when African Americans are confronted with a life stressor, they may possibly resort to spirituality strategies, which in turn possibly promote their level of social support and may counteract their feelings of low self-confidence, low self-esteem, and low self-efficacy and may help alleviate the deleterious effects of stress.

According to Lazarus and Folkman (1984), how a stressor is appraised influences the extent to which stress responses follow it. After a stressor has been appraised, the next step, if necessary, is coping. It is possible that when African Americans appraise life stressors as threatening, they resort to spiritual strategies that may promote their sense of control and social support, which might reduce the chance that they will develop symptoms of psychological distress, thereby providing for a more favorable mental health status.

Racial Identity–Coping

The moderating effect of racial identity between the relationship of life stressors and psychological distress has been supported in research. Studies show that the highest levels of psychological distress were observed in the group with the lowest levels of racial identity in the majority of the studies reviewed (Archibald, 2010; Franklin-Jackson & Carter, 2007; Pieterse & Carter, 2010; Sellers, Caldwell, Schmeelk-Cone, & Zimmerman, 2003; Sellers & Shelton, 2003). More importantly, Archibald (2010) provided evidence that the moderating effect of racial identity on psychological distress was present even after controlling for social support, sense of control, and demographic factors. To be more specific, although samples of African Americans who had higher levels of racial identity tended to have higher levels of social support and sense of control, the influence of racial identity remained.

Hence, it is probable that during the reappraisal phase of the life stress process, African Americans activate their active coping skills through their racial identity by accessing their beliefs, opinions, and attitudes with respect to the way they feel they should act, along with their evaluative judgment of their race, as identified by Sellers and Shelton (2003). Even further, at the point that African Americans begin the reappraisal phase, they opt for racial identity resources by identifying such things as their closeness to other African Americans; identifying positive traits of African Americans; and identifying the relevance of being African American.

Azibo (1989) suggests that the self-concept of African Americans seems to be engrained within their culture and their racial identity. This is perceived as being necessary for their optimal functioning and any deviation from this core self-concept may lead to more pathology among African Americans. Consequently, this self-concept seems to activate African Americans' active coping skills by allowing them to regulate the emotions related to the life stressors and also by allowing them to actively participate in activities that reduce or eliminate the impact of the life stressors. These active coping skills activated by their level of racial identity moderate the relationship between life stressors and psychological distress, and again, will tend to reduce the chance that they will develop symptoms of psychological distress and provide for a more favorable mental health status.

IMPLICATIONS

What has been presented would suggest that African Americans living in urban communities are at great risk for mental health issues but are faring far better than would be expected. This would be a simplistic conclusion to draw for what is a highly complex issue. It is clear that the stress-coping response may mediate the effects of stress exposures. However, the African American community is not homogeneous with regard to these protective forces in play. Indeed, in the urban communities of concentrated disadvantage, these coping characteristics may be less present. Even further still, the full assessment of well-being must be taken into account. One of the open areas of discussion and debate in the mental health community is whether or not the traditional diagnostic tools for mental disorders are culturally sensitive and relevant. Mental health is not as easy to assess because the assessment is usually grounded in value judgments that oftentimes differ among individuals and cultures (U.S. Department of Health and Human Services, 2001). In fact, Weare (2000) reported that "mental health is socially constructed and socially defined" (p. 12). Hence, a key to understanding mental health and mental illness is defining these terms in cultural contexts (U.S. DHHS, 2001).

A second issue is an understanding of mental health as a continuum (Figure 7.5), not merely the presence or absence of a disorder. Mental health and mental illness are not polar opposites, but should be considered as degree to which thoughts, moods, and behavior serve in the interest of daily functioning (U.S. DHHS, 2001). Viewing mental health from this perspective is important for consideration of both prevention and intervention strategies in addressing mental health.

The third issue to consider is whether or not the responses to stress manifest themselves in maladaptive ways that may be evidenced through rates of homicide in African American communities, gang involvement for youth, incidence of personal injury, and domestic violence (Hill & Cummings, 2013; Santrock, 2008; Smith, Daniels, & Akers, 2013). One important trend to consider is the increased rates of suicide among African American young adults, with suicide being the third leading cause of death among African Americans aged 15 to 24 years (CDC, 2011). Because the African American community is disproportionately young (32.9 years vs. 40.2 years for Whites and 37.4 years for the general population).

With such a complex set of influences on mental health status in the urban African American communities, it is important that the social work field strengthen its capacity and competency to respond. There has been a movement toward more collaboration and transdisciplinary interactions, which seems to reduce the mistrust from the community being served while increasing compliance and cooperation. The social work ecological

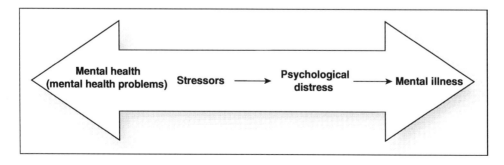

FIGURE 7.5 Mental health–illness continuum.

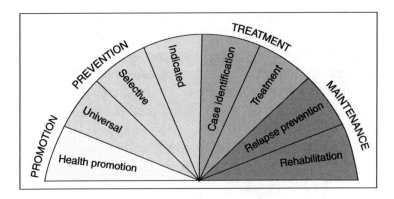

FIGURE 7.6 Mental health intervention spectrum.
Adapted from Institute of Medicine (1994, p. 23).

TABLE 7.1 PHSW Mental Health Prevention–Intervention–Treatment

CLASSIFICATION	TARGETS	EXAMPLE OF STRATEGIES
Health promotion	Target an entire population to increase knowledge of mental health risk reduction	Health fair about stress reduction
Universal	Eclectic and broad approach that targets risk factors of a whole population that has not been identified as currently at individual risk for developing mental disorders	Healthy relationship psychoeducational module as part of a university orientation course for all entering freshmen
Selective	Target a specific subgroup of a population who share common significant biopsychosocial risk factors for developing mental disorders	Peer support groups for African American adolescents whose mother and/or father were diagnosed with schizophrenia
Indicative	Target individuals at high risk for developing mental disorders due to current symptomatology by focusing on the risk and protective factors available to the individual	Information and referral to appropriate practitioners for African American adults diagnosed with cancer
Treatment	Target individuals whose symptoms meet the criteria for a diagnosable mental disorder	African American who meets criteria for a major depressive disorder is connected with an outpatient mental health clinic to participate in psychotherapy

PHSW, Public health social work.
Adapted from Institute of Medicine (1994).

theory-based practices serve as an important addition to the current public health practices. To address this issue, the discipline of social work will need to step into the fray with prevention and intervention strategies that examine this issue from both a theoretical and applied frame, as well as work in partnership with other disciplines, such as public health, to construct meaningful prevention and intervention strategies at all levels of interface.

The Institute of Medicine (IOM, 1994) developed a prevention classification based on Gordon's (1987) disease prevention classification and serves as a useful model for implementing appropriate prevention–intervention PHSW services. The IOM prevention model provides for a continuum of care that is divided into three parts: prevention, treatment, and maintenance (Figure 7.6).

This PHSW prevention–intervention model proposes that the most effective preventions–interventions are those that are appropriately matched to the population's level of risk (Table 7.1).

Prevention at any level is important for the future of PHSW services. However, it is understood that not all people in a specific population are at the same risk of developing health problems. Therefore, a consensus on what will be the determining factors for PHSW that will delineate where prevention versus intervention and treatment occur becomes crucial. This PHSW approach should be applied to meeting the mental health needs of urban communities as well as myriad health issues confronting them.

FOR FURTHER STUDY

Discussion Questions

1. What is the history of social work's relationship with public health? *Social work has been involved in public health practice since the early 20th century as social workers practiced their skills in the settlement houses.*

2. What are some of the shared values of social work and public health? *Enhancing social, economic, and environmental justice; eliminating disparities within and among populations; emphasizing underrepresented groups.*

3. What are some of the shared theories of social work and public health? *Examination of social systems' relations to health status; social epidemiology (public health). Ecological approach—person-in-environment (social work).*

4. What are some of the shared practices of social work and public health? *Strength perspective, empowerment, family centered, culturally proficient, team science.*

5. How can you develop a mental health promotion activity targeting depression among African Americans? *Target population as a whole to increase knowledge of depression risk reduction.*

6. Compare universal prevention, selective prevention, indicative prevention, and treatment intervention in the context of addressing African American's mental health status (depression). *Universal: eclectic and broad approach; selective: target a specific subgroup of African Americans; indicative: target African*

Americans at high risk of developing depression; treatment: target African Americans who have been diagnosed with depression.

Suggested Assignments

1. *Annotated bibliography assignment*—For this annotated bibliography assignment, you will prepare a descriptive list of 10 research sources specific to public health and social work followed by a brief 150-word descriptive and evaluative note for each.

   a. Use the American Psychological Association (APA) style format (or other style approved by your instructor to format sources);

   b. List in alphabetical order;

   c. Include sources related to social work and public health specific to urban environments;

   d. Include an annotation, or description of each source.

2. *Field assignment*—For this assignment, the class will be divided into two groups in which one group will visit the public health department within your specific city while the other group will visit a social work department within that same city catchment area. Each group will focus their inquiry on the following:

   a. Develop a 10-page group paper surrounding your experience at that particular agency (i.e., name of agency representative, discussion of current data surrounding the agency, interventions utilized by agency, and the groups observations and final thoughts);

   b. Present a class presentation of the groups' content of the visit;

   c. Discuss your assessment of how each agency does/does not fall within the parameters of the public health social work model discussed in class.

3. *Final reflection paper*—For this assignment, each student is expected to write a 10-page reflection paper, which would focus on the following:

   a. Your understanding of the public health social work model as discussed in class;

   b. Description of your community; and

   c. How the model would be implemented within your community and which agency(ies) you would utilize.

Suggested Readings

Marshall, J. W., Ruth, B. J., Sisco, S., Bethke, C., Piper, T. M., Cohen, M., & Bachman, S. (2011). Social work interest in prevention: A content analysis of the professional literature. *Social Work, 56*(3), 201–211.

McCave, E. L., & Rishel, C. W. (2011). Prevention as an explicit part of the social work profession. *Advances in Social Work, 12*(2), 226–240.

Moniz, C. (2010). Social work and the social determinants of health perspective: A good fit. *Health & Social Work, 35*(4), 310–313.

Ruth, B. J., Marshall, J. W., & Velasquez, E. E. M. (2013). Prevention in social work scholarship: A content analysis of Families in Society. *Families in Society, 94*(3), 182–185.

Ruth, B. J., & Sisco, S. (2008). Public health social work. In T. Mizrahi & L. E. Davis (Eds.), *Encyclopedia of social work* (20th ed.). New York, NY: Oxford University Press.

Sable, M. R., Schild, D. R., & Hipp, J. A. (2012). Chapter 4: Public health and social work. In S. Gehlert & T. Browne (Eds.), *Handbook of health social work*. Hoboken, NJ: John Wiley, pp. 64–99.

Siefert, K., & Butter, I. (1993). Incorporating race and gender into the curriculum. *Journal of Teaching in Social Work, 6*(2), 19–32.

Van Pelt, J. (2009). Social work and public health—Perfect partners. *Social Work Today, 9*(1), 28.

REFERENCES

American Psychological Association Presidential Task Force on Violence and the Family. (1996). *Violence and the family*. Washington, DC: Author.

Aponte, J., Rivers, R., & Wohl, J. (1995). *Psychological interventions and cultural diversity*. Boston, MA: Allyn & Bacon.

Archibald, P. (2010). *The role of spirituality and racial identity in the non-familial life stress process of African-Americans. Dissertation (DrPH)*. Baltimore, MD: Morgan State University.

Archibald, P., Dobson-Sydnor, K., Daniels, K., & Bronner, Y. (2013). Explaining African-Americans' depressive symptoms: A stress-distress and coping perspective. *Journal of Health Psychology, 18*(3), 321–331.

Azibo, D. A. (1989). African-centered theses on mental health and a nosology of Black/African personality disorder. *Journal of Black Psychology, 15*, 173–214.

Azibo, D. A. (2006). An African-centered rudimentary model of racial identity in African descent people and the validation of projective techniques for its measurement. *Humboldt Journal of Social Relations, 30*(1), 145–176.

Bharmal, N., Tseng, C.-H., Kaplan, R., & Wong, M. D. (2012). State-level variations in racial disparities in life expectancy. *Health Services Research, 47*, 544–555. doi:10.1111/j.1475–6773.2011.01345.x

Boyd-Franklin, N., Kelly, S., & Durham, J. (2008). African-American couples in therapy. In A. S. Gurman (Ed.), *Clinical handbook of couple therapy* (pp. 681–697). New York, NY: Guilford Press.

Broman, C. L. (1996). Coping with personal problems. In H. W. Neighbors & J. S. Jackson (Eds.), *Mental health in Black America* (pp. 117–129). Thousand Oaks, CA: Sage.

Brown, E. E., & Jackson, J. S. (2004). Age related issues among minority populations. In C. D. Spielberger (Ed.), *Encyclopedia of applied psychology* (pp. 79–90). Oxford, England: Academic Press.

Bureau of Justice Statistics. (2013). *Criminal victimization 2012: National crime victimization survey*. Washington, DC: Author.

Cameron, J., & Lalonde, R. (1994). Self, ethnicity, and social group memberships in two generations of Italian Canadians. *Personality and Social Psychology Bulletin, 20*, 514–520.

Centers for Disease Control and Prevention. (2013). *Web-based Injury Statistics Query and Reporting System (WISQARS)*. Retrieved from http://www.cdc.gov/injury/wisqars/leading_causes_death.html

Chatters, L. M., Taylor, R. J., Jackson, J. S., & Lincoln, K. D. (2008). Religious coping among African-Americans, Caribbean blacks and non-Hispanic whites. *Journal of Community Psychology, 36*(3), 371–386.

DeNavas-Walt, C., Proctor, B. D., & Smith, J. C. (2012). *U.S. Census Bureau, current population reports, P60–243, income, poverty, and health insurance coverage in the United States: 2011.* Washington, DC: U.S. Government Printing Office.

Department of Health and Human Services Healthy People 2020 Framework. Retrieved September 3, 2014, from http://www.healthypeople.gov/2020/Consortium/HP2020Framework.pdf

Edwards, K. L. (1999). African-American definitions of self and psychological health. In R. L. Jones (Ed.), *Advances in African-American psychology* (pp. 287–312). Hampton, VA: Cobb and Henry.

Eliassen, A. H., Taylor, J., & Lloyd, D. A. (2005). Subjective religiosity and depression in the transition to adulthood. *Journal for the Scientific Study of Religion, 44,* 187–199.

Ellison, C. G., Boardman, J. D., Williams, D. R., & Jackson, J. S. (2001). Religious involvement, stress, and mental health: Findings from the 1995 Detroit Area Study. *Social Forces, 80*(1), 215–249.

Fielding, J. E., Teutsch, S., & Breslow, L. (2010, December). A framework for public health in the United States. *Public Health Reviews, 32*(1), 174–189.

Franklin-Jackson, D., & Carter, R. T. (2007). The relationships between race-related stress, racial identity, and mental health for Black Americans. *Journal of Black Psychology, 33*(1), 5–26.

Geronimus, A. T., Hicken, M., Keene, D., & Bond, J. (2006). Weathering and age patterns of allostatic load scores among Blacks and Whites in the United States. *American Journal of Public Health, 96*(5), 826–833.

Glicken, M. D. (2011). *Social work in the 21st century: An introduction to social welfare, social issues, and the profession.* Thousand Oaks, CA: Sage.

Gordon, R. (1987). An operational classification of disease prevention. In J. Steinberg & M. Silverman (Eds.), *Preventing mental disorders: A research perspective* (pp. 20–26). Rockville, MD: Department of Health and Human Services, National Institute of Mental Health.

Hall, R. E. (2001). Identity development across the lifespan: A biracial model. *Social Science Journal, 38*(1), 119–124.

Halpern, D. (1993). Minorities and mental health. *Social Science and Medicine, 36*(5), 597–607.

Halstead, M., Johnson, S., & Cunningham, W. (1993). Measuring coping in adolescents: An application of the ways and coping checklist. *Journal of Clinical Child Psychology, 22,* 337–344.

Harburg, E., Erburt, J. C., Hauenstein, L. S., Chape, C., Schull, W. J., & Schork, M. A. (1973). Socioecological stress, suppressed hostility, skin color and black-white male blood pressure: Detroit. *Psychosomatic Medicine, 35,* 276–296.

Hasin, D. S., Goodwin, R. D., Stinson, F. S., & Grant, B. F. (2005). Epidemiology of major depressive disorder: Results from the National Epidemiologic Survey on Alcoholism and Related Conditions. *Archives of General Psychiatry, 62,* 1097–1106.

Hill, C. V., & Cummings, T. (2013). The multiple risks for U.S. Black males: A priority case for crimongenic disparities research. In E. Waltermaureur & T. Akers (Eds.), *Epidemiological criminology: Theory to practice,* pp.79–86. New York, NY: Routledge.

Holt, C. L., & McClure, S. M. (2006). Perceptions of the religion-health connection among African-American church members. *Qualitative Health Research, 16*(2), 268–281.

Hoyert, D. L., & Xu, J. (2012). *Deaths: Preliminary data for 2011. National vital statistics reports, vol. 61 No. 6.* Atlanta, GA: U.S. Department of Health and Human Services, Centers for Disease Control and Prevention.

Institute of Medicine. (1994). *Reducing risks for mental disorders: Frontiers for preventive intervention research.* Washington, DC: National Academy Press.

Jackson, J. S., Torres, M., Caldwell, C. H., Neighbors, H. W., Nesse, R. M., Taylor, R. J., . . . Williams, D. R. (2005). The national survey of American Life: A study of racial, ethnic and cultural influences on mental disorders and mental health. *International Journal of Methods in Psychiatric Research, 13*(4), 196–207.

Jang, S. J., & Johnson, B. R. (2004). Explaining religious effects on distress among African-Americans. *Journal for the Scientific Study of Religion, 43*(2), 239–260.

Johnson, R. L. (2002). Racial identity from an African-American perspective. *Journal of Cultural Diversity, 9*(3), 73–78.

Kessler, R. C., McGonagle, K. A., Zhao, S., Nelson, C. B., Hughes, M., Eshelman, S.,...Kendler, K. S. (1994). Lifetime and 12-month prevalence of *DSM-III-R* disorders in the United States. *Archives of General Psychiatry, 51*, 8–19.

Kessler, R. C., Mickelson, K. D., & Williams, D. R. (1999). The prevalence, distribution, and mental health correlates of perceived discrimination in the United States. *Journal of Health and Social Behavior, 40*, 208–230.

Kessler, R. C., & Wang, P. S. (2008). The descriptive epidemiology of commonly occurring mental disorders in the United States. *Annual Review of Public Health, 29*, 115–129.

Lazarus, R., & Folkman, S. (1984). *Stress, appraisal, and coping.* New York, NY: Springer Publishing.

Mattis, J. S., Eubanks, S., Zapata, A., Grayman, N., Belkin, M., Mitchell, N., & Cooper, S. (2004). Factors influencing religious non-attendance among African American men: A multi-method analysis. *Review of Religious Research, 45*, 386–403.

McGoldrick, M., Giordano, J., & Garcia-Preto, N. (2005). *Ethnicity and family therapy.* New York, NY: Guilford Press.

Mental Health America. (2006). Americans reveal top stressors: How they cope (Press Release). Alexandria, VA: Author. Retrieved from http:// www.nmha.org/index.cfm?objectid= ABD3DC4E-1372-4D20-C8274399C9476E26

Miranda, J., & Green, B. L. (1999). The need for mental health services research focusing on poor young women. *Journal of Mental Health Policy and Economics, 2*, 73–89.

National Association of Social Workers. (2006). Public health social work. Retrieved from http:// www.socialworkers.org/research/naswResearch/PublicHealth/default.asp

National Center for Health Statistics. (2012). *Health, United States, 2011: With special feature on socioeconomic status and health.* Hyattsville, MD. Author.

Nazroo, J. Y. (2003). The structuring of ethnic inequalities in health: Economic position, racial discrimination and racism. *American Journal of Public Health, 93*, 277–284.

Pargament, K. I., Kennell, J., William, W., Grevengoed, N., Newman, J., & Jones, W. (1988). Religion and the problem-solving process: Three styles of coping. *Journal for the Scientific Study of Religion, 27*, 90–104.

Pearlin, L. I. (2005). Some conceptual perspectives on the origins and prevention of social stress. In A. Maney & J. Ramos (Eds.), *Socioeconomic conditions, stress and mental disorders: Toward a new synthesis of research and public policy* (pp. 1–35). Washington, DC: Mental Health Statistical improvement Program, National Institute of Mental Health.

Pearlin, L. I., Lieberman, M. A., Menaghan, E. G., & Mullan, J. T. (1981). The stress process. *Journal of Health and Social Behavior, 22*, 337–356.

Pieterse, A. L., & Carter, R. T. (2010). The role of racial identity in perceived racism and psychological stress among Black American adults: Exploring traditional and alternative approaches. *Journal of Applied Social Psychology, 40*(5), 1028–1053.

Plummer, D. L., & Slane, S. (1996). Patterns of coping in racially stressful situations. *The Journal of Black Psychology, 22*(3), 302–315.

Popple, P. R., & Leighninger, L. (2004). *Social work, social welfare and American society.* Boston, MA: Allyn & Bacon.

Robins, L., & Reiger, D. A. (1991). *Psychiatric disorders in America: The epidemiologic catchment area study.* New York, NY: The Free Press.

Santrock, J. W. (2008). *Adolescence: Twelfth edition.* Boston, MA: McGraw-Hill Higher Education.

Schieman, S., Pudrovska, T., & Milkie, M. (2005). The sense of divine control and the self-concept: A study of race differences in late-life. *Research on Aging, 27*, 165–196.

Seaton, E. K. (2003). A validity study of the Index of Race-Related Stress Scale among African American adolescents. *Journal of Black Psychology, 29*, 292–307.

Sellers, R. M., Caldwell, C. H., Schmeelk-Cone, K. H., & Zimmerman, M. A. (2003). Racial identity, racial discrimination, perceived stress, and psychological distress among African-American young adults. *Journal of Health and Social Behavior, 43*, 302–317.

Sellers, R. M., & Shelton, J. N. (2003). Racial identity, discrimination, and mental health among African-Americans. *Journal of Personality and Social Psychology, 84*(5), 1079–1092.

Smith, S., Daniels, K., & Akers, T. (2013). The epidemiological criminology of child victimization: The evolution of hybrid gang families and violence. In T. Akers, R. Potter, & C. Hill (Eds.), *Epidemiological criminology: A public health approach to crime and violence* (pp. 118–127). New York, NY: Routledge.

Sussman, L. K., Robins, L. N., & Earls, F. (1987). Treatment seeking for depression by Black and White Americans. *Social Science and Medicine, 24*, 187–196.

Tayfun, T. M., & Asli, B. (2008). Impacts of urbanization process on men. *Anatolian Journal of Psychiatry, 9*, 238–243.

Turner, R. J., Wheaton, B., & Lloyd, D. A. (1995). The epidemiology of stress. *American Sociological Review, 60*, 104–125.

UN World Urbanization Prospects. (2008). The 2007 revision; the urban transformation of the developing world. *Science, 319*(5864), 761–764.

U.S. Census Bureau. (2011). *Census redistricting data (Public Law 94–171) Summary File, Table P1*. Washington, DC: Economics and Statistics Administration. Retrieved from https://www.census .gov/prod/cen2010/doc/pl94-171.pdf.

U.S. Department of Health and Human Services. (2000). *Healthy people 2010: With understanding and improving health and objectives for improving health* (2nd ed.). Washington, DC: Author.

U.S. Department of Justice. (2013). *Uniform crime reports: Hate crime statistics, 2012*. Washington, DC: Federal Bureau of Investigation.

Weare, K. (2000). *Promoting mental, emotional and social health: A whole school approach*. London, England: Taylor & Francis.

Wilson, W. J. (1987). *The truly disadvantaged*. Chicago, IL: The University of Chicago Press.

Windle, M. (1992). A longitudinal study of stress buffering for adolescent problem behaviors. *Developmental Psychology, 28*, 522–530.

World Health Organization. (1946). *Preamble to the Constitution of the World Health Organization as adopted by the International Health Conference*. Geneva, Switzerland: Publications of the World Health Organization.

CHAPTER 8

Exploring Urban Faith-Based–Social Work Community Collaboration for Mental Health Promotion in Urban African American Communities

Paul Archibald, Kevin Daniels, and Sandra Austin

The chapter identifies the spirituality factors that contribute to the mental health beliefs of Urban African Americans (UAAs). Subsequent sections present the collaborative role of UAA faith-based practitioners and urban social work (USW) practitioners in promoting mental health. The chapter concludes with a review of research on urban faith-based (UFB) mental health–promoting interventions and the role of USW practitioners in the process. It summarizes specific UFB health promotion models in action reviewing their adherence to the socioecological or multilevel model of behavior change with implications for social work practice in urban communities.

UAA SPIRITUALITY

Culture influences many aspects of the mental health status of UAAs. UAAs today share a varied culture that is shaped from historical African religions, slavery, and segregation (Boyd-Franklin, 1989; Frame & Williams, 1996; Mbiti, 1970; Nobles, 2004). The culture of UAAs has been shown to promote adaptive coping within the context of a mixture of values and practices (Lopez et al., 2002). One of the prominent values and practices that form UAA's cultural context is spirituality and religious beliefs and practices (Waites, 2008). Spirituality in the UAA helping tradition is a critical value deeply rooted in the African worldview and used by African Americans as a tool for survival and means for intergenerational advancement. African Americans tend to conceptualize spirituality in terms of positive values that are internalized and consistently manifested in their overall life behaviors and attitudes, and based on a personal relationship with God (Mattis, 2000). Spirituality in the African American culture is utilized to motivate and uplift African American people while providing hope and meaning during periods of exposure to life stressors (Martin & Martin, 2002).

African Americans report greater levels of religious and church involvement than the general population in the United States (Kosmin & Keysar, 2009) but those living in the urban environment present with differing levels of religious and church involvement. UAAs are less likely to report affiliating with any denomination or being a member of a church and attend religious services less frequently than their rural and suburban counterparts (Taylor, Chatters, & Levin, 2004). In the African American helping tradition, spirituality goes beyond the identified polar opposites or dichotomies of religion–spirituality, sacred–secular, religion–nonreligion, denominational–nondenominational.

The National Survey of American Life (NSAL), conducted from 2001 to 2003, shows that there were more than 40 religious denominations reported among African Americans. However, more than half of the African Americans are most likely to be affiliated with Baptist (51.1%), while 10.1% do not affiliate with a religious denomination, and 1% indicate affiliation with Muslim (Taylor et al., 2004). The American Religious Identification Survey (ARIS), conducted from February to November 2008, reported that 45% of African Americans indicated that they were affiliated with *Baptist*, which was inclusive of Southern Baptist, American Baptist, Free-Will, Missionary, and African American denominations; 15% indicated they were affiliated with Christian Generic, which was inclusive of Christian, Protestant, Evangelical/Born Again Christian, Born Again Fundamentalist, Independent Christian, Missionary Alliance Church, Nondenominational Christian; and 11% indicated that they were affiliated with *No Religious Denomination*, which was inclusive of no religion, Humanistic, Ethical Culture, Agnostic, Atheist, Secular (Kosmin & Keysar, 2009).

Although the UAA faith experience is heterogeneous in its nature, UAAs express their spirituality principally through the vehicle of the African American church (Richardson & June, 1997). Spirituality in the African Americans church is derived partly from the African slaves' need to develop their own places of worship and to maintain a strong sense of community (Moore, 1991). Whether or not African Americans are affiliated with an organized religion or church, whether Christian or Muslim, spirituality is an internalized and valued cultural norm. This internalized sense of spirituality is intergenerational in its nature as it is passed down through the generations (Cook & Wiley, 2000). The African American church also serves as an informal support network (Gurin, Hatchett, & Jackson, 1989; Taylor & Chatters, 1988) and a coping mechanism for many UAA communities as they are faced with family, economic, and social issues (Brashears & Roberts, 1996; Cook, 1993; McAdoo & Crawford, 1991; Moore, 1991; Taylor et al., 2004).

Spirituality Factors Related to UAAs' Attitudes Toward Mental Health

The spirituality factor and its relationship with UAAs' attitudes toward mental health service utilization have been researched over the past few years. It was initially found that AAs' high levels of involvement in the activities of African American faith-based organizations tend to greatly influence their utilization of formal mental health services in the community. Those with high levels of organizational religiosity sought mental health services from their faith-based leaders rather than from mental health practitioners. More recent research found that even those who identified with high levels of organizational religiosity did not seek any assistance, including faith-based leaders or mental health practitioners, when faced with mental health issues (Ayalon & Young, 2005).

However, findings reveal that there is a direct and significant positive relationship between spirituality and sense of control among African Americans. Those with high levels of spirituality seem to have an increased feeling of autonomy in reference to their level of mastery and understanding of perceived constraints and available resources, which in turn affect their perception of requiring mental health services (Archibald, Dobson-Sydnor, Daniels, & Bronner, 2013). Hence, when African Americans are confronted with a stressor, they resort to spirituality strategies that can promote their sense of control and may counteract feelings of powerlessness, thus alleviating the deleterious effects of the stressor, and decreasing the perceived need for treatment from secular practitioners (Barksdale & Molock, 2009; Cooper, Corrigan, & Watson, 2003; Holt & McClure, 2006; Taylor et al., 2004).

Consequently, UAAs are more likely to report higher levels of shame and embarrassment around mental illness influenced by the cultural expectation that they possess the inner capacity and strength to cope with life's difficulties. There is a cultural stigma of weakness connected to acknowledging the acceptance of a mental health issue that requires utilization of mental health services (Sanders-Thompson, Bazile, & Akbar, 2004). For instance, only 16% of African Americans who experienced a mental health disorder throughout their lifetime pursued any relief from their symptoms from a mental health practitioner (Breslau, 2005), and only 2.8% of African Americans experiencing a mood disorder actually pursued and received services from a mental health practitioner (Williams et al., 2007).

African Americans who chose to defy the norm and utilized mental health services described unfavorable attitudes about the services provided, returned for follow-up services less than their White counterparts, and were secretive about their mental health services (Diala et al., 2000). Some of the issues influencing their attitudes toward mental health utilization include the concern that White mental health providers were not culturally competent regarding African American issues (Sanders-Thompson et al., 2004).

African Americans reported feeling alienated from the dominant society, and their mistrust of mental health programs and mental health service providers is attributed to the mistrust of other systems that include the health care system, criminal justice system, and the entire government in general (Campbell et al., 2007; Whaley, 2001). Cultural mistrust has also been a prominent reason for the underutilization of traditional mental health services including participation in mental health–promoting interventions and participation in research endeavors that could enhance UAAs' mental health status. This cultural mistrust of the mental health system must be considered when mental health programs are being developed for the African Americans (Campbell et al., 2007).

URBAN FAITH-BASED ORGANIZATIONS' AND URBAN SOCIAL WORK PRACTITIONERS' HEALTH PROMOTION

The role of African American faith-based organizations and social workers in urban communities is not new—there is a plethora of literature that undergirds not only their presence but also their significance and impact (Caldwell, Chatters, Billingsley, & Taylor, 1995; Cnaan, Sinha, & McGrew, 2004; Collins, 2006; Martin & Martin, 2002; Schiele, 2000). Faith-based organizations based in urban environments have been a source of vitality and health promotion in the areas of coalition building, emotional uplift, educational and health services, financial sustenance, social activities, community and political advocacy, and equity, in that, at times they were the only source of social service provider care (Burris & Billingsley, 1994). Historically, discriminatory practices of the larger sociopolitical macrosystems in the United States forced the development of the early pioneering efforts of faith-based practitioners in the lives of those who live in urban cities (Mays & Nicholson, 1933). Community and political advocacy were instrumental in ensuring that the needs of community members were met—not only in providing the service itself but also ensuring that urban families received services equal to other groups (Schnieder & Lester, 2001). Since times of the antebellum, world wars, multiple economic contractions, civil rights, and to the present, advocacy among African American faith practitioners has been paramount to the uplifting and progress of urban residents and their communities or environments (Wilks, 2012).

Health promotion has also been an essential service of African American faith practitioners that has served urban communities. As early as the 1500s BC (Mesopotamian Era), through the Middle Ages, Renaissance, Enlightenment, to the present, faith-based institutions have had to play a significant role in the communal integrity for health promotion and against the health disparities that tend to pervade urban populations, even amid the challenges of imperialization, reformation, colonization, and the capitalization of America and beyond (Daniels & Archibald, 2013; Rosen, 1993). More specifically, African American faith-based practitioners such as Richard Allen and Denmark Vessey, among others, braved the early antebellum and Civil Rights Era providing housing, health care access, and mental health services in UAA communities. These efforts were critical in dismantling the historic stigmatization and lack of trust most urban populations had toward the greater service provider professions (Newman, 2009; Roberston, 2009). Since the enactment of the Affordable Health Care Act, the church, once again, is at the forefront of partnering and serving as a key change agent for a myriad of challenges faced by urban populations, as it navigates not only a new set of potentials and possibilities, but also challenges (De Marco et al., 2011).

Along with faith-based practitioners, social work practitioners have at their roots a history of caring and service provision for urban communities. The early pioneering work of the Settlement Movements—Jane Addams and Mary Richmond, among others—promulgated the work of charities and the beginnings of the field of social work among urban populations. In that earlier practice, social work (nonsectarian) and faith-based institutions (sectarian) served side by side in the area of pioneering change, but, eventually, social work organizations came to feel that the secular aspects of their practice was being subsumed by the religious sector, while the faith-based institutions feared that they were losing their edge in religious matters. Thus, the role of social work in the United States went through myriad changes—from indigenous precolonial times, sectarian religious origins (colonial period to early 20th century), professionalism and secularization (1920s–1970s), resurgence of interest in spirituality (1980s–1995), to transcending boundaries (1995–present)—see Table 8.1.

TABLE 8.1 Historical Phases in Connection Between Spirituality and American Social Work

PHASE	CHARACTERISTICS
One	Hundreds of indigenous cultures with spiritually based social welfare systems
Indigenous precolonial times	Discrimination, oppression, and mass destructive impacts from European colonial contact and expansion
Two	Primarily Christian and Jewish sectarian professional services
Sectarian origins (colonial period to early 20th century)	Sectarian ideologies in governmental services; beginnings of nonsectarian humanistic spiritual ideologies for social services
Three	Professionalization and secularization of social work ideologies and institutions
	Increased professional skepticism of religiously based social work; separation of church and state more strictly enforced in social service delivery; tacit religious ideologies continue in governmental social service delivery; sectarian private social service agencies and educational institutions continue; Beginnings of existential, humanistic, and new nonsectarian approaches to social work
Four	Continuation of private sectarian social work; calls for inclusion approach to spirituality; increasing diversity of religious and nonreligious spiritual perspectives in social work
Resurgence of interest in spirituality (1980–1995)	Rapid increase of related research, publication, and networking; beginnings of systematic international collaboration; return of attention to religion and spirituality in social work education
Five	Escalation of previous trends; general and context-specific definitions and research on spirituality refined; curriculum guidelines, courses, textbooks widely established; postmodern perspective increased; faith-based social services policies formalized
Transcending boundaries (1995–present)	Interdisciplinary and international networking and collaborations increased; empirical studies increased; whole earth perspectives on spirituality introduced

Adapted from Canda and Furman (2010).

With the unfortunate destabilization of the economy, under the recent Great Recession in America, there has been a resurgence of interest in the stability, sustainability, viability, and density of urban environments where people of color and those who live on the margins reside (McKernan, Ratclife, Steuerle, & Zhang, 2014; Pfeffer, Danziger, & Schoeni, 2013). According to recent statistics, most urban populaces have suffered tremendous decline and decentralization as a result of the Great Recession, which has resulted in an environment that has greatly impacted the housing market, employment, and market trends to the detriment of urban areas. According to Shapiro, Meschede, and Osoro (2013), the recession has further exacerbated the wealth gap between the rich and the poor and, thereby, leading to an already fragile urban existence that, historically, has implications for health and other socioeconomic concerns.

The household wealth gap doubled almost 22% between Whites and Blacks—the median household net worth for Whites was $110,729 in 2010, versus $4,995 for African Americans (Bayer, Ferreira, & Ross, 2013). African Americans among other minority groups, were systematically pushed into a housing crisis of epic proportions by the nation's biggest banks, to the extent that taking on bad mortgages practically decimated historical gains. This caused the loss of almost 600,000 public sector government jobs that were previously held by the majority of African Americans and people of color. To date, the unemployment rate (13.1%) for African Americans continues to be the highest among other racial groups, which underscores the continuing collective racial gulf among and between groups (U.S. Department of Labor Statistics, 2014).

However, mistrust within the social structure and poor therapeutic alliances affect UAAs' ability to be healthy and resilient in the face of such penetrating circumstances. Although taking into consideration the level of mistrust and poor therapeutic alliances along with the spirituality factors related to mental health, culturally responsive and competent faith-based health promotion (FBHP) programs have become increasingly more prevalent as the UAA church and other faith-based organizations have moved beyond just providing spiritual, economic, social, and political development to their members and the community. They have now added mental health promotion to their helping tradition regimen and engage in activities that help reduce health disparities (Braithwaite & Taylor, 2001; Campbell et al., 2007; Eng, Hatch, & Callan, 1985; Lasater, Becker, Hill, & Gans, 1997; Lincoln & Mamiya, 1990; Thomas, Quinn, Billingsley, & Caldwell, 1994).

Faith-Based Health Promotion

The FBHP model, also known as church-based health promotion (CBHP), serves as a public health social work modality in its role as an agent of health promotion and disease prevention (Campbell et al., 2007). FBHP can be broadly conceptualized utilizing a socioecological framework, which incorporates the complexity of the social support mechanisms of the urban Black church along with the significant historical role of spiritual and religious practices in the lives of UAAs. The FBHP model takes into consideration the wholistic person in environment, culturally, and contextually, while

TABLE 8.2 Socioecological Model and Faith-Based Health Promotion

LEVEL OF CHANGE	THEORETICAL APPROACHES AND TARGETS	EXAMPLE OF FBHP STRATEGIES
Intrapersonal	Individual characteristics that influence health behavior such as knowledge, attitudes, beliefs, affect, and past experiences	Tailored communications Motivational interviewing
Interpersonal/social network	Interpersonal and group influences, including formal and informal social networks and social support from family, friends, and church members to support healthy behaviors	Family programs Lay health advisers Support groups Witnessing/group testimonials Psychotherapy groups
Organizational	Policies, facilities, and organizational structures (e.g., standing committees such as health ministry), which may help promote–maintain recommended behaviors within the church	Pastor Leadership Church-sponsored education/ events Bulletin inserts Policy changes (e.g., foods served)
Environment/policy	Neighborhood, community, or governmental resources, institutions, policies, advocacy, media activities, or other activities that improve the supportiveness and availability of healthy options for church members	Farmers' markets Walking trails Community coalitions Increasing access to health care and low-cost screening/follow-up

FBHP, faith-based health promotion.
Adapted from Campbell et al. (2007); Glanz and Rimer (1997) .

providing culturally competent pedagogy needed to promote optimal and healthy life-styles (Markens, Fox, Taub, & Gilbert, 2002). Table 8.2 describes the characteristics of the types of changes and theoretical approaches that encompass the socioecological model and FBHP.

Historical Perspective of African American FBHP

The earliest charitable services occurred between 1882 and 1895 and involved the work of Reverend Thurman Tillman of the First African Baptist Church of Savannah who provided programs for delinquent youth in the neighborhood (Burris & Billingsley, 1994). During the period known as the National Negro Movement of 1915, public health issues were addressed in African American churches. In fact, from 1915 to 1950, Health Improvement Week was implemented in African American churches, during which they coordinated services with public health entities to disseminate information about preventable diseases among the African American community (Healthy People, 2000). By the 1920s, 97% of the African American churches provided community outreach programs (Mays and Nicholson, 1933). However, the African American church was unable to place social services as a top priority because its congregants were poor and there was not much funding that could be utilized for charitable causes (Montgomery, 1993).

In the 1970s, the increase in drug use and the explosion of an inexpensive drug eventually led African American churches in the 1980s to adopt a response to the crack epidemic that coincided with the HIV/AIDs epidemic. Jessie Jackson and many organizations such as the National Conference on African American Family/Community and Crack Cocaine brought attention to the need to address the issues and adopted the slogan, "Down with Dope, Up with Hope" (Pinn, 2002). Despite the slow response of the church, grassroots African American women's organizations actively addressed the AIDS epidemic by offering prevention education and resource referrals to African American clergy organizations and the women's church ministries (McLane-Davison, 2013). In 1989, Balm in Gilead, a nonprofit organization, collaborated with the Columbia University School of Public Health in providing technical assistance to African American churches. Balm in Gilead continues to keep HIV/AIDS in the forefront of the African American churches by offering an annual week of prayer for AIDS, and the church continues to respond to health issues impacting their congregants. Research universities, with support and funding from the Centers for Disease Control and Prevention (CDC) and National Institutes of Health (NIH), have collaborated with churches by conducting community-based participatory research (CBPR) to identify effective methods to address cancer, diabetes, cardiovascular diseases, smoking cessation, and obesity among African Americans (Austin & Claiborne, 2011; DeHaven, Hunter, Wilder, Walton, & Berry, 1994).

By the 1990s, the African American church was more engaged in community outreach (Lincoln & Mamiya, 1990). The African American faith-based leaders have been instrumental in supporting the formation of health committees composed of church members who are allied health professionals (i.e., nurses, health care administrators, and technicians) to conduct research in church settings with culturally congruent components that have included scripture verses, use of the culinary staff, and use of church space (Austin & Claiborne, 2011). In response to the growing issue of health disparities among African Americans, the websites of the National Baptist Conference, American Methodist Episcopal, and Church of God in Christ identify health ministries as a formal component of their churches' organization. In Catholic churches, faith-based nurses provide spiritual guidance with health education, information, and referral for parishioners on health matters (Sheehan et al., 2013).

UFB Health Promotion Models in Action

Six-Month Type II Diabetes Program

An example of how faith communities can become engaged in a health issue is an implementation of a 6-month type 2 diabetes program held in four African American Baptist churches in a Northeast city in the United States. This diabetes education program consisted of a one-half day community awareness session and a series of seven workshops followed by a focus group. During the community awareness session, attendees were informed about the health disparities among African Americans. Individuals who identified being diagnosed with type 2 diabetes were invited to enroll in the workshop series at one of the four participating African American churches. The 2.5-hour workshops were offered weekly for seven consecutive weeks. Three workshops focused on healthy eating, three focused on exercise, and one focused on the role of family and friends in supporting individuals diagnosed with type 2 diabetes. Participants self-reported becoming aware of behaviors and thought processes that permitted them to ignore self-care practices and improvements in management of diabetes and feeling empowered to manage their health (Austin & Claiborne, 2011). Although this was a small program, the larger impact on the African American community has resulted in churches instituting a weekly exercise program, walking group at a local mall, and an ongoing health promotion program.

Faith-Based Hip-Hop Psychotherapy Group

The Faith-Based Hip-Hop Psychotherapy Group (FBHH; Archibald, Daniels, & Cox, 2014) utilizes Niebuhr's Christ and culture framework (1951) and Travis and Deepak's (2011) individual and community empowerment (ICE) by integrating positive youth development (PYD) dimensions and empowerment (see Table 8.3). Familiar hip-hop music, themes, and values are examined during the group intervention to assist participants with uncovering and reexamining their negative beliefs and replacing them with more adaptive ways of viewing life events. The main objectives of the FBHH psychotherapy group are to: (a) teach participants how their thinking influences their behavior and relationship with self, others, and God; (b) facilitate cognitive restructuring through the use of culturally relevant music and lyrics; and (c) reduce the participants' tendencies to engage in self-serving cognitive distortions or thinking errors. Participants showed a decrease in their Individual and Community Risk score; a reduction in their cognitive distortions or thinking errors; and an increase in their ICE score.

TABLE 8.3 FBHH Sample Group Session (Archibald, Daniels, & Cox, 2014)

	WEEK 2: IT IS A HARD KNOCK LIFE
Objectives	Students will examine the impact that life choices have on constructing values Students will learn about challenges that have confronted other youth and how God intervened and/or assisted Students will begin to think about the impact that positive and negative experiences have on their lives
Activities	Have students create a time line based on their life, including any interventions by church or God, family, therapist, counselor…documenting anything that they identify as important (positive or negative) Allow a few students (those who are comfortable) to discuss their time line Hand out the lyrics and play the "song for the day." Students will process questions and share feelings and thoughts evoked by the song
Song	"Hard Knock Life—*Vol. 2,*" *Hard Knock Life* (Jay Z)

Intergenerational Life Stage Program

The Intergenerational Life Stage (ILS) Program, which integrates Dr. Gambone's intergenerational dialogues (Gambone, 2002) and Erikson's life stages (Erikson, 1959) with African American intergenerationality (Waites, 2008), brought together six generations (Silent, Baby Boomers, Generation Jones, Baby Busters, Millennials, and iGeneration), who participated in several dialogues (Archibald & Daniels, 2013). The main objectives of the intergenerational dialogues are to: (a) provide an opportunity for several generations of African Americans in a faith-based organization to engage in a face-to-face dialogue with each other on several themes in reference to spiritual, social, emotional, political, financial, and educational issues that they identified; (b) to exchange the perspectives and recommendations from each other on the themes and to address the concerns and issues presented; and (c) to agree on some key proposals and make recommendations on the main themes identified. Participants identified that the sessions broke down barriers between the generations by intentionally listening to the values of each generation, then challenging them to work together intergenerationally to come up with action steps that helped moved them toward common goals.

The Holistic Needs of African American Men Program

The Holistic Needs of African American Men (HAAM) program is a 14-week psychotherapy group that encompasses the historical approach of faith-based communities by aggressively and proactively utilizing a community outreach approach to recruiting African American men (Daniels & Archibald, 2011b). The goals of the HAAM Program are to: (a) support and nurture the HAAM; (b) provide information and resources that help African American men take control of their lives physically, spiritually, mentally, and economically; (c) provide a safe and culturally sensitive and appropriate environment for African American males to freely discuss their needs; and (d) assist African American men in utilizing the service delivery systems that are available to them in the community and beyond the community. The HAAM Program's theoretical framework is grounded in Clinebell's (1997) Seven Dimensions of Well-Being and Holistic Health due to the multiplicity of needs identified by African American men living in an urban environment. Participants reported an increased feeling of self-efficacy and autonomy in regard to their life challenges.

Levitical Cycle of Health Program

The Levitical Cycle of Health (LCOH) program is an 8-week psychotherapy group designed to promote positive mental and physical health among participants (Daniels & Archibald, 2011a). The theoretical foundation of the LCOH model is based on the CBHP model that recognizes the church as a public health social work conduit. The LCOH model is based on the spiritual Judeo–Christian framework called the *moedim* (celebration of life) found in the biblical book of Leviticus. The LCOH model was designed to be delivered in conjunction with an ongoing health ministry and health promotion. The overall goals of the LCOH model–program are: (a) to bring participants into a greater sense of self-awareness; (b) to help participants understand the importance of optimal health and disease prevention; (c) to help participants focus on the meaning, purpose, and value of their lives; (d) to help participants understand one's universal call to service, awareness, and purpose in one's own call to service, and fulfillment with one's self and call to service; and (e) to help participants understand how the link between their physical, emotional, mental, and spiritual state can potentially influence their optimal health. Participants noted an increased awareness of healthy practices, as well as the importance of the physical, emotional, mental, and spiritual aspects of their lives, and most important, the linkage between them.

IMPLICATIONS FOR SOCIAL WORK PRACTICE
IN URBAN ENVIRONMENTS

The transdisciplinary process of social work and faith-based organizations in promoting mental health among UAAs can provide a paradigm shift in the way mental health service is provided to African Americans in urban settings. The UFB organizations have come a long way from "Down with Dope, Up with Hope" in bringing attention to treating health issues. The African American faith-based setting has proven itself as a viable setting in which to provide health-promoting services and research that could enhance mental health services. The social work environment has also begun to acknowledge the significant importance of faith-based organizations in the process of culturally competent health promotion. UAA faith-based leaders and social work practitioners must begin the dialogue about faith-based and social work techniques, which can help to reduce the level of cultural mistrust. The themes developed from these dialogues can increase the legitimacy of the partnership between public mental health agencies and the African American church. In addition, it can help develop new nontraditional faith-based mental health promotion programs and evaluate existing faith-based mental health promotion models that integrate spirituality resources with public mental health resources. Keep in mind that health interventions that incorporate spiritual and cultural resources have been found to be very effective for African Americans (Campbell et al., 2007).

Faith Based Practitioners + Social Work Practitioners = FBHP

What is oftentimes not clearly delineated is that the helping traditions of providing assistance, guidance, and support to underrepresented populations are a common thread for the UAA church and the USW profession. Many in the UAA church do not value the role of urban secular social work interventions if it is void of spiritual components. On the other hand, many in the social work arena have difficulties acknowledging the significant contribution of the African American church to human services (Plante, 2008). Both the African American church and the social work profession share commonalities in reference to their scope of focus and influence, which should be utilized to develop strategies for collaborative community interventions. According to Cnaan, Sinha, and McGrew

(2004), the members within the African American church can be reached, increasing participation and support, through further collaborations with the social work profession. The UAA faith-based setting is a viable setting in which mental health promoting social work services and research that could enhance urban AAs' mental health status are provided. Garland and Yancey (2012) maintain that the faith-based setting possesses characteristics that are unique for social work practice. UAAs' health and mental health attitudes, beliefs, and behaviors are not developed outside of social systems. Hence, the facilitation of health promotion methods may be best assessed and influenced within a context of reciprocal social interaction of faith-based and the social work community. As UAAs are involved in faith-based organizations for social and psychological support, developing FBHP interventions utilizing, a transdisciplinary model of USW professionals and UFB professionals has the potential to reach a broader African American population with a greater potential for reducing mental health disparities (Taylor et al., 2004). Although there is a perception of competition among faith-based organizations and social work organizations due to the limited pool of public funding (Tangenberg, 2005), there is an ever-growing opportunity for the African American church and social work organizations to collaborate in an effort to provide community interventions that address the social ills that are faced by African Americans.

CASE STUDY

Frank Williams (37 years) and Shawna Williams (35 years) are an African American couple, who were referred by their pastor to an outpatient community mental health clinic—Destiny Health Services (DHS) for familial conflicts and abuse allegations. They have a 17-year-old son, Frank, Jr., and a 13-year-daughter, Shawntrice. They were married 2 years ago, although they have been living together for the past 12 years. They rent a two-bedroom apartment in an apartment complex where they have lived for 9 years. Shawna works as a day care provider and Frank works at a dairy production company as a blow-molder operator. Frank has been diagnosed with hypertension and has lower back issues, which seem to have been sustained from his work assignments. Shawna was diagnosed with diabetes this past year, but has not fully accepted the diagnosis. Both deny any alcohol, tobacco, and other drug (ATOD) use. Frank was arrested several times as a juvenile for assault and battery and for robbery. Shawna has no criminal history. They are very active in their Pentecostal church and attend church regularly as a family. Frank is an ordained deacon and serves on the Adjutant Ministry. Shawna sings on the praise team and is a member of the Hospitality Ministry. Their two children have been very active in the youth ministry although they have started to become ambivalent about attending church, and at times defiant (refusing to follow household rules). They have been attending this church for the past 8 years and enjoy the large network of friends that they identify with at the church.

(*continued*)

(*continued*)

DHS was contacted by the pastor of the church after Frank, Sr., and Shawna had been in pastoral counseling with him for 3 months. After it was reported that the conflicts in the home had increased to physical fights between Frank, Sr., and Shawna and between Frank and his son, Frank, Jr., the pastor decided that the services needed were beyond his scope of expertise. The pastor informed the therapist that he would like to receive updates on the progress of the Williams family. Frank initially became very angry at the pastor for the referral, but was able to de-escalate his angry feelings after he was provided with biblical–scriptural justification for the referral. He was also informed that DHS provided therapeutic services from both a secular and spiritual perspective. Shawna was ambivalent about the referral and deferred to her husband to make the decision about attending; they both reluctantly decided to attend.

During the intake session, when the social worker met with the family for the first time, both Frank, Sr., and Shawna were clearly angry at both the therapist and the pastor for being referred to therapy. They both felt that they had done nothing wrong and that they could have completed working the issues out with their pastor. Both Frank, Sr., and Shawna normalized the fighting as they both were witnesses to their parents fighting as well as being "beaten" by their parents. The parents stated that they loved each other and their children and felt that they worked hard to keep their family together. The therapist assessed for physical and emotional abuse to determine if child protective services (CPS) needed to be contacted.

The parents admitted that they have seen increased fighting in the household, which goes against all of their spiritual beliefs. They stated that they were having economic difficulties that have been adding to the strain in their relationship. They discussed past indiscretions by Frank, Sr., a subject that frequently leads to physical fights when it is brought up during an argument. They also stated that both of their children have become increasingly defiant both in the home and in school (refusing to follow adults' directives). Their children have begun to question their belief in God and have become more engrossed in secular activities. Frank, Sr., and Shawna both feel that their family is in this current predicament because they have done something against "God's will" for their lives. When this was explored further, they explained that they felt they may have committed a sin against God by not following "Biblical directives."

During the intake meeting, Frank, Sr., stated several times that he puts in overtime any time he can because money is "tight." Frank, Sr., explained that "tight" meant that he most times did not have enough to pay the bills in the house and provide for the other essential needs of the family. He expressed great concerns about having to attend the therapy sessions, as it would interfere with his overtime and interfere with his ability to bring in much needed income for the family. Shawntrice and Frank, Jr., were adamant that they did not need to attend any therapy sessions, but were not

(*continued*)

(continued)

willing to defy their parents' request that they attend. Shawna appeared anxious during the initial meeting and repeatedly asked if their church members would find out
about their having to come to therapy. The therapist assured her that the sessions were
confidential, and that they would be assisted through the process by developing a plan
that would be satisfactory to all involved. They were informed that it would be up to
them to complete those plans successfully. The therapist offered support through the
process and conveyed empathy around their response to the situation.

Together, the therapist and the Williams family discussed the plan for family treatment. It was decided that Frank, Sr., and Shawna would attend a 12-week positive parenting program (PPP), which also encompasses the spiritual parenting program (SPP)
along with weekly family sessions. This treatment modality encompasses the teaching
of techniques and skills to encourage parents to fulfill their role as the primary educators of their children. It utilizes both secular and spiritual readings and affirmations to
be utilized both in sessions and in the home. Mr. and Mrs. Williams will increase their
skills of encouraging, guiding, educating, and training their children "in the way that
they should go" while building on their current spiritual and practical development as
parents. The family sessions will utilize the ILS model in which the two generations—
Baby Busters (parents) and Millennials (children)—break down barriers between the
generations by intentionally listening to the values of each generation, and then challenging the generations to work together intergenerationally to come up with action
steps that can move the family toward common goals. The children, Frank, Jr., and
Shawntrice, would attend the family sessions coupled with an 8-week FBHH psychotherapy group to: (a) teach them how their thinking influences their behavior and relationship with self, others, and God; (b) facilitate cognitive restructuring through the
use of culturally relevant music and lyrics; and (c) reduce their tendencies to engage in
self-serving cognitive distortions or thinking errors.

In an effort to reduce some of the financial burden of the family attending
multiple sessions at the office, the SPP and the FBB is scheduled for the same day.
Also, the therapist offered to meet with the family at their home for the ILS family
sessions. Mr. and Mrs. Williams along with Shawntrice and Frank, Jr., agreed with
the plan as developed and assured the therapist that they would work really hard to
be compliant. They made it clear that they were still unsure about participating in
therapy, but were willing to give it a try because it was supported by their pastor.

FOR FURTHER STUDY

Suggested Assignments

1. What specific intervention strategies (skills, knowledge, etc.) should be used
   to address this family situation? *The pastor should make a referral to a social*

work practitioner; role-playing can be utilized to help family members view how each of them perceived their behaviors.

2. Which theory or theories can be used to guide your practice? *The strengths perspective and family systems theory can be utilized; focus on what resources the family had and how they could access the available resources (such as their spirituality) that had yet been untapped; and look at how the family interacted as a unit rather than as four separate individuals.*

3. What are the identified strengths of this family? *Frank, Sr., and Shawna loved each other and their children. There seemed to be a high level of spirituality among this family.*

4. What are the identified challenges faced by this family? *Economic restraints, health issues, intergenerational conflicts, unresolved anger and resentment, and the conflict between their spiritual beliefs and counseling from a practitioner who was not their pastor.*

5. What were the agreed-on goals to be met? *Attend parenting sessions, attend family session, and attend hip-hop psychotherapy group.*

6. Are there any issues of cultural competence that need to be address? *The Williams' culture around their spiritual beliefs and parenting should be considered. Their perspective based on their cultural lens must be considered when assessing this family.*

7. What local, state, or federal policies could affect this case? *If there were any "reasons to believe" that abuse occurred, the policies in reference to mandated reporting to Child Protective Services may come into play.*

8. Are there any legal or ethical issues present in this case? *The pastor requested to receive updates on the progress of the Williams' treatment. Ethically, the therapist may be torn between adherence to confidentiality and desire to maintain rapport with both family and pastor.*

9. How can evidence-based practice be integrated into this case? *The PPP is an evidence-based program to teach parenting skills; the SPP, IL, and FBHH are all research-informed modalities that are currently being tested.*

10. What was the relationship between the faith-based organization and social work agency? *The pastor made initial referral and the therapist acknowledged the spiritual beliefs of the Williams family and incorporated faith-based interventions in treatment; the pastor will need further education on the role of the therapist.*

Suggested Readings

Billingsley, A. (1999). *Mighty like a river: The black church and social reform*. New York, NY: Oxford University Press.

Boyd-Franklin, N. (2003). *Black families in therapy: Understanding the African American experience* (pp. 125–143). New York, NY: Guilford Press.

Boyd-Franklin, N., & Lockwood, T. W. (2009). Spirituality and religion: Implications for psychotherapy with African American families. In F. Walsh (Ed.), *Spiritual resources in family therapy* (2nd ed., pp. 141–155). New York, NY: Guilford Press.

Canda, E. R., & Furman, L. D. (2010). The meaning of spirituality. In E. R. Canda & L.D. Furman (Eds.), *Spiritual diversity in social work practice* 2nd ed. (pp. 59–95). New York, NY: Oxford University Press.

Frame, M. W. (2003). Chapter 10: Ethical considerations. In *Integrating religion and spirituality into counseling* (pp. 281–297). Pacific Grove, CA: Brooks/Cole.

Keller, R. R. (2000). Religious diversity in North America. In P. S. Richards & A. E. Bergin (Eds.), *Handbook of psychotherapy and religious diversity* (pp. 27–55). Washington, DC: American Psychological Association.

Koenig, H. G., McCullough, M. E., & Larson, D. B. (2001). *Handbook of religion and health*. Chapter 15 (pp. 214–228) and Chapter 25 (pp. 383–394). New York, NY: Oxford University Press.

Martin, E. P., & Martin, J. M. (2002). *Spirituality and the black helping tradition in social work*. Washington, DC: NASW Press.

Taylor, R., Chatters, M. L., & Levin, J. (2004). *Religion in the lives of African Americans: Sociological, psychological and health perspectives*. Thousand Oaks, CA: Sage.

REFERENCES

Archibald, P., & Daniels, K. (2013). *Utilization of an intergenerational life stage model to promote community-based mental health initiatives among urban African Americans in a faith based environment* (Unpublished manuscript). Baltimore, MD: Morgan State University.

Archibald, P., Daniels, K., & Cox, S. (2014). *The effects of a hip hop psychotherapy group on the risk reduction and spiritual enhancement of African-American youth attending church* (Unpublished manuscript). Baltimore, MD: Morgan State University.

Archibald, P., Dobson-Sydnor, K., Daniels, K., & Bronner, Y. (2013). Explaining African-Americans' depressive symptoms: A stress-distress and coping perspective. *Journal of Health Psychology, 18*(3), 321–331.

Austin, S., & Claiborne, N. (2011). Faith well collaborative: A community based approach to addressing type II diabetes disparities in an African American Community. *Social Work in Health Care, 50*(5), 360–375.

Ayalon, L., & Young, M. A. (2005). Racial group differences in help-seeking behaviors. *The Journal of Social Psychology, 145*(4), 391–404.

Barksdale, C. L., & Molock, S. D. (2009). Perceived norms and mental health help seeking among African American college students. *The Journal of Behavioral Health Services & Research, 36*(3), 285.

Bayer, P., Ferreira, F., & Ross, S. L. (2013). *The vulnerability of minority homeowners in the housing boom*. Working Paper 19020. Cambridge, MA: National Bureau of Economic Research.

Boyd-Franklin, N. (1989). Religion, spirituality, and the treatment of Black families. In N. B. Franklin (Ed.), *Black families in therapy: A multisystems approach* (pp. 78–83). New York, NY: Guilford Press.

Braithwaite, R. L., & Taylor, S. E. (2001). *Health issues in the Black community* (2nd ed.). San Francisco, CA: Jossey-Bass.

Brashears, F., & Roberts, M. (1996). The Black church as a resource for change. In S. L. Logan (Ed.), *The Black family: Strengths, self-help, and positive change* (pp. 181–191). Boulder, CO: Westview.

Breslau, J. (2005). Lifetime risk and persistence of psychiatric disorders across ethnic groups in the United States. *Psychological Medicine, 35*(3), 317.

Burris, J. C., & Billingsley, A. (1994). The black church and the community: Antebellum times to the present, case studies in social reform. *National Journal of Sociology, 8*(1–2), 25–47.

Caldwell, C. H., Chatters, L. M., Billingsley, A., & Taylor, R. J. (1995). Church-based support programs for elderly Black adults: Congregational and clergy characteristics. In M. A. Kimble, S. H. McFadden, J. W. Ellor, & J. Seeber (Eds.), *Handbook on religion, spirituality, and aging* (pp. 306–324). Minneapolis, MN: Augsburg Fortress.

Campbell, M. K., Hudson, M. A., Resnicow, K., Blakeney, N., Paxton, A., & Baskin, M. (2007). Church-based health promotion interventions: Evidence and lessons learned. *Annual Review of Public Health, 28*, 213–234.

Canda, E. R., & Furman, I. (2010). *Spiritual diversity in social work practice.* New York, NY: Oxford University Press.

Clinebell, H. J. (1997). Anchoring your well being: A guide for congregational leaders. Nashville, TN: The Upper Room.

Cnaan, R. A., Sinha, J. W., & McGrew, C. C. (2004). Congregations as social service providers: Services, capacity, culture, and organizational behavior. *Administration in Social Work, 28*(3/4), 47–68.

Collins, W. L. (2006). The black church as a practice resource: Networking on behalf of at-risk African American youth. *Journal of the North American Association of Christians in Social Work, 33*(2), 178–194.

Cook, D. A. (1993). Research in African American churches: A mental health counseling imperative. *Journal of Mental Health Counseling, 15*, 320–333.

Cook, D. A., & Wiley, C. Y. (2000). Psychotherapy with members of African American churches and spiritual traditions. In P. S. Richards, & A. E. Bergin (Eds.), *Handbook of psychotherapy and religious diversity* (pp. 185–209). Washington, DC: APA.

Cooper, A. E., Corrigan, P. W., & Watson, A. C. (2003). Brief reports: Mental illness stigma and care seeking. *The Journal of Nervous and Mental Disease, 191*(5), 339–341.

Daniels, K., & Archibald, P. (2011a). The levitical cycle of health: The church as a public health social work conduit for health promotion. *Social Work and Christianity, 38*(1), 88–100.

Daniels, K., & Archibald, P. (2011b). Merging community and faith-based organizations to empower African-American males. *Journal of Pastoral Care and Counseling, 65*(2), 1–6.

DeHaven, M. J., Hunter, I. R., Wilder, L., Walton, J. M., & Berry, J. (1994). Health programs in faith-based organizations: Are they effective? *American Journal of Public Health, 6*, 1030–1036.

De Marco, M., Weiner, B., Meade, S. A., Hadley, M., Boyd, C, Goldmon, M., . . . Corbie-Smith, G. (2011). Assessing the readiness of black churches to engage in health disparities research. *Journal of the National Medical Association, 103*(9 and 10), 960–967.

Diala, C., Muntaner, C., Walrath, C., Nickerson, K. J., LaVeist, T. A., & Leaf, P. J. (2000). Racial differences in attitudes toward professional mental health care and in the use of services. *American Journal of Orthopsychiatry, 70*(4), 455–464.

Eng, E., Hatch, J., & Callan, A. (1985). Institutionalizing social support through the church and into the community. *Health Education Quarterly, 12*(1), 81–92.

Erikson, E. H. (1959). *Identity and the life cycle. Part one. Psychological issues.* New York, NY: International Universities Press.

Frame, M. W., & Williams, C. B. (1996). Counseling African Americans: Integrating spirituality in therapy. *Counseling and Values, 41*(1), 116–128.

Gambone, J. V. (2002). *Together for tomorrow: Building community through intergenerational dialogue.* Crystal Bay, MN: Elder Eye Press.

Garland, B., & Yancey, G. (2012). Moving mountains: Congregation as a setting for social work practice. In T. Scales & M. Kelly (Eds.), *Christianity and social work* (4th ed., pp. 311–336). Botsford, CT: NACSW.

Glanz, K., & Rimer, B. K. (1997). *Theory at a glance. A guide for health promotion practice.* NIH Pub. No. 97—3896. Washington, DC: U.S. Department of Health & Human Service, National Cancer Institute, National Institutes of Health.

Gurin, P., Hatchett, S., & Jackson, J. (1989). *Hope and independence: Blacks' response to electoral and party politics.* New York, NY: Russel Sage Foundation.

Healthy People 2000. (1991). *National Health Promotion and Disease Prevention Objectives* (DHHS publication PHS 91–50212). Washington, DC: US Department of Health and Human Services.

Holt, C. L., & McClure, S. M. (2006). Perceptions of the religion-health connection among African-American church members. *Qualitative Health Research, 16*(2), 268–281.

Kosmin, B. A., & Keysar, A. (2009). *American Religious Identification Survey (ARIS) 2008. Summary report of the Leonard E. Greenberg Center for the Study of Religion in Public Life.* Hartford, CT: Trinity College.

Kramer, M., Rosen, B., & Willis, E. (1973). Definitions and distributions of mental disorders in a racist society. In C. Willie, M. Kramer, & B. Brown (Eds.), *Racism and mental health* (pp. 353–459). Pittsburgh, PA: University of Pittsburgh Press.

Lasater, T. M., Becker, D. M., Hill, M. N., & Gans, K. M. (1997). Synthesis of findings and issues from religious-based cardiovascular disease prevention trials. *Annals of Epidemiology, 7*(57), s47–s53.

Lincoln, C., & Mamiya, L. (1990). *The Black church in the African-American experience.* Durham, NC: Duke University Press.

Lopez, S. J., Prosser, E. C., Edwards, L. M., Magyar-Moe, J. L., Neufeld, J. E., & Rasmussen, H. N. (2002). Putting positive psychology in a multicultural context. In C. R. Snyder & S. J. Lopez (Eds.), *Handbook of positive psychology* (pp. 700–714). New York, NY: Oxford University Press.

Markens, S., Fox, S. A., Taub, B., & Gilbert, M. L. (2002). Role of black churches in health promotion programs: Lessons from the Los Angeles mammography promotion in churches program. *American Journal of Public Health, 92*(5), 805–810.

Martin, E. P., & Martin, J. M. (2002). *Spirituality and the Black helping tradition.* Washington, DC: NASW Press.

Mattis, J. S. (2000). African-American women's definitions of spirituality and religiosity. In African-American culture and identity: Research directions for the new millennium. *Journal of Black Psychology, 26*(1), 101–122.

Mays, B., & Nicholson, J. (1933). *The Negro's church.* New York, NY: Institute of Social and Religious Research.

McAdoo, H. P., & Crawford, V. (1991). The Black church and family support programs: The limits of individual efforts. *Journal of Health and Social Behavior, 25*, 406–423.

McKernan, M. M., Ratclife, C., Steuerle, E., & Zhang, S. (2014). *Impact of the great recession and beyond: Disparities in wealth building by generation and race.* Working Paper. Washington DC: Urban Institute.

McLane-Davison, D. (2013). The art of activist mothering: Black feminist leadership and knowing what to do. In D. Davis-Maya, A. D. Yarer & T. E. Perry (Eds.), *What My Press of America* (pp. 137–215). Lanham, MD: University Press of America.

Montgomery, W. E. (1993). *Under their own vine and fig tree: The African-American Church in the South, 1865–1900.* Baton Rouge: Louisiana State University.

Moore, T. (1991). The African American church: A source of empowerment, mutual help, and social change. *Prevention in Human Services, 10*, 147–167.

Newman, R. S. (2009). *Freedom's prophet: Bishop Richard Allen, the AME church and the Black founding fathers.* New York: New York University Press.

Niebuhr, H. R. (1951). *Christ and culture.* New York, NY: Harper Collins.

Nobles, W. (2004). African philosophy: Foundations of black psychology. In R. L. Jones (Ed.), *Black psychology* (4th ed., pp 23–26). New York, NT: Harper & Row.

Pfeffer, F. T., Danziger, S., & Schoeni, R. F. (2013). *Wealth disparities before and after the Great Recession.* Working Paper #13–05. Ann Arbor, MI: National Poverty Center.

Pinn, A. (2002). *The African American church in the post-civil rights era.* Maryknoll, NY: OrbisBooks.

Plante, T. G. (2008). What do the spiritual and religious traditions offer the practicing psychologist? *Pastoral Psychology, 56,* 429–444.

Richardson, B. L., & June, L. N. (1997). Utilizing and maximizing the resources of the African American church: Strategies and tools for counseling. In C. C. Lee (Ed.), *Multicultural issues in counseling: New approaches to diversity* (2nd ed., pp. 155–170). Alexandria, VA: American Counseling Association.

Roberston, D. (2009). *Denmark Vesey: The buried story of America's largest slave rebellion and the man who led it.* New York, NY: Random House.

Rosen, G. (1993). *A history of public health.* Baltimore, MD: Johns Hopkins Press.

Sanders-Thompson, V. L., Bazile, A., & Akbar, M. (2004). African Americans' perceptions of psychotherapy and psychotherapists. *Professional Psychology: Research and Practice, 35*(1), 19–26.

Schiele, J. H. (2000). *Human services and the Afrocentric paradigm.* New York, NY: The Haworth Press.

Schnieder, R., & Lester, L. (2001). *Social work advocacy: A new framework for action.* Belmont, CA: Brooks/Cole.

Shapiro, T., Meschede, T., & Osoro, S. (2013). *The roots of the widening racial wealth gap: Explaining the Black-White economic divide.* Waltham, MA: Institute on Assets and Social Policy, Brandeis University.

Sheehan, A., Austin, S., Brennan-Jordan, N., Frenn, D., Kelman, G., & Scotti, D. (2013). The impact of Parish nurses teaching defy diabetes healthy living classes in a faith-based community. *Journal of Christian Nursing, 30*(4), 244–247.

Tangenberg, K. M. (2005). Faith-based human services initiatives: Considerations for social work practice and theory. *Social Work, 50*(3), 197–206.

Taylor, R. J., & Chatters, L. M. (1988). Church members as a source of informal social support. *Review of Religious Research, 30*(2), 192–203.

Taylor, R. J., Chatters, L. M., & Levin, J. (2004). *Religion in the lives of African-Americans.* Thousand Oaks, CA: Sage.

Thomas, S. B., Quinn, S. C., Billingsley, A., & Caldwell, C. (1994). The characteristics of northern Black churches with community health outreach programs. *American Journal of Public Health, 84*(4), 575–579.

Travis, R., & Deepak, A. (2011). Empowerment in context: Lessons from hip-hop culture for social work practice. *Journal of Ethnic & Cultural Diversity in Social Work, 20,* 203–222.

U.S. Department of Labor Statistics. (2014). Employment status of the civilian noninstitutional population by sex, age, and race, 2013. Retrieved from http://www.bls.gov/cps/cpsaat05.pdf

Waites, C. (2008). *Social work practice with African American families: An intergenerational perspective.* New York, NY: Routledge.

Whaley, A. L. (2001). Cultural mistrust and mental health services for African-Americans: A review and meta-analysis. *The Counseling Psychologist, 29*(4), 513–531.

Wilks, T. (2012). *Advocacy and social work practice.* Maidenhead, England: Open University Press.

Williams, D. R., Gonzalez, H. M., Neighbors, H., Nesse, R., Abelson, J. M., Sweetman, J., & Jackson, J. S. (2007). Prevalence and distribution of major depressive disorder in African Americans, Caribbean Blacks, and Non-Hispanic Whites. Results from the National Survey of American Life. *Archives of General Psychiatry, 64,* 305–315.

CHAPTER 9

Urban Health: Four Issues of Concern

Linda Darrell and LaPricia Lewis Boyer

"In spite of all I've been through I still have joy," perhaps not a jubilant joy but joy nonetheless. Joy that I have made it in spite of it all. This may be an unorthodox way to open a chapter on health concerns within the urban community, but one must never overlook the strength, resolve, and resilient spirit with which many urban residents have faced debilitating effects of chronic illness. Chronic illness within the urban community impacts persons across gender and age. Chronic illness affects physical, psychological, and social development; educational processes; earning capacity; and longevity. Each of these issues creates opportunities for social workers to practice from a systemic perspective and to assist individuals, families, and communities at multiple levels.

This chapter is not meant to address the disenfranchised manner in which many residents are treated or receive services within urban communities. That information is provided in a multiplicity of public health research studies and reports. This chapter provides basic information on illnesses such as diabetes, hypertension, cardiovascular disease, and sickle cell anemia, which are but a few of the most prevalent and chronic purveyors of physical, psychological, and social disabling effects among African Americans in urban communities. Along with the physiological impact of these diagnoses, mental health challenges such as depression and anxiety are frequently serious side effects resulting in increased disabling consequences.

The first goal of this chapter is to provide awareness about the nature and prevalence of four of the most widespread disabling illnesses impacting members of the urban community through the provision of empirical data. The establishment of empirical data will demonstrate the preponderance of these illnesses among African Americans and other persons of color who make up the overwhelming majority of inner city residents.

The second goal is to provide information to social work clinicians to incorporate facts into the services they offer in an effort to educate individuals, families, and communities about these illnesses and their long-term effects, along with ways to help identify symptoms that are frequently overlooked, ignored, or denied by those most significantly impacted. The third goal is to offer social work clinicians practical ways to engage and empower community persons with help-seeking and positive problem-solving behaviors. These three goals will help empower individuals, families, and communities as they relate to increased health knowledge. Empowered individuals can become more proactive in the identification of familiar patterns of illnesses and their treatment as a way to decrease the debilitating consequences of minimally treated disorders within families.

Physical and mental illnesses impact all levels of health and well-being, and these four chronic illnesses seem to be the most pervasive, debilitating, and prominent within the urban community. This chapter provides an overview of each illness utilizing an inclusive life-span approach as a way to assist the urban social work clinician in understanding not only the significance of the illness on the individual but also the implications of the illness within the family and community. In order to provide consistency in the approach to each of the four chronic illness diagnoses, the chapter is laid out from genetically based diagnosis to those illnesses that may have a genetic marker but can perhaps be better managed or avoided through improved self-care.

Each diagnosis will include live web-based links, which will provide access to current information, exercises, and downloads. These downloads are derived from links that can be used as educational resources when developing individual or small-group discussions and/or trainings.

SICKLE CELL ANEMIA

What Is Sickle Disease?

Sickle cell anemia is the most common form of sickle cell disease (SCD). SCD is a serious disorder in which the body makes sickle-shaped red blood cells. Sickle-shaped red blood cells are shaped like a crescent, where normal red blood cells are disc shaped and look like doughnuts without holes in the center. Normal disc-shaped red blood cells move easily through the blood vessels; they contain an iron-rich protein called hemoglobin. This protein carries oxygen to and from the lungs to the rest of the body. Sickle cells contain abnormal hemoglobin called sickle hemoglobin, or hemoglobin S, which causes the cells to develop a sickle, or crescent, shape. Sickle cells are stiff and sticky, and they block blood flow in the blood vessels of the limbs and organs. Blocked blood flow can cause pain and organ damage. It can also raise the risk for infection (National Institutes of Health, National Heart, Lung, and Blood Institute, 2014).

Sickle cell anemia is a condition in which one's blood has a lower than normal number of red blood cells. Red blood cells are made in the spongy marrow inside the larger bones of the body. Bone marrow is always making new red blood cells to replace old ones. Normal red blood cells live about 120 days in the bloodstream and then die. They carry oxygen and remove carbon dioxide (a waste product) from our bodies. In sickle cell anemia, the abnormal sickle cells usually die within 10 to 20 days, and the bone marrow cannot make new red blood cells fast enough to replace the dying ones.

What Causes Sickle Cell Anemia?

Sickle cell anemia is an inherited disease, and people who have the disease inherit one gene from each parent. Some people have sickle cell trait (SCT) but not the disease because they have inherited one sickle hemoglobin gene from one parent and a normal gene from the other parent. Persons with SCT usually have few, if any, symptoms and lead normal lives. However, some people may have medical complications. People who have SCT can pass the sickle hemoglobin gene to their children (National Institutes of Health, National Heart, Lung, and Blood Institute, 2014).

Who Is Affected and How Are They Affected?

Sickle cell anemia is an inherited lifelong disease. Some people who have the disease have chronic pain or fatigue. Sickle cell is most common in people whose families come from Africa, South or Central America, Caribbean islands, Mediterranean countries, India, and Saudi Arabia. In the United States, it is estimated that sickle cell anemia affects 70,000 to 100,000 people, mainly African Americans. The disease occurs in about one out of every 500 African American births. Sickle cell anemia also affects Hispanic Americans. The disease occurs in more than one out of every 36,000 Hispanic American births. More than 2 million Americans have the SCT. The condition occurs in about one in 12 African Americans.

Sickle cell anemia is present at birth, but many infants do not show any signs until after 4 months of age. The most common signs and symptoms are linked to anemia and pain. Other signs and symptoms are linked to the complications of disease, such as shortness of breath, dizziness, headaches, coldness in the hands and feet, paler than normal skin or mucous membranes, and jaundice. Sudden pain throughout the body is a common symptom of sickle cell anemia. The pain is called a sickle cell crisis. Sickle cell crises often affect the bones, lungs, abdomen, and joints. Both children and adults who have sickle cell anemia may get infections easily and have a hard time fighting infections.

SCD in children can lead to hand–foot syndrome, which is caused by the sickle cell blocking the small blood vessels in the hands and feet in children, usually those younger than 4 years of age. Swelling often occurs on the back of the hands and feet and moves into the fingers and toes. One or both hands and/or feet might be affected at the same time. Another complication of SCD is a splenic crisis. The spleen is an organ in the abdomen that normally filters out normal red blood cells and helps fight infections. Because of the sickle shape of the red blood cells caused by the disease, the spleen may trap the red blood cells that should be in the bloodstream. This causes the spleen to grow large and leads to anemia. If the spleen traps too many red blood cells, blood transfusions may be needed until the body can make more cells and recover. Infants and young children who have damaged spleens are more likely to get serious infections that can kill them within hours or days. Bloodstream infections are the most common cause of death in young children who have sickle cell anemia. Getting treatment right away for high fevers (which can be a sign of a severe infection) also helps prevent death in infants and children who have sickle cell anemia. It is also important to get treatment right away for a cough, problems with breathing, bone pain, and headaches.

Developmental Issues

Scholars Thompson, Gustafson, Bonner, and Ware (2002) concluded that young children with SCD are at risk of neurocognitive impairment. They cite Brown, Armstrong, and Eckman (1993) in research, which demonstrates that children with SCD are at a high risk of neurocognitive deficits and poor academic performance associated with the complications of SCD, which include infarction of major cerebral arteries or microvascular systems, silent infarcts, and a chronic state of anemia and poor oxygen to the brain due to poor pulmonary function and oxygen saturation.

The high rates of morbidity and mortality associated with chronic anemia, vaso-occlusive events, and tissue damage resulting from obscured blood flow in SCD have a major impact on individuals and families with the disease and make it a significant public health concern (Ashley-Koch, Yang, & Olney, 2000). In the United States, approximately 83,000 adults and 30,000 children were hospitalized with an SCD discharge diagnosis in 2004 alone, generating estimated costs of almost $500 million (Steiner & Miller, 2006). In addition, as many as 3 million individuals in the United States carry SCT and although SCT is largely asymptomatic, it has been associated under certain conditions with an increased risk of serious adverse events, including sudden death during strenuous exercise, venous thromboembolism, and renal complications (Jordan et al., 2011). According to researchers Boyd, Watkins, Price, Fleming, and DeBaun (2005), in spite of the prevalence and serious burden of this genetic disorder, community knowledge regarding the inheritance pattern of SCD, knowledge of personal sickle cell status, and the health and reproductive implications of SCD and SCT remains inadequate.

Bearing in mind the serious consequences of SCD and SCT, social work clinicians must recognize the stress on patients, parents, and caregivers of persons diagnosed with this illness. Caregiver stress and distress have been linked with both less-optimal caregiver interactions and family functioning and lower child development competencies (Crnic & Greenberg, 1990). Thompson et al. (1994) and Thompson, Gustafson, Gil, Kinney, and Spock (1999) state that 13% to 20% of mothers of children with SCD have consistently high levels of psychological distress related to high levels of daily stress and family functioning characteristics with less supportiveness and more control. Considering the complexities of SCD and SCT, the opportunities for social work clinicians to provide educational and supportive services to parents and families of children impacted by this illness are numerous.

Social workers' knowledge of early assessments and interventions becomes most imperative in helping families to understand the significance of the illness as well as learning effective coping skills to allay the risk of developing a learned helplessness attributional style that would negatively affect parenting directly, as well as indirectly through impact on psychological distress (Thompson et al., 2002). With proper care and treatment, many people who have the disease can have improved quality of life and reasonable health most of the time. Because of improved treatments and care, people who have sickle cell anemia are now living into their 40s and 50s or longer (National Institutes of Health, National Heart, Lung, and Blood Institute, 2012).

The following link will enable individuals to access extensive information about SCD along with resources for education, assessment, and potential treatment options.

National Institutes of Health, National Heart, Lung, and Blood Institute: www .nhlbi.nih.gov/health/health-topics/topics/sca

DIABETES

What Is Diabetes?

Diabetes is caused when the body does not make enough insulin or cannot use it well. This causes high levels of glucose (blood sugar) to build up in the blood, which results in the body not working as it should. There are two types of diabetes. Type 1 diabetes occurs when the body stops making insulin. Type 2 diabetes occurs when some insulin is made but the body cannot use it well. Type 2 diabetes is more common. Information provided by the American Diabetes Association (2014a, b, c) states that, in most cases of type 1 diabetes, people need to inherit risk factors from both White parents because Whites have the highest rate of type 1 diabetes. Type 2 diabetes has a stronger link to family history and lineage than type 1, although it, too, depends on environmental factors. If there is a family history of type 2 diabetes, it may be difficult to figure out whether the diabetes is due to lifestyle factors or genetic susceptibility.

What Are the Risk Factors for Diabetes?

The American Diabetes Association (2014a, b, c) informs us that in most cases of type 1 diabetes, people need to inherit risk factors from both parents. However, researchers are also studying the environmental triggers for persons who are predisposed to diabetes but may not actually have the diagnosis. Type 1 and type 2 diabetes do have different causes, yet two factors are important in both. One inherits a predisposition to the disease, and then something in his or her environment triggers it. In type 1 diabetes, researchers believe cold weather may be a trigger. Type 1 diabetes develops more often in winter than in summer and is more common in places with cold climates. Two other triggers for type 1 diabetes are early diet including baby formula containing sugars and other food containing starches, sugars, and carbohydrates compared to breastfeeding and the impact of previous viruses.

Type 2 diabetes has a stronger link to family history and lineage, although, according to the American Diabetes Association (2014a, b, c), type 2 diabetes can also be dependent on environmental factors. Lifestyle also influences the development of type 2 diabetes. Obesity as a risk factor for type 2 diabetes is likewise prevalent in many families with members who have similar eating and minimal exercise habits.

The risks of children developing diabetes are different for both types of diabetes. In type 1 diabetes, the odds of your child developing diabetes are 1 in 17. For women with type 1 diabetes and their children being born before they were 25 years old, their children's risk is 1 in 100. The risk of children developing diabetes doubles if the parent develops diabetes before the age of 11 years. If both parents have type 1 diabetes, the risk is between 1 in 10 and 1 in 4. As indicated earlier, type 2 diabetes runs in families and is also linked to poor diet and a sedentary lifestyle. If your parent(s) have type 2 diabetes and you were diagnosed before the age of 50 years, the risk of the children developing diabetes is one in seven; if diagnosed after the age of 50 years, the risk is 1 in 13. Some researchers believe that a child's risk is greater when the parent with type 2 diabetes is the mother. If both parents have type 2 diabetes, the risk is one in two that the child will develop diabetes (American Diabetes Association, 2014a, b, c).

Who Is Affected and What Is the Impact?

According to the American Diabetes Association, diabetes is one of the most serious health problems that the African American community faces today. Compared to the general population, African Americans are disproportionately affected by diabetes (American Diabetes Association, 2014b, c). The statistical data provided in the National Diabetes Statistics Report (American Diabetes Association, 2014c) indicate that the prevalence of diabetes in 2012 was 29.1 million Americans, or 9.3% of the population. Diabetes was the seventh leading cause of death in the United States in 2010, with 69,071 death certificates listing it as the underlying cause of death, and a total of 234,051 death certificates listing it as an underlying or contributing cause of death. There are nine most prevalent complications and comorbid conditions due to diabetes that are debilitating and create major burdens for persons directly impacted and their families. These conditions are hypoglycemia; hypertension; dyslipidemia; cardiovascular disease; heart attacks; stroke; blindness and eye problems; kidney disease, which is the cause of renal failure; and amputations due to diabetes, caused by nerve damage. The cost of diabetes as documented in 2013 by the American Diabetes

Association is $245 billion, a 41% increase from a previous estimate of $174 billion in 2007, making diabetes a substantial burden on the economy of the United States in the form of increased medical costs and indirect costs from work-related absenteeism, reduced productivity at work and at home, reduced labor force participation from chronic disability, and premature mortality (American Diabetes Association, 2003). In addition to the economic burden that has been quantified, diabetes imposes high tangible costs on society in terms of reduced quality of life and pain, and suffering of people with diabetes, their families, and friends (American Diabetes Association, 2008).

Concerns regarding the impact of illness on young children are important to clinicians working with this population. Instructing families in a variety of methods addressing coping skills and self-management is an essential task for clinicians. This illness is noted to affect growth and puberty, in that, the impact of chronic illness affects biological, psychological, and social development as separate as well as interrelated domains (Suris, Michaud, & Viner, 2004). Maddux, Roberts, Sledden, and Wright (1986) state that cognitive and intellectual development is crucial to the child's ability to understand the relationship among behavior, health, and illness, and to make decisions about his or her health behavior. Psychosocial development is critical to the issue of individual responsibility in health behavior, and developmental issues for children were addressed in a study conducted by Band and Weisz (1990), who noted that a developmental perspective may be essential for an accurate understanding of children's adaptation to chronic illnesses such as diabetes. Additional research in this area is needed to increase the knowledge base of social work clinicians and other health care professionals to work collaboratively on behalf of this understudied population.

Social work clinicians, particularly in urban communities, have immense opportunities to engage persons impacted by diabetes and the multiple comorbid debilitating conditions through psychosocial treatment methods such as problem solving. Problem solving is an essential skill for effective diabetes self-management (Schumann, Sutherland, Majid, & Hill-Briggs, 2011), and successful problem-solving techniques may positively affect persons with diabetes, their families, and friends. Problem solving, which has its origins in the behavioral and cognitive basic sciences, is an identified intervention approach for behavior change (Schumann et al., 2011). There are many educational modules, such as "Just A Touch," which is a community-based program addressing issues related to nerve damage known as neuropathy. Another community-based program is Project Power, which provides resources for creating awareness about diabetes among members and families. Choose to Live is a diabetes awareness toolkit targeting African American women between the ages of 35 and 55 years. Each of these programs and many others can be accessed through www.diabetes.org/in-my-community/awareness-programs. Information about diagnosis, treatment, and management of diabetes can be accessed through agencies such as the National Institutes of Health (NIH), National Heart, Lung, and Blood Institute, which provides resources for community health workers. Information on the genetics of diabetes can be found at www.diabetes.org/diabetes-basics/genetics-of-diabetes.html.

CORONARY HEART DISEASE

What Is Coronary Heart Disease?

Coronary heart disease (CHD) is a disease in which a waxy substance called plaque (plak) builds up inside coronary arteries. These arteries supply oxygen-rich blood to your heart muscle. When plaque builds up in the arteries, the condition is called athero-sclerosis (ATH-er-o-skler-O-sis). The buildup of plaque over time can harden or rupture (break open) arteries causing them to weaken. Hardened plaque narrows the coronary arteries and reduces the flow of oxygen-rich blood to the heart (National Institutes of Health, National Heart, Lung, and Blood Association, 2014).

The causes of CHD are attributed to

1. High levels of cholesterol in the blood

2. Smoking

3. High blood pressure

4. High levels of sugar in the blood due to insulin resistance or diabetes

5. Blood vessel inflammation.

Plaque might begin to build up where the arteries are damaged. The buildup of plaque in the coronary arteries may start in childhood. Arteries narrowed and damaged from plaque buildup can cause chest pain or angina. If the plaque ruptures, blood fragments called platelets stick to the site of the injury. They may clump together to form blood clots. Blood clots can further narrow the coronary arteries and worsen angina. If a clot becomes large enough, it can mostly or completely block a coronary artery and cause a heart attack (National Institutes of Health, National Heart, Lung, and Blood Institute, 2014).

Who Is at Risk of CHD?

There are certain traits, conditions, or habits that raise the risk for developing CHD. The more risk factors you have, the more likely you are to develop a heart disease. The major risk factors for developing CHD are inclusive of the aforementioned chronic illnesses. The other risk factors are:

1. Unhealthy high levels of low-density lipoprotein (LDL; sometimes referred to as bad cholesterol) in the blood, caused by high-fat diets and lack of exercise, and low levels of high-density lipoprotein (HDL; good cholesterol). The target amount for bad cholesterol (LDL) in people with diabetes should be less than 100 mg/dL. The good cholesterol (HDL), which helps protect your heart and blood vessels, should be more than 40 mg/dL for men and more than 50 md/dL for a woman.

2. High blood pressure: Blood pressure is measured by two numbers; the systolic blood pressure is the first (or top) number. Systolic blood pressure is the amount of force exerted on the arteries when the heart beats, pumping blood. This number should be less than 140 mmHg. For people with diabetes or chronic kidney disease, this number should be less than 130 mmHg. The diastolic blood pressure is the force being exerted on the arteries between heartbeats, when the heart is at rest. This number should be less than 90 mmHg. For people with diabetes or chronic kidney disease, this number should be less than 80 mmHg.

3. Smoking can damage and tighten blood vessels, lead to unhealthy cholesterol levels, and raise blood pressure. Smoking can also limit the amount of oxygen that reaches the body's tissues.

4. Insulin resistance is a condition that occurs if the body cannot make its own insulin properly. Insulin is a hormone that helps move blood sugar into cells where it is used for energy. Insulin resistance may lead to diabetes.

5. Diabetes is diagnosed when the body's blood sugar level is too high because the body does not make enough insulin or does not use its insulin properly. There are tests that can be taken to provide information about one's blood sugar level. For persons with diabetes, the first test taken in the morning is called the fasting blood sugar. This test is taken before breakfast and can be taken on your own at home. The fasting blood sugar should be between 90 and 130 mg/dL. Persons with diabetes are frequently required to also test their blood sugar levels about 2 hours after eating. This will tell how the foods they ate changed their blood sugar level. Two hours after you eating, blood sugar should be less than 180 mg/dL.

6. Overweight or obesity are terms used to describe body weight. Being overweight or obese is a high-risk factor for developing diabetes and CHD. Being overweight or obese can limit one's ability to exercise, as well as build up bad cholesterol levels. A person's weight should be in proportion to his or her height and body type.

7. Lack of physical exercise can worsen risk factors for CHD, such as unhealthy blood cholesterol levels, high blood pressure, diabetes, and overweight or obesity.

8. An unhealthy diet can raise your risk for CHD. Foods high in salt (sodium), saturated fats and trans fats, cholesterol, and sugar can worsen other risk factors for CHD. The following information is added as a way to identify what a healthy diet might look like (National Institutes of Health, National Heart, Lung, and Blood Institute, 2014). A multicenter, randomized feeding study known as The Dietary Approaches to Stop Hypertension (DASH; Appel et al.,1997) sought to examine the effects of dietary factors on blood pressure control. According to the DASH study, efforts to reduce the prevalence of hypertension have focused on nonpharmacologic approaches to lower blood pressure, such as reducing the intake of salt, reduced alcohol consumption,

TABLE 9.1 Foods to Watch Out For If You Have Diabetes: DASH Diet

FOODS WITH HIDDEN SUGARS	TRADITIONAL SUGAR FOODS
Starches and carbohydrates (potatoes, rice, bread, pasta/noodle, beans, crackers)	Soft drinks, sodas, regular chocolates, candy, alcohol, beer
Fruits	Regular (sweetened) tea and punch mixes
Fruit juices, sweetened water	Sweetened desserts, pastries, cookies
Milk, coffee creamers	Regular candies
Drink plenty of water	

Source: Appel et al., 1997; Hill-Briggs et al., 2011. Adapted with permission.

and possibly the increase of potassium as nutritional approaches to prevent and treat hypertension (Appel et al., 1997). According to the results of this study, the DASH diet (see Table 9.1) consists of fruits, vegetables, and low-fat dairy products with reduced saturated fat, all of which demonstrated certain dietary patterns can favorably affect blood pressure in adults. (Appel et al., 1997)

The incidence of heart failure increases exponentially with age, with an overall lifetime risk of approximately 20%. Although heart failure is generally considered a disease of the elderly, it is notable that African Americans often experience an earlier onset of the disease (Braithwaite, Taylor, & Treadwell, 2009). According to Braithwaite et al. (2009), African Americans manifest a higher prevalence of the major risk factors for developing heart failure: hypertension, obesity, diabetes, and left ventricular hypertrophy. This information is supported by researchers who indicate that the higher risk of heart failure among African Americans is primarily related to the higher prevalence of hypertension, diabetes, and lower socioeconomic status (Loehr, Rosamond, Chang, Folsom, & Chambless, 2008). The inclusion of socioeconomic factors in the research conducted by Loehr et al. (2008) suggests the potential of access to quality health care and the effective diagnosis and management of risk factors (e.g., hypertension) as an important determinant of health disparities related to heart failure (Braithwaite et al., 2009).

A recent research study entitled Achieving Blood Pressure Control Together (ACT) seeks to educate persons with hypertension, diabetes, and cardiac disease to identify risks factors and to develop effective problem-solving skills to help decrease and perhaps ameliorate negative health outcomes (Ephraim et al., 2014). Utilizing a basic human thinking process such as problem solving in a nonthreatening therapeutic format can assist persons facing struggles of illness; self-management can be empowered to reduce their behavioral risks and transfer their knowledge to family members and friends. The ACT study used materials with a demonstrated efficacy in a population with diabetes mellitus adapted for a population with hypertension (Hill-Briggs et al., 2011). The problem-solving approach has its origins in the behavioral and cognitive basic sciences (Smith, 1991), and is an identified intervention approach for behavior change (D'Zurilla & Goldfried, 1971). Although problem solving is a counseling approach that may be incorporated within other intervention models, PST is a stand-alone intervention with a long-standing history (Schumann et al., 2011). PST can be utilized by social workers in the urban community as a way to engage persons in their own health management, thereby developing a sense of empowerment and positive self-care. More information on coronary artery disease can be found at www.nhlbi.nih.gov/health/health-topics/topics/cad.

HYPERTENSION

What Is Hypertension?

Hypertension is traditionally defined as a persistent systolic blood pressure of at least 140 mmHg and/or a diastolic blood pressure of at least 90 mmHg, or blood pressure that is controlled to guideline-recommended levels using antihypertensive medication (National Institutes of Health, National Heart, Lung, and Blood Institute, 2014). Hypertension is one of the several common devastating and treatable disorders that disproportionately affect African Americans. The chronic elevation of blood pressure in patients with hypertension predisposes them to cardiovascular disease complications such as stroke, myocardial infarction (heart attack), heart failure, and renal failure (Davis, Quarrels, & Gibbons, 2009).

Who Is Impacted by Hypertension?

According to Collins and Winkleby (2002), African Americans have some of the highest rates of hypertension in the world. Their study identified subgroups of U.S. African American women and men with particularly high and low rates of hypertension. Davis et al. (2009) provide statistical data, which state that the rates of adult hypertension have increased by an average of 5%, with an overall rate increasing from 24.4% in 1994 to 28.9% in 2004. This increase has been seen across gender and racial–ethnic groups. The rates of adult hypertension range from 27.1% among Mexican Americans and 27.4% among non-Hispanic Whites to 40.1% among non-Hispanic Blacks. Among African Americans, 40.8% of women and 39.1% of men have hypertension. Davis et al. (2009) indicate that hypertension shows up earlier in African Americans than in the general population, with hypertension rates that are twice as high for young African Americans as for their peers in other racial–ethnic groups. Ten percent of African American men from 18 to 29 years of age have hypertension, in comparison with 5.5% of White men and 3.5% of Mexican American men. This racial disparity is less pronounced among young women than young men. Rates of hypertension increase with age, culminating in rates of 83% in African American men and women aged 70 years or older. According to Fields et al. (2004), in a study to establish the preponderance of hypertension in the United States during 1999 to 2000, at least 65 million adults had hypertension. The total hypertension prevalence rate was 31.3%. This figure represents adults with elevated systolic or diastolic blood pressure, or using antihypertensive medications at a rate of 28.4%, and adults who otherwise by medical history were told by a physician or health professional that they had high blood pressure. Approximately 25 million women and 30 million men had hypertension. At least 48 million non-Hispanic White adults, 9 million non-Hispanic Black adults, 3 million Mexican American adults, and 5 million other adults had hypertension.

To this point, information on hypertension has focused on adults. Researchers Hansen, Gunn, and Kaelber (2007) address the issue of hypertension in children and adolescents. According to these researchers, hypertension is a common chronic disease in children. There is an estimated prevalence between 2% and 5% of pediatric hypertension. Hypertension in children has been shown to correlate with a family history of hypertension, low birth weight, and excess weight. With increasing prevalence of childhood weight problems, increased attention to weight-related health conditions including hypertension is warranted (Must et al., 1999). Researchers Ogden et al. (2006) and Strauss and Pollack (2001) have all conducted research in the area of obesity in the United States, particularly among children; their research provides evidence that suggests that blood pressure in children and adolescents is increasing in parallel with weight (Hansen et al., 2007). With multiple risks of increased obesity, limited access to fresh-food markets, negative influence of familial predisposition to hypertension, and inadequate education in urban communities about the hazards of these issues does not serve children or adolescents well.

IMPLICATIONS FOR THE FUTURE

Davis et al. (2009) address culture and family lifestyle behaviors of African Americans as significant in the development of efficacious interventions to ameliorate issues of obesity and compliance to health education and medical treatment. The resilience and salutatory aspects of African American communities provide excellent opportunities for programs aimed toward enhancing health. Furthermore, it has been suggested that culturally sensitive interventions for minority populations should pay attention to several important factors during planning and execution phases: (a) degree of family influence; (b) level of acculturation and identity; (c) differential family member acculturation leading to family conflict; (d) family migration and relocation history; (e) trauma, loss, and possible posttraumatic stress due to relocation; (f) work and financial stressors; and (g) language preferences and impediments due to English as a second language and level of literacy in the native language. These complex issues related to cultural sensitivity reinforce the importance of family-based interventions to address cardiovascular risk factor reduction (Davis et al., 2009). According to Davis et al. (2009), cardiovascular risk behaviors are learned early in life from family members. In contrast to efforts to promote behavioral change in high-risk adults, an alternative and potentially more effective approach is to begin teaching healthy lifestyle habits to young children before they form unhealthy habits that are resistant to change.

Social workers have major opportunities to intervene on micro, macro, and mezzo levels to support resilience and empower families in matters of health concerns, health education, and supportive services in urban communities. Social workers as active community organizers, culturally competent clinicians, and family practitioners can intervene with both in-school and after-school programs to provide appropriate educational tools in the development of exercise programs, and dietary and physical education information for children and adolescents. With increased activity, healthier diets, and less sedentary lifestyles, social workers working collaboratively with schools, community-based agencies, and churches may assist in lowering the potential increase of obesity among children and adolescents. The implementation of supplementary Internet activities, such as Wii games, may also aid in increased levels of family involvement during indoor as well as outdoor activities.

FOR FURTHER STUDY

Suggested Assignments

Assignment # 1: Awareness—Interview your family and develop a genogram that depicts the most prevalent illnesses within your family.

Assignment #2: Education—Visit www.nhlbi.nih.gov/health/health-topics/topics/sca. Identify educational, assessment, and treatment options that will assist you in your work with families in which SCD is a prevalent issue. Develop an educational tract that can be shared with families.

Assignment #3: Empowerment—Access www.diabetes.org/diabetes-basics/genetics-of-diabetes.html. Identify community-based resources that can be utilized in a group setting to inform community members about the genetics of diabetes. Obtain information from the library that will assist you in writing a small group plan to disseminate health information.

Suggested Readings

National Institutes of Health, National Heart, Lung, and Blood Institute: http://www.nhlbi.nih.gov/health/health-topics/topics/sca

American Diabetes Association—Genetics of diabetes: http://www.diabetes.org/diabetes-basics/genetics-of-diabetes.html

National Institutes of Health, National Heart, Lung, and Blood Institute—coronary artery disease: http://www.nhlbi.nih.gov/health/health-topics/topics/cad

REFERENCES

American Diabetes Association. (2003). Economic costs of diabetes in the U.S. in 2002. *Diabetes Care, 26(*3), 917–932.

American Diabetes Association. (2008). Economic costs of diabetes in the U.S. in 2007. *Diabetes Care, 31*(3), 596–615.

American Diabetes Association. (2014a). *Genetics of diabetes.* Retrieved from http://www.diabetes
.org/diabetes-basics/genetics-of-diabetes.html

American Diabetes Association. (2014b). *Live empowered/African American programs.* Retrieved
from http://www.diabetes.org/in-my-community/awareness-programs/african-american-
programs

American Diabetes Association. (2014c). *Statistics about diabetes: Overall numbers, diabetes and
prediabetes.* Retrieved from http://www.diabetes.org/diabetes-basic/statistics

Appel, L. J., Moore, T. J., Obarzanek, E., Vollmer, W. M., Svetkey, L. P., Sacks, F. M.,... Harsha, D. W.
(1997). A clinical trial of the effects of dietary patterns on blood pressure. *New England Journal
of Medicine, 336,* 1117–1124.

Ashley-Koch A., Yang, Q., & Olney, R.S. (2000). Sickle hemoglobin (Hb S) allele and sickle cell disease: A HuGE review. *American Journal Epidemiology, 151*(9), 839–845.

Band, E. B., & Weisz, J. R. (1990). Developmental differences in primary and secondary control
coping and adjustment to juvenile diabetes. *Journal of Clinical Child Psychology, 19*(2),
150–158.

Boyd, H. W., Watkins, A. R., Price, C. L., Fleming, F., & DeBaun, M. R. (2005). Inadequate community knowledge about sickle cell disease among African-American women. *Journal of the
National Medical Association, 97*(1), 62–67.

Braithwaite, R. L., Taylor, S. E., & Treadwell H. M. (Eds). (2009) *Health issues in the Black community.* San Francisco, CA: Jossey-Bass.

Brown, R. A., Armstrong, F. D., & Eckman, J. R. (1993). Neurocongitive aspects of pediatric sickle
cell disease. *Journal of Learning Disabilities, 26*(1), 33–45.

Collins, R., & Winkleby, M. (2002). African American women and men at high and low risk for
hypertension: A signal detection analysis of NHANES III, 1988–1994. *Preventive Medicine,
35*(4), 303–312.

Crnic, K. A., & Greenberg, M. T. (1990). Minor parenting stresses with young children. *Child
Development, 61*(5), 1628–1637.

Davis, S. K., Quarrels, R. C., & Gibbons, G. S. (2009). Hypertension in African American communities. In R. L. Braithwaite, S. E. Taylor, & H. M. Treadwell (Eds.), *Health issues in the Black
community* (pp. 234–258). San Francisco, CA: Jossey-Bass.

D'Zurilla, T. J., & Goldfried, M. R. (1971). Problem solving and behavior modification. *Journal of
Abnormal Psychology, 78*(1), 107–126.

Ephraim, P. L., Hill-Briggs, F., Roter, D. L., Bone, L. R., Wolff, J. L., Lewis-Boyer, L.,... Boulware,
L. E. (2014). Improving urban African Americans' blood pressure control through multi-level
interventions in the Achieving Blood Pressure Control Together (ACT) study: A randomized
clinical trial. *Contemporary Clinical Trials, 38*(2), 370–382.

Fields, L. E., Burt, V. L., Cutler, J. A., Hughes, J., Roccella, E. J., & Sorlie, P. (2004). The burden
of adult hypertension in the United States 1999 to 2000: A rising tide. *Hypertension, 44*(4),
398–404.

Hansen, M. L., Gunn, P. W., & Kaelber, D. C. (2007). Under diagnosis of hypertension in children and
adolescents. *JAMA, 298*(8), 874–879.

Hill-Briggs, F., Lazo, M., Peyrot, M., Doswell, A., Chang, Y. T., Hill, M. N.,... Brancati, F. L. (2011).
Effect of problem-solving-based diabetes self-management training on diabetes control in a low
income patient sample. *Journal of General Internal Medicine, 26*(9), 972–978.

Jordan, L. B., Smith-Whitley, K., Treadwell, M. J., Telfair, J., Grant, A. M., Ohene-Frempong, K.
(2011). Screening U.S. college athletes for their sickle cell disease carrier status. *American
Journal of Preventative Medicine, 41*(6S4), S406–S412. Doi:10.1016/j.amepre.2011.09.014

Loehr, L. R., Rosamond, W. D., Chang, P. P., Folsom, A. R., & Chambless, L. E. (2008). Heart failure incidence and survival (from the Atherosclerosis Risk to Communities Study). *American
Journal of Cardiology, 101,* 1016–1022.

Maddux, J. E., Roberts, M. C., Sledden, E. A., & Wright, L. (1986). Developmental issues in child health psychology. *American Psychologist, 41*(1), 25–34.

Must, A., Spadano, J., Coakley, E. H., Field, A. E., Colditz, G., & Dietz, W. H. (1999). The disease burden associated with overweight and obesity. *JAMA, 282*(16), 1523–1529.

National Institutes of Health, National Heart, Lung, and Blood Institute. (2012). *What is sickle cell anemia?* Retrieved from http://www.nhlbi.nih.gov/health/health-topics/topics/sca

National Institutes of Health, National Heart, Lung, and Blood Institute. (2014). *What is coronary artery disease?* Retrieved from http://www.nhlbi.nih.gov/health/health-topics/topics/cad

Ogden, C. L., Carroll, M. D., Curtin, L. R., McDowell, M. A., Tabak, C. J., & Flegal, K. M. (2006). Prevalence of overweight and obesity in the United States, 1999–2004. *JAMA, 295*(13), 1549–1555.

Schumann, K. P., Sutherland, J. A., Majid, H. M., & Hill-Briggs, F. (2011). Evidence-based behavioral treatments for diabetes: Problem-solving therapy. *Diabetes Spectrum, 24*(2), 64–69.

Smith, S., & Blankenship, S. (1991). Incubation and the persistence of fixation in problem solving. *American Journal of Psychology, 104*(1), 61–87. DOI:10.2307/1422851

Steiner C., & Miller, J. (2006). *Sickle cell disease patients in U.S. hospitals, 2004.* HCUP Statistical Brief #21. Rockville, MD: Agency for Healthcare Research and Quality. Retrieved from http://ncbi.nlm.nih.gov/books/NBK63489

Strauss R. S., & Pollack, H. A. (2001). Epidemic increase in childhood overweight 1986–1989. *JAMA, 286*(22), 2845–2848.

Suris, J. C., Michaud, P. A., & Viner, R. (2004). The adolescent with a chronic condition. Part 1: Developmental issues. *Archives of Disease in Childhood, 89*, 938–942.

Thompson, R. J., Gil, K. M., Gustafson, K. E., George, L. K., Keith, B. R., Spock, A., & Kinney, T. R. (1994). Stability and change in the psychological adjustment of mothers of children and adolescents with cystic fibrosis and sickle cell disease. *Journal of Pediatric Psychology, 19*(2), 171–188.

Thompson, R. J., Gustafson, K. E., Bonner, M. J., & Ware, R. E. (2002). Neurocognitive development of young children with sickle cell disease through three years of age. *Journal of Pediatric Psychology, 27*, 235–244.

Thompson, R. J., Gustafson, K. E., Gil, K. M., Kinney, T. R., & Spock, A. (1999). Change in the psychological adjustment of children with cystic fibrosis or sickle cell disease and their mothers. *Journal of Clinical Psychology in Medical Settings, 6*, 373–392.

CHAPTER 10

Inner City Blues: Social Work Practice With Urban Communities Impacted by HIV/AIDS

Denise McLane-Davison and Warren W. Hewitt

It happened 17 years too late, but it happened: the federal governments' first targeted effort at addressing HIV/AIDS in black communities. It's hard to understand how it took until 1998 for Congress to officially recognize the epidemic's disproportionate impact on African Americans— reality that was plainly visible from the epidemic's opening moments
—Wright, 2006, p. 9

AIDS was publicly recognized by the United States in 1981 after the Centers for Disease Control and Prevention (CDC) linked the disease to a fatal pneumonia found in five gay men in Los Angeles, initially calling it gay-related immune deficiency (GRID) or "gay cancer" (Cohen, 1999). Early public health assessments linked the spread of AIDS to the four "H's"—hemophiliacs, heroin addicts, Haitians, and homosexuals (Cohen, 1999; Wright, 2006). In 1984, HIV was termed as the virus that causes AIDS. However, it was not until September 17, 1985, that President Ronald Reagan finally acknowledged AIDS in a public address (Cohen, 1999; Wright, 2006).

Since the beginning of the 21st century, there has been overwhelming evidence that the HIV/AIDS epidemic has become increasingly concentrated in colorized communities, representing microepidemics (Nunn et al., 2014). According to CDC (2010) data, Blacks or African Americans (inclusive of Caribbean Americans, Africans, and other persons of the Black race who may or may not identify as African American) have the most severe burden of HIV of all racial–ethnic groups in the United States. Compared to other racial–ethnic populations, African Americans have a higher proportion of reported new HIV infections, higher rate of those living with HIV, and those ever diagnosed with AIDS. Although African Americans account for approximately 12% of the U.S. population, they account for 44% of all new HIV infections among adults and adolescents (aged 13 years or older; Centers for Disease Control and Prevention, 2014). Overall, CDC statistics show that:

- In 2010, men accounted for 70% (14,700) of the estimated 20,900 new HIV infections among all adult and adolescent African Americans. The estimated rate of new HIV infections for African American men (103.6/100,000 population) was seven times that of White men, twice that of Latino men, and nearly three times that of African American women (CDC, 2014).
- In 2010, African American gay, bisexual, and other men who have sex with men represented an estimated 72% (10,600) of new infections among all African American men and 36% of an estimated 29,800 new HIV infections among all gay and bisexual men. More new HIV infections (4,800) occurred among young African American gay and bisexual men (aged 13–24 years) than any other sub-group of gay and bisexual men (CDC, 2014).
- In 2010, African American women accounted for 6,100 (29%) of the estimated new HIV infections among all adult and adolescent African Americans. Most new HIV infections among African American women (87%; 5,300) are attrib-uted to heterosexual transmission of the virus. The estimated rate of new HIV infections for African American women (38.1/100,000 population) was 20 times that of White women and almost five times that of Hispanic/Latina women (CDC, 2014).

Complicating the heavy burden of HIV/AIDS in African American communities are the socioeconomic complexities of the epidemic that reaches beyond the outcomes of commonly associated behaviors such as unprotected sex and substance abuse (Nunn et al., 2014; Sutton et al., 2009). African American communities are typically confronted with multiple, co-occurring diseases and syndromes, which are a part of the larger public health conflagration. Systemic issues such as high rates of poverty; cumulative violence exposure (CVE; Kennedy, Bybee, & Greeson, 2014); low socioeconomic status (SES), posttraumatic stress disorder (PTSD); incarceration; transgenerational trauma (Reid et al., 2005; West-Otalunji & Conwill, 2010); sexual networks (Nunn et al., 2014); intimate part-ner violence and sexual assault; and disproportionate exposure to HIV/AIDS infection represent intersecting, overlapping, and interactive health, economic, and social welfare problems, which complicate efforts to define a coherent strategy (Nunn et al., 2014).

As evidence showed, multiple factors contribute to racial–ethnic health disparities, including socioeconomic factors (e.g., education, employment, and income); lifestyle behaviors (e.g., physical activity and alcohol intake); social environment (e.g., educa-tional and economic opportunities, racial–ethnic discrimination, and neighborhood and work conditions); and access to preventive health care services (e.g., cancer screening and vaccination) (Kennedy et al., 2014; Metezel & Roberts, 2014; Nunn et al., 2014; Roberts, 2011; Sotero, 2006).

Assessing HIV infection rates and AIDS diagnoses requires a comprehensive lens. Utilizing ecological and structural systems, rather than exclusively individual behaviors, provides an opportunity to impact sociohistorical, geographical, and structural racism that contribute to an ever-increasing pandemic of HIV/AIDS in communities of color, and specifically for African Americans (Metzl & Roberts, 2014; Nunn et al., 2014). HIV/AIDS work in urban communities requires a systemic examination of factors including historical experiences that are often overlooked because of the consistent focus on individual pathology and viewing HIV/AIDS through a moral lens.

AIDS: THE GREAT MAAFA

The concept of Maafa is derived from the Swahili term for disaster, terrible occurrence, or great tragedy (Ani, 1997). Maafa is a great disaster designed to dehumanize and/or destroy African people. It is not a single event in history, but an ongoing, strategic, intentional, and sophisticated continuous "process" of destruction. Maafa has been achieved through structural institutions such as slavery, imperialism, colonialism, invasion, oppression, dehumanization, and exploitation of persons of African ancestry throughout the African diaspora (Ani, 1997). To date, AIDS is the greatest public health Maafa that has threatened the continuation of the race of persons of African descent.

A History of Distrust

As a component of the great Maafa, there is a history of distrust between African Americans and the medical community, which stems mostly from ongoing violations of human rights (Collins, 2005; Nattrass, 2013; Stevenson, 1994). Numerous case studies during the 19th century revealed surgical procedures performed on female slaves without benefits of anesthesia. Even as late as the 20th century there are countless examples of different sectors of the population who continue to have their human rights violated. Prisoners, the mentally ill, and persons who are poor and disenfranchised, disproportionately representative of African Americans, have found themselves convenient subjects (Byrd & Clayton, 2000; Collins, 2005; Roberts, 1997; Skloot, 2010; Washington, 2008).

The Tuskegee Syphilis Study, conducted from 1932 to 1972, provides a poignant example of how government and public health saw the opportunity to better understand the natural course of syphilis by experimenting on a cohort of Black men who did not receive treatment. The government researchers deceived African American sharecroppers for 40 years about their receiving medical treatment for syphilis. This deceit eventually led to their deaths and to birth defects in their offspring. The study breached human ethics through blocking medical treatment to participants, even with the knowledge that no treatment would cause irrevocable harm (Clinton, 1997).

Kirp (1995) further advanced this conversation in his article, "Blood, Sweat, and Tears: The Tuskegee Experiment and the Era of AIDS," in which he described AIDS as a "metaphor for pervasive racism." HIV/AIDS is not exclusively a health issue, but a personal disease that has been politicalized. Access to health insurance, employment, housing, and education are but some of the social issues that can negatively impact a person's response to HIV/AIDS. Intimate relationships with family, friends, and sexual partners are equally affected by persons who are living with HIV, or at risk of becoming infected. Segments of America's population who have not been able to overcome other social ills in society are also ill equipped to respond to HIV/AIDS (Williams et al., 2003).

Other historical case studies of medical racism also exist as evidence of the Maafa. One of the most prominent cases was that of Henrietta Lacks, an African American mother and wife, who died from an aggressive cancer at the age of 30 years in 1951 after being treated in the segregated "Colored" ward of Johns Hopkins Hospital. A sample of her cancerous cell tissue was taken without her or her family's knowledge or consent. Her cells were named "He-La" using the first two letters of her first and last name. He-La cells, are unique in their ability to reproduce endlessly, and thus are considered the "work horse" of all cells. As the medical miracle unfolded, Henrietta's cells were given to medical researchers across the world for additional experimentation. This discovery, although medically significant, was not shared with the family until 30 years later, but this sharing of information was only accidental. The biomedical industry was launched and polio, HIV, human papilloma virus (HPV), and other significant medical advances have all birthed from Henrietta Lacks's tissue womb. Yet, to date, the family has not received monetary compensation for the use of their mother's body. On her death, Mrs. Lacks left five children behind, including a daughter who had been institutionalized for mental illness. This daughter had also been experimented on and harvested for medical advancement without the family's knowledge or consent (Roberts, 2011; Skloot, 2010).

Furthermore, the 1970s brought the eugenics movement in which doctors coerced hundreds of thousands of Black women to consent to sterilization as a condition for receiving other medical services (Roberts, 1997; Washington, 2008). Eugenics, from the Greek root meaning "good in birth," embraces the theory that intelligence and other personality traits are genetically determined and therefore inherited. Eugenicists advocate for the rational control of reproduction in order to improve society. The eugenics process is designed to lead to extinction of inferior groups (such as poor Whites, mentally impaired, and African Americans) through selective breeding (Washington, 2008). Therefore, they exert that "it is counterproductive to waste public charity on people who produced children with inferior qualities, arguing that the time may come when such persons would be considered enemies to the state" (Roberts, 1997, pp. 59–60). Thus, many Black women have been systematically coerced into sterilization, abortion, or court ordered to take contraception such as Norplant (Roberts, 2011).

In sum, the history of distrust predicated on examples such as the Tuskegee experiment, the eugenics movement, and the story of Henrietta Lacks that serve as historical case studies of Maafa and traumatic medical racism. These life stories speak to the ideological acceptance of ignoring, disregarding, and too often overriding the humanity of African Americans, without regard to intent to harm.

Waging War on Urban Communities

In 1982, President Ronald Reagan introduced the race-neutral term "The War on Drugs" as a means of "restoring order" in urban communities. This "War" was waged with laws and policies that called for "swift and just" punishment of individuals engaged in illegal activities, with special emphasis on inner city communities that were in economic turmoil. In the prior year, 1981, President Reagan made his first mention of AIDS. But, the introduction of harsh criminal penalties, lack of medical access, and absence of gainful employment created a triple threat for persons who were not able to escape (Alexander, 2010). The emergence of "crack cocaine," which flooded Black communities, also saw the increase of violent street gangs and crimes. Images of "crack addicted" babies and street arrests led the evening news on a daily basis and were also popularized through popular 1980s movies like "New Jack City" and "Boyz n the Hood." This imagery further fueled the conservative political mantra to "get tough on crime" while simultaneously linking crime, disease, and chaos with race, in particular, the Black community (Alexander, 2010).

Prosecutors unfairly targeted Black women, whom society viewed as undeserving (Robertson, 1995). Society is much more willing to condone the punishment of poor Black women who fail to meet the middle-class ideal of motherhood. In a study of pregnant women published in the *New England Journal of Medicine*, researchers found that "despite similar rates of substance abuse among white women (15.4 percent) and Black women (14.1 percent) during pregnancy, Black women were ten times more likely than whites to be reported to government authorities" (Roberts, 1997, pp. 59–60). Both public health facilities and private doctors were more inclined to turn in Black women than White women for using drugs while pregnant (Roberts, 2011). Targeting crack use during pregnancy unfairly singled out Black women for incarceration, placed their children in foster care, and greatly precipitated the further demise of the African American family. Although there were White women who were crack addicts, the public's image of the pregnant crack addict was decidedly Black. Singling out crack abuse users for severe punishment has a discriminatory impact that cannot be medically justified (Metzl & Roberts, 2014).

Simultaneously with the early days of the HIV/AIDS epidemic, the U.S. Department of Justice and other governmental agencies focused on drug trafficking or the "supply" side of the War on Drugs. Federal policy on drug abuse was centered on reducing the drug use by prosecuting and incarcerating those who used or sold illicit drugs. For the African American community, the immediate impact of this War on Drugs was on the large number of young African Americans being removed from their families and communities and ultimately incarcerated for prolonged periods of time. Accompanying this immediate impact were the second-order effects that were not anticipated. First, the removal of so many African American males sharply affected family gross income, which spiraled many single-parent families further into poverty. Second, the absence of African American male role models left maturation to chance, most notably for young sons, but also for young daughters. Third, with the systematic destruction of many of the "anti-poverty programs" of the Johnson era and the continuing effects of residential segregation, the only real venture capital available for community–economic development was through drug and gangs (Wyatt et al., 2013).

In essence, the "War on Drugs" became a cornerstone of the domestic policy agenda, as the HIV/AIDS epidemic encountered a quandary about how best to contain the growing number of new cases and where to place priorities. After ensuing deliberations and a great deal of political action, the connection to gay White men became the highest priority and subsequently the focus of the U.S. Department of Health and Human Services actions to address the HIV/AIDS epidemic. Although parenteral transmission of HIV through injection drug use (IDU) had been reported in the *Morbidity and Mortality Weekly Report* (*MMWR*) in 1981 as a major source of transmission of HIV, it did not receive the same attention or emphasis given to gay White men. Individuals injecting drugs were among the disenfranchised and those at the periphery of contemporary society. The Department of Justice had plans to control drugs that would benefit HIV by incarcerating drug users in prisons, thereby removing the threat from society.

Like the War on Drugs, however, there were also a number of second-order effects that were not anticipated. First, the connection of the War on Drugs and the HIV/AIDS epidemic did not become a matter of discussion at the highest levels of government, which often translates to insufficient resources. Second, the historically high rates of sexually transmitted infections in African American communities were the single most important risk factor for HIV transmission, which any casual examination of the epidemiological data would have demonstrated, especially in the Southern States (Biello et al., 2012; Doherty, Shiboski, Ellen, Adimora, & Padian, 2006). Third, aside from heroin, embodied in injection drug use, the use of other drugs was not considered to be of seminal importance. The failure to correctly assess the impact of crack cocaine in the African American community created a forum for infection far greater than the impact of men who have sex with men or IDUs (Edlin et al., 1994). Fourth, crack cocaine elevated African American women to positions as targets for criminal prosecution and incarceration, and further destabilized African American families by placing their children in foster care and only in some cases extended family. However, the intersection of HIV and crack was not readily apparent to the public health world, and consequently, the rates of infection among urban communities increased dramatically in the 1980s and 1990s (Lam, Wechsberg, & Zule; Litt & McNeil, 1997; Murphy & Rosenbaum, 1992). Finally, by placing young men in prisons where inmates having sex with other inmates was verboten, neither the criminal justice nor the public health systems were prepared when these young men returned home HIV positive and infected their wives and girlfriends (Conklin, Lincoln, & Tuthill, 2000; Khan et al., 2009).

REFRAMING AN OLD PROBLEM: SEMINOLE FRAMEWORKS

Black Feminist and Womanist Theories

Women in urban Black communities have been the anchors and foundations in the families and communities. As such, theories that speak to their significant roles are important for advancing work with HIV/AIDS. For instance, Black feminist thought (BFT; Collins, 2000; Gentry, Elifson, & Sterk, 2005; Roberts, Jackson, & Carlton-LaNey, 2000) introduces the sociological perspective that race and gender are neither distinctive, separate, nor conflictual in their approach to liberation from multiple social orders that seek to restrict Black women's humanity. Although Black women are certainly not homogeneous, there is a common bond of experience, precolonial and postcolonial, which produces a common thread of knowledge, which combines their experiences throughout the African diaspora. These ways of knowing are a continuous landscape of triumphs and struggle that produce a distinct voice. Her voice challenges privilege, status quo, patriarchy, ideology, and normative constructs that edit and silence "her story" (McLane-Davison, 2013; Norwood, 2013; Roberts, et al., 2000).

Similarly, Womanism (Alexander-Floyd & Simien, 2006; Collins, 2000; Littlefield, 2003) is recognized as a sister theory of Black feminism, and is often used synonymously. It too is concerned with the interlocking systems of oppression while introducing the compassion of women working and loving each other, regardless of sexuality. Alice Walker's definition of womanist argues, "a Womanist is a Black feminist"—an idea involving such "qualities as being challenging and bold, being inquiring, pushing and straining toward a special kind of maturity. The idea involves love, being relational, being committed to health and survival" (Gilkes, 1995, p. 36). When a womanist addresses an issue, she does so out of her dedication to the wholeness of the community. She has a community understanding of family, their survival is interdependent. On an individual level, there is a willingness to do what is necessary for the well-being of the family–community. Thus, gender is utilized as strength to activate social networks for collaboration and community building. A womanist preserves reciprocal relationships of equality and respect with men, including intimate partnerships, which implores that women and men be free to shape their own identities and to choose their own roles in the African American family–community's fight for survival and wholeness (Alexander-Floyd & Simien, 2006; Gilkes, 2000; Littlefield, 2003; Norwood, 2013).

Critical Race Theory

Critical race theory (CRT) resists the notion that, as a society, we are color-blind and race neutral, and that difference equates with deficit (Abrams & Moio, 2009). CRT, born out of legal and law studies, examines the historical, intentional, and multiple systems of oppression that inform social policy and shape the intellectual discourse of race privilege (Crenshaw, 2011; Zuberi, 2011). CRT recognizes six key tenets that frame the discussion regarding race: (a) racism is endemic to living in America and is so pervasive that it is invisible to those who benefit; (b) race is a social construct; (c) groups are racialized at the convenience of those in power, which is subsequently tied to worth; (d) racism is used to exploit materialism and psychic dominance; (e) race counters ahistorical accounts of events that mute, distort, and limit the experiences of oppressed groups; and (f) recognizes the complexity of the interlocking systems of oppression (Abrams & Moio, 2009; Zuberi, 2011).

CRT offers a mechanism for deconstructing and dismantling the previously described tenants, by offering counter stories and counterspaces (Crenshaw, 2011; Solorzano & Yosso, 2002; Zuberi, 2011). Counter storytelling is used to reposition voices of color and oppressed from the margins to the center. Their stories, which have been assigned as "other," are now the critical voice from which the story begins. These stories become the voice of resistance and reconstruction that oppose dominant assumptions of pathology and deficit, while insisting on inclusion of the lived experiences of people of color as "normal." Counterspaces become essential as physical and virtual space where power is generated as collective action and used to create safety barriers for persons of color. These safe spaces are used to inoculate and transform the experiences of racially oppressed groups by valuing, celebrating, and validating their voices (Solorzano & Yosso, 2002).

Structural Competency

Structural competency (Metzl & Roberts, 2014) represents a new perspective for addressing health disparities and individual behaviors. Emerging as an interprofessional model that accounts for comorbidity race and mental illness in historical context, it

> contends that many health-related factors previously attributed to culture or ethnicity also represent the downstream consequences of decisions about larger structural contexts, including health care and food delivery systems, zoning laws, local politics, urban and rural infrastructures, structural racisms, or even the very definitions of illness and health. (p. 674)

The definition of structural competency (Metzl & Roberts, 2014) further asserts that medical approaches and racial diversity practices that exclusively address individual biology, backgrounds, and patient–doctor communication, provides health professionals with incomplete information "to address the biological, socioeconomic, and racial impacts of upstream decisions on structural factors such as expanding health and wealth disparities" (p. 674).

Within this new theoretical framework, the authors (Metzl & Roberts, 2014) give credence to evidence-based research that confirms the impact of structural racism, including: (a) racial discrimination is linked to high levels of stress; (b) the positive correlation of high-stress and resource-poor environments contributions to transgenerational risk factors for disease; and (c) high poverty and social segregation as impairments of brain functioning. Documenting these medical advances, with their inclusion of structural racism, provides an alternative to assessing individuals that locates their health outside of personal pathology and race-based health. Furthermore, the theory of structural competency introduces a new perspective for understanding the interlocking systems of institutions, ideology, and policies that create negative health outcomes for particular populations.

Historical Trauma Theory

Historical trauma theory (Sotero, 2006), also a relatively new concept, posits that "populations historically subjected to long-term, mass trauma, such as colonialism, slavery, war, genocide, exhibit a higher prevalence of disease even several generations after the original trauma occurred" (p. 93). The theory, which was first introduced in the 1960s, focused on Jewish Holocaust and World War II survivors, and has been used most frequently to frame the experiences of American Indians–Alaskan Natives under colonization (Brave Heart, 2003), but also has been incorporated into studies with Palestinian, Cambodian, and African American communities (Sotero, 2006). The historical trauma theory is inclusiveness of three other theoretical frameworks:

Psychosocial theory—person-in-environment is also linked to physical and psychological stressors which not only create susceptibility to disease, but act as a direct pathogenic mechanism affecting biological systems in the body

Political/economic theory—structural determinants of health are influenced by intentional/unintentional power imbalances and class inequality

Social/ecological systems theory—acknowledges the multilevel and interlocking dynamics of life course variables in disease. (p. 94)

Inherent in the theory of historical trauma are four distinct assumptions that connect person and environment and past to present.

1. Mass trauma is deliberately and systematically inflicted on a target population by a subjugating and dominant population.

2. Trauma is not limited to a single catastrophic event, but continues over an extended period of time.

3. Traumatic events reverberate throughout the population, creating a universal experience of trauma.

4. The magnitude of the trauma experience derails the population from its natural, projected historical course resulting in a legacy of physical, psychological, social, and economic disparities that persists across generations. (pp. 94–95)

Race-related historical trauma has measurable and distinct outcomes, including links to health disparities, maladaptive social and behavioral patterns, cumulative and collective psychological and emotional injury, PTSD, perpetual and intergenerational cycles of trauma, maternal malnutrition, HIV/AIDS, chronic stress, and autoimmune diseases (Sotero, 2006), Posttraumatic slave disorder (PTSlaveryD; Reid, Mims, & Higginbottom, 2005). Brave Heart (2003) refers to "soul wound(s)" as a term to explain indigenous communities' unresolved grief as a result of cumulative subjugation to intentional environmental stimulus, such as discrimination, colonizing, and oppression.

Reframing the problem of racism is significant to understanding the cumulative impact of HIV/AIDS in the Black community and throughout the African diaspora. In the Progressive Era, the response to disease and discrimination was rooted in racial uplift, self-help, and mutual aid in the Black community. BFT and womanism conjoin race, gender, power, class, and sexuality to provide a multipronged framework for understanding these complex social constructs. CRT introduces racial oppression as an intentional and inherent consequence of American's culture, which is tied to economic gains for the dominant group. Structural competency disconnects race from health pathology and introduces health outcomes as the product of institutional racism, which is inherent, intentional, and structurally invisible. Finally, historical trauma theory, provides a comprehensive lens for framing race-based trauma through social–ecological systems theory, psychosocial theory, and political–economic theory giving us a multifaceted, multilevel, and cumulative means for understanding its historical, immediate, and future generational impact.

COMMUNITY AND GOVERNMENT RESPONSES

Uplift, Self-Help, and Mutual Aid

Strategies of uplift, self-help, and mutual aid have a robust and extended history in the Black community. During the Progressive Era (1890–1920), the terms "race men" and "race women" were given to individuals whose primary concern was the survival, uplift, and liberation of Black people. Their pattern of self-help developed from the Black extended family, which included four components: mutual aid, social–class cooperation, male–female equality, and prosocial behavior in children (Martin & Martin, 1985).

Race men and women were middle-class Blacks who were concerned with the moral and mental improvement of the race. These free Black leaders emphasized hard work, frugality, industriousness, education, sobriety, and similar virtues (Carlton-LaNey, 2001; O'Donnell, 1996). They saw these virtues as the means of upward mobility and strongly believed that "self-improvement would in itself raise Blacks from degradation" (Martin & Martin, 1985, p. 41). Individual Blacks who conformed to "respectable standards" of conduct that improved their minds, and worked hard, were considered to be "elevating the race" (Martin & Martin, 1985; Riggs 1994). Although seemingly motivated by self-interest, organizations like the National Association of Colored Women (NACW) also felt that helping the poor was their social responsibility and linked fate. "Lifting As We Climb" was their lived mantra of the social justice and ethical agenda movement, which insisted on socioeconomic advancement for the entire race, and executed in solidarity with the oppressed and impoverished masses (Carlton-LaNey, 2001).

Mutual aid groups such as the NACW were essential to the intergenerational transmission of traditional African values and the backbone of the Negro Health Movement. From 1890 to 1950, a period of legalized segregation, many African American saw their battle for improved health conditions as part of a political agenda for their human rights. African American activist and leadership endeavored to make their health needs a legitimate political concern for the United States despite their limited influence on government and public social policy; yet, they recognized that health care projects and activism were vital to community sustainability (Carlton-LaNey, 2001; Smith, 1995).

Needle Exchange

Although behavioral scientists have proven that HIV transmission can be significantly reduced among IDUs through needle-exchange programs, many states have banned the use of government funds to support the programs or made them illegal. Lawmakers banned federal funding for needle-exchange programs in 1988 at the height of the crack epidemic under the Reagan presidential administration as part of the "War on Drugs." Conservative Congress members have repeatedly extended this ban despite scientific evidence that supports the universal precautions associated with needle exchange as part of effective harm reduction measures. The Baltimore City Health Department is one of a handful of city and state-funded needle-exchange programs that have demonstrated consistent decrease in the numbers of HIV-injected drug use–related diagnosis. Most notably, over the past decade, there has been a decrease from 16% to 53% as of 2010. Health care agencies like the Baltimore City Health Department with high rates of HIV see the lack of needle-exchange programs as a missed opportunity to include individuals in drug treatment programs (Fritze, 2014).

In terms of the debate on substance abuse and drug addiction as a criminal activity or a public health issue, a few factors must be considered. First, there was no real connection made between the public health efforts to reduce transmission and the criminal justice system waging the war on drugs. Second, the opposition by the Office of National Drug Control Policy (ONDCP) and others in the criminal justice community to the legalizing of syringe exchange was likely a factor that impacted transmission of HIV in the African American community. Third, the impact of excess incarceration of Black men not only destabilized African American families by reducing the male role model and male's income, but it also created a forum for HIV transmission among African American women leading to increases in concurrent sexual relationships and greater out-of-marriage sex with other partners. Fourth, though a number of those in the drug treatment community recognized the need to address HIV by increasing the availability of drug treatment, the focus on criminalization of drug addiction ignored the salient public health implications (Alexander, 2010; Roberts, 2011).

A National Health Care Plan and HIV/AIDS Strategy

The sharp rise in the HIV/AIDS burden calls for increased efforts to combat the spread and impact of HIV/AIDS. On March 23, 2010, President Obama signed the Patient Protection and Affordable Care Act (ACA), which set into place a mechanism that provided consumer protections, private insurance reforms, Medicare reforms, health care marketplaces at the state level, and an overall effort to improve the health care system (Owens, 2012). This was a significant and hard fought battle for health reform advocates, who had tried for several decades to address the fragmented, underfunded, and illness–maintenance U.S. health care system. Historically, people living with HIV and AIDS have had a difficult time obtaining private health insurance and have been particularly vulnerable to insurance industry biases. The Ryan White HIV/AIDS Program has traditionally been the health care mechanism used to funnel monies to state and local government, and provide treatment resources. But, the ACA has sought to make considerable strides in addressing structural health-related disparities and biases, by advancing primary care and community-based care initiatives, as well as, the need for linguistic and culturally competent health workers. In particular, ACA aims to increase access to quality health care treatment and health education through a culturally proficient and skillfully trained allied health care workforce.

In July 2010, the Obama administration released the National HIV/AIDS Strategy (NHAS) for the United States, which represents an effort to refocus national attention on ending the domestic HIV epidemic (Owens, 2012). Goals for the NHAS sought to reduce new HIV infections, increase access to care and improve health outcomes for people living with HIV, and reduce HIV-related health disparities. According to the Owens (2012), the nation must adopt a more strategic and coordinated approach that utilizes a combination of effective HIV prevention interventions and stimulates innovation to develop additional effective scalable tools. NHAS structured a number of lofty goals to reduce new HIV infections, to increase access to health care and improve health care outcomes for people living with HIV, and to reduce HIV-related disparities and inequities. However, the expectations to achieve substantial outcomes with respect to these goals across the African American diaspora were not deemed to be a particularly important focus of the strategy. Low-hanging fruit and the politicization of the HIV/AIDS Strategy all but negated the much-needed focus on HIV transmission differences among African Americans. The lack of clear emphasis on the structural factors driving HIV or the African American–specific social determinants of health such as entrench, long-term poverty, residential segregation, and racism was weakly articulated, and virtually not addressed in NHAS public policy implementation (Friedman, Cooper, & Osborne, 2009).

The cookie-cutter approach to public health strategy and policy development predicted that the emphasis would concentrate on men who have sex with men and by extension on African American men who have sex with men. This public policy approach fostered greater division across the African American community creating a "them versus us" division that benefited none. Thus, although the NHAS embraced many of the strategic goals that had been a constant part of the discussion throughout the AIDS epidemic, it ignored the distinct differences that have existed in the nature of the epidemic in the African diaspora, in the African American South, among young African American men who have sex with men and young heterosexuals, and across the SES spectrum of the African American community. The NHAS failed in large measure because it did not try to understand the social milieu and the mechanisms for transmission of HIV, nor did it understand how limited the infrastructure is to address the NHAS goals in these communities.

SOCIAL WORK FRONT AND CENTER

In 1969, the National Association of Black Social Workers (NABSW) was created out of the historical Black Power Movement and the need to address the race-based policies and practices that disproportionately threatened the preservation and uplift of Black families, institutions, and communities. In their inception, they developed a *Code of Ethics* that implicitly acknowledges racism as a threat to their humanitarian, liberation, and survival. Within their brief, but thorough, *Code of Ethics* is a call to action by those engaged in the profession to assure that we address injustice at all levels "by any means necessary." NABSW unapologetically boast the need to address social injustices, including within the profession of social work, on behalf of those of African ancestry (Reid-Merritt, 2010).

> If a sense of community awareness is a precondition to humanitarian acts, then we as Black social workers must use our knowledge of the Black community, our commitments to its self-determination, and our helping skills for the benefit of Black people as we marshal our expertise to improve the quality of life of Black people. Our activities will be guided by our Black consciousness, our determination to protect the security of the Black community, and to serve as advocates to relieve suffering of Black people by any means.

> In America today, no Black person, except the selfish or irrational, can claim neutrality in the quest for Black liberation nor fail to consider the implications of the events taking place in our society. Given the necessity for committing ourselves to the struggle for freedom, we as Black Americans practicing in the field of social welfare, set forth this statement of ideals and guiding principles. (nabsw.org, 2014)

In 2007, the National Association of Social Workers (NASW) issued a comprehensive 31-page document that embraced racism as a significant and ever-present social and human justice issue. Under the leadership of NASW President Elvira Craig de Silva, a task force was convened, which produced "Weaving the Fabrics of Diversity." The following call to action was issued:

> What is key is that the social work profession and the systems through with the profession has evolved historically, into the present, is part of a larger society in which policies, resources, and practices are designed to benefit some groups significantly more than others, while simultaneously denying the existence of racism as a variable, except in its most extreme forms. The responsibility of individual social workers is to recognize that

structural racism plays out in their personal and professional lives and to use this awareness to ameliorate its influence in all aspects of social work practice, inclusive of direct practice, community organizing, supervision, consultation, administration, advocacy, social and political action, policy development and implementation, education, and research and evaluation. (NASW, 2007, p. 3)

At the core of NABSW and NASW is the significant charge of social justice. Thus the question remains, "What is the responsibility of social work in addressing HIV/AIDS a social justice issue?" and "Why do African Americans overwhelmingly bear the brunt of inner-city blues?" Various experts would argue that in our push after the 1960s Civil Rights Movement and with the passing of integration policies, economic and educational floodgates were opened that birthed a new middle class and ushered in inclusive language such as diversity. As a concept, diversity has been used to capture various forms of discrimination and oppression; yet, race has become stigmatized by its own family of origin. The legal system was used to address any intentional forms of racial discrimination, yet has eventually failed to address race-neutral language in policies that disenfranchise and disingenuously impact communities of color. Race has been swept under the rug and reintroduced in a color-blind, post-racial, and postelection of the first President of the United States acknowledging African Ancestry.

IMPLICATIONS FOR THE FUTURE

The following are future directions for addressing HIV/AIDS:

1. Acknowledge racism as a pervasive and systemic ideology that undergirds American institutions and society. Racism is a necessity for legitimizing and promoting various policies and laws that advantage one group at the cost of another.

2. Medical racism is a part of American history, which has been used to justify inhumane treatment toward people of color, inclusive of those of African ancestry. Inclusion of this acknowledgment is necessary for neutralizing those who have ignored serious violations of ethical behavior by admonishing them as "urban legends" and "conspiracy theories."

3. Acknowledgment that race is a social construct that is used to group humans with a common history and land of origin, while simultaneously assigning superior and inferior value to certain groups.

4. Community-based and interprofessional responses are keys to unraveling the interconnected and tangled systems that contribute to creating a blanket of despair and oppression for communities subjugated by institutional racism.

5. Embracing new theoretical frameworks that center the experiences of African Americans as the core of conversations that link them to strength and liberation.

6. Actively renew a "call to action" that addresses the pathology and inherent imbalances of structured power in systems that perpetuate racism.

7. A comprehensive HIV prevention plan must be inclusive of individuals' behavioral responses to sociohistorical geographical and structural racism.

HIV/AIDS in the African American community is tethered to the daunting challenge of racism in America. AIDS rates will not be reduced or eliminated without first acknowledging the interlocking systems of structural barriers that create overwhelming risk factors and inevitable gateways to HIV infection. There has been no appearance of a so-called Paul Revere challenged with the task of warning the African American community of the dangers posed by HIV. HIV, being a gay disease, set the tone for three decades of denial and indifference. Our failure to understand that our connectedness was our greatest strength, which brought us through the perils of the Civil Rights era, but which in the era of HIV became part of our peril. We should have circled the wagons, renewed our commitment to each other, and set about formulating an African American NHAS grounded on the principles outlined in the Nguzo Saba: Umoja (unity); Kujichagulia (self-determination); Ujima (collective work and responsibility); Ujamaa (cooperative economics); Nia (purpose); Kuumba (creativity); and Imani (faith). Such a plan of us and by us would have empowered us, a theme not present in the president's NHAS.

As urban social workers clinging to our roots for social justice and challenging policies that preclude self-determination, we must openly and honestly address systemic oppression at the personal and political level. Embracing HIV/AIDS as a human rights fight demands that we also examine the sociohistorical context that urban communities of color, particularly African Americans, have shouldered as a result of structural racism. Contemporary social work practice has insisted on licensure as a means of ensuring professional standards; yet, this focus has derailed us from confronting the political climate that continues to create generations of disenfranchised communities

FOR FURTHER STUDY

Suggested Assignments

Develop a Pinterest Board About HIV/AIDS

Pinterest (www.Pinterest.com) is a free downloadable website–mobile app that requires registration to use. You can upload, save, sort, and manage images—known as pins—and other media content (e.g., videos and images) through collections known as pinboards. Pinterest acts as a personalized media platform, storyboard, or digital scrapbooking.

1. You will create a personalized board thematically suited to the content of the chapter. You can develop content about a specific population (children; men; women and girls; lesbian, gay, bisexual, transgender, and queer [LGBTQ];

rural; urban; transcontinental) and/or specific political issues and policies (needle-exchange programs, housing, Americans with Disabilities Act [ADA], anonymous and confidential testing, World Bank, alternative and complementary medicine). You can use public or privacy settings or link your Pinterest board to other social media such as Facebook or Twitter.

2. You can browse the content of others on the main page. Users can then save individual pins to one of their own boards using the "Pin It" button, with Pinboards typically organized by a central topic or theme.

3. You can search for content outside of Pinterest, such as those at www.youtube .com, www.twitter.com, or www.facebook.com. Self-authored content such as short videos, music, and photos can also be uploaded as pins to your board.

4. There are several instructional videos at www.youtube.com that demonstrate basic steps of using Pinterest. However, unlike earlier versions of Pinterest, you don't have to be invited to use the board.

Benefits

1. Author driven and directed

2. Engages critical thinking

3. Endless opportunities for research and creativity

4. Encourages community and resource sharing

5. Integrates multiple media content

6. Curates and collects sustainable knowledge–content

7. Engages mobile technology devices (tablets, ipads, smartphones, computers).

Documenting Service Learning Project Using Digital Time Line

Join an AIDS service organization on a specific project in your community. This project may be a specific awareness day (i.e., World AIDS, Girls & Women, African American, HIV Testing Day, AIDS Walk); outreach service; policy/lobby day; or evaluation of a specific program. Before, during, and after the volunteer experiences, students should gather artifacts and photos (when permitted) of their process. Use the free social media tool www.dipity.com to develop a digital time line of their experience, including details of "the event."

What is Dipity?
Dipity is a free digital time-line website. Our mission is to organize the web's content by date and time. Users can create, share, embed, and collaborate on interactive, visually engaging time lines that integrate video, audio, images, text, links, social media, location, and timestamps.

Who is Dipity for?

Dipity time lines are for anyone who uses the Internet. Newspapers, journalists, celebrities, government organizations, politicians, financial institutions, community managers, museums, universities, teachers, students, nonprofits, and bloggers all use Dipity to create time lines.

Why use Dipity?

Dipity allows users to create free time lines online. Dipity is the fastest and easiest way to bring history to life with stunning multimedia time lines.

Benefits

1. Author driven and directed

2. Engages critical thinking

3. Endless opportunities for research and creativity

4. Encourages community and resource sharing

5. Integrates multiple media content

6. Curates and collects sustainable knowledge–content

7. Engages mobile technology devices (tablets, iPads, smartphones, computers).

Create a Culturagram Using the "Life Support" (2007) HBO Films

About the Film

In Brooklyn, New York, the former crack-addicted Ana Wallace is HIV positive and is a volunteer in the Life Support, an organization that promotes a fight against AIDS in the African American community. Ana wanders through the streets handing out condoms and helping people with AIDS through lectures and advice. She lives with her mate Slick, who has transmitted AIDS to her, and their little daughter Kim. She has lost the custody of her older daughter Kelly, who lives with her estranged mother Lucille. When Kelly's childhood gay friend Amare, who is sick and rejected by his sister Tanya, vanishes on the streets of Brooklyn, Ana seeks him out and tries to save him. Meanwhile, Lucille decides to move to Virginia with Kelly, and Ana reflects about her life and the relationship with Kelly. Written by Claudio Carvalho, Rio de Janeiro, Brazil.

The Culturagram is a family assessment tool developed to help social workers and others better understand families from different cultural backgrounds. It consists of a diagram with 10 different aspects. For the purpose of developing urban social work practice with Black families, ethnicity–racial identity–consciousness has been included.

- Location/migration/travel
- Legal status
- Time in community

- Language spoken at home and in the community
- Health beliefs
- Crisis events–impact
- Holidays and special events, family traditions, and rituals
- Cultural and religious/spirituality practices
- Values about education and work
- Values about family structure, power, myths, and rules
- Ethnic and racial identity-consciousness
- Culture is not a singular concept, a singular term.

Please visit http://socialworkpodcast.blogspot.com/2008/12/visual-assessment-tools-culturagram.html

Benefits

1. Increases integrated learning

2. Engages students in active learning

3. Applies a culturally sensitive assessment tool

4. Incorporates multiple media

5. Provides opportunity to incorporate foundational knowledge about problem solving, systems theory, empowerment, intersectionality, and help-seeking behaviors.

Suggested Readings

Alexander, M. (2010). *The new Jim Crow: Mass incarceration in the age of colorblindness*. New York, NY: The New Press.

Byrd, M. W., & Clayton, L. A. (2000). *An American health dilemma: A medical history of a African Americans and the problem of race: Beginnings to 1900*. New York, NY: Routledge.

Cohen, C. J. (1999). *The boundaries of African Americanness: AIDS and the breakdown of African American politics*. Chicago, IL: University of Chicago Press.

Collins, P. H. (2005). *Black sexual politics: African-Americans, gender, and the new racism*. New York, NY: Routledge.

Reid-Merritt, P. (2010). *Righteous self-determination: The Black social work movement in America*. Imprint Edition. Baltimore, MD: Black Classic Press.

Roberts, D. (1997). *Killing the African American body: Race, reproduction, and the meaning of liberty*. New York, NY: Pantheon Books.

Roberts, D. (2011). *Fatal invention: How science, politics, and big business re-create race in the twenty-first century*. New York, NY: The New Press.

Skloot, R. (2010). *The immortal life of Henrietta Lacks*. New York, NY: Random House.

Washington, H. A. (2008). *A notoriously syphilis-soaked race: What really happened at Tuskegee? Medical apartheid: The dark history of medical experimentation on black Americans from colonial times to the present* (pp. 157–189). New York, NY: Anchor.

West-Olatunji, C. A., & Conwill, N. (2010). *Counseling African Americans*. San Francisco, CA: Houghton Mifflin Company/Cengage.

Suggested Websites

The Sentencing Project: www.sentencingproject.org
Black AIDS Institute: www.blackaids.org
Centers for Disease Control and Prevention: www.cdc.gov

Suggested Viewing

PBS Frontline Series: www.pbs.org/frontline
"The Age of AIDS" (2006)
ENDGAME: AIDS in Black America (2012)
"Prison State" (2014)
Series producer and reporter Renata Simone.

The Immortal Life of Henrietta Lacks (2011), Yasmin Rammohan. http://chicagotonight.wttw
.com/2011/12/29/immortal-life-henrietta-lacks

Ms. Evers' Boys (1997). Anasazi Productions, Home Box Office

REFERENCES

Abrams, L. S., & Moio, J. A. (2009). Critical race theory and the cultural competence dilemma in social work education. *Journal of Social Work Education, 45*(2), 245–261.

Alexander, M. (2010). *The new Jim Crow: Mass incarceration in the age of colorblindness.* New York, NY: The New Press.

Alexander-Floyd, N. G., & Simein, E. M. (2006). Revisiting "What's in a name": Exploring the contours of Africana womanist thought. *Frontiers: A Journal of Women Studies, 27*(1), 67–89.

Ani, M. (1997). *Let the circle be unbroken: The implications of African spirituality in the diaspora.* New York, NY: Nkonimfo Publications.

Biello, K.B., Kershaw, T., Nelson, R., Hogben, M., Ickovics, J., & Niccolai, L. (2012). Racial Residential Segregation and Rates of Gonorrhea in the United States, 2003-2007. *American Journal of Public Health, 102*(7), 1370–1377.

Brave Heart, M. (2003). The historical trauma response among natives and its relationship to substance abuse: A Lakota illustration. *Journal of Psychoactive Drugs, 35*(1), 7–13.

Byrd, M. W., & Clayton, L. A. (2000). *An American health dilemma: A medical history of African Americans and the problem of race: Beginnings to 1900.* New York, NY: Routledge.

Carlton-LeNey, I. (Ed.). (2001). *African American leadership: An empowerment tradition in social welfare history.* Washington, DC: NASW Press.

Centers for Disease Control and Prevention. (2010). Heightened national response to the HIV/AIDS crisis among African Americans. Retrieved from http://www.cdc.gov/news/2007/03/hiv_african_americans.html

Centers for Disease Control and Prevention. (2014). 30 Years of HIV in African American communities: A timeline. Retrieved from http://www.cdc.gov/nchhstp/newsroom/docs/timeline-30years-hiv-african-american-community-508.pdf

Clinton, W. J. (1997). Remarks in apology to African Americans on the Tuskegee experiment. *Weekly Compilation of Presidential, 33*(20), 718–721.

Cohen, C. J. (1999). *The boundaries of African Americanness: AIDS and the breakdown of African American politics.* Chicago, IL: University of Chicago Press.

Collins, P. H. (2000). *Black feminist thought: Knowledge, consciousness, and the politics of empowerment* (2nd ed.). New York, NY: Routledge.

Collins, P. H. (2005). *Black sexual politics: African-Americans, gender, and the new racism*. New York, NY: Routledge.

Conklin, T. J., Lincoln, T., & Tuthill, R. W. (2000). Self-reported health and prior health behaviors of newly admitted correctional inmates. *American Journal of Public Health, 90*(12), 1939–1941.

Crenshaw, K. W. (2011). Twenty years of critical race theory: Looking back to move forward. *Connecticut Law Review, 43*(5), 1253–1352.

Doherty, I. A., Shiboski, S., Ellen, J. M., Adimora, A. A., & Padian, N. S. (2006). Sexual bridging socially and over time: A simulation model exploring the relative effects of mixing and concurrency on viral sexuall transmitted infection transmission. *Sexually Transmitted Diseases, 33*(6), 368–373.

Edlin, B. R., Irwin, K. L., Faruque, S., McCoy, C. B., Word, C., Serrano, Y., . . . Holmberg, S.D. & The Multicenter Crack Cocaine & HIV Infection Study. (1994). Intersecting Epidemics-crack cocaine use and HIV infection among inner-city young adults. *New England Journal of Medicine, 331*(21), 1422–1427.

Friedman, S. R., Cooper, H. L. F., & Osborne, A. H. (2009). Structural and social contexts of HIV risk among African Americans. *American Journal of Public Health, 99*(6), 1002–1008.

Fritze, J. (2014). Groups push to lift needle exchange ban in funding bill. *Baltimore Sun Newspaper*. Retrieved September 27, 2014, from http://articles.baltimoresun.com/2014–01-09/news/bs-md-needle-exchange-20140109_1_mikulski_drug_users_ban

Gentry, Q. M., Elifson, K., & Sterk, C. (2005). Aiming for more relevant HIV risk reduction: A Black feminist perspective for enhancing HIV intervention for low-income African American women. *AIDS Education and Prevention, 17*(3), 238–252.

Gilkes, C. T. (1995). We have a beautiful mother: Womanist musings on the Afrocentric idea. In C. J. Sanders (Ed.), *Living the intersection: Womanism and Afrocentrism in theology*. (pp. 21–43) Minneapolis, MN: Fortress Press.

Gilkes, C. T. (2000). *If it wasn't for the women*. New York, NY: Orbis Books.

Kennedy, A. C., Bybee, D., & Greeson, M. R. (2014). Examining cumulative victimization, community violence exposure, and stigma as contributors to PTSD symptoms among high-risk young women. *American Journal of Orthopsychiatry, 84*(3), 284–294.

Khan, M. R., Doherty, I. A., Schoenbach, V. J., Taylor, E. M., Epperson, M. W., & Adimora, A. A. (2009). Incarceration and high-risk sex partnerships among men in the United States. *Journal of Urban Health-Bulletin of the New York Academy of Medicine, 86*(4), 584–601.

Kirp, D. L. (1995). Blood, sweat, and tears: The Tuskegee experiment and the era of AIDS. *Tikkun, 10*(3), 50–54.

Lam, W. K., Wechsberg, W., & Zule, W. African-American women who use crack cocaine: A comparison of mothers who live with and have been separated from their children. *Child Abuse & Neglect, 28*(11), 1229–1247.

Litt, J., & McNeil, M. (1997). Biological markers and social differentiation: crack babies and the construction of the dangerous mother. *Health Care Women International, 18*(1), 31–41.

Littlefield, M. B. (2003). A womanist perspective for social work with African American women. *Social Thought, 22*(4), 3–17.

Martin, E. P., & Martin, J. M. (1995). *Black social work pioneers and the power of social work. In social work and the Black experience*. Washington, DC: NASW Press, pp. 23–45.

McLane-Davison, D. (2013). The art of activist mothering: Black feminist leadership and knowing what to do. In D. Davis-Maye, A. D. Yarber, & T. E. Perry (Eds.), *What my momma gave me: Conceptualizations of womanhood* (pp.137–159). Lanham, MD: University Press of America.

Metzl, J. M., & Roberts, D. E. (2014). Structural competency meets structural racism: Race, politics, and the structure of medical knowledge. *American Medical Association Journal of Ethics, 16*(9), 674–690.

Murphy, S., & Roenbaum, M. (1999). *Pregnant women on drugs: Combating stereotypes and stigma.* New Brunswick, NJ: Rutgers University Press.

National Association of Black Social Workers. (2014). *Code of ethics.* Retrieved from www.nabsw.org

National Association of Social Workers. (2007). Institutional racism and the social work profession: A call to action. Retrieved from www.socialworkers.org/diversity/institutionalracism.pdf

Nattrass, N. (2013). Understanding the origins and prevalence of AIDS conspiracy beliefs in the United States and South Africa. *Sociology of Health & Illness, 35*(1), 113–129.

Norwood, C. (2013). Perspectives in Africana feminism: Exploring expressions of black feminism/womanism in the African diaspora. *Sociology Compass, 7*(3), 25–236.

Nunn, A., Yolken, A., Culter, b., Trooskin, S., Wilson, P., Little, S., & Mayer, K. (2014). Geography should not be destiny: Focusing HIV/AIDS implementation research and programs on microepidemics in US neighborhoods. *American Journal of Public Health, 104*(5), 775–780.

O'Donnell, S. M. (1996). *Urban African American community development in the progressive era. African American Community Practice Models* (pp. 7–26). New York, NY: The Hawthorne Press.

Owens, A. P. (2012). The affordable care act: Implications for African Americans living with HIV. *Journal of Human Behavior in the Social Environment, 22*, 319–333.

Reid-Merritt, P. (2010). *Righteous self-determination: The Black social work movement in America.* Baltimore, MD: Inprint Editions-Black Classic Press.

Reid, O., Mims, S., & Higginbottom, L. (2005). *Post traumatic slavery disorder: Definition, diagnosis and treatment.* Philadelphia, PA: Xlibris Corporation.

Riggs, M. Y. (1994). *Awake, arise and act: A womanist call for Black liberation.* Cleveland, OH: Pilgrim Press.

Roberts, A., Jackson, M. S., & Carlton-LaNey, I. (2000). Revisiting the need for feminism and afrocentric theory when treating African American female substance abusers. *Journal of Drug Issues, 30*(4), 901–918.

Roberts, D. (1997). *Killing the African American body: Race, reproduction, and the meaning of liberty.* New York, NY: Pantheon Books.

Roberts, D. (2011). *Fatal invention: How science, politics, and big business re-crate race in the twenty-first century.* New York, NY: The New Press.

Robertson, J. A. (1995). Norplant and irresponsible reproduction. *Hastings Center Report, 25*(1), S23–S26.

Skloot, R. (2010). *The immortal life of Henrietta Lacks.* New York, NY: Random House.

Smith, S. L. (1995). *Sick and tired of being sick and tired: African American women's health activism in America, 1890–1950.* Philadelphia: University of Pennsylvania Press.

Solorzano, D. G., & Yosso, T. J. (2002). Critical race methodology: Counter-storytelling as an analytical framework for education research. *Qualitative Inquiry, 8*(1), 23–44.

Sotero, M. M. (2006). A conceptual model of historical trauma: Implications for public health practice and research. *Journal of Health Disparities Research and Practice, 1*(1), 93–108.

Stevenson, H. C. (1994). The psychology of sexual racism and AIDS: An ongoing saga of distrust and the "sexual other." *Journal of African American Studies, 25*, 62–80.

Sutton, M. Y., Jones, R. L., Wolitski, R. J., Cleveland, J. C., Dean, H. D., & Fenton, K. A. (2009). A review of the center of disease control and prevention's response to HIV/AIDS crisis among blacks in the United States, 1981–2009. *American Journal of Public Health, 99*(2), S351–S359.

Washington, H. A. (2008). *A notoriously syphilis-soaked race: What really happened at Tuskegee? Medical apartheid: The dark history of medical experimentation on black Americans from colonial times to the present.* New York, NY: Anchor, pp. 157–189.

West-Olatunji, C. A., & Conwill, N. (2010). *Counseling African Americans.* San Francisco, CA: Houghton Mifflin Company/Cengage.

Williams, D. R., Neighbors, H. N., & Jackson, J. S. (2003). Racial/ethnic discrimination and health: Findings from community studies. *American Journal of Public Health, 93*(2), 200–208.

Wright, K. (Ed.). (2006). *AIDS in blackface: 25 Years of an epidemic.* Los Angeles, CA: Black AIDS Institute.

Wyatt, G. E., Gomez, C. A., Hamilton, A. B., Valencia-Garcia, D., Gant, L. M., & Graham, C. E. (2013). The intersection of gender and ethnicity in HIV risk interventions and prevention. *American Psychologist, 68*(4), 247–260.

Zuberi, T. (2011). Critical race theory of society. *Connecticut Law Review, 43*(5), 1573–1591.

CHAPTER 11

Mental and Emotional Wellness Among African Americans in Urban Environments: What Do We Know? How Can We Improve Outcomes?

Rhonda Wells-Wilbon, Kenya Jones, and Thelma Rich

DEFINING MENTAL AND EMOTIONAL HEALTH AND WELL-BEING

Overview of Mental Illness

Being mentally healthy is a state of well-being that is often taken for granted. However, in the last decade, a growing number of children and adults, suffering from mental illness, have come to the public's attention. The sensationalized acts of violence, leading to homicide(s) or suicide, often result in public outcry to do something about the mentally ill, but many fail to realize these rare cases do not accurately represent the majority of the population of those suffering with various forms of mental illness. In fact, the National Alliance on Mental Illness (NAMI) reports that one in four American Adults suffer from mental illness (NAMI, http://www .nami.org/Learn-More/Mental-Health-Conditions). This ratio represents a population of men and women in society that are in full view, yet often they suffer in silence with mental health challenges that others may not be aware of. In some cases, the persons themselves may not actually know they are experiencing symptoms associated with mental illness. This represents a large number of untreated and often undiagnosed cases of mental illness.

In our efforts to define and understand mental wellness, it is difficult to fully understand what "wellness" looks like, without defining and understanding mental illness.

The Centers for Disease Control and Prevention defines mental illness as disorders that impact the regulation of "mood, thought, and/or behavior" (http://www.cdc.gov/mental health/basics/mental-illness.htm). Mental illness includes a wide range of mental health conditions—examples of mental illness include depression, anxiety disorders, schizophrenia, eating disorders, and addictive behaviors (Mayo Clinic, n.d.). It is believed that most adults suffer with mental health symptoms from time to time throughout their lifetime, but it is when behaviors become chronic and impede normal functioning that there is a cause for concern and, in many cases, intervention.

Although the overall need for addressing mental illness seems to be a growing public health concern, there are always diverse groups within any population that researchers rarely study. This chapter focuses on conditions and resources in urban environments that influence how mental wellness is experienced by African American urban dwellers. Having knowledge of unique and culturally diverse experiences and perspectives helps provide information that could improve resources and services for African Americans in urban environments.

What Is Mental and Emotional Wellness or Well-Being

In May 2014, the Office of the U.S. surgeon general, posted on its website four national prevention strategies to safeguard mental and emotional well-being.

1. Promote positive early childhood development, including positive parenting and violence-free homes.

2. Facilitate social connectedness and community engagement across the life span.

3. Provide individuals and families with the support necessary to maintain positive mental well-being.

4. Promote early identification of mental health needs and access to quality services.

These guidelines provide some direction on how to be prevention focused. Based on these guidelines, one could conclude that early childhood experiences, social involvement and connectedness, support and resources for mental health, and identification and quality services have been identified as the most important social dynamics associated with well-being.

The well-being of African Americans is not much different than what has been highlighted here. In traditional Africa, the way of life was grounded in spirituality and a relationship with God; this was central to the values and beliefs that guided daily behavior and interactions. This spiritual foundation coupled with a major commitment to a communal shared existence is the foundation on which people of African ancestry thrive.

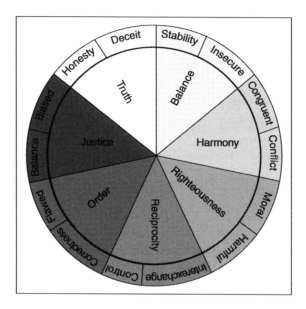

FIGURE 11.1 Asili Ma'at restoration model is a way to utilize the virtues of Ma'at to assist African Americans to mental health and well-being.

The virtues of Ma'at are grounded in seven core values centered around ethical and moral principles that governed ancient Egypt, which, if practiced as part of daily living, can lead to greater wholeness and support well-being as a way of life. The seven virtues are presented in Figure 11.1. These virtues can be observed throughout the African continent, and are central to the values and beliefs of the people, no matter the village, tribe, or ethnic heritage. The model was created as a foundation for building practice models that can be used to engage with people of African ancestry from a culturally relevant perspective, and was first introduced in another form in an article by Wells-Wilbon and Simpson (2009), but it is holistic enough that it can be used as a foundation for well-being for any group or population. For each virtue, two concepts have been assigned, one that embodies the positive nature of the virtue and one that embodies the negative nature of the virtue. The purpose of assigning these concepts is to help conceptualize the virtues and the potential capacity they may have in practice and in negotiating everyday living. The specific concepts chosen can be replaced with any other concept that embodies the virtues' positive or negative components, depending on the actual situation. This versatility helps define the depth of the virtues and how they may show up in the actions or quality of a person's character and the way they negotiate life. It also provides a foundation for helping to view wellness and sickness from an African centered perspective. A psychologically well person will experience life with these virtues primarily showing up in a way that brings light to the positive qualities of each virtue.

A CULTURAL LENS

What is lacking in current literature about African Americans and mental health is a real analysis of the true experiences of African Americans. There is a tendency to begin the conversation about the African American experience in the United States with the civil rights movement of the 1960s. There is a glossing over of the long historical experiences of people of African ancestry in this society that proceeded the civil rights movement. The Trans-Atlantic Slave Trade Database estimates that the Atlantic slave trade took around 12.8 million people from the continent of Africa between 1450 and 1900 (Lovejoy, 2012). Approximately 450,000 of those Africans eventually ended up in the United States. There is an international history rooted in laws, policy, economics, values, and racism that people do not want to discuss, but it has major implications not just for the mental health of African Americans and other people of African descent throughout the diaspora, but the current mental health status of all mankind. Here, the focus will remain on the well-being and mental health of African Americans, particularly those in urban settings.

To understand the psychological well-being of African Americans, the culture, values, and beliefs of Africa must be considered central to that analysis. These experiences that are passed from generation to generation in families, and practiced through communal interactions are the foundation on which societies are built. When this process is disrupted in the way the African American experience was disrupted there is a shift in the legacy of what is passed from generation to generation and the communal experience is also interrupted (Ani, 2001).

In the literature on child welfare and children in the foster care system, a common concern identified by mental health professionals is attachment disorder. Although the number of African American children in foster care has decreased over the past decade, from approximately 45% to 26% (Department of Health and Human Services (DHHS), 1913–1), the current website of Black Administrators in Child Welfare reports that among the children in foster care, there were still 31,000 waiting to be adopted in 2011. This is an area where African American social workers and other mental health professionals devote a great deal of their time and expertise. Attachment disorder is a concept that is used to define the experiences of children, who do not develop healthy bonding relationships with a primary caregiver (Shah, 2015). The end result can lead to mood and behavior disorders that impede relationships over the course of a lifetime (Shah, 2015). Although symptoms of attachment disorders are a major issue faced by children in the foster care system, perhaps this is not where this disorder began as a major problem of concern for African American people. The history of the transatlantic slave trade created dynamics in regular daily life for African Americans who were enslaved that could have created such crises around detachment that the residue still continues to impact the well-being of the descendants of such a systematic process of detaching and dehumanizing for economic gain and benefit.

A HISTORICAL PERSPECTIVE

Major Shifts in U.S. Mental Health Policy

The National Alliance on Mental Illness (NAMI) compiled a time line that traces the shifts in mental health policy. The first documented mental health policy was in London in 1247. It was not until 1817 that mental health was acknowledged in the public sphere in the United States, when the first asylum[1] was opened in Philadelphia based around principles of moral treatment for the mentally ill. In 1841, Dorothea Dix traveled in the country addressing the needs of the mentally ill; this raised concern for the mentally ill, and more than 30 mental hospitals were opened across the United States. In Illinois in 1867, the court ruled that a patient's insanity had to be determined by a jury, in a case where a husband was attempting to have his wife committed to a mental institution against her will.

In the first ruling in the U.S. Supreme Court on mental health in 1927, the court ruled that sterilization of defectives, including the mentally ill, was constitutional. The Durham Rule in the District of Columbia U.S. Court of Appeals in 1954 determined that if a person accused of crime was mentally diseased, the person was not responsible. It was later rejected because of the difficulty determining mental disease. The Community Mental Health Centers Act of 1963 led to the closure of many large state psychiatric hospitals. In 1966, the U.S. Court of Appeals in the District of Columbia ruled that patients in psychiatric hospitals had a right to receive treatment in the least restrictive settings.

It was not until 1975 that another major shift occurred. The U.S. Senate held hearings about the use of antipsychotic drugs in juvenile facilities for the developmentally disabled. In 1979, the NAMI was founded. In 1988, the Fair Housing Amendment Act prohibited housing discrimination based on physical and mental disabilities, and in 1990, the Americans with Disabilities Act was passed, prohibiting discrimination against people with physical and mental disabilities.

In 2004, DuPage County, Illinois, began the Mental Illness Court Alternative Program. The purpose was to redirect offenders, with a mental health diagnosis that was a contributing factor in the commission of the crime. This provided a sentencing alternative with the focus on integrated treatment services, thus diverting the offender from traditional prosecution.

In 2008, Congress passed the Mental Health Parity and Addictions Equity Act, requiring that insurance limits for mental illness coverage could be no more restrictive than those for physical health issues. The Patient Protection and Affordable Care Act of 2010 puts additional pressure on insurance companies and states to honor the Act passed by Congress in 2008, as many insurance institutions have continued to be out of compliance with this law.[2]

Historical Experiences of African Americans

The historical experiences of African Americans might lead one to expect African Americans to experience higher rates of mental health disorders, but according to two major studies, the Epidemiologic Catchment Area study (ECA) conducted in the 1980s and the National Comorbidity Survey (NCS), the rate of mental health symptoms and illness among African Americans is similar to that of other Americans, with some exceptions (Robins & Reiger, 1991). Although rates may be similar, the experiences of African Americans may not only be different from others, but it may even speak more clearly to the strength, resilience, and shear will to survive of African Americans, which few researchers and mental health professionals consider or acknowledge. Current mental health disparities are rooted in the historical experiences of African Americans, particularly as related to being excluded from participation in the larger society. A study of Medicare clients revealed disparities consistent with race-based discrimination (McBean & Gormick, 1994; Williams, 1998) exceptions (Kessler et al., 1994; Robins & Reiger, 1991). Some of the adverse experiences of African Americans that may influence mental health outcomes include more limited access to insurance and other financial resources, overrepresentation among higher need populations, and help-seeking behaviors that lead to preferring assistance from nonprofessional sources, to name only a few.

The teachings of Marimba Ani (2001) define the experience of African Americans who were sold into slavery and taken from their continent as the Maafa. "Maafa" is a Swahili term that means great disaster. From an African-centered perspective, the Holocaust would be considered the Jewish Maafa. Figure 11.2 is a functioning version of Ma'at, but it is post-Maafa. The distinction here is, the person is no longer functioning at his or her optimum level; therefore, resources and support from others are needed in order for the person to be well and experience wholeness.

Stigma in the African American community is greater than the broader society and accessible educational opportunities, to learn more about mental health may be limited. Research also indicates that African Americans may be misdiagnosed more often than

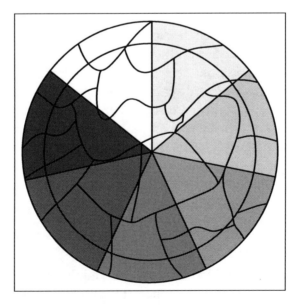

FIGURE 11.2 Asili Ma'at functioning model.

their White counterparts, thus increasing their bias and distrust of health professionals in general (Baker & Bells, 1999; Lawson & Lawson, 2013). Some of the experiences, indicators, and warning signs for Africans Americans are unique enough to warrant additional discussion.

Although the rate of African Americans with mental illness is said to be the same one in four as the larger population, there are many reasons that some African Americans may be at greater risk. There is distrust among African Americans of mental health services, thus African Americans are more likely to seek help from a primary care physician than to get care from a mental health specialist (Pingitore, Snowden, Sansone, & Klinkman, 2001). Additionally, a 2007 study (Bailey, R. K., Patel, M., Barker, N. C., Ali, S., & Jabeen, S., 2011) showed that 63% of African Americans believed that depression was a personal weakness, with 30% indicating that they would manage it themselves and only one third reported that they would take medication if recommended by a medical professional. There is some research indicating that African Americans may metabolize medications differently, and thus perhaps experience more side effects with higher doses of medication (Bradford, Gaedigk, & Leeder, 1998). This could lead to more noncompliance with taking medication (Swartz et al., 2014), but also more discussion within the African American community about medications and side effects. These discussions may influence African Americans and their unwillingness to take medication for psychological disorders such as depression and other more severe disorders. Other studies have indicated a relationship between mental illness among African Americans and higher incidence of somatization, which is the manifestation of actual physical illnesses (Robins & Reiger, 1991). There is some research that suggests that mental health disorders that go untreated could ultimately lead to a physical illness. If this is true, given what is known about African Americans and mental health treatment practices, they could be at greater risk for such physical health outcomes.

African Americans do share a common collective experience of racism and oppression and many African American families come from a historical experience of some economic hardship. Spirituality, religion, and a belief in God or some higher power, is a well-known source of strength for many African Americans. Resiliency and the capacity to overcome difficulty and hardships as a cornerstone for survival have been documented by researchers and human service professionals. But few address the question, at what cost?

THE URBAN ENVIRONMENT

Being a resident of an urban environment, has many benefits, particularly as it relates to access to variety and the newest information, products, services, and resources. However, research has shown that residing in an urban environment has some specific potential challenges and stressors, particularly for those who are economically disadvantaged. Some of the potential challenges to mental health associated with living in the inner city include (a) overcrowded conditions, (b) exposure to violence, and (c) inadequate resources. There are also conditions that may put urban dwellers at greater risk for stressors that can negatively impact mental health (Evans, 2003). For example, there are reports that urban residents do not get enough sunlight, which is reported to be associated with vitamin D deficiency, which researchers now believe can be associated with depression (Holick & Chen, 2008). These potential challenges have multiple layers, adding to the complexity of understanding each dynamic and its potential relationship with negative outcomes for various populations of urban dwellers. Within about 20 minutes of ultraviolet exposure in light-skinned individuals (three to six times longer for pigmented skin), the concentrations of vitamin D precursors produced in the skin reach an equilibrium, and any further vitamin D produced is degraded (Holick, 1995).

Social disparities are more prominent in urban environments and can increase the amount of stress faced by residents. According to Adli (2011), recent research has indicated greater risk for mental disorders among urban residents, a meta-analysis showed a 20% higher risk of developing anxiety disorders and a 40% higher risk of developing mood disorders, and longitudinal studies indicate that an urban upbringing and not epidemiological variables actually account for patients with schizophrenia and increases the risk of other mental disorders (Adli, 2011).

Long-term exposure to urban living without the benefit of having access to the best opportunities in the environment and community can lead to stress, social disorientation, and challenges for mental health. Long-term exposure without the interventions that are the right fit, could lead to what we describe in Figure 11.3 as the Asili Ma'at dysfunctional model. In this model, well-being has been seriously compromised and the person is no longer at an optimum or functioning level, but they are dysfunctional and wholeness does not exist.

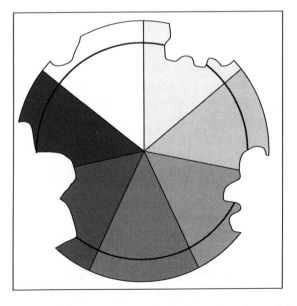

FIGURE 11.3 Asili Ma'at dysfunctional model.

Special Populations

The special populations highlighted subsequently represent many of those who experience mental health challenges. Research reveals many overlaps among the following populations, making it difficult to uncover cause and effect, but, at the core, these populations are at a greater risk of experiencing higher rates of mental illness. Being an urban dweller, in many cases, may add to the challenge. Comorbidity has been found in many research studies (Schwartz, Bradley, Sexton, Sherry, & Ressler, 2014).

Women

African Americans in general are misdiagnosed and undertreated for depression and African American women may be among those suffering the most. Because of stigma and not wanting to be considered weak, African American women often do not seek services or treatment they may in fact need. Although White women are more likely to have depression, African American and Caribbean women suffer greater severity and persistence with their depressive symptoms. Left untreated, these women can sink deeper and deeper into a black hole, and often without anyone knowing they are in fact suffering from depression.

Children

The research literature suggests that the longer a person resides in an urban setting, the more likely it is they will develop some form of mental illness. This puts children who grow up in urban environments at higher risk. African American children who grow up in urban environments can be particularly vulnerable. Some potential risk factors associated with children experiencing depression include (a) poverty, (b) malnourishment, (c) growing up in a child welfare system or foster care, and (d) exposure to violence. African American children represent approximately 45% of the foster care population, and are three times more likely than White children to live in poverty. Twenty-five percent of African American children exposed to violence display signs of posttraumatic stress. Overall, these challenges not only can lead to depression, they lead to an inability for the African American child to develop properly and thrive.

Homeless

African Americans only make up about 12% of the U.S. population, but represent 40% of those experiencing homelessness (Jencks, 1994). In a recent study, women in general were found to be more likely to be homeless pre- and post-incarceration and suffer from higher rates of mental illness and substance-use disorders (Fries, Fedock, & Pimlott-Kubiak, 2014).

Inmates

Prison inmates are at a greater risk of developing mental illness and African American men represent almost half of the prison population (Ditton, 1999). Although African Americans have lower rates of actual mental illness in prison than Whites, they are less likely to receive the mental health treatment and services needed (Ditton, 1999).

Survivors of Violence and Trauma

The study by Schwartz et al. (2014) on low-income African Americans in an inner city mental health clinic confirms the results from previous studies. Early childhood trauma was found to be correlated with many adult indicators of mental illness. These mental health challenges include substance use disorders, posttraumatic stress disorder (PTSD), and suicide attempts (Schwartz et al., 2014). Some gender distinctions among African American men and women with mental health disorders were discovered. Among the patients receiving clinic services, African American women had higher rates of sexual abuse and/or assault and African American men were more likely to have experienced military combat or assault with a weapon (Schwartz et al., 2014) and been exposed to various forms of trauma in the community.

In a study of 378 African American inner city youth, the researchers found a relationship between trauma caused by (a) physical abuse, (b) sexual abuse, and (c) transportation accidents and PTSD symptoms (Brown, T. H., Mellman, T. A., Alfano, C. A., & Weems, C. F. (2011)). Sleep fears and insomnia were identified as a major consequence of the traumatic experience for these youth.

Clinical Practice

The literature indicates that African Americans are more likely to seek health care services from African American professionals; there is a great need for more African Americans to be trained in mental health and various forms of clinical psychotherapy. African Americans only make up 2% of psychologists and psychiatrists and 4% of clinical social workers.

There is also a great need for more research specifically on African American populations to better understand some of the unique ways African Americans experience various mental disorders and treatment methods that better address their needs. Understanding medications and the impact they have on African Americans as well as various treatment modalities would be very important in closing the disparity gap around mental health.

Although it is true that alternative methods to address mental health symptoms, such as seeking out spiritual leaders and church ministries, are not always the best resource for African Americans, it does not erase the fact that this population utilizes religion and religious institutions at higher rates than they seek treatment from health and mental health professionals. Because this is true, mental health professionals interested in helping African American's must do a better job working with these institutions so that trained professionals can be a frontline resource in the place where African Americans are most likely to seek help.

Social Work Education

A course on mental health with an emphasis on urban environments is an opportunity to offer students a chance to gain knowledge specific to the conditions and experiences that make urban dwelling unique. When you shift the focus to more vulnerable populations such as African Americans, Latinos, homeless, poor, illegal drug users, unemployed, and children, there is a niche where social workers can have the greatest impact. Knowledge gained in practice courses, human behavior, diversity, and social and economic justice can serve as a foundation for building a learning environment where students can discuss, analyze, and process through the use of vignettes, role-plays, case studies, and technological devices that aid classroom learning.

Such a course should be designed to provide students with an in-depth knowledge base. This should include information on prevention and intervention with client systems experiencing or at-risk of experiencing problems in functioning around mental wellness. Students should showcase a demonstration of knowledge, values, skills, and strengths for effective practice where the delivery created has a dual approach that will cover how mental health in social work can enhance clients' developmental capacities, problem-solving, and coping skills and how this type of practice within an urban environment will emphasize culturally competent, compassionate professionals who can process service delivery systems effectively.

Students' capacity to demonstrate competent practice behaviors for work with urban populations can be assessed based on their ability to apply their knowledge, values, and skills with assignments such as video analyses, case study assessments, presentations on strength-based assessments, and group assignments. These assignments offer students a chance to engage with each other to advance their knowledge and skills when working in various settings. The course should emphasize the importance of understanding the client's experiences of oppression and unequal access to power within political, social, and economic institutions and organizations. This information is vital for appropriate assessment and intervention with urban African American clients experiencing social and economic injustices based on characteristics related to race, ethnicity, sexual orientation, culture, and gender.

Field Education

Field Education Programs at Schools of Social Work in urban communities are required to partner with social welfare agencies in both the public and private sectors, which offer mental health services to urban dwellers. Selected agencies should be committed to providing transformative learning opportunities for social work student interns placed in the agency for the field practicum experience. The partnership among field education, agencies, and students is where the program takes responsibility for preparing students to become effective and relevant urban social work practitioners for the 21st century.

Due to the increase in need for mental health services with urban populations, many agencies recognize that they cannot separate mental health issues from other social problems. More and more, there is a need for agencies to integrate mental health services along with housing, employment, child care, day care, after-school programs, family counseling, and other needed resources and services. There is also an increased need for psychiatric rehabilitation programs in urban areas. Field Education Programs in urban settings should be vigilant in increasing the number of mental health agencies available for student interns.

Students who work with African American clients in urban areas must utilize their knowledge of theories of human behavior, family systems, communities, and organizations. They must apply practice skills in identification, assessment, and treatment goals in order to enhance problem-solving skills and engage clients in active participation. Students are expected to become familiar with agency policies and procedures that affect agency service delivery, systems operations, and overall community involvement. During the field placement experience, students must demonstrate acquired social work skill sets, including but not limited to knowledge of policies, programs, and procedures, written and verbal communication skills, and critical and analytical thinking skills. All of the aforementioned skills are also intertwined, interwoven, and incorporated into motivational interviewing, assessment, and prevention methods.

Students' involvement and investment in working with clients with mental health challenges must be a reoccurring discussion due to the myriad of problems identified and needed to be solved. Almost every factor–facet of survival in the urban community either directly or indirectly points to the need for competency in mental health. Culturally competent social workers, who practice in urban settings, are required to be micro, mezzo, and macro practitioners. The environment itself is vast and multifaceted, and the social problems that urban dwellers face are not less challenging.

Field Education Seminar Courses

Field Education Seminar courses are a dynamic learning laboratory for students to express perceptions and insights gained from client contact–interactions and working with other agencies on behalf of their clients. The open forums created by the seminar experience include such topical areas as case management, theoretical frameworks, and techniques that are utilized in the agency setting to ably assist clients.

Students in seminars discuss the relationship between the variations in demographics, the communities understanding of mental illness or other social issues, whether a social stigma still exists regarding mental illness, and, if so, what are some of the ramifications? Students in different concentrations have an opportunity to discuss mental health problems with clients in their respective fields of practice, such as mental health issues across the life span (in children, adolescents, young adults, and middle and aged adults) and across systems (child welfare, schools, group homes, public, private, and nonprofit health systems, programs for the aged, etc.).

Implications for Job Placement

As students successfully complete these assignments in the field seminar course, it enhances their capacity to demonstrate their knowledge of the urban settings and use their practice skills in the agency. As a result, students are more prepared to meet the challenges of a social worker who practices in urban communities. Because of their unique capacity, students with this unique skill set are highly desired by agencies in urban environments. The student obtains employment and the agency inherits a well-trained employee. This is especially true in the mental health area. It is indicative of the students' level of advancement in providing services to this population and their demonstration of acquired practice skills. Students must have excellent interpersonal and communication skills, analytical and critical thinking, knowledge of human behavior, knowledge of health care resources and systems, and participate in learning current trends and patterns. Most vital is for the student to be personable and possess a passion for working in the community. Experience shows that the number of students interested in becoming entrepreneurs in the mental health area is increasing. Still others create agencies in partnerships with other colleagues, all who have had training to work in the urban community.

The goal of the Field Education Program is to prepare social work practitioners for work that meets the mission of its program; however, skills of urban practitioners can be used in other environments. The mental health social work practitioner is called to serve a population in urban settings that is not only vulnerable and often disenfranchised but also subject to frequent changes in priorities of all levels of government whether local, state, or federal, thus influencing resources and funding to combat social problems.

Training for Field Supervisors/What We Have Learned

During training sessions with field supervisors, it is inevitable that client behaviors emerge as a focus in providing quality services. Paramount among the topics discussed is conditions leading to mental health problems.

Supervisors working in urban public school settings who have predominantly African American children have explained that an overwhelming number of the children they work with cannot achieve academic success due to multiple environmental pressures. These pressures may include bereavement and grief and loss issues that have not been addressed stemming from community violence. Bullying may manifest into disruptive behaviors, self-esteem issues, and attitude outbursts. Incarceration, substance use disorders, and absence of biological parents from the home leave children bereft of support systems and trust issues emerge. Children may face homelessness and poverty.

Supervisors working in substance abuse prevention and recovery agencies cite that when mental health problems are not addressed, their programs experience soaring recidivism rates. In training, field supervisors attribute isolation from family and friends, relationship problems, unemployment, and underemployment as the prevailing issues that have a negative impact on their clients' progress.

Supervisors in public child welfare settings express agreement with these problem areas, and it is often true these various settings serve mutual clients. Mental health issues also affect the elderly and disabled. Among the issues most prevalent there is loss, declining physical health, loneliness, and making choices such as choosing to purchase food or medication due to limited income. Mental health services are very prevalent in service delivery systems in urban areas. Yet the need far exceeds the available resources—more are still needed. The challenge of preventing mental health issues within the African American population must be met with an even greater commitment from urban social work practitioners who have been trained by experts in the mental health field.

IMPLICATIONS

Although African Americans have a unique historical experience that has influenced their well-being, they come from a legacy of great resilience. Their historical resources, values, and beliefs are central to what helps them thrive and cannot be ignored when interventions and services are created and implemented for positive mental health outcomes.

There should be no question that African Americans in urban environments have an increased need for mental health services, access to outpatient mental health treatment programs, and prevention services. The need for mental health services is evident across the life span, from infants, toddlers, school-age children, adolescents, young adults, mature adults, to the elderly. No population is exempt. African Americans are also challenged by lack of access, disparities in treatment, labeling stigma, and environmental stressors. African Americans experience environmental stressors such as poor housing, violent neighborhoods and schools, and poverty. They are also affected by homelessness of families and children, substance abuse, HIV/AIDS, attention-deficit hyperactivity disorder, commonly referred to as ADHD, PTSD, and Alzheimer's disease, as discussed throughout the book. All of these factors contribute to mental health and mental illness concerns among African Americans living in urban environments.

The challenge is to bridge the gap between the cultural values, beliefs, and resources African Americans utilize and trust and the resources and expertise of trained mental health professionals. Neither can serve as the only solution when it comes to engaging and helping African Americans who face serious mental health symptoms and disorders. Culture sensitivity without bias must allow for the implementation of needed mental health services in such a way that African Americans who suffer with treatable mental health disorders, can come out of the shadows and get the help they not only need, but deserve.

FOR FURTHER STUDY

Suggested Assignments

- Assignments might include research papers, essays, individual and team oral presentations, process recordings, review of case studies, role-play, debates on current health policies, psychosocial assessments, social work practitioner interviews, and student-led seminar discussions. Any or all of these assignments can be tailored to expand and assess knowledge values and skills specific to mental health.
- Students can create a genogram, tracing family health conditions—using no less than three generations. This assignment provides students with information that assists them in assessing family issues and identifying problems. It also provides an opportunity to highlight patterns in urban communities.

- Students can do a reflection paper on the topic "Perceptions of Mental Health in the Urban Community," using the targeted population of their field placement.
- As a group assignment, students can be asked to work in teams to utilize their creativity, imagine they had received a grant in the amount of their choice, develop a mental health program for a population of their choice, conduct a needs assessment, and set up an implementation plan—community residents and community agencies must be engaged.
- Students can review films to strengthen and improve practice skills such as "Assessing ADHD in the Schools." Living with PTSD: Lessons For Partners Friends and Supporters," "Evidenced–Based Treatment Planning for Bipolar Order," and "Explaining PTSD: Lessons for Mental Health Professionals."
- Film presentations can be accessed through www.psychotherapy.net.
- These assignments allow the assessment of student abilities to apply their knowledge base and acquired skills to become a more effective practitioner in urban settings.
- The video analysis assignment can encompass more than assessing how mental health is portrayed through film. It can also have students examine and locate local community supports, as well as apply intervention tools and assessments from the movie analysis videos. Course topics can include *Diagnostic and Statistical Manual of Mental Disorders* (*DSM*) history and classification, the at-risk and underserved populations, and how the differences impact various groups. Also include social supports, societal conditions, impacts of gender, and physical health.

Several movies intensely discuss mental health in ways that social work students can understand. The following is a short list of popular films that address specific areas in mental health that can enhance classroom discussions.

One Flew Over the Cuckoo's Nest (1975): A historically acclaimed movie about mental health and treatment within psychiatric institutions.

Sybil (1976): A story about a young woman with a difficult childhood that develops alternate personalities to cope.

Fight Club (1991): Discusses several mental health issues consisting of insomnia as well as dissociative disorder by a young man and his encounters with people and consumerism.

The Fisher King (1991): Shares a story that includes both depression and posttraumatic stress disorder.

A Beautiful Mind (2001): Discusses true-life events of John Forbes Nash, Jr., a brilliant mathematician living with schizophrenia.

The Notebook (2004): Discusses the story of unconditional love of a man for his wife, despite her memory lapses from dementia.

Canvas (2006): Addresses how mental health impacts families.

Mr. Brooks (2007): A psychological thriller about a man living a secret life of compulsions.

The Soloist (2009): Shares a true-life story, which looks at schizophrenia and strengths and challenges that are encountered by family and friends of someone living with a mental health disorder.

Silver Linings Playbook (2012): Shares the story of a man recently released from a mental institution, who copes with bipolar disease while living with his family as well as encountering new people.

Suggested Readings

Barrio, C., Yamada, A. M., Hough, R. L., Hawthorne, W., Garcia, P., & Jeste, D. V. (2003). Ethnic disparities in use of public mental health case management services among patients with schizophrenia. *Psychiatric Services. 54*(9), 1264–1270.

Clark, R., Anderson, N. B., Clark, V. R., & Williams, D. R. (1999). Racism as a stressor for African Americans: A biopsychosocial model. *American Psychologist, 54*(10), 805.

Garland, A. F., Lau, A. S., Yeh, M., McCabe, K. M., Hough, R. L., & Landsverk, J. A. (2005). Racial and ethnic differences in utilization of mental health services among high-risk youths. *American Journal Psychiatry, 162*(7), 1336–43

Gary, T. L., Stark, S. A., & LaVeist, T. A. (2007). Neighborhood characteristics and mental health among African Americans and whites living in a racially integrated urban community. *Health & Place, 13*(2), 569–575.

Goldmann, E., Aiello, A., Uddin, M., Delva, J., Koenen, K., Gant, L. M., & Galea, S. (2011). Pervasive exposure to violence and posttraumatic stress disorder in a predominantly African American Urban Community: The Detroit Neighborhood Health Study. *Journal of Traumatic Stress, 24*(6), 747–751.

Robinson-Brown, D., & Keith, V. (Eds.). (2013). *In and out of our right minds: The mental health of African American women.* New York, NY: Columbia University Press.

Schwartz, A. C., Bradley, R. L., Sexton, M., Sherry, A., & Ressler, K. J. (2005). Posttraumatic stress disorder among African Americans in an inner city mental health clinic. *Psychiatric Services, 56*(2), 212–217.

Woods, S. W., Sullivan, M. C., Neuse, E. C., Diaz, E., Baker, C. B., Madonick, S. H.,…& Steiner, J. L. (2014). Best practices: Racial and ethnic effects on antipsychotic prescribing practices in a community mental health center. *Psychiatric Services, 54*(2), 177–186.

Young, J. L., Griffith, E. E., & Williams, D. R. (2003). The integral role of pastoral counseling by African-American clergy in community mental health. *Psychiatric Services, 54*(5), 688–92.

Zimmerman, M. A., Ramirez-Valles, J., & Maton, K. I. (1999). Resilience among urban African American male adolescents: A study of the protective effects of sociopolitical control on their mental health. *American Journal of Community Psychology, 27*(6), 733–751.

Suggested Websites

www.mentalhealth.gov
www.mentalhealthamerica.net
www.psychiatry.org
www.nami.org
www.uniteforsight.org

NOTES

1. An asylum is a refuge or shelter established for those suffering from mental illness. By 1904, about 150,000 people were housed in asylums in the United States.
2. This time line is documented in many sources, but the information gathered for this section came from a global time line on mental health on the National Alliance on Mental Health website on January 1, 2015. www.nami.org

REFERENCES

Adli, M. (2011, November). Urban stress and mental health. Retrieved from http://lsecities.net/media/objects/articles/urban-stress-and-mental-health/en-gb

American Psychiatric Association. (2013). *Diagnostic and statistical manual of mental disorders* (5th ed.). Washington, DC: Author.

Ani, M. (2001). *Yurugu: An African-centered critique of European cultural thought and behavior.* Washington, DC: Nkonimfo Publications.

Baker, F. M., & Bell, C. C. (1999). Issues in the psychiatric treatment of African Americans. *Psychiatric Services, 50*(3), 362–8.

Bradford, L. D., Gaedigk, A., & Leeder, J. S. (1998). High frequency of CYP2D6 poor and "intermediate" metabolizers in black populations: A review and preliminary data. *Psychopharmacology Bulletin,* [PubMed: 10513455]. 34797–34804.

Ditton, P. M. (1999). *Special report: Mental health and treatment of inmates and probationers.* Washington, DC: U.S. Department of Justice, Bureau of Justice Statistics.

Evans, G. W. (2003). The built environment and mental health. *Journal of Urban Health, 80*(4), 536–555.

Fries, L., Fedock, G., & Kubiak, S. P. (2014). Role of gender, substance use, and serious mental illness in anticipated postjail homelessness. *Social Work Research, 38*(2), 107–116.

Holick, M. F. (1995, March). Environmental factors that influence the cutaneous production of vitamin D (PDF). *The American Journal of Clinical Nutrition, 61*(3 Suppl.): 638S–645S.

Holick, M. F., & Chen, T. C. (2008). Vitamin D deficiency: A worldwide problem with health consequences. *The American Journal of Clinical Nutrition, 87*(4), 1080S–1086S.

Jencks, C. (1994). *The homeless.* Cambridge, MA: Harvard University Press.

Lawson, W. B., & Lawson, A. (2013). Disparities in mental health diagnosis and treatment among African Americans: Implications for the correctional systems. In B. Sanders, Y. F. Thomas, & B. G. Deeds (Eds.), *Crime, HIV and health: Intersections of criminal justice and public health concerns* (pp. 81–91). Dordrecht, The Netherlands: Springer Science + Business Media.

Lovejoy, P. E. (2012). *Transformations of slavery: A history of slavery in Africa.* London, England: Cambridge University Press.

Mayo Clinic. (n.d.). Retrieved from http://www.mayoclinic.org

Mbembe, A. (2001). *On the postcolony.* Berkeley: University of California Press.

McBean, A. M., & Gornick, M. (1994). Differences by race in the rates of procedures performed in hospitals for Medicare beneficiaries. *Health Care Financing Review, 15*(4), 77.

Pingitore, D., Snowden, L., Sansone, R. A., & Klinkman, M. (2001). Persons with depressive symptoms and the treatments they receive: A comparison of primary care physicians and psychiatrists. *International Journal of Psychiatry in Medicine, 31*(1), 41–60.

Robins, L., & Regier, D. A. (1991). *Psychiatric disorders in America: The epidemiologic catchment area study.* New York, NY: The Free Press.

Schwartz, A. C., Bradley, R. L., Sexton, M., Sherry, A., & Ressler, K. J. (2005). Posttraumatic stress disorder among African Americans in an inner city mental health clinic. *Psychiatric Services, 56*(2), 212–217.

Shah, N. S. (2015). Effects of attachment disorder on psychosocial development. *Student Pulse, 7*(02), 2/3.

Swartz, M. S., Swanson, J. W., Hiday, V. A., Borum, R., Wagner, H. R., & Burns, B. J. (2014). Violence and severe mental illness: The effects of substance abuse and non-adherence to medication.

Wells-Wilbon, R., & Simpson, G. M. (2009). Transitioning the caregiving role for the next generation: An African-centered womanist perspective. *Black Women, Gender & Families, 3*(2), 87–105.

Williams, D. R. (1998). African-American health: The role of the social environment. *Journal of Urban Health, 75*(2), 300–321.

CHAPTER **12**

The Magic of Aging in the Urban Environment

Margaret E. Pittman, Leeza M. Scheidt,
Merissa R. Munford, and Halaevalu F. Ofahengaue Vakalahi

I am the reason my ancestors survived, and I am proud to be a bridge for the next generation of survivors.

—Dr. Rhonda Wells-Wilbon, 2013

This introductory chapter provides an entry into the section on aging among African Americans in urban environments. Briefly discussed in this section are a broader portrait of older African American adults living in urban communities and selected issues of importance such as caregiving, intergenerational dynamics of urban families, and coping with grief and loss in urban communities. Although not exhaustive, these selections are intended to initiate further discussion on not only people and contextual challenges but also the strengths and powers of people in contexts, in which lies the magic of aging in urban communities.

OUR RESPONSIBILITY

As social workers across space, time, and cultures, we have taken an oath to advocate for, promote, and sustain healthy and functioning individuals, families, and communities across the life course. This is our collective responsibility as social workers especially to those who have paved the way—our elders—for present and future generations. To this end, we must stand with the aged for social and economic justice; to celebrate maturity, and to fight against racism, economic injustices, ageism, and all other isms that negatively affect the quality of life of our elders, particularly those in urban communities.

The stories and legacies of African American elders in urban communities deeply reflect social and economic justice work, advocacy for equity and equality, and other social movements that have positively impacted not only the African American diaspora but all people who live in urban settings. The aged have built magnificent cities filled with promises and often untapped resources for generations to come, and it is our responsibility to sustain those legacies and to ensure that people in our cities have the capacity to thrive and establish new legacies for the next generation of urban dwellers. As expressed by Yancey, Baldwin, Saran, and Vakalahi (2014), despite the overwhelming challenges of urban communities today, for our urban elders, it is their home and a place of refuge filled with unconditional love and acceptance of diverse histories and lived experiences. This sense of home, connection, love, and acceptance is the "magic" of aging in the urban environment.

THE URBAN CONTEXT AND MAJOR AGING ISSUES

In 2010, there were more than 3,500 urban areas in the United States, defined as areas that have been developed for commercial, residential, and other industrial uses. Urbanized areas consisted of 50,000-plus people and urban clusters consisted of at least 2,500 to 50,000 people (U.S. Census Bureau, 2010). Today, these urban cities or metro/metropolitan areas are often unfairly over-associated with negative experiences and perceptions such as prevailing poverty, disproportionate crime rates, segregation by socioeconomic status, and other struggles (Robert & Ruel, 2006). Although this is the story of many cities, the story tends to be cyclical in terms of periods of peace and prosperity as well as periods of poverty and struggles. Nonetheless, the convenience of the urban environment in relation to the availability and accessibility of resources within close proximity has also contributed positively to the independence in daily activities and overall quality of life of older adults (Oswald et al., 2007; Yancey et al., 2014).

The current "gerontological explosion" suggests that the majority of the U.S. population is aged 65 years and above, the first time in U.S. history for such a population shift (U.S. Census Bureau, 2010). The older adult population will reach about 72 million by year 2030, with many older adults living in urban settings (Bureau of Labor Statistics, 2008; Slack & Jensen, 2008). Consequently, this is the time to prepare urban social workers and related professionals to respond in culturally appropriate ways to the needs of this urban population. These urban elders come from various cultures around the world, bringing diverse lived experiences and perspectives, and live side-by-side facilitated by the convenience of urban environmental systems and structures. This increased trend in aging and urbanization is a global phenomenon (Masotti, Fick, Johnson-Masotti, & MacLeod, 2006); however, in the United States, older racial–ethnic minorities will increase by more than 200% by year 2030 (U.S. Census Bureau, 2010). For some of the largest urban communities in the United States, including Baltimore, Detroit, Jackson, and New Orleans, the predominant racial–ethnic group is African American, and they are aging (U.S. Census Bureau, 2010).

Major issues impacting many aging African Americans in urban environments include deteriorating housing amid decreased household income, and increased caregiving responsibilities for multiple generations as a result of incarceration and chronic health problems of those with primary responsibilities for caregiving (Simpson & Lawrence-Webb, 2009; Yancey et al., 2014). Likewise, these urban older adults are often challenged with accessing quality health care services in urban systems that, historically, have provided substandard care to African Americans and other ethnic–racial groups. These urban older adults are in dire need of accessing nutritious fruits and vegetables, but are plagued with the reality of food deserts and unaffordable prices when nutritious options are available. The lack of nutritional services for older adults, especially in urban settings (Charlton & Rose, 2001) and others concerning urban community conditions (Eisenhauer, 2001; Wolfe, Frongillo, & Valois, 2003), have contributed to ongoing nutritional deficiencies among urban older adults.

In addition, technology knowledge and skills have become important to older adults in urban environments as a means for accessing resources and communication with health care providers. Technology has become an important mechanism for maintaining relationships; dealing with isolation and loneliness; and a source of empowerment, independence, and being informed among urban older adults (Berridge, 2014). Moreover, contrary to popular beliefs, issues of sex and intimacy are of significance among the urban aging population, which require culturally sensitive responses from social work professionals in consideration of the reality of life-threatening diseases and illnesses resulting from risky behaviors that sometimes are linked to necessity and survival (Giunta & Jacobson, 2014).

The intersection of mental health, substance abuse, and HIV/AIDS among older adults in urban communities has become a major challenge requiring answers from professionals across disciplines, with social work in the lead (Yancey et al., 2014). Among urban older adults, substance abuse is the "invisible epidemic" (Ferrell & Sorocco, 2006), which has been exacerbated by the interaction of mixing drugs or alcohol and medication (Aira, Hartikainen, & Sulkava, 2005) often used as sleeping aids in response to difficulty sleeping, attributed to fear of certain conditions in urban neighborhoods (Johnson, 1997). Poverty, debilitating housing, and chronic socioeconomic problems have likewise contributed to mental health disorders and social isolation among urban older adults (Massey & Denton, 1993; Zheng et al., 2011). Although urban older adults are less likely to seek out mental health services, they are also often less distressed compared with their rural counterparts (Norris & Karlin, 2006; Uphold, Rane, Reid, & Tomar, 2005), perhaps because the urban communities, despite their challenges, also offer kin, family, and community support systems (Yancey et al., 2014). However, older ethnic–racial individuals in urban communities are also at a higher risk of contracting HIV/AIDS, particularly those who are exposed to drug trafficking and commercial sex trades (Ward, Disch, Levy, & Schensul, 2004).

SUPPORTS AND RESOURCES IN THE URBAN ENVIRONMENT

Notwithstanding the known challenges and struggles faced by the urban elders, the richness offered by the cultural diversity in urban communities can provide positive experiences for older adults. In a study by Chumbler, Cody, Booth, and Beck (2001), findings showed that urban older adults reported lower rates of functional limitations, cognitive impairment, and chronic health conditions compared with rural older adults. Urban older adults are also more resilient and astute in terms of awareness of their surroundings and appropriately managing risky situations (Yancey et al., 2014).

Furthermore, the collective and inclusive orientation, which facilitates the opportunity to access existing support systems in urban communities and neighborhoods, can also minimize isolation and loneliness (Burton, Mitchell, & Stride, 2011). For instance, the built environment is critical for the urban aging population because of their dependence on environmental systems and structures for accomplishing their daily activities (Yancey et al., 2014). The urban built environment includes public transportation, health and medical facilities, shops, and other amenities that can promote social interaction, physical activity, and community engagement among urban older adults (Burton et al., 2011; Clarke, Ailshire, Bader, Morenoff, & House, 2008; Li, Fisher, Brownson, & Bosworth, 2005).

In addition, the urban community offers opportunities for faith and civic engagement, which are important for the health and well-being of urban African American elders (Hodge, 2005). Faith and spirituality have been used for coping and as a source of hope and meaning among older adults across cultures (Hodge & Limb, 2010). Of historical significance to the urban African American community are the Black churches that served as a source of empowerment and justice, and provided for the bio-psycho-social-spiritual needs of African American older adults. It is the oldest and most influential institution by and for Black people; a resource that continues to be a necessity for the quality of life of today's urban African American older adults (Adkison-Bradley, Johnson, Sanders, Duncan, & Holcomb-McCoy, 2005; Martin & Martin, 2002). Also within the African American community is the structure of fictive kin, which is a magnificent aspect of the urban African American community that has greatly benefited urban older adults and their families in terms of caregiving, social interaction, and support systems (Yancey et al., 2014). Fictive kin includes the nonbiological relatives in one's social support network who become and play the role of a supportive family (Yancey et al., 2014).

WORKING WITH THE AGING POPULATION

Appropriately conceptualizing social work practice with the aging African American population in the urban environment is critical for promoting quality of life. That is, as discussed by Simpson, Giunta, and Vakalahi (2014), older adults represent intersectional and multidimensional lived experiences, cultures, histories, and sociopolitical worldviews that challenge mainstream linear approaches and theories. Responding to today's older adults, particularly African Americans in urban communities, requires not only an appreciation for differences but also embracing of commonalities (Nash, 2008) as a framework for grappling with aging issues at the individual, family, and community levels. In particular, intersectionality (Crenshaw, 1989, 1991; McCall, 2005), as a theoretical framework, calls for multiple levels of deconstruction of lived experiences; cross-disciplinary collaboration, social work and public health for example, in cocreating new approaches and theories with the understanding of the diverse backgrounds of urban older adults; accepting of multi-categorical identity even within groups; consideration of shared experience and shared history; and engaging older adults in both the processes and practices relative to aging in the urban community (Simpson et al., 2014).

Working with an urban African American aging population also requires passion, unwavering commitment, and most importantly, appropriate education and training. As such, among the many social work competencies and skills required for effectively working with older African American adults in urban communities some are listed as follows:

Core competencies and skills
- Passion for working with older adults, in this case, African Americans, in urban communities
- Ability to contextualize and navigate practice in urban community systems
- Use of cutting-edge knowledge and skills to address critical issues among urban African American older adults
- Appropriate knowledge and skills in providing services on grief and loss in the context of the urban environment
- Ability to work across disciplines, for example, social work and the law, to secure culturally appropriate services for urban African American older adults
- Working knowledge of older adult growth, development, and behaviors
- Working knowledge of relevant and culturally effective prevention and intervention for urban African American older adults
- Excellent verbal and written communication skills
- Appropriate social work educational background, problem-solving skills, and licensing
- Use of cultural and linguistic sensitivity and ability to work respectfully with older adults
- Possession of excellent assessment and decision-making skills (Ritter, Vakalahi, & Kiernan-Stern, 2009; Yancey et al., 2014).

MAKING A DIFFERENCE

Leeza M. Scheidt, MSW, LGSW, Central Region Manager, Meals on Wheels, Baltimore, MD
"As a psychology major going into my first semester of college, it didn't take long to realize that, although I loved counseling and studying human behavior, I wanted to do

more than just help others from an office. I wanted to be among the people I serve. To be next to them, in the trenches, seeing firsthand their circumstances and learning how their culture and environment have shaped their lives. When I first learned of the ever-expanding field of social work, it clicked that this was exactly the career choice for me.

"My love for older adults began in high school, working as a receptionist in a nursing home. My ability to have compassion for and build rapport with this specific population was always effortless for me and in essence made my decision to pursue gerontological social work an easy one. I obtained a bachelor's degree in Social Work from Southeastern University in Lakeland, FL, and later attended Morgan State University in Baltimore, MD, for a master's in social work, with a concentration in gerontology.

"While working and interning at Meals on Wheels of Central Maryland (MOWCM), I discovered from an in-house survey that 23% of the clients we served reported that the only person they see on a daily basis is the volunteer who delivers their meal. Learning this statistic led to the motivation to invent a simple tool, the isolation reduction plan (IRP), which could assess clients for isolation, depression (using the Geriatric Depression Scale), and suicidal ideation during routine home visits. Within the first month of implementation, the IRP discovered two clients who already had a plan in place to take their own lives, proving that this tool can actually save lives.

"Currently, I am the central region manager at MOWCM. After graduating with a master's of social work (MSW), I achieved an LGSW and was also proud to accept the 2013 Maryland Gerontological Association student award for the creation of the IRP. This tool is still being utilized within the MOWCM Client Services department, and now, any sign of moderate to severe isolation includes a referral into our targeted case management program with extensive follow-up."

MEETING URBAN NEEDS

Merissa R. Munford, MSW, LGSW, Founder of "Actively Aging to Perfection," Towson, Maryland

"I received a bachelor's of science degree in psychology and an MSW degree with a specialty in gerontology from Morgan State University. Since 2005, I have provided mental health services, case management, and community resource linkage to adults, children, adolescents, and their families throughout Maryland's nonprofit organizations and county agencies. My areas of expertise include anxiety, depression, relationship issues, grief support, trauma recovery, and crisis intervention. My service experiences include being therapist, social worker, senior service intern, computer instructor, entitlements coordinator, psychiatric rehabilitation coordinator, counselor, consultant, and case manager.

"Within the past 5 years, I have focused my work and passion on older adults, their loved ones, caregivers, and health care professionals in the capacity of a gerontological social worker providing therapy, advocacy, case management, computer education, General Educational Diploma (GED) prep, and counseling. I have provided supportive services to seniors at their homes, assisted-living settings, medical day programs, and nursing and retirement communities to ensure that the needs and concerns of elders are addressed.

"Currently, I am the founder and chief executive officer of "Actively Aging to Perfection" (AA2P). AA2P offers personalized care, counseling, and resources to the older adult or baby boomer population, their family members, health care professionals, and other care providers. It was created with a responsibility to give back to this population by investing in them as they have invested in me. I believe that each person seeks to live to his or her fullest potential and that this process will continue throughout each stage of a person's life."

IMPLICATIONS FOR THE FUTURE

Looking into a future filled with possibilities and also challenges among an ever-growing diverse group of older adults with lived experiences that expands the globe in terms of diverse cultures, social work professionals are called to action, to contribute to the revival and sustaining of the "magic" of aging in the urban environment. As referenced earlier, this magic of urban communities is indicative of the strengths of neighbors caring for each other; the strengths of grandmothers caring for their grandchildren while their children recover and organize their lives; the ever-present spiritual support of the Black churches not only for the African American older adults but also for all who seek refuge; the resilience of older adults in the face of inequity, inequality, and relentless poverty; and the collective advocacy of the community for access and availability of services and resources for residences from all ages as a reflection of the interdependence of older lives in urban communities. In essence, the strengths and challenges of urban communities spark the magic of aging in the urban environment, in the sense that challenges, individual or collective, give us purpose and meaning as well as test our strengths and resilience in the face of individual and collective adversity. This is the magic of aging in the urban environment.

FOR FURTHER STUDY

Suggested Assignments

Answers to issues impacting the lives of urban older adults are multifaceted. However, the literature and practice wisdom offer some basic answers to most of these issues. What do you know about aging in the urban environment? True or false. Explain.

1. Deprivation is an urban older adult phenomenon.

2. Sex and intimacy are important to urban older adults.

3. Urban older adults deteriorate faster mentally and physically.

4. The experience of urban older adults has much relevance in today's society.

5. Urban older adults want to be left alone.

6. Urban older adults are technologically savvy.

7. HIV/AIDS, substance abuse, and mental health issues are not problems among urban older adults.

8. The urban environment is lacking of social supports for the aging population.

9. Urban older adults are well represented in today's workforce.

10. Caregiving responsibilities of many urban older adults have doubled.

Suggested Readings

Administration on Aging. Retrieved from http://www.aoa.gov

African Americans and Aging. Retrieved from http://www.questia.com/library/science-and-technology/health-and-medicine/aging/african-americans-and-aging

African Americans in Gerontology. Retrieved from http://www.linkedin.com/company/african-americans-in-gerontology?trk=top_nav_home

Berkman, B. (2006). *Handbook of social work in health and aging*. New York, NY: Oxford University Press.

Gero-Ed Center. www.cswe.org/CentersInitiatives/GeroEdCenter.aspx

National Institute on Aging. Retrieved from www.nia.nih.gov

Vakalahi, H. F. O., Simpson, G. M., & Giunta, N. (Eds.). (2014). *The collective spirit of aging across cultures*. International perspectives on aging, 9. Spring Science and Business Media Publisher. New York, NY: Springer Science and Business Media.

REFERENCES

Adkison-Bradley, C., Johnson, D., Lipford Sanders, J., Duncan, L., & Holcomb-McCoy, C. (2005). Forging a collaborative relationship between the Black church and the counseling profession. *Counseling and Values, 49*, 147–154.

Aira, M., Hartiainen, S., & Sulkava, R. (2005). Community prevalence of alcohol use and concomitant use of medication—A source of possible risk in the elderly aged 75 and older? *International Journal of Geriatric Psychiatry, 20*, 680–685.

Berridge, C. (2014). Seeing the social in technology for older adults: Making the implicit explicit through a multidisciplinary lens. In H. F. O. Vakalahi, G. M. Simpson, & N. Giunta (Eds.), *The collective spirit of aging across cultures. International perspectives on aging* (Vol. 9, pp. 173–190). New York, NY: Springer Science and Business Media.

Bureau of Labor Statistics. (2008). *Spotlight on statistics: Older workers*. Washington, DC: U.S. Department of Labor. Retrieved July 12, 2013, from http://stats.bls.gov/spotlight/2008/older_workers/pdf/older_workers_bls_spotlight.pdf

Burton, E. J., Mitchell, L., & Stride, C. B. (2011). Good places for ageing in place: Development of objective built environment measures for investigating links with older people's wellbeing. *BMC Public Health, 11*(1), 839. doi:10.1186/1471-2458-11-839

Charlton, K. E., & Rose, D. (2001). Nutrition among older adults in Africa: The situation at the beginning of the millennium. *The Journal of Nutrition, 131*(9), 2424S–2428S.

Chumbler, N. R., Cody, M., Booth, B. M., & Beck, C. K. (2001). Rural-urban differences in service use for memory-related problems in older adults. *The Journal of Behavioral Health Services and Research, 28*(2), 212–221.

Clarke, P., Ailshire, J. A., Bader, M., Morenoff, J. D., & House, J. S. (2008). Mobility disability and the urban built environment. *American Journal of Epidemiology, 168*(5), 506–513. doi:10.1093/aje/kwn185

Crenshaw, K. (1989). Demarginalizing the intersection of race and sex: A black feminist critique of antidiscrimination doctrine, feminist theory, and antiracist politics. University of Chicago Legal Forum, 140, 139–167.

Crenshaw, K. (1991). Mapping the margins: Intersectionality, identity politics, and violence against women of color. *Stanford Law Review, 43*(6), 1241–1299.

Eisenhauer, E. (2001). In poor health: Supermarket redlining and urban nutrition. *GeoJournal, 53*(2), 125.

Ferrell, S. W., & Sorocco, K. H. (2006). Alcohol use among older adults. *The Journal of General Psychology, 133*(4), 453–467.

Giunta, N., & Jacobson, S. A. (2014). Aging, intimacy, and sex. In H. F. O. Vakalahi, G. M. Simpson, & N. Giunta (Eds.), *The collective spirit of aging across cultures. International perspectives on aging* (Vol. 9, pp. 87–110). New York, NY: Springer Science and Business Media.

Hodge, D. R. (2005). Spiritual ecograms: A new assessment instrument for identifying clients' spiritual strengths in space and across time. *Families in Society, 86*(2), 287–296.

Hodge, D. R., & Limb, G. E. (2010). Native Americans and brief spiritual assessment: Examining and operationalizing the Joint Commission's assessment framework. *Social Work, 55*, 297–307.

Johnson, J. E. (1997). Insomnia, alcohol, and over-the-counter drug use in old–old urban women. *Journal of Community Health Nursing, 14*(3), 181–188.

Li, F., Fisher, K. J., Brownson, R. C., & Bosworth, M. (2005). Multilevel modeling of built environment characteristics related to neighbourhood walking activity in older adults. *Journal of Epidemiology and Community Health, 59*, 558–564. doi:10.1136/jech.2004.028399

Martin, E., & Martin, J. (2002). *Spirituality and the black helping tradition in social work*. Washington, DC: NASW Press.

Masotti, P. J., Fick, R., Johnson-Masotti, A., & MacLeod, S. (2006). Healthy naturally occurring retirement communities: A low-cost approach to facilitating healthy aging. *American Journal of Public Health, 96*(7), 1164–1170.

Massey, D. S., & Denton, N. A. (1993). *American apartheid: Segregation and the making of the underclass*. Cambridge, MA: Harvard University Press.

McCall, L. (2005). The complexity of intersectionality. *Signs, 30*(3), 1771–1800.

Nash, J. C. (2008). Re-thinking intersectionality. *Feminist Review, 89*, 1–15.

Norris, M. P., & Karlin, B. E. (2006). Public mental health care utilization by older adults. *Administration and Policy in Mental Health and Mental Health Services Research, 33*(6), 730–736.

Oswald, F., Wahl, H. W., Schilling, O., Nygren, C., Fange, A., Sixsmith, A., … Iwarsson, S. (2007). Relationships between housing and healthy aging in very old age. *The Gerontologist, 47*(1), 96–107.

Ritter, J. A., Vakalahi, H., & Kiernan-Stern, M. (2009). *101 careers in social work*. New York, NY: Springer.

Robert, S. A., & Ruel, E. (2006). Racial segregation and health disparities between black and white older adults. *The Journals of Gerontology: Series B: Psychological Sciences and Social Sciences, 61B*(4), S203–S211. doi:10.1093/geronb/61.4.S203

Simpson, G. M., Giunta, N., & Vakalahi, H. F. O. (2014). 4th generational theories of intersection: Multicultural aging. In H. F. O. Vakalahi, G. M. Simpson, & N. Giunta. (Eds.), *The collective spirit of aging across cultures* (pp. 1–5). *International perspectives on aging* (Vol. 9). New York, NY: Springer Science and Business Media.

Simpson, G. M., & Lawrence-Webb, C. (2009). Responsibility without community resources: Informal kinship care among urban, low-income, African-American grandmother caregivers. *Journal of Black Studies, 39*(6), 825–847.

Slack, T., & Jensen, L. (2008). Employment hardship among older workers: Does residential and gender inequality extend into older age? *The Journals of Gerontology, 63B*(1), S15–S24.

Uphold, C. R., Rane, D., Reid, K., & Tomar, S. L. (2005). Mental health differences between rural and urban men living with HIV infection in various age groups. *Journal of Community Health, 30*(5), 355–375. doi:10.1007/s10900–005-5517-y

U.S. Census Bureau. (2010). American Fact Finder. Retrieved May 1, 2013, from www.census.gov/c2ss/www

Ward, E. G., Disch, W. B., Levy, J. A., & Schensul, J. J. (2004). Perception of HIV/AIDS risk among urban, low-income senior-housing residents. *AIDS Education and Prevention, 16*(6), 571–588.

Wells-Wilbon, R. (2013). *Tweetings @ doctor_rhonda*. Mustang, OK: Tate Publishing & Enterprises.

Wolfe, W. S., Frongillo, E. A., & Valois, P. (2003). Understanding the experience of food insecurity by elders suggests ways to improve its measurement. *The Journal of Nutrition, 133*(9), 2762–2769.

Yancey, K., Baldwin, T., Saran, A. R., & Vakalahi, H. F. O. (2014). City life: What a wonderful way of life—Aging in the urban environment. In H. F. O. Vakalahi, G. M. Simpson, & N. Giunta (Eds.), *The collective spirit of aging across cultures. International perspectives on aging* (Vol. 9, pp. 207–228). New York, NY: Springer Science and Business Media.

Zheng, X., Zhang, J., Song, X., Pang, L., Li, N., & Chen, G. (2011). Risk factors for depression in older adults in Beijing. *Canadian Journal of Psychiatry, 56*(8), 466–473.

CHAPTER 13

On Urban Ground: An Integrated Framework for Working With African American Grandparent Caregivers

Gaynell M. Simpson, Belinda Davis Smith,
and Dana Burdnell Wilson

Grandparents raising their grandchildren remains an important concern for service providers, administrators, educators, and policy advocates across local, state, and federal institutions. In the United States, the traditional role of grandparents in multigenerational household structures has transitioned from co-parenting or transitory caregivers to the permanent role of a primary caregiver. Ongoing and recent conditions influencing the primary assumption of care by African American grandparents include parental absence due to military deployment (Bunch, Eastman, & Moore, 2007); parental illness and mortality due to HIV/AIDS (Crewe, 2012; Joslin, 2002); drug abuse (Dowdell, 2004; Minkler & Roe, 1993); incarceration (Young & Smith, 2000); and community violence (Burnette, 1997; Simpson, 2008). Grandparents are caring for children who were abandoned, abused, or neglected and who were experiencing emotional and physical distress (Dowdell, 1995; Stinson, 2010). It is important to understand that not all grandparent caregivers are caring for those under distress. In some multigenerational families, grandparents co-reside with biological parents and assume the role of co-parenting grandparents (Cox, 2000) that has culturally positive attributes (Wells-Wilbon & Simpson, 2009).

In this chapter, we focus on grandparents and their grandchildren left behind in economically marginalized urban communities. With this group in mind, we examine the various types of grandparent households: multigenerational and skipped generational households of grandparent caregivers. We address the contemporary perspective of the normative cultural practices of these families and discuss the historical role of the helping tradition, which is central to sustaining African American families. Subsequently, we present an ecological system, strengths-based, and empowerment approach to illuminate how kinship care, education, and child welfare policies affect grandparents rearing grandchildren in low-income urban communities through an ecological perspective. We examine how service providers can collaborate with grandparents, community members, and key stakeholders in creating positive long-standing change at various levels. Finally, educational resources and sample assignments are included to guide leaders responsible for educating the next generation of urban social work practitioners.

MULTIGENERATIONAL AND SKIPPED-GENERATION HOUSEHOLDS

Grandparent caregivers were once described as a hidden segment of the U.S. caregiving population (Fuller-Thomson, Minkler, & Driver, 1997). The prevalence of grandparent caregiving was not fully captured until the role of grandparent caregivers was included in the U.S. decennial census of 2000 (Simmons & Dye, 2003). Findings from this report were the beginning of making the *invisible* role of grandparent caregivers *visible*. In a study utilizing the Census 2000 American Community Survey (ACS), comparing caregivers to non-caregiving peers revealed that 500,000 African American grandmother caregivers aged 45 years and older were estimated to be raising grandchildren (Minkler & Fuller-Thomson, 2005). Minkler and Fuller highlighted that close to half (47.1%) of the African American grandparent caregiver households consisted of skipped-generation households, without the co-residence of parents, aunts, or uncles. African American grandmothers were younger, female, less educated, and had limited economic resources compared to their caregiving peers (Minkler & Fuller-Thomson, 2005).

A report derived from the 2000 decennial census and the 2005 to 2011 ACS revealed dramatic increases in children co-residing with or primarily being cared for by grandparents following the economic recession of 2007. This recession was stabilized toward the end of the 2009 recession (Livingston, 2013). In 2011, the number of children living in a multigenerational household was 7.7 million, and 3 million of these children were being primarily cared for by their grandparents (Livingston). A disparate number of African American children co-resided with or are being cared for primarily by their grandparents compared to Asians, Whites, and Latinos (Livingston). In a multigenerational household structure, co-resident African American grandparents are more likely to be the primary caregivers (49%) and the duration of caregiving is longer (greater than 3 years). Grandparent caregivers are also more likely to be female (72%), less likely to be married (48%), and more likely to live below the poverty line (31%) compared to Latinos, Asians, and Whites (Livingston). Furthermore, in grandparent primary caregiving homes, the co-residing biological parent present most often is the mother, biological parent(s) are unmarried, they lack a high school degree, and they are unemployed compared to households with no grandparent caregiver present (Livingston).

Not surprisingly, grandparents are at the core of caregiving in African American families, and different generations living together is a common coping strategy often employed during difficult times (Hill, 2003; Stack, 1974; Waites, 2009). A major concern is that African American grandparent caregivers are disproportionately represented in the skipped-generation household, where a grandparent serves as the primary caregiver with no parent present compared to other racial–ethnic populations (Kochhar & Cohn, 2011; Livingston, 2013). Although the skipped generation is relatively small compared to the other household structures, it does reflect lack of family resources and a greater need for assessment and intervention (Simpson, 2008). Since skipped-generation households are not the normative cultural practice of African American families it indicates that accumulated social and economic conditions are changing the resilient structure and functioning of African American families (Simpson, 2009). The role of grandparents is important to family survival and the caregiving traditions of grandmothers remain central in serving as *"the mother"* to past, current, and future generations of family and community members (Jimenez, 2002; Carlton-LaNey, Hamilton, Ruiz, & Alexander, 2001; Wells-Wilbon & Simpson, 2009).

GRANDFATHER CAREGIVERS

Often, men as caregivers in African American families are overlooked (Simpson & Cornelius, 2007) and only a few studies have recognized their role as co-resident grandparent caregivers (Bullock, 2005, 2007; Hayslip & Kaminski, 2005; Keene, Prokos, & Held, 2012; Kolomer & McCallion, 2005; Minkler & Fuller-Thomson, 2005). During the years 2007 and 2009, males resided in multigenerational households at a higher percentage than their female counterparts (Lofquist, 2013). Even though co-residing grandparents are primarily women (64%), the remaining (36%) are men (Livingston, 2013). Married grandfathers in multigenerational homes when biological parents present are advantageous compared to those not married and without a multigenerational household (Keene et al., 2012). Similar to African American grandmother caregivers, single grandfather-headed households with no biological parent present are a vulnerable group (Keene et al., 2012).

In summary, skipped-generation households are smaller in number compared to multigenerational and are more at risk due to economically marginalized urban communities. Multigenerational families have become increasingly more prevalent, which is aligned with the long-standing history of forming multigenerational structured households. In the next section, we examine the traditional patterns of African American mobilization of kin networks before, during, and after slavery to provide care for children whose parents were either unable or unwilling to fulfill their parental responsibilities.

HISTORICAL TRADITIONS OF AFRICAN AMERICAN CAREGIVING

Seminal work by Hill (1972/2003), *The Strengths of Black Families*, underscores the significance of flexible family roles, accompanied by strong intergenerational ties as a cultural practice and strength among African American families. In African American families, it is normative behavior for family members, whether bonded by blood or fictive relations, to extend mutual aid and reciprocity to protect and sustain the family (Hill, 1997). In the groundbreaking book, *The Helping Tradition in the Black Family and Community*, Martin and Martin (1985) described the helping traditions of African American families as having their historic origins in the West African culture. The term "the helping tradition" was coined as a metaphor to describe a survival mechanism to endure the atrocities resulting from the dehumanizing experiences of slavery. It was customary for elderly slave women to provide child care to children who were too young to work, while their parents worked in the field or the masters' house (Hine, Hine, & Harrold, 2006; Martin and Martin, 1985). Even after slavery ended, assuming responsibility for children without parents was a cultural practice within an African American community. In fact, "other mothering" was a role assumed by African American women as a protective factor to inoculate family members against hardship resulting from political and economic disparities (Collins, 2000).

African American families consider the extended family as an integral part of the family unit, involving role flexibility among family members (Hill, 1997; Martin & Martin, 1985). Parents faced challenges and sometimes were unable to assume parental responsibility; grandparents have typically served as the buffer by providing custodial care (Everett, Chipungu, & Leashore, 2004; Gibson, 2014). The historical analysis of African American grandmothers (Jimenez, 2002) supports earlier scholars' conclusion that caregiving in an African American community was not restrictive to biological parents and was a collective endeavor inclusive of fathers and mothers, grandfathers and grandmothers, and aunts and uncles (Jones, 1985; Martin & Martin, 1985).

Caregiving Traditions Migrate From the South to North

During the Progressive Era and continued through World War I, the migration northward represents a pivotal milestone for the massive exodus of African Americans from the south to the north in search of better economic opportunities (Franklin & Moss, 1994; Martin & Martin, 1985). The expansion of northern factories and domestic opportunities contributed to African Americans' decision to migrate north. African Americans migrated in massive numbers to large cities and states, such as Maryland, Chicago, Pittsburgh, and New York (Franklin & Moss, 1994). Although migration declined during the Great Depression, a rapid increase occurred again during and after World War II.

World War II created a tremendous influx of African Americans into urban areas. Although families were separated geographically, the degree of connectedness and involvement with extended families was varied and maintained. African Americans migrated in large numbers to industrialized urban centers, in the hope of finding work and a better way of living (Franklin & Moss, 1994). However, as noted by Winston (1999), young males hired to work in the north were offered no provisions to bring their families. During this major out-migration of African Americans, the extended family was viable in assisting family members who were seeking employment. As noted by Jones (1985):

> Grandmothers cared for their children's children and all three benefited, the elderly women gained companionship and in, some cases, a measure of economic support; their children were free to search for jobs elsewhere, and the grandchildren lived under the watchful eye of a relative who was often as strict and as kind a person as she knew to be. (p. 228)

According to Hine et al. (2006), the migration to the north was often done separately, with fathers or mothers living separately and in search of employment opportunities and housing. This migration created a tremendous strain on the family, and grandparents served a viable role in providing caregiving. Commonly, children often remained "down south" with grandparents until their parents adapted to their new environment (Gibson, 2005). Commonly, extended family members served as a buffer to help new migrants become acclimated to urban life. Martin and Martin (2002) term this as a "collective approach" used as a protective mechanism to buffer the risk factors associated with living in a large and often impersonal environment. Martin and Martin further described the practice of "social class cooperation" as one that involved reaching back and helping extended family members regardless of social economic status. In general, extended family members and, specially, grandmothers played a viable role in providing support to their children and grandchildren particularly during times of migration for better opportunities.

Living in the City: Caregiving Traditions in Marginalized Urban Communities

During the period of civil rights and into the 1980s, African Americans experienced a heightened degree of economic success due to stable factory employment and an increase in the number of African American professionals and entertainers (Puckerin, 1984). Puckerin noted that the "level of education, political participation and material well-being approached that of the majority whites" (p. 4) compared to African Americans. However, African Americans' educational, political, and material achievements were not equal to Whites due to obstacles of legal segregation, discrimination, poverty, and racist governmental policies (Franklin & Moss, 1994). Although the Civil Rights movement provided an increase in social and economic opportunities for some middle-class African Americans, it did not provide much alleviation to families who were economically disadvantaged to escape the changing environment of the urban city. A seminal work by Newman (2006), *A Different Shade of Gray: Midlife and Beyond in the Inner City*, provided actual accounts of challenges endured by older, African Americans residing in marginalized inner cities.

The song, *Inner City Blues (Make Me Wanna Hollar)*, popularized by the legendary singer Marvin Gaye, captured the essence of the social and economic context of urban communities during this period. The out-migration of White and African American middle-class families into suburban communities followed by local businesses and large manufacturing plants created a rapid structural deterioration of institutional resources and marginalization of urban communities (Dunlap, Golub, & Johnson, 2006; Small & Newman, 2001). Low-skilled jobs in urban cities increasingly declined, which further compromised the economic well-being of many struggling African American families. Manufacturing jobs in the northeast and midwestern cities relocated to places such as the Sunbelt, suburban communities, and other countries. White communities relocated with businesses from which African Americans sought employment opportunities. According to Franklin and Moss (1994):

> Factories and shops that had once graced the central city and given it life as well as hope were shut down, began to deteriorate, and frequently were razed to make way for a new highway leading to the suburban industrial parks, shopping malls, and carefully zoned residential areas. (p. 470)

Consequently, African American families were left to work at jobs offering minimum wage or to rely on welfare services (Franklin & Moss, 1994).

In Wilson's groundbreaking books, *When Work Disappears: The World of the New Urban Poor* (1996) and *The Truly Disadvantaged: The Inner City, the Underclass, and Public Policy* (1987), he described how the civil rights movement created social, political, and economic opportunities for African Americans. Prior to the amelioration of restrictive covenants and special zoning laws that prevented the building of public housing in suburban communities, African Americans in large cities mostly lived in inner city neighborhoods. Once opportunities emerged, an unintended consequence of progress caused a devastating impact on the poor and disadvantaged in urban communities (Wilson, 1987, 2009). With the exodus of the African American middle class from the inner city, the poor, working poor, and vulnerable were left behind in resource-depleted communities. Consequently, drugs, gang activity, and violence escalated, creating a vicious cycle that devastated neighborhood resources, such as schools, hospitals, and community programs in urban communities. The devastation due to economic decline became far-reaching, significantly impacting the quality of life of residents in urban communities (Newman, 2006). Increasingly, underserved communities became a haven for the flourishing drug subculture and gang membership; leaving African American families in urban settings quite vulnerable. The most vulnerable were single mothers and older adults attempting to survive in cities where drugs and crime debased whole communities (Newman, 2006; Martin & Martin, 2002).

Near the end of the 20th century, a new generation of custodial caregivers emerged. The social problems debilitated the functional capacity of birth parents to assume parental responsibilities led to an increase in the number of custodial grandparents (Hill, 2003; McAdoo, 1982). Beginning in the 1980s and 1990s, families across the country were greatly impacted by the crack cocaine epidemic (Burton, 1992; Minkler & Roe, 1993); HIV/AIDS (Joslin, 2002); and community violence hampered family functioning (Simpson, 2009). The rise in teen-age pregnancies (Hardren, Clark, & Maquire, 1997), maternal incarceration (Krofpt & Yoon, 2006), abandonment, and mental illness (Dowdell, 1995) affected family functioning and child well-being. Child neglect significantly increased the need for grandparents to become primary caregivers (Sands, Goldberg-Glen, & Shin, 2009).

These social problems significantly impacted families and African Americans residing in impoverished inner city communities, and this impact was extensive and far-reaching. Simpson (2009) found that the skipped-generation households in marginalized, inner city communities were hampered by an accumulation of social and economic structural inequalities that have drained and depleted availability of viable family members and community resources to support caregiving traditions. Furthermore, systematic inequalities have created urban enclaves that are racially segregated, economically disadvantaged, and disconnected from city resources.

Poverty negatively obstructs African Americans and urban communities and destroys community resources, debilitates family functioning, and creates a strain on the caregiving traditions of African American families. The periods between the 1970s and the 1990s resulted in five major economic setbacks, which led to increased unemployment among African American families (Hill, 1998). African Americans were never able to recover from one slump before being hit by another recession (Hill, 1998, p. 20). As economic recessions continued, unemployment rates increased and societal conditions such as drug abuse, incarcerations, deaths related to community violence, worsened. It is during these times that an increase was witnessed in multigenerational households and grandmothers transitioned from co-parenting or transitory caregivers to a permanent role of primary caregiver especially in skipped-generation households with no biological parent present, or extended family present. Earlier grandparent caregiving studies documented daily stressors associated with caring for children experiencing emotional and/or physical problems due to the loss of a parent (Burnette, 1997; Burton, 1992; Heywood, 1999; Jendrek, 1994). Furthermore, findings from earlier studies suggested a high prevalence of depression among grandparent caregivers who care for their grandchildren on a full-time or part-time basis (Burton, 1992; Dowdell, 1995; Kelley, Whitley, Sipe, & Yorker, 2000; Minkler & Roe, 1993). Current social conditions maintained the findings of earlier studies regarding the health and mental health stressors experienced by grandparent caregivers. Kelly (2001) concluded that grandparents who reported psychological distress had fewer resources, less social support, and poor physical health conditions when compared to grandparents reporting minimal psychological distress. Despite the level of psychological distress experienced by caregivers, grandparents were not seeking or receiving mental health services (Emick & Hayslip, 1996). Lack of access and availability of services as well as stigma that accompanies mental health services continue to be barriers to help seeking.

In the following discussion, the authors present an ecological perspective to explain how kinship care, education, and child welfare policy affects grandparents rearing grandchildren in low-income urban communities. Furthermore, a discussion of the current literature on grandparents' psychosocial adjustment to caregivers in areas of mental and physical health is offered. The core concepts and principles from empowerment theory (Pinderhughes, 1983; Solomon, 1976) and social justice perspective (Pinderhughes, 1983) are presented to explain how service providers can collaborate with grandparents, community members, and key stakeholders in creating positive long-standing change at various levels having long-standing impact on grandparents and grandchildren.

AN INTEGRATED FRAMEWORK: ECOLOGICAL PERSPECTIVE, STRENGTHS PERSPECTIVE, AND EMPOWERMENT THEORY

The purpose of this section is to present an ecological framework (Bronfenbrenner & Morris, 1998) that is integrated with core concepts and principles from empowerment theory (Pinderhughes, 1983; Solomon, 1976) and the strengths perspective (Hill, 2003) to understand resilience and challenges of African American grandparent caregivers. Bridging across these paradigms is necessary to understand grandparents' historical and contemporary contextual experiences of caregiving, recognize and build on their strengths and resilience, and provide readers with tools for assessment and intervention with African American grandparent caregivers in low-income, urban communities.

At the core of an ecological perspective is a person-in-environment systems perspective which "posits that individuals are engaged in constant transactions with other human beings and with other systems in the environment and that these various persons and systems reciprocally influence each other" (Hepworth, Rooney, & Larsen, 2002, p. 3). An ecological systems perspective offers utility to help child welfare workers identify, assess, understand, and address the dynamic complexities and transaction between grandparent caregivers and the environment that have experienced oppression (Fong & Furuto, 2001). It provides a way to help social workers develop a better understanding of grandparent caregivers within the context of their social environment and the reciprocal interaction between the family system to include the grandparents, parents, and grandchildren. Considering the challenges and even the positive experiences grandparent caregivers in urban communities encounter, using an ecological perspective provides a framework to adopt a multifaceted and holistic approach to effectively work with grandparent kinship caregivers (Bronfenbrenner, 1998, Dannison, Smith, & Vacha-Haase, 1999).

The ecological perspective offers a multilayered approach to examine the relationships between and among the four levels of the environment within a social system: the microsystem, mesosystem, exosystem, and macrosystem (Bronfenbrenner & Garbarino, 1985). Simpson and Lawrence-Webb (2009) suggest that the ecological perspective provides a lens to understand grandmother-headed household as a micro-level entity based on the context of the community. The researchers further content that the microsystem involved grandmother-headed household consisting of the family relationship among members residing in the home including the grandmother, grandchildren, and adult children. Smith (2006) further asserts that "a core aspect of the micro perspective is that it examines individual functioning, motivation, intellectual and emotional capacities, the impact of life experiences, and the qualitative nature of the interactions between individuals and elements in the environment" (p. 30).

The microsystem highlights the grandparent caregiver as an individual, along with the transaction between the various people in their household or family system encountered on a daily basis that impact the caregiver's well-being and the family's functioning, requiring social workers to conduct ongoing assessments. Bronfenbrenner and Garbarino (1985) also posit that the mesosystem is the second level of the social environment and considered to have an intermediate level of influence filtered through the microsystem. Simpson and Lawrence-Webb also contend that the mesosystem considers the relationships among the grandparent caregivers, their adult children, and members of the household. Understanding external systems such as the child welfare system, social service agencies, the school system, and health care system may impact grandparents' role as caregivers. The exosystem is the third level of the social environment that considers neighborhood or community factors that may have an impact on grandparent caregivers. For example, residents in urban communities may be challenged by depleted resources, gangs, drug activity, community violence, homelessness, and substandard housing.

For grandparent caregivers employed in the workforce, balancing work responsibilities and access to day care or after-school enrichment programs are important to understand and help them. Social policy at the federal, state, and agency levels impacts funding stream and serves as a determinate of the availability of resources. To that end, the exosystem provides a framework to understand the extent to which external factors impact the microsystem in grandparent caregivers' households. The macrosystem level is the fourth level of the social environment and in broader societal ideologies such as laws, culture, values and beliefs, expectations, traditions. Waites, Macgowan, Pennell, Carlton-LaNey, and Wells (2004) highlight the importance of understanding the cultural context and dimensions of African American families. McCullough-Chavis and Waites (2008) suggest using cultural genograms to give consideration to the cultural heritage and influences in addition to intergenerational family values, patterns, transactions, and strengths. The macrosystem also provides a framework to understand how macro-level changes, such as Temporary Assistance for Needy Families, affect grandmother-headed households (micro-level entities) in urban communities.

An ecological perspective is enriched when it is integrated with an empowerment approach and a strengths perspective from the micro- through macro-levels. Since the 1970s, the social work profession has focused on culturally competent social work practice (Fong & Furuto, 2001). This increased attention to developing cultural competent practice and assessment is congruent with social work values and code of ethics. It is a necessary change in theoretical practice as the number of ethnic, racially diverse population is growing and thus places a greater demand on services received from social work practitioners (Saleebey, 1997). This also has resulted in a movement from a deficit approach to a strengths-based empowerment approach to respond to these demands (Pinderhughes, 1983; Saleebey, 1997). As presented in the study case of Ms. Jackson later, it is important to recognize that African American grandmothers are taking care of their grandchildren based on the needs of their family and not on the needs of the child welfare system. Traditionally and as currently reflected in the study case, grandmothers are often called on to meet the needs of their family members. Far too often, this is done under provisions of minimal support from informal and formal social support structures and at the risk of the caregivers' physical and emotional well-being. Implications for direct practice suggest that a strengths-based case-management approach, which includes culturally competent clinical tools and is built on a multidisciplinary and empowerment approach, is an important component in providing direct clinical services to African American grandmother caregivers and their families.

In the case of Ms. Jackson, treatment–intervention services need to be directed toward family members who provide support and not to those who may not be able to provide support because of drug addiction, medical conditions, or poverty. Social work clinical treatment–intervention plans generally focus on the parent(s) and child. Minimal attention is directed at extended kin or non-kin who may be possible sources of support. Providing direct services at the family system is important in working with African American grandmother caregivers. Far too often, when biological parents leave their children for the grandmother to rear, minimal to no services are provided to biological parents so that they can reunify with their child(ren). Social work services need to be interprofessional, holistic, and directed at the biological parents so that they can reunify with their children. Social workers can play an essential role in assisting biological parents in recovery from their addiction back into their role as mother and father. Social workers can help by assisting grandmothers with maintaining an open communication with parents during and after drug treatment programs. Intergenerational programs aimed at strengthening family units in grandparent-headed households have been recommended countless times by previous researchers (Glass & Huneycutt, 2002; Kelley & Yorker, 2001; Smith, 1994). Providing intergenerational support should include services directed at biological parents, extended kin, and family members who are potential sources of support for grandmothers who are caring for their grandchildren. Supporting the intergenerational survival of the entire family is important in meeting the needs of African American grandmother caregivers.

As witnessed in the study case, social support structures appeared to be resilient even when faced with severe social and economic conditions. Ms. Jackson has at least two family members to rely on for support. Capitalizing on this strength is imperative. Social workers could empower grandmother caregivers to mobilize additional resources from family members who are capable of providing support. Also, a restructuring of the type of support provided and increasing support to the grandmother caregiver by family members may be necessary. For example, in the case of Ms. Jackson, she is concerned about who will care for grandchildren if she dies as a result of her cancer. This suggests that a treatment plan should include a crisis support plan. This means that the service provider would discuss with the grandmother caregiver and her family members their availability to provide support during crisis. The goal is to encourage and assist family discussions so that family members can identify who will be available to assist the needs of the grandchild when a caregiver is hospitalized or should no longer be capable of assuming the role as a primary caregiver. This plan would include the names and contact information of family members who agree to provide crisis support. Furthermore, this family meeting could provide the clinician with an ongoing assessment of the availability of supportive resources in grandmother caregivers informal social support structures.

The roles of African American males are often not recognized or are unassessed during the intake, treatment, and planning processes of social work practice. In the case of Ms. Jackson, her brother, who is the great uncle to her grandchildren, can play a crucial role as a father figure and mentor. This lack of attention by service providers to collect information about the role of African American males, such as fathers, sons, brothers, uncles, and/or cousins, and the hesitancy of grandmother caregivers to provide information, is influenced by the historical practices within social welfare. African American families who relied on social services were often reluctant to speak about the presence of males in their life out of fear that their social services would be withdrawn. At the same time, service providers may assume male members are unavailable and fail to explore this area in-depth. First, it is important that social workers establish a trusting relationship with grandparent participants prior to obtaining information related to males and their level of participation. Second, social workers need to inform grandparent participants that this information cannot and will not be used against them in determining their receipt of social services. Social workers need to assure grandmother participants that this information is only used to assist them with accessing greater resources from within their informal social support structure.

Clinical interventions are needed for grandmother caregivers for their overall mental health and well-being. Ms. Jackson may be neglecting her own physical and emotional health needs to care for her grandchildren. Clinicians need to pay greater attention to directing services at the caregiver and ensuring that their emotional and health needs are adequately met. Social workers will need to fulfill the roles of advocator and boundary-role spanner for the needed resources grandmother caregivers require to raise their grandchildren. Such resources are accessible mental and physical health care, respite care, and economic provisions that should be sought at the legislative level in order to ensure federal policies and procedures are tailored to address the concerns of grandmother caregivers. Social workers can assist grandmother caregivers with negotiating the kinship care system so that they can receive a higher form of child care payment. Arrangements for respite services are needed so that grandmother caregivers can have a reprieve from the daily ongoing stress associated with caregiving. The caregiver's lack of supportive services is the reason an intervention is needed. These intervention programs should include agency-based, church-based, and voluntary organization–based programs.

A COLLECTIVE RESPONSE TO URBAN
GRANDPARENT CAREGIVING

As we study an urban community and organization, it is prudent to consider how the cyclical intersection of an urban environment and family interacts. According to Burton and Jarrett (2000), conventional wisdom implies that families play a major role in determining how urban environments impact the lives of their children. Burton and Jarrett (2000) found that family-level variables are more strongly associated with child outcomes than neighborhood-level variables. Ethnographic research using extended family models has provided crucial insights on how the composition of families mediates a neighborhood's effects on children. Burton and Jarrett (2000) also reported that a family's ability to be flexible and reassign roles as needed allowed them to function well even in high-risk environments. Interdependence and cooperation are critical, especially in disenfranchised neighborhoods.

Literature focusing on how children being raised by kin caregivers fare has the following common threads: They tend to be stable in fewer homes, more likely to live in their own neighborhoods, stay with their siblings, and have contact with their birth parents (Rubin et al., 2008). Their study demonstrated a protective effect on early behavioral outcomes. Johnson-Garner and Meyers (2003) sought factors contributing to the resilience of African American children being raised by kin caregivers. They used qualitative in-depth interviewing to study children who overcame adversity to adapt successfully, compared to those viewed as non-resilient. The Center for Law and Social Policy (CLASP) supports these finding as well, citing stability, placement with siblings, and fewer school changes. Casey and Hurley (2009) maintain that children with grandparents and other kin caregivers maintain attachment relationships and are buffered against the trauma of separation that is often experienced when children are placed outside of their families.

THE FAITH COMMUNITY

In discussing the African American helping tradition in social work, Martin and Martin (1985) discussed spirituality in terms of deep concern for collective well-being. They realized spirituality was "geared toward the promotion of community through Black communal solidarity and social support" (2002, p. 5). Historically, an African American church worked for the social betterment of African American community focused on uplifting an African American family. This tradition continues, with matters of the soul as well as social, economic, and political concerns addressed by the contemporary African American community church.

Faith and spirituality are important aspects of family life that are relevant to caregiving and the integral role of extended family. Stinson (2010), reflecting on her own experience as a grandparent caregiver, stated, "When I wonder why I am doing this, I go to my Bible. God chose me to do this because He felt I could do it. I try not to complain around my grandkids because it is not their fault. I took two of my grandchildren from the hospital because my daughter had left them there" (p. 2). As reflected in this statement, exploring one's faith, spirituality, and belief systems and how this influences decision making is important in maintaining perspective on caregiving (Congress & Gonzalez, 2012).

Social workers need to assess the level of organizational religious involvement among African American grandmother caregivers and need to have knowledge of the communal orientation of the African American church. Communal orientation relates to the tradition of the African American churches' involvement in social, political, and economic activities in the African American community (Lincoln & Mamiya, 1990). Working with organizations that serve African American grandmothers can be helpful in assessing and planning ways to educate religious leaders regarding the needs of grandparent caregivers and to assist with reestablishing ties between grandmother caregivers and the African American church. Social workers can identify church-sponsored outreach programs that assist with the provision of support and assistance to grandmother caregivers. For example, Grandmother's Day can be an avenue in which church leaders recognize grandmother caregivers and begin to develop church-sponsored programs to assist in meeting their needs. Such programs would include respite care, mentorship for grandchildren, and support (instrumental and material) for grandmother caregivers.

In situations of mixed religion and sometimes mixed ethnicity, families can acknowledge and determine how to engage different traditions (Parker et al., 2002). Social workers must consider the cultural significance of multigenerational families in the African American community, acknowledge the history of spirituality, strength, and perseverance, and seek to build on the advantages that these qualities provide (Waites, 2009). An Afrocentric worldview promotes communalism, spirituality, and their integral connection to African identity and community (Schiele, 2000). To the extent that an African American community has a collective identity that fosters sharing, cooperation, and social responsibility, caregiving by grandparents in this instance, could foster mutual dependence and collective strength.

Carlton-LaNey (1999) asserted that a focus on self-help and mutual aid became an institutionalized part of the African American community. "Overwhelmingly excluded from full participation in the U.S. social system and at the same time receiving limited responses to individual and social problems from White social workers, African Americans developed a dogged determination to take care of their own" (p. 312). Urban faith-based organizations as well as urban community organizations also provide needed resources and support for grandparents and other extended family members in their caregiving roles. The following project provides context for how self-help organizations have contributed to the stability of grandparent caregiving, even when resources are scarce.

FAMILY TIES PROJECT

The Family Ties Project is a citywide collaboration in Washington, DC, providing permanency and life-planning services to families affected by HIV/AIDS. It is a project of the Consortium for Child Welfare, an interprofessional collaboration of service providers. The mission of the Family Ties Project is to promote and preserve the well-being of children, youth, and families affected by HIV/AIDS by working with parents and caregivers to plan for the future care of their children. The project also advocates for public policies to improve life-planning options for parents and caregivers of Washington, DC.

The Family Ties Project multidisciplinary team provides comprehensive assessment, case collaboration, and wraparound services to families. They provide legal services for life planning including stand-by-guardianship, living wills, legal custody, adoption, and child support. Community mental health services are provided for crisis intervention, grief and bereavement, as well as family support services. Caregiver support groups, youth enrichment activities, HIV/AIDS awareness and education services, and prevention and reproductive health services are also provided. The Family Ties Project is a prime example of how urban community organizations and resources may be utilized to effectively address the challenges and meet the needs of urban extended families.

Generations United (2000) is a national organization that was convened to address the needs of grandparents who are primary caregivers for their grandchildren, now numbering 2.7 million in the United States. Initially formed from national organizations previously focused on serving either seniors or children, GU has reached across the generations, establishing a National Center on Grandfamilies to address policy and practice issues related to grandparent caregivers. Grandparent caregiver organizations have evolved at the neighborhood, local municipal, state, and national levels. Social workers as advocates have these resources to connect with, to make sure that federal and state legislation and regulations favor the families who struggle to care for their kin. It is the local organizations that are most associated with the needs of the grandparent caregivers in their communities and strive to address those needs, whether in the form of resources, support and education groups, assistance with respite, or help in navigating legal issues.

IMPLICATIONS FOR THE FUTURE

In this chapter, authors have proposed an urban ecological framework for targeted assessment and multilevel interventions aimed at the biopsychosocial–spiritual; history, culture, race–ethnicity context of caregiving; physical and built community–environment, physical health and functional outcomes of grandparent caregivers. As social workers contemplate the cultural norms and traditions of the urban community, and further address the need for public policy priorities to include grandparent caregiving as a strength of the African American family to be upheld and supported, consideration should be given to how grandparent caregiving actually addresses the challenge of disproportionate separation of African American children from their families (Bent-Goodley, 2011). According to Bent-Goodley, this practice of kin caregiving could be proposed as a strategy to reduce the contributing factors and problems that result in placing African American children at risk of separation from their homes. As kin caregiving helps to preserve families and maintain connections and traditions, even in difficult circumstances, respecting and supporting it as an indigenous response outside of formal child welfare policy is a strategy that should be embraced, allowing family values and culture to be passed on. Bent-Goodley (2011) describes this practice as evidence that there is an organized response to needs that persist in the community, and that African American children are valued and considered integral to the preservation of the community. In conclusion, an ecological perspective integrated with a strengths-based and empowerment approach is crucial for intervening with grandparent caregivers. This approach provides social workers with tools for identification of presenting problems from the micro- through the macrosystems. It recognizes family resiliency, challenges weakening family ties, and addresses cultural factors underlying African American families.

FOR FURTHER STUDY

Suggested Assignments

Study Case of Ms. Jackson

Course assignment developer: Belinda Davis Smith, PhD

Family background: Geraldine Jackson is a 58-year-old African American woman who resides in a large, northeastern city. She has lived in the city and in her neighborhood for the past 25 years. She has three adult children; Michael, Jr. (37), Samantha (35), and Simeon (33). Geraldine was married to Michael, Sr. They divorced after 12 years of marriage and Michael remarried and moved to Florida with his new wife. He provided child support, but did not maintain emotional contact. Ms. Jackson loves her children and feels that she spent much of her young life parenting and making sacrifices. Being the oldest sibling in her family, she has provided care to both of her parents who passed away earlier this year. Also she has helped her daughter, Samantha, a single parent who is on the verge of having her children removed and placed in a foster care. Ms. Jackson realized that she would have to help her daughter and granddaughter to keep her family intact.

Samantha Jackson is a 35-year-old high school graduate with 2 years of college. At age 20, she dropped out of college to give birth to her daughter Monique. Although she never married the father, they lived together for 2 years after the birth of their daughter. Eventually they broke up and Samantha started dating again. Later, she met Malik Maudester and gave birth to two more children. Malik was a drug dealer who introduced Samantha to drugs. Initially, she was a recreational user, but when Malik was gunned down Samantha was left to raise her children without a father present in the home. As a result, Samantha became increasingly depressed and began to increase her drug usage, eventually becoming addicted to heroin. Although she was very loving toward her children, Malik's murder caused her to become more depressed. However, she never sought any mental treatment. Samantha strongly believed that mental health services were for "crazy people" and that her faith was enough to help her overcome stressors. However, she self-medicated with drugs and her ability to assume parental responsibility was significantly compromised.

Child protective services conducted investigations and supportive family preservation services were put in place. Samantha appeared to be responsive to working with a social worker and her mother, Geraldine participated in the Family Group Conferencing meetings. Things were appearing somewhat stable and the case was closed. However, once Samantha lost her job as a receptionist for a law firm, she went from job to job. Furthermore, her addiction to drugs was spiraling out of control. To support her habit, she became involved with a credit card scheme that led to her arrest and sentencing to jail for 7 years. To keep Samantha's children together, Geraldine agreed to take the children in and become a full-time parent again.

Monique is 15 years old and the firstborn child of Samantha. As a young child, Monique frequently witnessed her mother use drugs and sometimes she did not have food to provide for them. She also helped to care for her two younger siblings. Monique loved her mother, but resented her grandmother for arguing with her mother. When Samantha went to prison, Monique was 11 years old and at the beginning stage of adolescence. Her world tumbled down and suddenly she had to move in with her grandmother, whom she loved but had mixed feelings about. By the time she was 14 years old, she began to hang out with some girls who seemed to know their way around. She began skipping school, obtained a fake identification card, and started smoking marijuana. During this period, she met an older guy and had her first sexual encounter. Just like the conflict between her mother and grandmother, Monique and Geraldine frequently argued too. Things at home and school were becoming increasingly worse and most of all, Monique missed her mother tremendously. Recently, the family came to the attention of the school social worker because of Monique's behavior and academic performance.

Presenting problem: For the past 27 years, Geraldine has worked with a city government agency as an administrative assistant and although her salary was modest, she managed to raise her children with some help from her ex-husband while they were growing up. However, when her child support ended several years ago, she started working an extra part-time job as a customer service representative for a retail store during holiday seasons. When her grandchildren came to live with her, Geraldine was thrust with the responsibility of parenting all over again. It has not been easy at all. Financially she is struggling and she is unable to work her second job during the holidays due to her responsibilities to the children. She resides in a three-bedroom house in a community comprised of homeowners and renters living in row houses located in a working-class neighborhood. Since moving there 25 years ago, she has seen the demise of the community, where resources have been depleted, the crime rate has escalated due to increased involvement with youth gang activities, and the neighborhood has become transient.

The responsibility of parenting again has been mired with challenges. For example, Geraldine was recently diagnosed with breast cancer and her blood pressure is continuously high. She is concerned about who will take care of her grandchildren if she does not recover. Monique, now aged 15 years, has a 25-year-old boyfriend who is encouraging her to engage in prostitution to earn money. She is unwilling to listen to her grandmother and refuses to participate in the youth group at church. Geraldine tried to have family meetings, but Monique refuses to participate and says that her grandmother is the cause of her mother's failure. Given the paucity of resources in the community, Geraldine is very concerned about her granddaughter as well as her other grandchildren. She is worried that Monique's behavior will influence the other children and it may be just a matter of time before they, too, get out of control. So far, the two younger children are obedient doing well in school, and are actively involved with the youth group at their church.

Geraldine is feeling tremendous pressure from the responsibility and disappointed that her own hopes and dreams have once again been placed on hold. Sometimes she feels that it is just too much and she feels like giving up, but her strong faith and her extended and church family have been very supportive and help her to combat the fatigue and depressive symptoms she experiences from becoming a parent again. She is no longer able to consider attending school, and her dating life no longer exists. Geraldine's brother and sister have offered to help, but Geraldine feels reluctant to receive support.

As the social worker, you are responsible for beginning the intervention process by conducting an assessment. Subsequently, you are responsible for the following:

1. Identify the presenting problems within the family, school, and community (Educational Policy and Accreditation Standards (EPAS) 2.13, 2.1.10).

2. Utilize an integrated framework to assess the family strengths and challenges (EPAS 2.1.8, 2.1.10).

3. What universal developmental task do you need to understand about adolescence and middle adulthood (EPAS 2.1.7)?

4. Identify and describe cultural factors present (EPAS 2.1.4)?

5. How does the family communicate (EPAS 2.1.3, 2.1.4)?

6. What social work values are important to consider when working with this family? (EPAS 2.1.1., 2.1.2).

7. Based on your assessment, what goals would you develop to work with this family? (EPAS. 2.1.9, 2.1.0)?

Using Various Web-Based Instructional Resources

Institution: Morgan State University
Department: School of Social Work
Course Title: Social Work 620 Urban Social Work Practice With the Aged and their Families
Developer: Gaynell M. Simpson, PhD

Web resources
NIH Senior Health (http://nihseniorhealth.gov)
The National Library of Medicine (NLM), National Institutes of Aging
(http://www.nlm.nih.gov)

Research, Education, and Outreach Community Project

This project consists of three activities: (a) research a health topic related to aging; (b) examine and critique your topic from an ecological perspective; (c) coordinate and conduct a community-based educational session with older adults in Baltimore, Maryland. A Blackboard discussion forum will be provided to assist students with online consultation and questions related to this independent project.

Step 1: Select an aging topic of interest focused on caregiving and health in urban communities. The topic of interest must be selected from the following online resource: http://nihseniorhealth.gov

Step 2: Conduct a preliminary review of the literature. After reading information about your topic of interest, develop a research area of inquiry about this topic (e.g., what are the stressors associated with caring for a family member with Alzheimer's?). To help with developing a research inquiry, research your topic using online databases and journal articles. Use the United States National Library of Medicine (NLM), National Institutes of Health: http://www.ncbi.nlm.nih.gov/pmc/

Step 3: Conduct a comprehensive review of the literature. Now it is time to develop your practice paper.

Step 4: First Draft of Research Paper. This draft is not graded. You are provided detailed and critical feedback. The following headings are required:

Title page

Abstract

Introduction (topic and research inquiry)

Background/prevalence (clearly define the social problem, prevalence in society, and implications for aging and minorities of color). Discuss why the issue you have raised is important.

Body of paper (subheadings will vary depending on your topic): Your literature review will reflect your understanding of this problem. Provide appropriate American Psychological Association (APA) citations.

Practice implications: Describe types of interventions–recommendations for selected topic of interest (what are the coping skills and resources available to assist family caregivers?).

Education/electronic resources: This area is essential because you are going to educate consumers and service providers about ways to address the topic of interest. You are encouraged to use case examples (must cite source); online tools and resources (must be user-friendly to consumers/providers); handouts.

References: use APA style format.

Step 5: Submit final research, education, and training. Final submission is due and this will be graded. This is your final grade for the research–paper project.

Step 6: Create a draft presentation of education and training. Present preliminary draft of research, education, and training presentation. Receive feedback from professor and peers. This informational/training PowerPoint presentation must be directed toward consumers and/or service providers. Utilize online resources to assist with creating an informative and interesting informational training presentation.

The online communications Resource for Grantees of The John A. Hartford Foundation. http://www.bandwidthonline.org

Examine data, image, stories, and messages. Look under the tab "how do I" for help with preparing PowerPoint.

Step 7: Final Community Research, Education and Training Projects. This is moving your paper from a research practice to an applied community-based setting. This first step is to identify and secure a community-based setting where you can conduct a poster presentation focused on older adults. Your presentation will be evaluated by your audience members, fellow students, and professor.

Suggested Readings

Bene, S. B. (2010). African American grandmothers raising grandchildren: A phenomenological perspective of marginalized women. *Journal of Gerontological Nursing, 36*(8), 1–39. doi:10.3928/00989134–20100330-01

Bertera, E., & Crewe, S. (2013). Parenthood in the twenty-first century: African American grandparents as surrogate parents. *Journal of Human Behavior in the Social Environment, 23*(2), 178–192. doi:10.1080/10911359.2013.747348

Carr, G. F., Hayslip, J. B., & Gray, J. (2012). Feature article: The role of caregiver burden in understanding African American custodial grandmothers. *Geriatric Nursing, 33*, 366–374. doi:10.1016/j.gerinurse.2012.03.004

Carthron, D. L., Johnson, T. M., Hubbart, T. D., Strickland, C., & Nance, K. (2010). "Give Me Some Sugar!" The diabetes self-management activities of African-American primary caregiving grandmothers. *Journal of Nursing Scholarship, 42*(3), 330–337. doi:10.1111/j.1547–5069.2010.01336.x

Cox, C. (2002). Empowering African American custodial grandparents. *Social Work, 47*(1), 45–54.

Crowther, M. R., Ford, C. D., & Peterson, T. (2014). A qualitative examination of barriers for urban and rural custodial grandparents. *Journal of Intergenerational Relationships, 12*(3), 241. doi: 10.1080/15350770.2014.929938

Dilworth-Anderson, P., Williams, I. C., & Gibson, B. E. (2002). Issues of race, ethnicity, and culture in caregiving research: A 20-year review (1980–2000). *Gerontologist, 42*(2), 237–272.

Dunifon, R. (2013). The influence of grandparents of the lives of children and adolescents. *Child Development Perspectives, 7*(1), 55–60. doi: 10.1111/cdep.12016

Dunlap, E., Golub, A., & Johnson, D. B., (2006). The severely-distressed African American family in the crack era: Empowerment is not enough. *Journal of Sociology and Social Welfare, 33*(1), 115–139.

Gibson, P. A. (2014). Grandmother caregiver-in-chief continues the tradition of African American families. *Affilia: Journal of Women & Social Work, 29*(3), 298. doi:10.1177/0886109913519794

Gibson, P. A., & McGlynn, C. (2013). Enough is enough: Grandmother caregivers' strategies for mitigating out-of-school suspensions for African–American youth. *Children & Youth Services Review, 35*(11), 1836—1842.

Kelch-Oliver, K. (2011). The experiences of African American grandmothers in grandparent-headed families. *The Family Journal, 19*(1), 73–82.

Kelley, S. J., Whitley, D. M., & Campos, P. E. (2013a). Psychological distress in African American grandmothers raising grandchildren: The contribution of child behavior problems, physical health, and family resources. *Research in Nursing & Health, 36*(4), 373. doi:10.1002/nur.21542

Kelley, S. J., Whitley, D. M., & Campos, P. E. (2013b). African American caregiving grandmothers: Results of an intervention to improve health indicators and health promotion behaviors. *Journal of Family Nursing, 19*(1), 53—73. doi:10.1177/1074840712462135

Lee, S., Colditz, G., Berkman, L., & Kawachi, I. (2003). Caregiving to children and grandchildren and risk of coronary heart disease in women. *American Journal of Public Health, 93*(11), 1939–1944.

Lindsey, M., Chambers, K., Pohle, C., Beall, P., & Lucksted, A. (2013). Understanding the behavioral determinants of mental health service use by urban, under-resourced Black youth: Adolescent and caregiver perspectives. *Journal of Child & Family Studies, 22*(1), 107—121. doi:10.1007/s10826-012-9668-z

Loper, A., Phillips, V., Nichols, E., & Dallaire, D. (2014). Characteristics and effects of the co-parenting alliance between incarcerated parents and child caregivers. *Journal of Child & Family Studies, 23*(2), 225—241.

Minkler, M., & Fuller-Thomson, E. (2005). African American grandparents raising grandchildren: A national study using the Census 2000 American Community Survey. *Journals of Gerontology, 60B*, S82—S92.

Musil, M. C., Gordon, N. L., Warner, C. B., Zauszniewski, J. A., Standing, T., & Wykle, M. (2010). Grandmothers and caregiving to grandchildren: Continuity, change, and outcomes over 24 months. *The Gerontologist, 51*(1), 86–100.

Nancy, P., & Burnett, D. (2003). Grandparents as family caregivers: Lessons for intergenerational education. Social Work Faculty Publications. Paper 9. Retrieved from http://scholarworks.gsu.edu/ssw_facpub/9

Pew Research. (September 9, 2010). *Since the start of the great recession, more children raised by grandparents.* Retrieved January, 2014, from http://pewsocialtrends.org/files/2010/10/764-children-raised-by-grandparents.pdf

Rubin, M. (2013). Grandparents as caregivers: Emerging issues for the profession. *Journal of Human Behavior in the Social Environment, 23*(3), 330–344.

Stinson, D. L. (2010). This ain't something you can pray away: Grandparents raising grandchildren, a photovoice project. *Journal of Health Care for the Poor and Underserved, 21,* 1–25. Retrieved from https://www.press.jhu.edu/journals/journal_of_health_care_for_the_poor_and_underserved

Whitley, D. M., Kelley, S. J., & Campos, P. E. (2013). Promoting family empowerment among African American grandmothers raising grandchildren. In B. J. Hayslip, G. C. Smith, B. J. Hayslip, & G. C. Smith (Eds.), *Resilient grandparent caregivers: A strengths-based perspective* (pp. 235–250). New York, NY, US: Routledge/Taylor & Francis Group.

REFERENCES

Bent-Goodley, T. (2011). *Regulating the lives of children: Kinship care as a cultural resistance strategy of the African American community: Social welfare policy, regulation and resistance among people of color.* Thousand Oaks, CA: Sage.

Bronfenbrenner, U., & Garbarino, J. (1985). *Extrafamilial factors in child abuse and neglect and their prevention.* Paper presented at the State Conference on Child Abuse and Neglect, Albany, NY.

Bronfenbrenner, U., & Morris, P. A. (1998). The ecology of developmental processes. In W. Damon & R. Learner (Eds.), *Handbook of child psychology* (5th ed., pp. 993–1027). New York, NY: John Wiley.

Bullock, K. (2005). Grandfathers and the impact of raising grandchildren. *Journal of Sociology & Social Welfare, 32*(1), 43–59.

Bullock, K. (2007). Grandfathers raising grandchildren: An exploration of African American kinship networks. *Journal of Health & Social Policy, 22*(3/4), 181–197. doi:10.1 300/J045v22n0312

Bunch, S. G., Eastman, B. J., & Moore, R. R. (2007). A profile of grandparents raising grandchildren as a result of parental military deployment. *Journal of Human Behavior in the Social Environment, 15*(4), 1–12.

Burnette, D. (1997). Grandparents raising grandchildren in the inner city. *Families in Society, 78*(5), 489–499. doi:101606/1044–3894818

Burton, L. M. (1992). Black grandparents rearing children of drug-addicted parents: Stressor, outcomes, and social service needs. *The Gerontological Society of America, 32*(6), 744–751.

Burton, L. M., & Jarrett, R. L. (2000). In the mix, yet on the margins: The place of families in urban neighborhood and child development research. *Journal of Marriage and the Family, 62*(4), 1114–1135. Retrieved from http://www.ncfr.org/jmf

Carlton-LaNey, I. (1999). African American social work pioneers' response to need. *Social Work, 44,* 311–322.

Carlton-LaNey, I., Hamilton, J., Ruiz, D., & Carleton Alexander, S. (2001). "Sitting with the sick": African American women's philanthropy. *Affilia, 16*(4), 447–466.

Casey, K., & Hurley, M. (2009). *Supporting kinship care: Research and strategies to promote and fund placement with relatives* (pp. 1–38). Washington, DC: Public Consulting Group.

Collins, P. (2000). *Black feminist thoughts: Knowledge, consciousness, and the politics of empowerment.* New York, NY: Routledge.

Congress, E. P., & Gonzalez, M. J. (Eds.). (2012). *Multicultural perspectives in social work practice with families* (3rd ed.). New York, NY: Springer Publishing Company.

Cox, C. B. (2000). *To grandmother's house we go and stay: Perspectives on custodial grandparents.* New York, NY: Springer.

Crewe, S. E. (2012). Guardians of generations: African American grandparent caregivers for children of HIV/AIDS infected parents. *Journal of Family Strengths, 12*(1). Retrieved from http://digitalcommons.library.tmc.edu/jfs/vol12/iss1/4

Dannison, L. L., Smith, A. B., & Vacha-Haase, T. (1999). Grandparents as parents: An ecological approach to programming. *Michigan Family Review, 4*(1), 37–48. Retrieved from http://hdl.handle.net/2027/spo.4919087.0004.105

Dowdell, E. B. (1995). Caregiver burden: Grandmothers raising their high risk grandchildren. *Journal of Psychosocial Nursing, 33*(3), 27–30.

Dowdell, E. B. (2004). Grandmother caregivers and caregiver burden. *Journal of Maternal Child Nursing, 29*(5), 299–304.

Dunlap, E., Golub, A., & Johnson, D. B. (2006). The severely-distressed African American family in the crack era: Empowerment is not enough. *Journal of Sociology and Social Welfare, 33*(1), 115–139.

Emick, M. A., & Hayslip, B. (1996). Custodial grandparenting: New roles for middle-aged and older adults. *International Journal of Aging and Human Development, 43*(2), 135–154.

Everett, J. E., Chipungu, S. P., & Leashore, B. (Eds.). (2004). *Child welfare revisited: An Africentric perspective* (pp. 77–93). New Brunswick, NJ: Rutgers University Press.

Fong, R., & Furuto, S. (2001). *Culturally competent practice: Skills, interventions, and evaluations.* Needham Heights, MA: Allyn & Bacon.

Franklin, J. H., & Moss, A. A. (1994). *From slavery to freedom: A history of African Americans*. New York, NY: Alfred A. Knopf.

Fuller-Thomson, E., Minkler, M., & Driver, D. (1997). A profile of grandparents raising grandchildren in the United States. *The Gerontologist, 37*(3), 406–411.

Generations United. (2000). *Grandparents and other relatives raising grandchildren: Grassroots concerns and solutions from across the United States*. Washington, DC: Author.

Gibson, P. A. (2005). Intergenerational parenting from the perspective of African American grandmothers. *Family Relations, 54*(2), 280–297.

Gibson, P. A. (2014). Grandmother caregiver-in-chief continues the tradition of African American families. *Affilia: Journal of Women & Social Work, 29*(3), 298–309. doi:10.1177/0886109913519794

Glass, C. J., & Huneycutt, T. L. (2002). Grandparents raising grandchildren: The courts, custody, and educational implications. *Educational Gerontology, 28*(3), 237–251.

Harden, A. W., Clark, R. L., & Maquire, K. (1997). *Informal and formal kinship care*. Washington, DC: U.S. Department of Health and Human Services.

Hayslip, B., Jr., & Kaminski, B. J. (2005). Grandparents raising their grandchildren. *Marriage & Family Review*, Taylor & Francis, 147–169. doi:10.1300/J002v37n01_10. Retrieved from http://www.tandfonline.com/doi/abs/10.1300/J002v37n01_10

Hepworth, D. H., Rooney, R. H., & Larsen, J. A. (2002). *Direct social work practice: Theory and skills* (6th ed.). Pacific Grove, CA: Wadsworth Publishing.

Heywood, E. C. (1999). Custodial grandparents and their children. *Family Journal, 7*(4), 367–373.

Hill, R. B. (1972). *The strengths of black families*. New York, NY: Emerson Hall.

Hill, R. B. (1998). Understanding black family functioning: A holistic perspective. *Journal of Comparative Family Studies, 29*(1), 15–26.

Hill, R. B. (2003). *The strengths of black families* (2nd ed.). Lanham, MD: University Press of America.

Hine, D. C., Hine, W. C., & Harrold, S. (2006). *The African-American odyssey*. Upper Saddle River, NJ: Pearson Prentice Hall.

Jendrek, M. P. (1994). Grandparents who parent their grandchildren: Circumstances and decisions. *The Gerontologist, 34*(2), 206–216.

Jimenez, J. (2002). The history of grandmothers in the African American community. *Social Services Review, 76*(14), 523–551.

Johnson-Garner, M. Y., & Meyers, S. A. (2003). What factors contribute to the resilience of African American children in kinship care? *Child and Youth Care Forum, 32*, 255–269.

Jones, J. (1985). *Labor of love, labor of sorrow: Black women, work, and the family from slavery to the present*. New York, NY: Basic Books.

Joslin, D. (2002). *Invisible caregivers: Older adults raising children in the wake of HIV/AIDS*. New York, NY: Columbia University Press.

Keene, J., Held, B., & Prokos, A. (2012). Grandfather caregivers: Race and ethnic differences in poverty. *Sociological Inquiry, 82*(1), 49–77. doi:10.1111/j.1475–682X.2011.00398

Kelley, S. J., Whitley, D., Sipe, T. A., & Yorker, B. C. (2000). Psychological distress in grandmother kinship care providers: The role of resources, social support, and physical health. *Child Abuse & Neglect, 24*(3), 311–321.

Kelley, S. J., & Yorker, B. C. (2001). A multimodal intervention for grandparents raising grandchildren: Results of an exploratory study. *Child Welfare, 80*(1), 27–50.

Kelly, E. M. (2001). Female, young, African-American and low income. *Feminism and Psychology, 11*(2), 152–156.

Kochhar, R., & D'Vera, C. (2011). Fighting poverty in a tough economy, Americans move in with their relatives. Pew Social and Demographic Trends Publication. Retrieved from http://www.pewsocialtrends.org/files/2011/10/Multigenerational-Households-Final1.pdf

Kolomer, S. R., & McCallion, P. (2005). Depression and caregiver mastery in grandfathers caring for their grandchildren. *International Journal of Aging & Human Development, 60*(4), 283–294.

Kropt, N. P., & Yoon, E. (2006). Grandparents raising grandchildren: Who are they? In B. Berkman & S. D'Ambruoso (Eds.), *Handbook of social work in health and aging* (pp. 355–362). New York, NY: Oxford.

Lincoln, C. E., & Mamiya, L. H. (1990). The black church in the African American experience. Durham, NC: Duke University Press.

Livingston, G. (2013). At grandmother's house we stay: One-in-ten children are living with a grandparent. Pew Research Center's Social & Demographic Trends Project. Retrieved from http://www.pewsocialtrends.org/2013/09/04/at-grandmothers-house-we-stay/

Lofquist, D. A. (2013). Multigenerational households: 2009–2011. American Survey Briefs. U.S. Census Bureau. Retrieved from www.census.gov/prod/2012pubs/acsbr11–03.pdf

Martin, E. P., & Martin, J. M. (1985). *The helping tradition in the Black family and community.* Washington, DC: National Association of Social Workers.

Martin, E. P., & Martin, J. M. (2002). *Spirituality and the Black helping tradition.* Washington, DC: NASW Press.

McAdoo, H. (1982). Stress absorbing systems in black families. *Family Relations, 31*(4), 479–488.

McCullough-Chavis, A., & Waites, C. (2004). Genograms with African American families: Considering cultural context. *Journal of Family Social Work, 8*(2), 1–19.

Minkler, M., & Fuller-Thomson, E. (2005). African American grandparents raising grandchildren: A national study using Census 2000 American Community Survey. *The Journal of Gerontology, 60B*(2), 82–92. doi:10.1093/geronb/60.2582

Minkler, M., & Roe, M. K. (1993). *Grandmothers as caregivers: Raising children of the crack cocaine epidemic* (Vol. 2). Newbury Park, CA: Sage.

Newman, K. (2006). *A different shade of gray: Midlife and beyond in the inner city.* New York, NY: The New Press.

Parker, M. W., Bellis, J. M., Bishop, P., Harper, M., Allman, R. M., Moore, C., & Thompson, P. (2002). A multidisciplinary model of health promotion incorporating spirituality into a successful aging intervention with African American and White elderly groups. *The Gerontologist, 42*(5), 406–415.

Pinderhughes, E. (1983). Empowerment for our clients and ourselves. *Social Casework, 31,* 331–337.

Puckerin, G. (1984). America's black middle class: A progress report. *Wilson Quarterly Report, 3,* 3–4.

Rubin, D., Downes, K., O'Reilly, A., Mekonnen, R., Xianqun, L., & Localio, R. (2008). The impact of kinship care on behavioral well-being for children in out-of-home care. *Archives of Pediatric and Adolescent Medicine, 162*(6), 1–14.

Saleebey, D. (1997). *The strengths perspective in social work practice* (2nd ed.). White plains, NY: Longman.

Sands, R. G., Goldberg-Glen, R. S., & Shin, H. (2009). The voices of grandchildren of grandparent caregivers: A strength–resilience perspective. *Child Welfare League of America, 88*(2), 25–45.

Schiele, J. H. (2000). *Human services and the Afrocentric paradigm.* Binghamton, NY: The Haworth Press.

Simmons, T., & Dye, J. L. (2003). Grandparents living with grandchildren: 2000. Retrieved July 8, 2013, from http://www.census.gov/prod/2003pubs/c2kbr-31.pdf" \t "pmc_ext" www.census.gov/prod/2003pubs/c2kbr-31.pdf

Simpson, G. (2008). A qualitative perspective of family resources among low income, African American grandmother-caregiver. *Journal of Gerontological Social Work, 51*(1–2), 19–41. doi:10.1080/01634370801967539

Simpson, G. M., & Cornelius, L. (2007). Overlooking African American males: Urban African American grandmother caregivers' reliance on family members. *Journal of Human Behavior in the Social Environment, 5,* 149–170. doi:10.1300/J137v15n01_08.

Simpson, G. M., & Lawrence-Webb, C. (2009). Responsibility without community resources: Informal kinship care among low-income, African American grandmother caregivers. *Journal of Black Studies, 39*(6), 825–847. doi:10.1177/0021934707303631

Small, M. L., & Newman, K. (2001). Urban poverty after the truly disadvantaged: The rediscovery of the family, the neighborhood, and culture. *Annual Review of Sociology, 27,* 23–45.

Smith, A. (1994). African American grandmothers' war against the crack-cocaine epidemic. *Arete, 19*(1), 22–26.

Smith, B. D. (2006). *An examination of contextual factors that influence permanency decisions in the public child welfare system* (Unpublished doctoral dissertation). Howard University, Washington, DC.

Solomon, B. B. (1976). *The empowerment tradition in American social work.* New York, NY: Columbia University Press.

Stack, C. B. (1974). *All our kin: Strategies for survival in a black community.* New York, NY: Harper Torchbook.

Stinson, D. L. (2010). This ain't something you can pray away: Grandparents raising grandchildren, a photovoice project. *Journal of Health Care for the Poor and Underserved, 21,* 1–25. Retrieved from https://www.press.jhu.edu/journals/journal_of_health_care_for_the_poor_and_underserved

Waites, C. (2009). Building on strengths: Intergenerational practice with African American families. *Social Work, 54*(3), 278.

Waites, C., MacGowan, M. J., Pennell, J., Carlton-LaNey, I., & Weil, M. (2004). Increasing the cultural responsiveness of family group conferencing. Advancing child welfare practice. *Social Work, 49*(2), 291–300.

Wells-Wilbon, R., & Simpson, G. M. (2009). Transitioning the caregiving role for the next generation: An African-centered womanist perspective. *Black Women, Gender & Families, 3*(2), 87–105.

Wilson, W. J. (1987). *The truly disadvantaged: The inner city, the underclass, and public policy.* Chicago, IL: The University of Chicago Press.

Wilson, W. J. (2009). *More than just race: Being black and poor in the inner city.* New York, NY: W.W. Norton.

Wilson, W. J. (1996). *When work disappears: The world of the new urban poor.* New York, NY: Knopf Doubleday Publishing Group.

Winston, C. A. (1999). Self-help for grandmothers parenting again. *Journal of Social Diseases and the Homeless, 8*(3), 157–163.

Young, D. S., & Smith, C. J. (2000). When moms are incarcerated: The needs of children, mothers, and caregivers. *Families in Society, 81*(2), 130–141. doi:10.1606/1041-3894.1007

CHAPTER 14

Coping With Loss and Grief in Urban Communities

Tanya L. Sharpe and Margaret E. Pittman

This chapter discusses the complexities of coping with loss and grief in urban communities whose experiences are often associated with forms of loss as a result of chronic violent crimes and victimization; natural and human-made disasters; unanticipated death (e.g., homicide, infant mortality, and other health-related disparities); and chronic intangible loss, such as loss of control, hope, trust, and self-worth. Whether chronic tangible or intangible losses are experienced, the response to loss results in some form of grief (Walsh, 2012). Grief is the general term used to describe the various cognitive, emotional, physical, and behavioral reactions that may surface, in any combination, after a loss (Doka, 1998; Jeffreys, 2011; Walsh, 2012; Worden, 2009).

Although the circumstances surrounding a loss and the resulting grief reactions may differ considerably, it is common knowledge, that loss and grief are both common individual and collective experiences (Walsh, 2012). And yet, research detailing loss and grief among urban, diverse, marginalized, and vulnerable populations (e.g., African American, elderly) is limited (Laurie & Neimeyer, 2008). Understanding the full range of loss and grief experienced by diverse urban communities requires the expansion of definitions, meanings, and the lenses through which loss and grief are examined.

LOSS

Loss is a normal part of everyday life, individually and collectively (Doka & Davidson, 1998; Jeffreys, 2011). Everyone, regardless of ethnicity, age, gender, race, culture, socioeconomic status, intelligence level, or physical ability, will experience some type of loss and exhibit grief reactions. Jeffreys (2011) defines loss as a change that results from the severing of an attachment even if the change is perceived as helpful or is welcomed. For example, relocation by choice can simultaneously produce feelings of delight and accomplishment while also producing feelings of loss. Although one welcomes the opportunity to relocate for the purpose of pursuing and making what is expected to be a better life, loss is also a part of this transition because familiar friends, traditions, and even the route traveled to work no longer exist. Those routine places, events, and people that provided stability, security, and support are no longer readily available, and such losses may be grieved.

Experiencing loss at the community level also affects the grieving process of individuals as a collective body. For example, in urban communities where incidents of unanticipated death (e.g., homicide, drug overdose) are high, community residents must grieve the loss of safety in neighborhoods and the prosperous possibilities for murdered youth and neighbors, and create alternative support networks and resources that can help communities function and prosper.

Types of Loss

More often than not, loss is associated with a death or dying (e.g., terminal illness, suicide, homicide violence, motor vehicle accident). These types of losses are referred to as tangible losses. In addition, there are also many other forms of losses including a bevy of non-death-related situations, occurrences, or events that one experiences during a lifetime. These losses can include but are not limited to feelings and experiences of loss that result from absent parents, amputation of limbs, cancer diagnoses, chronic unemployment, discrimination, divorce, eviction, loss of security, medical and mental health challenges, and so on (Herrmann, 2011; Jeffreys, 2011; Walsh, 2012; Worden, 2009). Such losses are often referred to as symbolic or intangible losses. Symbolic or intangible losses may not be recognized by the griever or by society at the same degree as death and other tangible or actual losses. However, the impact of symbolic or intangible losses can warrant reactions similar to those losses experienced as a result of death and dying (Jeffreys, 2012; Walsh, 2012).

Loss in Urban Communities

An urban community consists of a large number of people who live in close proximity to one another in a city. Urban communities are typically associated with high levels of poverty, socioeconomic deprivation, isolation from equitability career advancement opportunities, limited standardized housing, and high levels of crime and victimization often referred to as community-level deprivation. Community deprivation includes both material and social aspects. Material deprivation relates to insufficient diet; health–health care; clothing; and environmentally sound communities and can be measured based on financial income and fiscal, physical, and mental health outcomes. On the other hand, social deprivation relates to limited access and the unequal distribution of social networks and resources that help to sustain and support healthy communities such as adequate housing and access to educational and employment opportunities (Townsend, 1987). Shaw (1979) suggests that there are three types of deprivation: household, opportunity, and mobility. Household deprivation is defined as the unmet needs of communities such as inadequate shelter in safe environments. Opportunity deprivation refers to a lack of employment and quality educational opportunities. Mobility deprivation concerns accessibility to services and facilities that support and allow for the probability of social advancement. What is most important about the many forms of deprivation is understanding the increased impact that it has on urban communities' habitual experiences with loss specific to opportunities for personal and collective mobility and advancement.

One need only consider the recurrent incidents of community violence (e.g., homicide violence, crime, and victimization) structural (e.g., racism, discrimination), environmental (e.g., pollution), and systemic socioeconomic challenges (e.g., limited employment and quality educational opportunities), which can often lead to psychological trauma, brought about by living in marginalized urban neighborhoods, to understand loss in urban communities. These multiple, co-occurring types of loss that take place in urban areas suggest that the vast majority of urban communities throughout the United States do not just experience loss, but they experience repeated symbolic and tangible incidents of loss that can best be classified as traumatic (Anda et al., 2006; Cloitre et al., 2009; Dong et al., 2004; Pynoos et al., 2009; Sims et al., 1989). Chronic traumatic experiences such as these can often lead to dramatic ruptures in individuals' and communities' psychosocial development, sense of safety, security, and trust (Gardner, 1971; Parson, 1994; van der Kolk, 1987) across the life span.

Loss Across the Life Span

In addition to habitual traumatic loss experienced in urban racial and ethnic communities, individuals across the life span often experience multiple victimization or polyvictimization as a result of chronic exposure (direct or indirect) to violent victimization and/or loss due to health and aging. For instance, young and middle-aged children and adolescents who are exposed to various types of crime or trauma on a chronic basis, can exhibit grief reactions such as hypervigilance, social isolation, and so on, that compromise their cognitive, emotional, and behavioral development (Walsh, 2012). The same holds true for middle age to older adults. Urban-dwelling older adults (aged 65 years and older) experience losses that are common to those in their birth cohort who reside in other types of communities. Losses common to older adults include but are not limited to the loss of independence, loss of income, loss of social support, loss of role identity, loss of physical and cognitive abilities, loss of self-worth, loss of independent housing, and the death of a spouse, child, friend, or other loved ones (Herrmann, 2011;

Tomaka, Thompson, & Palacios, 2006; Walsh, 2012; Williams, Sawyer Baker, Allman, & Roseman, 2007). Moreover, they experience these types of multiple losses in rapid succession, often referred to as loss pileup (Jeffreys, 2011; Walsh, 2012; Williams et al., 2007). The characteristics of chronic traumatic loss for urban communities can add a layer of complication to the grieving process experienced by older adults coping with loss related to aging.

GRIEF

Grief is characterized by a multifaceted response to loss, particularly to the loss of someone or something to whom or which a bond was formed (Kastenbaum, 2001). Although used interchangeably, it is important to note that grief is the reaction to loss, while bereavement refers to the state of loss (Doka, 1989a; Parkes, 1999). Individuals can experience grief in a myriad of ways. Individuals may experience emotional reactions such as anger, guilt, and helplessness; cognitive reactions such as an inability to concentrate, disbelief, and depersonalization; and behavioral reactions such as hyperactivity or withdrawal (Doka, 2002; Kubler-Ross & Kessler, 2005).

Grief Reactions

Common reactions to death and dying and symbolic or intangible losses consist of thoughts of disbelief, preoccupation, and confusion and feelings of shock, numbness, sadness, anger, guilt, relief, loneliness, and anxiety (Kubler-Ross & Kessler, 2005; Walsh, 2012; Worden, 2009). For some, the grief reactions may be slight, barely noticeable to the griever, and for others, grief reactions can be extreme taking the form of sleeplessness or appetite disturbances and disorganization. More moderate grief reactions may appear in the same or different areas, such as overt displays of anger and feelings of helplessness. Individuals may experience intense behavioral, cognitive, or physical grief reactions as a result of loss. There may be intense behavior changes, such as variations in crying patterns, disturbances to sleep and appetite routines, increased sighing, differences in levels of concentration, and increased or decreased desires and opportunities for social interaction. Physical changes and challenges may also occur in those who have experienced a loss, including chest and throat tension, lethargy, nausea, shortness of breath, weak or achy muscles, and dry mouth (Walsh, 2012).

Beyond the psychological and physical manifestation of grief is the spiritual domain wherein survivors attempt to make sense of the loss. When a loss occurs, it is common to utilize spiritual resources (e.g., faith) as a means of coping with the loss, or to question or deviate from long-held spiritual beliefs because the loss challenges one's security, stability (Walsh, 2012; Worden, 2009), and sense of meaning and understanding of the world and how one operationalizes oneself within it (Sharpe, 2008; Sharpe & Boyas, 2011). However, as mentioned earlier, variations in the levels of intensity differ with each griever and with each experience of loss. Grief reactions to traumatic loss are influenced by several factors, including the unique meaning of the loss, the strength and nature of the attachment to the person or object, the circumstances surrounding the loss (e.g., homicide violence vs. natural causes), reactions and experiences of earlier loss, the temperament and adaptive abilities of the individual and their sphere influence, the presence and support of family and other informal and formal support systems, cultural and spiritual beliefs and practices, and general health and lifestyle practices of the grieving individuals (Parkes, 1999; Rando, 1986; Redmond, 1989).

Although it is typical that grief reactions will decrease and disappear, given time and support, there are times however, when the expected grief reactions increase in intensity, duration, or both, causing complex challenges and/or extended anguish in the life functioning of an individual. That is, the initial reactions experienced at the onset of the loss have not decreased, but have remained the same or have increased with the passing of time. This is not the expected trajectory of grief and thus is referred to as complicated or prolonged grief (Worden, 2009).

Complicated or Prolonged Grief

Research suggests that there is no specific time frame for the cessation of grief. Complicated or prolonged grief develops when one has a protracted response to grief and experiences complex challenges adapting to the loss(es) (Rando, 1993; Walsh, 2012; Worden, 2009). Complicated or prolonged grief is influenced and impacted by a variety of factors. In Doka's (1989b) seminal work, he created the term "disenfranchised grief" to refer to those losses deemed by society as unacceptable to acknowledge and or discuss, such as the absence and loss of an immediate family member due to incarceration, homicide, or suicide. Losses of this type are no less painful than a socially acceptable loss, however the inability to openly acknowledge, discuss, and receive support for these types of losses can exacerbate grieving, especially because one of the most important factors in the healing process is the ability to speak and to have someone quietly listen. There are several factors, which influence the manner in which one adapts to a loss and the longevity of the grief response. For example, being repeatedly exposed to violent and traumatic experiences even when not directly affected by them such as living in neighborhoods where violence is most frequently witnessed. Being a part of a high profile or intensely public loss can inhibit the healing process and lead to prolonged grief because the grievers are continuously reliving the loss through excessive media coverage and repeated broadcast of the details. In addition, the quantity and types of psychosocial stressors co-occurring with a loss can have a profound impact on the length, type, and level of grief reaction. For instance, in communities where homicide violence is pervasive, several factors can influence grief reactions including the unanticipated and violent nature of the death, self-blame related to being unable to protect their loved one from harm, funeral service costs, and so forth (Sharpe, 2008; Sharpe & Boyas, 2011).

In summary, grief and loss are assured experiences in human existence, though we do battle with their inevitability. Despite this ubiquity, it is a phenomenon conceived and dealt with differently, depending on several sociocultural constructs. The experience of every loss is distinct to the individual experiencing the loss even when the experience is shared with another (Kübler-Ross & Kessler, 2005). The diverse nature of loss and grief is apparent because of its complex and interrelated exposure to the sociocultural practices, expectations, and experiences of coping with various types of loss. A plethora of research on loss and grief focuses on the mental suffering, physical effects, and spiritual challenges of individuals and populations coping with symbolic loss, death, and dying (Archer, 1999; Parkes, 1999; Rando, 1991; Worden, 1991). Lost in translation is the sociocultural transformation that takes place among communities experiencing chronic and collective loss. The sociocultural transformative context of grieving can best be understood when experiencing loss as a result of urban trauma.

Urban Community Grief

Understanding individual grief responses and the aforementioned sociocultural factors that influence grief reactions provides instrumental insight into the construct of collective or community grief. Particularly when considering the concentrated and pervasive nature of community deprivation, incarceration, and homicide violence that are found in urban communities. When traumatic loss occurs in urban communities, community members search for an explanation of what occurred and guidance relevant to how to best deal with the loss from internal community members (e.g., family, friends, faith-based resources) most familiar with what and how the community has experienced and been impacted by the loss (Castle & Phillips, 2003). Thus, urban community grief reactions are illustrated through community-based ritual and cultural practices (Bryant, 2003). Ritual practice grief reactions, such as prayer vigils, and makeshift street memorials, allow victims to collectively identify the meaning of the loss and grieve in a way that is understood and accepted by other community members. Cultural grief reactions consist of the use of social institutions as a means to create stability and a sense of order to what is often a chaotic situation. Culturally informed strategies used to manage grief in disenfranchised urban communities that have unequal access to formal support systems often involves faith-based institutions, family, and fictive kin who provide support as a collective body (e.g., comfort, funeral expense, caregiving). It is important to note that ritual and cultural are not mutually exclusive grief reactions—they are interrelated and one does not exist without the other (Bryant, 2003). In addition, while it is typical that grief reactions will decrease and disappear given time and support, there are times when the expected grief reactions increase in intensity, duration, or both, causing complex challenges and/or extended anguish in the life functioning of an individual. This is not the expected trajectory. However, for marginalized, disenfranchised communities of color, disproportionately vulnerable to incidents of urban traumatic loss, grief experiences are chronic and therefore prolonged and complicated (Doka, 2002; Worden, 2009).

COPING WITH URBAN TRAUMATIC LOSS AND GRIEF

Understanding coping with loss and grief in urban communities is particularly relevant to social work practice with African Americans in urban environments because African Americans are much more likely than Whites to be living in communities that are geographically and economically isolated from equitable economic opportunities, quality services, and institutions that families need to thrive. These disparities have left African Americans across the life span disproportionately vulnerable to incidents of urban trauma in the form of chronic tangible loss experienced through high rates of crime and violence and intangible loss such as community (e.g., material and social) deprivation. Moreover, the aforementioned disparities not only contribute to the experience of loss in urban communities, they often challenge the scarce resources available to cope with the grief reactions that are frequently illustrated throughout urban communities in response to chronic traumatic loss (Myers, 1982, 1989).

Research indicates that grief is a social construct and differences exist between cultures relative to how grief is shaped and managed (Neimeyer, Prigerson, & Davies, 2002; Rosenblatt, 1988; Walter, 1999). Multidisciplinary research has consistently emphasized the importance of considering both universal- and cultural-specific aspects of coping (Moore & Constantine, 2005; Wong, Wong, & Lonner, 2006). For example, relation-focused coping has been examined (Lyons, Mickelson, Sullivan, & Coyne, 1998; O'Brien & DeLongis, 1996) and linked with non-Western, collectivistic cultures (Wong et al., 2006) such as those found in Africa, Asia, and Latin America (Markus & Kitayama, 1991). Collectivistic cultures place greater value and emphasis on relational coping strategies such as seeking help and support from family and friends than engagement in formal supports such as counseling and medication (Moore & Constantine, 2005). Whereas, individualistic cultures are most often affiliated with Western civilization and embrace coping strategies that include assertive self-disclosure, confrontation, open expression of personal thoughts, and feelings consistent with problem-focused and emotion-focused coping (Moore & Constantine, 2005). The interdependent coping style of collectivistic cultures also places an emphasis on shielding family members from harm for fear of over-burdening them. Moreover, urban communities collectively coping with traumatic loss, have a fear of being stigmatized further and are often reluctant to share their problems with others outside of the community due to a lack of trust in systems that have a proven history of mistreating populations of color (Williams & Williams-Morris, 2000).

Understanding coping with traumatic loss for urban communities requires a fundamental understanding of race-based structural inequality and its influence on the disproportionate amount of traumatic loss experienced in urban communities, the manner in which grief manifests itself, and the resources that are utilized to cope with the loss (McGuffey, 2010, 2013; Sharpe, 2014).

IMPLICATIONS FOR THE FUTURE

Although instruments to assess community loss exist (Abramovitz & Albrecht, 2013), there are no instruments designed to assess the influence of urban traumatic loss on community grief and coping strategies. For this reason, an assessment of community subsystems (e.g., informal support networks; extended family; community health systems; spiritual, educational, economic, and cultural institutions and practices) is recommended, using multiple tools (e.g., coping, complicated grief inventory, urban stress, impact of events, trauma, loss) that are culturally normative and have adequate reliability and validity for measuring specific subsystem impacts. For example, in the absence of valid instruments, it is important that assessing for past and current losses become a routine part of the social work biopsychosocial and spiritual assessment process within various agency settings. Conducting a loss history audit (Jeffreys, 2011), which is designed to document the events and the degree of healing associated with past losses to determine the impact that previous losses might have on current losses would be helpful in understanding the impact of collective and chronic trauma on loss and grief reactions. Moreover, "loss history" information could be useful to educate laypersons and other professionals about how to provide best resources and services to individuals and communities who have experienced chronic varied types of losses over the life span.

In addition, law enforcement and those working in the judicial systems perform better when they understand how to interact most effectively with those who suffer from chronic trauma and experienced historical and contemporary cultural trauma as a result of race-based structured inequality. Federal and local first responders (e.g., law enforcement, emergency medical technicians) are trained to help communities during natural and man-made episodic disasters that are traumatic and create community loss experiences. However, there are little to no services offered and no federal personnel trained to adequately address the loss suffered in and by urban communities due to chronic factors such as community deprivation, violent crime, oppression, and isolation. The grief reactions of both communities mirror one another, but the services available to assist each community are diametrically different. For this reason, the phenomena of community loss and grief must be expanded and included in disaster-related culturally sensitive trainings in order to help communities heal and flourish from a lifetime of constant trauma.

A major implication for understanding loss and grief among urban communities is that faith-based institutions are more effective in fostering spiritual, emotional, and relational wellness when leaders and parishioners understand how to more effectively come alongside those who have suffered trauma. In addition, educators provide more meaningful classroom experiences when they understand the challenges of urban trauma and create trauma-informed strategies for social and emotional learning. Moreover, social workers will be better equipped to address loss and grief when graduate programs require an introductory loss and grief course as part of the graduate core curriculum. Newly licensed social workers will become more effective as practitioners when they are aware of various losses experienced by individuals and communities and learn to assess expected grief reactions that individuals experience and communities exhibit based on sociocultural experiences.

Although there are several tools used to conduct appropriate assessments with individuals in an effort to help those suffering to refrain from, address, and understand the maladaptive behaviors used to cope with loss, it is quite the contrary for communities. There is a dearth of appropriate assessment tools that can be used to assess and comprehend the level and intensity of community loss and grief. For this reason, it is imperative that future research focus on discovering and recording grief reactions and the adaptive and maladaptive coping strategies that communities, as systems, demonstrate when reacting to episodic and chronic trauma and loss.

FOR FURTHER STUDY

Suggested Assignments

Roberta's House: Hope for an Urban Community

Roberta's House, founded in 2007, is a grief and loss nonprofit organization in Baltimore, Maryland, with the focus of restoring children and families to a place of wholeness as they experience grieving the loss of a loved one through the development of healthy coping skills that lead to positive outcomes. The core value of Roberta's House is HOPE; *H*onoring the memory of those who have died by *O*ffering opportunities to learn *P*ositive and *E*mpowering grief experiences.

Roberta's House is built on three generations of experience of a family that, for more than 50 years, has embodied the notion of community support and outreach and the many Baltimore residents who have been touched by and benefited from these efforts. The March Family, of March Funeral Homes, spearheaded the development of Roberta's House.

Roberta's House is a family-centered program where professional and community volunteers provide services at no cost to the entire community. Services are available to the whole community with opportunities for volunteer training, school support, professional seminars and workshops, and bereavement ministry support and development. Roberta's House offers a number of programs to empower the community at large and assist its residents in the journey to healing. One such program, the Homicide Survivors Transformation Project, is a bereavement support group for African Americans aged 18 and over, whose family members were victims of homicide in urban, low-income communities in the Baltimore Metropolitan area (Roberta's House, 2010). The Project, which is funded by the Maryland Governor's Office of Crime Control and Prevention, was codeveloped and evaluated by the chapter's author, Dr. Tanya Sharpe.

For more information visit: http://robertashouse.org

Study Case 1

On Saturday, August 9, at approximately 12 p.m., Mike Brown was murdered by a police officer in Ferguson, Missouri, becoming the latest in a line of Black men targeted and killed at the hands of law enforcement. Following his death, the people of Ferguson began to protest, as did people all over the country. Even without the mainstream media's presence, people continued to protest. Many demonstrations (although peaceful), have been were filled with sadness, anger, rage, and disappointment toward an institution that was supposedly designed to "protect and serve" its citizens.

1. How do incidents such as these impact urban communities?
2. What type of community loss and grief reactions can we anticipate from this experience?
3. What type of intervention would you recommend to help communities safely grieve with this loss?
4. What social work policy, research, and practice recommendations would you make that address this form of community loss and grief?

Study Case 2

Jorobe Shine is a 19-year-old male who resides in an urban neighborhood. He is the son of a Caucasian mother, Jolene Shine, and an African American father, Rob Battle, who are cohabitating. They have resided in an impoverished inner city neighborhood in a row house owned by Jorobe's grandmother, Ms. Patterson, who is wheelchair bound. Jolene has been a heroin abuser on and off for the last 10 years and currently uses in the house next door to the family home. Rob has been incarcerated several times during Jorobe's life.

Jorobe, although 19, is in his junior year of high school because he was retained in his freshman year due to an extended absence. During the ninth grade, he was shot in the leg by a stray bullet while walking to the corner take-out restaurant to get dinner. His recovery was slow due to the lack of access to adequate physical therapy services needed. This was the first time Jorobe was the direct victim of a major crime, however, he has witnessed neighborhood crime on a consistent basis and regular crime in his high school even though the schools in the neighborhood use metal detectors as an attempt to keep the students safe. Many of his classmates and their family members have regularly heard gunshots, been victims of crimes (stabbings, bullying, and victims of gang initiations), and perpetuated or witnessed crimes. One of Jorobe's friends was murdered while they were playing ball together at the local basketball court.

The neighborhood is comprised of row houses in various states of disrepair and various levels of occupancy. The residents of the neighborhood are owners, renters, and trespassers. Many of the houses are vacant and boarded up, including the houses on either side of Jorobe's house. The house on the left was badly burned by someone attempting to conceal a murder and the house remains uninhabitable. The house on the right is rented to a young man who allows the home to be used by neighborhood dealers and users of illegal drugs who frequently engage in verbal altercations and physical fights and leave drug and alcohol paraphernalia on the steps of both Jorobe's and the renter's houses.

The neighborhood is economically deprived. Most of the residents are unemployed or underemployed and using creative and sometimes illegal ways to generate additional income. It is located in a food desert and is socially isolated. Most residents have unpredictable or no personal transportation at all, instead relying on sporadic public transportation or staying within the neighborhood and using take-out food and corner stores to meet their needs.

1. Identify the chronic incidents of trauma in the urban community and discuss

   a. The impact on the community.

   b. The impact on the family members and family unit.

2. Develop a community assessment

   a. Identify and discuss the various types of losses and deprivation experienced by the community.

   b. Identify and discuss the strengths of the community.

3. Discuss the similarities and differences between symbolic and actual losses.

4. Identify and discuss the losses experienced by the family as a system and as individuals.

5. Categorize and discuss the expected grief reactions for each family member.

6. Identify and discuss the factors that affect grieving for each family member.

7. Discuss the core principles of relational coping; how would the strategies help the family cope with loss and grief in the urban community.

8. Discuss the similarities and differences between individualistic and collectivistic coping strategies.

Core Competencies Assignments

The Council on Social Work Education (CSWE) uses the Educational Policy and Accreditation Standards (EPAS) to accredit baccalaureate- and master's-level social work programs. EPAS supports academic excellence by establishing thresholds for professional competence. It permits programs to use traditional and emerging models of curriculum design by balancing requirements that promote comparability across programs with a level of flexibility that encourages programs to differentiate.

1. Educational Policy and Accreditation Standards (EPAS) *2.1: Student Introductions and Loss and Grief Word Association*
   Students will introduce themselves using the first letter of the first name to explain a term, feeling, concept, and so on, that is associated with loss and grief.

2. *Pre- and Post-Quiz*
   EPAS 2.1.1: Identify as a professional social work and conduct oneself accordingly:
   On the first day of class before and readings, have students define the chapter concepts, that is, loss, grief, victimization, community deprivation, and so on.

3. *Loss accumulation and active listening*

   a. In teams, allow each student to select Jenga Blocks or River Rocks, equal to the amount of losses they feel comfortable in disclosing to the team and eventually the class.

   b. Using examples from mainstream media (current newspaper, Internet articles, etc.) that discuss an urban community's experience with grief and loss (e.g., community violence, loss of housing, closing of a facility), ask student teams to review an article and list the types of loss experienced by that community.

   Loss accumulation reflection
   EPAS 2.1.1: Identify as a professional social work and conduct oneself accordingly:
   Loss accumulation reflection, demonstration, and discussion of numerous losses *(actual and tangible) that have accumulated*:

   a. Discuss how the losses may have impacted community functioning

   b. Categorize and discuss some of the possible community grief reactions

4. *Active listening*
   EPAS [2.1.10(a)], assess [2.1.10 (b)], intervene [2.1.10 (c)], and evaluate [2.1.10 (d)] individuals, families, groups, organizations, and communities
   EPAS 2.1.3: Apply critical thinking to inform and communicate professional judgments
   Active listening is one of the most important social work skills and equally important in working with those who are experiencing or have experienced grief.

   a. Ask each team to report back to the larger classroom group, explaining the (a) (article) community experience with loss; (b) how the losses may have impacted community functioning; (c) discuss some of the possible community grief reactions; and (d) discuss what factor might influence community grief reactions.

   b. After each team is given the opportunity to present their findings to the larger group, the entire class should reconvene to discuss ways that social workers can best asset each community group that was presented in managing the grief experienced as a result of the identified loss. All recommendations must consider the sociocultural context of the community, utilize a strength-based perspective, and be community based.

Suggested Readings

Danesh, H. B. (2008). Creating a culture of healing in multiethnic communities: An integrative approach to prevention and amelioration of violence-induced conditions. *Journal of Community Psychology*, *36*(6), 814–832.

Kropf, N. P., & Jones, B. L. (2014). When public tragedies happen: Community practice approaches in grief, loss, and recovery. *Journal of Community Practice*, *22*(3), 281–298.

Murphy, P. A., & Price, D. M. (1998). Dying and grieving in the inner city. In K. J. Doka & J. D. Davidson (Eds.), *Living with grief: Who we are, how we grieve* (pp. 113–1200). New York, NY: Routledge.

Roberta's House Family Grief Support Center. Retrieved from http://www.robertashouse.org

Sharpe, T. L. (2015). Understanding the sociocultural context of coping for African American family members of homicide victims: A conceptual model. *Trauma, Violence & Abuse*, *16*(1), 48–59.

Vakalahi, H. F. O., Simpson, G. M., & Giunta, N. (Eds.). (2014). *The collective spirit of aging across cultures: International perspectives on aging*. New York, NY: Springer Science + Business Media.

REFERENCES

Abramovitz, M., & Albrecht, J. (2013). The community loss index: A new social indicator. *Social Service Review*, *37*(4), 677–724.

Anda, R. F., Felitti, V. J., Bremner, J. D., Walker, J. D., Whitfield, C., Perry, B. D., & Giles, W. H. (2006). The enduring effects of abuse and related adverse experiences in childhood. *European Archives of Psychiatry and Clinical Neuroscience, 256*, 174–186.

Archer, J. (1999). *The nature of grief: The evolution and psychology of reactions to loss*. London, England: Routledge.

Bryant, C. D. (2003). *Handbook of death and dying*. Thousand Oaks, CA: Sage.

Castle, J., & Phillips, W. L. (2003). Grief rituals: Aspects that facilitate adjustment to bereavement. *Journal of Loss and Trauma, 8*(1), 41–71.

Cloitre, M., Stolbach, B. C., Herman, J. L., van der Kolk, B., Pynoos, R., Wang, J., & Petcova, E. (2009). A developmental approach to complex PTSD: Childhood and adult cumulative trauma as predictors of symptom complexity. *Journal of Traumatic Stress, 22*, 399–408.

Doka, K. (1989a). Grief. In R. Kastenbaum & B. Kastenbaum (Eds.), *Encyclopedia of death* (p. 127), Phoenix, AZ: The Oryx Press.

Doka, K. (Ed.). (1989b). *Disenfranchised grief: Recognizing hidden sorrow*. Lexington, MA: Lexington Books.

Doka, K. (Ed.). (2002). *Disenfranchised grief: New directions, challenges, and strategies for practice* (pp. 61–77). Champaign, IL: Research Press.

Doka, K. J., & Davidson, J. D. (Eds.). (1998). *Living with grief: Who we are, how we grieve*. New York, NY: Routledge.

Doka, K. J., Davidson, J. D., & Gordon, J. D. (1998). *Living with grief: Who we are, how we grieve*. New York, NY: Routledge Press.

Dong, M., Anda, R. F., Felitti, V. J., Dube, S. R., Williamson, D. F., Thompson, T. J.,…Giles, W. (2004). The interrelatedness of multiple forms of childhood abuse, neglect, and household dysfunction. *Child Abuse & Neglect, 28*, 771–784.

Gardner, W. I. (1971). *Behavior modification in mental retardation*. London, England: University of London Press.

Herrmann, A. F. (2011). Losing things was nothing new: A family's story of foreclosure. *Journal of Loss and Trauma: International Perspectives on Stress & Coping, 16*(6), 497–510.

Jeffreys, J. S. (2011). *Helping grieving people: When tears are not enough. A handbook for care providers* (2nd ed.). New York, NY: Taylor & Francis.

Kastenbaum, R. J. (2001). *Death, society, and human experience* (7th ed.). Boston, MA: Allyn & Bacon.

Kübler-Ross, E., & Kessler, D. (2005). *On grief and grieving: Find the meaning of grief through the five stages of loss*. New York, NY: Simon & Schuster.

Laurie, A., & Neimeyer, R. A. (2008). African Americans in bereavement: Grief as a function of ethnicity. *Omega, 57*, 173–193.

Lyons, R. F., Mickelson, K. D., Sullivan, M. J., & Coyne, J. C. (1998). Coping as a communal process. *Journal of Social and Personal Relationships, 15*, 579–605.

Markus, H. R., & Kitayama, S. (1991). Culture and the self: Implications for cognition, emotion, and motivation. *Psychological Review, 98*, 224–253.

McGuffey, C. S. (2010). Blacks and racial appraisals: Gender, race and intraracial rape. In J. Battle & S. Barnes (Eds.), *Black sexualities: Probing powers, passions, practices and policies* (pp. 273–298). New Brunswick, NJ: Rutgers University Press.

McGuffey, C. S. (2013). Rape and racial appraisals: Culture, intersectionality, and Black women's' accounts of sexual assault. *Du Bois Review, 10*, 1–22.

Moore, J. L., & Constantine, M. G. (2005). Development and initial validation of the collectivistic coping styles measure with African, Asian, and Latin American international students. *Journal of Mental Health Counseling, 27*, 329–347.

Myers, H. F. (1982). Stress, ethnicity, and social class: A model for research with Black populations. Ethnic minority research: Research trends and directions. In E. Jones & S. Korchin (Eds.), *Minority mental health* (pp. 118–147). New York, NY: Praeger.

Myers, H. F. (1989). Urban Stress and mental health in Black youth: An epidemiologic and conceptual update. In R. Jones (Ed.), *Black adolescents* (pp. 123–152). Berkeley, CA: Cobb & Henry.

Neimeyer, R. A., Prigerson, H. G., & Davies, B. (2002). Mourning and meaning. *American Behavioral Scientist, 46*, 235–251.

O'Brien, T. B., & DeLongis, A. (1996). The interactional context of problem-, emotion-, and relationship-focused coping: The role of the Big Five personality factors. *Journal of Personality, 64*, 775–813.

Parkes, C. M. (1999). *Bereavement: Studies of grief in adult life*. London, England: International Universities Press.

Parson, E. A. (1994). Inner city children of trauma: Urban violence traumatic stress response syndrome U-VTS and therapists' responses. In J. P. Wilson & J. D. Lindy (Eds.), *Countertransference in the treatment of PTSD* (pp. 157–178). New York, NY: Guilford.

Pynoos, R. S., Steinberg, A. M., Layne, C. M., Briggs, E. C., Ostrowski, S. A., & Fairbank, J. A. (2009). DSMV PTSD diagnostic criteria for children and adolescents: A developmental perspective and recommendations. *Journal of Traumatic Stress, 22*, 391–398.

Rando, T. A. (1986). A comprehensive analysis of anticipatory grief: Perspectives, processes, promises, and problems. In T. A. Rando (Ed.), *Loss and anticipatory grief*. Lexington, MA: Lexington Books.

Rando, T. A. (1991). *How to go on living when someone you love dies*. New York, NY: Bantam.

Rando, T. A. (1993). *Treatment of complicated mourning*. Champaign, IL: Research Press.

Redmond, L. M. (1989). *Surviving: When someone you know was murdered*. Clearwater, FL: Psychological Consultations and Educations Services Ltd.

Rosenblatt, P. (1988). The social context of private feelings. *Journal of Social Issues, 44*, 67–78.

Sharpe, T. L. (2008). Sources of support for African American family members of homicide victims. *Journal of Ethnic & Cultural Diversity in Social Work, 17*, 197–216.

Sharpe, T. L. (2015). Understanding the sociocultural context of coping for African American family members of homicide victims: A conceptual model. *Trauma, Violence & Abuse, 16*(1), 48–59.

Sharpe, T. L., & Boyas, J. (2011). We fall down: The African American experience of coping with the homicide of a loved one. *Journal of Black Studies, 42*, 855–873.

Shaw, J. M. (1979). *Rural deprivation and planning.* Norwich, England: Geobooks.

Sims, D. W., Bivins, B. A., Obeid, F. N., Horst, H. M., Sorensen, V. J., & Fath, J. J. (1989). Urban trauma: A chronic recurrent disease. *Journal of Trauma, 29*(7), 940–946.

Tomaka, J., Thompson, S., & Palacios, R. (2006). The relation of social isolation, loneliness, and social support to disease outcomes among the elderly. *Journal of Aging and Health, 18*, 359–384.

Townsend, P. (1987). Deprivation. *Journal of Social Policy, 16*(2), 125–146.

van der Kolk, B. A. (1987). The drug treatment of post-traumatic stress disorder. *Journal of Affective Disorders, 13*, 203–213.

Walsh, K. (2012). *Grief and loss: Theories and skills for helping professionals.* Upper Saddle River, NJ: Pearson.

Walter, T. (1999). *On bereavement: The culture of grief.* Philadelphia, PA: Open University Press.

Williams, B. R., Sawyer Baker, P., Allman, R. M., Roseman, J. M. (2007). Bereavement among African American and White older adults. *Journal of Aging Health, 19*, 313–333.

Williams, D. R., & Williams-Morris, R. (2000). Racism and mental health: The African American experience. *Ethnicity & Health, 5*(3–4), 243–268.

Wong, P. T. P., Wong, L. C. J., & Lonner, W. J. (2006). *Handbook of multicultural perspectives on stress and coping.* New York, NY: Springer Publishing.

Worden, J. W. (2009). *Grief counseling and grief therapy: A handbook for the mental health practitioner.* New York, NY: Springer Publishing.

Worden, J. W. (1991). Grief counseling and grief therapy: A handbook for the mental health practitioner (2nd ed.). New York, NY: Springer Publishing.

CHAPTER **15**

Youth Violence—An Overview: Prevalence and Intervention Strategies to Address Violence Among Urban African American Youth

Rhonda Wells-Wilbon, Von E. Nebbitt, and Margaret Lombe

More than a decade ago Gibbs and Huang (2003) argued that African American youth were our nation's most vulnerable population of youth. They are disproportionately overrepresented in the juvenile justice system and disproportionately underserved by community-based mental health service providers (Coalition for Juvenile Justice, 2000; Juvenile Justice Evaluation Center Online, 2005). In addition to these challenges, African American youth living in urban communities are at a higher risk of being exposed to community violence, as witnesses and victims, than their White and Latino counterparts (Aisenberg & Herrenkohl, 2008; Garbarino, Hammond, Mercy, & Yung, 2004). It is important to note that homicide has been their leading cause of death for more than four decades (Singh, 2010).

Historically, violence has been pervasive in urban African American communities. For example, violence among African American youth nearly tripled between 1984 and 1993 (Singh, 2010). This spike in youth violence was followed by a number of local, state, and national interventions; fortunately, youth violence has been on a downward trend since the late 1990s. Despite reductions in youth violence, burgeoning research on the causes and correlates of youth violence and government efforts to curb youth violence, African American youth in urban settings still experience the lion's share of youth violence (i.e., witnesses and victims). These youth also experience many of the hardships (e.g., elevated mental health symptoms, substance use, sex-risk behavior, and suppressed immune functioning) that exposure to violence leaves in its wake.

Understanding and reducing youth violence are important for a number of reasons. First, in 2010, about 6% of high school students reported not going to school on 1 or more days because they felt unsafe at school or on their way to and from school (Centers for Disease Control and Prevention [CDC], 2010). Second, approximately 700,000 young people aged 10 to 24 years are treated in emergency departments each year for injuries sustained due to violence-related assaults (CDC, 2009). Third, on average, 16 persons between the ages of 10 and 24 years are murdered each day in the United States (CDC, 2009). In addition to causing injury and death, youth violence affects communities by increasing the cost of health care, reducing productivity, decreasing property values, and disrupting social services (Mercy, Butchart, Farrington, & Cerdá, 2002). Miller, Fisher, and Cohen (2001) estimated the direct and indirect cost of youth violence at approximately $6.6 billion annually.

In this chapter, we address the prevalence of youth violence in the lives of African Americans. Specifically, drawing on the existing literature on youth victimization by violence, we discuss current evidence on violence among African American youth in urban settings. Following this, we review research on violence exposure among African American youth in two specific domains, including the community and household. Finally, interventions to reduce violence in urban African American youth are reviewed.

CONCEPTUALIZING YOUTH VIOLENCE

The World Health Organization (WHO) defines violence as the intentional use of physical force or power, threatened or actual, against oneself, another person, or against a group or community, that either results in or has a high likelihood of resulting in injury, death, psychological harm, maldevelopment, or deprivation (Krug, Mercy, Dahlberg, & Zwi, 2002). Drawing from this definition, youth violence can be said to be acts intended to cause physical harm against youth who may be perpetrators, direct or indirect victims, bystanders, witnesses or familiar with victims, or are cognizant of or anxious about the potential for violence (Trickett, Durán, & Horn, 2003). As noted earlier, youth living in urban neighborhoods tend to have a higher likelihood of being exposed to violence. Despite this, experiences of violence may occur through various modalities (e.g., media, hearsay, victimization); hence, violence often extends beyond urban localities.

PREVALENCE OF EXPOSURE TO YOUTH VIOLENCE

The actual rate of exposure to violence among African American youth in urban locations remains largely unknown. Indeed, many forms of violence, such as bullying, daily urban hassle, and sexual assaults, may go undetected and/or unreported. However, evidence from the CDC, and social commentators suggest that the rate of violence in this population is quite high. For example, in 2010, the National Center for Injury Prevention and Control (NCIPC) at the CDC (CDC/NCIPC, 2013) reported that homicide is the second leading cause of death for young people aged 15 to 24 years. That year, 13 youth on an average, lost their lives to violence each day (CDC/NCIPC, 2013). During that time frame, homicide was the leading cause of death among African American youth. It is important to note that homicide has been the leading cause of death for African American youth since 1967 (Singh, 2010). In 2006, homicide rates among non-Hispanic, African American males, 10 to 24 years of age (62.2 per 100,000), were three times higher than those among Hispanic males (21.5 per 100,000) and 20 times higher than those among non-Hispanic White males (3.4 per 100,000; CDC/NCIPC, 2009). More recent data indicate that the racial disparity in homicide rates have remained relatively stable over time (CDC/NCIPC, 2013).

Data on youth exposure to nonfatal violence indicate patterns similar to youth homicide. From 1993 to 2003, youth (12–17 years of age) were 2.5 times more likely than individuals 18 years and older to be victims of nonfatal violent crimes. Compared with adults, youth aged 12 to 17 years were twice as likely to be robbery or aggravated assault victims, 2.5 times as likely to be victims of a rape or sexual assault, and almost three times as likely to be victims of a simple assault (CDC/NCIPC, 2013; Snider & Sickmund, 2006). As indicated earlier, African American youth in urban locations were more likely to be the victims of nonfatal violence (CDC/NCIPC, 2013). Data from the National Crime Victimization Survey found that African American youth experience the highest rates of serious nonfatal violent crime. Furthermore, the disparity in serious nonfatal violence has remained consistent for the last decade (White & Lauritsen, 2012). There is also a common agreement in the youth violence literature that being an older African American male adolescent is associated with higher exposure to violence (Buka, Stichick, Birdthistle, & Earls, 2001; Fitzpatrick & Boldizar, 1993; Richters & Martinez, 1990).

YOUTH VIOLENCE ACROSS DOMAINS

Youth Violence and the Urban Context

Few phenomena are more inextricably linked than violence, race, and place. Evidence suggests that violence in the United States is often concentrated in relatively small geographical locations. This spatial divide in violence is nationwide and enduring (Peterson & Krivo, 2010). Evidence also points to the a between residential segregation and violence, especially in urban minority communities (Massey & Denton, 1998). Using national data that include nearly 9,000 neighborhoods in 87 cities, Peterson and Krivo (2010) found that African American communities experience violent crime at a rate five times higher than White communities. These findings suggest an engrained relationship between residential segregation and violence. Accordingly, child and adolescent exposure to violence is extremely pronounced in urban centers. For example, Chicago has led the nation in assaults and homicides; however, approximately one quarter of this violence occurred on 3% of the land mass: primarily in areas where African American families are highly represented (Chicago Police Department: CompStat, 2013). Morenoff, Sampson, and Raudenbush (2001) reported significant associations among concentrated poverty, residential segregation, and neighborhood homicide rates. Peterson and Krivo (2010) found that the strongest predictors of neighborhood violence were low socioeconomic status (SES), being predominantly African American, and sharing borders with low-SES neighborhoods. In many urban areas, it is not poverty per se but correlates of poverty (e.g., drug sales, urban blight, high joblessness, and gang activity) that account for most neighborhood violence. For example, although gang violence has been on a downward trend, gang violence still accounts for a significant portion of youth violence and homicides (Harrel, 2005). Community violence and gang violence are only two forms of victimization that urban African American youth encounter.

The faces of violence, both as victims and perpetrators and across social domains, are all too often urban African American youth (http://www.cdc.gov/injury/). In addition to experiencing community violence, they also witness events such as violence, crime, and abuse in their home and at schools. Furthermore, African American youth are likely to suffer or experience several types of victimization in a relatively short time span (i.e., within 1 year). These African American youth, referred to as poly-victimized youth, are at particularly high risk of experiencing lasting physical, mental, and emotional problems.

Household Violence

Finkelhor, Turner, Ormrod, and Hamby. (2009) estimated that 16.3% of youth 17 years of age and younger have witnessed some form of interadult violence in their homes, which amounts to 4.6 million youths experiencing household violence each year. In 2010, an estimated 2.8 million children lived in households where one family member aged 12 years or older were victims of violence, which equates to 3.9% of all children aged 12 years or younger witnessing some form of violence in their home each year (Truman & Smith, 2012). Childhood exposure to household violence was greatest in households with annual incomes of less than $15,000 and families living in disadvantaged urban areas (Truman & Smith, 2012). Domestic violence rarely occurs in the absence of other forms of household violence (Appel & Holden, 1998; Dong et al., 2004; Margolin et al., 2009). Youth who have witnessed domestic violence are more likely to be physically and emotionally abused (Zolotor, Theodore, Coyne-Beasley, & Runyan, 2007). Although the rates of overlap between domestic violence and child victimization fluctuate across studies, there is agreement that domestic violence is a risk factor for child victimization by household violence (Holt, Buckley, & Whelan, 2008).

Community Violence

Scholars (Pinchevsky & Wright, 2012) have noted that community violence is closely linked to household violence. This observation is noteworthy and may be suggestive of a link between victimization by household violence and living in low-income urban communities. Indeed, there is evidence suggesting this link. For example, researchers in geography, criminology, and public health have observed a relationship between community context and violence at the household level (Raghavan, Mennerich, Sexton, & James, 2006). Data from the National Survey of Families and Households support the hypotheses that economic disadvantage at the community level was related to the likelihood of experiencing household violence (Benson, Fox, DeMaris, & Van Wyk, 2003; Fox & Benson, 2006). Other scholars, (e.g., Browning, Leventhal, & Brooks-Gunn, 2005; Dembo, Belenko, Childs, & Wareham, 2009) have also reported the link between community or contextual variables and household violence. Some of this research has in fact focused on youth sexual activity, crime involvement, and health outcomes. Furthermore, the seminal work of Sampson, Raudenbush, and Earls (1997) point to concentrated contextual disadvantage as a strong predictor of violence; further bolstering the case for a consideration of community characteristics and concentrated disadvantage as risk factors for individual domestic violence.

Although the aforementioned literature does not focus specifically on African American youth, the fact that most household violence occurs within low-income families living in disadvantaged neighborhoods would suggest that urban African American youth are probably exposed to the lion's share of household violence. Moreover, for many of these youth, particularly those living in poor urban areas, violence is woven into the fabric of their daily lives. They are likely to experience violence as witnesses, victims, and/or even perpetrators. In fact, existing evidence suggests that more than 80% of youth living in urban localities have witnessed community violence; many of them (about 70% of them) report being victims of community violence (Kliewer, Lepore, Oskin, & Johnson, 1998).

School Violence

A prominent form of youth violence is school violence, a multifaceted problem, which can take many forms including bullying, slapping or hitting, gang violence, and even assault (with or without a weapon). Evidence suggests that school violence is widespread. For example, data from a nationally representative sample of youth (Robers, Zhang, Truman, & Synder, 2011) indicate that a significant number of youth, about 20%, had been bullied on school property and 16% had been bullied electronically during the 12 months before the survey; about 15% indicated that they had been in a physical fight on school property during the survey year; about 6% failed to go to school on 1 or more days in the 30 days prior to the survey because they felt unsafe at school or on their way to or from school; others (5.4%) reported carrying a weapon (gun, knife, or club) on school property on one or more days in the 30 days before the survey; and about 7.4% reported being threatened or injured with a weapon on school property one or more times in the 12 months prior to the survey.

Risk factors associated with school and youth violence are many and complex. They include community and environmental vulnerabilities; prior history of violence;

drug, alcohol, or tobacco use; affiliation with delinquent peers; poor family functioning; and school disengagement.

Although school violence does not necessarily result in serious injury, it warrants attention in that it has been linked to emotional and behavioral problems as well as anxiety, depression, disruptive, and aggressive behavior; substance use; and school disengagement (Cooley-Quille, Boyd, Frantz, & Walsh, 2001; Fowler, Tompsett, Braciszewski, Jacques-Tiura, & Baltes, 2009). These factors may have profound effects on a youth's development into early adulthood and beyond. To help curb the negative correlates of youth violence, a number of preventive intervention strategies have been implemented to prevent and reduce youth violence and intervene in the lives of youth who are victims of violence.

PREVENTIVE INTERVENTIONS

Community-Level Interventions

Much of the research currently in place as well as treatment, and preventive interventions tend to focus mainly on perpetrators of youth violence. With the growing evidence on the negative consequences of exposure to violence, attention is beginning to be focused on youth exposed to violence as witnesses and victims, or both, and interventions to help them adjust.

As mentioned earlier, the 1990s witnessed drastic increases in youth violence. In response to this increase in youth violence, and the mass murders of Columbine, the federal government initiated the National Campaign Against Youth Violence (NCAYV). NCAYV is a private, nonprofit organization formed by a diverse group of political, business, academic, and grassroots leaders at the White House Summit on Children, Violence, and Responsibility. With the support of the White House and a bipartisan board of directors, the Campaign sought to engage the general public and the private sector in violence reduction. NCAYV provided grants to public and private agencies to host gang summits, to produce peace murals, and to engage youth in the process of reducing youth violence. Unfortunately, NCAYV does not have a documented evaluation; furthermore, this initiative was not extended beyond the Clinton administration. Still, the NCAYV model may provide insights into how public–private collaborations can be used to address the issue of youth violence.

CeaseFire is another program developed in response to dramatic increases in youth violence during the 1990s. CeaseFire is a component of the Cure Violence Health Model (CVHM). CVHM uses a public health approach to mitigate and interrupt urban violence. It uses the three basic components used to reverse epidemic disease outbreaks. (a) interrupting transmission of the disease; (b) reducing the risk of the highest risk; and (c) changing community norms. CeaseFire works with, and trains, members of urban communities (i.e., individuals they call "violence interrupters") in its efforts to reduce violence. Interrupters are normally ex-gang members or community leaders. Violence interrupters prevent shootings by identifying and mediating potentially lethal conflicts in the community, and following up to ensure that the conflict does not reignite. Also, interrupters and community outreach workers work with youth and adults at highest risk of using violence to mitigate their use of violence. These outreach workers talk to those at highest risk about the costs of using violence and help them to obtain social services such as job training and drug treatment. CeaseFire has several published evaluation, which indicate positive effects on reducing youth violence. Related to this are gun buyback programs aimed at eliminating guns from the streets (Hammond & Arias, 2011).

Another intervention worth mentioning is Canada's model that was initiated in Harlem in the 1990s and has been replicated in many urban communities. The place-based model aims at educating children and rebuilding communities by transforming neighborhoods struggling with issues of poverty, poor health, failing schools, and high crime rates. It utilizes the following five core principles:

- Serve an entire neighborhood comprehensively and at a scale to create a "tipping point" and definitively shift the culture of the community.
- Create a pipeline of coordinated, best-practice programs to give children and families seamless support from birth through college.
- Build community among residents, institutions, and stakeholders in order to create a healthy, positive environment where children can thrive.
- Evaluate program outcomes and create a feedback loop to provide managers with real-time data and strengthen services.
- Cultivate an organizational culture of success rooted in passion, accountability, leadership, and teamwork.

School-Level Interventions

With the goal of reducing and ultimately eliminating violence, churches, community and civic organizations, and school systems have developed and implemented a wide range of interventions—ranging from escort services for children in crime-rich neighborhoods, after-school programs to keep children off the streets, anger management, and emotion regulation programs to antibullying programs (CDC, 2009; Sanderson & Richards, 2010). We provide an overview of programs that have been effective in curbing youth violence at schools subsequently.

The Safe Passage program is implemented through Chicago Public Schools with the stated goal to provide safer conditions for students while traveling to and from schools for classes, extracurricular activities, and after school programs. The program is premised on the assumption that a student's safety and perception of safety impacts his or her school attendance and academic performance. The Safe Passage program is designed to provide safe routes to students in order to increase attendance and decrease violent incidents involving students. The Safe Passage program employs community watchers to create safe passages for students to go to and from school. Community watchers are deployed throughout designated routes to supervise students traveling to and from school; in addition to community watchers signs are also posted along Safe

Passage routes. Community watchers beginning working 1 hour before the morning bell and work until 30 minutes after the morning bell; on the other hand, they patrol approximately 3.5 hours after the school's dismissal bell. Although a formal external evaluation of the Safe Passage program has not been conducted, Chicago public school is boasting double digit reductions in school-related youth violence.

Other school-based interventions that have had success in reducing and/or preventing, youth violence include universal violence prevention programs delivered to all students in a school or grade level. The focus is to help youth develop social skills such as emotional self-awareness and control, problem solving, conflict resolution, and teamwork. Other interventions within the context of the school have focused on multiple stakeholder groups, bringing together parents and educators. The primary goal of such interventions is to improve family relations and lower the risk for violence by children. These programs educate parents about child development and teach skills to communicate and solve problems in nonviolent ways. Alongside these are mentoring programs that utilize community assets. These intend to provide a young person with a caring adult—a young person is paired with an adult who can serve as a positive role model and help guide the young person's behavior.

This section is in no way a comprehensive overview of violence prevention interventions. However, in our opinion, these programs may have utility given their appeal to both public and private partnerships to address youth violence primarily, but not exclusively, among urban African American youth.

IMPLICATIONS

The risk factors for African American youth associated with exposure to violence in urban communities has major consequences. Although the negative consequences are often well known, there is still limited community supports and interventions in place for urban youth. Additionally, few helping professionals are willing to work with youth, because they are seen as a hard to reach population. Feedback from those who do work closely with African American youth suggest that this population is reluctant to go to social workers and other helping professionals, and would more likely seek help from peers, parents, and other adults such as coaches. Given this knowledge, social workers should work more closely with parents, coaches, and other adults that youth would likely seek out, to equip them with the information and resources they need, so that they can provide the best assistance for the youth who confide in them and come to them for guidance and advise. Additionally, the research suggests that poor family functioning is a significant risk factor for young people. Working more closely with families so that they can remain intact and receive needed supports and interventions is something those interested in youth must advocate for on their behalf. Because long-term and repeated exposure to violence is also known to be a major challenge for urban youth, more community-based violence prevention programs and models must be developed and implemented at the community level.

Most important, valuing African American youth by learning how to engage them through the vehicles they use themselves such as music, poetry, sports, films, clubs, and shopping malls are examples of activities youth enjoy. And these are also the places to meet youth in a space where they feel the most free to be their authentic selves. Contrary to popular belief, today's young people are smart and creative but most are waiting for direction so they can find their way. Going to these places versus the traditional places social workers meet with the clients they serve is so important, especially when engaging this hard to reach population. It is imperative to go to the places they frequent and learn new skills and new approaches that truly meet them where they are in their space of need, with the right resources that can help them get healthier. Rethinking social work curriculums and developing models that are culturally sensitive and African centered, is the real work needed to engage African American urban youth.

FOR FURTHER STUDY

Suggested Assignments

Violence Preventi   on

Assignment 1: Please view the documentary, "*The Interrupters*" on Public Broadcasting Service (*PBS*) *Frontline*. Following is the link to the film. Please address the following questions in completing the critical response paper. If the hyperlink does not open on your computer, then search Google for "PBS Frontline" and "the interrupters," which will provide you with the PBS *Frontline* link to watch the film. In addition to the critical analysis, you will be asked to respond to a Blackboard discussion (class discussion), which will be posted after the due date.

www.pbs.org/wgbh/pages/frontline/interrupters/

1. Briefly summarize the documentary.

2. Can we address violence in Baltimore (your urban city) using the approach being used in the documentary. Why or Why not?

3. What is your critical analysis of the social issue (violence) being raised and the prevention/interventions addressing the issue?

4. What are the challenges/barriers in addressing violence in Chicago and other urban areas? Your response should focus on social, political, economic, cultural, and psychological dimensions.

5. Can this program be funded in Baltimore (your urban city)? What would be the challenges in implementing this program in your community? How would you implement it? Who would be involved? How would you know it is effective?

Assignment 2: This assignment will require you to select a recent incident of violence in an urban community. Summarize the incident by providing information on the setting, social class, race, and gender of the individual involved. Address the following questions in your critical analysis. How do you think the race and gender of the perpetrator(s) and victims(s) impacted the reporting of the incident? Do you think the incident was reported with any bias? Do you think the response would be different if the person was of another gender, race, or social class? Why or why not? Please use two empirical articles on social determinants of violence in supporting your stance (see Suggested Readings).

Assignment 3: For this assignment you will evaluate an evidence-based practice model addressing violence prevention in urban communities. You can select an evidence-based practice model on your own or you can utilize the link that follows to the National Registry on Evidence-Based Practice. Please answer the following questions:

www.nrepp.samhsa.gov

1. Summarize the intervention.

2. Would the intervention be appropriate for a population group you are interested in working with? Why or why not?

3. Would the intervention be appropriate for urban communities?

4. Is the intervention applicable across race, class, gender, age, culture, and setting? Why or why not?

5. How would you implement the intervention in your community? What would be the pros and cons?

Suggested Readings

Banyard, V. L. (2008). Sexual violence: Current perspectives on prevention and intervention. *Journal of Prevention & Intervention in the Community, 36*(1–2), 1–4.

Banyard, V. L., Moynihan, M. M., & Plante, E. G. (2007). Sexual violence prevention through bystander education: An experimental evaluation. *Journal of Community Psychology, 35*(4), 463–481.

Banyard, V. L., Eckstein, R. P., & Moynihan, M. M. (2010). Sexual Violence Prevention The Role of Stages of Change. *Journal of Interpersonal Violence, 25*(1), 111–135.

Banyard, V. L., Moynihan, M. M., & Crossman, M. T. (2009). Reducing sexual violence on campus: The role of student leaders as empowered bystanders. *Journal of College Student Development, 50*(4), 1–12.

Bend-Goody, T. (2004). Perceptions of domestic violence: A dialogue with African American families. *Health and Social Work, 29*, 307–317.

Borges, A. M., Banyard, V. L., & Moynihan, M. M. (2008). Clarifying consent: Primary prevention of sexual assault on a college campus. *Journal of Prevention & Intervention in the Community, 36*(1–2), 75–88.

Burstyn, J., Bender, G., Casella, R., Gordon, H. W., Guerra, D. P., Luschen, K. V.,...Williams, K. (2001). *Preventing violence in schools.* Mahwah, NJ: Lawrence Erlbaum. In-depth look at school violence programs (grades K–12). www.routledge.com

Coloroso, B. (2009). *The bully, the bullied, and the bystander: From preschool to high school—how parents and teachers can help break the cycle* (Updated ed.). New York, NY: Harper Collins. Investigates the relationship between bullies and their victims (grades K–12). www.harpercollins.com

Conoley, J., & Goldstein, A. (2004). *School violence intervention.* New York, NY: The Guilford Press. Analysis of school violence and proactive interventions (grades K–12). www.guilford.com

Cornell, D. (2006). *School violence: Fears vs. facts.* Mahwah, NJ: Lawrence Erlbaum. Case studies used to illustrate assessment and interventions (grades K–12). www.routledge.com

Espelage, D. (2010). *Bullying in North American schools.* Florence, KY: Routledge. Research-based book on violence in schools (grades K–12). Retrieved from www.routledge.com

Garbarino, J., & Delara, E. (2003). *And words can hurt forever: How to protect adolescents from bullying, harassment, and violence.* New York, NY: Free Press (grades 7–12). www.freepress.net

Gerler, E. (2004). *Handbook of school violence.* New York, NY: Haworth Press. General presentation of interventions and strategies (grades K–12). www.haworthpress.com

Langman, P. (2010). *Why kids kill.* New York, NY: Palgrave Macmillan. Case studies of ten school shooters and what created the shooting scenarios, along with intervention ideas. http://www.palgrave.com

Lassiter, W., & Perry, D. (2009). *Preventing violence and crimes in America's schools.* Santa Barbara, CA: Praeger. A clear approach to what works and what doesn't in preventing violence.

Lee, V. (2003). Domestic violence: Confusing abuse with manhood. *Afro-American Red Star, 111*(13), A5.

Lieberman, J. (2008). *School shootings.* New York, NY: Kensington. Studies the life of Kip Kinkel and offers insights into prevention and intervention (grades 7–12). www.kensingtonbooks.com

Moynihan, M. M., & Banyard, V. L. (2008). Community responsibility for preventing sexual violence: A pilot study with campus Greeks and intercollegiate athletes. *Journal of Prevention & Intervention in the Community, 36*(1–2), 23–38.

Prothrow-Stith, D., Oliver, J., & Chery, J. (2005). *Peacezone Curriculum Series.* Champaign, IL: Research Press. Program for teaching social relationships. www.researchpress.com

Sexton-Radek, K. (2004). *Violence in schools.* Westport, CT: Praeger. Academic explanation of the history and treatment of violence in schools. www.praeger.com

Simmons, R. (2011). *Odd girl out: The hidden culture of aggression in girls.* New York, NY: Harcourt Books. Understanding the culture of aggression in girls. www.harcourtbooks.com

Thomas, R. M. (2009). *Violence in America's schools.* Lanham, MD: Rowman and Littlefield. Discusses escalation in violence, motivation, and interventions. www.rowmanlittlefield.com

Twemlow, S., & Sacco, T. (2011). *Preventing bullying and school violence.* Washington, DC: American Psychiatric. Examines the range and complexity of school violence. www.appi.org

REFERENCES

Aisenberg, E., & Herrenkohl, T. (2008). Community violence in context: Risk and resilience in children and families. *Journal of Interpersonal Violence, 23*(3), 296–315.

Appel, A. E., & Holden, G. W. (1998). The co-occurrence of spouse and physical child abuse: A review and appraisal. *Journal of family psychology, 12*(4), 578–599.

Benson, M. L., Fox, G. L., DeMaris, A., & Van Wyk, J. (2003). Neighborhood disadvantage, individual economic distress and violence against women in intimate relationships. *Journal of quantitative criminology, 19*(3), 207–235.

Browning, C. R., Leventhal, T., & Brooks-Gunn, J. (2005). Sexual initiation in early adolescence: The nexus of parental and community control. *American Sociological Review, 70*(5), 758–778.

Buka, S. L., Stichick, T. L., Birdthistle, I., & Earls, F. J. (2001). Youth exposure to violence: Prevalence, risks, and consequences. *The American Journal of Orthopsychiatry, 71*(3), 298–310.

Centers for Disease Control and Prevention. (2009). Web-based Injury Statistics Query and Reporting System (WISQARS [Online]). National Center for Injury Prevention and Control, Centers for Disease Control and Prevention (producer). Retrieved from http://www.cdc.gov/injury/wisqars/index.html

Centers for Disease Control and Prevention. (2010). Youth risk behavioral surveillance-United States, 2009. *Morbidity and Mortality Weekly Report, 59*(No. SS-5).

Centers for Disease Control and Prevention. (2012). Youth risk behavior surveillance-United States, 2011. *Morbidity and Mortality Weekly Report, Surveillance Summaries, 61*(no.SS-4). Retrieved from www.cdc.gov/mmwr/pdf/ss/ss6104.pdf

Centers for Disease Control and Prevention, National Center for Injury Prevention and Control. (2013). Web-based Injury Statistics Query and Reporting System (WISQARS [online]). Retrieved April 22, 2013, from www.cdc.gov/injury/wisqars

Chicago Police Department: Compstat. (2013). Retrieved from https://portal.chicagopolice.org/portal/page/portal/ClearPath/Internal%20Affairs%20Division/Reports/Annual%20Reports/2013%20Year%20End%20Summary.pdf

Coalition for Juvenile Justice. (2000). *Handle with care: Serving the mental health needs of young offenders.* Annual report. Washington, DC: Coalition for Juvenile Justice.

Cooley-Quille, M., Boyd, R. C., Frantz, E., & Walsh, J. (2001). Emotional and behavioral impact of exposure to community violence in inner-city adolescents. *Journal of Clinical Child Psychology, 30*(2), 199–206.

Dembo, R., Belenko, S., Childs, K., & Wareham, J. (2009). Drug use and sexually transmitted diseases among female and male arrested youths. *Journal of behavioral medicine, 32*(2), 129–141.

Dong, M., Anda, R. F., Felitti, V. J., Dube, S. R., Williamson, D. F., Thompson, T. J., . . . Giles, W. H. (2004). The interrelatedness of multiple forms of childhood abuse, neglect, and household dysfunction. *Child abuse & neglect, 28*(7), 771–784.

Finkelhor, D., Turner, H., Ormrod, R., & Hamby, S. L. (2009). Violence, abuse, and crime exposure in a national sample of children and youth. *Pediatrics, 124*(5), 1411–1423.

Fitzpatrick, K. M., & Boldizar, J. P. (1993). The prevalence of depression among low-income African American youth. *Journal of Consulting and Clinical Psychology, 61*, 528–531.

Fowler, P. J., Tompsett, C. J., Braciszewski, J. M., Jacques-Tiura, A. J., & Baltes, B. B. (2009). Community violence: A meta-analysis on the effect of exposure and mental health outcomes of children and adolescents. *Development and Psychopathology, 21*(1), 227–259.

Fox, G. L., & Benson, M. L. (2006). Household and neighborhood contexts of intimate partner violence. *Public health reports, 121*(4), 419–427.

Garbarino, J., Hammond, R., Mercy, J., & Yung, B. R. (2004). Community violence and children: Preventing exposure and reducing harm. In K. I. Maton, C. J. Schellenbach, B. J. Leadbeater, & A. L. Solarz (Eds.), *Investing in children, youth, families, and communities* (pp.13–30). Washington, DC: American Psychological Association.

Gibbs, J. T., & Huang, L. N. (2003). Children of color: Psychological interventions with culturally diverse youth. San Francisco, CA: Jossey-Bass Press.

Hammond, W. R., & Arias, I. (2011). Broadening the approach to youth violence prevention through public health. *Journal of prevention & intervention in the community, 39*(2), 167–175.

Harrell, E. (2005). *Violence by gang members, 1993–2003* (Bureau of Justice Statistics, NJC 208875). Washington, DC: U.S. Department of Justice.

Holt, S., Buckley, H., & Whelan, S. (2008). The impact of exposure to domestic violence on children and young people: A review of the literature. *Child abuse & neglect, 32*(8), 797–810

Juvenile Justice Evaluation Center Online. (2005). *Disproportionate Minority Contact, 2005.* Retrieved March 1, 2007, from http://www.jrsa.org/jjec/programs/dmc/index.html

Krug, E. G., Mercy, J. A., Dahlberg, L. L., & Zwi, A. B. (2002). The world report on violence and health. *The lancet, 360*(9339), 1083–1088.

Kliewer, W., Lepore, S. J., Oskin, D., & Johnson, P. D. (1998). The role of social and cognitive processes in children's adjustment to community violence. *Journal of consulting and clinical psychology, 66*(1), 199–209.

Margolin, G., Vickerman, K. A., Ramos, M. C., Serrano, S. D., Gordis, E. B., Iturralde, E., . . . Spies, L. A. (2009). Youth exposed to violence: Stability, co-occurrence, and context. *Clinical child and family psychology review, 12*(1), 39–54.

Massey, D. S., & Denton, N. A. (1998). The elusive quest for the perfect index of concentration: Reply to Egan, Anderton, and Weber. *Social Forces, 76*(3), 1123–1133.

Mercy, J., Butchart, A., Farrington, D., & Cerdá, M. (2002). Youth violence. In E. Krug, L. L. Dahlberg, J. A. Mercy, A. B. Zwi, & R. Lozano (Eds.), *World report on violence and health* (pp. 25–56). Geneva, Switzerland: World Health Organization.

Miller, T. R., Fisher, D. A., & Cohen, M. A. (2001). Costs of juvenile violence: Policy implications. *Pediatrics, 107*(1), E3.

Morenoff, J. D., Sampson, R. J., & Raudenbush, S. W. (2001). Neighborhood inequality, collective efficacy, and the spatial dynamics of urban violence. *Criminology, 39*(3), 517–559.

Peterson, R. D., Krivo, L. J., & Hagan, J. (2010). *Divergent social worlds.* New York, NY: Russell Sage Foundation.

Pinchevsky, G. M., & Wright, E. M. (2012). The impact of neighborhoods on intimate partner violence and victimization. *Trauma, Violence, & Abuse, 13*(2), 112–132.

Raghavan, C., Mennerich, A., Sexton, E., & James, S. E. (2006). Community violence and its direct, indirect, and mediating effects on intimate partner violence. *Violence Against Women, 12*(12), 1132–1149.

Robers S., Zhang J., Truman J., & Synder T. D. (2011). Indicators of school crime and safety, National Center for Education Statistics, U.S. Department of Education, and Bureau of Justice Statistics, Office of Justice Programs, U.S. Department of Justice. Washington, DC, 2010. Retrieved from http://nces.ed.gov/pubs2012/2012002.pdf

Sampson, R. J., Raudenbush, S. W., & Earls, F. (1997). Neighborhoods and violent crime: A multilevel study of collective efficacy. *Science, 277*(5328), 918–924.

Sanderson, R. C., & Richards, M. H. (2010). The after-school needs and resources of a low-income urban community: Surveying youth and parents for community change. *American Journal of Community Psychology, 45*(3–4), 430–440.

Singh, G. K. (2010). *Youth mortality in the United States, 1935–2007: Large and persistent disparities in injury and violent deaths.* A 75th Anniversary Publication. Health Resources and Services Administration, Maternal and Child Health Bureau. Rockville, Maryland: U.S. Department of Health and Human Services.

Trickett, P. K., Durán, L., & Horn, J. L. (2003). Community violence as it affects child development: Issues of definition. *Clinical Child and Family Psychology Review, 6*(4), 223–236.

Truman, J. L. & Smith, E. L. (2012). *Prevalence of violent crime among households with children, 1993–2010* (Bureau of Justice Statistics, NJC 238799). Washington, DC: U.S. Department of Justice.

White, N., & Lauritsen, J. L. (2012). Violent crime against youth, 1994–2010. *Office of Justice Programs, Bureau of Justice Statistics, NJC, 240106.*

Zolotor, A. J., Theodore, A. D., Coyne-Beasley, T., & Runyan, D. K. (2007). Intimate partner violence and child maltreatment: Overlapping risk. *Brief Treatment and Crisis Intervention, 7*(4), 305–321.

CHAPTER 16

Providing Culturally Sensitive Interventions With Urban African American Victims of Intimate Partner Violence

Yvonne V. Greene and Marni N. Seyyid

The discussion of intimate partner violence (IPV) can be controversial. Highly debatable and charged questions often arise in the beginning of these conversations as to why the abused person remains in the relationship. Compounding the complexity of these discussions is the variance in opinions regarding the definition of IPV. This difference of opinion regarding IPV often centers around two areas: the nature of the acts that constitute "violence" and the type of relationships that qualify as "domestic" (Garner & Fagan, 1997). As such in recent years, the definition of IPV has expanded to include other forms of violence such as the abuse of elders, children, and siblings as well as violence between same-sex partners and male victims of violence.

The issue of IPV, occurring specifically within the African American community, has long been a hot-button topic replete with all manner of finger-pointing and head-scratching by public health and mental health researchers, policy makers, criminal justice officials, and frontline helping professionals weighing in on the causes and the appropriate remedies. No matter what group is debating the topic, they should acknowledge the unique cultural factors at play in order to understand the dynamics of IPV among this population and to provide culturally responsive interventions. Although research supports the general assessment that IPV occurs across all ethnic groups, socioeconomic statuses, religions, and geographical areas, for African American women, violence (and IPV) is reported at greater levels by the media, law enforcement, and health care personnel (Neville & Pugh, 1997). Oftentimes, the dialogue regarding IPV in the African American community has reported incidence and prevalence rates in ways that exacerbate already existing stereotypes and misconceptions about African American individuals and African American culture as a whole (Anda & Beccerra, 2000). As such, violence and abuse related to African American women still remain relatively understudied, despite calls for greater inclusion of African American women in IPV research.

Compounding this issue for African American women is the fact that although survey research and arrest records indicate that the numbers of battered African American women are significant, battered African American women as a group are often obscured and ignored because of their race, gender, class, and victim statuses (Henneburg, 2000). African American women who are victims of abuse by intimate partners often remain invisible to the general public or are further victimized by service institutions and helping professionals charged with providing refuge and assistance.

This chapter is designed to enhance the reader's knowledge as it relates to African American women who seek help from social work professionals as a result of abuse by male, African American intimate partners. This chapter delineates and discusses the universal issues that all women in battering relationships face; however, the authors propose that there are some unique cultural dynamics that must be addressed and incorporated into practice as well as in the educational curricula of social work students who will one day intervene with these women in various urban social work service settings.

The chapter further explores some of the core differences that exist for urban African American women in violent intimate relationships. It will specifically address within a cultural context: the unique bond between African American males and females as it relates to shared race-related lived experiences; the role of community and religion and how these experiences and expectations may directly affect urban African American women's decision to report IPV; characteristic responses from service institutions and helping professionals; and ultimately, her decision to seek and receive help. Additionally, strategies for providing effective, culturally responsive interventions that recognize and appreciate these differences are shared.

Last, the authors suggest that violence and abuse as it relates to urban African American women still remains a relatively under-investigated topic, despite calls for greater inclusion of urban African American women in the studies of IPV. Consequently, this paucity of research results in little attention being focused on the interpersonal dynamics of violence as it relates to urban African American women. As social work educators and practitioners, the implications of this missing knowledge is profound. This chapter is designed to raise awareness of the continuing need to develop curricula and create field placement settings that acknowledge these trends and respond to the needs of this at-risk population.

OVERVIEW OF INTIMATE PARTNER VIOLENCE

Universal

IPV is a pattern of abuse involving threatening or controlling behavior imposed on a person by a loved one without regard for his or her rights, feelings, body, or health (http://www.cdc.gov/violenceprevention/intimatepartnerviolence/index.html).

The terms "intimate partner violence" and "domestic violence" have been used interchangeably in the literature. However, IPV is a broader expression than domestic violence because it includes any adults involved in an intimate relationship, whether or not the parties reside together. This term includes same-sex domestic partners (legally married or not) and covers children who are injured during violent episodes. Therefore, for the purposes of this chapter, the term "intimate partner violence" or the acronym IPV is used, except in instances of citing or quoting a study in which the study author's meaning would be changed by the use of this term. Overwhelmingly, men are the perpetrators of IPV.

Recent data show that the incidence and prevalence rates of IPV continue to increase annually (American Institute on Domestic Violence, 2005). A collaborative study conducted by the Tjaden and Thoennes (2000) reported that former husbands, cohabitating partners, boyfriends, or dates victimized 64% percent of the women who reported being raped, physically assaulted, and/or stalked since the age of 18 years. Battering of women by men is more likely to occur inside the home. In fact, battering accounts for more injuries to women than car accidents, muggings, and rapes combined. During 2006, men committed 4.8 million acts of violence against women, including 1,544 murders (Centers for Disease Control and Preventions [CDC], 2006, as cited in Smith, 2008). In fact, current and/or former husbands, boyfriends, or dates victimized 33% of all female homicide victims (USA Today, 2003, as cited in Smith, 2008). These data provide support for the hypothesis that systems responsible for treating, prosecuting, and advocating for victims and perpetrators of IPV lack the proper tools and resources to do so effectively enough to reduce the impact of IPV on American society.

Among African American–Urban Populations

The Bureau of Justice Statistics (BJS) relates that among women, being Black, young, divorced or separated, earning lower incomes, living in rental housing, and living in urban areas were all associated with higher rates of intimate partner victimization between 1993 and 1998 (Rennison & Welchans, 2000). For the purpose of this chapter, we use the following definition of urban: relating to a city with a dense population and/or vertical geographical setting; an environment where the economy is based on manufacture, service, and sales, but not agriculture; and a place where there is a specific culture that arises from living in close proximity to others.

Rankin, Saunders, and Williams (2000) offered that attachment style, social support, sense of belonging, and depression are risk factors (previously identified in the battering literature resulting from studies conducted using Caucasian men) that are especially salient for African American men. Furthermore, African American men face violence, racial inequities, helplessness, hopelessness, frustration, and devaluation; as a result, they exist in an overall climate of alienation. Living in this climate, coupled with the stress of having fewer resources to gain and maintain the basic necessities of life (employment status or quality), may contribute to displaced anger against society. The researchers suggest that displaced anger in African American men may manifest itself in violence against intimate partners.

Smith (2008) echoed the findings of Rankin et al. (2000) in his report that, because of the impact of institutionalized racism, African American men may have a greater need to exert control and influence over members of their own household—particularly, their female intimates. Smith cites a study by Ehrensaft and Cohen (2003) that reports that "experiencing child abuse doubles one's risk" for committing IPV, but stresses that "witnessing violence in childhood triples one's risk for growing up to become a batterer."

The debate over the prevalence of IPV continues between African American and Caucasian research communities. African American researchers attempt to dispel negative stereotypes about African Americans as generally more violent in their interactions with each other, while Caucasian researchers maintain that socio-economic factors play a significant role in the prevalence of IPV. Either way, the problem of IPV among African American men and women is significant enough to warrant specific, targeted interventions grounded in African American culture to improve efficacy.

CULTURALLY COMPETENT PRACTICE

Definition

Cultural competence as it relates to social work practice mandates the recognition and respect of differences among ethnic groups and the impact those differences have on the intervention process. It challenges the practitioner to "think outside of the box" and explore creative and innovative ways to intervene within a cultural framework. In doing so the clinician begins to recognize and understand the dynamics of difference and the need to provide delivery of services that acknowledges, addresses, and respects those differences. Additionally, the ability of the practitioner to understand their own cultural issues and biases and how these impact the intervention process is essential (Garner & Fagan, 1997).

Culturally competent practice recognizes that culture shapes an individual's experiences and is demonstrated by both the acceptance of and respect for differences, which is preferable to "tolerance" of those differences. Optimally, this type of practice should be utilized by individuals, organizations, and systems in their interventions. Implementing culturally competent practice is a necessary and ongoing process.

The culturally competent practitioner recognizes that diversity exists both *within* and *between* cultures, combines general knowledge about various cultures with specific information provided by the individual, and incorporates an awareness of one's biases and prejudices. Paramount in providing culturally competent practice is the practitioner's development of the ability to engage clients who are culturally different in ways that respect and appreciate difference. This development requires that the interventionist presents as accepting, genuine, and courteous when addressing the lived experiences of their clients. Practitioners who give equal value to others' worldviews are better able to engage clients in ways that put them at ease quickly and successfully (McPhatter, 1997). As such the client develops a feeling of validation and the practitioner is better able to provide culturally relevant services. This capacity building on the part of the interventionist results in asking and listening to what culturally diverse people say about their needs, and we attend and respond to their views about how to approach resolution (McPhatter, 1997).

Significance

Within the urban community there exist unique cultural aspects that the competent helping professional must respect and understand in order to provide services that truly meet the needs of urban African American women in IPV relationships. These cultural components if not understood and incorporated often result in disengagement of the client, disconnect in the therapeutic relationship, and often a lack of appreciation for the coping strategies utilized by the urban African American women in IPV relationships living in urban areas. Oftentimes, the practice approaches and interventions utilized in work with both the African American woman and the urban community are influenced by personal biases of providers that seem to view their clients through a lens of pathology and disorganization, disregarding and not utilizing the strength and resilience that clients may possess.

Clinical Relevance

Within the context of the urban community, African American women are challenged with a plethora of dynamics, which can often influence decision making regarding their reporting and help-seeking behaviors. As with other racial or ethnic groups, there exists a set of cultural norms and mores that distinctly characterize the makeup and functioning of the subsystems within the community. The African American inhabitants of these urban communities play a significant role in the creation of the "mood" of the environment, which affects the ways the dynamics of IPV are played out as it relates to disclosure, reporting, and help-seeking behavior.

These cultural dynamics are infused at the micro-, mezzo-, and macro-levels. As a result, the culturally competent helping professional must understand the following: (a) how urban communities and their African American inhabitants relate to one another, how they view their community, how they respond to those outside of their community, as well as how they address the issues facing members of their community; (b) practice approaches must be interprofessional and inclusive of community members' input regarding services; (c) interventions cannot be one-dimensional in nature and applied without consideration for special circumstances and individual client needs; (d) both African American women and the urban communities in which they dwell must be viewed from a more holistic standpoint; (e) how institutional racism and lack of trust may influence reporting habits and help/service-seeking behavior; (f) how urban African American people define family (nuclear, extended, and fictive); and (g) how and why spirituality and religiosity are used as coping mechanisms.

Certainly, there cannot be a discussion of urban communities without recognizing that there exist challenges regarding the violent and economic conditions that are prevalent in these communities. However, in spite of these conditions, it is imperative that the conversations still include the strength and resiliency that is interwoven throughout these communities that is often overlooked when practitioners do not incorporate the aforementioned cultural components as integral aspects of the helping process. Appreciating the unique look of urban communities and the ever-evolving dynamics is paramount and key in providing intervention goals that match services. The achievement of culturally competent practice is only as successful as the practitioner's willingness to incorporate an enlightened consciousness that involves a fundamental process of reorienting one's primary worldview (McPhatter, 1997). It is then that the helping professional truly begins to welcome into the therapeutic relationship the diverse experiences of others and how their lived experiences affect both perceptions of their environment and those with whom they interact.

SOCIETAL PERCEPTIONS OF AFRICAN AMERICAN WOMEN AND MEN

Historical View

The Black family and Black community are similar to those of the larger society in that caregivers tend to rear and respond to boys and girls differently. However, there are two methods or concurrently active "tracks" of socialization: practices that teach children socially appropriate gender roles as well as those that teach African American children how to get along in the context of a generally accepted reality, status, and condition of African American people in America and the world. This dual socialization, according to gender and station, is consistent with W. E. B Du Bois's famous quote: "One ever feels his twoness—as an American, a Negro; two souls, two unreconciled strivings; two warring ideals in one dark body, whose strength alone keeps it from being torn asunder" (Du Bois, 1903).

According to this "twoness," African American boys are rewarded and celebrated for being larger, faster, more athletic, and more aggressive. These boys are trained at home and at (community-based) school that assertiveness is the way to get what you want—even if people are disturbed or frightened temporarily by your behavior. This is their gender-based training. Paradoxically, these same boys are taught that behaving aggressively outside the Black community, could be met with misunderstanding, violence, and even death (Birns, Cascardi, & Meyer, 1994; Carr & Mednick, 1988). This is a station-based training.

African American girls are also socialized according to seemingly opposing realities: their gender-based training, which requires softness, nurturing, submissiveness to men, and other traditionally assigned feminine roles and attributes are juxtaposed with their station-based training—an expectation or requirement that they act as lionesses to gatekeep the safety, stability, and sanctity of the Black family and thus the Black community (Dove, 1998; Lee, Sanders-Thompson, & Mechanic, 2002; Martinson, 2001; Neville & Pugh, 1997; Simien, 2004). Black girls are routinely fed the conflicting messages that they should be beautiful, kind, generous, knowledgeable, but submissive; modest and virtuous; and not too outspoken. But at the same time, Black women are taught that they should be confident and self-sufficient, flexible in their interpretation of right and wrong, and ready to fight at a moment's notice (for child, man, family, or community), because African American women have been tasked with safeguarding the Black family.

Nah Dove attributes this dual construction of heterosexual relationships among African American women and men and its resultant conflict to a concept she calls the "Clash of Cultures" (1998) that resulted from the integration of African peoples (culturally rooted in matriarchy, agrarianism, collectivism) into Western society (undergirded by patriarchy, nomadism, and hierarchy). As a result of the dual tracks of socialization applied to African American women and men outlined earlier in the chapter, men and women may develop a two-tier relationship with each other: an in-community relationship (that which they share with the African American community and family members) vs. out-community relationship—the one they share with the larger community. This compartmentalization is not to be confused with the usual layer of secrecy or shame that is synonymous with IPV sufferers wherein they are required to keep secret everything (including the abuse) that happens within household for reasons of safety–stability of the home. There is a greater weight or level of importance imposed on the secrecy as if it carries with it a more profound dependence and/or demonstration of loyalty, especially for children and female victims.

Dove offers that the in-community orientation of Black families remains one of shared duties among men and women and an orientation toward the greater good, particularly as it relates to the attainment and maintenance of economic stability. However, the process of assimilation and the need to coexist with and survive in the larger society, with its orientation toward devaluation of women and Black people as a whole, may force African American men and women to develop an out-community orientation that creates a sort of relational alter-ego. This alter-ego (or dysfunctional male–female relationship identity) or out-community tendency created by the clash of cultures, in the context of so many other disparate and difficult societal conditions, may create dysfunctional in-community inclinations and be a crucial component of IPV behavior among African American heterosexual intimates. This dysfunctional in-community thrust (or role oversimplification) is often manifested by the "Super Woman" and the "Super Stud."

"Super Woman" Versus "Super Stud"

Super Woman

The myth of the African American "Super" woman dates back to and incorporates the African American woman's earliest tasks in America: that of enslaved laborer (at par with and shoulder to shoulder with Black male slaves); nurturer and caregiver for all (White as well as Black) children; keeper of the household (both the slaveholder's household and her own meager dwellings); provider of sisterhood and support for other women; supplier of additional workers for the slave system; deliverer of sexual favors both to Black and White men; and protector of the slave community (Giddings, 1984; Hemphill, 2008; Hill, 2005, 2011; Hooks, 1981, 1992; Kusmer & Trotter, 2009; Welsing, 1991; Winbush, 2001). Through abolition, Reconstruction, the Industrial Revolution, the Great Migration, and into the 21st century, the myth has remained fairly stable.

The myth of the African American "Super" woman dictates that the African American woman must, through the combination of her assigned in-community (between herself and others in the African American community) and out-community (between herself and those outside the African American community) roles, be simultaneously and congruently the tough-as-nails gatekeeper of the African American family and community and intelligent, resilient, and flexible enough to endure all that the majority society may throw at her while securing all manner of resources to sustain her family–community (Simien, 2004). Because the African American woman is expected to do so much, she is cast as indestructible and self-sufficient. She is not expected to need care or attention similar in type or intensity to other women (Hooks, 2000).

Many African American women find themselves attempting to fulfill the mandated role of gatekeepers of the African American community (despite their own internal objections), because that expectation has been such an integral part of their socialization. African American women in urban environments describe a constant communication and reinforcement of the message that the African American community is wholly dependent on the caregiving and protection of the African American woman (Lee, et al., 2002; Martinson, 2001; Neville & Pugh, 1997; Simien, 2004). This message is delivered in all the places and spaces that urban African American women congregate: the family, school, church, sororities, supermarkets, clothing stores, and beauty shops via media, African American men, the larger society, and other African American women.

As a result of these gatekeeping obligations and a healthy paranoia based on a general distrust of the criminal justice and health care systems, as well as the expectation that they should "handle their business," African American women do not generally discuss personal problems (including incidents of IPV) with anyone other than a close "sister-friend" (Lee, et al., 2002; Martinson, 2001; Neville & Pugh, 1997). African American women victims of IPV report feeling the burden of preserving and protecting the Black family, maintaining allegiance to the Black community as a whole, and perpetuating the image of the "strong Black woman."

Super Stud

Some studies cite sex-role socialization of African American men as an important factor in the development of battering behavior of men toward their female intimates. For example, Black barbershops are well-known as information hubs, neighborhood political think tanks, and social centers. They are also institutions of sex-role socialization for African American men (Taubman, 1986; Wright & Calhoun, 2001). It is for this reason that Clyde Franklin (1985) conducted a groundbreaking qualitative study of sex-role interactions in urban Black barbershops in the Chicago area. He posited that this early (most Black boys begin receiving haircuts by age 3 years); habitual (most customers visit the barbershop at an average of every 2 weeks); and long-lasting (Black men tend to be extremely loyal to their barbers; many clients of the studied barbershop had been so for as much as 20–25 years) exposure to the masculine negotiations in Black urban barbershops, put the Black barbershop at par with the Black family, the Black church, and school as an institution of socialization for Black men—especially regarding sex-role socialization.

Franklin (1985) points out that two of the most interesting features of barbershop "negotiations" (conversations) are that they are clearly visible to all negotiators and bystanders and nonverbal communication plays a significant role in the process. The topic of discussion does not matter so much as does the posturing. However, Franklin did note that nearly three quarters of the conversations were about sex roles (i.e., perceptions of men who help with housework, working mothers, infidelity, fatherhood, the nature of homophobia) and several sex-role stereotypes were perpetuated and reinforced (i.e., "by nature" men are polygamous; women must take care of the children).

Dr. Franklin noted that women were often referred to as "bitches," "whores," "cunts," and the like. Sexual encounters were often described in great detail, to the delight of young male customers (as evidenced by their giggles and smiles). Franklin wrote:

> Learning that "men" are violent toward each other is not the only aspect of the male role that Black male youth may receive from barbershop negotiations in settings such as the one discussed. Young Black boys also can learn that violence toward women is permissible under certain conditions...consistent with the above are the constant sexualizations of male-female relationships, the persistent use of sexual epithets and stereotypes to define women, and the tacit endorsements of discriminating policies toward women—all of which teach young Black males dominance, aggression, and violence toward Black women and women in general. (Franklin, 1985, p. 13)

Franklin (1985) provides us with valuable insight into one mechanism for sex-role socialization that may contribute to IPV among African American intimates—the Black barbershop. However, other institutions impact the developmental course of African American men.

Smith (2008) explained that there are two components of the "male role" for African men—as previously described—that of the breadwinner and that of the "sexual conquistador." Respondents in Smith's 2008 study described threats to these roles as "triggers" for IPV. Smith (2008) reasons that structural factors impact the African American man's capacity to fulfill both his roles: decreased economic opportunity threatens the African

American man's capacity to fulfill the breadwinner role, thereby making him less attractive as a mate. As he seeks alternative methods to increase his earning potential, the incarceration looms large threatening his freedom as well as his ability to fulfill his male role.

Smith (2008) suggests that the role of the breadwinner and the sexual conquistador so rigidly and thoroughly undergird the masculine identity of the African American man that there is little room for negotiation in their minds, the minds of their partners or the larger African American community. Smith contends that this construction of African American masculinity is a structural and institutional response to the structural and institutional response of racism. Smith recommends further examination of the systems of socialization at work in the African American community.

The Super Woman, Super Stud, and the Risk of IPV

The influence of those previously described dual tracks of socialization for African American women and men living in urban areas is enduring. Researchers have reported that even when African Americans attain a level of affluence and move out of urban areas, they still return to the community fairly regular—on average, once weekly—to "check-in" with friends, family members, and the like (Diamond, 1999; Pattillo-McCoy, 1999; Villemez, 1980;). They may visit, eat, shop, get their hair done, or care for family members in need. During these visits, messages of prescribed roles for African American men are reinforced. Interestingly, African American members of the "middle class" are less likely than Whites to leave urban areas, because pockets of housing for African American working-class and middle-class citizens are less likely to exist. That is, African Americans need to make quite a bit more than their White counterparts to upgrade their housing, (Pattillo-McCoy, 1999; Villemez, 1980). If women and men continue to live in the urban environment, those messages of socialization replay incessantly. Therefore, African American women and men may become locked into a cycle of enacting approved roles based on their gender and station (ethnicity and socioeconomic status [SES]).

Smith (2008) concluded that every Black man living in the United States is susceptible to engaging in battering as a response to threats and challenges to their masculine identities—particularly, the challenges they may face in terms of providing for their families (or breadwinning)—and the types of violence that African American men perpetrate are more severe because of their increased exposure to structural and institutional inequality that "adds to the weight they unload on their female partner."

Many authors suggest that standing in the gap for absent men (financially and logistically) has caused Black women to be less emotionally available to Black children. Bell Hooks suggested that the core of the modern-day love and familial relationship between African American men and women has been retarded by the residual effects of the burden (real or perceived) Black women have felt for shoring up the Black community. She writes:

> Usually adult males who are unable to make emotional connections with the women they choose to be intimate with are frozen in time, unable to allow themselves to love for fear

that the loved one will abandon them. If the first woman they passionately loved, the mother, was not true to her bond of love, then how can they trust that their partner will be true to love. Often in their adult relationships these men act out again and again to test their partner's love. While the rejected adolescent boy imagines that he can no longer receive his mother's love because he is not worthy, as a grown man he may act out in ways that are unworthy and yet demand of the woman in his life that she offer him unconditional love. This testing does not heal the wounds of the past, it merely reenacts it, for ultimately the woman will become weary of being tested and end the relationship, thus reenacting the abandonment. This drama confirms for many men that they cannot put their trust in love. They decide that it is better to put their faith in being powerful, in being dominant. (Hooks, 2000)

Smith (2008) reports that African American boys witness violence in their homes and internalize it as a conflict strategy—a way to manage the household and preserve control (even if the violence hurts them or another loved one). Using Walker's Cycle of Violence (1979), Smith outlines a slightly different process from that put forward by Gunderson and Dutton involving family of origin violence and the use of battering behavior in Black men. He posits that marginalized African American men have developed alternative ideologies that take into account their specific realities. As a result, African American men (in large numbers) subscribe to the thinking that their masculinity is tied to and measured by their capacity to provide financially for their families and their ability to exert sexual influence over their female intimates.

Smith (2008) reports that, within the context of their intimate relationships, African American men must successfully perform the roles of "breadwinner" and "sexual conquistador." He explains that life in general for African American men is tantamount to Walker's (1979) tension-building phase, where each day he encounters scrutiny, hostility, reduced opportunity, and high levels of alienation in the world. When the African American man perceives a threat to either of his two core roles within his household, he may respond with violence—activating the acute battering phase. Finally, realizing that he has hurt and alienated his only ally (the African American female intimate), the African American man sets about acts of contrition in hopes of regaining intimacy with his mate. This stage is Walker's honeymoon phase. Once intimacy is restored, the cycle begins again.

UNIQUE CULTURAL CHALLENGES FACED BY AFRICAN AMERICAN WOMEN IN VIOLENT INTIMATE RELATIONSHIPS AND BARRIERS TO REPORTING

Bond With African American Men

Both the African American woman and her male counterpart have been exposed to overt and covert, individual and institutional racism and discrimination although experienced and internalized by each in different ways. Both are aware that the legal system has been infused with racial and discriminatory practices against African Americans especially those of lower socioeconomic status living in urban settings as compared to their White, affluent rural or suburban counterparts (Walker, 1991). These experiences and the complex socialization of African American men and women have helped to bond them in secrecy and dysfunction.

Exposure to the historical and contemporary patterns of racial and gender oppression may cause African American males to adopt manhood roles that condone resorting to violence as a means of resolving disputes often resulting in an increased risk of committing acts of IPV (Hampton, Oliver, & Margarian, 2003). For the African American female this adaptation in men can result in more reluctance to report acts of violence fearing that the likelihood of such reporting will result in harsher treatment and continued stereotyping of African American men. Well aware of the portrayal of African American men in the media and their treatment by law enforcement and the courts, African American women delay involving others in their battering and do not want to be one more person to "bring her man down." Therefore, the socialized understanding and consent among African American women to participate in the duality and secrecy—to govern their relationships according to these two tracks of established norms is ever active. This may be one factor contributing to hesitation among African American women who hesitate to "call the man" when they are victims of IPV.

Influence of the African American Family (Nuclear, Extended, or Fictive) and Community

The term "family" within African American households and urban communities will often include those persons related through birth (nonfictive kin) and those considered "family" because of established and long-standing close bonds (fictive kin). These subdivisions of family are the major elements of the extended family and in both historical and contemporary times have played a significant role in the survival of urban African Americans (Martin & Martin, 1985). As such, the African American extended family as a caregiving institution in urban areas still plays a pivotal role in the learned behaviors of its members and their interactions with the wider society. Few urban African Americans would put the welfare of nonkin and strangers on par with that of kin or family (Martin & Martin, 1985). Strangers are not trusted and the interactions with helping professionals are often viewed through a lens that has been tainted with experiences of institutional racism.

Socialization as it relates to the Black family is an important component in understanding the identity and decision-making strategies of the abused woman. Often there is intense loyalty to family and strong views regarding respecting the privacy of member and not "airing one's dirty laundry" with outsiders. Although this strong bond often has proven to be positive, it can also prove to be a hindrance for the abused women when it comes to disclosing the violence. She may be concerned that sharing such information may cause already overburdened and taxed family members or friends to feel a sense of pressure to "take sides." Additionally, the interconnectedness of the family bonds may be grounded in agreements regarding the exchange of financial and/or emotional support. These close ties often make it difficult for African American women to disclose the abuse for fear that these supports will be withdrawn or negatively impacted.

Within urban communities, families (fictive and nonfictive) may often reside within close proximity to one another either geographically or interact with one another at multiple levels, such as in places of worship, social events, and informal family and/or neighborhood gatherings. Although often providing supportive elements, this can also provide challenges when IPV occurs and cause interactions and relationships to become strained. Those supportive networks become compromised and women often find themselves vacillating between remaining silent and reporting. It is not uncommon for families to have experienced long histories of IPV within the family and in some ways this "family secret" may become normalized with participants becoming desensitized to its affects. Often this desensitizing is coupled with the urban families' continual exposure to other types of violence within their own environments; sometimes resulting in a minimization, justification, and/or acceptance of the violence.

Influence of "Faith," Religion, and Spirituality

Another influential presence within the African American culture is the role faith, religion, and spirituality have and continue to play in the African American community. For the African American woman her reliance on her "faith" has been instrumental in coping with a multiplicity of problems. She has often been viewed as the cornerstone of the church typically comprising the majority of the congregation. The principles of her "faith" may indeed cause her to focus on the need to forgive and reconcile because "God can heal the relationship." As such her strength to endure in the abusive relationship and her faith for the healing of the relationship must be understood within its cultural and spiritual context and not automatically interpreted by helping professionals as a lack of insight or willingness to engage in counseling.

The African American woman of faith does, however, find herself in a precarious position, as she struggles to reconcile the violent secret reality of her household with the best possible image of the Black family. She risks shame and possible rejection from the church should she choose to disclose the violence. She may be further conflicted if indeed her batterer is a member of the church or worse, one of the ministry leaders. The unspoken messages that are communicated within the church as well as the sometime misinterpretation of scripture (i.e., Colossians: 18–21; Corinthians I 7: 14–16; Ephesians 4:21–33; Ephesians 5) has been used to justify continued abuse at the hands of a violent partner. These misinterpretations of scripture suggest that women are to be submissive and quiet and as a result many abused women have suffered in silence. Although the Black church has been renowned for providing support and care for the community and each other, when it comes to IPV (and other issues involving women i.e., sexual harassment) the church as a whole has been curiously silent (Martinson, 2001). Additionally, many churches, like other service institutions, still view the crime of IPV as "family business" and as such provide little to no support in congregations for women that are silently suffering at the hands of their abusers.

The African American IPV victim may fear that disclosure of the abuse will bring shame to her (immediate and extended) family, her partner, and her church community. One prevalent message from the African American church to these women seems to be that there will be all manner of respect, admiration, and praise for their testimony following the IPV ordeal. However, it appears that the church still struggles with providing real-time support during the actual occurrence of the violence and her subsequent attempts to find assistance. This communication is consistent with the overt and covert teachings of the Black church that undergird the station-based socialization of Black women as the protector of the image of the Black man, the Black family, and the Black community. In this way, in order to be seen as a "strong spiritual person who can through faith endure all," urban African American women are encouraged to endure the violence in silence. Thus, urban African American women in abusive relationships may find their faith to be either a support or a stumbling block when contemplating whether the church will ultimately provide refuge from the abuse.

Places of worship within urban communities are increasingly faced with supporting congregants as they struggle to manage issues impacting urban dwellers such as polysubstance abuse, economic inequities, health issues, and "street" violence. These faith-based institutions often provide congregants with spiritual, emotional, and concrete supports through various ministries, outreach efforts, support groups, clothing, and food pantries. However, as it relates to IPV, creating faith-based interventions that address IPV is limited (Bent-Goodley, 2006). This lack of conversation presents a unique opportunity in urban communities to begin dialogues with congregants about sustainable and realistic goals to eradicate IPV in African American households. Places of worship are highly visible, relatively numerous and seated directly within the urban enclave—giving them the appearance of being (physically) accessible to urban African American women victims of IPV; however, the communication from faith-based institutions regarding IPV is often deficient, unclear, and/or absent altogether, making their defense of IPV victims less accessible. Despite the uncertain response, African American women still may turn to their faith-based community to address IPV before they consult mental health, social service, law enforcement, or medical providers (Adams & Fortune, 1995; Bent-Goodley, 2001). Barring all other interventions, the physical access that the Black church has to urban African American female IPV victims continues to provide the richest opportunity for partnerships between faith-based organizations, social workers, and other helping professionals working within urban communities to address the violence.

These intersecting dynamics that both the African American male and female urban dwellers experience may lead to a guarded trust of police, law enforcement, and other helping professionals who may not be willing to acknowledge and incorporate into their interventions the lived experiences of African Americans, both within a historically and contemporary context. This lack of understanding may alienate families dealing with IPV and further perpetuate the cycle of IPV, which can continue from generation to generation.

IMPLICATIONS FOR SOCIAL WORK PRACTICE

During intervention with victims of domestic abuse, the presence or lack of support networks is a key aspect to consider when formulating treatment goals and safety plans. Clinicians know that with regard to IPV, personal or family embarrassment often leads to secrecy even when support systems are present. African Americans are generally very private, especially with regards to "family business." Historically, there has been hesitancy in sharing sensitive information with those outside of one's race due to an abiding fear that it will be misinterpreted and/or misused. Understanding the makeup of the family system and appreciating the role of formal and informal relationships within that system has proven to be key in providing effective treatment with African Americans. In working with the African American female, attention has to be given to her ambivalence in even seeking help outside of the family and her concerns regarding their opinion should she tell them about the violence. Clinicians should be well aware of and closely attend to the potential impact disclosure of the abuse could have on urban African American women clients experiencing IPV. For some, sharing such closely held "family secrets" could put them at even greater risk for scrutiny and criticism from the family; withdrawal of community support as well as further/increased violence at the hands of the abuser. This could further diminish her already limited options for safety.

In providing culturally competent intervention with regard to IPV, clinicians must address the experiences women have had with other helping institutions. In IPV situations legal institutions and health care are two key systems with which women are most likely to become involved. The effective clinician must explore with the women of color what her past experiences and interactions with these systems have been. It is from those experiences that she begins to form ideas about the helpfulness and receptiveness of these institutions in dealing with issues that are of particular significance to her situation. Black women are very sensitive to the ability of these institutions to respectfully address issues that are unique to their experiences. Culturally ineffective interventions oftentimes influence women's decision to file charges against the abuser as well as help seeking actions.

If the woman's experiences with these systems have been less than favorable or tainted with discrimination, she may indeed rethink her decision to seek future help. An internalized belief that important systems are not likely to understand or be helpful affects the women's decision to stay, to report the abuse, or to seek help from agencies that are designed to provide help to victims of IPV.

Culturally competent practice recognizes that minority victims of IPV have unique needs based on unique experiences that mandate unique interventions. These interventions must encapsulate those cultural influences and mores that are important and influential in the lives of the client. Although every woman who suffers at the hands of abuse shares the commonality of pain, differences exist as to how, when, and if they see their situation as changeable. Practice must address these differences in real, viable, and culturally meaningful ways. If not the clinician does little more than perpetuate silent suffering and rising statistics.

CASE STUDY

Sharon is a 23-year-old, single, African American woman. She has one son, aged 5 years. They live in a two-bedroom apartment in the city. Sharon is employed as a hair stylist. She received her Associate of Arts degree from the community college with further aspirations to continue her education at a 4-year institution.

Sharon and the father of her son have been together for 7 years. The history of the abuse began shortly after they started dating and was primarily verbal. The violence quickly escalated and became physical in nature shortly after the birth of the couple's son. Sharon has been to the emergency room several times for injuries resulting from physical abuse at the hands of her boyfriend. On only one of those emergency room visits did any helping professional screen for IPV.

Sharon's boyfriend was arrested on a drug charge and subsequently incarcerated for 3 years. During that time she maintained regular contact with him via phone calls and occasional visits. She also maintained regular contact with the family of her boyfriend, often taking her son to visit with them several times a month. At no time during this separation did Sharon consider leaving her boyfriend nor did she disclose the abuse to anyone in her support system. She has been praying about her situation and considered speaking with the pastor of her church but decided against it because she did not want to embarrass her mother, who has been a lifelong member and serves on several church boards and ministries within the church. Her mother is also well known within the community as a former teacher and now principal of a local high school. Sharon's mother has been divorced for 10 years from Sharon's father, who was verbally abusive. Sharon has had sporadic contact with her father since her parents' divorce. Additionally, several members of her boyfriend's family live in the same neighborhood as her mother and attend the church as well.

Shortly after her boyfriend's release from jail, the physical abuse continued and has resulted in one additional emergency room visit and a two-night stay at a shelter for battered women. Sharon is concerned that if she reports the abuse, another charge could "land him in jail again" and he could lose the part-time job he has secured since he exited prison. Sharon has never filed formal charges against her boyfriend, has never disclosed the abuse to family or friends, and currently is planning to marry him in the near future.

Discussion

- Sharon's decisions regarding her situation have in many instances been based on a history of interaction both internal and external to her family system. The verbal and nonverbal messages communicated to her from

(continued)

(continued)

various sources, the secrecy with which she has kept the abuse, her own nuclear family's abusive history, and the conflicted sense of loyalty toward her abuser have all impacted upon her actions.

- In providing services to her, the culturally competent practitioner must delve into the meanings behind and ramifications of all aspects of her situation. The significance of "protecting" her abuser and how that emanates out of a shared history of systemic oppression is key in providing meaningful intervention. The cultural significance of the relationships of the family—both blood relatives and fictive kin—must be explored.

- The need to keep some secrets because of embarrassment and the cultural and often generational transmitted belief that one cannot trust those outside the family, especially if they are of another racial group, must be addressed. Additionally, the significance of religion in Sharon's life and the role it plays in coping and decision making must be incorporated in setting realistic and life applicable goals.

Questions

1. What does the word "urban" mean to you?

2. How might Sharon have a conversation with her pastor about the state of her relationship, particularly as she looks to get married?

3. How might Sharon talk with her mother about her situation? Is Sharon's mother's experience different from or similar to hers? Why or why not?

4. What does it mean to "handle your business" as an African American woman living in an urban community?

5. What are the benefits of Sharon's continuing to keep the IPV in her relationship a secret?

6. You are a lifelong neighborhood friend of Sharon. One day she pulls you aside and tells you everything. What do you say? What do you do?

7. Why would Sharon need to protect her boyfriend? Do African American men need protection? Why or why not?

8. How might helping professionals employ cultural competence with Sharon if she sought help? How might individual biases keep helping professionals from adhering to agency protocols?

9. What types of multidisciplinary approaches could be utilized with African American women based on your understanding of what "urban" is?

FOR FURTHER STUDY

Suggested Assignments

1. Visit Local DV/IPV shelters and inquire about their programs and services. Ask specifically what they do to imbue their interventions with cultural competence and how they ensure those who need their services get access to the agency?

2. While at the shelter ask what items and/or assistance they are lacking. Organize a team of people to address that need: whether it is a clothing drive or a storytelling afternoon for the children who live at the shelter.

3. Film a 5-minute PSA for use with children ages 5 to 10, wherein you explain what DV/IPV is and how to stay safe if it is happening in your home or community.

4. Invite local leaders of various/different religious organizations, health care organizations, police/legal departments, and so on, to discuss DV/IPV interventions are addressed. Develop a culturally sensitive interdisciplinary strategy/plan that might be utilized on your campus with students who may be in a DV/IPV relationship based on the information you receive.

5. Show the DVD *For Colored Girls Who Have Considered Suicide When The Rainbow is Enuff*. Develop a treatment plan for the character in the DV/IPV relationship.

Suggested Readings

Cleage, P. (1997). *What looks like crazy on an ordinary day*. New York, NY: Harper Collins.

Dove, N. (1998). *African mothers: Bearers of culture, makers of social change* (pp. 101–102). Albany: State University of New York Press.

Franklin, C. W. (1985). The black male urban barbershop as a sex-role socialization setting. *Sex Roles, 12*(9/10), 965–979.

Potter, H. (2008). *Battle cries: Black women and intimate partner abuse*. New York: New York University Press.

Shange, N. (2010). *For colored girls who have considered suicide when the rainbow is enuf*. New York, NY: Simon & Schuster.

REFERENCES

American Academy of Experts in Traumatic Stress, Inc. (1996). *Prevalence of domestic violence*. Retrieved October 27, 2005, from http://www.aaets.org/arts/art8.html

American Institute on Domestic Violence. (2005). *Domestic violence in the workplace statistics*. Retrieved October 27, 2005, from http://www.aidv-usa.com/Statistics.htm.

de Anda, D., & Becerra, R. M. (2000). An Overview of "Violence: Diverse Populations and Communities." *Journal of Multicultural Social Work, 8,* 1–14.

Bent-Goodley, T. (2001). Eradicating domestic violence in the African-American community: A literature review, analysis, and action agenda. *Trauma, Violence, and Abuse,* 316–330.

Bent-Goodley, T. (2006). Domestic violence and the Black church. In R. Hampton & T. Gullotta (Eds.), *Interpersonal violence in the African-American community* (pp. 107–119). New York, NY: Springer.

Birns, B., Cascardi, M., & Meyer, S. L. (1994). Sex-role socialization: Developmental influences on wife abuse. *American Journal of Orthopsychiatry, 64*(1), 50–59.

Burke, A. C., & Clapp, J. D. (1997). Ideology and social work practice in substance abuse settings. *Social Work, 42*(6), 552–562.

Carr, P. G., & Mednick, M. T. (1988). *Sex role socialization and the development of achievement motivation in black preschool children.* Washington, DC: Academic Computing Services, Howard University.

Diamond, E. (1999). From the project on religion and urban culture. *Research Notes, 2*(5), 1–8. Indianapolis: The Polis Center Press at Indiana University/Purdue University.

Dove, N. (1998). *African mothers: Bearers of culture, makers of social change* (pp. 101–102). Albany: State University of New York Press.

Du Bois, W. E. B. (1903/1996). *The souls of black folk* (p. 5). New York, NY: Viking Penguin.

Ehrensaft, M. K., Cohen, P., Brown, J., Smailes, E., Chen, H., & Johnson, J. G. (2003). Intergenerational transmission of partner violence: A 20-year prospective study. *Journal of Consulting and Clinical Psychology, 71*(4), 741–753.

Franklin, C. W. (1985). The black male urban barbershop as a sex-role socialization setting. *Sex Roles, 12*(9/10), 965–979.

Garner, J., & Fagan, J. (1997). *Victims of domestic violence.* California: Sage.

Giddings, P. (1984). *When and where i enter.* New York, NY: Quill/William Morrow.

Hampton, R., Oliver, W., & Margarian, L. (2003). Domestic violence in the African American community: An analysis of social and structural factors. *Violence and Victims, 9,* 533–557.

Hemphill, A. F. (2008). *The Black female crisis & the politics of love in Black America.* Baltimore, MD: Publish America.

Henneburg, M. (2000). *Bureau of justice statistics: At a glance.* Washington: U.S. Department of Justice Statistics.

Hill, A. (2011). *Reimagining equality: Stories of gender, race and finding home.* Boston, MA: Beacon Press.

Hill, S. A. (2005). *Black intimacies:* a *gender perspective on families and relationships.* Oxford, UK: Alta Mira Press.

Hooks, B. (1981). *Ain't I a woman. Black Women and Feminism.* Boston, MA: South End, p. 665.

Hooks, B. (1992). Yearning: Race, gender, and cultural politics. *Hypatia, 7*(2), 177–187.

Hooks, B. (2000). *Feminism is for everybody: Passionate politics.* Cambridge: South End Press.

Hooks, B. (2004). *The will to change: Men, masculinity and love.* (pp. 65). New York, NY: Atria Books.

Jackson, S. F. (2003). *Batterer intervention programs: Where do we go from here?* Washington, DC: National Institutes of Justice.

Kusmer, K. L., & Trotter, J. W. (Eds.). (2009). *African American urban history since World War II.* Chicago, IL: University of Chicago Press.

Lee, R. K., Thompson, V. L., & Mechanic, M. B. (2002). Intimate partner violence and women of color: A call for innovations. *American Journal of Public Health, 92*(4), 530–534.

Martin, J., & Martin, E. (1985). *The helping tradition in the Black family and community.* Washington, DC: National Association of Social Workers.

Martinson, L. M. (2001). An analysis of racism and resources for African American female victims of domestic violence in Wisconsin. *Wisconsin Women's Law Journal, 16*, 259–285.

McPhatter, A. (1997). Cultural competence in child welfare: What is it? How do we achieve it? what happens without it? *Journal of Policy, Practice, and Program*, 255–276.

National Institutes of Justice. (2002). *Batterer intervention: Where do we go from here? Workshop notes* (pp. 1–15). Washington, DC: NIJ.

Neville, H. A., & Pugh, A. O. (1997). General and culture-specific factors influencing African American women's reporting patterns and perceived social support following sexual assault. An exploratory investigation. *Violence Against Women, 3*(4), 361–381.

Pattillo-McCoy, M. (1999). *Black picket fences. Privilege and Peril among the Black.* Chicago, IL: University of Chicago Press.

Rankin, L. (1998). The effect of interpersonal relatedness on partner abuse as mediated by hopelessness and depression in African American males. *Dissertation Abstracts International.* Ann Arbor, MI, USA: UMI No. 9840632.

Rankin, L., Saunders, D., & Williams, R. (2000). Mediators of attachment style, social support and sense of belonging in predicting woman abuse by African American men. *Journal of Interpersonal Violence, 15*(10), 1060–1080.

Rennison, C. M. & Welchans, S. (2000). *Intimate partner violence* (Bureau of Justice Statistics, IJC 178247). Washington, DC: U.S Department of Justice.

Simien, E. (2004). Gender differences toward black feminism among African Americans. *Political Science Quarterly, 119*(2), 315–338.

Smith, E. (2008). African American men and intimate partner violence. *Journal of African American Studies, 12*(2), 156–179.

Taubman, S. (1986). Beyond the bravado: Sex roles and the exploitive male. *Social Work, 31*(1), 12–18.

Tjaden, P., & Thoennes, N. (2000). *Full report of the prevalence, incidence, and consequences of violence against women.* Washington, DC: National Institute of Justice & The Center for Disease Control and Prevention.

Villemez, W. J. (1980). Race, class and neighborhood: Differences in the residential return on individual resources. *Social Forces, 59*(2), 414–430.

Walker, L. (1979). *Battered woman.* Denver, CO: Perennial.

Walker, L. E. (1991). Post-traumatic stress disorder in women: Diagnosis and treatment of battered woman syndrome. *Psychotherapy: Theory, Research, Practice, Training, 28*(1), 21.

Welsing, F. C. (1991). *The Isis papers: The keys to the colors.* Chicago, IL: Third World Press.

Winbush, R. A. (2001). *The warrior method: A parents' guide to rearing healthy black boys.* New York, NY: Amistad.

Wright, E., & Calhoun, T. C. (2001). From the common thug to the local businessman: An exploration into an urban African American barbershop. *Deviant Behavior: An Interdisciplinary Journal, 22*, 267–288.

CHAPTER 17

Substance Use Prevention in the Urban Environment

Anthony Estreet

The purpose of this chapter is to provide social work professionals with the knowledge and tools to effectively teach and discuss the topics of substance use prevention within the urban environment. Through gaining a more thorough understanding of substance use prevention, social workers can effectively make contributions that can help inform public health policy as well as develop new prevention programs and/or strengthen existing programs that specifically address the needs of the identified population, ultimately ensuring that services are available to all individuals who need them.

SUBSTANCE USE PREVENTION

Prevention program should address all forms of drug abuse, alone or in combination, including the underage use of legal drugs (e.g., tobacco or alcohol); the use of illegal drugs (e.g., marijuana or heroin); and the inappropriate use of legally obtained substances (e.g., inhalants), prescription medications, or over the counter drugs. (National Institute on Drug Abuse [NIDA], 2003a, p. 2)

The concept of substance abuse prevention has been around for many years and there are a wide variety of models and explanations used to support the continued need of prevention efforts. However, to thoroughly provide effective knowledge in this content area, one must start at the beginning with an understanding of the concept of prevention.

Substance use prevention is a concept that has traditionally been associated with the adolescent population. This is due largely in part to the notion that substance use disorders are often initiated during the adolescent development period, which is marked by periods of experimentation (drugs, alcohol, and other risky behaviors; NIDA, 2001). This prevention perspective aimed at young people is often inclusive of educating youth about the harmful effect of initiating use and ways to avoid and resist substance use. However, this approach to prevention is only one of the ways prevention can be conceptualized. Over the years, the notion of prevention has been expanded to include additional age-groups and strategies to complement the educational approach, in addition to culturally competent goals. To effectively understand prevention models and those programs aimed at prevention, the overall methods and goals must be taken into consideration.

MODELS OF SUBSTANCE USE PREVENTION

One particular model used to explain prevention efforts was proposed in the early 1990s by the Institute of Medicine (IOM)'s subcommittee for the prevention of mental disorders (Kumpfer & Baxley, 1997; Mrazek & Haggerty, 1994). This model is used as a targeted population approach at three defined levels: universal, selective, and targeted. Those prevention programs classified as universal are designed to provide large coverage to the general public or to entire populations that have not been identified based on individual risk (i.e., urban communities, athletes, high school students). In contrast, selective prevention programs target their efforts at those individuals who are identified as a higher risk group. The risk level can range from imminent to lifetime risk factors. These selective programs may focus on individuals who are involved in gangs or those who demonstrate academic problems (i.e., excessive truancy, poor academic performance, suspensions, and fighting), or those who reside in high-risk neighborhoods. The last level within this model consists of indicated prevention programs that are designed and targeted at individuals who have demonstrated signs of problem development. This could include youth who currently use or have experimented with tobacco, alcohol, and other drugs, and adults who engage in behaviors such as purchasing substances for minors, driving under the influence (DUI), or driving while intoxicated (DWI; NIDA, 1997).

As the field of prevention research continues to evolve, so does the conceptualization of prevention and the understanding of prevention models. The model proposed by the IOM has since been adapted by Weisz, Sandler, Durlak, and Anton (2005), which contributed an additional level of "health promotion/positive development" to the IOM three-level model and also clearly delineated between prevention and treatment efforts (Table 17.1). This adapted model is of particular importance because it highlights the continuum of interventions aimed at addressing substance use–related issues. The early stage of the continuum consists of prevention efforts that can be targeted based on individual, family, and community needs. However, if the prevention efforts are unsuccessful, then the next phase of intervention needs to be initiated, which consists of various treatment options discussed later. In addition to the prevention models previously discussed, another model (which may be more familiar) used to classify prevention programs is that proposed by Leavell and Clark during the 1940s, also known and commonly referred to

TABLE 17.1 Definitions of Prevention and Treatment

Prevention levels	Level 1	• Health promotion/positive development strategies target an entire population with the goal of enhancing strengths so as to reduce the risk of later problem outcomes and/or to increase prospects for positive development.
	Level 2	• Universal prevention strategies are approaches designed to address risk factors in entire populations of youth—for example, all youngsters in a classroom, all in a school, or all in multiple schools—without attempting to discern which youths are at elevated risk.
	Level 3	• Selective prevention strategies target groups of youth identified because they share a significant risk factor and mount interventions designed to counter that risk.
	Level 4	• Indicated prevention strategies are aimed at youth who have significant symptoms of a disorder, but do not currently meet diagnostic criteria for the disorder.
Treatment level	Level 5	• Treatment interventions generally target those who have high symptom levels or diagnosable disorders at the current time.

Source: Weisz et al., 2005, p. 632.

as the public health model (Goldston, 1987). This particular model is similar to the one proposed by the IOM in that it uses a three-level system: primary, secondary, and tertiary, which examines the goals of prevention programs, but it differs in the regard that it accounts for levels of drug use, which is an important factor to consider when discussing prevention efforts.

Within this model, programs that are aimed at individuals who are yet to try alcohol, tobacco, or other drugs or who have experimented minimally with a specific substance are classified as primary prevention programs. These programs would likely focus on continued abstinence among the identified population and are also informational in regard to the potential effects of initiating substance use. Secondary prevention programs should then be conceptualized as those programs designed and targeted at individuals who are more "advanced" in their drug use experimentation. These individuals may have tried a particular identified drug or multiple drugs in question without serious consequences and may not be candidates for formal treatment at this point. The goal of secondary prevention programs is to prevent the escalation of the identified substance use. This includes using more dangerous substances, developing additional ways to use, or using more of the identified substance(s) they are already experimenting with. The last level within the public health model differs in that the prevention efforts within this stage occur following the treatment of the substance use disorder (commonly referred to as recovery). Tertiary prevention programs, such as relapse prevention, aim to prevent the recurrence of the substance use and to assist with restoring optimal health status and a high level of wellness.

All of the identified prevention models discussed earlier have been tested within the field of substance use prevention and treatment. These models have been the basis for developing and evaluating existing prevention programs that have been implemented across various age groups and identified populations. Now that we have an understanding of the three different prevention models, we will explore substance use prevention frameworks and their effectiveness at a variety of levels.

SUBSTANCE ABUSE PREVENTION FRAMEWORKS

On their initial inception within the substance abuse arena, prevention programs have primarily been targeted at the child and adolescent population, and were largely based on anecdotal and subjective evidence and lacked theoretical foundations. However, this has changed vastly over time and has resulted in the ongoing development and refinement of theoretical frameworks that can be used to explain the rationale and goals of the prevention program. These prevention efforts have very early roots and can be traced back to the 1960s, a time when substance use by young people was on the rise. This rise prompted a response in drug prevention efforts that increased the amount of information about the use of drugs and the harmful effects of such use. This increase in information was a direct result of societal influences and the existing antidrug programs during that period, which were already provided to the adolescent population within the school system. Many of the major prevention approaches used over the past few decades are summarized in Table 17.2.

One of the theoretical frameworks more frequently used to develop prevention programs in this arena is the social influence model. This particular model was developed in the mid-1970s and was originally used for smoking prevention. Since then, the model has been adopted within the substance use prevention field and was a major component of school-based prevention efforts during the 1990s (Abadinsky, 2013). The social influence model consists of three major components that contribute to the overall effectiveness. The first component consists of psychological inoculation, which operates under the hypothesis that, through slow incremental exposure to positive drug social influences, individuals exposed to the model will develop a tolerance and resistance to more powerful drug messages (typically in high school) as they progress through the adolescent development period.

Another major component of the social influence model is that of normative education. Research has demonstrated that adolescents typically overestimate the prevalence of drug and alcohol use among their peer group and adults. As a result, this perception leads to an inaccurate assumption that the majority of adolescent and adults use drugs and alcohol. The social influence model is designed to correct this misinformation and to provide adolescents with accurate information through a variety of methods. The final component consists of training on resistance skills. One of the main hypotheses within this model is that adolescents begin to use substances due to an increased lack of knowledge about how to resist or refuse substances, or the overall lack of confidence to resist peer pressure.

Through the use of this model, participants are then provided with skills to resist influences from peers and other influences (media, family, etc.). The resistance skill

TABLE 17.2 Overview of Major Preventive Approaches for Substance-Using Adolescents and Their Parents

INTERVENTION	FOCUS	METHODS
Traditional information dissemination	Increase knowledge of drugs and consequences of use to promote antidrug attitudes	Didactic instruction, discussion, audio/visual presentations, posters, etc.
Fear arousal	Dramatize the risks linked to tobacco, alcohol, and drug use	Dissemination of clear, unambiguous messages that drugs are dangerous
Moral appeals	Cast substance abuse prevention in moral or ethical frameworks	Lectures about the evils of smoking, drinking, and using drugs
Effective education	Increase self-esteem, responsibility, decision making, interpersonal growth, using little or no information; offer alternatives to drug use to reduce boredom and sense of alienation	Didactic instruction, discussion, experiential activities, and group problem-solving community services; and vocational training centers
Psychological resistance skills	Increase social influence awareness to smoking, drinking, or using drugs; develop resistance skills; increase substance users' knowledge of immediate negative consequences	Resistance skills training; behavioral rehearsal; extended practice homework; use of older peer leaders
Personal and social skills training	Increase decision making, personal behavior change, anxiety reduction, communication, social and assertive skills; application of generic skills to resist substance-use influences	Class discussion; cognitive-behavioral skills training (instruction, demonstration, practice, feedback, and reinforcement)

Source: Skiba, Monroe, and Wodarski (2004, p. 347).

training aspect of the model typically focuses on three types of resistance skills: increasing awareness of media influences, recognition of high-risk situations, and refusal skills. The overall effectiveness of this approach has been shown to reduce initiation to marijuana and alcohol use by 30% to 50%; however, booster sessions are needed or results deteriorate in 3 years (Botvin, 2000).

One such existing prevention program that utilizes the social influence model is the life skills training (LST) program. This school-based program, which promotes skill development (social resistance, self-management, and general social skills) and avoidance of substance use, is targeted for ages 13 to 17 years; however, there are adapted programs for students in both elementary and middle schools. Utilizing the IOM model of prevention, this program is categorized as a universal prevention approach, which aims at preventing alcohol, tobacco, and marijuana use and violence. As indicated in the social influence model, this program's effectiveness is achieved by targeting the major factors (social and psychological) that promote the initiation of substance use and other risky behaviors. Moreover, the LST program addresses multiple risk factors while also enhancing protective factors. The LST program promotes resilience among its participants through the development of necessary personal and social skills, which increases the participant's capacity to navigate developmental tasks. The LST program uses facilitated discussion, structured small group activities, and role-playing scenarios to stimulate participation and promote the acquisition of skills (Botvin & Griffin, 2004).

The LST program has undergone extensive research investigation over the past 20 years, which has consistently reported similar findings across the board. In a series of randomized, controlled studies (which include two large trials), results have continually demonstrated statistically significant reductions in smoking, alcohol use, and marijuana use of 50% or more in students receiving the LST program when compared with the control groups. Additionally, the LST program has been used effectively across multiple geographic locations, particularly urban populations as well as various racial–ethnic populations, which supports the notion of the utilization of culturally and age-appropriate prevention programs (Botvin, Griffin, Diaz, & Ifill-Williams, 2001).

PROMISING CULTURALLY SPECIFIC PREVENTION FRAMEWORK: AFROCENTRIC THEORY

The social work profession has continued to move in a direction that consistently recognizes the importance of cultural competence and sensitivity (Gilbert, Harvey, & Belgrave, 2009). Given this shift, the emergence of the Afrocentric theory as an emerging best practice framework for the development of prevention and intervention programs has been increasingly accepted within the profession. The Afrocentric theory "is a complementary, holistic perspective that emerged as a response to traditional theoretical approaches that failed to consider the worldviews of historically oppressed populations" (Gilbert et al., 2009, p. 243). The Afrocentric theory promotes the worldviews and existence of African Americans, which include their historical trauma and collective disenfranchisement as a result of slavery and racial disparities. As such, this theoretical framework utilizes a distinct set of guiding principles or values (Ma'at and *Nguzo Saba*), which are incorporated into the prevention or intervention program.

One value system often discussed within the Afrocentric theory is that of Ma'at, a culturally specific philosophy, which encourages the development of one's sense of self or spiritual essence (Parham, 2002). This value system, as expressed through the *Nguzo Saba* (seven principles: unity, self-determination, collective work and responsibility, cooperative economics, purpose, creativity, and faith), represents "the minimum set of values African Americans need to rescue and reconstruct their lives in their own image and interest and build and sustain an Afrocentric family, community and culture" (Karenga, 1996, p. 543). As a prevention framework, the values associated with the Afrocentric theory when incorporated into prevention programs have been found to promote behavioral changes within the population and additionally create changes through community empowerment and sense of purpose among African Americans (Harvey & Hill, 2004).

In a review of Afrocentric drug preventions and interventions, researchers indicated three major components of this promising prevention framework: (a) the incorporation of values, specifically communalism and spirituality, increases protective factors and resilience while decreasing risk factors; (b) to reduce societal pressures and increase positive sense of self and community, components should emphasize the current state of the African American community; and (c) the utilization of Afrocentric programming, such as projects and activities that highlight culturally relevant historical examples, is an important aspect to promote one's positive sense of self (Chipungu et al., 2000).

One such program that utilizes this approach is the *MAAT Afrocentric Adolescent and Family Rites of Passage Program*. This program was developed for African American adolescents aged 11.5 to 14.5 years and their families with the specific goals to "reduce the incidence and prevalence of substance abuse and antisocial attitudes and behaviors" (Harvey & Hill, 2004, p. 65). Rooted heavily in the Afrocentric principle of Ma'at, this strengths-based, family-centered program utilized after-school programming, family empowerment and enhancement activities, as well as individual and family counseling. Results of a multiyear study indicated that participants demonstrated significant increases in self-esteem and knowledge about substance abuse. Moreover, the study indicated increases in parenting skills, racial identity, cultural awareness, and community involvement. Although the latter findings were not statistically significant, they do provide a strong argument for further development and extensive research replication of the Afrocentric framework and the prevention approaches that utilize these critical components and values. Through consistent evaluative and replicable approaches, Afrocentric prevention programs can begin moving closer to meeting the criteria for evidence-based practices (Schiele, 2000).

SUBSTANCE USE PREVENTION MOVES TOWARD EVIDENCE-BASED PRACTICES

Given the lack of research support showing effectiveness of a non-evidence-based program, there was a shift in the mid-1990s largely due to public criticism regarding the ineffectiveness of existing prevention programming in addition to changes in the governmental funding structure (Petrosino, Turpin-Petrosino, & Finckenauer, 2000). As a result, the substance use prevention field increased emphasis on theoretically sound empirically based prevention approaches that resulted in significant increases in transferability across programs. Since the adoption of evidence-based practices, the substance abuse prevention field has become a more unified theoretically based discipline (Sloboda et al., 2009). Given this shift toward evidence-based prevention programs (EBPs), the NIDA (2003b) has outlined the following prevention principles (Table 17.3), which should be taken into consideration when discussing, planning, and implementing community-based drug abuse prevention programs within an urban environment. As indicated by the NIDA, these principles offer a rigorous structure, which can be used to evaluate and reevaluate programs aimed at prevention efforts among urban African American youth.

TABLE 17.3 National Institute on Drug Abuse: Preventing Drug Use Among Children and Adolescents

Principle 1—Prevention programs should enhance protective factors and reverse or reduce risk factors.

Principle 2—Prevention programs should address all forms of drug abuse, alone or in combination, including the underage use of legal drugs (e.g., tobacco or alcohol); the use of illegal drugs (e.g., marijuana or heroin); and the inappropriate use of legally obtained substances (e.g., inhalants), prescription medications, or over-the-counter drugs.

Principle 3—Prevention programs should address the type of drug abuse problem in the local community, target modifiable risk factors, and strengthen identified protective factors.

Principle 4—Prevention programs should be tailored to address risks specific to population or audience characteristics, such as age, gender, and ethnicity, to improve program effectiveness.

Principle 5—Family-based prevention programs should enhance family bonding and relationships and include parenting skills; practice in developing, discussing, and enforcing family policies on substance abuse; and training in drug education and information. Family bonding is the bedrock of the relationship between parents and children. Bonding can be strengthened through skills training on parent supportiveness of children, parent–child communication, and parental involvement.

Principle 6—Prevention programs can be designed to intervene as early as preschool to address risk factors for drug abuse, such as aggressive behavior, poor social skills, and academic difficulties.

Principle 7—Prevention programs for elementary school children should target improving academic and social-emotional learning to address risk factors for drug abuse, such as early aggression, academic failure, and school dropout. Education should focus on the following skills: self-control, emotional awareness, communication, social problem-solving, and academic support (especially in reading).

Principle 8—Prevention programs for middle or junior high and high school students should increase academic and social competence with the following skills: study habits and academic support, communication, peer relationships, self-efficacy and assertiveness, drug resistance skills, reinforcement of anti-drug attitudes, and strengthening of personal commitments against drug abuse.

Principle 9—Prevention programs aimed at general populations at key transition points, such as the transition to middle school, can produce beneficial effects even among high-risk families and children. Such interventions do not single out risk populations and, therefore, reduce labeling and promote bonding to school and community.

Principle 10—Community prevention programs that combine two or more effective programs, such as family-based and school-based programs, can be more effective than a single program alone.

Principle 11—Community prevention programs reaching populations in multiple settings—for example, schools, clubs, faith-based organizations, and the media—are most effective when they present consistent, community-wide messages in each setting

Principle 12—When communities adapt programs to match their needs, community norms, or differing cultural requirements, they should retain core elements of the original research-based intervention which include structure (how the program is organized and constructed); content (the information, skills, and strategies of the program); and delivery (how the program is adapted, implemented, and evaluated).

(continued)

TABLE 17.3 National Institute on Drug Abuse: Preventing Drug Use Among Children and Adolescents   (*continued*)

Principle 13—Prevention programs should be long term with repeated interventions (i.e., booster programs) to reinforce the original prevention goals. Research shows that the benefits from middle school prevention programs diminish without follow-up programs in high school.

Principle 14—Prevention programs should include teacher training on good classroom management practices, such as rewarding appropriate student behavior. Such techniques help to foster students' positive behavior, achievement, academic motivation, and school bonding.

Principle 15—Prevention programs are most effective when they employ interactive techniques, such as peer discussion groups and parent role-playing, that allow for active involvement in learning about drug abuse and reinforcing skills.

Principle 16—Research-based prevention programs can be cost-effective. Similar to earlier research, recent research shows that for each dollar invested in prevention, a savings of up to $10 in treatment for alcohol or other substance abuse can be seen.

One of the most recognizable yet controversial prevention programs that has felt the ongoing demand for evidence-based practice is the Drug Abuse Resistance Education (DARE) program. The DARE program's approach to prevention based on the social influence model utilized a curriculum, which was typically taught to adolescents during their fifth grade year and often incorporated elements of information dissemination, effective education, as well as social influence approaches to the prevention of substance use. This program's most notable component was that the information was being disseminated by a uniformed police officer. Despite the key elements within the program, DARE was highly criticized due to consistent research studies reporting only short-term effectiveness in the areas of substance-related knowledge, attitudes, and behaviors. Since its inception, DARE has undergone many changes and adaptations to the original model (Abadinsky, 2013).

The DARE program of today still begins when the youth enters the fifth grade. On program initiation, students are provided with opportunities to engage in decision making around high-risk, low-gain choices. Additionally, there is an increased focus on resisting peer pressure and other influences in the areas of substance use and other high-risk behaviors. Added to the curriculum in 2009, the DARE program has incorporated the *Keepin' it REAL* curriculum, which is an evidence-based multicultural program designed to help students assess the risks associated with substance abuse, enhance decision making and resistance strategies, improve antidrug normative beliefs and attitudes, and reduce substance use. This curriculum begins in the sixth grade, with booster sessions during grades 7, 8, and 12 (Substance Abuse and Mental Health Services Administration [SAMHSA], 2006). Currently, the research regarding the DARE program is unclear about the lasting effects of the prevention approach; however, this program has withstood the test of time and is continually evolving in its efforts to prevent the incidence and prevalence of drug use among adolescents.

PREVENTION PROGRAMS THAT WORK

Substance abuse prevention within the urban environment is an important area for social workers to focus on. The adage "an ounce of prevention is worth a pound of cure" is relevant given that the development of substance use disorders is preventable. The more that we know about prevention, the more we can advocate for additional funding for effective programs, which leads to a greater effect on the clients we serve overall. As such, this section reviews existing substance abuse prevention programs that are promoted as evidence-based programs. Table 17.4 provides a brief overview of selected programs and their target populations. These programs can be found on the *National Registry for Evidenced Based Programs and Practices.*

TABLE 17.4 Evidence-Based Practice Programming

PROGRAM NAME (IOM LEVEL OF PREVENTION)	AGES (Y)	SETTING	FOCUS OF INTERVENTION
Brief strategic family therapy (indicated)	6–12 13–17	Home or outpatient	The program seeks to prevent, reduce, and/or treat adolescent behavior problems such as drug use; improve prosocial behaviors such as school attendance and performance; and improve family functioning, including effective parental leadership and management.
Strengthening families program (all 3 levels)	6–12 13–17 18–55	Home or school	The program seeks to help drug-abusing parents improve their parenting skills and reduce their children's risk for subsequent problems.
Project ALERT (universal and selective)	13–17	School	Program that focuses on alcohol, tobacco, and marijuana use. It seeks to prevent adolescent nonusers from experimenting with these drugs, and to prevent youths who are already experimenting from becoming more regular users or abusers.
SPORT prevention plus wellness (universal)	13–17	School/ community	A motivational intervention designed for use by all adolescents, integrates substance abuse prevention with health promotion to help adolescents minimize and avoid substance use while increasing physical activity and other health-enhancing habits, including eating well and getting adequate sleep.
Project SUCCESS (all 3 levels)	12–18	School/ community	To prevent and reduce substance use among students of 12 to 18 years of age. Strong focus on students attending alternative high schools.

IOM, Institute of Medicine.

PREVENTION PROGRAM HIGHLIGHT

Hip-Hop 2 Prevent Substance Abuse and HIV (*H2P*; Turner-Musa, Rhodes, Harper, & Quinton, 2008) is a unique technology-driven evidence-based program, which incorporates the hip-hop culture into substance use and risky sexual behavior prevention messages. This prevention program uses the cultural competence perspective, risk and protective framework, social development theory, and social learning theory and strategies to promote change around attitudes and behaviors related to substance use and HIV risk. Additionally, this program curriculum is modeled after two existing evidence-based programs, which are Project SUCCESS and Becoming a Responsible Teen (BART). The H2P program is categorized as both *universal* and *selective* prevention approaches according to the IOM prevention model. The H2P program is a school-based prevention approach, which focuses on students aged 13 to 17 years. The H2P curriculum consists of 10 two-hour sessions, which focus on the development of self-efficacy, resistance, and conflict resolution skills. Additionally, students are challenged to clarify their own norms and beliefs about substance use and risky sexual behaviors (Table 17.5).

The H2P curriculum is broken up as follows: sessions 1 to 4 are completed after school and provided participants with education on drugs, HIV or AIDS, healthy alternatives, positive communication, and decision-making skills related to positive and negative characteristics of hip-hop. H2P sessions 5 to 10 emphasize on substance use prevention, positive lifestyle messages, resistance skills, and additional education on sexual behavior and occur during a 3.5-day-long camp, which consists of classroom-time and structured free-time activities.

Evaluative research conducted on the overall effectiveness of the H2P program found that students who participated in the intervention demonstrated a significant increase in the perception of risk associated with using marijuana. Additionally, posttest follow-up demonstrated that students who participated in the H2P program continued to have negative beliefs toward drug and alcohol use. Most of these beliefs diminished at 6-month follow-up with the exception of negative beliefs toward marijuana (Turner-Musa et al., 2008).

TABLE 17.5 Hip-Hop to Prevent Substance Use and HIV Logic Model

H2P COMPONENTS	PROXIMAL OUTCOMES	DISTAL OUTCOMES
10-session Substance Abuse/ HIV prevention program • Provide general knowledge about healthful practice and harmful effects of alcohol and other drugs via hip-hop • Improve substance abuse resistance skills • Improve accuracy in peer norms in substance abuse	• Improve knowledge and self-efficacy skills • Norms clarification • Accurate perception of risk associated with substance abuse and inappropriate sexual behaviors • Negative attitudes toward substance abuse and risky sex	• Decrease in substance use and HIV risk behaviors

Given the cultural appropriateness of this intervention, it could be a beneficial tool to incorporate into existing prevention programs or a stand-alone program within urban environments. Research has demonstrated that "among African American urban youth, popular music, such as hip-hop, has been shown to play a significant role in decision-making and behavioral choices. Hip-hop is a form of expression that, for many youth, is a way of life. It is a complex system of values and ideas that include music, song, poetry, film, and fashion. At its best, hip-hop is a "voice for the voiceless" and relates messages that reflect real-life experiences for those growing up in impoverished or underpowered environments" (Turner-Musa et al., 2008, p. 353).

Substance use prevention as a field is one that is ripe with opportunities for creativity and to affect the lives of the many populations served by the social work profession. As previously indicated, there are a variety of prevention models, frameworks, and practices, which can be utilized to effect change within the urban community. Given the fact that the evidence-based practices represent the gold standard for interventions among researchers and practitioners, it is important to consider which prevention approach would be best suited for the goals of the individual, family, school, or community.

When discussing prevention efforts in regard to substance use among various populations, social workers should be at the forefront of the conversation given the unique person-in-environment perspective, which focuses on empowerment and strength-based approaches. Social workers within the urban environment often encounter complex interwoven issues. These complex issues, such as substance use and other high-risk behaviors, provide unique opportunities to use effective prevention strategies. Through the careful selection and implementation, social workers can address prevention and other related issues at various levels (individual, family, and community). Additionally, given the comprehensive systems that often operate within the urban environment, social workers can involve multiple stakeholders through the development of cooperative relationships. Research has demonstrated that the most successful prevention programs are comprehensive in terms of curriculum and often address multiple issues (Botvin, 2000).

IMPLICATIONS FOR SOCIAL WORK

Given the wide variety of service settings and clients who are encountered by social workers, there is an inherent duty to contribute to a larger arena of substance use disorder prevention at all three levels of social work (micro, mezzo, and macro). Within the micro level, social work professionals interact with clients at various stages of development from early infancy through older adulthood. Given these opportunities, social work professionals can engage in early screening and prevention efforts, which would assist in early detection or delay the onset of a substance use problem. As discussed in this chapter, a large majority of prevention efforts are targeted at school-age youth. This provides a unique opportunity for social workers to work with the highlighted programs from the chapter or to adopt any number of EBPs to assist with decreasing the overall incidence of substance use among youth. Furthermore, there is an existing opportunity across the life span to implement prevention efforts. Within the older population, there has been an increase in the misuse of prescription medications. Social workers who practice with this population could adapt and use a targeted approach to address this increase.

Although the micro aspects of social work contribute to direct client contact within the context of prevention efforts, the mezzo level of social work practice can provide similar effects but from a larger agency perspective. For example, social work agencies can adopt prevention practices and implement them across the board, which would provide a greater effect than the micro approach. Social work agencies could provide training and technical assistance to entire school districts to adopt and implement additional evidence-based substance use disorder prevention programs. As demonstrated in this chapter, an example of this was the DARE program. Initially implemented in a California school district, DARE and other similar programs have been adopted and integrated into many school district curriculums nationwide. Moreover, large-scale implementations of prevention programs additionally help the larger communities where the programs are being used.

The macro-aspect of social work practice as it relates to substance use prevention is the ongoing opportunity for social workers to engage in the policy and funding decision-making process. Research has demonstrated that despite the fact that substance use disorders are completely preventable, less than 3% of funding efforts go toward the combination of prevention, treatment, and research, which is minimal when compared with other problematic health behaviors. Social workers have a duty to increase advocacy and lobbying efforts to increase the awareness and the practicality of utilizing and increasing substance use prevention efforts. From a policy and funding position, one could assert that prevention costs are far lower than treatment and intervention cost overall. Increased efforts in the area of policy and funding regarding substance use prevention would have a significant impact on society by possibly decreasing the need for increased and complex treatment options, which often are incurred as a result of the development of a substance use disorder.

FOR FURTHER STUDY

Suggested Assignments

Chapter Objectives

1. Describe the various levels of prevention and the goals for each identified level.

2. Describe the historical shift in substance abuse prevention from unstructured approaches to more evidence-based practices.

3. Give examples of prevention programs that can be utilized at various levels.

4. Identify effective EBPs that have been utilized in the field and supported by the SAMHSA.

Review Questions

1. What are the three levels of prevention as identified by the IOM prevention model? Explain the goals of each identified level.

2. Examining the prevention model proposed by Weisz et al. (2005), what are some of the advantages of this approach? Why?

3. How does the IOM model of prevention differ from the Public Health model of prevention?

4. Compare and contrast three major preventive approaches.

5. Discuss the importance of the Afrocentric theory in relationship to culturally appropriate prevention programs.

6. Select one of the identified EBPs and evaluate it using the 16 principles identified by the NIDA.

7. Discuss the pros and cons of the DARE program and what did research indicate about the overall effectiveness? How did the DARE program respond?

Additional Assignments

1. Conduct an assessment of ongoing prevention programs within an identified school or community. Select one of the prevention approaches and critique it using the 16 NIDA principles for effective EBPs. How does it compare? What suggestions would you make to increase the overall effectiveness and enhance service delivery?

2. Evaluate an identified community or school and conduct a need assessment in regard to substance use prevention. Using the gathered information, visit SAMHSA's *National Registry of Evidence-based Programs and Practices* and select two programs that best fit the needs of the identified community or school. Develop a mock proposal and implementation strategy for the identified prevention programs.

Suggested Readings

Agabio, R., Trincas, G., Floris, F., Mura, G., Sancassiani, F., & Angermeyer, M. C. (2015). A systematic review of school-based alcohol and other drug prevention programs. *Clinical Practice and Epidemiology in Mental Health: CP & EMH, 11*(Suppl. 1 M6), 102–112.

Capuzzi, D., & Gross, D. R. (2014). *Youth at risk: A prevention resource for counselors, teachers, and parents.* New York, NY: John Wiley & Sons.

Cronce, J. M., & Larimer, M. E. (2011). Individual-focused approaches to the prevention of college student drinking. *Alcohol Research & Health: The Journal of the National Institute on Alcohol Abuse and Alcoholism, 34*(2), 210–221.

Harvey, A. R. & Hill, R. B. (2004) Africentric youth and family rites of passage program: promoting resilience among at-risk African American youths. *Journal of Social Work, 49*(1), 65–74.

Hawkins, J. D., & Catalano, R. F., Jr. (1992). *Communities that care: Action for drug abuse prevention*. San Francisco, CA: Jossey-Bass.

Hawkins, J. D., Oesterle, S., Brown, E. C., Monahan, K. C., Abbott, R. D., Arthur, M. W., & Catalano, R. F. (2012). Sustained decreases in risk exposure and youth problem behaviors after installation of the Communities That Care prevention system in a randomized trial. *Archives of Pediatrics & Adolescent Medicine, 166*(2), 141–148.

Hecht, M. L., Marsiglia, F. F., Elek, E., Wagstaff, D. A., Kulis, S., Dustman, P., & Miller-Day, M. (2003). Culturally grounded substance use prevention: An evaluation of the keepin' it R.E.A.L. curriculum. *Prevention Science: The Official Journal of the Society for Prevention Research, 4*(4), 233–248.

Miller-Day, M. A., Alberts, J., Hecht, M. L., Trost, M. R., & Krizek, R. L. (2014). *Adolescent relationships and drug use*. New York, NY: Psychology Press.

Monti, P. M., Colby, S. M., & O'Leary, T. A. (Eds.). (2012). *Adolescents, alcohol, and substance abuse: Reaching teens through brief interventions*. New York, NY: Guilford Press.

Resnicow, K., Soler, R., Braithwaite, R. L., Ahluwalia, J. S., & Butler, J. (2000). Cultural sensitivity in substance use prevention. *Journal of Community Psychology, 28*(3), 271–290.

Ringwalt, C. L., Ennett, S., Vincus, A., Thorne, J., Rohrbach, L. A., & Simons-Rudolph, A. (2002). The prevalence of effective substance use prevention curricula in U.S. middle schools. *Prevention Science: The Official Journal of the Society for Prevention Research, 3*(4), 257–265.

REFERENCES

Abadinsky, H. (2013). *Drug use and abuse: A comprehensive introduction* (7th ed.). Belmont, CA: Wadsworth, Cengage Learning.

Botvin, G. B. (2000). Preventing drug abuse in schools: Social and competence enhancement approaches targeting individual-level etiologic factors. *Addictive Behaviors, 25*(6), 887–897.

Botvin, G. J., & Griffin, K. W. (2004). Life skills training: Empirical findings and future directions. *Journal of Primary Prevention, 25*(2), 211–232.

Botvin, G. J., Griffin, K. W., Diaz, T., & Ifill-Williams, M. (2001). Drug abuse prevention among minority adolescents: Posttest and one-year follow-up of a school-based preventive intervention. *Prevention Science: The Official Journal of the Society for Prevention Research, 2*(1), 1–13.

Chipungu, S. S., Herman, J., Sambrano, S., Nistler, M., Sale, E., & Springer, J. F. (2000). Prevention programming for African American youth: A review of strategies in CSAP's national cross-site evaluation of high-risk youth programs. *Journal of Black Psychology, 26,* 360–385.

Gilbert, D. J., Harvey, A. R., & Belgrave, F. Z. (2009). Advancing the Africentric paradigm shift discourse: Building toward evidence-based Africentric interventions in social work practice with African Americans. *Social Work, 54*(3), 243–252.

Goldston, S. E. (Ed.). (1987). *Concepts of primary prevention: A framework for program development*. Sacramento, CA: California Department of Mental Health.

Harvey, A. R., & Hill, R. B. (2004). Afrocentric youth and family rites of passage program: promoting resilience among at-risk African American youths. *Social Work, 49*(1), 65–74.

Karenga, M. (1996). The Nguzo Saba (the seven principles): Their meaning and message. In M. K. Asante & A. S. Abarry (Eds.), *African intellectual heritage: A book of sources* (pp. 543–554). Philadelphia, PA: Temple University Press.

Kumpfer, K. L., & Baxley, G. B. (1997). *Drug abuse prevention: What works?* Rockville, MD: National Institute on Drug Abuse.

Mrazek, P. J., & Haggerty, R. J. (Eds.). (1994). *Reducing risks for mental disorders: Frontiers for preventive intervention research*. Washington, DC: The National Academies Press.

National Institute on Drug Abuse. (1997). *Drug abuse prevention for at-risk groups.* Washington, DC: U.S. Department of Health and Human Services.

National Institute on Drug Abuse. (2001). *Lessons from prevention research.* Washington, DC: NIAAA.

National Institute on Drug Abuse. (2003a). *Drug addiction treatment methods.* Rockville, MD: NIDA.

National Institute on Drug Abuse. (2003b). *Preventing drug abuse among children and adolescents: A research based guide for parents, educators, and community leaders.* Washington, DC: U.S. Department of Health and Human Services.

Parham, T. A. (2002). *Counseling persons of African descent.* Thousand Oaks, CA: Sage Publications.

Petrosino, A., Turpin-Petrosino, C., & Finckenauer, J. O. (2000). Well-meaning programs can have harmful effects! Lessons from experiments of programs such as scared straight. *Crime & Delinquency, 46*(3), 354–379. doi: 10.1177/0011128700046003006

Schiele, J. H. (2000). *Human services and the Afro-centric paradigm.* Binghamton, NY: Haworth Press.

Skiba, D., Monroe, J., & Wodarski, J. S. (2004). Adolescent substance use: Reviewing the effectiveness of prevention strategies. *Social Work, 49*(3), 343–353.

Sloboda, Z., Stephens, R. C., Stephens, P. C., Grey, S. F., Teasdale, B., Hawthorne, R. D., . . . Marquette, J. F. (2009). The Adolescent Substance Abuse Prevention Study: A randomized field trial of a universal substance abuse prevention program. *Drug and Alcohol Dependence, 102*(1–3), 1–10.

Substance Abuse and Mental Health Services Administration, National Registry of Evidence-based Programs and Practices (NREPP). *Keepin' it REAL program* (2006). Retrieved August 29, 2014, from http://www.nrepp.samhsa.gov

Turner-Musa, J. O., Rhodes, W. A., Harper, P. T., & Quinton, S. L. (2008). Hip-hop to prevent substance use and HIV among African-American youth: A preliminary investigation. *Journal of Drug Education, 38*(4), 351–365.

Weisz, J. R., Sandler, I. N., Durlak, J. A., & Anton, B. S. (2005). Promoting and protecting youth mental health through evidence-based prevention and treatment. *The American Psychologist, 60*(6), 628–648.

CHAPTER 18

Substance Use Treatment Approaches in the Urban Environment

Anthony Estreet

This chapter reviews and discusses the current system of care for those with substance use disorders. Given that the social work profession spans across many different areas, this chapter starts with screening for possible substance use disorders and then moves into the treatment process. To better understand and address the needs of the identified individuals and their families, it is necessary to have a working knowledge about treatment options and how the system of care operates. During the course of this chapter, a description of multiple treatment approaches and theoretical frameworks are discussed in the context of addressing substance use disorders within the urban environment.

According to the Center for Substance Abuse Research (CSAR), less than 3% of federal and state substance abuse spending goes to prevention, treatment, or research (Miller & Hendrie, 2008). These critically low numbers are problematic given the fact that substance use disorders continue to remain at critical levels within the United States (Substance Abuse and Mental Health Services Administration [SAMHSA], 2011). Substance use treatment is a major issue that social workers can address through the use of a variety of prevention and intervention approaches (Wells, Kristman-Valente, Peavy, & Jackson, 2013). At the core of the issue is the ongoing problematic use of legal and illegal substances, which are often associated with significant negative outcomes (Centers for Disease Control and Prevention, 2010). According to the National Survey for Drug Use and Health, approximately 23 million people aged 12 years and older were found to have used illicit drugs within the month prior to the administration of the survey (SAMHSA, 2011). Moreover, an estimated 22 million individuals met the criteria for substance dependence or abuse in the past year (SAMHSA, 2011).

The issue of substance use disorders is of concern to social workers because the consequences of substance use disorders, while directly affecting individuals and society, have an additional negative effect on family functioning and frequently affects those vulnerable populations that are often served by the profession (Burke & Clapp, 1997). Social workers encounter a variety of individuals who meet criteria for either substance abuse or dependence in a large variety of settings such as HIV/AIDS treatment, nursing homes, domestic violence, and trauma centers, as well as work with immigrant populations (Bass, Linsk, & Mitchell, 2007; Cohen et al., 2009; Epelbaum, Trejo, Taylor, & Dekleva, 2010; Kane & Green, 2009; Thomas & Bennett, 2009). According to research, approximately 75% of social workers working in the United States encounter substance abusing clients either through referral or through the provision of substance abuse treatment (Rapp, Li, Siegal, & DeLiberty, 2003).

TREATMENT FOR SUBSTANCE USE DISORDERS

The following section describes important components of the substance use disorder treatment system of care. Understanding the treatment of care system is especially important for social workers working in the urban environment with individuals who may require substance use disorder treatment. Consequently, given the makeup of most urban environments (ease of access and availability of multiple legal and illegal substances), the potential for needing some level of substance abuse treatment increases exponentially when compared to that of suburban and rural environments (SAMHSA, 2009). This section reviews levels of care as well as effective treatment components to consider while evaluating potential treatment services for your clients.

Social workers who primarily work in the urban environment will, without a doubt, come in contact with a client that has used or is currently using alcohol or other drugs (Mason & Posner, 2009). Unless substance use disorder treatment is your specialization, a referral to another provider or agency would be the most appropriate response. Some of the questions that should be asked when considering referral options are:

- What level of care will my client need?
- How severe are the symptoms?
- What if they are reluctant to go to treatment?
- What type of treatment is utilized? Is it culturally appropriate or a good match?

These are all relevant questions, and rest assured that social work professionals are not the only ones faced with such challenging questions. Fortunately, researchers and practitioners who are not experts in the substance use disorder treatment field have access to an evidence-based practice approach, which can assist social workers in getting their clients to treatment in a way that respects "where they are" in the process and also utilizes the person-in-environment approach, which is the cornerstone approach of the social work profession (Burke & Clapp, 1997).

This evidence-based approach previously mentioned is a model known as screening, brief intervention, and referral to treatment (SBIRT), which has been developed and utilized among health care professionals to assist with getting clients to the appropriate intervention needed (Babor et al., 2007). The SBIRT model consists of three major components:

Screening—The social worker assesses their client for risky substance use behaviors using a selected standardized screening tool. These screening tools can be agency selected and can be as comprehensive as deemed necessary to cover the full spectrum of risky substance use to diagnosable substance use disorders.

Brief intervention—The social worker engages the client in a time limited nonjudgmental manner (usually one to two sessions) showing the results of the screener and discussing risky substance use behaviors. This is an opportunity for the social worker to provide advice, increase motivation to decrease or avoid substance use, or to teach substance avoidance and/or refusal skill, which could decrease the negative consequences often associated with continued use. It is important to note that this is not a lecture about their substance use but more so a show of concern about what is going on with their using behavior.

Referral to treatment—Based on the screening tool results, the social worker provides a referral for additional treatment (including brief treatment) for clients who are determined to be in need of additional services. Given the nature of substance use disorders, it may be best to make the referral call with the client and establish the appointment prior to them leaving your office. Once the social worker has successfully made the referral to treatment, it is important to follow-up with the client to ensure that they make their scheduled appointment.

As illustrated in Figure 18.1, the SBIRT model is an approach that provides the social worker with three possible outcomes following their use of a selected screening tool (Table 18.1). If the screening tool indicates no abnormal or problematic substance use, the social worker would not provide any intervention at this point, however could

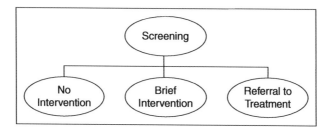

FIGURE 18.1 SBIRT decision-making model.

TABLE 18.1 Selected Substance Use Disorder Screening Tools

SCREENING TOOL	POPULATION	PURPOSE
Cut down, angry, guilty, eye opener-adapted to include drugs (CAGE-AID)	Adolescents and adults	The CAGE-AID modifies the CAGE questions for use in screening for drugs other than alcohol. Like the CAGE, the CAGE-AID focuses on lifetime use, although individuals who are drug dependent may screen positive, individuals who are at risk may not.
Adolescent Drug Involvement Scale (ADIS)	Adolescents	The ADIS is a 13-item self-report instrument designed to differentiate between heavier, more problematic drug users and users less involved in drug use and experiencing fewer problems related to their use.
Drug Abuse Screening Test (DAST)	Adolescents and adults	The DAST was designed to provide a brief instrument for clinical and nonclinical screening to detect drug abuse or dependence disorders. It is most useful in settings in which seeking treatment for drug use problems is not the patient's stated goal.
Alcohol Use Disorder Identification Test (AUDIT)	Adults	The AUDIT was developed to identify persons whose alcohol consumption has become hazardous or harmful to their health. The AUDIT takes less than 2 minutes to administer.
Alcohol, Smoking and Substance Involvement Screening Test (ASSIST)	Adults	The ASSIST is an 8-item questionnaire developed to detect psychoactive substance use and related problems among primary care patients. The ASSIST provides information about: the substances people have ever used in their lifetime; the substances they have used in the past 3 months; problems related to substance use; risk of current or future harm; level of dependence; and injecting drug use.
Car, Relax, Angry, Friends, Forget, Friends/Family, Trouble (CRAFFT)	Adolescents	This instrument is a brief test for screening alcohol and other drugs use in adolescents.
Substance Abuse Subtle Screening Inventory (SASSI)	Adolescents and adults	The SASSI is a brief self-report, easily administered psychological screening measure that is available in separate versions for adults and adolescents. The Adult SASSI-3 helps identify individuals who have a high probability of having a substance dependence disorder. The Adolescent SASSI-A2 is designed to identify individuals who have a high probability of having a substance use disorder, including both substance abuse and substance dependence. The SASSI includes both face valid and subtle items that have no apparent relationship to substance use. The subtle items are included to identify some individuals with alcohol and other drug problems who are unwilling or unable to acknowledge substance misuse or symptoms associated with it.
Michigan Alcohol Screening Tool (MAST)	Adolescents and adults	The MAST is one of the most widely used measures for assessing alcohol abuse. The measure is a 25-item questionnaire designed to provide a rapid and effective screening for lifetime alcohol-related problems and alcoholism. It is also useful in assessing the extent of lifetime alcohol-related consequences.

recommend ongoing screening with a primary care physician or at regular intervals while engaging with the social worker. If the screening tool indicates mild to moderate abnormal or problematic substance use, the social worker could utilize a brief intervention approach, which identifies and discusses results from the screening tool and possible short-term goals to change problem behaviors. If the screening tool indicates moderate to severe abnormal or problematic use, the social worker would then provide a brief intervention with the goal of encouraging the client to seek a more formalized treatment approach (referral to treatment). One of the most important aspects to consider when working with a client that has a history of use or is currently using substances is the potential for further harm (i.e., withdrawal symptoms, potential for overdose, harm to self or others [Driving while intoxicated-DWI/Driving Under the influence-DUI]). The use of the SBIRT model can assist social workers with getting their clients to the next phase of treatment intervention (Babor et al., 2007).

According to a multisite study conducted by Madras et al. (2009), which examined the SBIRT model and substance use at intake and 6-month follow-up, it was indicated that individuals who were exposed to the SBIRT model demonstrated significant decreases in substance use at 6-month follow-up. Moreover, Agerwala and McCance-Katz (2012) indicated that the SBIRT model is a flexible approach, which can be integrated and utilized in a variety of settings. Their article highlights successful integration of this approach in setting such as: hospital emergency settings, primary care centers, office- and clinic-based practices, and other community settings. Additionally, this approach can be used for specialized population such as children and adolescents (Babor et al., 2007). Research, which examines both the integration and the effectiveness of this model in decreasing substance use, is important given the ongoing and known consequences of continued substance use. Given the often fragmented system of care associated with substance use disorder treatment, social workers should use an integrated approach for the coordination of services to ensure that the identified client is able to access and benefit from all recommended services. An important element to consider during the referral to treatment and coordination of care phase is the process of treatment and the various levels of care (Abadinsky, 2013).

LEVELS OF SUBSTANCE USE DISORDER TREATMENT

When thinking about treatment options, it is best to use an approach that emphasizes the continuum of care model (which allows for increases and decreases in treatment based on progress or lack thereof) that is often available to most individuals needing substance use treatment (McNeece & DiNitto, 2011). Levels of care can be determined by a variety of methods and the most commonly used tool for this process is the American Society of Addiction Medicine, Patient Placement Criteria-2nd Revision (ASAM-PPC-2R; Stallvik & Nordahl, 2014). Each of the various levels of care as determined by the ASAM-PPC-2R (Tables 18.2 and 18.3) indicates the increasing levels of intensity

TABLE 18.2 American Society of Addiction Medicine—Patient Placement Criteria Assessment Dimensions

ASSESSMENT DIMENSIONS	ASSESSMENT AND TREATMENT PLANNING FOCUS
1. Acute intoxication and/or withdrawal potential	Assessment for intoxication and/or withdrawal management. Detoxification in a variety of levels of care and preparation for continued addiction services.
2. Biomedical conditions and complications	Assess and treat co-occurring physical health conditions or complications. Treatment provided within the level of care or through coordination of physical health services.
3. Emotional, behavioral or cognitive conditions and complications	Assess and treat co-occurring diagnostic or sub-diagnostic mental health conditions or complications. Treatment provided within the level of care or through coordination of mental health services.
4. Readiness to change	Assess stage of readiness to change. If not ready to commit to full recovery, engage into treatment using motivational enhancement strategies. If ready for recovery, consolidate and expand action for change.
5. Relapse, continued use or continued problem potential	Assess readiness for relapse prevention services and teach where appropriate. If still at early stages of change, focus on raising consciousness of consequences of continued use or problems with motivational strategies.
6. Recovery environment	Assess need for specific individualized family or significant other, housing, financial, vocational, educational, legal, transportation, child care services.

within the treatment continuum (Mee-Lee, Shulman, Fishman, Gastfriend, & Griffith, 2001). This can better help social workers understand their client's severity in terms of usage but also the intensity of care and what you can expect your clients to receive in terms of services. The ASAM-PPC-2R criterion is used as a standard language to assess severity of use and need for treatment (Fishman & Kaminer, 2013). This criterion utilizes six dimensions, which are rated from mild to severe based on the client's current level of functioning. Each of the dimensions of the ASAM-PPC-2R is used to evaluate and assess critical biopsychosocial aspects, which can then be used to inform the assessor and the treatment program of the immediate clinical needs and concerns (Stallvik & Nordahl, 2014). This is also a critical component, which can be (and often is) utilized to determine and authorized the requested level of care based on the managed care organization's (MCO's) authorization procedures.

Following the comprehensive assessment, placement at the appropriate level of care should take place based on the findings from the placement criteria. These levels of treatment options include: (a) detoxification, (b) inpatient, (c) residential, (d) partial hospitalization, (e) intensive outpatient, and (f) traditional outpatient.

TABLE 18.3 ASAM-PPC-2R Levels of Care

ASAM-PPC-2R LEVELS OF CARE	LEVEL	SAME LEVELS OF CARE FOR ADOLESCENTS EXCEPT LEVEL III.3
Early intervention	0.5	Assessment and education for at-risk individuals who do not meet diagnostic criteria for substance-related disorder
Outpatient services	i	Less than 9 hours of service per week (adults); less than 6 hours per week (adolescents) for recovery or motivational enhancement therapies/strategies
Intensive outpatient	ii.1	9 or more hours of service per week (adults); 6 or more hours per week (adolescents) to treat multidimensional instability
Partial hospitalization	ii.5	20 or more hours of service per week for multidimensional instability not requiring 24-hour care
Clinically managed low-intensity residential	iii.1	24-hour-structure with available trained personnel; at least 5 hours of clinical service per week
Clinically managed med-intensity residential	iii.3	24-hour care with trained counselors to stabilize multidimensional imminent danger. Less intense milieu and group treatment for those with cognitive or other impairments unable to use full active milieu or therapeutic community
Clinically managed high-intensity residential	iii.5	24-hour care with trained counselors to stabilize multidimensional imminent danger and prepare for outpatient treatment. Able to tolerate and useful active milieu or therapeutic community
Medically monitored intensive inpatient	iii.7	24-hour nursing care with physician availability for significant problems in Dimensions 1, 2, or 3. Sixteen hours per day counseling ability
Medically managed intensive inpatient	IV	24-hour nursing care and daily physician care for severe, unstable problems in dimensions 1, 2, or 3. Counseling available to engage patient in treatment.

ASAM-PPC-2R, the American Society of Addiction Medicine, Patient Placement Criteria-2nd Revision.

DETOXIFICATION PROGRAMS

The process of detoxification can vary depending on the individual and the type of substance that they have become dependent on. Detoxification programs are typically needed when a physiological dependence has developed as a result of ongoing use and withdrawal symptoms appear when the substance use is reduced or terminated. It is important to note that not all drugs will produce significantly distressful withdrawal symptoms and many clients will be able to "detox" on their own during their treatment process. Consequently, individuals who use substances such as alcohol, benzodiazepines, and opioids may require medical assistance for withdrawal symptoms and are most common for the use of detoxification programs. The level of care (hospital, inpatient, or outpatient) required for detoxification services will be dependent on factors evaluated during the comprehensive substance use assessment.

INPATIENT TREATMENT

Inpatient treatment programs are typically utilized for those individuals who require the highest level of care for substance use disorders. This level of care provides ongoing 24/7 supervision and intensive clinical and medical services. Individuals at this level of care are required to engage in treatment services that restrict their access to the outside world aside from scheduled family visitation and/or clinical sessions. Individuals that participate at this level of care are exposed to intensive treatment services, which are provided ongoing throughout the treatment day. These services are highly structured and often performed by clinical personnel. Previously, this level of care typically lasted from 28 days to up to 6 weeks depending on insurance coverage. Given the ongoing financial demands and criticism with this level of care, there has been a significant decrease in the amount of time covered by insurance companies, which can range anywhere from 3 to 28 days.

RESIDENTIAL TREATMENT

Residential treatment programs are aimed at providing services to individuals with higher severity substance use disorders. This level of care typically provides ongoing substance use disorder treatment services (6 months to a year or more) while also providing stable housing, which individuals utilize during their treatment duration. Residential programs consist of dwellings such as halfway houses, missions, and therapeutic communities. These programs are highly structured with policies and procedures as well as residential staff, which provide ongoing monitoring to assist with maintaining drug-free environments. Residential programs often utilize 12-step programs as part of the treatment approach and often have sanctions for individuals who are unable to remain abstinent.

PARTIAL HOSPITALIZATION TREATMENT

Partial hospitalization also known as day treatment is the highest level of outpatient treatment services. This level of care typically runs for 4 or more days per week for long periods of time each session (typically 6–8 hours). The partial hospitalization program is utilized by those individuals who may have recently been discharged from a higher level of care, are not able to function at lower levels of treatment due to severity of symptoms, or those who are awaiting a spot at residential or inpatient treatment. Individuals who are referred to this level of care often have ongoing co-occurring (substance use and mental health) disorders, which require much more intensive services. These services are often packaged together during the day and typically include substance use education, relapse prevention, communication skills, educational/vocational training services, independent living skill, hygiene, and so on.

INTENSIVE OUTPATIENT TREATMENT

Intensive outpatient programs (IOP) have increasingly become the treatment modality of choice by the individuals that utilize them and by managed care organization that provide reimbursement for related treatment services. IOP provide services to clients who often find it difficult to participate in inpatient treatment because of other obligations such as work, family, school, and so on. Individuals who participate in IOP are expected to attend treatment multiple sessions throughout the week for 2 to 3 hours each session. This level of care is typically prescribed for 10 to 12 week durations with the intention of stepping down to the next level of care, which is outpatient treatment.

TRADITIONAL OUTPATIENT TREATMENT

Outpatient treatment programs are nonresidential-type programs, which can occur in a variety of settings. Individuals at this level of care receive comprehensive assessments, treatment, and recovery services provided by a qualified treatment professional. Individuals who participate at this level of treatment receive ongoing regularly schedule sessions, which focus on a variety of aspects such as (substance use, family issues, education or vocation, legal issues, mental health, medical, and socialization). These regularly scheduled sessions are typically prescribed in accordance with the policies and regulations as defined by the agency and generally taper off as progress is achieved.

There are a wide variety of approaches (therapy, medication, nontraditional, etc.) that can be used to treat substance use and related disorders. Research has continuously demonstrated that individuals who engage in substance use disorder treatment have been found to have better outcomes than those who do not participate in treatment. According to the Pearson et al. (2012), the following is a National Institute of Drug Abuse (NIDA) list of components (Table 18.4) that are considered as principles of effective treatment.

Given the complex nature of substance use disorders within the urban environment, it is important that social workers are aware of the prevention and treatment resources within their area. Through the creation of community partnerships and the development of a trusting therapeutic relationship with your client, social workers can become the catalyst for change to assist individuals who are struggling with substance use disorders. It is important to note that in most cases, multiple treatment episodes are needed to sustain the continued progress of your client (McNeece & DiNitto, 2011).

TABLE 18.4 National Institute of Drug Abuse: Principles for Effective Treatment

1. *Addiction is a complex but treatable disease that affects brain function and behavior.* Drugs of abuse alter the brain's structure and function, resulting in changes that persist long after drug use has ceased.

2. *No single treatment is appropriate for everyone.* Treatment varies depending on the type of drug and the characteristics of the patients. Treatment matching is a critical component and should be based on an individual's particular problems and needs.

3. *Treatment needs to be readily available.* Because drug-addicted individuals may be uncertain about entering treatment, taking advantage of available services the moment people are ready for treatment is critical.

4. *Effective treatment attends to multiple needs of the individual, not just his or her drug abuse.* To be effective, treatment must address the individual's drug abuse and any associated medical, psychological, social, vocational, and legal problems.

5. *Remaining in treatment for an adequate period of time is critical.* The appropriate duration for an individual depends on the type and degree of the patient's problems and needs.

6. *Behavioral therapies—including individual, family, or group counseling—are the most commonly used forms of drug abuse treatment.* Behavioral therapies vary in their focus and involve addressing a numerous aspects of the client's treatment.

7. *Medications are an important element of treatment for many patients, especially when combined with counseling and other behavioral therapies.*

8. *An individual's treatment and services plan must be assessed continually and modified as necessary to ensure that it meets his or her changing needs.* A patient may require varying combinations of services and treatment components during the course of treatment and recovery. A continuing care approach provides the best results, with the treatment intensity varying according to a person's changing needs.

9. *Many drug-addicted individuals also have other mental disorders.* Because drug abuse and addiction often co-occur with other mental illnesses, patients presenting with one condition should be assessed for the other(s).

10. *Medically assisted detoxification is only the first stage of addiction treatment and by itself does little to change long-term drug abuse.* Patients should be encouraged to continue drug treatment following detoxification. Motivational enhancement and incentive strategies, begun at initial patient intake, can improve treatment engagement.

11. *Treatment does not need to be voluntary to be effective.* Sanctions or enticements from family, employment settings, and/or the criminal justice system can significantly increase treatment entry, retention rates, and the ultimate success of drug treatment interventions.

12. *Drug use during treatment must be monitored continuously, as lapses during treatment do occur.* Knowing their drug use is being monitored can be a powerful incentive for patients and can help them withstand urges to use drugs.

13. *Treatment programs should test patients for the presence of HIV/AIDS, hepatitis B and C, tuberculosis, and other infectious diseases as well as provide targeted risk-reduction counseling, linking patients to treatment if necessary.* Targeted counseling focused on reducing infectious disease risk can help patients further reduce or avoid substance-related and other high-risk behaviors.

EVIDENCE-BASED TREATMENT APPROACHES

On entering any treatment program, clients will be introduced to a variety or treatment approaches. These approaches can include but are not limited to medication-assisted treatment (MAT), 12-step model, as well as a wide array of psychosocial treatment approaches such as motivational enhancement therapy (MET) and cognitive behavioral therapy. This section of the chapter identifies and reviews selected treatment approaches that have shown positive outcomes in the addictions treatment field.

Medication-Assisted Treatment

When discussing MAT, many people initially think of commonly known medications such as methadone or antabuse. Both of these medications are still used in treatment approaches currently however, there have been many more added for the benefit of assisting clients with detoxification and/or continued treatment and recovery. On the basis of this approach, medication is used to target the pharmacological effects of the identified drug and even more recently have been able to reduce overall cravings (Boone et al., 2004). Currently, there are a few medications that can be utilized as a treatment approach depending on the identified drug of choice. For example, individuals that have been struggling with an opioid use disorder could benefit from medication such as methadone, buprenorphine, naloxone (Narcan), and naltrexone (oral or injectable). These selected medications fall into two categories: antagonist and agonist and can be used at various stages of treatment.

Opioid antagonists have been defined as medications that can be used to block or counteract the effects of opioids. The medications bind to the receptor sites and "occupy" the receptor therefore preventing the activation of the receptor site by opioids (Boone et al., 2004). This is best demonstrated with the medication naltrexone in either the oral or injectable form. Naltrexone can be used as an ongoing approach to opioid treatment when taken daily (oral) or monthly (injectable). Research has demonstrated that naltrexone has increased patients' adherence to abstinence and treatment at far greater rates than the typical treatment as usual approach (Maisel, Blodgett, Wilbourne, Humphreys, & Finney, 2013). In some instances (case of an overdose), the medication (naloxone) can be used to remove opioids from the receptor site therefore decreasing the effects of the overdose (Centers for Disease Control and Prevention [CDC], 2012; Doe-Simkins, Walley, Epstein, & Moyer, 2009). Both naloxone and naltrexone have been used as precursors for the use of the next form of MAT-opioid agonists.

Opioid agonists (methadone and buprenorphine [Suboxone, Subutex]) are synthetic medications that have a similar makeup to the identified drug (Boone et al., 2004). According to research (Roux et al., 2013), these substances produce analgesic and sedative effects similar in nature as other opioids such as heroin or prescription medications. These medications when used appropriately have been shown to decrease illicit substance use and increase retention and adherence among participants (Hser et al., 2014). Additionally, these medications have an added benefit of decreasing the psychological dependence, which is often associated with continued use and one of the main identified factors for continued use (Hser et al., 2014). Used as a treatment approach, individuals are prescribed a specified dosage of the medication and consistently monitored for adverse effects. Once the ideal dose has been identified that allows the person to function to the best of their ability, they are said to be on a maintenance dose. This approach to treatment is often used in conjunction with ongoing clinical or behavioral therapy to increase the overall effectiveness (Boone et al., 2004).

Additional forms of MAT include nicotine replacement therapy (NRT) such as nicotine gum, transdermal patch, inhaler, nasal spray, and medications such as Zyban (bupropion) and Chantix (verenacline). These NRTs have been shown effective in reducing the overall withdrawal symptom-related smoking cessation (Etter & Stapleton, 2006). Additionally, there have been medications used for alcohol use disorders. These medications are acamprosate calcium (Campral), antagonist medications such as naltrexone (oral or injectable; Revia, Depade, Vivitrol), as well as a version-based medication disulfiram (Antabuse), which have been evaluated by the Food and Drug Administration (FDA) and have demonstrated effectiveness for addressing alcohol dependence (Weiss & Kueppenbender, 2006). As previously mentioned, while MAT can be used as a standalone treatment, it is best if combined with ongoing clinical treatment. Research has demonstrated that the use of MAT improves treatment outcomes such as increased retention rates, decreased substance use, decreased hepatitis and HIV infections, decreased criminal behaviors and involvement, increased employment, and improved birth outcomes for patients (Boone et al., 2004; Hser et al., 2014).

Psychosocial Treatment Approaches

Psychosocial treatment approaches are the ongoing basis for substance use disorder treatment (Mason & Posner, 2009; Waldron & Turner, 2008; Wells et al., 2013). Under this approach, various treatment approaches can be used and combined in a variety of treatment setting and modalities such as individual, group, or family sessions. These particular approaches are selected by the treatment provider and/or program and implemented as a means to assist the client with decreasing the amount of psychosocial dysfunction that they may be experiencing as a result of the substance use (Schaeffer, Saldana, Rowland, Henggeler, & Swenson, 2008; Wells et al., 2013). There are many psychosocial approaches that can be utilized in treatment. As such, this section focuses on some of the more established evidence-based practices that have shown effective treatment outcomes among a variety of populations and are also classified as relatively brief interventions. According to research conducted by (D'Onofrio & Degutis, 2004), the following elements have been identified as necessary components of a majority of brief interventions, which have been shown to produce change in the substance using population:

- *Feedback*: Give feedback on the risks and negative consequences of substance use. Seek the client's reaction and listen.
- *Responsibility*: Emphasize that the individual is responsible for making his or her own decision about his/her drug use.
- *Advice*: Give straightforward advice on modifying drug use.
- *Menu of options*: Give menus of options to choose from, fostering the client's involvement in decision making.

- *Empathy*: Be empathic, respectful, and nonjudgmental.
- *Self-efficacy*: Express optimism that the individual can modify his or her substance use if they choose. Self-efficacy is one's ability to produce a desired result or effect.

Transtheoretical Model—Stages of Change

The transtheoretical model (TTM) of change is a behavioral change approach, which was originally developed for the promotion of smoking cessation and overall health behavioral change and has more recently been applied to change behaviors within the substance use disorder population (DiClemente, Nidecker, & Bellack, 2008). The TTM is an integrated approach that allows clients to assess and establish their level of commitment to the change process or current stage of change. This is an integrated approach, which incorporates a variety of constructs from other theories. Central to this approach is the process by which individuals modify a problem behavior (i.e., substance use disorder) or acquire a positive behavior (abstinence). The TTM asserts that individuals progress intentionally through a change cycle based on informed decision making and can enter or exit the change process at various points within the stages of change (DiClemente, Schlundt, & Gemmell, 2004). Change is then facilitated through ongoing cognitive and behavioral processes that an individual is guided through during their treatment episode. These 10 processes are often associated with the model: (a) consciousness raising, (b) dramatic relief, (c) self-reevaluation (d) environmental reevaluation, (e) social liberation, (f) self-liberation, (g) helping relationships, (h) counterconditioning, (i) reinforcement management, and (j) stimulus control. As an important note, some of these processes work better at certain stages of changes.

Central to the TTM approach is the assumption that individuals who enter into the behavioral change event typically move through various stages of change (DiClemente, Schlundt, & Gemmell, 2004). In this approach, individuals progress through the following six stages: precontemplation, contemplation, preparation, action, maintenance, and termination. In substance use disorder treatment, the stage of termination is not often used given the fact that treatment and recovery from addiction is an ongoing and continuous process, which should consistently be worked on. With this in mind, maintenance is usually the final stage that is discussed within this model for substance use disorders. As a part of an ongoing treatment, clinicians will use a variety of intervention strategies to assist the client with progressing to their next stage with the goal of achieving and maintaining the identified change in behavior. The following is a brief description of the six stages of change:

1. *Precontemplation*—In this stage, people are often unaware that a problem exists or is having negative consequences. Some people in this stage may not initially see the benefits of engaging in any behavioral change efforts.

2. *Contemplation*—In this stage, people recognize that a problem may exist and are willing to consider the pros and cons of changing their behavior. Overall

ambiguity could still exist at this point however more consideration is given to the problem than in the previous stage.

3. *Preparation*—In this stage, people are preparing to begin their behavior change. They are establishing small goals of commitment and have a strong belief that their behavioral change will be positive and lead to healthier life.

4. *Action*—In this stage, behavioral change cycle has begun and plans have been made to continue progression.

5. *Maintenance*—In this stage, the initial behavioral change has been continuous and sustained for at least 6 months. The goal is for continuous sustainment indefinitely (substance use disorder treatment). Relapse prevention is a key component in this stage.

6. *Termination*—In this stage, people are certain that their behavioral change is permanent. Concerns for relapse have diminished and there is no desire to revert back to old behaviors. As previously mentioned, this stage is typically not used with substance use disorder treatment.

MOTIVATIONAL ENHANCEMENT THERAPY

According to Crits-Christoph et al. (2009), MET is a psychosocial counseling approach that seeks to evoke from clients their own motivation for change. Central to this approach is the resolution of ambivalence toward change (i.e., stopping drug use, or engaging in treatment). This approach is markedly different from a 12-step approach in which the change is much quicker, internally motivated, and does not rely on a stepwise approach to treatment or recovery (Miller, 1994).

Key to the MET approach is the time-limited approach, which typically consists of four carefully planned and individualized treatment sessions. The first session (week 1) consists of the clinician providing feedback in regards to the initial assessment. This is a key session where the clinician elicits motivation from the clients while also encouraging a self-evaluation of current substance using behaviors (Miller, 1994). During this session and subsequent sessions, the clinician often uses motivational interviewing (MI) techniques to increase internal motivations and development of a plan for change. This plan for change often includes identification of coping skills and relapse prevention for high-risk situations. Subsequent sessions (weeks 2, 6, and 12) in this approach focus on monitoring and reviewing progress, as well as encouraging continued progress or sustaining behavioral change. Treatment duration within this approach is about 90 days or 12 weeks.

The MET approach is consistent with social work principles in that it is a client-centered empowerment approach, which starts where the client is (Wells et al., 2013). This therapeutic approach has the basic assumption that the client is responsible for change and that the clinician's job is the creation of additional opportunities for the client to enhance their motivation and commitment to change. Through the use of the stage of change model within the MET approach, clinicians can address where a client currently is in the cycle of change and assist the person in moving through the stages toward successful sustained change. Rollnick and Miller (1995) identified five main principles, which will assist the client with progressing through the change process:

1. *Express empathy*—The clinician communicates respect for client. Takes on a supportive but knowledgeable consultant role.

2. *Develop discrepancy*—The clinician seeks to enhance and focus client on where he or she is and where he or she wants to be.

3. *Avoid argumentation*—The clinician is not judgmental and does not force diagnostic labels on the client. Use alternate techniques to elicit motivation.

4. *Roll with resistance*—The clinician does not meet resistance head on. Uses alternate means to "roll with" any negative momentum with the goal of shifting and increasing motivation.

5. *Support self-efficacy*—The clinician will support and encourage client's ability to meet change goals.

As previously mentioned, the MET approach is considered a brief treatment approach and as such, MET requires fewer clinical sessions when compared to other approaches. This is especially useful with clients that have history of treatment failure (dropout), managed care payment (reduced sessions), or nonformalized treatment approach (primary care setting). MET has been shown to be beneficial in a variety of treatment settings and diverse populations. Research on MET has demonstrated the approach's overall effectiveness (Crits-Christoph et al., 2009; Wells et al., 2013). More specifically, MET has been used successfully with alcohol- and cannabis-dependent clients (Walker, Roffman, Stephens, Wakana, & Berghuis, 2006), as well as combined with alternative approaches such as cognitive behavioral therapy (CBT), which has also demonstrated significant positive outcomes (Walker et al., 2011). Consequently, research related to the effectiveness of MET for use with other substances such as opioids have resulted in ambiguous findings. Overall, MET has been shown as an effective treatment approach and is currently registered as an evidence-based practice approach.

COGNITIVE BEHAVIORAL THERAPY

CBT is another brief intervention that is often used in substance use disorder treatment. One of the most appealing aspects about this treatment approach is the versatility that it provides to clinicians and treatment programs. CBT has a wide variety of uses for substance use treatment and can be applied to individual, group, and family settings (Abadinsky, 2013; Walters & Rotgers, 2011).

In its original inception for substance use disorder treatment, CBT was typically a method utilized to prevent relapse (McNeece & DiNitto, 2011). This approach has since evolved to include utilization with substance use prevention, treatment, recovery, and relapse prevention. CBT is an approach that provides clients with skills that can be used over time even when treatment is complete. Clients are able to identify and correct problematic thinking and behaviors through the use of a variety of skills, which can be used to address substance use issues as well as additional psychosocial issues often present with substance-related issues (Abadinsky, 2013; Walters & Rotgers, 2011).

One of the benefits of this particular approach is the fact that it is not one specific approach but rather a collection of techniques/skills utilized with the underlying theme that substance use disorders are learned behaviors and as such can be unlearned with the proper techniques (Abadinsky, 2013). Some of the techniques used include examining the pros and cons of continued drug use, craving awareness and management, functional analysis, as well as avoidance skills especially in regard to high-risk situations or dealing with drug-using family or peers (McHugh, Hearon, & Otto, 2010; Windsor, Jemal, & Alessi, 2014).

Some of the more well-known approaches that utilize CBT are MI, contingency management (CM) or motivational incentives, and relapse prevention (Lundahl, Kunz, Brownell, Tollefson, & Burke, 2010). As previously mentioned, when discussing MET, a client's motivation to participate in treatment and to commit to behavioral change is imperative to successful treatment outcomes. However, the use of MI as a CBT approach has demonstrated significant results in raising awareness and increasing motivation while also decreasing ambivalence toward change among the substance using population (Miller, 1994). MI can be utilized in both group and individual settings as well as in combination with other treatment approaches such as MET and MAT (Wells et al., 2013).

Another approach that can be classified as CBT is the use of CM, which is more recently known as motivational incentives. This approach has shown efficacy in countering some of the effects often associated with substance use. The main idea behind CM/motivational incentives is the reinforcement of positive treatment outcomes such as abstinence, treatment attendance, and/or participation. This approach has been supported by numerous treatment studies (Wells et al., 2013); however, the ongoing long-term sustainability by community treatment programs has not been investigated to a large degree and is often cited as a barrier to more utilization of this approach outside of research funding.

Relapse prevention (RP) has also been identified as a much needed skill or technique within the CBT approach (Miller, 1994). This particular skill teaches clients how to anticipate high-risk patterns of their substance use through a functional analysis approach. By assisting clients with proper planning and identification of high-risk situations, the client can then be better prepared through practice with the clinician to deal with these situations. RP has a large focus on developing coping skills, behavioral strategies to avoid triggers, building problem solving, and drug refusal skills in addition to challenging the client's previous beliefs about drug-using situations and the risks associated with them (McHugh, Hearon, & Otto, 2010).

As previously mentioned, CBT as a brief intervention for substance use disorder treatment, has demonstrated consistent and ongoing effectiveness across populations (Abadinsky, 2013). Research has also indicated that skills obtained through the CBT approaches remain following treatment (McHugh, Hearon, & Otto, 2010). Although CBT can be used as a stand-alone treatment, it can also be used in conjunction with other treatment approaches such as MAT and self-help groups.

AFROCENTRIC PARADIGM AS AN EMERGING TREATMENT APPROACH FOR AFRICAN AMERICANS

Research has indicated that African Americans have experienced the greatest consequences from engaging in illicit substance use when compared to their white counterparts (SAMHSA, 2011). Consequently, research has indicated that African Americans are also significantly less likely to seek out treatment for their substance use disorder and additionally believe that they are less likely to benefit from a formalized treatment approach when compared to their White counterparts (Jackson, Stephens, & Smith, 1997). One of the consistently stated barriers to initiation and engagement in substance use disorder treatment among African Americans is the lack of treatment, which specifically addresses sociocultural factors that are often experienced by this diverse population (Longshore, Grills, Annon, & Grady, 1998). As such, research and practitioners alike have been advocating for the development of more culturally diverse and sensitive treatment approaches (Hodge, Jackson, & Vaughn, 2012).

One emerging treatment approach that has been moderately tested in the research and the social work practice arena is that of the Afrocentric paradigm (Schiele, 1996). The Afrocentric approach, is a quality of thought and practice rooted in the cultural image and human interests of African people (Schiele, 1996). Some of the key elements of this approach are the strong emphasis of spirituality, harmony with nature, rites of passages, interconnectedness with previous generations, self-identity and dignity, and the overall respect for traditions (Jackson et al., 1997).

Longshore, Grills, Annon, and Grady (1998) developed an intervention called the Engagement Project (EP), which was based on Afrocentric principles and incorporated the stages of change approach. As a brief treatment intervention, the EP model "attempts to engage clients in a psychosocial process conducive to recovery from illicit drugs" (Longshore et al., 1998, p. 320). Through the use of a brief intervention approach, focused dyadic counseling, and MI skills, the EP model combines a strong culturally sensitive Afrocentric framework into each aspect of the intervention (intake process, a meal, video, and a 30-minute counseling session), which is guided by the *Nguzo Saba*. The end result of this approach is to make a successful referral for the participant to receive additional services. This approach is similar to the SBIRT model discussed in the beginning of the chapter. The EP model is unique in that it targets substance users who have never been in treatment and were possibly in the precontemplation or contemplation stages of change.

Additional support for the use of the Afrocentric approach with substance use disorders has demonstrated treatment approaches with both adolescent males (Kalonji, 2014; Liddle, Jackson-Gilfort, & Marvel, 2006) and women (Poitier, Niliwaambieni, & Rowe,

1997). Moreover, the Afrocentric approach for substance use disorders has been adapted to both inpatient residential and outpatient treatment (Jackson et al., 1997). Culturally appropriate treatment options for addressing substance use disorders is an important area for expansion in both program development and research. Given the dearth of information currently available in regard to treatment, program options, and research, which extensively evaluates the overall effectiveness of the program should be prime areas of focus, especially given the large number of minorities that are affected by continued substance use disorders.

IMPLICATIONS FOR SOCIAL WORK PRACTICE

According to the 2014 National Drug Control Strategy, President Barack Obama furthered a national approach, which moved away from the previous "war on drugs" model to a strategy that focuses on evidence-based public health and safety reforms. As such, the focus on this chapter is to encourage the use of evidence-based treatment approaches, which provide social workers with the ongoing opportunity to meet the goals of the proposed drug strategy, which include: (a) strengthening efforts to prevent drug use in our communities through education; (b) expand access to treatment for Americans struggling with addiction; (c) breaking the cycle of drug use, crime, delinquency, and incarceration; and (d) support Americans in recovery by lifting the stigma associated with those suffering or in recovery (Office of National Drug Control Policy, 2012).

According to Burke and Clapp (1997), "the social work profession has a unique role in preventing and treating alcohol and other drug (AOD) problems" (p. 552). Within the context of micropractice, social workers have the ability to implement and lead the adoption of the SBIRT model into a large variety of settings from school to older adult-assisted living settings. This provides the opportunity to engage in substance use screening across the life span and to intervene given the outcome of the screening. This model also prepares the micro-level practitioner to directly respond to the increasing need for early identification of substance use disorders. As demonstrated in this chapter, the substance use treatment arena can be complex in regard to access, navigation, and treatment approaches. Social workers are charged with ensuring that appropriate referrals are made on behalf of their clients. In this regard, the social worker must be an active collaborator within the substance use disorder treatment environment. The National Association of Social Workers' *Code of Ethics* charges each individual in the social work profession to ensure ongoing competency in identified practice areas. Given the high number of social workers that come into contact with clients that may use (experimentally or continuous) substances, it is imperative for social workers to become more familiar with the substance use disorder treatment system. Moreover, the National Drug Control Strategy speaks directly to one of the goals, which is paramount to the social work profession and code of ethics. Eliminating social injustices, by providing more education around substance use disorders, treatment, and recovery social work professional can assist and alleviate the existing stigma around individuals in treatment and recovery services. Given the unique, "person-in-environment" perspective used within the field, social work professionals have an increased opportunity to effect change within a large range of social work settings in which they encounter the substance abusing population (McNeece & DiNitto, 2005).

Within the context of mezzo practice, social work administrators should ensure that they are incorporating the SBIRT model into their existing agency screening and assessment process. Social work agencies provide a vast array of services, which include but are not limited to homelessness, domestic violence, trauma, poverty, foster care involvement, criminal justice involvement, and mental health issues. According to research, a large majority of clients experiencing these issues have some degree of substance use, which could interfere with their ongoing use of social work services. Social work administrators have the ability to ensure that each employee is competently trained to screen and make necessary referral when indicated. This approach could significantly increase access to treatment, which is directly consistent with the 2014 National Drug Control Strategy. Additionally, social work administrators can begin to increase their overall service prevention, which could include evidence-based practices specific to substance use disorders such as MAT. Social work professionals and administrators have an opportunity to advance the discussion around treatment approaches (including culturally based approaches) and how best to assist the substance-using population, which has been known to heavily access social work-related services.

From the macropractice perspective, social workers can increase awareness around the increased need for policies that support substance abuse treatment approach rather than punitive criminal justice approaches. As previously discussed, substance use disorders are in public health concerns, which require ongoing treatment. Consequently, federal funding is not at a level that is consistent with the current and ongoing need for effective substance use disorder treatment. Research has demonstrated ongoing needs for longer treatment stays and in most cases, client need multiple treatment episodes. Social workers are key to providing ongoing advocacy, research, and support around increasing access to those in need. Moreover, with the ongoing changes in health care, substance abuse treatment is of major concern and is at is greatest need for advocacy for parity. Social workers have an opportunity to use information from this chapter and other resources to develop and create social action within urban environments, which often have the greatest concentration of individuals with substance abuse issues.

FOR FURTHER STUDY

Suggested Assignments

1. Students should conduct a needs-based assessment at their agency to determine the current screening and assessment techniques used, percent of the population encountered exhibiting substance using behaviors, and how many referrals made to substance use treatment agencies. Students should then

evaluate the current techniques to determine appropriateness for screening of substance use disorders. They should make recommendations as needed to address their findings.

2. Students should identify a substance use treatment center in their community. They should contact the treatment center to conduct an interview to determine the following information:

a. Type of treatment setting

b. Population served

c. Treatment approaches used

d. Do they offer specialized treatment, if so, what kind?

e. Duration of treatment at each level of care if applicable

f. Insurance accepted

g. Process for making a referral

Suggested Readings

Barbosa, C., Cowell, A. J., Dowd, W. N., Landwehr, J., & Bray, J. W. (2013). Cost to conduct screening, brief intervention, and referral to treatment (SBIRT) in healthcare settings. *Addiction Science & Clinical Practice, 8*(1), A7.

Bart, G. (2012). Maintenance medication for opiate addiction: The foundation of recovery. *Journal of Addictive Diseases, 31*(3), 207–225.

Hser, Y. I., Evans, E., Grella, C., Ling, W., & Anglin, D. (2015). Long-term course of opioid addiction. *Harvard Review of Psychiatry, 23*(2), 76–89.

Hser, Y. I., Evans, E., Huang, D., & Anglin, D. M. (2014). Relationship between drug treatment services, retention, and outcomes. *Psychiatric Services, 55*(7), 767–774.

Joe, G. W., Simpson, D. D., Dansereau, D. F., & Rowan-Szal, G. A. (2014). Relationships between counseling rapport and drug abuse treatment outcomes. *Psychiatric Services, 52*(9), 1223–1229.

Jones, H. E., Finnegan, L. P., & Kaltenbach, K. (2012). Methadone and buprenorphine for the management of opioid dependence in pregnancy. *Drugs, 72*(6), 747–757.

Maisel, N. C., Blodgett, J. C., Wilbourne, P. L., Humphreys, K., & Finney, J. W. (2013). Meta analysis of naltrexone and acamprosate for treating alcohol use disorders: When are these medications most helpful? *Addiction, 108*(2), 275–293.

McCormack, R. P., Gauthier, P., McClure, B., Moy, L., Hu, M., Pavlicova, M.,...Rotrosen, J. (2015). Do chief complaints allow targeting of SBIRT in the emergency department? *Drug & Alcohol Dependence, 146*, e201.

McLellan, A. T., Curtis, B. L., & Meitiner, H. (2014). Implementing screening and brief intervention in public schools: Feasibility and proof of concept. *Drug & Alcohol Dependence, 140*, e142.

Osborne, V., Benner, K., Snively, C., Vinson, D., & Horwitz, B. (2012). Teaching screening, brief intervention, and referral to treatment to social work students. *Addiction Science & Clinical Practice, 7*(1), A64.

Pitts, S., & Shrier, L. A. (2014). Substance abuse screening and brief intervention for adolescents in primary care. *Pediatric Annals, 43*(10), 412.

Satre, D. D., McCance-Katz, E. F., Moreno-John, G., Julian, K. A., O'Sullivan, P. S., & Satterfield, J. M. (2012). Using needs assessment to develop curricula for screening, brief intervention, and referral to treatment (SBIRT) in academic and community health settings. *Substance Abuse, 33*(3), 298–302.

Van Wormer, K., & Davis, D. (2012). *Addiction treatment.* New York, NY: Cengage Learning.

Vendetti, J., McRee, B., Hernandez, A., & Karuntzos, G. (2013). Screening, brief intervention, and referral to treatment (SBIRT) implementation models and work flow processes: Commonalities and variations. *Addiction Science & Clinical Practice, 8*(1), A79.

REFERENCES

Abadinsky, H. (2013). *Drug use and abuse: A comprehensive introduction* (7th ed.). Belmont, CA: Wadsworth, Cengage Learning.

Agerwala, S. M., & McCance-Katz, E. F. (2012). Integrating screening, brief intervention, and referral to treatment (SBIRT) into clinical practice settings: A brief review. *Journal of Psychoactive Drugs, 44*(4), 307–317.

Babor, T. F., McRee, B. G., Kassebaum, P. A., Grimaldi, P. L., Ahmed, K., & Bray, J. (2007). Screening, brief intervention, and referral to treatment (SBIRT): Toward a public health approach to the management of substance abuse. *Substance Abuse, 28*(3), 7–30.

Bass, M., Linsk, N. L., & Mitchell, C. (2007). Training substance abuse counselors about HIV medication adherence. *Journal of HIV/AIDS & Social Services, 6*(1–2), 139–159. doi:10.1300/J187v06n01_09

Boone, M., Brown, N. J., Moon, M. A., Schuman, D. J., Thomas, J., Wright, D. L., & American Institutes for Research, W. D. (2004). *Clinical guidelines for the use of buprenorphine in the treatment of opioid addiction.* Treatment improvement protocol (TIP) series, 40. Rockville, MD: Substance Abuse and Mental Health Services Administration.

Burke, A. C., & Clapp, J. D. (1997). Ideology and social work practice in substance abuse settings. *Social Work, 42*(6), 552–562.

Centers for Disease Control and Prevention. (2010). Youth risk behavior surveillance—United States, 2009. *Morbidity and Mortality Weekly Report, 59*, SS-5. Retrieved from http://www.cdc.gov/mmwr/pdf/ss/ss5905.pdf

Centers for Disease Control and Prevention. (2012). Community-based opioid overdose prevention programs providing naloxone—United States, 2010. *Morbidity and Mortality Weekly Report, 61*(6), 101.

Cohen, L. R., Tross, S., Pavlicova, M., Hu, M., Campbell, A. N., & Nunes, E. V. (2009). Substance use, childhood sexual abuse, and sexual risk behavior among women in methadone treatment. *The American Journal of Drug and Alcohol Abuse, 35*(5), 305–310. doi:10.1080/00952990903060127

Crits-Christoph, P., Gallop, R., Temes, C. M., Woody, G., Ball, S. A., Martino, S., & Carroll, K. M. (2009). The alliance in motivational enhancement therapy and counseling as usual for substance use problems. *Journal of Consulting and Clinical Psychology, 77*(6), 1125–1135.

DiClemente, C. C., Nidecker, M., & Bellack, A. S. (2008). Motivation and the stages of change among individuals with severe mental illness and substance abuse disorders. *Journal of Substance Abuse Treatment, 34*(1), 25–35. doi:10.1016/j.jsat.2006.12.034

DiClemente, C. C., Schlundt, D., & Gemmell, L. (2004). Readiness and stages of change in addiction treatment. *American Journal on Addictions, 13*(2), 103–119. doi:10.1080/10550490490435777

Doe-Simkins, M., Walley, A. Y., Epstein, A., & Moyer, P. (2009). Saved by the nose: Bystander-administered intranasal naloxone hydrochloride for opioid overdose. *American Journal of Public Health, 99*(5), 788–791. doi: 10.2105/AJPH.2008.146647

D'Onofrio, G., & Degutis, L. C. (2004). Screening and brief intervention in the emergency department. *Alcohol Research and Health, 28*(2), 63.

Epelbaum, C., Trejo, E., Taylor, E., & Dekleva, K. (2010). Immigration trauma, substance abuse, and suicide. *Harvard Review of Psychiatry, 18*(5), 304–313. doi:10.3109/10673229.2010.511061

Etter, J. F., & Stapleton, J. A. (2006). Nicotine replacement therapy for long-term smoking cessation: A meta-analysis. *Tobacco Control, 15*(4), 280–285.

Fishman, M., & Kaminer, Y. (2013). The case for placement criteria for adolescent substance use disorder. *Journal of Addiction Prevention, 1*(1), 1–4.

Hodge, D. R., Jackson, K. F., & Vaughn, M. G. (2012). Culturally sensitive interventions and substance use: A meta-analytic review of outcomes among minority youths. *Social Work Research, 36*(1), 11–19. doi:10.1093/swr/svs008

Hser, Y. I., Saxon, A. J., Huang, D., Hasson, A., Thomas, C., Hillhouse, M.,...Ling, W. (2014). Treatment retention among patients randomized to buprenorphine/naloxone compared to methadone in a multi-site trial. *Addiction, 109*(1), 79–87. doi:10.1111/add.12333

Jackson, M. S., Stephens, R. C., & Smith, R. L. (1997). Afrocentric treatment in residential substance abuse care: The Iwo San. *Journal of Substance Abuse Treatment, 14*(1), 87–92.

Kalonji, T. (2014). The Nguzo Saba & Maat, a path for self-reconstruction and recoveredness: Exploring a Kawaida paradigm for healing addiction in the Black community. *Journal of Pan African Studies, 7*(4), 195–210.

Kane, M. N., & Green, D. (2009). Substance abuse by elders and self-enhancement bias. *Educational Gerontology, 35*(2), 95–120. doi:10.1080/03601270802349494

Liddle, H. A., Jackson-Gilfort, A., & Marvel, F. A. (2006). An empirically supported and culturally specific engagement and intervention strategy for African American adolescent males. *American Journal of Orthopsychiatry, 76*(2), 215.

Longshore, D., Grills, C., Annon, K., & Grady, R. (1998). Promoting recovery from drug abuse: An Africentric intervention. *Journal of Black Studies, 28*, 319–333.

Lundahl, B. W., Kunz, C., Brownell, C., Tollefson, D., & Burke, B. L. (2010). A meta-analysis of motivational interviewing: Twenty-five years of empirical studies. *Research on Social Work Practice, 20*(2), 137–160.

Madras, B. K., Compton, W. M., Avula, D., Stegbauer, T., Stein, J. B., & Clark, H. W. (2009). Screening, brief interventions, referral to treatment (SBIRT) for illicit drug and alcohol use at multiple healthcare sites: Comparison at intake and six months. *Drug and Alcohol Dependence, 99*(1–3), 280–295. doi:10.1016/j.drugalcdep.2008.08.003

Maisel, N. C., Blodgett, J. C., Wilbourne, P. L., Humphreys, K., & Finney, J. W. (2013). Meta analysis of naltrexone and acamprosate for treating alcohol use disorders: When are these medications most helpful? *Addiction, 108*(2), 275–293.

Mason, M. J., & Posner, M. A. (2009). Brief substance abuse treatment with urban adolescents: A translational research study. *Journal of Child & Adolescent Substance Abuse, 18*, 193–206. doi:10.1080/10678280902724184

McHugh, R. K., Hearon, B. A., & Otto, M. W. (2010). Cognitive-behavioral therapy for substance use disorders. *The Psychiatric Clinics of North America, 33*(3), 511.

McNeece, C. A., & DiNitto, D. M. (2011). *Chemical dependency: A systems approach* (4th ed.). Boston, MA: Pearson Education/Allyn and Bacon.

Mee-Lee, D., Shulman, G. D., Fishman, M., Gastfriend, D. R., & Griffith, J. H. (Eds.). (2001). *ASAM patient placement criteria for the treatment of substance-related disorders, second edition-revised (ASAMPPC-2R)*. ChevyChase, MD: American Society of Addiction Medicine.

Miller, T., & Hendrie, D. (2008). *Substance abuse prevention dollars and cents: A cost-benefit analysis*. DHHS Pub. No. (SMA) 07–4298. Rockville, MD: Center for Substance Abuse Prevention, Substance Abuse and Mental Health Services Administration.

Miller, W. R. (1994). *Motivational enhancement therapy manual: A clinical research guide for therapists treating individuals with alcohol abuse and dependence* (Vol. 2). Rockville, MD: DIANE Publishing.

Pearson, F. S., Prendergast, M. L., Podus, D., Vazan, P., Greenwell, L., & Hamilton, Z. (2012). Meta-analyses of seven of NIDA's *Principles of drug addiction treatment. Journal of Substance Abuse Treatment, 43*(1), 1–11. doi:10.1016/j.jsat.2011.10.005

Poitier, V., Niliwaambieni, M., & Rowe, C. L. (1999). A rite of passage approach designed to preserve the families of substance-abusing African American women. *Child Welfare Perspectives: Serving African American children, LXXVI*(1), 169–191.

Rapp, R. C., Li, L., Siegal, H. A., & DeLiberty, R. N. (2003). Demographic and clinical correlates of client motivation among substance abusers. *Health & Social Work, 28*(2), 107–116.

Rollnick, S., & Miller, W. R. (1995). What is motivational interviewing?. *Behavioral and Cognitive Psychotherapy, 23*(04), 325–334.

Roux, P., Sullivan, M. A., Cohen, J., Fugon, L., Jones, J. D., Vosburg, S. K.,...Comer, S. D. (2013). Buprenorphine/naloxone as a promising therapeutic option for opioid abusing patients with chronic pain: Reduction of pain, opioid withdrawal symptoms, and abuse liability of oral oxycodone. *Pain, 154*(8), 1442–1448.

Schaeffer, C. M., Saldana, L., Rowland, M. D., Henggeler, S. W., & Swenson, C. C. (2008). New initiatives in improving youth and family outcomes by importing evidence-based practices. *Journal of Child & Adolescent Substance Abuse, 17*(3), 27–45.

Schiele, J. H. (1996). Afrocentricity: An emerging paradigm in social work practice. *Social Work, 41*(3), 284–294.

Stallvik, M., & Nordahl, H. M. (2014). Convergent validity of the ASAM criteria in co-occurring disorders. *Journal of Dual Diagnosis, 10*(2), 68–78. doi:10.1080/15504263.2014.906812

Substance Abuse and Mental Health Services Administration. (2011). *Results from the 2010 National Survey on Drug Use and Health: Summary of national findings*. NSDUH Series H-41, HHS Publication No. (SMA) 11–4658. Rockville, MD: Author.

Substance Abuse and Mental Health Services Administration, Office of Applied Studies. (2009). *National Survey of Substance Abuse Treatment Services (N-SSATS): 2008. Data on substance abuse treatment facilities*. DASIS Series: S-49, HHS Publication No. (SMA) 09–4451, Rockville, MD: Author.

Thomas, M. D., & Bennett, L. (2009). The co-occurrence of substance abuse and domestic violence: A comparison of dual-problem men in substance abuse treatment and in court-ordered batterer program. *Journal of Social Work Practice in the Addiction, 9*, 299–317. doi:10.1080/15332560903084457

Waldron, H. B., & Turner, C. W. (2008). Evidence-based psychosocial treatments for adolescent substance abuse. *Journal of Clinical Child & Adolescent Psychology, 37*(1), 238–261. doi:10.1080/15374410701820133

Walker, D. D., Roffman, R. A., Stephens, R. S., Wakana, K., & Berghuis, J. (2006). Motivational enhancement therapy for adolescent marijuana users: A preliminary randomized controlled trial. *Journal of Consulting and Clinical Psychology, 74*(3), 628. doi:10.1037/0022–006X.74.3.628

Walker, D. D., Stephens, R., Roffman, R., DeMarce, J., Lozano, B., Towe, S., & Berg, B. (2011). Randomized controlled trial of motivational enhancement therapy with nontreatment-seeking adolescent cannabis users: A further test of the teen marijuana check-up. *Psychology of Addictive Behaviors, 25*(3), 474. doi:10.1037/a0024076

Walters, S. T., & Rotgers, F. (Eds.). (2011). *Treating substance abuse: Theory and technique*. New York, NY: Guilford Press.

Weiss, R. D., & Kueppenbender, K. D. (2006). Combining psychosocial treatment with pharmacotherapy for alcohol dependence. *Journal of Clinical Psychopharmacology, 26*(6), S37–S42. doi:10.1097/01.jcp.0000248604.58305.b3

Wells, E. A., Kristman-Valente, A. N., Peavy, K. M., & Jackson, R. T. (2013). Social workers and delivery of evidence-based psychosocial treatment for substance use disorders. *Social Work and Public Health, 28,* 279–301. doi:10.1080/19371918.2013.759033

Windsor, L. C., Jemal, A., & Alessi, E. J. (2015). Cognitive behavioral therapy: A meta-analysis of race and substance use outcomes. *Cultural Diversity & Ethnic Minority Psychology, 21,* 300–313.

CHAPTER 19

Educating Social Workers in a Client-Centered Defense Practice

Lori James-Townes and Marquis Chandler

As society continues to struggle with the correct balance between the latest "tough on crime" laws and sentencing policies, social workers are utilized increasingly to assist defense attorneys in identifying services, treatment, causation, and offender culpability while offering alternatives to incarceration. These social workers are providing a specialized service. This type of specialized social work service originates from the broad practice of forensic social work. Over the past 80 years, the forensic field has evolved, which led to the growth of forensic social work in various practice settings. According to the National Association of Forensic Social Work:

> Forensic social workers provide services in the legal field. This specialty practice area can be found in both the criminal and civil courts. Forensic social workers may provide services in the juvenile and adult justice arenas. Criminal justice policy and legislative development would also encompass services provided by forensic social workers (National Organization of Forensic Social Work, 2014).

Social workers, researchers, and mental health professionals who practice in the criminal justice arena have become valuable contributors to populations of people struggling with oppression and the accompanying challenges of incarceration (Maschi & Killian, 2011). Interestingly, the practice of advocating for imprisoned individuals began as early as the 1700s, when two social workers (Howard and Fry) initiated visiting inmates in England's jails and prisons (Roberts & Springer, 2007). While Fry was more interested in lending aid and goods to prisoners, Howard was more concerned with improving the overall prison conditions (Siegal & Brandon, 2011). This marked the beginning of private social work intervention in prisons. Social workers, even during the 18th century, were aware that providing social work services to the prison population required a wide variety of services and interventions. This focused type of social work service became even more vital as the United States became the world leader in the practice of incarcerating her citizens (Maur, 1995).

TWO PROFESSIONS: SERVING THOSE DISPROPORTIONATELY IMPACTED BY OVER-INCARCERATION

According to the Bureau of Justice Statistics (Carson & Golinelli, 2014), Blacks and Latinos are imprisoned at much higher rates than Whites. The disparity in prison demographics shows that those residing in urban communities with larger minority populations face a greater risk of falling under the influence of the criminal justice system (Freudenberg, 2001). The same research by Freudenberg (2001) showed that those residing in urban environments are at an increased risk of developing mental health–related issues because of their increased likelihood of being exposed to violence, neglect, poor paternal involvement, and poverty. Traditional sentencing practices that fail to take these issues into consideration will most likely continue to yield high rates of incarceration and recidivism. However, data show that when we raise the court's competency in regard to individuals living under oppressive conditions, we will see a reduction in incarceration rates (Page & Whetstone, 2014). This implies that when the right information and suggestions are presented in court, judges are more likely to consider alternatives to incarceration such as drug treatment, therapy, restitution, community services, and so forth. Social workers are trained to provide this information and insight.

Providing appropriate treatment (mental health and substance abuse), job training, social support, and treatment plans to individuals within the criminal justice system (offenders, victims, or survivors) has been a focus and concern to the social work professional since its inception (Roberts & Springer, 2007). Despite the vast research in the area of forensic social work, it has only been recently that reports have begun to examine and discuss the need for and use of social workers in public defender offices in the United States. Social workers who work in public defender offices are working in a defense-based setting. Defense-based representation is a term adopted by public defenders as they embrace and exercise holistic representation. This is also known as "client centeredness or holistic representation" practice. As described by Clark and Savner (2010), client-centered defense offices seek to employ a multidisciplinary team, which includes a diverse group of attorneys, social workers, investigators, and other defense team members who "respect their clients' wishes and goals, and work together to ensure that the dignity of every client is honored." Public defenders who do not utilize this model are viewed as ineffective because they fail to employ social workers who are key components in the team (Clark & Savner, 2010).

Requiring the presence of social workers in public defender offices makes perfect sense. Why? First, because public defenders can (as stated in their mission) only represent the poor and disenfranchised, and this is the same clientele being serviced by social workers in other settings. Therefore, the shared mission to provide holistic representation shared by social workers and public defenders creates a working relationship that merges well to meet the needs of the indigent clients they represent. Second, there is a clear link between minorities living in poverty and the criminal justice system. Poor people and people of color are incarcerated at higher rates than their counterparts (Alexander, 2010). However, this phenomenon exists not because they are committing more crimes, but it is simply because they are more likely to be arrested, charged, and detained (Alexander, 2010). Finally, because public defender clients have to fall below the federal poverty line to be eligible for services, they come to court with a variety of issues, barriers, and inflictions that impede or contribute to their criminal and delinquent lifestyles. Social workers are hired to explain, mitigate, and/or remove those things that contribute to incarceration and re-offending. Judges in the criminal and juvenile courts, private attorneys, and sentencing professionals have recognized the unparalleled value that social workers bring to poor people's representation (Walker & Miller, 2013).

THE MARYLAND OFFICE OF THE PUBLIC DEFENDER: SERVING THE URBAN COMMUNITY

The state of Maryland has been committed to this population for over a century, which is evident by the establishment of *The Prisoners' Aid Association of Maryland*, which opened in 1896 (Roberts & Springer, 2007).[1] In keeping with this tradition of providing basic representation to those charged of crimes and offenses, the General Assembly established the State of Maryland Office of Public Defender (MOPD) in 1971, following the Supreme Court decision of *Gideon v. Wainwright*.[2] As public defenders develop legal strategies that promote the most positive litigation and sentencing outcomes for their clients, highly skilled social workers work in like-minded partnership with them, unearthing, scrutinizing, and evaluating valuable client information. This crucial information, when presented to courts, offers evidence-based support for alternative, life-affirming sentencing plans designed to help MOPD clients change the course they are on and remain out of the prison pipeline in the future.

MOPD defines "indigent" as those individuals who are eligible based on an assessment of their disposable income and net worth as compared to the cost to obtain private counsel. The MOPD determines the eligibility of adults by review of their income, expenses, and net worth (Copper & DeWolfe, 2014). MOPD determines the eligibility of all juveniles by the financial status of their parents or legal guardians. Any juvenile whose parent or legal guardian refuses to provide legal representation is automatically provided legal representation through the MOPD. This is a statewide uniform standard.

> MOPD considers 6 factors in determining eligibility: disposable net income, nature and extent of assets, nature of offense, length of proceedings, effort and skill required to gather pertinent information, other foreseeable expenses. (Copper & DeWolfe, 2014)

With a stated mission to provide "superior legal representation to the indigent," MOPD relies heavily on the expertise of two groups of professionals: public defenders and social workers. Attorney Jonathan Rapping stated, "Public defenders are doing the most important civil rights work of our generation because the greatest abuses that happen to poor people and people of color are occurring in our criminal justice system."[3] If you agree with Jonathan Rapping's assessment, then you must concede that the social workers who are working hand in hand with public defenders are doing important civil rights work.

The MOPD statewide Social Work Division has become an essential component of the agency's mission. According to the annual statistics compiled by the MOPD, the Litigation Support Division and Baltimore City social work teams comprised of no more than eight social work staff and an average of 15 interns provided services to more than 300 adult and juvenile cases in Baltimore City in 2013 (Copper & DeWolfe, 2014). Baltimore City (District 1) is only one of the agency's 12 districts. MOPD has several statewide divisions that are supported by the Litigation Support Division social workers and interns, including Mental Health, Children in Need of Assistance, Appellate, Aggravated Homicide, and Collateral Review Divisions. MOPD attorneys handled more than 67,000 cases statewide in 2012 (Copper & DeWolfe, 2014).

Social workers collaborate with one another, attorneys, investigators, mental health professionals, educators, family members, and anyone else who may provide insight pertaining to the lives of their clients. The Social Work Division has been able to enhance team collaborations with attorneys through staffing practices, internal collaborations, external social work experts, intern placements, and quality trainings. It is through the social work divisions that the office is able to provide evidenced-based data measuring the impact of nonattorney involvement. As a result of social work services, clients who may otherwise be incarcerated are given the opportunity to mitigate the issues that contributed to their criminal or delinquent behaviors. Social workers can identify their clients' specific needs and ensure that services are put in place to avoid recidivism, and make recommendations that lead to release, services, and/or reduced sentences.

Judges frequently rely on the social workers to provide them with reports or testimony that provides the court with options for dispositions. For example, court-requested sentencing plans that provide alternatives to incarceration can increase the client's motivation to be successful. Some judges have also become accustomed to having social workers present in court, and have expressed frustration when no social worker is available to assist clients in desperate need of intervention and treatment. This is recognized as a positive shift in court culture.

MOPD has created a culture that recognizes the need for team representation, which has become evident as every office and division in the agency regularly seeks the support of social work assistance. MOPD social workers provide a wide array of services on behalf of MOPD clients. Criminal defense offices, such as Maryland's, which employ social workers, are able to save thousands of dollars in unbudgeted cost for outside experts and services (James-Townes, 2011).

In addition to services provided to clients, attorneys, and the courts, social workers also directly contribute to successful outcomes (James-Townes, 2011). Reunification of parents and children will indirectly defray the cost of short- and long-term foster care placements. MOPD social workers abet efforts to reunify and strengthen clients' families in order to construct a foundation of support once a client returns home. Efforts to build family support can help reduce the likelihood of recidivism in the future. MOPD social workers likewise reduce funds spent on private or paneled attorneys and experts by handling critical functions that would otherwise consume an inordinate number of attorneys' billable hours. The same is true for costlier mental health experts (James-Townes, 2011). The training modules and support provided to the social workers have made the MOPD a model program for other public defender offices across the country.

MOPD: A NATIONAL MODEL

The value of having social workers as part of the public defender defense team in MOPD has been recognized for quite some time. As such, the office has maintained social work staff for more than 20 years. The training model developed by the MOPD Social Work Division thus secures quality services to clients by training interns and staff to meet clients' legal, social, and daily needs, while reducing the barriers to repeated or continued incarceration.[4] In order to be effective, MOPD social workers must understand the barriers their clients face and use their specialized skills and tools to help advocate for this at-risk population they serve. Thus, proper training of social work staff and interns has to be a priority for public defender offices. Proper training contributes to quality representation and is required given this specialized setting and population. Proper defense-based training includes:

- Conducting life history investigation
- Numerous client interviews
- Interviews of others who can add to social history (parents, siblings, neighbors, providers, etc.)
- Consulting with other professionals
- Reviewing reports, documents, records, and research
- Reviewing material for past services, incarcerations, and impediments to success
- Creating theme-based reports and drawing conclusions that reflect the client's social history
- Incorporating and creating demonstrative evidence and aids
- Possible testimony

TRAINING THE DEFENSE-BASED SOCIAL WORKER

The MOPD created a model to train social workers requiring that each staff and intern receive training tailored to the duties they are required to perform. The training program is an essential component of providing unprecedented social work services to clients

TABLE 19.1 The Duties that Social Workers Are Required to Perform

Interview clients and apply social work principles and techniques to assist clients who suffer from coexisting health, mental health, substance abuse, and/or other social adjustment factors.	Provide therapeutic social work counseling, crisis counseling, and ongoing treatment to clients with chronic health or mental health conditions and other presenting social adjustment factors, such as substance abuse, physical or developmental disability, or communicable disease. Provide crisis counseling to the client's family members on an as-needs basis.
Provide psychosocial assessments and remediation plans and makes treatment recommendations for clients.	Participate in multidisciplinary teams; provide updates to the attorney assigned to the case, client, and approved family members.
Provide case management services and act as a liaison to community organizations and residential programs to develop and coordinate after-care plans for special-needs clients scheduled for release from correctional or detention facility or transitional services for clients at various stages of the adjudication process.	Prepare written reports and recommendations; Present information or testify in court at the direction of an assistant public defender; may provide expert testimony in court proceedings.

represented by the office as traditional social work education is only geared toward understanding causes of problems and issues related to the clients served. Simple advocacy of "client's best interest" is not the focus in the legal setting, as social workers must adhere to the "client's expressed interest" while addressing underlying causation. This defense-based social worker role requires a specific set of duties as demonstrated in Table 19.1. This social worker's primary responsibility requires him or her to provide forensic social work services, including mitigation to clients charged with crimes or delinquent offenses and creating a defense strategy in partnership with the public defender.

When creating materials, reports, and opinions to the courts, the attorney prior to presentation must approve them. This is required based on legal rules of evidence and standards of practice. When social workers are asked to develop alternatives to incarceration, such alternatives must satisfy the court's concerns (e.g., public safety, punishment, and reduced chances of recidivism). Social workers are also asked to identify and recommend additional experts if needed, and assist in the development of strategies for each stage of the case. It is important that defense-based social workers understand and appreciate their roles.

To ensure a proper understanding and appreciation for defense-based social work, the training program focuses on several areas of competencies: understanding mitigation, report writing, interviewing, understanding the importance of collateral information, testimony, and working as an agent of a defense counsel. The social workers also act as a liaison among the attorney, the client, and the client's family and/or significant others. Social workers' testimonies, written reports, and demonstrative aids must be thoroughly accurate and compelling to emotionally reach defense attorneys, prosecutors, probation officers, judges, juries, and/or other decision makers.[5] This is important because they are

TABLE 19.2 Mitigation as Defined by The Judicial Conference of the United States (1998)

Mitigation is based on a very thorough investigation of the offender's life, as well as his or her family history. Only after a leave-no-stone-unturned approach is the counsel in a position to marshal effectively a powerful case for life, as well as defuse the government's arguments for death. The counsel requires the assistance of others to complete this task successfully. Again, a mitigation specialist conducts the life history investigation. Mitigation covers an enormous array of issues, but it begins with the individual's family history. Mitigation necessarily focuses on the offender in relation to his or her family for the simple fact that families shape the child in ways that profoundly affect and sometimes control adult behavior.
Family behavior patterns and effects are multigenerational and passed from one generation to the next as certainly as genetic factors such as eye color and height are passed along. Healthy development of children depends on family relationships, and unhealthy development reflects family practices and values. The quality of the attachments to parents and other members of the family during childhood is central to how the child will relate to and value other members of society as an adult. Each mitigating factor contributes to the mosaic of a person's life. Although understanding the family dynamic is the first step, it is not exclusive in its power to explain an offender's behavior.
Family influences must be considered along with psychiatric and neurologic deficits, developmental disabilities, medical diseases, compromised intellectual functioning, and cultural and ethnic influences. The offender's actions surrounding the offense should be viewed against the backdrop of his social history. A thorough, reliable social history assists the jury and court in understanding how the offender's experiences in the world affected his or her behavior. No list of specific factors can adequately describe the diverse elements of mitigation, whether or not related to the offense for which the offender is on trial. The possibilities of mitigation are limitless.

required to make decisions concerning outcomes, services, and sentences. To prepare social workers for the type of advocacy required in criminal defense settings, the trainings has to be specifically geared to answer four questions:

1. How did the client become involved in the offense?

2. Why did this client become involved in the offense?

3. What sentence can be imposed to reduce the risk of recidivism?

4. What reason is there to think that the behavior will not recur?

Understanding Mitigation

The aforementioned questions are typically answered when effective mitigation is developed. To produce a quality report, defense-based social workers must be able to understand and put into context for the court the client's life story and most importantly mitigating circumstances (Table 19.2). There are three major areas that social workers focus on to highlight the mitigating factors in their clients' lives:

1. Explaining the process: The process that resulted in the client's involvement in the criminal or juvenile justice system.

2. Humanizing the client: The ability to utilize the client's life experiences through the presentation of his or her life history.

3. Finding humanity: The ability to reveal the client's humanity by finding uniqueness in his or her life history.

Written Social Histories, Mitigation Reports, and Testimonies

The curriculum for training at the MOPD also ensures that social workers are able to clearly present a client's social history through common themes as expressed in written reports, testimonies, or both. Table 19.3 outlines the goals and skill sets incorporated into the training model.

Evaluation Methods and Tools

Evaluation methods and tools used by defense-based social workers, such as mitigation reports, biosocial histories, genograms and times, and others have become effective tools that clearly communicate the client's history during court proceedings. The biopsychosocial approach is helpful in creating recommendations for treatment, alternatives to incarceration, and release planning (Abrahamsen, 2014). Two important tools used to advocate for individuals charged with criminal offenses are assessments and evaluations. The biopsychosocial assessment highlights major events and risk and protective factors that have contributed to the client's legal problems. Forensic social workers utilize these tools specifically to describe clients' life experiences by providing detailed and

TABLE 19.3 Initial Training Goals and Outcomes

GOALS	OUTCOMES
Provide an opportunity to learn about the MOPD and its mission of indigent defense.	Participants will have a concrete understanding of defense-based advocacy through hands-on and experiential training.
Give participants an opportunity to enhance forensic skills.	Participants will develop motivational interviewing techniques and the ability to review records and conduct investigations appropriately.
Enhance advocacy skills using creative teaching techniques.	Participants will develop the ability to identify and create persuasive and creative visuals to support representation and mitigation themes.
Help participants incorporate best practice approaches.	Participants will have enhanced creative report writing and testimony abilities.

MOPD, Maryland Office of Public Defender.
Source: James-Townes, 2011.

specialized narrative and life history evaluations (Walker & Miller, 2013). Evaluations are also sought from experts who are retained to provide expert opinions concerning a particular risk or set of risk factors.

The work produced by the social workers in MOPDs requires them to present a client's social history through common themes that should be compelling, persuasive, emotional, and powerful, while shedding light on the client's current legal situation. Interviews from multiple sources are required for background information. Therefore, the team must make sure to interview individuals who can reflect on various areas of the clients' life, and who can corroborate the information shared by the client and his or her closest relatives. For example, it is not unusual to interview teachers, neighbors, classmates, and others.

Preparing to Testify

A major component of social workers in the criminal defense field is testimony. Judges call on social workers often to obtain their expert opinion, resources, insight, and suggestions. Testimony is another mechanism defense-based social workers use to advocate for their client. However, the testifying social worker's finding and opinions must be shared with the attorney prior to taking the stand. The attorney must agree that the testimony would be beneficial to the client. Types of demonstrative evidence used in some cases include but are not limited to genograms, letters, research, reports, videos, time lines, photos, and articles. To be an effective expert witness, a forensic social worker must be thoroughly prepared and understand the purpose of his or her presence in court each time he or she takes the stand. This area of expertise is a vital part of defense-based training. Some helpful hints for expert testimony are listed as follows:[6]

1. Know what others are saying, opening and closing statements, mitigation factors, and others.

2. Master the art of testimony through proper training and support. Testimony should be consistent with the overall theme of mitigation or defense. Be prepared—irrespective of skill level—and make time to review the questions being asked by the defense attorney.

3. The defense team should decide what type of written documents you will prepare in conjunction with your testimony. In this discussion, you should consider:

   a. What is the risk of providing your full findings in advance?

   b. In some jurisdictions, the court may require a full report, but the attorney should know the rules of evidence and prior notice of expert opinion.

   c. Is information corroborated?

   d. Will the report box you in?

   e. Will report aid in your testimony?

4. Be prepared with material, aids, and visuals; these must be approved by the counsel.

5. Talk to other witnesses and family so that you are aware of their testimony.

6. Know your sources.

7. Time lines are helpful and could be used to aid your testimony or as demonstrative aids.

8. Know your client's story—tell the story whenever you can within your testimony.

9. Teach as you go along.

10. It is a dance—wait for your turn and pattern your answers accordingly.

11. Whether on direct examination or cross-examination, think before you speak.

12. It is almost always better for there to be a short pause before you answer a question than for you to give a bad answer.

13. Silence is golden.

14. Ordinarily, you will not want to volunteer any additional information.

15. Sometimes, on cross-examination, you may be able to give more information (but be careful).

16. The opposing counsel may ask you to assume facts and explain how your opinion would change if those facts were true—you should practice these scenarios with the defense counsel.

17. Avoid isn't-it-true traps—listen carefully to the questions. Use silence when needed.

18. It is okay to answer, "I don't know," or ask for the question to be repeated.

19. Try to make your testimony understandable, and avoid technical jargon.

20. Use aids and visuals (referred to as demonstrative aids).

Ethical Considerations

There are aspects of traditional social work practice that do not apply to defense-based practices. There are many ethical dilemmas and implications to consider. In defense offices, all staff members are considered agents of the attorney—including social workers, investigators, secretaries, receptionists, interns, law clerks, and paralegals. Traditional social work education does not address the role of the social worker as employees, consultants, or experts in criminal litigation and representation. Therefore, this topic is included in the MOPD training program through lecture, role-plays, and case study scenarios. Attorneys must request assistance before a social worker can begin involvement in the case. A unique aspect of criminal defense work requires an understanding that the social worker and attorney roles are inherently different. Social workers who are employed in criminal defense offices are a part of the defense team during each stage of the case, including criminal proceedings, pre- and posttrial, and/or sentencing proceedings.

Typically, social workers are more involved in sentencing and plea negotiations because this is the proceeding where judges and prosecutors are informed of the client's social histories and life stories. Telling the client's story is an integral part of deciding the imposed sentence. However, social workers, by accepting employment in this legal setting, have chosen to assist attorneys in advancing the client's views to the court, but they do not "represent" a client. Guidelines for the social worker's role in criminal litigation are found in constitutional mandates, case laws, and attorney professional rules, not in the social work codes of ethics.

The National Association of Social Workers' *Code of Ethics* (2014) does not specifically address a social worker's role in the legal context, and this area of practice remains unique and is not comparable to other areas of traditional social work. However, the Sixth Amendment Right to Counsel addresses the Right to Effective Assistance, which extends to the entire defense team. This requires that the social worker remain loyal even if he or she disagrees with the "expressed interest" of the client. Being effective requires that defense-based social workers be competent in the areas of criminal law and court procedures. Because social workers are agents of the attorneys who seek their services, they must adhere to *that* state's jurisdictional rules regarding "Attorney Client Privileged Information." Every defense attorney and defense-based social worker must be aware of the law that requires social workers to adhere to mandated reporting requirements. Non-defense-based social workers are required to report if they suspect child abuse or believe that a vulnerable adult is in grave danger of abuse or harm. In other words, in any other setting, the law requires that social workers report any knowledge of abuse or neglect; however, in the criminal defense arena of some states and jurisdictions, they are protected by the law and/or court decisions that state that they are not mandated to report, because they are an agent of the attorney and covered by the attorney–client privilege.

Social workers in the state of Maryland operate under the authority of the *Pratt v. State* case;[7] a case decided in the Maryland Court of Special Appeals. The court found that the communications between the client and the defense-hired psychiatrist formed the basis of that expert's opinion and were therefore protected by the attorney–client privilege. That protected information was presented at the trial originally. The higher court reversed the trial court's ruling that allowed the privileged testimony at the original trial. This ruling would set the precedent. Consequently, agents of the attorney seen as defense team members are not mandated to report, nor can they dishonor privileged communication obtained from their clients. Therefore, in the MOPD setting, privilege is not confined to communications between attorney and client, but includes communications made with all agents (staff and experts) employed or retained by the office. Public defender offices across the country are joining together through various associations to address this issue in the hope of creating a national standard of practice that specifically addresses defense-based social workers.[8]

IMPLICATIONS FOR THE FUTURE

Social workers in criminal defense offices, especially public defender offices, are a vital resource. The impact not only has a quality-of-life value, but the services provided by MOPD social workers are notable, as they contribute significantly to reduced incarceration, especially in urban communities. MOPD social workers are able to and often do provide in court testimony during juvenile, adult, appellate, and reentry hearings. Each time they assist with a case successfully and judges base their disposition based on their involvement, it decreases the costs associated with utilizing expensive external mental health experts, days of incarceration, extended detention stays, and other collateral consequences associated with the practice of over-incarceration (Carson & Golinelli, 2014; James-Townes, 2011). In the landmark case of *Wiggins v. Smith*, attorneys argued that social workers should have been used to save the life of Mr. Wiggins. In the opinion rendered by the court, they noted the availability of social workers in Maryland and the importance of using them in such cases to tell defendants' stories.[9] Mr. Wiggins's sentence was overturned. Therefore, the court supported and validated the role of the forensic social worker. The MOPD has established itself as an agency that prepares the social work staff and interns for the challenges and uniqueness of defense-based representation.

Consequently, social workers have a tremendous and direct impact on their clients' future. The reports, insight, and testimony they provide in the criminal and juvenile courts assist judges every day as they decide the outcome of the cases before them. Judges in Maryland have become accustomed to relying on the social work staff within MOPD to provide vital client history information and recommendations. It is becoming more and more evident that successful training contributes significantly to the success that defense-based social workers are able to achieve on behalf of their clients. As such, they are providing an unbelievable service to their clients, the defense attorneys, the criminal justice system, and society at large.

FOR FURTHER STUDY

Suggested Assignments

Ethical Scenarios: Mandatory Reporting

Scenario 1: In the initial meeting, the client tells the social worker that he has minor children living with his girlfriend (the children's biological mother), who are routinely neglected by their mother, an active drug user. In fact, the client's arrest is directly related to his providing assistance to his children. The girlfriend is absent from the home for days at a time and the children, aged 9 and 14 years, are left to care for themselves. The social worker is immediately concerned about the safety of the children. What should the social worker do?

Questions to consider:

1. What is the social worker's obligation to report?

2. Does it matter what type and how many substances are used?

3. What should the social worker do if he/she observes direct evidence of neglect and current drug use during an interview at the home of the girlfriend?

4. What areas should the social worker investigate before disclosing this information?

Scenario 2: John, 45 years old, has had a serious addiction problem with heroin for more than 15 years. He has been arrested for selling heroin. He tells you that it was a small amount sold so that he could just make enough money to buy what he needed for his own addiction. His addiction has taken over his entire life. He tells you that he has a 10th-grade education and has only worked under the table. He is asking that you help him find an inpatient treatment program so that he can work toward recovery. You have found a treatment bed and a well-respected program, and his mother has agreed to pay the initial admission fee. On the day of court, you present a written recommendation to the court and speak on his behalf. The judge decides to let John go to the program as a condition of probation; however, if John does not follow through, he will be sentenced to 15 years. The next day, you receive a phone call from the program informing you that John has not arrived. His mother also calls you and wants her money back. What do you do?

Scenario 3: Charles is a defendant and you have been assigned to prepare a psychosocial report and background investigation. Charles is charged with rape and sexual offenses against a 10-year-old girl who is friends with his daughter. You interview both of Charles's children. His son, aged 12 years, refuses to make eye contact and does not discuss his father with you. His daughter, aged 11 years, tells you that her dad visits her bed at night. She wants to tell you more about him but is having a hard time. What do you do?

Scenario 4: An assistant public defender has given you a referral for a client to come up with a community-based treatment program. You complete your assessment with a recommendation of community-based services, and you have made referrals to these programs. On the court date, the assistant public defender tells you that the case is going to be dismissed and that you are not needed in the court. What would you say to the assistant public defender? These are answers to ethical scenarios based on Maryland's rules:

Ethical answer #1: The social worker does not report him for failure to report to the facility—this is a function of probation; it is not the social worker's role to report him; the money issue is between his mother and the program.

Ethical answer #2: The social worker should excuse him/herself and call his/her supervisor for direction; continue to gather information about the situation; understanding that he/she would not report this to local child protective services (CPS) without the client's permission; understanding the attorney–client privilege.

Ethical answer #3: The social worker should understand that the case no longer exists and unfortunately services are not necessary. The social worker may approach the client on the side to determine whether he/she is interested in further help.

Case Study: Ms. David's Story

Ms. David is a 45-year-old female who has a significant history of mental illness, substance abuse, homelessness, and criminal convictions for assaults, traffic violations, drug possession, and prostitution. She requested the services of the public defender when she was again charged with prostitution and a violation of probation. She was receiving Social Security Insurance and Medical Assistance. Ms. David required multiple services, including case management; mental health; substance abuse treatment; stable housing; medication monitoring; and ongoing assistance with daily living skills such as budgeting, decision making, and accessing service delivery systems in the most efficient way. She was on probation and court ordered to various treatments. The probation conditions presented problems because supervision fees and charges for urinalyses were taking a significant amount of her monthly check. In fact, the prostitution charges were an effort to earn money to pay expenses. Ms. David had never been employed and began prostituting as a means to earn money and pay her supervision fees.

Social work interventions and recommendations to the court:

1. She was assessed as disabled by the Social Security Administration.

2. She was referred to and accepted by the local assertive community treatment (ACT) team. The team has its own psychiatrist, case manager, therapists, and housing specialists.

3. She received comprehensive services including assistance with housing.

4. Terms of her probation were modified to include waiving of supervision fees, acknowledging inability to work, and identifying current treatment plan.

5. The social worker was able to negotiate that the probation officer and the substance abuse treatment program use results from one test weekly rather than two separate tests and share the information.

6. The court and probation agent were educated regarding:

   a. Ms. David's psychiatric condition and her medication needs;

   b. Supplemental Security Income (SSI) criteria, limited income, limits of medical insurance, and

   c. Requested to have her probation modified due to her limitations.

Outcome: The client called occasionally to report her successes, such as getting her own place to live, graduating from drug treatment, and then to identify completion of probation. Recent check indicates one charge being dismissed on appeal to the circuit court.

Case Study: Social History of Mike Doe

Mike Doe was born on January 17, 1988, at St. Joe's Hospital in West Baltimore, Maryland. Mike's mother, Martha, painfully disclosed that she conceived Mike after being violently raped by Rob. Martha was merely 12 years of age and Rob was 21 years old, when she gave birth to Mike. Martha recalls no birth complications during the delivery of Mike. After the rape, there was no contact between Martha and Rob. Mike is now charged with attempted murder and possession of a deadly weapon. It should be noted that Martha never disclosed her traumatic event to anyone prior to her initial interview with the social worker at the MOPD. She offered the information as a way to provide insight into Mike's juvenile delinquent behavior, mentioning that it may be possible that he knew something was wrong (meaning their relationship or lack of bonding with him as a child as compared to the other children). Martha states that when she gave birth to Mike, she was living with her parents. In addition to dealing with the trauma of rape and teenage parenting, Martha had to cope with the disappointment of her parents and family, who believed and still believe that she consented to the sexual encounter that caused her to become a teenage mother. She continued to live in the home with her parents despite her father's obvious disappointment. During this time, she took a passive role in raising Mike. Mike believed that his grandmother was his mother (he called her mom) and he called Martha by her first name, although he could not phonetically pronounce it correctly. Her mother died unexpectedly when Mike was 3 years old. Martha was 16 years old when her mother died, and she was forced to do something she had not done before: take an active role in raising Mike.

Mike Moves to East Baltimore

Raising Mike was difficult for Martha because she had not yet processed the emotional impact of the rape and how it affected her relationship with her son. She was scarred by the rape and found it difficult to love Mike, who was a constant reminder that her innocence had been violently violated. Searching for independence from what remained of her family after her mother's death, Martha moved out of the only home Mike ever knew into an apartment with two women. She eventually moved into her own place in City Homes Housing Projects. Mike attended School 116 on Atlas Street, and the first building they lived in was the 1000 Building. Despite her good intentions of providing for herself and Mike, the City Homes Housing Projects was a violent and scary place to live in, and Mike was exposed to drugs, violence, and other risks.

Single Parenting

In December 3, 1994, Malcolm Doe was born. Martha had no substantial relationship with Malcolm's father. When they met, Malcolm's father was unemployed and recently released from prison. Mike's second sibling, his sister Mary, was born 1 year later. Mary has a different father from Malcolm, and Martha had no substantial relationship with

Mary's father. At the tender age of 7 or 8 years, Mike longed for the stability of his grandfather's home and would catch public transportation to west Baltimore and visit him on a daily basis. He often took his baby brother, Malcolm, with him. Mike described his grandfather as a kind man who was a chronic alcoholic. When Mike arrived at the home, his grandfather was typically "drunk" and Mike would clean him and put him to bed. He felt that he had to stay with him to protect him. Mike resided with his grandfather during several periods of his childhood. He does not believe that his grandfather was an alcoholic prior to his grandmother's death.

Martha Marries James J.

Martha began to date James J. when Mike was approximately 7 or 8 years of age. According to Martha, James moved in with the family after he was released from prison and they married soon after. He moved in with the family prior to them marrying and assumed the role as husband and stepfather to Martha's three children, including Mike. Medical records indicate that James had a severe heroin addiction, which began in 1958 and continued to spiral out of control during Mike's childhood.

Extreme Domestic Violence and Witnessing of Violence

Martha admits that Mike did witness a lot of abuse that she suffered at the hands of James There were also times when Mike would try to protect her and argue with his stepfather. As Mike became older, he became more outraged with James's abusive behavior. Just like all the other traumatic events that occurred in this family, the abuse was never discussed. It should be noted that the abuse suffered by Martha at the hands of her husband was severe, requiring several hospitalizations. Records indicate that she received frequent medical attention, which included treatments for nose injuries, including nose surgery, eye injuries, stab wounds, and multiple contusions. It is no coincidence that Mike's first encounter with the juvenile justice system coincides with the onset of Martha's relationship with James There is no evidence of family intervention to effectively treat the level of pathology and damage occurring during this time period within this family.

Excerpts from Johns Hopkins Hospital Medical Reports:

Reason for referral: Assessment and review of records at the request of XX, Esq. for disposition.
Summary: Client mental health disorders since the age of 12 and prescribed eight (8) psychopharmacological medications (ranging from anti-depressants, stimulants, anti-anxiety's and one anti-psychotic). Client recently has been diagnosed with Neurodevelopment Disorder associated with Pre-Natal Alcohol Exposure (ND-PAE), by Dr. A.

Despite her obvious denial of the chaos and violence in many areas of her life, Martha did realize that Mike's behavior coincided with the onset of the abuse in the home. Martha recalls one particular incident when she was sitting in her car after her husband had assaulted her. Mike came home and saw that her face was swollen and bloody. She went on to explain that Mike became very angry and went to confront his stepfather. She was very afraid of what Mike might do, but when Mike arrived at the bedroom, James was unconscious on the bed from the drugs he had injected. Martha admitted that she never discussed the abuse but that Mike was deeply affected and always felt that he had to protect her. As the abuse worsened, Mike's behavior worsened. Mike continued to run away from home and school, and this contributed to his extensive delinquent behavior in juvenile commitments.

Reports From Siblings

It is important to note that Mike's brother Malcolm confirms all reports of physical abuse. Malcolm also remembers that Mike was a great provider for his three younger siblings. He fondly remembers Mike picking them up from the babysitter, taking them home, and feeding them. Malcolm even recalls Mike combing Nikki's hair when she was young. He mentioned that, most of the time, Mike would put all of the children on the bus to get home. It should be noted that Mike is only 4 years older than Malcolm, so he was very young (8 or 9 years of age) when he took responsibility of his younger brothers and sister.

Drug and Alcohol Abuse

At the tender age of 11 years, Mike was exposed to drug use when he was forced to watch his stepfather, James, inject himself intravenously with heroin. Mike's drug and alcohol use began at the tender age of 10 years. At this time, he began experimenting with alcohol, usually vodka, as well as heroin and marijuana. By the age of 14 years, he was using heroin intravenously, a behavior copied from his stepfather. As a child, Mike would receive drugs from older friends, both male and female. Mike did not like the feeling heroin gave him. "It made me feel out of control." Therefore, he discontinued his relationship with her and discontinued his heroin use for approximately eight years. However, he began using other drugs more heavily, such as cocaine, alcohol, and marijuana.

Mike continued his drug use while incarcerated. He reported sporadic intravenous use of heroin. In 1985, on his release, he began to use cocaine intravenously. Around this time, Mike realized that he was addicted. According to Mike, he used cocaine, marijuana, and alcohol daily.

It is important to note that Mike's drug use started at the age of 10 years and continued throughout his adult life, up until the time of his arrest for this offense. Mike was not able to remain abstinent even though that was his intention during several periods in his life. Mike never received any substance abuse treatment while in the community. Interviews with various persons confirm that Mike, Mary, Malcolm, and Randy have all used drugs as well as participated in the selling of drugs. Malcolm also has a history of drug abuse and according to him, a history positive for criminal behavior and at least one adult conviction. Mike's grandfather was an alcoholic as was his stepfather.

Questions for Mike's Case

1. What risk factors are present in Mike's life during the following stages:

   a. Prenatal

   b. Juvenile

   c. Young adult

   d. Adult

2. What services would you recommend for him pretrial, during incarceration, and postrelease?

3. What services would you recommend for his family?

4. What demonstrative aids would you use to assist in telling Mike's story?

Suggested Readings

Agnew, R. (1992). Foundation for a general strain theory of crime and delinquency. *Criminology, 30*(1), 47–87.

Barker, R. L., & Branson, D. M. (1993). Forensic social work: Legal aspects of professional practice. New York, NY: The Hawthorne Press.

Bergen-Cico, D., Haygood-El, A., Jennings-Bey, T., & Lane, S. (2014). Street addiction: A proposed theoretical model for understanding the draw of street life and gang activity. *Addiction Research and Theory, 22*(1), 15–26. doi:10.3109/16066359.2012.759942

Dudley, R. G., & Leonard, P. B. (2008). Getting it right: Life history investigation as the foundation for a reliable mental health assessment. *Hofstra Law Review, 36*, 963–987.

Griffin, G. (2012). Using a trauma informed approach in juvenile justice institutions. *Journal of Child & Adolescent Trauma*, 271–283.

Haney, C. (1994). Social context of capital murder: Social histories and the logic of mitigation. *Santa Clara Law Review, 35*, 547.

Harper, C. C., & McLanahan, S. S. (2004). Father absence and youth incarceration. *Journal of Research on Adolescence, 14*, 369–397.

Herman, J. L. (1997). *Trauma and recovery*. New York, NY: Perseus Books.

Hirschi, T., & Gottfredson, M. (1983). Age and the explanation of crime. *American Journal of Sociology, 89*, 552–584.

Johnson, R., & Dobrzanska, A. (2005). Mature coping among life-sentenced inmates: An exploratory study of adjustment dynamics. *Corrections Compendium, 30*(6), 8–9.

Kentucky Department of Public Advocacy (2005). *Mental health and experts manual*, (8th ed.). Frankfort, KY: Kentucky Department of Public Advocacy.

Miller, J. G. (1995). Criminal justice: Social work roles. In R. L. Edwards (Ed.), *Encyclopedia of social work* (19th ed., pp. 653–659). Washington, DC: NASW Press.

Pierce, C. T., Gleasonwynn, P., & Miller, M. G. (2001). Social work and law: A model for implementing social services in a law office. *Journal of Gerontological Social Work, 34*(3), 61–71.

Schnapp, W. B., & Cannedy, R. (1998). Offenders with mental illness: Mental health and criminal justice best practices. *Administration and Policy in Mental Health, 25*(4), 463–466.

van der Kolk, B. A., McFarlane, A. C., & Weisaeth, L. (Eds.). (1996). *Traumatic stress: The effects of overwhelming experience on mind, body, and society*. New York, NY: Guilford Press.

Williams, W. I. (2006). Complex trauma: Approaches to theory and treatment. *Journal of Loss and Trauma, 11*(4), 321–335.

NOTES

1. The director of St. Paul's Church in downtown Baltimore provided food and other assistance to men leaving the penitentiary.
2. The landmark Supreme Court decision, *Gideon v. Wainwright*, which declared the Sixth Amendment right to counsel in criminal cases, applies to the state and local governments throughout the country. Over the past 40 years, the agency (MOPD) has grown from an office of 72 lawyers and 17 locations to 570 lawyers, 320 support staff, 28 social workers, and more than 35 social work interns (annual average) serving more than 50 locations and presenting more than 234,000 cases a year.
3. Jonathan Rapping is an associate professor at Atlanta's John Marshall Law School, but is on a leave of absence as he devotes much of his time to working in MOPD, teaching Maryland's public defenders to better serve their poor clients amid "crushing" caseloads and is among the 2014 MacArthur Foundation "genius" grant recipients. This statement was made during an interview.
4. The Social Work Division has expanded its scope to include a Social Work Intern Program, which has fostered mutually beneficial partnerships. The division utilizes interns from every accredited social work program to assist with social work caseloads, coordinate trainings, provide policy and procedural input, and conduct research. As a result of the intern program, the office has been able to lead the way in the creation of a provocative, training program for social work interns interested in the forensic social work practice.
5. Demonstrative aids are used during testimony in sentencing and negotiation proceedings to tell the client's story.
6. The list was created by Lori James-Townes; MOPD Social Work Training Program (2012).
7. *Pratt v. State*: 39 Md. App. 442 (1977) 387 A.2d 779; *Margaret Melton Pratt v. State of Maryland*. No. 857, September Term, 1977; Court of Special Appeals of Maryland.
8. The National Association of Public Defender and the National Legal Aid and Defender Association have each established committees to implement a national standard for mandatory reporting for social workers in criminal defense settings.
9. Opinion noted in the Supreme Court decision in the case of *Wiggins v. Smith*, Warden et al.; Certiorari to the United States Court of Appeals for the Fourth Circuit; No. 02–311. Argued March 24, 2003—Decided June 26, 2003.

REFERENCES

Abrahamsen, S. (2014). *Risk factors for criminal behavior: A biopsychosocial study* (Unpublished doctoral dissertation). University of Oslo, Norway.

Alexander, M. (2010). *The new Jim Crow: Mass incarceration in the age of color blindness.* New York, NY: The New Press.

Carson, A., & Golinelli, D. (2014). *Prisoners in 2012: Trends in admissions and releases, 1991-2012.* Washington, DC: U.S. Department of Justice: Office of Justice Program—Bureau of Justice Statistics.

Clark, M., & Savner, E. (2010). *Community oriented defense: A stronger public defender.* New York, NY: Brennan Center for Justice.

Code of Ethics of the National Association of Forensic Social Work. (2014, October 8). *National Association of Social Work*. Retrieved from http:/www.socialworkers.org

Copper, C., & DeWolfe, P. (2014). *Fiscal year 2014 annual report*. Baltimore, MD: State of Maryland Office of Public Defender.

Freudenberg, N. (2001). Jails, prisons, and the health of urban populations: A review of the impact of the correctional system on community health. *Journal of Urban Health: Bulletin of the New York Academy of Medicine, 78*, 214–235.

James-Townes, L. (2011). *Social worker's role in representing critically impacted populations: A report for secretary Foster*. Baltimore, MD.

Maschi, T., & Killian, M. L. (2011). The evolution of forensic social work in the United States: Implication for 21st century practice. *Journal of Forensic Social Work, 1*, 8–36.

Maur, M. (1995). Americans behind bars: A comparison of international rates of incarceration. *Prison Journal, 75*, 113–123.

National Organization of Forensic Social Work. (2014). Retrieved July 10, 2014, from http://nofsw .org

Page, J., & Whetstone, S. (2014). *Beyond the trial: The disproportionate imprisonment of African Americans. In teaching race and anti-racism in contemporary America*. Netherlands: Springer.

Roberts, A., & Springer, D. (2007). *Social work in juvenile and criminal justice settings—third edition*. Springfield, MA: Charles C. Thomas.

Siegal, L., & Brandon, W. (2011). *Juvenile deliquency*. Belmont, CA: Wadsworth.

Walker, R. C., & Miller, J. (2013). *The Kentucky Department of Public Advocacy Social Work Alternative Sentencing Program*. Lexington: University of Kentucky Center on Drug and Alcohol Research .

CHAPTER 20

Urban Gangs: Epidemiological Criminology as a Theoretical Framework for Social Work Practice

Kevin Daniels, Stacy A. Smith, Paul Archibald, and Timothy Akers

The study of criminology as an interdisciplinary science is not new to social work literature, in that there is a plethora of studies that substantiate the collaborative biopsychosocial and environmental role social workers play within the criminal justice system as it relates to navigating the multiple dimensions of law enforcement, adjudication/courts, and corrections (Campbell & Hudson, 2007; Shapiro & Hassett, 2012; Smith, Daniels, & Akers, 2013). Clearly, social workers continue to play significant micro–, mezzo–, and macro–level-related roles as frontline direct service providers, staff, or administrators. Social workers are particularly instrumental in shaping the development of public policy as it relates to crime as a violation of criminal law, and critically understanding the financial and human developmental impacts of such policies on the conditions within urban communities (Criminal Justice Social Work, 2008; Roberts & Springer, 2007; Zastrow & Kirst-Ashman, 2010). Social work serves to bridge the gap between public health and criminal justice and its subsequent impact on the lives of African Americans; however, the existing literature is still relatively new within the corridors of social work, specifically concerning the full breadth and depth of urban gangs (Smith et al., 2013). To that end, in this chapter, we examine the African American urban environment and enclaves in a quest to identify the nexus among criminal behaviors as documented in the social work literature. Through this effort, the reader is challenged to examine closely the geospatial and global origins and complexities of gang activity, contextualizing the dynamics of urban gangs within the context of social science theories. Lastly, the reader is encouraged to consider the growth of hybrid families and epidemiological criminology as a theoretical framework or paradigm, in which social work practice is driven more by evidence-based interdisciplinary science, and less by operations-based outcomes.

AFRICAN AMERICAN URBAN SETTINGS AND CRIMINAL BEHAVIOR

The resilience of African American families in urban settings has persisted despite a historical legacy of slavery and indentured servitude in the United States, a legacy which evidently began to fuel the pathological self-concept and stereotyping that has perpetuated the subjugation of the urban environments and hamlets in which they live (Bernstein & Umbreit, 2002; Campbell & Hudson, 2007; Lewis & Trulear, 2008; Santrock, 2008). Moreover, the sustained levels of racial and structural segregation, housing redlining, limited access to health care options, and barriers to education and employment opportunities have created the environment that appears to have proliferated not only the disintegration of urban families and internalized rage, but also the foundation for criminogenic activity that have not only psychosocial consequences but also public health implications (Akers, Potter, & Hill, 2013; Braithwaite & Taylor, 2001; Hill & Cummings, 2013).

In terms of sources of possible risk for particular negative outcomes, according to the Bureau of Justice Statistics (2009) and the U.S. Census Bureau (2010), among African Americans 69.3% of births were to women who were unmarried compared to a striking 31.7% for their White counterparts. Likewise, compared to other ethnicities, there is a high mortality rate among young Black men as a result of homicide and drugs—11% of African American males compared to 3.5% of Latino males and 1.7% of White males in their late 20s and early 30s—as well as being disproportionately behind prison bars. The Drug Policy Alliance (2009) statistics are replete with disparities of those African Americans who are convicted as a result of drug offenses, in that though comprising approximately 13% of drug users, they account for approximately 59% of drug-related convictions. Moreover, the recent "Great Recession" of 2008 to 2009, caused by macroeconomic corporate entities, along with the housing sector, and other government taxation in the financial and housing sectors and amalgamated the destabilization and decentralization of urban families. These concurrent activities historically are not only critical factors as social determinants of criminal activity, but they have also given rise to the prevalence of collaboration among urban criminal gangs in their formation and sustainability today (Akers et al., 2013; Fitch, 2013; Merton, 1968; National Urban League, 2009; Spergel, 1995).

THE GEOSPATIAL AND GLOBAL ORIGINS OF GANG ACTIVITY

Even though criminal gang activity has seen a proliferation in the United States, with a migratory flow dating back to circa 1783, its reach has always been geospatially global in nature. Earlier members of gangs were primarily European immigrant groups that migrated to America from Europe, primarily from Germany, Great Britain, and Scandinavia, typically settling in urban slums (Howell & Moore, 2010). Between 1820 and 1920, a large wave of European Jews, Irish, Italians, and Poles migrated to the United States seeking a better life as America's cities were experiencing massive industrialization. According to Bost (1994), the immigrants were low-skilled and low-wage earners who were competing for better economic opportunities. Spergel (1995) contends that the genesis of gangs among immigrant groups emerged to serve as enforcers for labor union officials and local politicians. These gangs also provided protection from conditions resulting from the limitation of resources and the stress of adaptation in a new environment. Thus, urban communities became the landscape for the emergence of gang activity in the United States (Blakemore, Mayo, & Blakemore, 2007; Egley & Howel, 2013).

Seeking a better life after slavery, African Americans participated in the "great migration" leaving the deep South in search of a better life in the North (Frazier & Lincoln, 1974; Lincoln & Mamiya, 1990; Martin & Martin, 2003). However, Hill (1999) posits that African Americans migrated to urban communities in two waves, 1915 to 1929 and 1940 to 1950. Bost (1994) argues that the early gangs among African Americans date back to the 1920s in Los Angeles, California, hence becoming more organized during the 1950s and 1960s (Blakemore et al., 2007). Cureton (2009) further describes how African American migration to urban communities was laden with institutional racism resulting in structural inequalities that further excluded Blacks from achieving the "American Dream," and it is the historical boundaries of this context that gave rise to gang activity.

Since these early years of migration, accompanied by scarce resources and systemic conditions that perpetuated inequalities and inequities, gangs have become a social norm of the landscape of modern society. In 2011, the National Youth Survey reported that there were 29,000 gangs, 782,500 gang members, and 3,300 jurisdictions with problems associated with gang involvement (Office of Juvenile Justice and Delinquency Prevention [OJJDP], 2011). On the other hand, OJJDP (2011) reports that homicides related to gangs decreased from 2,020 in 2010 to 1,824 in 2012, clearly indicating that the well-being of the community is still challenged contentiously. These findings also showed that gangs are still mostly concentrated in urban communities. Even though the demographics of communities shift over time, Hispanic/Latino (45%) and African American/Black (39%) currently represent the largest racial and ethnic groups involved with gangs (Egley & Howel, 2013). According to Blakemore, Mayo, and Blakemore (2007), youth gangs and their propensity to become involved with delinquent behavior are extensive and far-reaching, especially for residents of underserved communities. Consequently, the safety and well-being of individuals, families, and communities are impacted tremendously. In many instances, residents have become prisoners in their homes, living in constant fear that they may become victims of gang activities. Furthermore, distrust of law enforcement, accompanying fear of retaliation have become a normative reaction to gang violence. As a result, the plethora of gang violence in urban communities calls forth the need to better understand the role social work occupies as the nexus and bridge between public health and criminal justice.

CONTEXTUALIZING THE DYNAMICS
AND COMPLEXITIES OF URBAN GANGS

Theoretically, the intersection and nexus between criminology and gang behavior has been posited by social science theories for decades, such as in *the theory of differential association* (Van Wormer & Besthorn, 2011), which asserts that criminal behavior is the result of a learning process that stems primarily from small, intimate groups such as family, neighborhoods, peer groups, and friends. Merton, on the other hand, proposed *anomie theory* (Merton, 1968), which considers delinquent behavior as the result when an individual or gang is prevented from achieving high status goals in a society. Another theory is *deviant subcultures theory*, which asserts that some groups have developed their own attitudes, values, and perspectives that support criminal activity (Miller, 1958). *Control theories* assume that all people would naturally commit crimes and therefore must be constrained and controlled by society from breaking the law (Zastrow & Kirst-Ashman, 2010).

With respect to youth gangs specifically, they are classified into four types: criminal, conflict, retreatist, and cult/occult. The primary goal of criminal gangs is material gain through criminal activities. *Conflict gangs* are turf oriented and will engage in violent conflict with individuals or rival groups that invade their neighborhood or that commit acts that they consider degrading or insulting (Van Wormer & Besthorn, 2011). *Retreatist gangs* focus on getting "high" or "loaded" on alcohol, cocaine, marijuana, heroin, or other drugs, while *occult gangs* are involved in a secret or hidden belief in the supernatural so that they can have or acquire supernatural powers (VanWormer & Besthorn, 2011; Zastrow & Kirst-Ashman, 2010).

All told, the gang problem in the United States, as tracked by the National Youth Gang Surveys (NYGS), continues to affect a large number of jurisdictions, both large and small. Since the early 2000s, not only has every large city (population more than 100,000) in the United States experienced gang problems in some form or another, so too have a majority of suburban counties and a sizeable number of smaller cities and rural counties (Ackeer, Johns, & Selkirk, 1997; Braithwaite et al., 2001; Egley & Howel, 2013; Roberts & Springer, 2007). Because gangs have been spreading like a disease, such entities as the National Institutes of Health have prioritized research on gang-identified youth and adults. As early as the 1980s, gang violence has been seen as a growing and serious public health and criminological concern (Akers et al., 2013; Smith et al., 2013).

EVOLUTION OF THE HYBRID GANG FAMILY

In 1994, a professor of sociology from the University of Wisconsin, Larry L. Bumpass, conducted a study on, "The Changing Character of Stepfamilies" (Bumpass, Raley, & Sweet, 1994). In this study, he stated that approximately half of the 60 million children under the age of 13 in the United States were living with one biological parent and that parent's partner. He also indicated that nearly half of all women, not only mothers, were likely to live in a stepfamily relationship, solidifying the fact that the nation had already become families of step individuals or blended families. The most critical issue, both then and now, is that the schools of thought in psychiatry, psychology, and social work did not and still do not provide relevant methods on how to effectively apply family dynamics to family situations (i.e., like those with violent youthful offenders and gang involvement) when creating interventions to address various family needs (Bumpass et al., 1994).

As stated above, Bumpass et al. (1994) clearly presented that people are living in families that share both biological and fictive ties (i.e., step families). This aligns with Billingsley's (1999) description that families no longer reflect what was once called the "normal family" or the traditional meaning of nuclear family. Equipped with this knowledge, the current authors conducted a case study on violent youthful offenders and gangs in Baltimore, Maryland, exploring the notion of family hybrids, which are families composed of biological and fictive ties. One major finding of this study was that most if not all of the families had social, emotional, and economic needs to be filled that were associated with an absent role, usually that of an absentee father being filled by a gang proxy, meaning a gang member or promulgator; hence the coining of the term hybrid gang family (Garland & Yancey, 2012; Smith et al., 2013).

As illustrated in the conceptual model of the hybrid gang family, the family structure and roles evolved over time as a consequence of micro-, mezzo-, and macro-level conditions (Figure 20.1). As discussed in the literature, in what is known as traditional families, the father (male role) is seen as the protector and provider who ensures that the family's needs are met. In hybrid gang families, typically the families that fit the characteristics of this family structure are biological female-led and the father or male role is filled by the gang proxy. It is critical to note that youths join gangs for social acceptance, protection, and financial support. Mothers (females, as some are led by biological female family members such as grandmothers, aunts, etc.) of gang members, who in most cases were teen mothers, represent the biological tie to the youth and either accepted the youth's behavior or indoctrinated the youth to gangs for safety and financial assurance. Because of a mother's socioeconomic status, she may be unable to fulfill the demands lead a youth to join a gang. Because of this vulnerability, the door is opened for a gang to fill the absentee father's role to protect and provide in an alternative manner, thus supporting the origination of the hybrid gang or blended family. Blended families leave the door open for youth to be coreared and predisposed to the gang's perverse version of family ideologies and violent influence. This type of rearing, via the hybrid gang family composition, leads to the cultivating of violent youthful offenders (Smith et al., 2013).

In the best of all worlds, the family as an agency of socialization and informal social control would be the best "first line of defense" against the gang problem (Knox, 1994, as cited by Smith et al., 2011). Therefore, in order to address the gang problem, the challenges and concerns of the family must be addressed first, reinforcing the need for

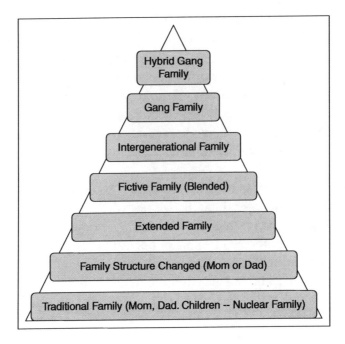

FIGURE 20.1 Evolution of the hybrid gang family.

more hard and quantifiable data regarding gangs' relationships to family and the many factors involved with this phenomenon. With a foundation visibly laid out, the stage has been set for a further collaborative look into epidemiological criminology as a theoretical framework in social work practice.

EPIDEMIOLOGICAL CRIMINOLOGY AS A THEORETICAL FRAMEWORK IN SOCIAL WORK PRACTICE

The interdisciplinary theoretical framework of epidemiological criminology is at the intersection and nexus between epidemiology and criminology, public health and criminal justice theories, and methods and practice. As a result, the epidemiological criminology paradigm serves as an emerging theory with the underpinning of new epistemological thought (Akers & Lanier, 2009). Epidemiological criminology, for example, considers the effects of social conditions on a society relative to health and crime, thereby directly complementing the unique and blended role of the social work profession with respect to its values, skills, and knowledge base.

According to Akers and Lanier (2009), sociologist Emile Durkheim was the first to discuss the intersection between crime in society and the public health medical sector, explore the similarities and differences between the two disciplines, and see it as an indicator for the health of a society. The epidemiological criminology model frames an analysis that can (and has) been used to compartmentalize primary (before behavior occurs), secondary (at-risk behavior that's at a tipping point), and tertiary (the aberrant behavior has already occurred) perspectives on how to attack, target, and embrace the best of what works, especially in understanding the dynamics of youth. Evidently, throughout the decades social work within urban settings have provided interventions that have incorporated individual counseling (micro), family and organizational interventions (mezzo), and community outreach (macro), which is consistent with the interdisciplinary epidemiological criminology model (Akers et al., 2013).

Each approach, theory, and paradigm discussed herein has served to take into consideration the breadth and depth of societal and health ills and to include both health and criminal disparities and social inequities (Waltermaurer & Akers, 2013). Yet it would be remiss to not reframe how contemporary urban settings choose to structure their interventions, both endogenously and exogenously. The epidemiological criminology model is a strategic approach to the gang epidemic or pandemic within a biopsychosocial and environmental disparities perspective, which is consistent with social work conceptual frameworks and practice theories (Egley & Howel, 2013; Smith et al., 2013). The growing concern of urban populations (and now a growing concern for rural communities) is the continuing plague of gang violence. These environments, based on historical trends shared previously, can incubate and cultivate gang activities.

Specifically, biopsychosocial and environmental disparities must be viewed, first and foremost, from the context of both the individual and collective. That is, urban settings have long seen how malnourished, abused, and neglected children are subject to a sort of "epigenetic" environmental alteration in their personality and outlook on life. Their environmental exposure can, at times, affect their individual biology, psychological makeup, and even their social interactions (Byers, 1999). Collectively, these are the dynamics that directly impact gang morphology. In other words, within the epidemiological criminology framework, it is noted that an analysis and intervention must, without question, take into account the biopsychosocial and environmental determinants that directly and indirectly impact the health and well-being of the child, family, and community.

As illustrated in Figure 20.2, the epidemiological criminology model has many dimensions. The biopsychosocial and environmental factors directly impact the tipping point between healthy behavior and criminal behavior. Meaning that there exists a push–pull continuum between the health–crime nexus. Social work practice and literature notes that a healthy behavior can tip or slide toward more criminal or deviant behavior due to any number of factors that take into account the biomedical and behavioral disparities. Figure 20.2, for example, shows that disparities can range from the more physiological (biomedical) to the behavioral, whereby data can show that differences can and do exist between youth who choose and do not choose to participate in gang-related violence (Akers et al., 2013).

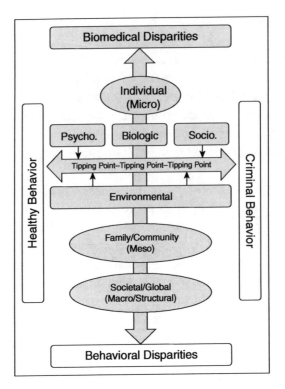

FIGURE 20.2 Epidemiological criminology model.

Source: Revised and adapted from Potter and Akers (2010);
Waltermaurer and Akers (2013).

EVIDENCE-BASED PRACTICE WITHIN URBAN SETTINGS

To illustrate how the epidemiological criminology model has been applied, a team of faith-based leaders, community organizers, and researchers at Morgan State University developed the "B'MORE" model targeting gang violence prevention. Specifically, the team learned through experience. In witnessing other programs around the city of Baltimore and in studying the Chicago Ceasefire model and various approaches, the team learned through experience that an exclusive public health approach to gang violence prevention is likely to have little to no effect, and can actually be more detrimental to the health and well-being of the population and community. In sharp contrast, a multidose response (Figure 20.3) that takes into account public health, criminal justice, social work, education, and many other interventions are essential and critical if measurable impact on youth behavior is to occur (Akers et al., 2013; Smith et al., 2013; Waltermaurer & Akers, 2013).

To contextualize the B'MORE model, the team organized a series of focus groups whereby youth participated as both members of known gangs, such as MS-13, BGF, Crips and Bloods, and as youth who were at risk of becoming affiliated. To facilitate participant recruitment for the 9-week pilot program, the facilitators made an

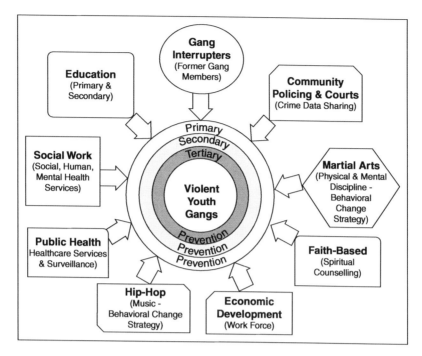

FIGURE 20.3 Health Care Services & Surveillance model
for gang violence prevention.

Source: Revised and adapted from Smith, et al. (2013).

announcement and extended an invitation in community association meetings located in the Westside of Baltimore City, where most of the families in the identified catchment area meet the preidentified risk factors. Twenty participants between the ages of 10 and 16 were selected to participate in the pilot study. All of the participants were African American, 10 girls and 10 boys. Prior to beginning the pilot study, the participants met with the facilitators for an orientation in which the program was fully explained and participants were asked to complete the informed consent with their parent(s) or guardian. During the first week, the participants were given seven categories of open-ended questions based on the epidemiological criminology framework and specifically designed to explore respondents' attitudes and beliefs about their understanding of the impact of gang engagement on their own well-being and that of their families and communities.

Qualitative responses were analyzed using a content analysis process to identify common themes. First, inductive analysis of the data was used from which patterns, themes, and categories emerged. To maintain objectivity, the two investigators developed systematic open-coding schemes independently; then both schemes were compared for similarities and differences. After convergence and discrepancy were analyzed, a level of reliability was determined by measuring the coded data for inter-coder agreement to the extent to which the two coders assigned the same code to each theme, thus allowing salient themes to be identified from the data.

Some of the thematic issues extracted from the youth focus groups included, for example, issues around "powerlessness"; "media encouraged violence"; "gang as family"; "many expressed disdain for violence but blamed larger systems for being hypercritical thereby leaving communities to do what they needed to do to survive"; "many saw the church as an answer in serving as a conduit between these larger systems and urban communities"; and "some didn't see the nexus between physical and mental health."

To combat these issues, community-based team members, academicians, and faith-based leaders began a series of interventions that responded to the multiple factors that impacted the lives of the youth. This served as a nine-step youth gang violence multidose epidemiological criminology framework response that would intervene in the behavior of the youth. This response targeted stopping youth violence and lawlessness while providing education and empowerment tools through lectures and workshops that would, in theory and practice, help teach them the importance of family, community, and self.

CASE STUDY: C-GANGS

Need and Background

Nationally, the United States has seen unprecedented, comorbid events through an increase in gun violence, stemming from individual acts of violence or mass shooting, and an increase in the number of gang-related violence and gang membership. Invariably, the violence that occurs is not foreign to our communities, but rather, is directly located within our neighborhoods, thereby impacting children, families, schools, businesses, and government agencies, among others. These tragic and impacting events and changes have plagued the nation. Yet our analytical response has been suspect from the context of evidence-based science, policy, and behavioral changes. Thus, this entails close analysis and examination of behavioral, epidemiological, criminological, and policy data. In effect, there are no integrative and interdisciplinary systems of analysis that can help scientists, policy makers, and behavioral and biomedical clinicians more effectively understand these relationships. Most recently, the president of Morgan State University scripted an OpEd piece in the campus community and recent newsprint, that guns and gun violence require a greater commitment by the academic community in our quest to help recommend fair and reasonable policies to help protect people and neighborhoods.

Proposed Activities

To address these challenges and gaps in our analytical capabilities, Morgan State University's School of Social Work and other academic programs have been developing a new and innovative national center of excellence to address these gaps in our

(continued)

(*continued*)

science and policy research. The center under development is titled *Center for Gun Analysis and Neighborhood Gang Studies (C-GANGS)*. The C-GANGS is being developed based on the Epidemiological Criminology Model through the efforts of Dr. Anna McPhatter, LCSW (dean, School of Social Work); Dr. Tim Akers (assistant vice president for Research Innovation & Advocacy); Dr. Kevin Daniels, LGSW (associate professor, School of Social Work); Stacy Smith, MSW (PhD candidate, School of Social Work); and Dr. Paul Archibald, LCSW-C (assistant professor, School of Social Work). C-GANGS is structured to address the scientific, policy, clinical, and academic needs of neighborhoods, the State of Maryland, and the nation.

Structure

The center is being structured around four main cores: (a) science and research, (b) policy and practice, (c) education and evaluation, and (d) neighborhood outreach. Each core has a unique mission and focus, charged with providing the best evidence-based data for decision making, teaching, learning, and behavioral change.

1. *Science and research core*—Conduct high-quality, evidence-based research that blends strong statistical and mathematical models with well-established theoretical grounding. This core will focus primarily on evidence-based research related projects. Specifically, the science and research core will comprise interdisciplinary researchers who will approach gun analysis and neighborhood gang studies from the context of epidemiological criminology. The researchers will consist of public health and epidemiologists, criminal justice and criminologists, social and behavioral sciences such as social workers, health scientists, physicians, medical epidemiologists, and anthropologists—all with a targeted focus on integrative and evidence-based outcomes. That is, this core will examine how data can be integrated across different surveillance systems of monitoring and tracking behaviors, to include technologies and techniques used in merging disparate data systems, as in the case of informatics.

2. *Policy and practice core*—Conduct policy and best practices research that can be used by policy makers, legislators, and practitioners who are responsible for implementation, constitutional enforcement, and safety. This core will focus on evidence-based policy analysis and best practices. Specifically, the policy and practice core will conduct, produce, and disseminate research that can be immediately carried out and used by policy makers and practitioners who are responsible for

(*continued*)

(*continued*)

implementation-related activities. This core will examine legislative and philanthropic policies, advocacy positions, and practice-based approaches and outcomes to make evidence-based recommendations for policy and practice shifts or changes. Endemic to this core will be a focus on evidence and not advocacy. It will be science-based policy and practice research in order to be objective and unbiased in the findings.

3. *Education and evaluation core*—Conduct educational and evaluation studies that can be used by educators, evaluators, and students to more effectively understand the difference between evidence-based policy versus biased teaching and learning. The education and evaluation core will serve as the training core for academics, policy makers, and practitioners in need of refresher training, certifications, and continuing education units. This core is vital as the mechanism for teaching and learning. The education and evaluation core will focus on classroom instruction as well as formative, summative, and impact evaluations. This core will further work toward the establishment of joint degrees in the area of epidemiological criminology. Courses will range from high school to college level, and include others outside academia. New course materials will be produced under this core and disseminated when teaching interdisciplinary and evidence-based science.

4. *Neighborhood outreach core*—Disseminate findings that can be readily used by neighborhoods that are charged with the safety and security of their families, homes, schools, religious organizations, and businesses, among others. The neighborhood outreach core's sole aim is to directly engage neighborhood residents and neighborhood representatives in order to seek their input when carrying out community-based participatory research. In addition, this core will serve as the outreach core to help in making direct contact with residents for home assessments, active engagement in research, and seeking resident input. This course is the C-GANGS anchor when engaging community as it is pivotal to ensure that data collected is valid and accurately representative of the community.

Collaborations–Collaborators

In short, the C-GANGS Center will establish some of the nation's first interdisciplinary and interprofessional collaborations, whereby academics, students, police, public health, courts, corrections, health care providers, and social and human service professionals will all work to coordinate new ways of examining the relationship among guns, gangs, and neighborhood violence throughout the city of Baltimore, the state of Maryland, and the nation.

IMPLICATIONS FOR SOCIAL WORK

As stated earlier, the helping traditions of providing assistance, guidance, and support to vulnerable populations are a common thread for the social work profession. Indeed, the practices of criminal justice and public health are better served when the social work profession serves as a bridge that links these two seemingly disparate disciplines. The collaborative nature of each sector is uniquely positioned in the urban community to serve as a catalyst between community and the social work profession. The initial results of the B'MORE pilot study indicate that this service delivery practice model has several key implications for practice that social workers, educators, public health and criminal justice professionals, and faith-based organizations could consider when working with urban populations on gang violence.

- Criminal justice and public health institutions and organizations could seek to partner with social workers more actively when seeking to intervene and provide preventive strategies with at-risk populations on gang violence, especially via the B'MORE model of epidemiological criminology.
- Urban communities (i.e., organizations) could be further undergirded in its grassroots approach to the ongoing proliferation of gang violence by utilizing the professional skill sets of the social workers.
- Beyond this particular study, further research could provide ongoing measures and outcomes with the relationship and significance of community organizations and the academy in alleviating violence in urban communities;
- Educationally, the B'MORE model can be taught to an emerging cohort of generalist social work students in providing community engagement with urban populations.
- Macro-constituents and lawmakers at a policy level can utilize the results to institute policies that reflect and support collective entities that will economically and socially benefit from the alleviation of gang violence.

Discussion Questions

1. What specific intervention strategies (skills, knowledge, etc.) should be used to address criminal behavior in urban settings?
   Epidemiological Criminology Model approach utilizing social work interventions.

2. Which theory or theories can be used to guide your practice?
   Epidemiological Criminology Model coupled with social work theories.

3. What are the identified strengths of this model?
   Transdisciplinary in its approach.

4. What are the identified challenges faced by this model?
Community, academic, and policy maker buy-in.

5. What were the agreed-upon goals to be met?
Urban communities undergirded in its grassroots approach to the ongoing proliferation of gang violence by utilizing the professional skill sets of the social workers.

6. Are there any issues of cultural competence that need to be addressed?
The perspective based on the community's cultural lens must be considered.

7. What local, state, or federal policies could affect this case?
Lawmakers at a policy level institute policies that reflect and support the alleviation of gang violence.

8. Are there any legal or ethical issues present in this case?
Debate over whether behaviors of youth gangs are nuisances or true criminality.

9. How can evidence-based practice be integrated into this case?
The B-MORE model is a research-informed modality that is currently being tested.

10. What was the relationship between criminology and social work?
Criminal justice and public health institutions and organizations seek to partner with social workers more actively when seeking to intervene and provide preventive strategies with at-risk populations surrounding gang violence.

FOR FURTHER STUDY

Suggested Assignments

1. *Annotated bibliography assignment* —For this annotated bibliography assignment, you will prepare a descriptive list of 10 research sources specific to urban environments followed by a brief 150-word descriptive and evaluative paragraph examining the relevance, accuracy, and quality of the sources cited. You will:

   a. Use the American Psychological Association (APA) style format (or other style approved by your instructor to format sources);

   b. List in alphabetical order;

   c. Include sources related to your epidemiological criminology specific to urban environments;

   d. Include an annotation, or description of each source.

2. *Field assignment*—For this assignment, the class will be divided into two groups in which one group will visit the public health department within your

specific city while the other group will visit a correctional facility within that same city catchment area. Each group will focus their inquiry on the following:

a. Develop a 10-page group paper surrounding your experience at that particular agency (i.e., name of agency representative, discussion of current data surrounding the agency, interventions utilized by agency, and the groups observations and final thoughts);

b. Present a class presentation of the groups' content of the visit;

c. Discuss your assessment of how each agency does/does not fall within the parameters of the epidemiological criminology model discussed in class.

3. *Final reflection paper*—For this assignment, each student is expected to write a 10-page reflection paper, which would focus on the following:

a. Your understanding of epidemiological criminology model as discussed in class;

b. Description of your community; and

c. How the model would be implemented within your community and which agency(s) you would utilize.

Suggested Readings

Frye, V., & O'Campo, P. (2011). Neighborhood effects and intimate partner and sexual violence: Latest results. *Journal of Urban Health, 88*, 187–190.

Last, J. M. (1988). *Dictionary of epidemiology* (2nd ed.). New York, NY: Oxford University Press.

Loue, S. (1999). *Forensic epidemiology: A comprehensive guide for legal and epidemiology professionals*. Carbondale, IL: Southern Illinois University Press.

Loue, S. (2002). *Case studies in forensic epidemiology.* New York, NY: Kluwer Academic/Plenum.

Petit, B. (2012). *Invisible men: Mass incarceration and the myth of Black progress.* New York, NY: Russell Sage Foundation.

Pinchevsky, G. M., & Wright, E. M. (2012). The impact of neighborhoods on intimate partner violence and victimization. *Trauma Violence Abuse, 13*, 112–132.

Potter, R. H. (2008). *Epidemiological criminology and criminological epidemiology: Macro to micro, with an emphasis on the meso.* Paper presented at the 136th Annual Conference of the American Public Health Association, San Diego, CA.

Potter, R. H., & Akers, T. A. (2010). Improving the health of minority communities through probation public health collaborations: An application of the epidemiological criminology framework. *Journal of Offender Rehabilitation, 49*, 695–609.

Public Health Law Office. (2012). *Forensic epidemiology 3.0 training curricula.* Atlanta, GA: Centers for Disease Control and Prevention (CDC). Retrieved November 20, 2012, from www2a.CDC .gov/phlp/phel.asp

Vaughn, M. G., Delisi, M., Beaver, K. M., Perron, B. E., & Abdon, A. (2012). Toward a criminal justice epidemiology: Behavioral and physical health of probationers and parolees in the United States. *Journal of Criminal Justice, 40*, 165–173.

REFERENCES

Ackeer, A., Johns, D., & Selkirk. B. (April, 1997). (No title). Video presentation on gangs. School of Social Work, University of Georgia.

Akers, T. A., & Lanier, M. (2009). Epidemiological criminology: Coming full circle. *American Journal of Public Health, 99,* 397–402.

Akers, T. A., Potter, R. H., & Hill, C. V. (2013). *Epidemiological criminology: A public health approach to crime and violence.* San Francisco, CA: Jossey-Bass.

Bernstein, G., & Umbreit, M. (2002). Side effect of welfare law: The no-parent family. *The New York Times,* A1.

Billingsley, A. (1999). *Mighty like a river: The Black church and social reform.* New York, NY: Oxford University Press.

Blakemore, J. L., Mayo, Y. Q., & Blakemore, G. M. (2007). *African-American and other street gangs: A quest for Identity (revisited). Human behavior in the social environment from an African American perspective* (2nd ed.). Binghamton, NY: Haworth Press, Inc.

Bost, D. (1994, November 19). *Gang prosecution.* San Diego County District Attorney's Office, Special Presentation.

Braithwaite, R. L., & Taylor, S. E. (2001). *Health issues in the Black community.* San Francisco, CA: Jossey-Bass.

Bumpass, L. L., Raley, R. K., & Sweet, J. A. (1994). *The Changing character of stepfamilies: Implications of cohabitation and nonmarital childbearing* (NSFH Woking Paper No. 63). A National Survey of Families and Households, Working Paper. Madison: WI: University of Wisconsin–Madison. Retrieved from http://www.ssc.wisc.edu/cde/nsfhwp/nsfh63.pdf

Bureau of Justice Statistics. (2009). *Prison and jail inmates at midyear 2008.* Washington, DC: U.S. *Department of Justice.* Retrieved from http//www.ojp.usdoj.gov/bjs/pub/pdf/pim08st.pdf

Byers, T. (1999). Role of epidemiology in developing nutritional recommendations: Past, present, future. *American Journal of Clinical Nutrition, 69*(6), 1304S–1308S.

Campbell, M. K., & Hudson, M. A. (2007). Church-based health promotion interventions: Evidence and lessons learned. *Annual Review of Public Health, 28,* 213–234.

Criminal Justice Social Work. (2008). *Criminal and youth justice social work.* Retrieved from www.cjsw.ac.uk

Cureton, S. R. (2009). Something wicked this way comes: A historical account of Black gangsterism offers wisdom and warning for African American leadership. *Journal of Black Studies, 40,* 347–361.

Drug Policy Alliance. (2009). *Race and the drug war.* Retrieved from http//www.drugpolicy.org/communities/race/

Egley, A., Jr., & Howel, J. (2013). *Highlights of the 2011 National Youth Gang Survey Fact Sheet.* Washington, DC: Office of Juvenile Justice and Delinquency Prevention.

Fitch, L. O. (2013). *The church: Surviving the recession.* Retrieved June 2013 from http://ourweekly.com/news/2013/Jun/06/church-surviving-recession/

Frazier, E. F., & Lincoln, C. E. (1974). *The Negro church in America. The Black church since Frazier.* New York, NY: Schocken Books.

Garland, B., & Yancey, G. (2012). Moving mountains: Congregation as a setting for social work practice. In T. Scales & M. Kelly (Eds.), *Christianity and social work, 4th ed.* (pp. 311–336). Botsford, CT: NACSW.

Hill, C. V., & Cummings, T. (2013). *The multiple risks for U.S. Black males. epidemiological criminology.* New York, NY: Routledge.

Hill, R. B. (1999). *The strengths of black families: Twenty-five years later.* Lanham, MD: University Press of America.

Howell, J. C., & Moore, J. P. (May, 2010). *History of street gangs in the United States. The National Gang Center bulletin.* Washington, DC: Office of Juvenile Justice and Delinquency Prevention, Bureau of Justice Assistance, Department of Justice.

Lewis, C. E., Jr., & Trulear, H. D. (2008). Rethinking the role of African American churches as social service providers. *Black Theology: An International Journal, 6*(3), 343–365.

Lincoln, E. C., & Mamiya, L. W. (1990). *The Black church in the African-American experience.* Durham, NC: Duke University Press.

Martin, E. P., & Martin, J. M. (2003). *Spirituality and the Black helping tradition.* Washington, DC: NASW Press.

Merton, R. K. (1968). *Social theory and social structure* (Enlarged ed.). New York, NY: The Free Press.

Miller, B. W. (1958). Lower class culture as a generation milieu of gang delinquency. *Journal of Social Issues, 14,* 5–19.

National Urban League. (2009). *The state of Black America 2009: Message to the president.* New York, NY: National Urban League Press.

Office of Juvenile Justice and Delinquency Prevention (OJJDP). (2011). *Easy access to Juvenile Court Statistics: 1985–2010.* Retrieved August 2013 from http://www.ojjdp.gov/ojstatbb/ezajcs/

Potter, R., & Akers, T. A. (2010). Improving the health of minority communities through probation-public health collaborations: An application of the epidemiological criminology framework. *Journal of Offender Rehabilitation, 49*(8), 595–609.

Roberts, A., & Springer, D. (2007). *Social work in juvenile and criminal justice settings* (3rd ed.). Springfield, IL: Thomas.

Santrock, J. W. (2008). *Adolescence* (12th ed.). New York, NY: McGraw-Hill Higher Education.

Shapiro R. J., & Hassett, K. A. (2012). *The economic benefits of reducing violent crime: A case study of 8 American cities.* Retrieved from http://www.americanprogress.org/issues/economy/report/2012/06/19/11755/the-economic-benefits-of-reducing-violent-crime

Smith, S., Daniels, K., & Akers, T. A. (2013). The epidemiological criminology of child victimization: The evolution of hybrid gang families and violence. In E. Waltermaurer & T. A. Akers (Eds.). *Epidemiological criminology: Theory to practice.* London, UK: Routledge Frontiers of Criminal Justice.

Spergel, I. (1995). *The youth gang problem.* New York, NY: Oxford University.

U.S. Census Bureau. (2010). *Income, poverty, and health insurance coverage in the United States: 2009.* Retrieved from http://www.census.gov/prod/2010pubs

Van Wormer, K., & Besthorn, F. H. (2011). *Human behavior and the social environment: Groups, communities, and organizations (macro level).* New York, NY: Oxford University Press.

Waltermaurer, E., & Akers, T. A. (2013). *Epidemiological criminology: Theory to practice.* London, UK: Routledge Frontiers of Criminal Justice.

Zastrow, C., & Kirst-Ashman, K. (2010). *Understanding human behavior and the social environment* (8th ed.). Belmont, CA: Brooks/Cole.

CHAPTER 21

Research With Urban African American Adolescents and Emerging Adults: Implications for Quasi-Community-Based Participatory Research and Community Action Research

M. Taqi Tirmazi, Von E. Nebbitt,
Kim Dobson Sydnor, and Dawn Thurman

The overall well-being and health of African American urban youth have received significant attention over the last several decades. However, much of the research has been from a deficit-oriented perspective (Cabrera et al., 2013) and has lacked the inclusion and engagement of urban African American adolescents and emerging adults in the research process. Engagement of community participants in developing research provides varying perspectives, which allow us to examine risk and resilience and gain insight on emerging trends. Although rigor in research designs and analyses continues to improve and evolve, engaging urban African American adolescents and emerging adults in the research process remains a challenge (Breland-Noble, Bell, Burriss, & Poole, 2011). Traditionally relied-on research approaches lack genuine and authentic academic and community-based partnerships and face challenges in generalizability. In addition, traditional research approaches lack rapport and trust among academic and community members who are needed to mitigate challenges related to reducing response error and conducting sustainable research. This chapter provides a theoretical and research framework in conducting research with urban African American adolescents and emerging adults in urban settings with a special focus on public housing developments. Due to the tremendous influence of the socio-ecocultural[1] factor in urban communities, employing a quasi-community-based participatory research and community action research approach guided by a socioecocultural perspective and acculturation theory is recommended in addressing the risk and resilience among African American adolescents and emerging adults.

CONTEXT FOR CONDUCTING RESEARCH AMONG AFRICAN AMERICAN URBAN YOUTH

According to the U.S. Census Bureau (2010), almost 86% of all African American families reside in urban communities with 40% living below the poverty line. Although African Americans make 14% of the U.S. population, they represent more than 45% of the families in public housing developments (Nebbitt, Williams, Lombe, McCoy, & Stephens, 2014; Public and Indian Housing Information Center, 2013; U.S. Census Bureau, 2010). African Americans represent upward of 90% of families living in public housing developments in some urban cities (Washington, DC, Chicago, Baltimore; Nebbitt et al., 2014; Public and Indian Housing Information Center, 2013). Scholars (Attar, Guerra, & Tolan, 1994; Bennett & Miller, 2006; Nebbit et al., 2014; Turner & Avison, 2003) suggest that low-income urban youth, especially in public housing communities, are at heightened risk for stressful life experiences that impact their overall health and well-being. Public housing development in urban communities are often faced with challenges associated with social, environmental, and economic stressors (Davies, 2006; Morales & Guerra, 2006; Nebbitt et al., 2014; U.S. Census Bureau, 2010; Wells, Mance, & Tirmazi, 2010; Youngstrom, Weist, & Albus, 2003). Despite the precarious circumstances faced by many African American adolescents and emerging adults living in public housing communities, many proceed to live productive lives and are able to thrive, engage in successful behaviors, and develop adaptive skills. Oftentimes, public housing development and urban communities are associated with negative stereotypes that impede objective research agenda (Wells et al., 2010). In addition, research bias, stereotypes, and stigma often ignore the varying differences and strengths in urban neighborhoods (Leviton, Snell, & McGinnis, 2000; Wells et al., 2010) especially in public housing developments. Although there has been sustained research examining the experiences of African American adolescents and emerging adults over the past several decades, there has been limited research exploring the perceptions of life experiences among this population group (Nebbitt et al., 2014). Thus, when conducting research among African American adolescents and emerging adults in urban communities and public housing, it is essential to include their perspective in the research process while being aware of the influence and intersectionality of socioecocultural factors associated with their overall well-being and health.

SOCIOECOCULTURAL AND ACCULTURATION THEORY

Scholars (Black & Krishnakumar, 1998) explain that the fundamental structure of urban life confines a vast number of people to a small area, which can lead to psychosocial risks (Wells et al., 2010). Public housing developments in many instances can produce high levels of stress, lack of support for prosocial behavior, disintegration, and exposure to deviance while fostering resiliency such as adultification, communal supports, self-efficacious behavior, and strong sense of identity. Due to the tremendous role of social, environmental, and cultural factors in public housing communities, a socioecocultural perspective provides a useful guide in exploring the impact of risk and resiliency among African American adolescents and emerging adults in public housing communities and urban communities. A great deal of research has focused on addressing the deleterious effects of urbanization on youth (Fitzpatrick & Boldizar, 1993; Margolin & Gordis, 2000; Rosario, Salzinger, Feldman, & Ng-Mak, 2003). In addition, research examining the experiences of African American urban youth has utilized a deficit perspective (Cabrera et al., 2013). However, theorists explain that living in poor and segregated neighborhoods, such as in urban public housing communities, can have a simultaneous inhibitive and promotive impact on adolescents' development (García Coll et al., 1996; Nebbitt, Lombe, Yu, Vaughn, & Stokes, 2012). Examining the lives of urban youth from a socioecocultural model accounts for key social, cultural, and communal factors that accentuate the strengths while still accounting for the associated risks within multiple systems. Although ecological system perspective posits the interplay between the individual and environment, a greater emphasis can be placed on sociocultural factors in urban communities, especially in public housing developments.

Bronfenbrenner's (1989) ecological perspective provides a useful structure to address the experience of urban adolescents and emerging adults. Brofenbrenner (1989) defines the ecological perspective as:

> the scientific study of the progressive, mutual accommodation, through the life course, between an active, growing human being, and the changing properties of the immediate settings in which the developing person lives, as is affected by the relations between these settings, and by the larger contest, in which the settings are embedded. (p. 188)

This interaction and accommodation takes place throughout an individual's life. The ecological approach considers both the interrelationship of the growing organisms and the continuously changing social and physical environment. As urban communities continue to gentrify and public housing developments evolve and transform, adolescents and young adults must also continue to adapt and adjust to the environmental shifts and interactions. These interactions between the individual (urban youth) and the environment (home, school, and community) produce "experiences" that dictate adaptive strategies impacting overall well-being.

The ecological perspective consists of four ecological systems: microsystem, mesosystem, exosystem, and macrosystem. For adolescents, the microsystem is made up of a familiar, often close, and intimate social network of interpersonal relationships including direct face-to-face interactions (Muss, 1996), such as home, family, school, sport teams, peer groups, clubs, religious institutions, and so on. The microsystem plays a critical role in the development as experiences in family, school, community, and so on serve as predictive factors in deciding the adaptive strategies for urban adolescents and emerging adults. The mesosystem comprises the linkages and processes that occur among multiple settings containing the developing person such as the relationship between home and school, school, workplace, and so on (Muss, 1996). The exosystem include relationships between school and neighborhood groups, mass media, the school board, local government, transportation system, religious institutions, civic groups, and so on (Muss, 1996). The macrosystem consists of the interconnectedness of the microsystem, mesosystem, and exosystem of a given culture, subculture, or other social structure that relates to the developmentally belief systems, resources, lifestyle, opportunity structures (Bronfenbrenner, 1989). The macrosystem is made up of key aspects of a general culture, political, social, legal, religious, economic, educational values, and public policy, which are all reflective of a societal blueprint (Muss, 1996). In urban communities specifically public housing developments, a great emphasis needs to be placed on cultural and social factors and values as these communities are uniquely organic with traditional and contemporary ideologies, paradigms, and perspective that shape life experiences and adaptation. Public housing developments often exist in silos and are associated with stereotypes and stigma. Therefore, an acculturative perspective may be useful in understanding why certain segments are segregated and marginalized while others segments may be assimilated and integrated.

Although much of the past research using acculturation theory has been used to study the experience of immigrants, it may be a useful model to understand the experience and adaptation of urban adolescents and emerging adults in urban communities, especially in public housing developments. Many urban communities and public housing developments have historically dealt with negative stigma and stereotypes. In addition, public housing developments within urban communities have been viewed to be isolated environments viewed from xenophobic perspectives by outsiders. When examining the experience of adolescents and emerging adults, one may find their experience and place in society parallels that of first and second generation immigrants as they are often grouped as "others" rather than "us" or "we." In addition, many health outcomes and disparities are similar to individuals in developing countries rather than their peer counterparts. In the United States, scholars (Phinney, Berry, Veddar, & Liebkind, 2006) explain that acculturation is an expansive concept that is associated with the subsequent changes that occur as a result of intercultural contact (Berry, 1997; Gordon, 1964; Graves, 1967). Acculturation theory refers to changes in an individual's behavior, social activities, thinking patterns, values, and self-identity as a result of contact with another culture (Gordon, 1964). Furthermore, Berry (1986) explains that "acculturation" is a term that has been defined as cultural change that results from continuous, firsthand contact between two distinct cultural groups. One can argue that urban communities, specifically public housing developments, have a distinct culture that is in constant interaction with the larger culture. Berry further states that in another formulation acculturation was defined by the Social Science Research Council (1954) as,

> culture change that is initiated by the conjunction of two of more autonomous cultural systems. Acculturative change may be the consequence of direct cultural transmission; it may be derived from non-cultural causes, such as ecological or demographic modification

induced by an impinging culture; it may be delayed, as with internal adjustments following upon the acceptance of alien traits or patterns; or it may be a reactive adaptation of traditional modes of life. Its dynamics can be seen as the selective adaptation of value systems, the processes of integration and differentiation, the generation of developmental sequences, and the operation of role determinants and personality factors. (p. 26)

Phinney et al. (2006) explain that acculturation derives from acculturation strategies, which are based on individual decisions on the level of intercultural contact. They further state that scholars had initially viewed acculturation strategies to be one dimensional, with an individual deciding to become assimilated or maintain his or her own ethnic culture. However, acculturation strategies are presently viewed to be two dimensional, wherein an individual can have intercultural contact and maintain his or her own culture as well (Phinney et al., 2006).

Acculturation attitudes are deconstructed into four distinct types: integration, assimilation, separation, and marginalization (Berry, 1986). Assimilation strategy is often referred to when an individual decides to relinquish maintaining practices of his or her ethnic culture but indulge in the mainstream culture by attempting to transition into the mainstream society (Berry, 1986; Phinney et al., 2006). Integration strategy is when an individual holds on to his or her cultural integrity and maintains his or her ethnic culture but also decides to transition into a host culture and to become an integral part of the larger society (Berry, 1986; Phinney et al., 2006). Separation strategy implies that an individual selects to maintain his or her ethnic culture while deciding not to interact with mainstream culture, preferring a self-imposed withdrawal from the larger society (Berry, 1986; Phinney et al., 2006). Marginalization strategy refers to when an individual decides not to maintain his or her ethnic culture of origin and not participate in the mainstream culture (Berry, 1986; Phinney et al., 2006). Individualism strategy refers to an individual's feeling that it does not matter which culture he or she participates in because it is his or her personal feelings and choice that matter the most. It is important to note that acculturation leads to bilateral outcomes between two cultures—not only are urban adolescents and emerging adults impacted by the intercultural contact but the mainstream culture is also impacted by Black youth culture.

Berry (2001) suggests that individuals have four strategies or options in dealing with their host society: integration, assimilation, separation, and marginalization. The host society has four options or strategies as well: multiculturalism, melting pot, segregation, and exclusion. Although multiculturalism is often the ideal strategy for urban youth, the dominant group varies in its preference of multiculturalism and melting pot. In order to decrease tensions there have to be low levels of prejudice and discrimination as well as a mutual tolerance and acceptance of the similarities and differences among urban communities in public housing and larger mainstream society. Additionally, both groups must have a level of attachment to and identify with the larger group (Berry & Kalin, 2001). Not only are communities as a whole impacted, but the residing people from the host community will have to adapt to the cultures that immigrants bring as well. In multicultural societies such as the United States, the integration strategy can be pursued (Berry & Kalin, 2001); however, integration cannot be achieved just because a society is multicultural as there are systematic structures and policies that perpetuate segregation and marginalization. Assimilation is preferred when the mainstream society aims to achieve a melting pot strategy (Berry, 2001; Phinney et al., 2006). Separation is preferred when the mainstream society aims to achieve segregation (Berry, 2001; Phinney et al., 2006). Lastly, marginalization is preferred when the mainstream society seeks to achieve exclusion (Berry, 2001; Phinney et al., 2006). Therefore, it is important to understand the socioecocultural factors that influence the overall acculturation of urban adolescents and emerging adults as it plays a significant role in their overall sense of adaptation and well-being. Using research approaches within a community and personal framework that is built on strengths will foster solutions to address health disparities due to marginalization in many urban and public housing communities.

COMMUNITY-BASED PARTICIPATORY RESEARCH AND PARTICIPATORY ACTION RESEARCH

Community-based participatory research (CBPR) is a useful approach in conducting research with urban communities and in public housing developments. CBPR has emerged in health-related research over the last decade. The WK Kellogg Foundation Community Health Scholars Program (2012) defines CBPR as a "collaborative approach to research that equitably involves all partners in the research process and recognizes the unique strengths that each brings. CBPR begins with a research topic of importance to the community, has the aim of combining knowledge with action and achieving social change to improve health outcomes and eliminate health disparities." It is similar to participatory action research, which functions not only as a means of knowledge production, but also as a tool for education and development of consciousness as well as mobilization for action (Rubin & Babbie, 2014). The two research approaches heavily rely on the utilization and involvement of the community and individuals under study. The National Institutes of Health (NIH) Office of Behavioral Health and Social Science Research (2015) defines CBPR as an "applied collaborative approach that enables community residents to more actively participate in the full spectrum of research (from conception with a goal of influencing change in community health, systems, programs or policies." CBPR aims to foster an equitable partnership between the community members and researchers to integrate knowledge and action for social change and addressing health disparities (NIH, 2015). Hartwig, Calleson, and Williams (2006) explain that keywords concepts of CBPR are "collaborative," "equitably," "partners," "combining knowledge with action," and "achieving social change." Similarly, Green (2003) defines participatory research as systematic inquiry, which included partnering with individuals impacted by the issue being studied in addressing education, action, and change. Tandon (1988) further states that "Participatory research attempts to present people as researchers themselves in pursuit of answers to the questions of their daily struggle and survival" (p.7).

CBPR and Community Action Research (CAR) both recognize the importance of developing collaborative and equitable partnerships in addressing social change. Although CBPR seems to focus on involving the community at each phase of the research process, Participatory Action Research (PAR) places more focus on action and change as the researcher becomes a resource to the community under study. There is a growing recognition that "traditional" research approaches have failed to solve complex health disparities (Hartwig et al., 2006). Traditional researchers often complain about challenges in trying to recruit participants and these challenges are often a result of community members feeling that researchers have used them and taken findings away for the researchers benefit, with the community being left with no direct benefit (Hartwig et al., 2006). CBPR and PAR approaches to research foster trust and rapport among researchers and communities, which lay the foundation for more insightful and equitable research. Although a number of researchers have advanced principles for CBPR, scholars (Israel, Schultz, Parker, & Becker, 1998; Minkler & Wallerstein, 2008) suggest eight key principles of CBPR that are widely used:

- Recognizes community as a unit of identity
- Builds on strengths and resources within the community
- Facilitates collaborative partnerships in all phases of the research
- Integrates knowledge and action for mutual benefit of all partners
- Promotes a colearning and empowering process that attends to social inequalities
- Involves a cyclical and iterative process
- Addresses health from both positive and ecological perspectives
- Disseminates findings and knowledge gained to all partners

Researchers should be aware that CBPR principles should not be imposed but be considered in developing an equitable partnership in conducting research. Although it is ideal to apply the CBPR principles in conducting research with African American urban youth, specifically in public housing, researchers should be aware that not all the principles will be successfully applied in each study because each community and public housing developments is uniquely different. In the example that follows we share our lessons learned from conducting several quasi-CBPR and PAR projects in public housing developments in urban communities. Through our research experience, we find that a quasi-CBPR and PAR approach has been effective in working with African American adolescents and emerging adults in public housing developments. Our community engagement and methodology is published in the book titled *Adolescents in Public Housing: Addressing Psychological and Behavioral Health.*

Following are some lessons learned from applying a quasi-CBPR and PAR approach:

- Being genuine and showing respect is paramount as participants in public housing can sense when researchers are not being authentic and respectful of their community and culture.

- Researchers must be aware of the reputation of their institution in the community and how the reputation may lead to apprehension and skepticism about participating in research studies.
- Trust and rapport are essential. However, trust and rapport take various forms of engagement, which require time and genuine commitment. In addition, there are layers of trust within public housing communities. Moving from one layer to the next requires time and rapport with social networks in public housing's communities.
- Successful development of research hypotheses often occurs during informal personal dialogue involving one-on-one engagement rather than through community advisory boards, research advisory boards, or other formal boards. Due to the nature of topics being addressed, youth in public housing feel more comfortable sharing their stories and insight while being involved in the research process through informal means.
- The research process often requires the research team to be reflective of the population race, gender, and culture. However, race and gender does not always translate to understanding the experience of a cultural group, therefore, cultural sensitivity, cultural humility, and urban competence, sensitivity, and awareness are essential.
- Informal leaders buy in from adolescents and emerging adults is just as if not more important than formal leaders. Researchers must be aware and sensitive about the relationships between formal and informal leaders. Although most of our research has found a healthy relationship between formal and informal leaders, there have been cases where there are biases and tensions between formal leaders and participants in the study.
- Participants want researchers to be a resource in addressing various issues. Our research has found that many young people need to be linked to resources such as job placement, health care, housing, education, literacy, tattoo removal, substance abuse counseling, mental health, and social services. The participants in our study expect us to be a resource or connect them to resources while being researchers at the same time.
- Mixed methodology is highly successful. Although quantitative research in many cases provides greater generalizability with a larger sample, takes less time, and can be cost effective, participants often have a story to tell, and using qualitative data collection techniques focusing on individuals at a one-on-one level provides greater insight about emerging and hidden issues that are not gathered through quantitative means and/or via qualitative focus group data collection approaches.
- Participants expect being rewarded on an individual level and community level. Our research has found that participants expect and appreciate being compensated for their participation individually, however, they are just as excited when the community benefits as well. Our research has facilitated health fairs and cookouts and donated recreational equipment, which has brought the community together and helped us in building a stronger partnership.

- Dissemination of knowledge must occur at multiple levels and through multiple means. Our research has found that the importance of giving formal presentations at conferences and community organizations is important, but presenting the findings with concrete suggestions is just as important to the community and participants. Our research has also found that presentations on findings need to occur in multiple settings that may include parents in one session, youth in one session, or male and female in individual sessions.

IMPLICATIONS

As mentioned earlier, a great deal of past research focusing on African American adolescents and emerging adults has used a deficit approach with traditional methodologies. This chapter discusses the importance of conducting a quasi and/or hybrid CBPR and PAR approach within a socioecocultural approach to address the experience of African American urban adolescents and emerging adults. The implication for conducting CBPR and PAR is to foster trust.

FOR FURTHER STUDY

Suggested Assignments

Provide an overview of a CBPR proposal for a project addressing a social issue among African American urban adolescents. The mini proposal should include an introduction and background; significance of the problem; research questions and hypotheses; brief review of the literature; strategies for community engagement and applying CBPR principles; proposed methodology; and implications for research, practice, and policy.

Identify a CBPR project to observe in your community and address the following questions. What CBPR principles stand out in the project? How did the researchers apply the CBPR principles? Were all the principles applied? How was the community involved? What are the strengths and limitations of the CBPR project?

Suggested Readings

Bermúdez Parsai, M., Castro, F. G., Marsiglia, F. F., Harthun, M. L., & Valdez, H. (2011). Using community based participatory research to create a culturally grounded intervention for parents and youth to prevent risky behaviors. *Prevention Science: The Official Journal of the Society for Prevention Research, 12*(1), 34–47.

Buchanan, D. R., Miller, F. G., & Wallerstein, N. (2007). Ethical issues in community-based participatory research: Balancing rigorous research with community participation in community intervention studies. *Progress in Community Health Partnerships: Research, Education, and Action, 1*(2), 153–160.

Flicker, S. (2008). Who benefits from community-based participatory research? A case study of the Positive Youth Project. *Health Education & Behavior: The Official Publication of the Society for Public Health Education, 35*(1), 70–86.

Hicks, S., Duran, B., Wallerstein, N., Avila, M., Belone, L., Lucero,...Hat, E. W. (2012). Evaluating community-based participatory research to improve community-partnered science and community health. *Progress in Community Health Partnerships: Research, Education, and Action, 6*(3), 289–299.

Israel, B. A., Schulz, A. J., Parker, E. A., Becker, A. B., and Community-Campus Partnerships for Health. (2001). Community-based participatory research: Policy recommendations for promoting a partnership approach in health research. *Education for Health (Abingdon, England), 14*(2), 182–197.

Israel, B. A., Schulz, A. J., Parker, E. A., & Becker, A. B. (1998). Review of community-based research: Assessing partnership approaches to improve public health. *Annual Review of Public Health, 19*, 173–202.

Israel, B., Eng, E., Schulz, A., Parker, E., (2013). *Methods of community based participatory research* (2nd ed.) San Francisco, CA: Jossey-Bass.

Kaplan, S. A., Ruddock, C., Golub, M., Davis, J., Foley, R., Devia, C.,...Calman, N. (2009). Stirring up the mud: Using a community-based participatory approach to address health disparities through a faith-based initiative. *Journal of Health Care for the Poor and Underserved, 20*(4), 1111–1123.

Minkler, M., & Wallerstein, N. (Eds.). (2008). *Community based participatory research for health: From process to outcomes* (2nd ed.). San Francisco, CA: Jossey-Bass.

Muhammad, M., Wallerstein, N., Sussman, A., Avila, M., & Belone, L. (2014). Reflections on researcher identity and power: The impact of positionality on community based participatory research (CBPR) processes and outcomes. *Critical Sociology.*

Wallerstein, N., & Duran, B. (2010). Community-based participatory research contributions to intervention research: The intersection of science and practice to improve health equity. *American Journal of Public Health, 100 Suppl 1*, S40–S46.

Wilson, N., Dasho, S., Martin, A., Wallerstein, N., Wang, C., & Minkler, M. (2007). Photo voice: The youth empowerment strategies (yes!). *The Journal of Early Adolescence, 27*, 241.

NOTE

1. Socioecocultural is a term that we decided to coin as it places an emphasis on the social, ecological, and cultural context of urban youth. Generally, the term ecological or socioecological is used, however, we feel that the cultural context of African American youth encompasses unique and pervasive urban factors which play a critical role in their sense of self and belongingness to their community.

REFERENCES

Attar, B. K., Guerra, N. G., & Tolan, P. H. (1994). Neighborhood disadvantage, stressful life events, and adjustment in urban elementary school children. *Journal of Clinical Child Psychology, 23*, 391–400.

Bennett, M. D., & Miller, D. B. (2006). An exploratory study of the Urban Hassles Index: A contextually relevant measure of chronic multidimensional urban stressors. *Research on Social Work Practice, 16*, 305–314.

Berry, J. W. (1986). The acculturation process and refugee behavior. In C. L. Williams & J. Westinmeyer (Eds.), *Refugee mental health in resettlement countries* (pp. 25–37). Washington, DC: Hemisphere Publishing Corp.

Berry, J. W. (1997). Immigration, acculturation and adaptation. *Applied Psychology, 46,* 5–68.

Berry, J. W. (2001). A Psychology of immigration. *Journal of Social Issues, 57*(3), 615–631.

Berry, J. W., & Kalin, R. (2001). Multicultural policy and social psychology: The Canadian experience. In S. Renshon & J. Duckitt (Eds.), *Political psychology in cross-cultural perspective* (pp. 263–284). New York, NY: Macmillan.

Black, M. M., & Krishnakumar, A. (1998). Children in low-income, urban settings. Interventions to promote mental health and well-being. *The American Psychologist, 53*(6), 635–646.

Breland-Noble, A. M., Bell, C. C., Burriss, A., Poole, H. K., and The AAKOMA Project Adult Advisory Board. (2012). The significance of strategic community engagement in recruiting African American youth & families for clinical research. *Journal of Child and Family Studies, 21*(2), 273–280.

Bronfenbrenner, U. (1989). Ecological systems theory. In R. Vasta (Ed.), *Annals of child development: Six theories of child development-Revised formulations and current issues* (pp. 187–249). London, UK: JAI Press.

Cabrera, N., Beeghly, M. J., Brown, C., Casa, J., Palacios, N.,...Rodriguez, J. (2013). Social policy report: Positive development of minority children. *Society for Research in Child Development, 27*(2), 2–27.

Davies, G. (2006). *Crime, neighborhood, and public housing.* New York, NY : LFB Publishing.

Fitzpatrick, K. M., & Boldizar, J. P. (1993). The prevalence and consequences of exposure to violence among African American youth. *Journal of the American Academy of Child and Adolescent Psychiatry, 32,* 424–430. doi: 10.1097/00004583-199303000-00026

García Coll, C., Lamberty, G., Jenkins, R., McAdoo, H. P., Crnic, K., Wasik, B. H., et al. (1996). An integrative model for the study of developmental competencies in minority children. *Child Development, 67*(5), 1891–1914.

Gordon, M. M. (1964). *Assimilation in American life.* New York, NY: Oxford University Press.

Graves, T. (1967). Psychological acculturation in a tri-ethnic community. *South-Western Journal of Anthropology, 23,* 337–350.

Green, L. W. (2003). Tracing federal support for participatory research in public health. In M. Minkler & N. Wallerstein (Eds.), *Community based participatory research for health.* San Francisco, CA.

Hartwig, K., Calleson, D., & Williams, M. (2006). Unit 1: Community-based participatory research: Getting grounded. Examining community-institutional partnerships for prevention research group. Developing and sustaining community-based participatory research partnerships: A skill-building curriculum. Retrieved from http://www.cbprcurriculum.info/

Israel, B. A., Schulz, A. J., Parker, E. A., & Becker, A. B. (1998). Review of community-based research: Assessing partnership approaches to improve public health. *Annual Review of Public Health, 19,* 173–202.

Leviton, L. C., Snell, E., & McGinnis, M. (2000). Urban issues in health promotion strategies. *American Journal of Public Health, 90*(6), 863–866.

Margolin, G., & Gordis, E. B. (2000). The effects of family and community violence on children. *Annual Review of Psychology, 51,* 445–479.

Minkler, M., & Wallerstein, N. (2008). *Community based participatory research for health: From process to outcomes* (2nd ed.). San Francisco, CA: Jossey-Bass.

Morales, J. R., & Guerra, N. G. (2006). Effects of multiple context and cumulative stress on urban children's adjustment in elementary school. *Child development, 77*(4), 907–923.

Muss, R. E. (1996). *Theories of adolescence* (6th ed.). McGraw-Hill Humanities/Social Sciences/ Languages

National Institutes of Health (NIH), Office of Behavioral Health and Social Science Research. (2015). *Community based participatory research*. Retrieved from http://obssr.od.nih.gov/scientific_areas/methodology/community_based_participatory_research

Nebbitt, V. E., Lombe, M., Yu, M., Vaughn, M. G., & Stokes, C. (2012). Ecological correlates of substance use in African American adolescents living in public housing communities: Assessing the moderating effects of social cohesion. *Children and Youth Services Review, 34*(2), 338–347.

Nebbitt, V. E., Williams, J. H., Lombe, M., McCoy, H., & Stephens, J. (2014). Descriptive analysis of individual and community factors among African American youths in urban public housing. *Social Work, 59*(3), 231–241.

Phinney, J., Berry, J. W., Vedder, P., & Liebkind, K. (2006). The acculturation experience: Attitudes, identities, and behaviors of immigrant youth. In J. W. Berry, J. S. Phinney, D. L. Sam, & P. Vedder (Eds.), *Immigrant youth in cultural transition: Acculturation, identity, and adaptation across national contexts* (pp. 71–116). Mahwah, NJ: Lawrence Erlbaum Associates, Inc.

Public and Indian Housing Information Center. (2013). *Inventory Management System (IMS)/PIH Information Center (PIC)*. Retrieved from http://portal.hud.gov/hudportal/HUD?src=/program_offices/public_indian_housing/systems/pic

Rosario, M., Salzinger, S., Feldman, R. S., & Ng-Mak, D. S. (2003). Community violence exposure and delinquent behaviors among youth: The moderating role of coping. *Journal of Community Psychology, 31*(5), 489–512.

Rubin, A., & Babbie, E. (2014). *Research methods for social work* (8th ed.). Brooks /Cole, Belmont: CA: Wadsworth.

Tandon, R. (1988). Social transformation and participatory research. *Convergence, 21*(2/3), 5–18.

Turner, R. J., & Avison, W. R. (2003). Status variations in stress exposure: Implications for the interpretation of research on race, socioeconomic status, and gender. *Journal of Health and Social Behavior, 44*(4), 488–505.

U.S. Census Bureau. (2010). *Population projection program*. Retrieved from http://factfinder.census.gov/home/staff/main.html

Wells, A., Mance, G. A., & Tirmazi, M. T. (2010). Mental health in the realm of primary prevention. In L. Cohen, V. Chavez, & S. Chehimi (Eds.), *Prevention is primary: Strategies for community well-being.* (pp. 371–396). San Francisco, CA: Jossey-Bass.

WK Kellogg Foundation Community Health Scholars Program. (2012). *Definition of community-based participatory research*. Retrieved from http://www.kellogghealthscholars.org/about/community.php

Youngstrom, E., Weist, M. D., & Albus, K. E. (2003). Exploring violence exposure, stress, protective factors and behavioral problems among inner-city youth. *American Journal of Community Psychology, 32*(1–2), 115–129.

CHAPTER 22

Leadership and Administration of Systems in Urban Settings

Colette Walker Thomas and Jarrell J. McRae

Have you ever undergone an experience where you were asked, "Would you prefer to work individually or within a group?" Ask yourself, were you being asked individually about your preference, or were you being asked as a part of a group? Personally, you should have a good idea of your own strengths and weaknesses. Knowledge of self can drive a person toward individual success, or to understand that there is power in numbers and seek allies for collective success. The same process creates leaders and active leadership abilities within people.

Leadership in many ways is an internal process that is manifested in one's desire to have an impact on or persuade a person or group. In micro-level social work we learn that one must build a therapeutic rapport with a client in order to build the client–clinician relationship. Within marketing and business development the same idea exists. Gaining stakeholder or consumer buy-in or trust is a form of leadership. One must be able to gain the trust and loyalty of a group of individuals to assist in the achievement of a set goal (Bunker, Hall, & Kram, 2010; Chrislip & Learson, 1994; Denhardt, Denhardt, & Aristigueta, 2009; Hays, Kearney, & Coggburn, 2009; Starling, 2010). Thus, it is important to explore the correlation between the skills for building a client relationship and ideal leadership abilities.

1. A social worker must be empathetic toward the client and his or her needs while also maintaining ethical and legal boundaries.

2. A social worker must be an active listener and supportive of the client through the process of communicating issues and concerns clearly.

3. A social worker must support autonomy throughout the process in order to ensure that the client gains personal breakthrough independently.

4. A social worker must be sure to not offend the client with both verbal and nonverbal gestures.

5. A social worker must let the client set the goals and projected outcomes to ensure the client's investment in treatment.

These are but a few core goals a social worker hopes to achieve in the first three to four sessions with a new client. Transferring these ideals to a more macro clientele, for example, a clinical director for a major mental health facility must be able to:

1. Understand the mission and vision of the organization to ensure all decisions meet the standards of the mission and vision.

2. Translate the goals of the organization to staff to ensure buy-in and commitment to the set goals and tasks.

3. Support staff to ensure their investment in the organization as well as to promote the staff members' professional growth.

4. Exude and model appropriate communication, both verbally and nonverbally, to support a positive work environment.

5. Appropriately guide both clinical practice while also keeping the ethical standards to maintain clear professional boundaries between staff and management.

DEFINITIONS

Key terms that are used throughout the chapter are as follows:

Macro practice—The application of social work practice through administrative venues. The macro–social work administration develops and guides organizations through change and development by using a "big picture" approach to impact policy, procedures, and practice that benefit clients (Chrislip & Learson, 1994; Denhardt, Denhardt, & Aristigueta, 2009; Starling, 2010).

Leadership—The ability to motivate and inspire others to believe in and execute the vision and mission set forth. "Leadership is everyone's business. Leadership is not a place" or position; "it is a process" (Goldsmith & Beckhard, 1996, p. 108). This definition implies that the title "Leader," "CEO," "Executive Director," or "President" does not in and of itself make someone deemed effective in the role. Moreover, this definition gives the true leader the ability to share the expectations of guiding macropractice.

Organizational culture—"the set of values, norms, guiding beliefs and understanding that is shared by members of an organization and taught to new members as a correct way to think, feel, and behave" (Daft, 2010, p. 374).

MACRO PRACTICE AS AN URBAN SOCIAL WORK LEADER

Macro social work, an interesting and unique sector of the profession of social work, offers practitioners the opportunity to guide large organizations, advocate in political arenas, and impact both consumers and public policy. Although macro social work is a fascinating field, many budding social work students and professionals shy away from this arena. Guiding practices for consumers on a large scale in terms of policy and practice can be a daunting task, but it is also very rewarding in terms of its correlation with public and private organizational management, program evaluation, and implementation as well as policy creation and analysis. Over the years, there has been a call and an expressed need for social workers to assume urban leadership positions such as executive director or director of large human service sectors. Yet, with the lack of interest from social workers, individuals with business administration or public administration backgrounds assume many of these leadership positions (Chrislip & Learson, 1994; Denhardt, Denhardt, & Aristigueta, 2009; Starling, 2010).

The issue grows even more serious when assessing the low number of leaders of color who assume leadership positions. Considering that the majority of client populations being served in urban environments are people of color and of low socio-economic status, the contrary exists when it comes to social service leadership. For example, many prominent child welfare agencies located in Baltimore City are headed by non-minority leaders. The client demography for these agencies is majority African Americans. There are other daunting reasons for social workers to be less than thrilled about leading large urban social service agencies, including the navigation of a challenging political system, lack of readily available resources, the inability to attract qualified and committed staff and the public scrutiny of unfortunate situations such as fatalities.

So, what are the basics of macro social work and why is it important for new social work students to aspire to this field? In connecting the dots, students are familiar with the concept of client-centered services; however, when speaking about macro social work, who are your clients? As a macro social worker the client is the policy and procedure that impact the individual who makes up the overall system and those who implement the policy. Therefore, the concept of client-centered service delivery does not change at the tertiary level, but it morphs into a larger concept of service delivery. For example, an assistant director who is asked to introduce a new policy to a program area has to ask himself or herself several questions:

1. What is the best method to present the information?
2. What are the key changes that the policy will address?
3. Which area of the program will be most impacted?
4. How will organizational culture be assessed to ensure that the appropriate changes are made to the desired policies?
5. How will we address and measure policy effectiveness?

Grappling with these questions, the assistant director has completed a needs assessment in order to ensure that appropriate methods are used to deliver information in a meaningful manner and ensure correct implementation. That is,

- In question number 1, the urban leader will need to assess what form of communication should be used so that the consumer and staff receive the policy, understand the purpose of the policy, thus obtaining buy-in for the policy from all parties. A policy directive is only as good as those who believe in it and will execute it. A policy loses its impact if the target audience does not understand its true intent.
- In question number 2, the urban leader is assessing the changes that need to occur for more effectiveness in a particular subject or policy area. Why are we making these changes? What is broken or missing in the existing policy? The leader is determining, based on data from the organization, that a shift in practice needs to occur for more effective service delivery in a particular area.
- In question number 3, the urban leader is drilling down to who will be directly and indirectly impacted by the policy changes or initiatives. The urban leader needs to assess how this will impact the client base, staff, working patterns, and the community at large. The urban leader should expect that any policy directive that is initiated under his or her administration will impact clients and staff for years as it relates to practice. Therefore, no policy should be created as a quick fix to long-term issue. The policy should be relevant for future practice as well as current practice.
- In question number 4, the urban leader is assessing organizational culture and paradigm shifts in practice to adapt to the policy directives. As the urban leader works to set the expectations and the organizational culture through a clear vision and value base, the staff will begin to see the parallel process between the leader and the work.
- In question number 5, the urban leader is assessing the effectiveness of the policy directive. Unlike question number two where the urban leader is assessing whether the policy is being implemented, in this question the urban leader must determine whether the policy made a positive difference in the subject area for which it was intended. This is a critical point for the leader to determine whether there needs to be a change of course or an enhancement of what has already begun.

GUIDING ORGANIZATIONAL CHANGE

Organizations are in constant change and evolution. For caseworkers and families, these changes are usually gradual but expected. Every couple of years an organization may undergo a major system-wide change that will impact service delivery and case worker performance. These changes may be driven by external factors such as state-wide performance base contracting (PBC), child welfare performance outcomes or rate reform/funding. Internal factors such as a redesign of service delivery, new database system, and change in board expectation will also impact organizational change. How the urban leader understands the impact of the organizational change and how he or she selects to implement the changes will have a significant impact on how clients and caseworkers receive the changes (Bunker, Hall, & Kram, 2010; Goldsmith & Beckhard, 1996; Salacuse, 2006).

The urban leader must be clear in the purpose of the change and ensure that he or she aligns the change with the mission and vision of the organization. This may be easier said than done when expectations are set without input from the organizational leader, but rather from the governing board or state or federal government. However, the leader cannot blame others for the change but own the "change" and develop a clear blueprint for success (Bunker, Hall, & Kram, 2010).

Case Study 1: Urban Organizational Decision Making

You are the director of the child welfare program of a local social service agency. The program functions as a traditional child welfare service, which includes child protective services, foster care, and independent living services. During a regular day at the office, you are alerted by one of your social workers that a child has died. The child is currently in the care and custody of your department of social services. After receiving the police report you discover that the child died due to physical abuse, possibly inflicted by a biological child of the foster parent. Because of the nature of the case, major publicity is given to this story, subjecting the case to both television news and local periodicals. The state governing agency for child welfare policy and practice now intervenes and asks for a plan of action and a full investigation on both the practices of the foster parents and the local social service program, which you manage.

1. What will be your first action step?

2. Who will you partner with to review practices within your program and ensure that an unbiased assessment of services and policy implementation is conducted?

3. How will you triage the concerns of your staff, foster parents, biological children in the home, social worker assigned to both the foster family, and the biological family of the deceased child?

4. Name and describe three pros and cons of the scenario and those which you believe will have a real impact of the program you manage and the series you provide.

5. Name three different endeavors that you believe will restore faith on your assigned program and assist all parties impacted to find resolve and move forward.

The death of any client in any mental health or human service setting can be devastating. However, death in an urban setting is more likely to occur due to inconsistency between service capacity and a larger service area as well as the lack of education and enduring poverty. Though a very sensitive and disheartening ordeal to undertake, a human service supervisor or manager must have the ability to practice empathy. Empathy includes an understanding of secondary trauma to ensure support for the assigned social worker, agency staff, and the family. Remember the concepts of micro, mezzo, and macro social work practice. Despite being identified as a leader, one is also a social worker with the responsibility over the agency. The caseload of a human service leader includes not only the identified clients under his or her program, but also the social workers and other assigned staff that deliver services.

As a leader, refrain from allowing anxiety or stress to impact decision making, which often indirectly model negative behaviors to staff. Maintaining your professionalism and upholding appropriate social work practices in terms of triaging major incidents, will send a nonverbal message to staff that you are addressing the issue at hand and you are confident that the situation will gain a positive resolution. No leader knows the true outcome of negative occurrences regarding client services. However, high profile and extremely negative situations shape and mold leaders and provide an experience that is rarely gained through matriculation of any master or doctoral program. The first step to overcoming a strenuous and extremely high profile case is to believe in your leadership's ability and the staff that provide services. There must be an inherent core belief that your staff is capable and competent to carry out their assigned task as the social worker.

The scenario discusses the death of a client who allegedly was physically abused by a youth, which caused injuries and lead to the death of the child. The leader's initial step will be to have an emergency meeting with the assigned social worker, supervisor, and the quality and compliance manager. The meeting should be formulated to help you understand the case in its entirety. Most agencies have media controls, which will typically prevent the front line worker from being in the cross fire of interviews. However, when leaders are responding to media questions or state officials, supervisory personnel and/or caseworker personnel are not present. A leader of any program needs to be an expert in not only policy and practice, but the endeavors of his or her workers to triage normal case issues. Knowledge of cases will help you as a leader to track trends and begin to mold practices through policy implementation and accountability to ensure quality service delivery at every interaction.

WORKING WITHIN SYSTEMS: QUALITY SERVICE DELIVERY VERSUS ORGANIZATIONAL EXPECTATIONS

As the federal government becomes more selective with funding as it relates to programs such as Title IV-E, the expectations and monitoring by state agencies have significantly increased. Many state child welfare agencies have undergone a PBC process for providers, which will directly impact the very existence of a program or agency. The PBC is implemented as a report card to include the elements of a monthly safety report, Child and Adolescent Needs and Strengths (CANS) completion, as well as being on the state referral hold, known as a "hot list." Provider leaders have indicated that because of the attention given to completing different data fields, the quality of service delivery has been challenging. Leadership has been extremely challenged in balancing both fiscal business expectations, with quality clinical performance.

Urban leaders have special challenges in that there are many providers saturated in the urban environment. This saturation causes providers to be extremely competitive for the same resources both in staff talent and funding. Urban programs constantly have to reinvent themselves to be more marketable to those who fund services. The conflict in that may be that those providers may not be specializing in anything, but generalizing in a variety of things. This lack of urban specialization could have a direct impact on the client population that is being served.

Even a chief executive officer (CEO) has to report to someone above him or her, usually a governing board or board of directors and board president. The board of directors' responsibility is to oversee a private or public organization to include fiduciary responsibility and to assist in setting policy and administrative procedures and hire and evaluate the organization's key leadership. To that end, social work leaders often must educate the board on social services, state regulations, and how they impact business, client population, and the politics of doing business in a particular region, county, or state (Chrislip & Learson, 1994; Hays, Kearney, & Coggburn, 2009).

There are many competing attributes for working with both nonprofit and for profit agencies. Nonprofit agencies allow for grant funding in addition to federal funding. Moreover, the nonprofit leader can solicit private dollars such as an annual giving fund or gifts in kind. Funds are limited and resources can be difficult to ascertain for additional support in areas that are specified in state regulations.

For-profit agencies are forbidden to raise funds or receive most grant funding; however, for-profit agencies are typically funded by corporate funders. The downside to for profit is the accountability to the board and their lack of knowledge about the work. The social work leader spends a significant amount of time educating the board on the work and the purpose of the work. The board is focused on financial stability and possible expansion.

A social work leader is often faced with the challenges of balancing quality outcomes with revenue expectations, whether imposed by the funders or by the government. Social work leaders must learn not only the basic business skills, but the advance business skills for effective macro-leadership. This unique leader knows not only the state regulations for caring for a particular client population, but also knows the business regulations for operations.

URBAN LEADERS LEADING WITH GRACE

The term *servant leadership* may sound like a buzz word these days, but the ability to lead with grace and a sense of compassion is an art and a gift. The true leader recognizes that they are only as effective as the team they lead and the outcomes that the team achieves. Gratitude, for the privilege to serve those less fortunate is the key to being effective in the industry of urban social service administration. The minute the leader loses sight of why they are in this business, is the moment when the work is no longer effective.

Leading with *Grace* is the ability to admit when one is wrong and not feel judged; being able to make the difficult decisions that will invariably impact someone; being able to treat each person with dignity and respect despite how they may be treating the leader or the business; allowing the team to grow and perhaps leave the nest that has been created. Leading with *Grace* is the ability to set aside one's ego, and to allow for others to grow and develop under one's leadership so that they can execute the agency vision and mission. Leading with *Grace* is knowing that the work that one does is *God Driven*, not self-serving and self-promoting.

Social work is not a field that most people randomly fall into, but are rather drawn to the profession because of a personal experience or interaction with a social worker. Social work is often referred to as a God Driven job, many are called but few are chosen. Social work is both emotionally and physically challenging and oftentimes not monetarily rewarded. However, every year schools of social work all around the country admit hundreds of students, who believe that they have received the calling. For many students the true test comes when they are face with field practicums that challenge their ability to impact change. Social work leaders accept the challenge of serving the student and client population and the educators and staff that lead the work.

ORGANIZATIONAL CULTURE AND LEADERSHIP

The social work leader sets the tone of the culture of the organization through the mission and vision that the leader puts forth. A leader that fails to implement a clear vision for the agency will breed a negative culture for both the clients and team. On the other hand, a leader who is clear with the agency vision and supportive of achieving the vision will breed a healthy and positive culture that will have the confidence of both its staff and clients alike. The bottom line is that the top leader sets the tone of how employees will function from day to day. According to Leading at a Higher Level, "A compelling vision creates a strong culture in which the energy of everyone in the organization is aligned. This results in trust, customer satisfaction, an energized and committed workforce, and profitability. Conversely, when an organization does not live up to its stated values, employee and customer trust and commitment erode, negatively impacting all aspects of the bottom line" (Blanchard, 2011, p. 25).

As stated earlier, the social work leader must not only be clear about the vision, but be clear about the core values that guides the leader's work. The leader must stick to those core values that he or she has set for himself or herself as it relates to the work—a personal code of ethics. Every social worker should be guided not only by a professional code of ethics, but also standards of values and ethics. These ethics for the leader should start with how one intends to lead and guide the team.

A fundamental basic value of leadership and customer service is the golden rule of always treating people as one would like to be treated. Simply put, placing oneself in the role of one's staff or client helps one connect better to the work. Not only does a leader need to be concerned with the clinical services, but also the aesthetics of the building and programs offered. The question then is: Would a child entering that program connect it to a feeling of safety and home?

A second value is to always maintain the dignity and respect of everyone. Leaders often encounter situations that challenge sensibilities and human nature. It is important to keep in mind that a leader is always being observed by others on how he or she handles the most challenging of situations. Thus, leaders must refrain from being in a position of losing one's "cool." It is in these moments of controversy and challenge that true leadership prevails. Likewise, the ability to terminate people who are failing to perform and maintain their dignity and respect is an art form.

A third value of leadership is to never believe that one is the only expert in the room. Oftentimes, leaders feel that, as the head of the organization, they are charged with being the expert on all matters. This could not be further from the truth. A leader's expertise lies in the ability to set a vision and a mission for the organization and maintain its finances and grow and sustain the organization. A good leader trusts that the team they lead and the staff are the experts of the work. That is why an effective leader with proven results can lead almost any area of work regardless of their educational or credentialed background.

A fourth value is to know that others are capable of resolving the problem. An effective leader encourages its employees to problem solve prior to bringing the issue to the leader's attention. This encourages the employees to think more macro and be engaged in problem solving. Moreover, it reduces the dependency that the employees tend to have with leaders that require a micromanagement style.

NAVIGATING RESOURCES IN AN URBAN COMMUNITY

As discussed earlier in this chapter, financial resources for urban environments are scarce and highly competitive, while the needs for this population continue to soar. According to the Child Welfare Outcomes 2008 to 2011 Report to Congress produced by the Children's Bureau, a decline in Title IV-E funding has caused state systems to be challenged in providing services. During 2008 to 2011 the report states that 25 states (48%) improved in their ability to triage cases of child victims experiencing a reoccurrence of child maltreatment within a 6-month period; whereas 22 states (42%) decreased in their ability to prohibit child victims from experiencing a reoccurrence of child maltreatment within a 6-month period. Although every state programming may differ, federal mandates are still the primary focus of ensuring the safety, permanency, and well-being of youth. Therefore, based on the report, many states failed to meet the overall case management, clinical, and therapeutic needs to support the decrease in recidivism, or youth reengaging in the child welfare system.

Although many of the primary issues may not be economically based in terms of implementing best practices to ensure success, the overarching concern is the lack of financial resources to support implementation of best practices as well as support for youth and families in need. The report further stated that Title IV-E Legislation and Policy has been amended several times to ensure funding for foster care, adoptive resources, as well as kinship resources. However, with the growing need for services due to a large but steady number of individuals with a low socioeconomic status, public and private social agencies continue to see a high need for services with little funding to support the appropriate service delivery.

Urban programs operating in a postrecession environment have the unique challenge of battling other programs for financial resources. Many federal, state, and private funding sources evaporated following 9/11 as funds for the Department of Health and Human Services (HHS) and Administration for Children and Families (ACF) were deferred to support war efforts and homeland security. The trickle-down effect was that a mass recession occurred, which impacted private funding sources. The world of social services was impacted significantly through both private donations and public funding.

Case Study 2: Navigating Urban Resources

A program manager in an urban public sector of social services experiences a budget cut for a vulnerable adult program under his or her supervision. The program manager is forced to transfer five caseworkers to new assignments in the organization to balance the budget. After the budget cut, a pilot program funding totaling $150,000 to support a family kinship program is provided to the program manager. The pilot is geared toward decreasing the number of children transferring into foster care from the family preservation service area. Although supportive funds have been filtered into the child welfare program, the adult services area is lacking necessary funding to drive supportive services for older adults and other vulnerable adult population within the region.

Given the growing aging population and number of elder abuse reports that occurred within the last fiscal year, the program manager knows that service delivery in the area of vulnerable adults is a key deliverable for the region. The program manager reviews the utilization policy for the allotted funds to the child welfare program. The program manager learns that $75,000 of the funds are dedicated to the hiring of three temporary caseworker staff to investigate reports of alleged neglect or abuse, determine if a home is viable for the child to remain in the family home, and provide 3 to 6 months of case management services to stabilize the family to ensure that the child remains in the family placement. The

(continued)

(*continued*)

other $75,000 is allocated to providing short-term emergency services to families in need. The program manager decides that the vulnerable adult program can benefit from the additional funding source. Think about it:

1. Do you agree with the decision made by the program manager to support the vulnerable adult program via the pilot program funding source?

2. Based on the program manager's decision, how would you move forward with implementing the allocated funds to support the reestablishment of the vulnerable adults program while also implementing the family/kinship program? Address the following areas of concern:

    • Staff
    • Program goals
    • Evaluation
    • Outcomes

3. What barriers would you expect to face? Why?

4. Knowing that the service delivery funding is $75,000 for an entire fiscal year, how would you monitor spending and what key services would you provide? Why?

5. Why is it important to identify data elements and track outcomes of the vulnerable adult program?

Our discussion began with the decision of the program manager to utilize the pilot program funding to support the vulnerable adult program. The vulnerable adult program funding was cut due to a lack of data that supported the need for funding the overall program. Funding for the adult program supports five full-time staff members as well as supportive funds to implement emergency services when necessary. The pilot program, although child welfare driven, provides you the opportunity to retain three of the five caseworkers that were transferred. The three caseworkers will have the knowledge to assess families for neglect and/or abuse of a human being, which can be transferred to a child welfare continuum. The question becomes is this misuse of program funds? Every urban human service leader will be faced with the dilemma of quality service delivery versus fiduciary concerns. Based on society, political agendas, and other environmental factors, the economical status of a nation, state, or local government can be altered. Therefore, it is imperative that a leader be innovative as well as strategic when utilizing funds and implementing services. A strategic leader is not only concerned with local issues, but also national and world issues as these issues ultimately impact the local government budget. An innovative leader understands the need and the policy-driven endeavors, which support ongoing service delivery. The innovative leader evaluates the program and envisions creative avenues to move services forward even in times of economic woes.

IMPLICATIONS FOR THE FUTURE

Urban social work leaders are faced with many challenges that are unique to the urban environments as described in this chapter. The role of urban leaders in today's climate is to set the vision that will assist the agency, customers, and staff in navigating through financial funding dilemmas, political land mines, and changing expectations of federal and state governing bodies.

Encouraging social workers of color to become urban leaders of human service agencies is essential to the viability of service delivery as it relates to understanding the populations served. Disproportionality or the overrepresentation of people of color is widespread in urban social service agencies. However, despite the large numbers of individuals of color within urban areas of service delivery, there continues to be a large disparity in leader of color. Furthermore, there continues to be a trend of leaders guiding practices with a nonhuman service or social work educational backgrounds. Having leadership that understands and can empathize with the population will yield better treatment outcomes. Therefore, the need for human service professionals to aspire for leadership roles is imperative in this postrecession era, as our nation begins to redefine and reenvision service delivery to combat 21st-century social issues.

Although schools of social work graduate hundreds of students per year, on average, most students shy away from macro practice, and desire micro or direct practice. Schools of social work will have to do a better job making the argument for macro practice and giving the students the tools for leadership. Urban communities are depending on people with social work skills to become the community change agents and policy advocates.

FOR FURTHER STUDY

Suggested Assignments

1. *Leadership portfolio*—Develop a leadership portfolio that describes your philosophy or theory of leadership practice. Include principles, values, knowledge, and skills applicable to leadership and administration of social service systems. This portfolio will *evolve* with time and experience. However, the basic components of this assignment will include a current resume; a few paragraphs about your ideas and assumptions about social work leadership; a leadership assessment (decision making, processing information, interacting with people, strengths, challenges, etc.) using a formal or informal tool; your philosophy about social work leadership based on your professional and personal experiences; and your leadership plan (goals and aspirations).

2. *Policy practice forum*—Attend a social work policy practice forum including National Association of Social Workers (NASW) or Council on Social Work Education (CSWE) lobbying sessions and write a one-page paper on implications for social work leadership.

3. *Leadership training resource list*—In small teams, create a resource list of existing leadership training opportunities specifically for developing social work leaders and administrators. The list may include local, national, or international opportunities.

Suggested Readings

Allen, S. A., & Vakalahi, H. F. O. (2013). My team members are everywhere! A critical analysis of the emerging literature on dispersed teams. *Administration in Social Work, 37*, 1–8.

Bass, B. M. (1998). *Transformational leadership*. Mahwah, NJ: Erlbaum.

Brody, R. (2004). *Effectively managing human service organizations*. Thousand Oaks, CA: Sage.

Claiborne, N. (2004). Presence of social workers in nongovernment organizations. *Social Work, 49*(2), 207–218.

Coley, S. M., & Scheinberg, C. A. (2008). Proposal writing: Effective grantsmanship. Thousand Oaks, CA: Sage.

Gellis, Z. D. (2001). Social work perceptions of transformational and transactional leadership in health care. *Social Work Research, 25*, 17–25.

Howard, L. W., & Dougherty, T. W. (2004). Alternative reward strategies and employee reactions. *Compensation & Benefits Review, 36*(1), 41–51.

Levi, D. (2010). *Group dynamics for teams*. Thousand Oaks, CA: Sage Publications.

Mizrahi, T., & Berger, C. S. (2001). Effect of a changing health care environment on social work leaders: Obstacles and opportunities in hospital social work. *Social Work, 46*(2), 170–182.

Northouse, P. G. (2010). *Leadership: Theory and practice*. Thousand Oaks, CA: Sage.

Spencer, P. C., & Munch, S. (2003). Client violence toward social workers: The role of management in community mental health programs. *Social Work, 48*(4), 532–544.

REFERENCES

Blanchard, K. (2011). *Leading at a higher level*. Upper Saddle River, NJ: BMC.

Bunker, K. A., Hall, D. T., & Kram, K. E. (2010). *Extraordinary leadership: Addressing the gaps in senior executive development*. San Francisco, CA: John Wiley & Sons.

Chrislip, D. D., & Learson, C. E. (1994). *Collaborative leadership*. Danvers, MA: John Wiley & Sons.

Daft, R. L. (2010). *Organizational theory and design* (10th ed.). Mason, OH: South-Western Cengage Learning.

Denhardt, R. B., Denhardt, J. V., & Aristigueta, M. P. (2009). *Managing human behavior in public and non profit organizations*. Thousand Oaks, CA: Sage.

Goldsmith, M., & Beckhard, R. (1996). *The Drucker Foundation: The leader of the future*. San Francisco, CA: Jossey-Bass.

Hays, S. W., Kearney, R. C., & Coggburn, J. D. (2009). *Public human resource management: Problems and prospects*. New York, NY: Pearson Education.

Salacuse, J. W. (2006). *Leading leaders*. New York, NY: Amacom.

Starling, G. (2010). *Managing the public sector*. Boston, MA: Wadsworth.

CHAPTER 23

Urgency and Advocacy for Organizational Change in Urban Public School Settings: A Social Work Perspective on Meeting the Needs of African American Children

Claudia Lawrence-Webb

At one time, the passion for learning and embracing education as a pathway to understanding the world around us was an avenue to strive for one's personal dreams and secure one's future. It was viewed as a means of escaping the negative aspects of life. Those who were fortunate to secure it were more successful in maneuvering and using their environments to their personal advantage. It was clearly set aside for the elite. Those unable to secure an education became the population of low-skilled workers necessary for the establishment of a prosperous manufacturing nation that relied on such individuals to keep the economy going. The juxtaposition of education in this manner has become a strategy and trend that has consistently played out over the historical development of the United States as a world power (Dewey, 1902, 1997). However, with the advent of technology and the global economy, the nation must revisit the role of education as a tool for maintaining the United States in a position of power so that it can equally compete with other nations and secure its status in the distribution of world resources. We can no longer send a message that education is not critical to the larger scheme of what is taking place globally (Smith, 2013).

Public educational institutions by the very nature of their bureaucratic structure appear to be challenged in an environment in much need of educational creativity. It is not that this structure did not produce creative young people who could be critical thinkers, analyze their surroundings, and come up with brilliant solutions for addressing world problems. But, it is the nature of how concepts and ideas are being taught to engage in such rigorous practices and interventions that allow this activity to take place and the context in which young people are evolving that requires examination.

Young people today are impacted by numerous social conditions that did not exist before—high rates of violence, low rates of marriages, high rates of divorce, highly mobile families, economic structure perpetuating two parent working families, and so on (Sullivan & Artiles, 2011). The constant adjustment and readjustment to the evolving nature of society makes it hard for the educational system to keep pace when it is encapsulated in such a restrictive organizational model of bureaucracy (Sahlberg, 2011). This model also has serious implications for the outcomes of schools and whether they are nimble enough to capitalize on the rapid changes taking place. This chapter discusses the historical nature of education in public schools, the legislative framework that it occupies, and its impact on the delivery of educational services and minority student populations residing in urban environments.

What does this have to do with education in urban settings? It has everything to do with education in urban settings as the majority of urban settings are educational locales where tax bases are low, where the majority of minority students receive their education and where resources and educational supports are scarce and in some instances nonexistent (Kozol, 1991, 2005; Ravitch, 2000). Young individuals coming from such environments are often ill prepared to effectively participate in the larger economy due to limited educational resources in their school settings (Blanchett, 2009; O'Connor & Fernandez, 2006). As a result, it is paramount that educational resources and opportunities be made available to everyone.

The current state of education is in flux, under attack, and seems to be off its course in terms of what is being taught, how it is being taught, and the overriding purpose of education (Weingarten, 2014). The debate seems to be: Is education for the liberation of people so that they can truly understand the world in which they live, how it impacts them, and how to alter its influence for the better of all (Friere, 1972), or is it to support the current democratic institutional structures (Dewey, 1997) in place that may or may not always work to improve the lives of those who comprise it regardless of their station in life? One of the most important things we know about education is that it takes one away from one's roots and exposes you to things that you sometimes could not have imagined existed. Once you learn something new, it will forever change how you view the world. That is why education is so critical, it teaches you to reexamine and question the world in which one lives.

STRUCTURE OF PUBLIC U.S. EDUCATION SYSTEM

Compulsory public education for everyone is a relatively new concept even in the United States. It was not until the 1930s that education became *nationally* compulsory. Furthermore, it was not until the 1960s that the federal government felt the need to establish a Department of Education for consultation and oversight to state and local education systems (U.S. Department of Education, 2011). Public educational institutions have a top-down structure that branches out to the state and local governments. The process starts at pre-K, kindergarten, elementary/middle, and high school levels of education. Schools usually have a state and district headquarters that disseminate information to local school districts and make recommendations for meeting certain basic guidelines for educating students. There is a lot of flexibility to locals for how they want to do things, but the rigidity comes in at the local levels of implementation. It is often politics that dictate what happens at this level fed by those in power making decisions for a few. Different associations and societal groups can influence this process by using their advocacy skills and persuasion of local and state school boards to entertain and promote what they perceive to be important in the process. It is at these varying levels that parents exact their influence about the educational dynamics, policies, and structures impacting their children (www.ed.gov/about/offices/list/ous/international/usnei/edlite-index.html).

How did we end up in this state of mass confusion and constant political debate about the role of education? It is quite interesting how the debate is framed in terms of a national discussion, especially when the federal government has little power to influence what happens in education, because education in the United States is decentralized, meaning that its very nature is really determined at the state and local levels (U.S. Department of Education, 2013). The U.S. Department of Education can make recommendations to states and locales about what they think is most critical to successful educational outcomes. However, the implementation of policies are left to the discretion of each state except for the legislation passed by Congress and deemed to be so fundamental to the process of educating students that every jurisdiction must meet certain basic requirements of the tenets of legislation (www.ed.gov/about/offices/list/ous/international/usnei/edlite-index.html). It is this relationship between the federal government and state or local governments that contribute to the discrepancies and disparities between what students learn in their educational process from state to state.

Johnathan Kozol (1991, 2005) and Ravitch (2000) make this abundantly clear when they discuss how education is funded from state to state and locale to locale. This funding model determines which students are at greater advantages for excellent versus mediocre educational outcomes. It is no secret that local and state tax bases determine how education looks in every district in the country. The greater the tax base and commitment to excellent educational outcomes, the greater the advantage to individual students. Unfortunately, the opposite is also true, resulting in educational outcomes that truly negatively impact not just individual students, but the larger society in terms of what the next generation can contribute and give back to their communities in light of their limited knowledge, skills, and preparation to carry the baton forward in society.

HISTORICAL EVOLVEMENT OF EDUCATION IN THE UNITED STATES

The early school systems within the United States were influenced by the teaching of French and German philosophers such as Rousseau and Frobrel (Dewey, 1902; Friedrich Froebel Timeline, 1998–2008; Mirel, 2011). Early principles of education believed in preparation of young men for the challenges of life with an emphasis on religion and vocational skills. The goal was to teach basic reading skills that would enable individuals to read the Bible so that they would be moral in their rearing of their children and families (Tate, 2014). Friedrich Wilhelm Froebel, founder of kindergarten, and Rousseau advocated that education should emphasize education of students in early childhood to promote natural growth and development and for children to use their own creativity to explore the world in a way that would propel them toward their evolution of becoming productive adult citizens (Friedrich Froebel Timeline, 1998–2008; Hirsch, 2009; Krogh, 1997; Shapiro, 1983; Tate, 2014).

Historically, the one-room school house, for the most part, no longer exists as it had in the past. There are not many locations of such institutions. For many Whites and minority groups in the United States, this is where it all started, a structure to provide a means for producing moral citizens and a necessary workforce for industry (Hirsch, 2009; Mirel, 2011). Although African Americans were at one time denied educational access due to slavery, even within the harsh system of slavery, African Americans still managed to pursue their dreams of education by illegal means and sometimes with the help of benevolent groups and societies like the Quakers and other abolitionist groups. One could be killed for reading, writing, or engaging in arithmetic calculations (The African American Struggle Through the U.S. Educational System, 2008–2009; Blanchett, 2009; Morris & Morris, 2000; Wilbur, Gabraldi, & Reed, 1991). Like Paolo Friere (1972), the liberation of people must come through an educational process.

According to the U.S. Department of Education (2014), the U.S. education system is not based on one, or even a few, framework laws. Instead, there are a wide variety of federal, state, and local laws, plus court decisions and regulations that define various aspects of our decentralized system. In addition, there are rules and policies adopted by educational associations, individual schools, and institutions that often have legal status with respect to matters within their competence (U.S. Department of Education, 2014). This type of framework contributes to a great deal of variant educational outcomes among and across student populations at various educational levels. This is clearly visible in the K–12 levels of education. What students acquire and learn during these years often influence a lifetime of outcomes with respect to occupational and lifelong economic impact (Kozol, 2005; Loewenberg & Forzani, 2011). This is particularly disturbing for minority and/or urban populations who are rapidly becoming statistically the majority group in society (Kozol, 1991).

A recent segment on a National Public Radio (NPR) broadcast (2014) and NBC News (2014) outlets reported that the United States is quickly losing ground as the preeminent nation for being number 1 in many areas including education. This is supported by research of the Program in International Student Assessment (PISA). "PISA's goal is to assess students' preparation for the challenges of life as young adults. PISA assesses the application of knowledge in mathematics, science, and reading literacy to problems within a real-life context" (Organization for Economic Co-operation and Development [OECD], 1999). In an international review of reading, math and science literacy, "eighteen education systems had higher average scores than the United States in all three subjects." The 18 education systems are: Australia, Canada, Chinese Taipei, Estonia, Finland, Germany, Hong Kong-China, Ireland, Japan, Liechtenstein, Macao-China, the Netherlands, New Zealand, Poland, Republic of Korea, Shanghai-China, Singapore, and Switzerland. The U.S. states of Massachusetts and Connecticut also had higher average scores than the United States in all three subjects (National Center for Educational Statistics, See Tables M4, S2, and R2 at http://nces.ed.gov/surveys/pisa/pisa2012/pisa2012highlights_1.asp).

URBAN POPULATIONS AND EDUCATIONAL POLICIES

Where do urban populations fall out in this scenario? Although public school systems nationwide are still predominantly White (58%), minorities are gaining in numbers (41%). However, private schools are far more dominated by White student populations (75%; National Center for Educational Statistics [NCES], 2012). In light of all of these data, minorities continue to be disproportionately represented in urban areas regarding enrollment and as students who are still behind in making the same gains in these areas as their White counterparts. From 1993 to 2003, minorities increased as a proportion of public school enrollment, with schools in central city areas experiencing the most growth in the percentage of minority students (NCES, 2014).

Data from the National Center for Education Statistics (2005) also indicate that minorities comprised about 33% of the U.S. population with the largest group being Hispanic (16%) and African Americans (12%). In addition, the majority of Blacks and Hispanics attended urban public schools with 75% minority enrollment. Since the Brown versus Board of Education court case in 1954, public school systems nationwide have struggled with circumventing its ideal concept of integration and equal access to education (Blanchett, 2009). Clearly, integration has not worked to the degree in which it was envisioned as demonstrated by the segregated school systems in the central parts of urban cities that are currently in place and by the increased numbers of White students attending private and charter schools (Sixty years after Brown v Board, PBS News, May 2014).

In addition to these statistics, minority populations, especially African American males are disproportionately represented in the identification and provision of Special Education Services as it relates to Individuals with Disabilities Education Act referred to as IDEA (O'Connor & Fernandez, 2006; Sullivan & Artiles, 2011).

The educational policies currently being debated and implemented, the rise of minority populations in the United States and the changes in the global economy are intricately integrated with the larger context of the educational outcomes of American students and their futures. Education is fundamental to creating individuals who can influence and change the world's implementation and application to world problems. Minority populations in the United States sit at the center of this process. How we educate our young have dire implications for how our world will look in the future and how we will promote mankind.

One of the most devastating policies to negatively impact education and put the U.S. educational system on a down spiral was the No Child Left Behind Act (Ravitch, 2000). This legislation had an impact on how students are taught and what they are taught. The highly driven concept of testing was central to the legislation and resulted in children being taught to the test as opposed to children being taught to think and analyze. Instead of being taught the knowledge and skill to analyze information to take the test and feel confident in that knowledge and analysis, students are being taught the questions to the test and how best to take the test to answer the questions. As a result, the rote learning taking place to memorize answers to the test has not been good for students (Weingarten, 2014). Now, three new ideas floating to reestablish a system teaching students the necessary skills of critical thinking and being analytic are the Common Core Curriculum (Loewenberg & Forzani, 2011; Minnici, 2014), preschool and early childhood learning initiatives (Sahlberg, 2011), and Race to the Top initiatives to monitor and track the educational process of what is being taught, its effectiveness, and the effectiveness of those teaching the information (Darling-Hammond, 2014; Loewenberg & Forzani, 2011).

A reevaluation of the implementation of the No Child Left Behind Policy needs to be reexamined as research (Kozol, 2005; Ravitch, 2000) indicates that it had the most negative impact on minority populations in urban areas and contributed to the highly disproportionate dropout rate and increased rate in the referral of African American students to special education services. Meeting the imposed requirements of No Child Left Behind was an impossible task when, at the same time, public schools were experiencing a lack of economic support by jurisdictions and legislatures, decreased teaching resources as older teachers began to retire, shortage of new teachers taking their place and a societal trend of reduced supports to families in need of a variety of community resources (Sullivan & Artiles, 2011; Woodard, 2013). At the same time as these events and societal changes have been taking place, there has been a negative wave of sentiment toward teachers and minorities (Cowan, 2014; Weingarten, 2014).

PERCEPTION OF TEACHERS IN URBAN ENVIRONMENTS

Currently teachers are viewed negatively in terms of their roles as public servants. No longer is teaching viewed as an esteemed profession imbued with the trust of educating the nation's children. The atmosphere at times has become venomous. Teachers are blamed for everything from student attendance to failure of students to achieve academically (Christodolou, 2014; Ravitch, 2000; Smith, 2014). According to one recent report on NPR Broadcast (2014), teachers lack the understanding of urgency necessary for pushing students to strive for the higher levels of academic achievement and to teach at such levels.

The perception of "other people's children" as discussed by Delpit (1998) seems to permeate and influence the commitment levels of teachers in terms of their responsibility to students. The often detached relational connections between teachers and students send a message that students are not genuinely cared for by their teachers, as if they were their own children. The concept of seeing a student as an extension of the teacher does not appear to be a concept embraced by some of the more current teachers. Somewhere along the way, this idea became lost in the fast pace environment emphasizing testing and outcome data (Darling-Hammond, 2014; Weingarten, 2014).

Nowhere is this felt more than among minority populations, which, according to research, "need a nurturing, supportive environment" (Morris & Morris, 2000), as it contributes to the ability to succeed academically (Obiakor, 2001). Often minority students are coming from school environments that have been dismally under-resourced in terms of their physical structure, supplies and equipment, staffing and access to academic programs like Advanced Placement (AP) classes (Bestor, 1985; Loewenberger & Forzani, 2011). As a result, students are poorly prepared to transition from one level of schooling to the next, toward high school graduation and then college or the world of work. As older teachers retire and younger teachers replace them, new teachers are often unprepared for some of the experiences and challenges they may encounter in the urban setting (Obiakor, 2001). They are predominantly White, inexperienced, and ill prepared for how to handle what they often view as hostile, resistant, and disruptive students who are unable or unwilling to focus on in class tasks and completion of assignments (Willingham, 2011). Their teacher education may be limited as some are coming from Teach for America, which has a brief training program on becoming a teacher, and others are coming from 4-year education programs that have not fully prepared them for the challenges of the urban school environment (Loewenberg & Forzani, 2011; Minnici, 2014; Mirel, 2011).

Such preparation often does not include a full understanding of limited resources, constant shifts in teaching curriculums and methodologies, emphasis on the science of teaching versus the art of teaching, limited mentoring by older teachers as many are retiring, young administrative staff, impact and complexity of the home and community environment on students, inconsistent parental support in the educational process of students due to employment or other personal life issues affecting the parent(s), and the difficulty that some students have in managing their own behavior in the class and school environment (Kea, Campbell, & Bratton, 2003; Willingham, 2011). Building teacher capacity in this area requires revamping the education programs responsible for preparing teachers, so that they incorporate this information, learn about the culture of students living in urban environments, and teaching strategies that can be employed to motivate, inspire, and address any behavioral issues as they come up in the classroom and school context. The nuts and bolts of how to handle the dynamics of urban education and genuinely connect with students in urban settings is a skill that needs to be taught and developed (Cowan, 2014; Obiakor, 2001; Smith, 2014).

In addition, there seems to be a backlash toward minority students with respect to immigration, reverse racism, and a lack of commitment and urgency with regard to the situation (Day-Vines, 2000). In light of the many variables impacting student ability to learn, process, and retain information (Minnici, 2014; Willingham, 2011) in a way that challenges them, is it not feasible and important to entertain the concept that societal changes and lower parental involvement play some role in student attendance, achievement, and success (Darling-Hammond, 2014)? Students are aware of the significant differences between some of their schools and those of their White counterparts (Loewenberg & Forzani, 2011). No longer are students in the dark regarding the discrepancies with respect to environments, resources, teachers, and access to advance programs, they can go online and see the stark comparisons. Knowing has a negative impact on the psyche of students. Despite the stark differences, many minority students strive to achieve to the best of their ability regardless of the situation. Those who are resourceful enough to cobble together whatever resources are available and create support systems that incorporate their parents, families, school, and community environmental supports can sometimes find the means to be successful academically and pursue their long-term goals of additional education/training or employment. This should not be the total responsibility of the student, but a community responsibility to provide the supports, high expectations, rigorous curriculum, and school activities necessary to encourage and promote students in reaching their highest academic potential.

BUILDING EDUCATIONAL CAPACITY

One of the most important actions that can take place organizationally in education today is to build capacity of staff, administration, and parents. It is their dedication and commitment that will make the real difference. What do we mean by building capacity? For sure, the field of education is being and has been negatively impacted by the political changes and initiatives of making education a science instead of an art. The science perspective unfortunately through legislative and policy development has emphasized quantity versus quality of education, tracking, and scientifically documenting the efficiency of education versus its effectiveness (Mirel, 2011; Weingarten, 2014). Many feel that the scientific perspective emphasizes paperwork, numbers, and outcomes. Teachers feel that if school systems would allow them to be creative in teaching and allow students to take the time to explore, examine, analyze, and experience the world through a guided and less highly structured process, the results of what is possible in terms of the academic achievements of students is limitless (Cowan, 2014). This process is one that has served us well. It only requires the integration of technology in the teaching process that will support it. Teachers are asking how the art of teaching became the science of teaching.

Some of this has been influenced by new technological interventions and their application and utilization within the profession. Clearly, it challenges students and teachers in ways we could not have imagined prior to their inventions. How technology is used in the classroom, goes back to how teachers and educational systems choose to employ them within the teaching arena (Smith, 2014). Will they be used only for scientific data collection of test scores, to track teachers and their effectiveness, to compute the savings and costs of education, or to provide a tool and opportunity for teachers to be creative and challenge the creativity, curiosity, and passion for learning and to also broaden their passion and love for teaching?

How education is delivered and provided, its role, function, and perspective needs to change as the world is changing. In the United States, serious questions are being raised about the discrepancies, inadequacies, inequalities, and the inequity of education across populations and especially with respect to the urban environment. It is time to evaluate where we have been, where we are, and where we hope to go in the future. It is no secret that American society as we currently know is moving toward a society in which minorities and people of color who are marginally excluded will become the dominant population groups. This is relevant because they will be the individuals to whom the baton will be given for the next generation. The present bifurcated system of education will make it challenging to sustain our own culture and compete in the global economy. We must invest in education at all levels, K–12 and beyond that supports the expression of different perspectives and constructive debate, while utilizing the talents of our diverse population of students to forge a new image and maintain a healthy respect among world nations. This can only occur if we prepare our children for the future. That means all of our children; from those in the poorest of rural environments to those in the most challenging of urban areas.

This will require boldness in terms of embracing all diversities and integrating and embedding diversity throughout the curriculum, hiring practices of teachers and administrations, expanding and developing community partnerships that will provide a support to students of all classes, races, genders, and beliefs (Okiabor, 2000; Simon, Gold, & Brown, 2002). Financially investing in education across local jurisdictions so that tax dollars are equitably disseminated across the different jurisdictions in a state would denote strong support of education. The quality of one's education should not be determined on which side of the tracks one lives (Cowan, 2014).

It is only when we as a society have the will to say no to the disparities in education attributed to racial disparities and poor tax bases, the philosophy of the science of teaching over the art of teaching, and the complexity of educational systems that sometimes lose sight of their central mission of educating all of society's populations that perhaps such indifferences can be addressed (Sullivan & Artiles, 2011). It is only when we take a more holistic perspective of supporting the family and the community in which schools sit through community centers attached to schools can we assist students and families struggling with securing the basics for survival (food, clothing, and shelter; Simon et al., 2002). Another avenue for addressing the concerns of education and those of urban populations is to become integrated within the communities by school administration attending community meetings and building partnerships with community leadership, parents, neighbors close to the school, and surrounding businesses.

One of the most critical things about building capacity is establishing relationships. Too often, educational systems in urban areas are so large that the communication between it and the communities in which schools sit is disjointed and often fragmented because of its enormity. Each school should designate a member of the school community to assume the role of the community liaison for the school. Often, many resources are underutilized by schools because they never make a connection with those in the community in which they sit. Recently, a teacher and an administrator were cited for their ability to turn around the lives of students and the school community because they rolled up their sleeves, went out in the community to meet with parents and to greet students as they came to school in the morning (NBC News, 2014). Outreach is one of the most useful endeavors in which a school can engage to make a difference in the lives of students, especially urban students as they have been known to view institutions (schools) included as not sensitive or really invested in helping them to be successful (Day-Vines, 2000). Not only is the institution detached, but sometimes the staff and administration is just as detached. For students, this detachment may impact their motivation to come to school. Depersonalization has no place in the field of education when your responsibilities require being able to make a human connection that will develop young productive citizens and positive human beings who can contribute to society (Cowan, 2014).

Another area for capacity building that will be central to urban environments will be the training of staff and administration in integrating technology within the educational environment (Minnici, 2014). Although minority students living in urban areas are behind in their ability to utilize technology in a way that enhances their understanding of the world, it has only been recently through the advent of smart phones that students have the world at their fingertips. Many students are light years beyond some of their teachers in their use of technology because this is the generation that is growing up with all the advances of technology in everyday products for home and personal use.

The integration of these technologies in schools due to lack of funding and poor infrastructure in school buildings has an education system that is struggling to keep up with the daily trends and upgrades. In the classroom setting, the broad use of technology in urban school settings is far from what it should be and students being educated without this knowledge are far behind their peers in better financed districts where resources are more plentiful. If urban students are to compete with their peers, they must be given access to communication tools so vital to society and its economy (Smith, 2014; American Federation of School Administrators, 2013). Finding a balance between overuse and underuse of technology is paramount to preparing students for future employment and its broadening use in everything from using an oven, TV, and washing machine to how one's phone or car operates. Building the technological capacity of staff and students in the educational arena is the foundation of how the world will communicate in the future. Everything will be assisted by the use of technology.

According to the latest data from Motivational Educational Entertainment (MME, 2002), there is extremely high Internet access (96%) by urban youth, at work, school, or home. Many (68%) are accessing the Internet through high-speed connections like cable, Digital Subscriber Line (DSL), or wireless. A national survey of more than 1,500 African American and Hispanic teens and young adults revealed that this group is highly connected, tech savvy, and brand loyal. However, only about half of those with access indicated that it was through a home computer. A 2008 survey found that males used the Internet to access sports information at a much higher rate than females (18%:1%), while female participants were more likely to use the Internet for schoolwork (23%:11%; www .meeproductions.com/ICT/ICTPressRelease.pdf). The research was conducted to aid service providers and institutions like schools to understand how to better communicate with urban youth and to create messages and outreach that reflect the ideals, culture, and environmental realities of urban youth. Schools need to take note of such research in developing curriculum and integrating aspects of technology in teaching the common core and preparing urban youth for the future (Smith, 2014).

Schools of Education need to collaborate with Schools of Social Work to assist them with understanding and developing programs of teaching that incorporate strategies for how to address difficult behaviors in the classroom setting and enhance classroom management skills to support teaching (Kea et al., 2003). This collaboration can also help teachers to understand how mental health issues, home, and community environments have a direct impact on a student's ability to be prepared and focus on the learning environment. It will also help teachers to incorporate classroom techniques that will help teachers to embed activities that reframe and utilize the negative behaviors in which students engage through changed perceptions of the behavior and positive interventions (Sugai, O'Keeffe, & Fallon, 2012; Willingham, 2011).

IMPLICATIONS FOR THE FUTURE

Social workers must be reminded of their roles as advocates and grassroots organizers. Education is a human service profession in need of change. Social workers should join with teachers in reframing education as a catalyst for human change, which has serious implications for the long-term humanity of society. It will be critical for social workers to support and assist teachers and administration in reclaiming teaching as an art not a science. The quality of education must be the focus point of intervention. Not how many tests have been completed but how students humanly connect to understanding the world around them through exploration and examination through an educational process (Weingarten, 2014). We have forgotten that students are not widgets and should not be treated as such. They are not objects of manufacturing but living organisms that are constantly evolving in the context of their environments.

As social workers, we can assist urban schools as well as their students, teachers, and administration in implementing strategies from an organizational and clinical perspective. We are trained and equipped to utilize a skill set that embraces understanding a person in environment; implementing theoretical frameworks and empirically based interventions such as response to intervention (RTI) and positive behavioral intervention and supports (PBIS); engaging and promoting social justice through restorative practices; providing guidance in developing cultural sensitivity of learning how to work and understand the mass changes in the cultural and racial makeup of students; and finding ways to employ techniques of behavioral management in the classroom context and larger school environment. We can also advocate what is in the best interest of the child educationally by engaging in political activities that support strong educational policies that serve to undergird future generations. The role of school social workers continues to expand as more community-based schools are being established. As in past history, the role of school social workers continues to be an intricate part of the school environment and serves to support the academic achievement and success of all students through the home/school/ community connection.

What are our ethical and professional responsibilities as social workers, educators, and community members to address these discrepancies, disparities, and conditions negatively impacting students and public institutions of education? Will public education continue to exist at this rate? Do we sit by idly and hope that the pendulum swings back or do we help to stabilize the situation? Will we evolve into a system where everyone has to pay for an education from pre-K through 12th grade? Will charter schools become the dominant structure for educating students? How will the landscape look? The discussion is a very serious one as evidenced by the perspectives on both sides of the debate. The bottom line is that children in this country belong to all of us and in this land where we strive for equality and equity, all should be treated with dignity, respect, and have fair and equal access to a free and appropriate education.

FOR FURTHER STUDY

Suggested Assignments

The following are some suggested assignments and readings that may be beneficial to broadening the knowledge and understanding of the topic discussed in the chapter.

1. Research information on the common core standards and assess their applicability to its utilization in the development of students in urban settings.

2. Visit three different urban school programs (pre-K program, traditional school, charter school, etc.) and speak with students who participate in these programs. Complete a comparison of a student's perception of his or her program to what is anecdotally written about such programs.

3. Interview a teacher working in an urban school setting and share with the class through an oral or written presentation his or her perceptions about students, changes in education, and how these factors impact his or her teaching.

4. Attend a conference for educators to learn what the latest trends are in education.

5. Identify what school systems are implementing in urban areas to address disproportionality of African American males in special education.

6. Conduct a debate with others in your class on what is the real purpose of education.

7. Shadow a school social worker for a day to find out what social workers do in the school setting.

8. Research the role of the Department of Education in your area.

Suggested Readings

About Pedagogy of the Oppressed (n.d.). Retrieved May 20, 2014 from www.pedagogyoftheop pressed.com/about

Alexander, M. (2010). *The new Jim Crow: Mass incarceration in the age of colorblindness*. New York, NY: The New Press.

Anderson, K. A., Howard, K. E., & Graham, A. (2007). Reading achievement, suspensions, and African American males in middle school. *Middle Grades Research Journal, 2*(2), 43–63.

The Civil Rights Project. (2014). Retrieved November 16, 2014, from http://civilrightsproject.ucla.edu/

Closing the Achievement Gap Research Brief (October 27, 2003). Retrieved May 30, 2014 from http://www.educationpartnerships.org

Delpit, L. (2006). *Other people's children: Cultural conflict in the classroom*. New York, NY: W. W. Norton and Company, Inc.

Flowers, L. A. (2007). Recommendations for research to improve reading achievement for African American students. *Reading Research Quarterly, 42*(3), 424–428.

Flowers, T. A., & Flowers, L. A. (2007). Factors affecting urban African American high school students' achievement in reading. *Urban Education, 43*(2), 154–171.

Hrabowski, F. A., Maton, K. I., & Greif, G. L. (1998). *Beating the odds: Raising academically successful African American males*. Oxford, England: Oxford University Press.

Historical Timeline of Public Education in the United States (2014). Retrieved May 21, 2014, from https://www.raceforward.org/research/reports/historical-timeline-public-education-us

Hrabowski, F. A., Maton, K. I., Greene, M. L., & Geoffrey, G. L. (2002). *Overcoming the odds: Raising academically successful African American young women*. New York, NY: Oxford University Press.

Kozol, J. (2005). *The shame of the nation: The restoration of apartheid schooling in America*. New York, NY: Broadway Books.

Leonard, J., & Hill M. L. (2008). Using multimedia to engage African American children in classroom discourse. *Journal of Black Studies, 39*(22). Originally published online March 28, 2007.

Lesaux, N. K., Vukovic, R. K., Hertzman, C., & Siegel, L. S. (2007). Context matters: The interrelatedness of early literacy skills, developmental health, and community demographics. *Early Education and Development, 18*(3), 497–518.

Noguera, P. A. (2003). The trouble with Black boys: The role and influence of environmental and cultural factors on the academic performance of African American males. *Urban Education, 38*, 431.

Ravitch, D. (2010). *The death and life of the great American school system: How testing and choice are undermining education*. New York, NY: Basic Books.

Ravitch, D. (2013). *The reign of error: The hoax of the privatization movement and the danger to America's public schools*. New York, NY: Knopf.

Rousseau, J. J. (1972). *Emile: Or on education*, trans. New York, NY: Allan Bloom (Basic Books).

Watkins, A. F. (2002). Learning styles of African American children: A developmental consideration. *Journal of Black Psychology, 28*(3), 3–17.

Williams, S. M., & Callins, T. (2007). Creating culturally responsive literacy programs in inclusive classrooms. *Intervention in School and Clinic, 42*, 195–197.

Willie, C. V., Garibaldi, A. M., & Reed, W. L. (1991). *The education of African Americans*. Boston, MA: Auburn House.

REFERENCES

The African American Struggle Through the U.S. Educational System. (2008–2009). Retrieved April 21, 2014, from https://historyengine.richmond.edu/episodes/view

American Federation of School Administrators. (2013). Expanded broadband access set for school districts. *The leader: A newsletter of the American federation of teachers, American Federation of School Administrators* (Vol. 76, p. 17). Washington, DC: American Federation of School Administrators.

Bestor, A. (1985). *Educational wastelands: The retreat from learning in our public schools.* Urbana: University of Illinois Press.

Blanchett, W. J. (2009). A retrospective examination of urban education: From Brown to the resegregation of African Americans in special education—it is time to "go for Broke." *Urban Education, 44*(4), 370–388.

Christodoulou, D. (Spring 2014). Minding the knowledge gap. *American educator: A quarterly journal of educational research and ideas in teacher evaluation: The importance of teaching content/professional development on the classics* (Vol. 38, pp. 27–33), No. 1. Washington, DC: American Federation of Teachers.

Cowan, L. (Spring 2014). Teaching and its spiritual power. *American Educator: A quarterly journal of educational research and ideas in teacher evaluation: The Importance of teaching content/professional development on the classics* (Vol. 38, pp. 38–39), No. 1. Washington, DC: American Federation of Teachers.

Darling-Hammond, L. (Spring 2014). One piece of the whole: Teacher evaluation as part of a comprehensive system for teaching and learning. *American educator: A quarterly journal of educational research and ideas in teacher evaluation: the importance of teaching content/professional development on the classics* (Vol. 38, pp. 4–13), No. 1. Washington, DC: American Federation of Teachers.

Day-Vines, N. (Winter 2000). Ethics, power and privilege: Salient issues in the development of multicultural competencies for teachers serving African American children with disabilities. *Teacher Education and Special Education, 23*(1), 3–18.

Delpit, L. D. (Aug 1988). The silenced dialogue: Power and pedagogy in educating other people's children. *Harvard Educational Review* 58, 280–298.

Dewey, J. (1902). *The child and the curriculum.* Chicago, IL: University of Chicago Press.

Dewey, J. (1997) *Democracy and education: An introduction to the philosophy of education.* Chicago, IL (Reprint): Free Press.

Epperly, J. (2014, May 15). *UCLA report finds changing U.S. demographics transform school segregation landscape 60 years after Brown v Board of Education (the Civil Rights Project).* Retrieved from UCLA, The Civil Rights Project website: http://civilrightsproject.ucla.edu/news/press-releases/2014-press-releases/ucla-report-find

Friedrich Froebel Timeline. (1998–2008). Retrieved May 30, 2014, from http://www.froebelweb.org/webline.html

Friere, P. (1972). *Pedagogy of the oppressed.* London, UK: Penguin Press.

Hirsch, E. D., Jr. (2009). *The making of Americans: Democracy and our schools.* New Haven, CT: Yale University Press.

Kea, C. D., Campbell, G. D., & Bratton, K. (2003). Culturally responsive assessment for African American students with learning and behavioral challenges. *Assessment for Effective Intervention, 29*(1), 27–38.

Kozol, J. (1991). *Savage inequalities: Children in America's schools.* New York, NY: Harper Perennial.

Kozol, J. (2005). *The shame of the nation: The restoration of apartheid schooling in America.* New York, NY: Random House.

Krogh, S. L. (1997). *Educating young children infancy to grade three.* (6th ed.). New York, NY: McGraw-Hill Inc.

Loewenberg, B. D., & Forzani, F. M. (Summer 2011). Building a common core for learning to teach: And connecting professional learning to practice. *American educator: A quarterly journal of educational research and ideas in rethinking teacher preparation: A bold plan to blend pedagogy and content knowledge* (Vol. 35, pp. 17–21), No. 2. Washington, DC: American Federation of Teachers.

Minnici, A. (2014). The mind shift in teacher evaluation: Where we stand and where we need to go. *American educator: A quarterly journal of educational research and ideas in teacher evaluation: The importance of teaching content/professional development on the classics* (Vol. 38, pp. 22–26), No. 1. Washington, DC: American Federation of Teachers.

Mirel, J. (2011). Bridging the widest street in the world: Reflections on the history of teacher education. *American educator: A quarterly journal of educational research and ideas in rethinking teacher preparation: A bold plan to blend pedagogy and content knowledge* (Vol. 35), No. 2. Washington, DC: American Federation of Teachers.

Morris, V. G., & Morris, C. L. (2000). *Creating caring and nurturing educational environment for African American children.* Westport, CT: Bergin and Garvey.

National Center for Educational Statistics (NCES). (2006). Digest of Education statistics, 2005. Retrieved from http://nces.ed.gov/pubsearch/pubsinfo.asp?pubid=2006030

National Center for Educational Statistics (NCES). (2012). Retrieved April 19, 2014, from http://nces.ed.gov/surveys/pisa/pisa2012highlights

National Public Radio Broadcast. (May 2014). *The US falls behind in academic achievement.* Arlington, VA: Corporation for Public Broadcasting.

NBC News. (May 2014). *International comparison of the US trends on educational achievement.* New York, NY: NBC News Broadcast.

Obiakor, F. E. (2001). Multicultural education: Powerful tool for preparing future general and special educators. *Teacher Education and Special Education, 24*(3), 241–255.

O'Connor, C., & Fernandez, S. D. (2006). Race, class and disproportionality: Re-evaluating the relationship between poverty and special education placement. *Educational Review, 35*(6), 6–11.

Organization for Economic Co-Operation and Development (OECD). (1999). *Monitoring student knowledge and skills: A new framework for assessment.* Paris, France: OECD Publications.

Ravitch, D. (2000). *Left back: A century of failed school reforms.* New York, NY: Simon and Schuster.

Sahlberg, P. (Summer 2011). The professional educator: Lessons from Finland. *American Educator: A quarterly journal of educational research and ideas in rethinking teacher preparation: A bold plan to blend pedagogy and content knowledge* (Vol. 35), No. 2. Washington, DC: American Federation of Teachers.

Simon, E., Gold, E., & Brown, C. (2002). Case study: Austin interfaith. Strong neighborhoods, strong schools. *The indicators project on education organizing.* Cross City Campaign for Urban School Reform, Chicago, IL.

Sixty years after Brown v Board, school segregation isn't yet American history of education. (May 16, 2014). *PBS News Hour education coverage is part of American graduate: Let's Make It Happen, a public media initiative made possible by the Corporation for Public Broadcasting.* Retrieved from http://www.pbs.org/newshour/bb/60-years-brown-v-board-school-segregation-isn't-yet-american-history/

Smith, M. (2013). Noted educator inspires optimism. *The leader: A newsletter of the American federation of teachers, American federation of school administrators* (Vol. 76, p. 16). Washington, DC: Winter.

Shapiro, M. (1983). *Childs garden.* University Park, PA: Penn State University Press.

Sugai, G., O'Keeffe, B., & Fallon, L. (2012). A contextual consideration of culture and school-wide positive behavior support. *Journal of Positive Behavior Interventions, 14*(4), 197–208.

Sullivan, A. L., & Artiles, A. J. (2011). Theorizing racial inequality in special education: Applying structural inequity theory to disproportionality. *Urban Education, 46*(6), 1526–1552.

Tate, B. (2014). *A history of education timeline.* Retrieved May 20, 2014, from http://www.tiki-toki.com/timeline/entry/56733/A-History-of-Education-Timeline/

U.S. Department of Education. (2005). *Statistical report: Condition of education [NCES].* Washington DC: Author.

U.S. Department of Education. (2011). *Statistical report on academic achievement of US students.* Washington, DC: Author.

U.S. Department of Education. (2013). *Statistical report on the condition of education [NCES].* Washington DC: Author.

U.S. Department of Education. (2014). An overview of the U.S. Department of Education. Retrieved May 20, 2014 from http://www2.ed.gov/about/overview/focus/what_pg2.html

Weingarten, R. (2014). Teaching and learning over testing. *American educator: A quarterly journal of educational research and ideas in teacher evaluation: The importance of teaching content/ professional development on the classics* (Vol. 38, p. 1), No. 1. Washington DC: American Federation of Teachers.

Willingham, D. T. (Summer 2011). Can teachers increase students' self-control? *American educator: A quarterly journal of educational research and ideas in rethinking teacher preparation: A bold plan to blend pedagogy and content knowledge* (Vol. 35, pp. 22–27), No. 2. Washington DC: American Federation of Teachers.

Woodward, D. (2013). The time is right for community leadership. *The leader: A newsletter of the American federation of teachers, American federation of school administrators* (Vol. 76, p. 2). Washington, DC: Winter.

CHAPTER 24

Policies That Impact Urban Communities

Tricia Bent-Goodley

This chapter examines three policy areas that impact urban communities. Using an intersectional and resistance framework, education, violence, and family issues are explored. The chapter discusses the necessity of using an intersectional and culturally informed strategy of examining policy in urban communities. Implications for social work practice are provided in the areas of educational policy standards, social work teaching, and action.

POLICIES THAT IMPACT URBAN COMMUNITIES

Policy impacts all areas of our lives. From education to public recreation, health, and criminal justice, social policy shapes critical issues that we negotiate each day. Policy and urban communities, particularly those with a large proportion of African Americans, continue to face pervasive racist and discriminatory issues while also negotiating new challenges. One could write this chapter from the perspective of all that is wrong in urban communities. However, using an Afrocentric approach to understanding how urban policy has shaped the lives of African American communities requires that one examine not just the disparate impact but also the strengths evidenced in these communities to address the continued oppression being experienced. Policies that have impacted urban communities are too numerous to mention in one chapter. Therefore, this chapter specifically focuses on three urban policy areas—education, violence, and family.

FRAMEWORK

The framework that is being utilized to examine policies and urban communities must be grounded in cultural specificity. Most policies are written as a form of regulation and enforcement. Policy is rarely developed using the strengths of any population; let alone those in urban communities. Therefore, to examine these policies and the impact that they have had on urban communities, one must utilize frameworks that illuminate the complexity of the urban African American experience. Because policy making is often driven from the standpoint of regulation, it is important to understand Schiele's framework of examining regulation and resistance (Schiele, 2010) as it connects with urban policy. Essentially, it is argued that policy has been used to control communities, particularly those that are poor and oppressed. Yet, despite these efforts, communities have used resistance as a way to fight policies that have been detrimental to their communities. It is vital then that this framework is utilized to understand both how policy has shaped the urban African American experience and how the community has collectively fought back to preserve itself. It is noted that resistance comes in many forms. Resistance can come from protest but it can also come through silent organizing. These diverse forms of resistance are both strengths and empowerment based. They are rooted in cultural tradition and history. Honoring the voices of those in the collective movement while simultaneously connecting with the cultural anchors that have been used to sustain the community, resistance is rooted in the ability of communities to use cultural strongholds to withstand those tangible and intangible assaults experienced daily.

An additional framework that is utilized in this chapter is intersectionality. "From an intersectionality viewpoint, targeted policies are often as ineffective as general policies in that both fail to address multiple identities and within-group diversity" (Hankivsky & Cormier, 2010, p. 219). Intersectionality is an emerging theory that has not often been used in policy. However, intersectionality helps us to better understand the complexity of experiences, issues, and circumstances (Murphy, 2009). They allow us to focus on multiple perspectives simultaneously, and not to examine issues from a singular linear perspective. Understanding policy and urban communities requires utilization of an intersectional lens. It is not any singular issue that weighs down communities. Instead, it is the multiplicity of persistent issues that relentlessly converge to negatively impact African American families and communities (Crenshaw, 1989). Thus, this chapter uses intersectionality as an additional framework to examine these complex issues.

Case Study

In the summer of 2014, communities around the country and nations around the world watched Ferguson Missouri residents' outrage over the killing of an 18-year-old African American male. It was not just the killing of this young man that struck the

(continued)

(continued)

nerve of the community. It was the fact that this community continues to experience racial oppression and inequity for many years (Cobb, 2014). This community watched as 67% of its population was African American; yet 83% of its police force and city council was White (Capeheart, 2014). This community rallied to bring attention to the disparities within their community. They came together to express their outrage and to bring attention to the racism and discrimination experienced especially by African American males across the nation. Ferguson then became symbolic of something much larger than this small community. It opened up discussion and dialogue about the experiences of African Americans, particularly African American males with the criminal justice system. It allowed African American men to tell the story of how negative stereotypes not only impact their daily lives but also have ended many of their lives. It allowed African American mothers to share how such violence and inequity impacts them as women, girls, and communities as well. Therefore, what happened in Ferguson is much bigger than this one incident. It was a reflection of how policies in urban African American communities have impacted these communities and it uncovered the frustration and fear of those having to navigate these environments. What stood out for many was the limited response of social workers providing leadership on these issues. Although there were social workers working on the ground to bring peace in this community, there was a limited response from the profession in bringing attention to the dynamics leading to what took place in Ferguson and continuing to keep the issues at the center of discussion following this issue has been noticeably minimal. The social work profession's roots are centered in social justice and human rights and yet, in this moment, social work was limited in bringing attention to these experiences, and furthering solutions to advance human rights and social justice in urban communities. Many social workers could not understand the swelling of outrage and anger that was being expressed in Ferguson and among some in their own communities. Some not only could not understand it but even expressed disagreement with the community's response. To understand urban policy, social workers must be willing to acknowledge how social and economic injustice has impacted communities.

EDUCATION, VIOLENCE, AND FAMILIES: INTERSECTIONS AND RESISTANCE

To understand how education, violence, and family policy impact African American urban communities, one must understand an issue at the center of these areas—economics. Although African Americans compose 12% of U.S. population, 25.8% live below the poverty rate (Macartney, Bishaw, & Fontenot, 2013). African Americans are three times more likely to be poor than Whites. African American children are three times more likely than White children to live in areas of concentrated poverty (Children's Defense Fund, 2014). The unemployment rate is twice as high among Blacks as compared to

Whites (Bureau of Labor Statistics, 2013). In 2009, the median household income for Whites was $62,545 and for Blacks was $38,409 (U.S. Census Bureau, 2012). Poverty, disparate incomes, wealth inequity, and food insecurity are growing in Black communities across the nation. One cannot ignore how these issues intersect with education, violence, and family structure.

The public education system has experienced vast challenges in the education of children in urban communities, especially Black males (Blanchett & Waynne, 2007; Ferguson, 2001). African American boys and girls are both more likely to be suspended and expelled from school compared to other groups of children. In fact, Black children are suspended and expelled at a rate three times higher than White students (U.S. Department of Education, 2014). African American children have lower graduation rates and disparately do not meet math and reading literacy goals at grade level (Gabriel, 2010). Educational systems have become spaces where children and parents have to fight to preserve the spirit of their boys from teachers and school systems that do not understand them. Frustrated with systems that are either diminishing their potential or not responding to their needs, Black children often check out of their own education. Black families struggling with economic pressures, addiction, violence, and/or the daily stressors of negotiating oppressive environments, do not often provide the checks and balances needed to sustain Black children within their school environment. Parents may not feel prepared to confront teachers about these experiences. With low parental involvement, these schools lack accountability needed to ensure equity in education. Educational systems are further challenged by the multiple bio psychosocial needs of children that they are either ill prepared or not prepared to address (Hart, Hodgkinson, Belcher, Hyman, & Cooley-Strickland, 2013; Sanchez, Lambert, & Cooley-Strickland, 2013). The multiplicity of these issues makes education much more complicated to address in urban communities.

Unfortunately, school systems also become safe havens for children who live in communities where there is growing violence and homes where violence is often way too common (Lormand et al., 2013). Access to guns has become a way to resolve problems in communities (Braga et al., 2012; Papachristos & Wildeman, 2014; Wilkinson, McBryde, Williams, Bloom, & Bell, 2009). The violence experienced within these communities is both alarming and reflective of broader societal issues. One cannot simply address the violence without understanding where it comes from. Gun violence has become an all too common way of resolving conflicts (Spano & Bolland, 2013). The proliferation of guns in urban communities creates a recipe for disaster. The ease by which guns can be obtained is reflective of a system that disregards the lives of Black children. Simultaneously, children are often left to fend for themselves in their communities. They lack the parental influence, adult guidance, and intentional socialization that make it permissible to resolve problems with guns. The proliferation of guns coupled with these challenging issues makes access and limited controls a ticking time bomb. In addition to gun violence in urban communities, violence in the home is pervasive (Reed et al., 2009). Children are often confronted with the realities of witnessing domestic violence in the home (Benson, Wooldredge, Thistlethwaite, & Fox, 2004; Thompson & Massat, 2005). Three to ten million children witness domestic violence annually. These children become susceptible to lower school participation and progress, increased mental health issues, poorer health outcomes, and an increase for criminal and juvenile justice activity. One study found 70% of young men in a juvenile facility were there as a result of trying to protect their mother from an abusive father or boyfriend. Although there is no certainty that youth exposed to domestic violence in the home will themselves experience or perpetrate abuse, it is clear that there is a negative impact that can be seen in increases in youth homelessness, substance abuse, educational dropouts, and poorer mental health (Acevedo, Lowe, Griffin, & Botvin, 2013). In addition to the children, victim survivors of domestic violence face increased risks for poorer health and mental health, increased exposure to criminal justice settings, homelessness, and lower employment outcomes. Girls are often victims of sexual assault even before reaching high school. These experiences with trauma often go unaddressed and unchecked by those who are most in a position to do something about it (Kennedy, Bybee, Kulkarni, & Archer, 2012; Miller, 2008; Teitelman, Ratcliffe, Morales-Aleman, & Sullivan, 2008; Walsh, Koenen, Aiello, Uddin, & Galea, 2014). Consequently, domestic and sexual violence become an issue that warrants serious attention in urban communities.

BUILDING ON STRENGTHS, RESILIENCY, AND AFRICAN AMERICAN CULTURAL VALUES

Despite these many challenges, complicated and interconnected in nature, African Americans continue to thrive and grow. Although strained, African Americans continue to evidence mutual-aid societies to support each other through difficult times. Organizations continue to flourish in the community to provide concrete and emotional needs. Civic organizations continue to provide an organizing force in urban communities. African Americans continue to grow and lean on extended family to deal with life's challenges. The extended family is strained in that there is more mobility within the community whereby persons are living away from home and immediate family networks. Yet, these extended family systems continue to assist with daily challenges. Persons continue to adopt fictive kin and create new family systems that are there to provide mutual aid and support (Richardson, 2012). African Americans continue to use their spirituality and religion as a source of hope and change (Bent-Goodley, 2014; Paranjape & Kaslow, 2010). Although the literature often distinguishes between spirituality and religion, many African Americans view the two as interconnected and not separate notions. They continue to use their faith-based communities to help address such issues, while also strengthening their spirituality to respond to various stressors. Black churches continue to have important relevance in the community. Increasingly, these churches are developing interventions to address social and public health issues. They are creating systems to address social ills through ministries and other community-based programs. Many faith-based communities continue to provide food, clothing, and other services to congregants and persons within the community. These strongholds, that continue to be utilized daily, are notable mechanisms that are created and recreated in communities and are rooted in cultural strengths.

IMPLICATIONS

A final implication, beyond social work education, is that all social workers need to grow their knowledge and skill in working in urban communities. Social workers are called to utilize social justice frameworks and to advance human rights, regardless if they are working in clinical or macro-settings. It is vital that social workers use their knowledge to serve as advocates that address the disparities and challenges being experienced in urban communities. Social workers are often on the ground in their communities. They are aware of many of the ways that disparate treatment impacts the community. Thus, social workers are strategically positioned to address these issues, bring greater awareness, and mobilize communities to act. Social workers must use this strategic position in advancing change in urban communities.

Social policy in urban communities is complex. Yet, there are opportunities to address these issues and find lasting solutions for change. Working with community strengths and resilience, social workers can support new advances and equitable change within urban settings. It is vital that practitioners see these communities as partners in fostering social change.

The current Council on Social Work Education (CSWE) Educational Policy and Accreditation Standards (EPAS) require that schools address issues of diversity, social justice, and human rights. Being able to address issues impacting urban communities is a component of implementing these EPAS standards. Developing urban-centered competencies is necessary to ensure that these social work education standards are measurable and adhered to within diverse forms of practice. Competencies that could be developed could include the following:

1. Knowledge of intersectionality in theory, practice, policy, and research.

2. Ability to utilize intersectionality in conducting policy-related analysis.

3. Examination of policy issues in urban settings to include knowledge of educational systems, criminal justice systems, environmental issues, family and child welfare policies, housing, social services, and spatial analysis.

4. Knowledge of urban gentrification as a social justice issue.

5. The ability to identify strengths within urban settings.

6. The ability to assess resilience, risk, and protective factors.

7. Knowledge of trauma-informed practice strategies.

8. Ability to engage in trauma-informed practices.

9. Examination of historical and contemporary forms of oppression and discrimination in urban communities.

10. Knowledge of research strategies and the historical context of conducting research in urban settings.

11. The ability to conduct research in urban settings.

FOR FURTHER STUDY

Suggested Assignments

Recognizing the key role of social work educators in furthering this information, social work educators can utilize intersectionality within the classroom in the form of classroom exercises, assignments, and service learning experiences. Following are ways in which social work educators can develop assignments that can assist with growing students' knowledge and ability to engage in practice within urban communities:

1. *Paper assignment*: Identify an issue faced by urban communities (i.e., education, health, neighborhood violence). Using an intersectional approach, conduct an analysis of the issue. Be sure to define intersectionality. Discuss the multifaceted and intersectional components of the issue. Include at least three intersectional areas in your analysis. This assignment should be between five to seven pages using the American Psychological Association (APA) style. Include citations that support your assertions in the paper.

2. *Historical analysis*: Identify an issue faced by urban communities (i.e., education, health, neighborhood violence). Provide a historical analysis of the issue. Trace the issue over time within urban communities. For this analysis, students can choose to focus on a specific urban community. Examine policies that have impacted the community over time as it connects with the identified issue. In addition to examining records, reports, and other documents, students are encouraged to talk with residents to obtain qualitative information to both inform and strengthen their historical analysis. This assignment should be between 16 and 18 pages using the APA style. Include citations that support your assertions in the paper.

3. *Community town hall meeting*: Identify a policy issue faced by a local urban community. Convene a community town hall meeting that brings attention and awareness to this policy issue in the community. Develop strategic partnerships with local stakeholders. Work collaboratively to identify persons needed to participate in the town hall meeting. Develop appropriate marketing mechanisms to promote the event and encourage attendance. Identify and administer an evaluation to determine the effectiveness of the town hall meeting. Prepare a report with findings and recommendations that can be shared with public officials to address the identified policy issue.

4. *Policy brief*: Develop a policy brief that specifically examines an urban policy issue in your local community. In five to six pages, present an overview of the policy issue. Utilizing an identified policy framework, provide information on the impact of the policy issue on the urban community. You must ensure that recommendations provided include cost-effective approaches. Select two to three papers that can be shared with local public officials on the policy issue identified.

5. *Community mapping and assessment*: Engage in a community needs assessment that also includes mapping of formal provider systems. Utilization of Geographical Information Systems (GIS) is highly recommended in conducting this mapping activity.

Suggested Readings

Davis, K. E., & Bent-Goodley, T. B. (2004). *The color of social policy*. Alexandria, VA: CSWE Press.

Dill, B. T., Zambrana, R., & Collins, P. (2009). *Emerging intersections: Race, class and gender in theory, policy and practice.* New Brunswick, NJ: Rutgers University Press.

Picower, B., & Mayorga, E. (2015). What's race got to do with it? How current school reform policy maintains racial and economic inequality. New York, NY: Peter Lang Publishing Group.

Schiele, J. H. (2010). *Social welfare policy: Regulation and resistance among people of color.* Thousand Oaks, CA: Sage Publications.

Robers, D. (2002). *Shattered bonds: The color of child welfare.* New York, NY: Basic Civitas Books.

REFERENCES

Acevedo, B. P., Lowe, S. R., Griffin, K. W., & Botvin, G. J. (2013). Predictors of intimate partner violence in a sample of multiethnic urban young adults. *Journal of Interpersonal Violence, 28*(15), 3004–3022.

Benson, M. L., Wooldredge, J., Thistlethwaite, A. B., & Fox, G. L. (2004). The correlation between race and domestic violence is confounded with community context. *Social Problems, 51,* 326–342.

Bent-Goodley, T. B. (2014). *By grace: The challenges, strengths and promise of African American marriages.* Washington, DC: NASW Press.

Blanchett, W. J., & Wynne, J. (2007). Reframing urban education discourse: A conversation with and for teacher educators. *Theory Into Practice, 46,* 187–193.

Bureau of Labor Statistics. (2013, October). *Labor force characteristics by race and ethnicity, 2012.* Washington, DC: Author. Retrieved November 14, 2014, from http://www.bls.gov/cps/cpsrace2012.pdf

Capeheart, J. (2014, September 5). Three troubling things exposed by the Ferguson police shooting of Michael Brown. *The Washington Post.* Retrieved November 14, 2014, from http://www.washingtonpost.com/blogs/post-partisan/wp/2014/09/05/three-troubling-things-exposed-by-the-ferguson-police-shooting-of-michael-brown

Children's Defense Fund. (2014). *The state of America's children: 2014.* Washington, DC: Author.

Cobb, J. (2014, August 17). A movement grows in Ferguson. *The New Yorker.* Retrieved November 14, 2014, from http://www.newyorker.com/news/news-desk/movement-grows-ferguson

Crenshaw, K. (1989). Mapping the margins: Intersectionality identity politics, and violence against women of color. *Stanford Law Review, 43,* 1241–1301.

Ferguson, A. A. (2001). *Bad boys: Public schools in the making of Black masculinity.* Ann Arbor, MI: University of Michigan Press.

Gabriel, T. (2010, November 9). Proficiency of Black students is found to be far lower than expected. *The New York Times.* Retrieved November 14, 2014, from http://www.nytimes.com/2010/11/09/education/09gap.html?_r=0

Hankivsky, O., & Cormier, R. (2010). Intersectionality and public policy: Some lessons from existing models. *Political Research Quarterly, 64,* 217–229.

Hart, S. L., Hodgkinson, S. C., Belcher, H. M., Hyman, C., & Cooley-Strickland, M. (2013). Somatic symptoms, peer and school stress, and family and community violence exposure among urban elementary school children. *Journal of Behavioral Medicine, 36*(5), 454–465.

Kennedy, A. C., Bybee, D., Kulkarni, S. J., & Archer, G. (2012). Sexual victimization and family violence among urban African American adolescent women: Do violence cluster profiles predict partner violence victimization and sex trade exposure? *Violence Against Women, 18*(11), 1319–1338.

Lormand, D. K., Markham, C. M., Peskin, M. F., Byrd, T. L., Addy, R. C., Baumler, E., & Tortolero, S. R. (2013). Dating violence among urban, minority, middle school youth and associated sexual risk behaviors and substance use. *The Journal of School Health, 83*(6), 415–421.

Macartney, S., Bishaw, A., & Fontenot, K. (2013, February). Poverty rates for selected detailed race and Hispanic groups by state and place: 2007–2011. *American Community Survey Briefs.* Washington, DC: U.S. Department of Commerce. Retrieved November 14, 2014, from http://www.census.gov/prod/2013pubs/acsbr11-17.pdf

Miller, J. (2008). Violence against urban African American girls: Challenges for feminist advocacy. *Journal of Contemporary Criminal Justice, 24,* 148–162.

Murphy, Y. (2009). *Incorporating intersectionality in social work practice, research, policy and education.* Washington, DC: NASW Press.

Papachristos, A. V., & Wildeman, C. (2014). Network exposure and homicide victimization in an African American community. *American Journal of Public Health, 104*(1), 143–150.

Paranjape, A., & Kaslow, N. (2010). Family violence exposure and health outcomes among older African American women: Do spirituality and social support play protective roles? *Journal of Women's Health (2002), 19*(10), 1899–1904.

Reed, E., Silverman, J. G., Welles, S. L., Santana, M. C., Missmer, S. A., & Raj, A. (2009). Associations between perceptions and involvement in neighborhood violence and intimate partner violence perpetration among urban, African American men. *Journal of Community Health, 34*(4), 328–335.

Richardson, J. (2012). Beyond the playing field: Coaches as social capital for inner-city adolescent African-American males. *Journal of African American Studies, 16,* 171–194.

Sanchez, Y., Lambert, S., & Cooley-Strickland, M. (2013). Adverse life events, coping and internalizing and externalizing behaviors in urban African American youth. *Journal of Child & Family Studies, 22,* 38–47.

Schiele, J. H. (Ed.). (2010). *Social welfare policy: Regulation and resistance among people of color.* Thousand Oaks, CA: Sage Publications.

Spano, R., & Bolland, J. (2013). Disentangling the effects of violent victimization, violent behavior, and gun carrying for minority inner-city youth living in extreme poverty. *Crime & Delinquency, 59,* 191–213.

Teitelman, A. M., Ratcliffe, S. J., Morales-Aleman, M. M., & Sullivan, C. M. (2008). Sexual relationship power, intimate partner violence, and condom use among minority urban girls. *Journal of Interpersonal Violence, 23*(12), 1694–1712.

Thompson, T., Jr., & Massat, C. R. (2005). Experiences of violence, post-traumatic stress, academic achievement and behavior problems of urban African-American children. *Child & Adolescent Social Work Journal, 22,* 367–393.

U.S. Census Bureau. (2012). *Income, expenditures, poverty and wealth.* Washington, DC: Author. Retrieved November 14, 2014, from http://www.census.gov/compendia/statab/2012/tables/12s0697.pdf

U.S. Department of Education. (2014, March). *Civil rights data collection: Data snapshot school discipline.* Washington, D.C.: Author. Retrieved November 14, 2014, from http://www2.ed.gov/about/offices/list/ocr/docs/crdc-discipline-snapshot.pdf

Walsh, K., Koenen, K. C., Aiello, A. E., Uddin, M., & Galea, S. (2014). Prevalence of sexual violence and posttraumatic stress disorder in an urban African-American population. *Journal of Immigrant and Minority Health/Center for Minority Public Health, 16*(6), 1307–1310.

Wilkinson, D. L., McBryde, M. S., Williams, B., Bloom, S., & Bell, K. (2009). Peers and gun use among urban adolescent males: An examination of social embeddedness. *Journal of Contemporary Criminal Justice, 25*, 20–44.

Index